# THE MASTER MUSICIANS

# BEETHOVEN

*Series edited by Stanley Sadie*

# THE MASTER MUSICIANS

# BEETHOVEN

*Barry Cooper*

OXFORD
UNIVERSITY PRESS

# OXFORD

UNIVERSITY PRESS

Great Clarendon Street, Oxford OX2 6DP

Oxford University Press is a department of the University of Oxford.
It furthers the University's objective of excellence in research, scholarship,
and education by publishing worldwide in

Oxford New York

Athens Auckland Bangkok Bogotá Buenos Aires Calcutta
Cape Town Chennai Dar es Salaam Delhi Florence Hong Kong Istanbul
Karachi Kuala Lumpur Madrid Melbourne Mexico City Mumbai
Nairobi Paris São Paulo Shanghai Singapore Taipei Tokyo Toronto Warsaw
and associated companies in Berlin Ibadan

Oxford is a registered trade mark of Oxford University Press
in the UK and in certain other countries

Published in the United States
by Oxford University Press Inc., New York

© Barry Cooper 2000

The moral rights of the author have been asserted

Database right Oxford University Press (maker)

First published 2000

British Library Cataloguing in Publication Data

Data available

Library of Congress Cataloging in Publication Data

Data available

ISBN 0–19–816598–6

1 3 5 7 9 10 8 6 4 2

Typeset by Hope Services (Abingdon) Ltd.
Printed and bound in Great Britain
on acid-free paper by
Biddles Ltd
Guildford and King's Lynn

*For Hugh, Paul, Rachel, and Simon*

# Preface

Books in the Master Musicians series have customarily been divided into two main parts—life and work. Only after much consideration has this structure been abandoned here, in favour of a continuous chronological narrative.[1] Such an approach is particularly advantageous in the case of Beethoven, since most of his life was devoted to his works and centred around them. It might even be said that his composing life was his real life, the true home for his mind, and the embodiment of his spiritual development, whereas mundane activities of daily life were of marginal concern for him.

Most of Beethoven's regular occupation consisted of sketching and drafting his compositions, and large quantities of these sketches survive. Thanks to the researches of Douglas Johnson, Alan Tyson, Robert Winter, Sieghard Brandenburg, and many others,[2] far more is known now than as little as twenty years ago about this aspect of his life, and in any balanced biography his sketches and autograph scores should occupy a prominent place. The sketches pose a particular problem for a life-and-works study, since there has been much debate about whether they are primarily of biographical or analytical significance. In fact, they shed much light on both his life and his works, bridging the gap between them. For instance, when it is noted that Beethoven added the first bar of the slow movement of the 'Hammerklavier' Sonata at a very late stage, thereby forging both a link from the end of the previous movement and also subtle motivic connections (rising 3rd followed by falling 3rd) with the first two movements, the observation is both biographical and analytical.

An integrated approach to Beethoven's life and works also allows works to be seen in their immediate historical and musical context, and has been tried successfully by several writers—most recently Konrad Küster (1994) and William Kinderman (1995).[3] These two authors, however, concentrate

[1] Some of the general problems of the relationship between life and works are discussed in Dahlhaus, *Beethoven*, 1–10 (for full reference to this and all literature cited, see Appendix D).

[2] See JTW and individual articles by Brandenburg.

[3] Küster, *Beethoven*; Kinderman, *Beethoven*.

mainly on the works. The present study, while placing more emphasis on biography, stresses those aspects of Beethoven's life that impinge most closely on his musical output. The aim has been to bring music and biography as close together as possible, so as to reveal the interconnections between the two more fully than in previous biographies.

The published sources available as the basis for an overall account of Beethoven are today innumerable, and have greatly multiplied even since the last Master Musicians *Beethoven* was completed by Denis Matthews in 1984. Mention has already been made of the large number of recent sketch studies, which have been supplemented by facsimiles of several of the sketchbooks. Beethoven's conversation books are also now available right up to December 1826 (by which time he had effectively ceased composing).[4] And, even since work on the present book was begun, new editions of many of Beethoven's works have appeared, with detailed critical commentaries and background information, as part of the Beethovenhaus's Complete Edition currently in progress; a new English translation of letters to Beethoven has been issued by Theodore Albrecht; and the long-awaited Beethovenhaus edition of his complete known correspondence has finally appeared. It will be some years before all this material is thoroughly correlated and absorbed into a new picture of Beethoven, and the present book is therefore in some ways only a provisional assessment, unable to take full account of these new publications.

The information that emanated from the enormous number of slightly earlier studies—those from the 1970s and 1980s—has intensified the problem of what to omit from a single-volume general study of Beethoven. Selecting material for inclusion or omission is perhaps the most difficult decision facing the writer of such a book, and it surfaced repeatedly in the present volume. The general principle of placing emphasis on the interface between life and work has been modified by several other considerations, including the aim of including all material of exceptional significance, and a disproportionate amount of material that has not previously received due attention. This approach has also been applied to the music itself: instead of a routine and systematic summary of each work discussed, only some of its most important features and innovations are outlined, along with subtleties that have been largely overlooked.

The main outlines of Beethoven's life have been known ever since they were painstakingly assembled over several decades by Alexander Wheelock Thayer in the late nineteenth century. Of the various editions of his path-breaking biography, the most useful and accessible for English readers is that by Elliot Forbes, first published in 1964,[5] which includes much post-Thayer material. Thayer's work has formed the foundation for all subsequent biographies including the present one, and where no source of information is provided here for biographical details, they generally derive

[4] See BKh.    [5] See TF.

from Thayer–Forbes. Much other material has also been incorporated, however, necessitating more footnotes than is usual in a Master Musicians book. Moreover, not everything found in Thayer–Forbes is reliable. Much of it is based on recollections and memoirs by a number of individuals of greatly varying degrees of trustworthiness. Chief scoundrel is Anton Schindler, an associate of Beethoven's during the 1820s and an early biographer. Schindler related a large number of stories about Beethoven and his music, but most have proved to be either completely or partly false. He even inserted numerous entries in Beethoven's conversation books after the composer's death, in order to enhance his own reputation; these entries, some of which were presented as genuine in Thayer–Forbes, were identified as fabrications only in the 1970s. Thus anything reported by Schindler must be assumed to be doubtful or false, unless supported by independent evidence (in which case, Schindler's contribution is redundant). This is especially true of his numerous anecdotes about the meaning of Beethoven's music. There is no evidence that Beethoven ever passed on to him any special insights on this subject, and wherever it has been possible to test Schindler's veracity on the matter, it has been shown to be false. Schindler's apparently fictional stories are among the most widely circulated about Beethoven's music: the claim that the opening of the Fifth Symphony denotes Fate knocking at the door; that the Sonata, Op. 31 No. 2, has some connection with Shakespeare's *The Tempest*; that the Triple Concerto was composed for Archduke Rudolph; that the slow movement of the *Pastoral* Symphony was written near Heiligenstadt and contains a fourth bird-call; and that the second movement of the Eighth Symphony was based on a canon in honour of Johann Maelzel's metronome (Schindler even composed the canon in question!).

Several other writers cited by Thayer, such as Friedrich Rochlitz, Johann Schenk, and Louis Schlösser, also now appear to have fabricated their anecdotes, while even Carl Czerny is often unreliable, especially in his dating of Beethoven's late works. Other accounts are of uncertain reliability, such as Gottfried von Breuning's report that Beethoven was once arrested as a tramp (though there is no reason to doubt this one); exception must be made, however, for those by Franz Wegeler and Ferdinand Ries.[6] They claimed to have made efforts to eliminate anything they did not know to be true, and their accounts are often corroborated by evidence that they could not have encountered.

In view of such varying levels of reliability, all material has been re-examined as thoroughly as is feasible, both to assess its validity and also to take into account newer discoveries and hypotheses. This re-examination has even extended to English translations of German material, notably Beethoven's letters. Although citations of letters refer, for convenience, to the letter number in the standard translation by Emily Anderson, her actual

---

[6] They were first published by Wegeler and Ries in *Biographische Notizen über Ludwig van Beethoven* in 1838, with a supplement by Wegeler in 1845. English translation in WR.

translations have not been strictly retained where scrutiny of the German text suggested that some alternative phraseology would be preferable.[7] The same applies to other references to English translations of German documents. As for music texts, these have been taken mainly from the old Complete Edition (*GA*), but other editions or sources have been compared where the text was suspected to be inaccurate. Sketch transcriptions, too, have generally been compared against Beethoven's original notations.

From this critical reassessment it emerges that surprisingly little is known for certain about Beethoven. Much is based on the accumulation of a weight of data that merely renders certain conclusions almost inescapable, others fairly probable, and others highly speculative or dubious though not impossible. I have generally avoided including this third category, though by doing so have risked omitting significant facets of Beethoven's life.[8] The first two categories have been accepted only with due caution. If, in the ensuing pages, there are unusually frequent appearances of words such as 'apparently', 'evidently', and 'it seems that', these should be regarded as reminders of our frequent lack of certainty. The problem is well illustrated by research on Beethoven's 'Immortal Beloved'; the evidence that she was Antonie Brentano is stronger than the evidence for many other widely held assumptions about Beethoven's life, yet it has been attacked vigorously in recent years by those who will not accept anything short of certain proof, which is unlikely to emerge.

As for musical observations by previous writers, while these are generally true at a purely factual level, it is often uncertain whether the features noted had any significance for Beethoven; hence I have concentrated here on features that are likely to have been an integral part of his compositional intentions rather than chance by-products. Distinguishing these two categories, however, is likely to remain contentious.

In the course of this re-examination of Beethoven's life and music, many new conclusions have been reached. These cover such diverse issues as his relationships with Haydn, with Josephine Deym, and with his sister-in-law Johanna, the originality of his earliest works, the genesis of his First Symphony and the *Prometheus–Eroica* theme, and the origins of the name 'Elise' in his famous *Für Elise*. Admittedly, most of these conclusions represent merely the balance of probability rather than certainty, but together they modify many details in the received image of Beethoven. They do not, however, alter our perception of his greatness as both man and composer—except, perhaps, by enhancing it: despite much sniping from twentieth-century critics, his reputation as a giant among composers remains intact as we enter the twenty-first century.

---

[7] Anderson's edition of *The Letters of Beethoven* (1961) remained the best until the recent appearance of the Beethovenhaus edition mentioned above.

[8] Cf. Solomon, *Beethoven*, which by contrast includes many fascinating psychological speculations about Beethoven's mental and emotional make-up. These present a fuller, though not necessarily more accurate, image of the composer.

It is impossible today to give an adequate account of the many facets of Beethoven's life and work within a single volume. The limitations of the present study, however, would be many times greater but for the enormous amount of research carried out by earlier writers whose names appear above and in the Bibliography. To them I owe a deep debt of gratitude. Also to be thanked are the numerous individuals with whom I have had fruitful discussions and/or correspondence on a wide range of aspects of the subject, including Theodore Albrecht, Otto Biba, Sieghard Brandenburg, Anne-Louise Coldicott, Peter Davies, Jonathan Del Mar, Tia De Nora, William Drabkin, Owen Jander, Susan Kagan, Joseph Kerman, William Kinderman, Lewis Lockwood, Nicholas Marston, William Meredith, Julia Moore, Maynard Solomon, Glenn Stanley, Marie-Elisabeth Tellenbach, Alan Tyson, Jos van der Zanden, and Petra Weber-Bockholdt. Thanks are due to all the libraries in which I have worked, and particularly those that have provided me with access to original source material, including the Beethoven-Archiv, Bonn; the Ira F. Brilliant Center for Beethoven Studies in San Jose; the Gesellschaft der Musikfreunde in Vienna; the Musikabteilung of the Staatsbibliothek zu Berlin, Preussischer Kulturbesitz; the Bibliothèque Nationale, Paris; and the British Library, London. Finally I am especially grateful to my wife Susan, for reading the penultimate draft of the book and making many useful suggestions, as well as for all her support throughout the project.

Barry Cooper
*Manchester, 1999*

# Contents

# Illustrations

# Abbreviations

(See Appendix D for full references)

| | |
|---|---|
| A- | Letter no. in Anderson, ed., *Letters* |
| Alb- | Item no. in Albrecht, ed., *Letters* |
| BB- | Item no. in Brandenburg, ed., *Beethoven: Briefwechsel* |
| *BeJb* | *Beethoven-Jahrbuch* |
| BF | *Beethoven Forum* |
| *BJo* | *Beethoven Journal* |
| BKh | Köhler *et al.*, *Ludwig van Beethovens Konversationshefte* |
| BN | *Beethoven Newsletter* |
| GA | *Gesamtausgabe* |
| Hess | Item no. in Hess, *Verzeichnis* |
| JAMS | *Journal of the American Musicological Society* |
| JTW | Johnson, Tyson, and Winter, *The Beethoven Sketchbooks* |
| KH | Kinsky (completed Halm), *Das Werk Beethovens* |
| ML | *Music & Letters* |
| MQ | *Musical Quarterly* |
| MT | *Musical Times* |
| N-I | Nottebohm, *Beethoveniana* |
| N-II | Nottebohm, *Zweite Beethoveniana* |
| NA | *Neue Ausgabe* |
| SGA | *Supplemente zur Gesamtausgabe* |
| SV | Item no. in Schmidt, 'Verzeichnis' |
| T- | Item no. in Solomon, 'Tagebuch' |
| TDR | Thayer, *Ludwig van Beethovens Leben* |
| TF | Forbes, ed., *Thayer's Life of Beethoven* |
| WoO | Werk ohne Opuszahl (work without opus no. as listed in KH) |
| WR | Wegeler and Ries, *Remembering Beethoven* |

# 1

# Young genius (1770–83)

Some composers are born into a family where composition already has an established place, or where younger members of the family turn to composition in years to come. Others are the only members of their family who ever take up the activity. Ludwig van Beethoven comes very definitely in the latter category. Apart from one or two half-hearted attempts by his brother Carl, not one of Beethoven's family took any interest in composition. His ancestors, who came from the vicinity of Mechelen (Malines) in what is now Belgium, were mostly tradesmen of various types, and his name suggests that they lived at one time at or near a beet farm, although this etymology has been questioned. Beethoven had no known descendants, but those of Carl have included workers on the railways, in the post office, in the building industry and so on, with no sign of a composer among them.

Nevertheless, Beethoven did have a more musical background than some composers. His grandfather Ludwig senior or Louis (1712–73) had shown musical promise from an early age, as both a singer and keyboard player in Mechelen, and after brief musical appointments in Louvain and Liège made the important move to Bonn, on the Rhine, in 1733, to take up a post as a court musician to the Elector of Cologne, being employed chiefly as a bass singer. Here he was sufficiently successful to become Kapellmeister (director of court music) in 1761. Meanwhile his son Johann (c. 1740–92), the father of the composer, had also shown musical inclinations; he, too, was appointed in his turn as court musician in 1764, having already given considerable service as a treble, alto, and latterly tenor. To describe Johann as simply a 'tenor', as is often done, is to give him less than due credit. In addition to being a professional singer at the court, he was a successful teacher of clavier (piano or harpsichord) and singing, a capable violinist, and could play the zither.

When he was not performing in Bonn, Johann often travelled to nearby places such as Cologne and Koblenz. On one of these trips, to Ehrenbreitstein near Koblenz, he met his future wife Maria Magdalena Keverich (1746–87). She was the daughter of the kitchen overseer at the palace of Ehrenbreitstein, who had died in 1759. She had then married one Johann Leym on 30 January 1763, while she was still only sixteen, and had given birth to one son (who died in infancy) before Leym himself died on

28 November 1765, leaving her a widow before she was nineteen. There is no indication of musical traditions in her family. However, her cousin Anna Margaretha had married a violinist named Johann Konrad Rovantini some years earlier, and the couple had moved to Bonn when he was appointed court musician there in 1764. This may even have provided the link through which Johann van Beethoven came to meet the widowed Maria Magdalena; in any case it was not wholly surprising that she, following her cousin's example, should accept a marriage proposal from a court musician from Bonn. She and Johann were married at the Church of St Remigius in Bonn on 12 November 1767. Her cousin had meantime been widowed herself in 1766, and was doubtless glad to have relatives living nearby again. Indeed Frau Rovantini's son Franz Georg, who was about nine years old when his father died, later lived in the Beethovens' house for a time.

The family surroundings, then, provided a sound if not ideal environment for a young composer. So, too, did the city of Bonn. Beethoven once referred to it as 'a small unimportant town', maintaining that he had achieved what he had done almost entirely by his own efforts.[1] Small it was, with a population of barely 10,000; but, as in the late twentieth century, its importance greatly exceeded its size. For centuries it had been the official seat of the Archbishop Elector of Cologne, an ecclesiastical and political position of considerable luxury surrounded by an extensive court. By the eighteenth century, patronage of the arts by such a court was automatically expected, and the combined needs of church, theatre, concert room, and ballroom provided employment for many musicians. Although the level of financial support for musicians varied with the economic climate, the amount and variety of music performed there would have been enough to stimulate any potential composer. From 1761 the Elector was Maximilian Friedrich, who later became Beethoven's first patron. He was assisted by his minister Kaspar Anton von Belderbusch, and the Beethovens seem to have enjoyed the personal support and confidence of both men.

After their marriage and a brief honeymoon back in Ehrenbreitstein, Johann and Maria Magdalena van Beethoven settled in the rear portion of house No. 515 in Bonngasse, the Beethovenhaus (No. 20) as it is now known. The house was almost opposite one occupied by a fellow musician at court named Johann Ries (1723–84), while further up the street lived another musician—the young horn player Nikolaus Simrock, who later founded a music publishing firm. About the same time as Johann's move, his father, Ludwig, who had been living for many years in a house owned by a family named Fischer, moved next door to the Ries family. He had initially been opposed to Johann's marriage and may not have been present at the wedding, but his opposition did not last and he was evidently anxious to remain close to Johann. About a year and a half after the marriage, Maria Magdalena gave birth to her second and Johann's first son, on 1

---

[1] A-90.

April 1769 or thereabouts. On 2 April he was christened Ludwig Maria, but he died after only six days.

Her third son—the composer—was conceived about a year later; he was born on 16 December 1770 and christened Ludwig the following day. There is no documentary proof of his date of birth, which has been the subject of some debate even today, but several later witnesses concur that it was the 16th.[2] Since it was the custom to baptize babies within twenty-four hours of birth, he was more likely to have been born towards the end of the 16th than in the early hours of the morning. Not only were the exact date and time of birth not recorded, but even the year was soon forgotten, and there has been much confusion since. Johann generally referred to Beethoven's age as one year less than it really was, either through an inattentiveness that was not uncommon in those days, or as a deliberate deception to enhance his child's reputation; later Beethoven himself came to believe he was born in 1772, even to the extent of 'correcting' an official baptismal certificate. These ancient errors have long been put right, but there is a modern error still prevalent: writers all too often refer to Beethoven's age in a particular year by deducting 1770 from that year, disregarding the fact that, for example, almost throughout 1780 he was only nine years old.

Of the composer's first three years after birth, next to nothing is known. His maternal grandparents were both dead, and his father's mother Maria Josepha (née Poll, *c.* 1714–75) was living in seclusion as an alcoholic. The Kapellmeister grandfather, however, visited the family often from across the road, and won a high place in the young child's affection and admiration. Beethoven kept a portrait of his grandfather throughout his life, and remembered him clearly. The first great tragedy in the composer's life was therefore the death of Ludwig senior on 24 December 1773, only eight days after the child's third birthday. Shortly afterwards the Beethovens moved from Bonngasse to Dreieckplatz, where his brother Caspar Carl Anton (named after the Elector's minister Belderbusch, his baptismal sponsor) was born in 1774; thence the family moved back to the Fischers' house in the Rheingasse where Beethoven's grandfather had formerly lived. This move enabled the Fischers' son Gottfried (1780–1864) many years later to record numerous events in the young composer's life which either he or his sister Cäcilia had witnessed in the 1770s and 1780s.[3] It was here that Beethoven's brother Nikolaus Johann was born in October 1776. Their mother later gave birth to three more children, but all died before the age of three.

Outstanding musical gifts are generally evident from an early age, and father Johann, being a musician himself, had noticed them in his son by the

[2] These include Johann Albrechtsberger, writing in 1796, and an assistant in the publishing firm of Beethoven's friend Nikolaus Simrock, who wrote the date on an obituary notice in 1827; see Albrecht and Schwensen, 'Birthday'. The date also appears on the lithograph printed at the beginning of the first Beethoven biography, published by J. A. Schlosser in 1827.

[3] See Schmidt-Görg ed., *Des Bonner Bäckermeisters*.

time of the move to the Fischers'. Before long he was teaching the boy the piano, with Beethoven reportedly being stood on a bench as he was still too small to reach the keyboard otherwise. Another report mentions that when he was no more than four years old he sometimes sat on his father's knee to play while his father sang, and that he would abandon his playmates to hear his father's playing. The age at which he began to take a serious interest in music is mentioned by Beethoven himself, in a document of 1783 that was no doubt prepared with the assistance of his father or other adults: 'From my fourth year, music began to become the foremost of my youthful occupations.'[4] His 'fourth year' was literally when he was aged three, but Beethoven consistently used this type of expression to denote one year later, so here he meant the age of four. And since his age was generally misrepresented by a year during his childhood, he probably meant five, and the year 1776. This was, therefore, about the time when he first had formal lessons from his father, on piano and violin, at the house in the Rheingasse. He was never considered an infant prodigy, unlike Mozart, Samuel Wesley and William Crotch, all of whom were roughly contemporary with him; and not a note of his compositions was written at his birthplace.

Once he had begun learning, however, his genius quickly became apparent, through a combination of his own natural ability and his father's very rigorous teaching, which was so severe that it sometimes brought the boy to tears. The daily lessons and the large amounts of practice he was forced to do soon paid off handsomely. By the age of seven he was delighting the court with his playing, and was ready for his public debut, which took place at a concert in Cologne on 26 March 1778, beginning at 5 p.m. Note the date in early spring; note the time in the late afternoon. Both were to be significant again, at the very end of his life. The concert was put on by his father, who presented two of his pupils: 'Mdlle. Averdonc, court contralto, and his little son of six years. The former will have the honour to contribute various fine arias, the latter various clavier concertos and trios.'[5] Concertos were in those days published in such a way that they could be played as solos without orchestra, since a reduction of the orchestral parts was incorporated into the keyboard part. They were not the virtuosic display pieces typical of the nineteenth century, but were still among the most difficult types of keyboard music; one would not have expected a child of seven (even an able one) to perform more than a few simple airs or rondos, and so Beethoven's performance must have appeared remarkable. As for the performance of 'trios', this is more puzzling, unless there were other performers not mentioned in the concert announcement.

While he was learning music from his father, he began attending the local school, where he remained until the age of ten or eleven. He did not mix very well with the other children or even learn much, by all accounts, and his studies concentrated on Latin—evidently at the expense of arithmetic,

---

[4] A-D1.     [5] See TF, 57.

for he never progressed as far as learning basic multiplication. As for his mother, she taught him morals. She was a very good, pious woman, much loved and honoured, who knew how to give and receive. Beethoven always insisted he acquired his lifelong desire for virtue as a child: 'From childhood on, my heart and soul were full of the tender feeling of goodwill'; 'From childhood on, I learnt to love virtue'; 'From my earliest childhood my zeal to serve our poor suffering humanity . . .'; 'From childhood my greatest happiness and pleasure have been to be able to do something for others.'[6] It was probably his mother, more than anyone, who inculcated in him these feelings. Very serious in character, she was hardly ever seen to laugh; her earnestness rubbed off on Beethoven's music, which was observed by contemporaries to be generally more serious than normal. She also recognized the value of suffering. Fischer reports her as saying: 'Without suffering there is no struggle, without struggle no victory, without victory no crown.'[7] This sounds almost like a motto for Beethoven's own life and work. His mother was, however, less concerned with externals, for there are reports of his often appearing dirty and untidy; this untidiness, too, persisted throughout his life.

There is no indication from his earliest years of any bent towards composition. For Beethoven, this grew initially out of instinctive desires for extemporization. Fischer relates that Beethoven sometimes extemporized during his violin practice, and when told off by his father on one occasion, played the notes again and said, 'But isn't that beautiful?' Johann replied that Beethoven was not yet ready for that sort of thing. Before long, however, he judged the time was ripe for instruction in the elements of composition. This was in about 1779, by which time Beethoven had made so much progress on the piano and violin that his father could bring him no further.

Several new teachers were found for him. Violin (and probably viola) lessons were taken over by his second cousin Franz Rovantini, who had followed his own late father as a violinist in the court orchestra. Beethoven also began learning the organ with a Franciscan friar, Willibald Koch, and was soon deputizing for him and the organist at the Minorite Church. Instruction in thorough-bass (as the first steps in composition) and keyboard was entrusted to the elderly court organist Gilles van den Eeden (c.1710–82). (Fischer mentions one Santerrini as Beethoven's new teacher, but this is evidently a gross corruption of a half-remembered name.) Johann soon concluded, however, that van den Eeden was not the right person for the task, and turned instead to Tobias Pfeiffer. Pfeiffer (or Pfeifer) had not long been in Bonn, having arrived in the summer of 1779, and was a young man of about twenty-eight—an oboist, singer, and pianist who occasionally also played the flute and perhaps composed. He was a very colourful, though somewhat unstable, character and Beethoven is said to have made good progress with him, but he left Bonn within about a year.

[6] Heiligenstadt Testament (1802); letters A-139 (1807), A-334 (1811), and A-1306 (1824).
[7] Schmidt-Görg ed., *Des Bonner Bäckermeisters*, 62.

Fortunately, a much more able musician had meantime settled in Bonn—Christian Gottlob Neefe (1748–98), a native of Chemnitz, Saxony, who took over Beethoven's instruction. It was in October 1779 that Neefe, the music director at a theatre company in Frankfurt, moved to a similar position in a company in Bonn that had been set up the previous year under the Elector's patronage. In its first season (1778–9) this company had produced little of musical interest, but now under Neefe the musical side was rapidly expanded. Performances in 1779–80 included operas and related genres by Monsigny, Hiller, Benda, and Neefe himself; the following season added works by Grétry, Paisiello, and others, and in 1782–3 the programmes included Mozart's recently written *Die Entführung aus dem Serail*. Beethoven must have heard many of these performances and probably took part in them on the violin or viola.

In 1781 Neefe applied to succeed the elderly van den Eeden as court organist, and duly did so on the latter's death in June 1782, although he continued to hold his theatre post. Precisely when he took over instruction of Beethoven in piano, thorough-bass, and composition is not known. Most likely, however, the lessons began immediately after Pfeiffer's departure in 1780. Neefe was already an established composer, albeit never a great one, writing mainly stage works, songs, and keyboard music. He was able to further Beethoven's musical education to a greater extent than any other member of the Electoral court, and Beethoven was eternally grateful. In 1793, after Beethoven had left Bonn, he wrote to Neefe: 'I thank you for your advice which you so often gave me as I progressed in my divine art. If some day I become a great man, you too will have a share in it.'[8] Prophetic words! For, despite all Neefe's compositions, he is now chiefly remembered as Beethoven's teacher. Perhaps his most significant and lasting influence on Beethoven's compositional attitudes was his view that musical ideas should be related to and based on the natural course of human feelings.

At the time of van den Eeden's death in 1782, Neefe was just about to embark on an extended absence with the theatre company. By now, however, he was sufficiently confident of Beethoven's abilities to leave him to carry out the duties of court organist until his own return. The duties were relatively light since the Elector was away, but it was nevertheless a big responsibility for such a young boy.

From the same year we see the first evidence of Beethoven's efforts in composition. He had probably begun writing down his musical ideas some time earlier, and in 1815 he referred to the 'habit I formed in childhood of feeling obliged to write down my first ideas immediately',[9] but only one work is known to date from as early as 1782. This is a set of nine variations for piano on a march by Ernst Christoph Dressler (WoO 63). Publication was arranged by Neefe, and the work was printed by Goetz in Mannheim.

[8] A-6.  [9] A-558.

It may seem unreasonable to expect anything that is not derivative in the work of an eleven-year-old, yet several signs of truly Beethovenian originality are evident. First is the high level of technique demanded. Although the work is technically easy compared with some of his later piano music, it is more difficult than most piano music of the 1780s, with awkward semiquaver or demisemiquaver figuration often prevalent. The awkwardness is itself striking: commonplace figures are used with slight deviations which prevent the figures falling neatly under the fingers, yet these deviations are of musical origin and are not present for display purposes. The variety of figures used, even within single variations, shows an unusually fertile imagination, while the amount of slurs and staccato marks in semiquaver figuration is also noteworthy, since articulation marks are relatively infrequent in music of this period. Another significant feature is the key, C minor, which gives the march a funereal character that was very unusual in sets of variations at the time (none of Mozart's independent sets, and only one of C. P. E. Bach's, is in any minor key). The key was to become particularly characteristic for Beethoven; and as in so many of his later C minor works, the music bursts unexpectedly into C major near the end, with a bravura final variation featuring rapid semiquaver runs. The work's biggest flaw is its lack of proper continuity, so that the sense of progress and direction created by the key-scheme and the carefully arranged sequence of variations is somewhat undermined: each half of each variation comes to a sudden halt, including the final variation which would have concluded more satisfactorily with some kind of coda. These were features that Beethoven was to work on energetically in later years.

If this really was Beethoven's first composition, it is an extremely impressive beginning, and it may have taken some time (and some advice from Neefe) to reach its final version. But why did Beethoven use a funeral march? Was there some personal reason, or did he just have a morbid fascination with death? Any attempt to answer these questions is bound to be speculative, and one must also remember that Dressler's theme, the source of which has not been traced, was described on Beethoven's title page simply as a march, not a funeral march. Nevertheless, the piece may well have been written partly as a personal memorial to a much-loved fellow musician. The man in question is Franz Rovantini, who died after a short illness in September 1781. As a second cousin, he was one of Beethoven's closest relatives outside his immediate family, since Beethoven had no living aunts, uncles, or first cousins. An outstanding violinist, Rovantini had been living with the Beethovens in the Fischer house for some years, and had been giving Beethoven violin lessons. He had been the sponsor at the baptism of both of Beethoven's latest siblings, Anna Maria Franziska (born and died 1779) and Franz Georg (born 1781), and both had been named after him. Thus he had become like an elder brother to Beethoven, and was particularly close since both were musicians. Indeed the two of them, along with Beethoven's father, had journeyed around several local towns that summer

(1781), visiting various musicians and music-lovers, and were always well received. Rovantini was also renowned for his goodness and piety, and was widely loved and admired. His death in the prime of life at the age of twenty-four was certainly a great shock to the family, and to Beethoven in particular. A composition based on a funeral march and written only a few months later would have been a fitting memorial to the man. The Rovantini connection would also explain why the final variation was in the major: the lamentation of the funeral has given way to celestial bliss, with the ascent into heaven portrayed by rising scales (Ex. 1.1), as was to be done explicitly by Beethoven, years later, at the words 'Et ascendit' in his *Missa solemnis*.

Ex. 1.1 WoO 63, Var. 9

A few months after the variations were published, Neefe sent a communication dated 2 March 1783 to Carl Friedrich Cramer's *Magazin der Musik*, in which he described the musical scene and personnel at the Elector's court in Bonn. The whole document is extremely illuminating, but the section on Beethoven is most relevant here:

Louis van Betthoven [*sic*], son of the above-mentioned tenor, a boy of eleven, and of most promising talent. He plays the clavier very skilfully and with power, sight-reads very well, and to put it in a nutshell: he plays chiefly *Das wohltemperirte Clavier* of Sebastian Bach, which Herr Neefe put into his hands. Whoever knows this collection of preludes and fugues in all the keys (which one might almost call the *non plus ultra*) will know what that means. Herr Neefe has also, as far as his other duties permit, given him an introduction to thorough-bass. Now he is training him in composition, and for his encouragement has had printed in Mannheim 9 variations for clavier by him on a march. This young genius deserves support so that he can travel. He would surely become a second Wolfgang Amadeus Mozart, if he continued as he has begun.[10]

Several passages here are worthy of comment. Firstly, Neefe already recognized Beethoven as a boy of exceptional promise, especially on the keyboard. Secondly, the reference to Bach is interesting. *Das wohltemperirte Clavier* was still unpublished, but copies emanating from pupils were circulating in manuscript and the collection was clearly seen as containing some of the most difficult keyboard music yet written. Neefe had

---

[10] TF, 66.

for a time studied music in Leipzig, where Bach had lived and where his name was still renowned; he was thus able to transmit to Beethoven an early admiration for Bach's music, although there is no obvious evidence of Bachian influence in the Dressler Variations. Neefe also indicates that the amount of composition teaching he had given Beethoven by that date was limited. Beethoven had in fact learnt composition mainly through osmosis, by hearing other music, in the same way that a child learns its native language. He wrote in later life: 'As for mistakes, so far as I am concerned I have really never had to learn that. Even as a child I had such delicacy of feeling that I exercised it without knowing that it had to be thus or could be anything else.'[11] The wonderfully prophetic reference to Mozart is perhaps the most interesting remark of all. It shows that Mozart was already a household name in Bonn as the archetypal young genius and already great composer, even though he was still only twenty-seven and most of his finest works had yet to be written; Mozart, not Haydn or even Bach, was held up as the model for Beethoven to emulate. Finally, Neefe's thinly veiled plea to the Elector to provide funds for travel is noteworthy. Several other young musicians had already been supported in this way: Rovantini and another violinist (Christoph Brandt) had been to Berlin and Dresden; Helene Averdonk, who had shared the platform with Beethoven on his debut in 1778, studied in Koblenz later that year; and Franz Ries (1755–1846), son of the court musician Johann Ries mentioned earlier, had visited Vienna for six months in the same year. He had returned as a highly accomplished violinist, and became Beethoven's violin teacher after the death of Rovantini. Beethoven, however, was presumably considered still too young for travel, for it was not until he was sixteen that he was funded to go to Vienna.

During 1783 Beethoven made rapid progress in composition, and before the end of the year more works had been published. First was a short, conventional song, 'Schilderung eines Mädchens' (Portrait of a Maiden), in which the beloved is referred to by the archetypal name 'Elise'. This song appeared in a music journal (*Blumenlese für Klavierliebhaber*) published in Speier by Heinrich Bossler, and on the following pages appears a Rondo in C for piano (WoO 48), unattributed but almost certainly also by Beethoven. A short two-voice fugue for organ (WoO 31) which remained unpublished probably also dates from about this time.

Far more significant, however, was a set of three piano sonatas (WoO 47) printed by Bossler that autumn, with a dedication to Elector Maximilian Friedrich dated 14 October 1783, the date when they were also first advertised. In the previous twenty years sonatas had become established as the most important and elevated form of piano music, and were usually published in sets of three or six. It says much for Beethoven's ambition and seriousness of purpose that he opted for this form so early, rather than contenting himself with more variations and rondos. The dedicatory letter,

[11] A-39 (date uncertain).

which begins with the remark that he had been concentrating on music since his 'fourth year', continues:

I have now reached my eleventh year; and since then my Muse in hours of dedication has often whispered to me: 'Try it and write down for once the harmonies of your soul!' Eleven years—I thought—and how would I look as a composer? And what would men experienced in the art say about it? I was almost shy. But my Muse wished it—I obeyed, and wrote.[12]

Already at this age, Beethoven clearly had a sense of compulsion to compose, despite the absence of any family tradition in the field. The letter goes on to describe the sonatas as 'the first-fruits of my youthful works', and they were evidently his first substantial product; but he later annotated his own copy of the volume, emphasizing that they were not his first work: 'Even before this work there appeared my Variations in C minor, as also songs in a Bossler journal.'[13]

These are full-sized, three-movement sonatas, and impressive by any standards; for a twelve-year-old they are astonishing. In style they are closer to the Mannheim school of orchestral music than to either C. P. E. Bach's sonatas or those of Haydn and Mozart, but no close models have been found. The first one, in E flat, has an energetic opening with off-beat accents typical of the later Beethoven, and as in the Dressler Variations the articulation of the semiquavers is unusually detailed. Articulation marks are also prevalent in the second movement, and towards the end Beethoven has actually revised the articulation by manuscript alterations to his own copy—an early example of his tendency never to be fully satisfied with the final version of any work. The main theme of the second movement is closely related to that of the first; this was a procedure that Beethoven repeatedly used throughout his life, but the connection is far more obvious here than in later examples, where it is often extremely subtle. The rondo finale has plenty of technical difficulties and a striking episode in C minor, but it ends rather too abruptly.

The second sonata, in F minor, is perhaps the most original of the three, especially its first movement which begins with a slow introduction; this is followed by an Allegro based on falling scales, but the slow, introductory material returns unexpectedly, in B flat minor, just before the recapitulation, resulting in a highly original structure. This and the overall mood clearly foreshadow Beethoven's *Pathétique* Sonata. The third sonata is in D major to contrast with the flat keys of its two predecessors. Its middle movement is a minuet with six variations, the fourth of which has extremely rapid demisemiquaver figuration that is scarcely playable at a normal minuet speed. The finale, however, is headed 'scherzando', suggesting a humorous mood that was to become very common in Beethoven's music.

---

[12] A-D1.    [13] This copy is now in the British Library, London, Add. MS 41631.

The three sonatas are not without their weaknesses, chief of which is, once again, insufficient sense of continuity; changes from one section to the next are often awkward, and the problem is only really overcome in the finale of No. 3. Nevertheless these sonatas show many fine and original touches, and an emphasis on orchestral style that suggests Beethoven was already looking towards composing symphonies. The custom of severing them from their thirty-two successors, by disregarding them in the standard numbering system and omitting them from supposedly complete editions and recordings of Beethoven's piano sonatas, is quite unjustifiable. There is far less distance between these three sonatas and those of Op. 49 than between the latter and the 'Hammerklavier'.

Before the end of 1783, Neefe's desire that Beethoven should travel had been fulfilled, but the journey to Holland was essentially a private one and there is no evidence that it was subsidized by the Elector. The circumstances surrounding the trip are related by Fischer.[14] Franz Rovantini had a sister, Anna Maria Magdalena, who was employed by a rich widow as a governess in Rotterdam. When Beethoven's mother informed her of Rovantini's death in 1781, she became anxious to visit his grave in Bonn, and eventually did so in autumn 1783, staying about a month and doing much sightseeing accompanied by Beethoven, his mother, or his father. A return visit by the Beethovens was arranged; Johann was unable to go, and so Beethoven went with his mother. During their journey down the Rhine, the weather was so cold that his mother reportedly held his feet in her lap to prevent frostbite. They stayed in Rotterdam for some time, and Beethoven played in several great houses there, astonishing people with his ability. He also performed on the piano at the Royal Court in The Hague, some ten miles away, on 23 November, and was paid 63 florins—far more than anyone else listed at the event. Nevertheless, he returned dissatisfied with the rewards, describing the Dutch as penny-pinchers and vowing not to go to the Netherlands again.

The real significance of the visit is that this was one of very few long journeys that Beethoven ever made. Whereas the young Mozart had been taken to many countries by his father, this was Beethoven's only foreign trip as a child, and his father was not even with him. Thus claims by Thayer and others that Johann attempted to promote Beethoven as a prodigy (and deliberately falsified his age) in order to make money lack foundation. Although, as the Dutch trip shows, Johann could clearly have done this quite successfully, any such efforts were half-hearted and short-lived. Like Johann, Beethoven both as a youth and in later life was very happy visiting places in the locality; but his cold feet on the Rhine boat may be emblematic of psychological cold feet over longer journeys. Despite the generosity of the Royal Court in The Hague, and the enjoyable time he and his mother

---

[14] Schmidt-Görg ed., *Des Bonner Bäckermeisters*, 64–7. Fischer does not give a date, and Thayer believed the trip to have taken place in 1781; but a little-known document published in 1965 proves that it was in late autumn 1783 (see Alb-3).

had with Anna Maria, his rewards from the great houses of Rotterdam were evidently insufficient to overcome his distaste for foreign places. His song 'Urians Reise um die Welt' (Urian's Journey round the World), Op. 52 No. 1, which relates a ludicrous journey to far-flung parts of the globe, is musical evidence of his attitude, and may even have been stimulated by his Dutch visit. The song has not been precisely dated but was noted by Wegeler as one of Beethoven's earliest works.

Even if Beethoven was not wholly enthusiastic about the trip, however, he returned to Bonn with an enhanced reputation at home and abroad. His absence from the Elector's court for a period had done him more good than harm. Soon he was to gain the reward of a full appointment there.

# 2

# Adolescence (1784–9)

In February 1784, not long after Beethoven's return from the Netherlands, Bonn suffered a disastrous flood such as periodically befalls the Rhineland towns. The Fischer house in the Rheingasse lay close to the river, and both the Fischers and the Beethovens were in some danger, but they were eventually rescued with ladders. This alarming experience evidently made a deep impression on Beethoven, and the flood may have destroyed his early manuscripts, for hardly any survive from before this date; but it does not seem to have affected his subsequent music.

By this time he was beginning to attract attention as a young composer, and visitors sometimes came to the Fischer house to see him or hear him play. Unfortunately the owner of the house, Theodor Fischer, was a master baker and needed to sleep during the afternoon so as to be able to work during the night; the noise generated by the visitors and music was liable to disturb his sleep, and this was one reason why the Beethovens eventually moved out of the house (which was also becoming too cramped for the growing family), about 1785.[1] They moved to a house in Wenzelgasse, conveniently, for Beethoven, close to the Minorite Church where he sometimes played the organ. Apart from one or two brief spells, this house remained his home until he left Bonn for good in 1792.

At court, meanwhile, his position changed rapidly in 1784. His ability on the organ and as a repetiteur in the theatre had been noticed, as had his father's declining ability to provide for his family. Accordingly he was appointed assistant organist at the end of February. Then on 15 April Elector Maximilian Friedrich died and was immediately succeeded by Maximilian Franz (1756–1801). This had many short- and long-term consequences. The theatre company was promptly dismissed, placing Neefe's position in peril. After some debate he was retained, however, as court organist, with a salary of 200 florins per year, while a figure of 150 florins was settled for Beethoven. This was not a large sum, but his duties were not onerous and seem to have left him plenty of time for studying, practising and, most important, composing.

---

[1] Schmidt-Görg ed., *Des Bonner Bäckermeisters*, 68–71.

The new Elector was the youngest of Empress Maria Theresa's sons, and therefore a man of great influence. Her eldest son, Joseph II, was by that time Emperor of Austria and the Holy Roman Empire, whose seat was in Vienna, and he had set up a programme of liberal reform based on the philosophies of the Enlightenment. Maximilian Franz promoted similar ideas in Bonn, and supported the arts and education, most notably by founding the University of Bonn in 1785. The university attracted several important writers and philosophers, and rapidly became a hotbed of Enlightenment ideals in the 1780s; indeed some of the professors were soon being regarded as dangerously radical or Protestant in outlook. Beethoven was just at that very impressionable age when philosophical ideas are most likely to be influential, and it was through this intellectual environment that his political views were shaped—in particular his hatred of all forms of tyranny and oppression. The seeds of his *Fidelio*, *Egmont*, and the Napoleonic elements of the *Eroica* were sown here in Bonn.

Another intellectual current was provided by a society known as the Order of Illuminati, founded in 1781, which aimed to improve man's moral character and support and promote knowledge independent of the Church—ideas closely related to freemasonry. Neefe was a leading member of the Bonn branch, and it may well have coloured Beethoven's religious views: although he was a firm believer in an all-powerful, all-loving God, he seems to have had little time for the clergy or for organized religion, and his preference for personal prayer rather than ritualized worship might be regarded as Protestant. It is striking that he composed next to nothing for the Church, either in Bonn (where he actually played the organ for services) or later, apart from his two great masses. The Order of Illuminati ceased to operate by 1785, but its ideas lived on, and many of its members regrouped to form the *Lesegesellschaft* (Literary Society) in 1787.

Further nourishment for the intellectually hungry Beethoven was provided by new friends. It was in 1784, or a little earlier, that he became associated with a young medical student named Franz Wegeler (1765–1848), who shortly afterwards introduced him to a family named von Breuning. The father, Emanuel Joseph, had died along with several others in a fire at the electoral palace in January 1777, but his brother Lorenz had then come to Bonn to support the widow, Helene (1750–1838), who lived in the same house as her brother Abraham von Kerich. The two men assisted her in bringing up her four children: Eleonore (1771–1841), Christoph (1773–1841), Stephan (1774–1827) and Lorenz or Lenz (1777–98).[2] When Eleonore and Lorenz were needing a piano teacher, Wegeler introduced Beethoven to them, and he was soon being treated, like Wegeler, as one of the family. (Wegeler eventually became an actual member of the family when he married Eleonore in 1802.) The family was well-to-do and highly

---

[2] These dates are sometimes given incorrectly: Gerhard, Stephan's son, states that Christoph was born in 1771 and Eleonore in 1772 (see Breuning, *Memories*, 24), and the error is repeated in TDR, i. 226–7.

cultured, and it was here that Beethoven was introduced to the delights of German literature (especially poetry), for which he acquired a life-long love, reflected in his numerous Lieder and the finale of the Ninth Symphony. Here, too, he became acquainted with Classical literature, and his subsequent devotion to Homer is widely attested. The atmosphere seems to have been more stimulating and easy-going than in Beethoven's own home, where his too-strict father was by now increasingly turning to alcohol; and as the adolescent Beethoven grew increasingly independent, he spent days and even many nights at the Breunings' house.

Little of this background is reflected in Beethoven's compositions of 1784. His study with Neefe presumably continued, and two more works were printed by Bossler in *Neue Blumenlese*—again a rondo and a song. The Rondo in A (WoO 49) has a surprisingly complex structure and it shows Beethoven already coming to terms with the problem of providing a work with a satisfactory conclusion—one that somehow rounds off or sums up what has gone before. Whereas his Dressler Variations and sonatas had simply stopped when they reached their natural conclusion, here Beethoven provides a sizeable coda that reintroduces the most striking idea from the episodes—a fortissimo arpeggio motif in the key of C major—and reconciles it with the tonic key.

The song, 'An einen Säugling' (To an Infant), provides the first clear hints about Beethoven's religious beliefs. The text Beethoven chose, by J. von Döhring,[3] portrays an infant as unaware that the person who nourishes him is his mother, just as we do not perceive our Provider, who will shortly make Himself known if we are pious and believe. Here is an early embodiment of Beethoven's concept of the 'loving Father' of his Ninth Symphony, expressed in language sufficiently simple to appeal to a twelve- or thirteen-year-old, who had watched his own mother nursing her children (the song may have been composed before the death of Beethoven's baby brother Franz Georg on 16 August 1783).[4]

Far more significant musically than either the rondo or the song is Beethoven's earliest known orchestral work, a piano concerto in E flat (WoO 4), which was possibly stimulated by a piano concerto in G by Neefe published in 1782. It is assumed to date from 1784, since the manuscript describes Beethoven as aged twelve. Unfortunately only the piano part survives, in a copyist's hand with numerous alterations by Beethoven. The orchestral tutti sections, however, have been incorporated into it, with fairly full indications of instrumentation that have enabled a tentative reconstruction to be made.[5]

---

[3] Not by Wirths as suggested in *GA*; see KH, 571.

[4] The suggestion in Solomon, *Beethoven*, 24, that the song's references to an unknown father should be related to alleged doubts on Beethoven's part about his own paternity seems far-fetched.

[5] Ed. Willy Hess (Kassel, 1961). Some aspects of this reconstruction and orchestration have been criticized for being uncharacteristic of early Beethoven.

Obviously it is difficult to judge the worth of a concerto from such fragmentary material, but certain features stand out. As usual with the young Beethoven, the piano part bears extensive articulation marks which demonstrate his great attention to detail. It is also strikingly virtuosic, with bravura figuration in all three movements, sometimes exceeding that which Mozart demanded in his concertos: in the first movement Beethoven uses not just semiquaver runs but semiquavers in parallel thirds for the right hand alone while the left is otherwise occupied (bars 195–210); and in the second movement, after the strings have stated a Larghetto theme mainly in quavers, the piano launches into extensive runs in demisemiquavers, hemidemisemiquavers and even, at one point, semi-hemidemisemiquavers! (Mozart rarely goes beyond demisemiquavers in comparable movements.)

The work is cast in the three-movement structure that had been the norm since the time of Vivaldi, but its first movement is somewhat diffuse thematically. In classical concertos, the first movement normally used a complex blend of ritornello form and sonata form. Beethoven retains this broad outline more or less intact, but his use of the themes is not very disciplined and much of the solo writing is mere figuration. In particular, the relationship between the recapitulation and the exposition is very loose, and much thematic material is left undeveloped. The second and third movements, however, with their simpler structure, have a clearer sense of organization. Beethoven evidently became dissatisfied with the work before long, for he never considered it for publication as far as is known. Nevertheless, like the sonatas of the previous year, it is an ambitious and far from unsuccessful attempt at coming to grips with one of the most important musical genres.

Various composers are claimed to have influenced these very early works, including C. P. E. Bach, Johann Sterkel, Georg Wagenseil, Neefe himself, and the Mannheim school, as well as Mozart and Haydn.[6] Certainly Beethoven was familiar with some of their music and absorbed it almost subconsciously into his own. Many of the similarities between their works and his, however, may be fortuitous, while with others the connection is not very close. No single model is predominant, and his music already exhibits many features that are apparently original.

If Beethoven wrote other works in 1784, they are either lost or undatable now, but from the following year come three substantial piano quartets (WoO 36), as well as a short minuet for piano (WoO 82). Again the dates are not confirmed, and there is no early source material for the minuet, but the handwriting in the quartets resembles that of Beethoven's annotations to the concerto and cannot be much later than it. The title page of the quartets shows that his casualness about his age was already present: after writing 'aged 14' he altered the figure to '13', providing further evidence that there was no grand conspiracy to hide his true age, but genuine uncertainty.

[6] See, for example, Schiedermair, *Der junge Beethoven*, 270–82.

The autograph, which most likely reflects the order of composition, places the C major quartet first, followed by those in E flat and D, but the first edition (published posthumously in 1828) moved the C major quartet to the end of the group, where it has remained in subsequent editions and catalogues.

Mozart was by now undeniably the prime influence, and evidently remained his favourite composer until Beethoven encountered the music of Handel after moving to Vienna. Neefe had already held up Mozart as a model in his printed notice of 1783, the year in which Beethoven must have heard Mozart's *Entführung* in Bonn. And reports of Mozart's piano concertos of the early 1780s could have prompted Beethoven to turn to the genre, although he would have had difficulty obtaining scores of them since they had not yet been published. In the Piano Quartet in E flat the allusion to Mozart is unmistakable. The model is the Violin Sonata in G, K. 379, composed and published in Vienna in 1781. Mozart's sonata has an unusual form: it begins with an Adagio in which the first part only is repeated, with the second part ending on the dominant and leading into an Allegro in the tonic minor in triple time; then the finale consists of a cantabile *thema* in the major followed by five variations (one in the tonic minor) and a reprise of the theme, plus a short coda. All these features are preserved exactly by Beethoven in WoO 36 No. 1, except that there are six variations instead of five. And lest one suspect that the similarity of structure is purely fortuitous, Beethoven begins his work with an Adagio theme almost identical to Mozart's.

Rather than emphasizing the similarities, however, it is more rewarding to see the ways in which Beethoven attempted to build on Mozart's model and not just imitate it. On the principle that a pygmy sitting on a giant's shoulders can see further than the giant, Beethoven was evidently using Mozart's music (and what better?) as a lever to raise his own artistic designs; and although his effort cannot match Mozart in terms of elegance and sophistication, there are a number of ways in which he overtly attempts to surpass his model, in addition to the obvious devices of using more instruments and one extra variation.

First there is the length. Since the two works correspond exactly in terms of metre, tempo, and repeats, bar numbers are for once a meaningful comparison: Mozart's movements contain 49, 192, and 129 bars, while Beethoven's contain 69, 196, and 144. His later propensity for composing on an unprecedented scale can already be sensed. Secondly, the level of technical difficulty in the piano part is in several places greater in Beethoven than Mozart: for example, in the opening Adagio, as in the slow movement of his concerto of the previous year, Beethoven uses note values twice as short as Mozart's, and in the two following movements there are also several places where the unconventional figuration places considerable demands on the pianist. One cannot help suspecting that, even at the age of fourteen, Beethoven was technically a more advanced pianist than Mozart. Another noteworthy feature is the dynamic range. Mozart does not use *ff*, *pp* or *fp* at all in K. 379, whereas Beethoven uses all of them several times in the quartet, greatly heightening its dramatic intensity in a manner so typical of his later works.

One of the most striking features about this quartet, however, is the key of the Allegro. Whereas Mozart used his characteristic G minor to create tension and pathos, Beethoven adopted E flat minor—a key hardly ever used before (although Beethoven had of course encountered it in Bach's *Das wohltemperirte Clavier*). The use of so many of the piano's black notes gives a more muted tone quality than, say, E minor, and the intonation would have been different in the days before equal temperament, while the notes of the string instruments lack the resonances provided by their open strings. The overall result is an unusually dark sound, and the fact that Beethoven exploited such a strange key is evidence of the extraordinary acuteness of his ear at this date, as well as an early sign of his fondness for the bizarre. This is an unmistakably Beethovenian movement and arguably the best in the whole set; its powerful, driving rhythms, sharp dynamic contrasts and incessant sense of urgency and seriousness mark a new and original sound in the Classical style, and one that was to be greatly exploited in his later music.

In the finale, both composers include a variation in the tonic minor, recalling the key of the Allegro, but Beethoven also recalls the Allegro theme itself by using arpeggio figuration that is clearly related to it, thereby providing an additional unifying element in a way that was to become so characteristic of his later music. This variation also displays an intense, unmistakably Beethovenian, emotional power far beyond anything in the Mozart sonata, with an *ff* marking, a sudden *p* near the middle, and thunderous left-hand demisemiquavers for the piano almost throughout (Ex. 2.1). Beethoven's desire for innovation continued right to the end of the movement. Whereas Mozart has a plain reprise of the *thema* after the last variation, Beethoven uses a varied reprise at a faster speed, enriching the texture and making other minor modifications. Finally, in the coda, where Mozart continues with the four-square phrase structure, Beethoven introduces two three-bar phrases to provide variety and contrast.

The other two quartets in the set, in D and C, also use ideas derived from Mozart violin sonatas—K. 380 in E flat and K. 296 in C respectively.[7] Yet here the similarities are even less conspicuous, while there are marked differences in character, with Beethoven making much greater use of dramatic contrast. Mozart's style was being assimilated as an additional resource in Beethoven's compositional palette, rather than as a direct model, and he instinctively used it to colour his own music without any further efforts at direct imitation. Indeed, there were occasions in his later sketches where he

---

[7] The three Mozart sonatas that provided ideas for Beethoven's quartets were all published together in his set of violin sonatas Op. 2, which contained K. 376, 296, and 377–80 in this order.

**Ex. 2.1** WoO 36 No. 1/III, Var. 5

seems to have noticed a too strong Mozartian influence only after drafting an idea, and it is likely that other cases where similarities have been observed were also unintentional. He continued to learn from Mozart's music long after his student days, copying out and studying relevant passages when composing quartets, dramatic music, and even the *Missa solemnis*. As in the E flat piano quartet, however, the Mozart style was never his only resource—he always attempted to go beyond where Mozart left off and introduce something innovative.

Beethoven's next known composition is a Trio in G for piano, flute, and bassoon (WoO 37). After a chamber work for piano and strings, one for piano and wind instruments would be a natural successor for an aspiring composer. On the back of the autograph score he gave his age as '4i', but it can be assumed he meant 'four–teen' (he commonly reversed the digits of such figures).[8] Allowing for the one year that was normally deducted from his age, he was therefore fifteen and the year was 1786 when he wrote it. The trio was allegedly written for members of the family of Count Friedrich von Westerholt, who was chief equerry to the Elector. The count could play the bassoon, while one of his sons played the flute and some of the count's servants were also wind players. Meanwhile the count's elder daughter, Maria Anna (1774–1852) was learning the piano with Beethoven, who later (about 1788–9) fell in love with her.[9] The difficulty of the piano part in the trio suggests that it could not have been written for a twelve-year-old—or indeed for anyone except Beethoven himself. As Maria von Westerholt's technique advanced, however, she probably played the trio with her family, and this would account for descendants of the family claiming that the work was composed for them. Beethoven may also have played the work with his new friend Anton Reicha, a Czech composer and flautist who had moved to Bonn in 1785, and with one of the several bassoonists now at the court.

The trio, which betrays the influence of Mozart almost throughout, is in three movements, the middle one being an Adagio in G minor and the finale a set of variations. Although the piano predominates, the wind writing is very idiomatic and there are some lovely passages for the bassoon in its tenor register, especially in the Adagio, where it soars up to B flat and even C above middle C. The technical difficulties in the piano (and the wind parts) arise chiefly from awkward figurations that often use large leaps, whereas the textures remain relatively simple, as in his previous works. By now the problem of disjointedness that had appeared in some of Beethoven's earlier works had been largely overcome, and the music proceeds smoothly from one section to the next; most strikingly, the slow

[8] Johnson, *Beethoven's Early Sketches*, i. 245. The age is not quoted in KH.
[9] She was his second girl friend, his first being Jeanette d'Honrath from Cologne, who used to visit the Breuning family. The date of Beethoven's brief liaison with Maria Anna von Westerholt can be deduced from Wegeler's reference to it: he indicates that he heard about it only indirectly, and he was absent from Bonn from September 1787 to October 1789.

movement even leads into the finale without a break—a device so common in middle-period Beethoven works but rare before 1800. The development section in the first movement, however, is somewhat brief and makes little attempt to develop the exposition material. Indeed the trio as a whole, despite much attractive melodic writing, provides no evidence that Beethoven had mastered the art of motivic development, which was to become such a hallmark of his later style.

The combination of piano, flute, and bassoon also features in another work written about the same time (Hess 13). Only a fragment of this ambitious piece survives, headed 'Romance cantabile', in which the three instruments form a concertante group accompanied by an orchestra of first and second violins, first and second violas, bass (cello and perhaps double bass), and two oboes. It is clearly the middle movement of a larger work, for there are four empty staves at the bottom of the score each marked 'Romance tacet', presumably applying to horns and trumpets that had played in the previous movement. The Romance is in E minor, with a second section in E major; unfortunately the manuscript breaks off after only four bars of the major section, but there is no reason to suppose the rest of the work, including a finale probably in G major, was not written. Its date can be deduced by external means: the paper type is the same as in part of the autograph of the Trio, WoO 37, and the handwriting is very similar.[10]

Here, then, is Beethoven's largest work yet, at least in terms of orchestral size, as well as his first known attempt at writing for oboes and brass. It was surely composed for, and performed at, the Bonn court, where all the instruments named or implied could by this time be found. Indeed it was probably played several times, since the manuscript contains a number of compositional revisions enriching the texture, in a slightly later hand. The score also contains a number of sketches in a later hand (*c.* 1790?) in the blank staves at the bottom, and their presence may provide the reason why Beethoven bothered to preserve the manuscript when he moved to Vienna. Among these sketches is a cadenza in G for piano that could conceivably be for the lost first movement of the concertante, but apart from this we have no further clues about a work that was surely a major milestone in Beethoven's compositional development.

From the following three years, 1787–89, even less of Beethoven's compositional activities appears to survive. It is, of course, possible that he virtually abandoned composition during this period, for his everyday cares increased considerably, as we shall see, and he is known to have gone through a number of silent phases during his life when he felt unable to commit much to paper. But to be silent for so long, and at such an early age, seems improbable. Far more likely, he simply abandoned or mislaid most of his

---

[10] Johnson, *Beethoven's Early Sketches*, i. 245. Handwriting and paper studies by Johnson have produced an approximate date of composition for a large number of Beethoven's early works to 1798.

compositions from this period in later years, and they gradually disappeared. Either way, however, it is difficult to measure his progress, from the very limited material that can be dated to these years.

None the less, his development up to the beginning of 1787 had been sufficient to induce the Elector at last to approve and subsidize a journey to Vienna to study composition with Mozart. Details of the arrangements and costs are completely lacking; but the journey could not have taken place without the financial assistance of the Elector, who some years later could still remember the 'debts' that had resulted from the visit.

Beethoven set out from Bonn towards the end of March 1787, reaching Munich on 1 April and Vienna about six days later (Easter Eve). No documents survive relating to the meeting of the two great composers—all we have is second-hand anecdotes of uncertain reliability. Mozart is reported to have been extremely impressed by Beethoven's extemporization, and to have told bystanders: 'Keep your eyes on him; some day he will give the world something to talk about.'[11] Ries says that Beethoven regretted never hearing Mozart play, but Czerny claims that Beethoven did hear him and that his playing was 'choppy', with no legato. Most likely, then, Beethoven heard Mozart's playing, perhaps during a theory lesson, but never attended a performance as such.

Shortly after arriving in Vienna, Beethoven received news that his mother was ill, and so after a stay of barely two weeks he set out on the long road back to Bonn, passing through Munich on 25 April. He reached Bonn to find his mother very ill, and she died of consumption on 17 July. 'She was such a good, lovable mother to me, and my best friend,' he wrote later that year.[12] Her death placed many extra family burdens on Beethoven, which increased in the ensuing years, as his father declined further into alcoholism while his two younger brothers still needed support. Meanwhile her baby daughter Margaretha, who had been born in May 1786 and was the last of Beethoven's siblings, did not survive her mother by many months, passing away on 25 November 1787; and Beethoven himself was unwell for many months after his return from Vienna, suffering from what he described as asthma and melancholia, which would certainly have impeded compositional activity.

Whether Beethoven gained much from his brief encounter with Mozart is uncertain. Did he resolve to write a grand symphony, and a new piano concerto, as a result of the meeting? And what about Mozart? Was his next work, the String Quintet in G minor (K. 516, completed in May), written in an ultra-serious vein due to his encounter with this earnest, forceful youth; and did he venture into the remote key of E flat minor in both the first and third movements of the quintet after being struck by Beethoven's impressive quartet movement in that key? Whatever their cause, all these effects can certainly be observed.

[11] TF, 87.   [12] A-1.

The new symphony was to be in C minor, the same key as the Dressler Variations. (If Rovantini was commemorated in the variations, then surely nothing less than a symphony would suffice for Beethoven's own mother.) All that survives is a single draft on two staves, headed 'Sinfonia' and 'presto', which progresses till nearly the end of the exposition before petering out into short sketches.[13] Its date is uncertain, but the handwriting is in a transitional form that strongly suggests it comes from this dark age between 1786 and 1790.[14] Beethoven's piano quartet movement in E flat minor was still very much in his mind when he began this symphony, for the first nine notes of its opening theme are identical apart from their key. This is the first of many cases where he effectively discarded an earlier work, and then used it as a repository of material for new ones (the C major Quartet, WoO 36 No. 3, was to be used in a similar way). Beethoven evidently realized that the quartet as a whole was too close to Mozart to permit publication, and yet it contained some music that was too good to be wasted.

What is striking about the quartet movement and the symphony draft is the way the same opening theme is subsequently handled. As a genre, the symphony had developed into a grand, public form in which, especially with the Mannheim school of composers, the emphasis was on continual development and transition, even within the exposition, so as to create a broad sweep in the music; the sonata and quartet, by contrast, tended to concentrate on building a series of small motifs connected much more loosely. The movement in E flat minor was actually the most 'symphonic' among Beethoven's childhood works (which is probably why he chose it as the basis for his symphony draft), but the development of the main theme is much tighter and more rigorous still in the symphony draft. During the transition before the second subject, for example, the main theme (Ex. 2.2a) is fragmented, developed, heard in sequence, and thoroughly 'explored' (Ex. 2.2b) in a manner that was to become so characteristic of the Beethoven style. Even in the contrasting second subject, which makes use of a descending scalic figure, the arpeggio shape of the first subject is very conspicuous in augmentation in the bass line, heightening the sense of continuity and unity. The cohesion and the skill at motivic development evident here show a remarkable advance on his earlier music, and if the movement was ever completed, it must have seemed an outstanding achievement to those in the Bonn court.

The new concerto that Beethoven began during this period is also known only from a single leaf, and again the handwriting suggests the period 1787–9.[15] The leaf exhibits a ten-stave score, of which the lowest two staves have been filled with nine bars of piano figuration while the upper eight,

---

[13] 'Kafka' Miscellany (SV 185), f. 70. See Kerman ed., *Miscellany*, ii. 175–6, for a complete transcription.

[14] Johnson, *Beethoven's Early Sketches*, i. 222.

[15] 'Fischhof' Miscellany (SV 31), f. 15. See Johnson, *Beethoven's Early Sketches*, i. 366; ii. 71–3.

**Ex. 2.2** Hess 298

intended for the orchestra, have been left blank. The key of the concerto is B flat major, like his Second Piano Concerto, Op. 19, and its thematic material is sufficiently similar to Op. 19 to suggest that this itself was the work being composed, although it was comprehensively overhauled in later revisions. Which part of the movement is represented on the Bonn leaf has been a puzzle. Both the cadenza and the development section have been suggested, but a cadenza would not have been written out with blank orchestral staves above (in fact it would not have been written out at all but improvised), and the harmonic direction is wrong for the development section. The clue to the true location of the fragment is provided by an extended, unresolved 6–4 chord of F major, implying a delayed but emphatic cadence in that key; such an event almost invariably occurs only at the end of the solo exposition, before a central tutti in F. Indeed, a harmonic progression very similar to that in the nine-bar fragment occurs at just this point in Op. 19 (bars 173–9), although the melodic details are completely different.

Whatever the relationship of the fragment to Op. 19, its crucial significance is that it demonstrates unequivocally that Beethoven was composing a new piano concerto at some point during the period 1787–9, to follow the one in E flat of 1784, and that he reached at least as far as the end of the exposition in full-score format, with the leaf in question evidently being replaced by a revised version before the orchestral parts could be inserted. In all probability the work was completed and performed in Bonn at that time. Since the leaf survives by pure chance (it was saved so that its blank spaces could be used later for other sketches), it must be concluded that much else besides the concerto was probably lost from this period.

Other works apparently dating from this time include a Prelude in F minor (WoO 55), two Preludes in C major (Op. 39), and possibly some of the eight songs that later appeared in Beethoven's Op. 52 collection. For the F minor prelude, a copy now lost is reported to have borne the annotation 'aged 15', implying that it was probably composed in 1787; meanwhile the C major preludes exist in a copy which Beethoven himself dated 1789. The three preludes suggest that he had turned for inspiration, at least temporarily, from Mozart to Bach—no doubt encouraged by Neefe. The F minor one sounds perhaps the most Bachian of all his compositions, with its incessant quaver movement, three-part counterpoint, rigorous adherence to an obbligato style, and typically Baroque figuration. The C major preludes are only slightly less Baroque in style and figuration. Here Beethoven takes up Bach's systematic use of keys in the '48', but does so within a single piece. Each of the preludes modulates through the entire circle of fifths (using just the major keys); and in the second prelude, having done this once Beethoven does so again much more rapidly, changing key twelve times in as many bars, in a slightly ludicrous attempt to progress from where Bach left off. Beethoven may have written several other Bachian preludes (and perhaps some fugues too) during this period, but none survives. The C major preludes were published in December 1803 and the F minor in January 1805, all during a period when Beethoven was digging out early works for publication. But for this activity, these preludes might not have survived either.

Thus Beethoven's musical occupations evidently continued more or less unabated after the death of his mother, although details are scanty. They received a great boost in late January 1788 with the arrival in Bonn of Count Ferdinand Waldstein (1762–1823). Waldstein, a cultured man who was admitted to the Bonn *Lesegesellschaft* almost immediately and soon became one of its leading members, had the rare advantage of being extremely rich and extremely musical, and is even said to have advised Beethoven on how to improvise variations on a theme.[16] He rapidly recognized Beethoven's ability and discreetly supplemented his meagre income from time to time. The Beethovens' resources had been considerably depleted by the composer's visit to Vienna and his mother's lengthy illness, and Waldstein's support was doubtless much needed. In fact Waldstein seems to have become Beethoven's leading patron during his last few years in Bonn.

[16] WR, 19–20.

Another stimulus to Beethoven's development came with the reopening of the opera theatre in Bonn in 1789. After Maximilian Franz had disbanded the theatre of his predecessor, temporary arrangements for a reduced season had been made in subsequent years, but now the activities were put on a firm footing again. Over a dozen operas were produced in the early months of 1789, including Mozart's *Die Entführung* and works by Salieri, Grétry, Cimarosa, and others; and the following season (13 October 1789 to 23 February 1790) included Mozart's *Le Nozze di Figaro* and *Don Giovanni*, which had been composed as recently as 1786 and 1787 respectively. Beethoven would have participated in all these works as a member of the orchestra, and was thus able to experience some of the latest and greatest operatic works of the time. It is perhaps surprising that his own involvement in writing music for the stage was so slow to develop. He was, however, learning the dramatic power of such music, and would shortly put that understanding to good use.

# 3

# Farewell to Bonn (1790–2)

By 1790 the number of musicians at the Electoral Court in Bonn had swollen to forty-nine. Beethoven and Neefe were the organists, while Beethoven was also listed as one of the four viola players. Nobody was officially listed as a composer, but several were capable, while one of the basses acted as principal copyist. Beethoven's physical appearance as an adult was described thus by Fischer: 'Short in stature, broad in the shoulders, short neck, large head, round nose, dark brown complexion; he always bent forward slightly when he walked. In the house he was called The Spaniard, even as a boy.'[1] This description is borne out by others and by various portraits from later in life.

Beethoven's activities, which are poorly documented for the years 1787–9, with few known compositions, become much clearer from 1790. His output from then on was profoundly affected by the deaths of two men in faraway Vienna that year: Emperor Joseph II and Prince Nikolaus Esterházy, who died on 20 February and 28 September respectively. In the first case the effect was immediate and direct; in the second it was long-term and wholly indirect. When news of Joseph II's death reached Bonn on 24 February, the electoral court there went into mourning at once, with the remainder of the opera season being cancelled. Four days later the young poet Severin Anton Averdonk (brother of the girl who had shared the stage at Beethoven's debut in 1778) presented to the *Lesegesellschaft* a newly written text for use as a commemorative cantata, and the task of composing the music was entrusted to Beethoven. The choice of composer is significant, for it provides further evidence that his talent had been recognized, and that he must therefore have written far more in the previous three years than now survives, for otherwise someone else such as Neefe or Reicha would surely have been chosen.

The performance of the *Cantata on the Death of Emperor Joseph II* (WoO 87) was due to take place on 19 March, but was cancelled two days beforehand for 'various reasons'. A glance at what Beethoven composed reveals what some of the reasons must have been. The most striking feature is perhaps the size of the work—nearly 800 bars, scored for double wind,

---

[1] TF, 72.

horns, strings, chorus, and soloists. This makes it both longer and larger than any known earlier work by him. To compose a work of this size in under nineteen days would be extremely difficult for any composer, especially as time would have had to be allowed for copying parts and rehearsal. Thus it seems unlikely that the work was ready in time. Beethoven was clearly unwilling to compromise his standards in order to produce something usable, for the setting is on a conspicuously elaborate scale, with much repetition of the words, lengthy instrumental interludes, and fairly full scoring in each of the six movements.

Even if Beethoven did miraculously complete the cantata in time, the performers would have found it extremely difficult compared with what they were accustomed to. There is little use of standard figurations that could easily be sight-read, or of straightforward and predictable melodic lines. Instead the melodies are often angular, with widespread chromaticism and several very awkward leaps for both voices and instruments, while several of the rhythmic patterns are confusing to look at or to execute. The bass aria 'Da kam Joseph', in particular, demands a formidable vocal technique and a range of over two octaves. The cantata's difficulties are not of the showy variety but are integral to Beethoven's grand and complex design, and they greatly enhance the expression of the words by stretching the bounds of convention. He had clearly learnt much from the dramatic style of the operas in which he had been participating, and now put that knowledge to good use in music that is highly dramatic in character. He also had great sympathy for the ideas in the text, and affection for Joseph II himself. Not only was the emperor the brother of Beethoven's own patron, but he had been an enlightened reformer who appealed greatly to the liberal intellectual climate in Bonn. Thus the combination of Beethoven's personal feelings and his recent experiences in opera provided the right ingredients for an outstanding work that is undoubtedly one of the finest and most original of his early period. Two passages in the cantata also have close links with the music of his opera, *Fidelio* (see Chapter 9).

Beethoven's originality is evident right from the opening, with the words 'Todt! Todt!' ('Death! Death!'), which is perhaps inevitably in C minor. One of the most notable features of his style in general is how he often manipulates different registers for expressive purposes, in ways that draw attention to the contrast between them. No previous composer had exploited register as a compositional parameter to anything like the same extent, and the opening bars of this cantata provide a highly prophetic and striking example of his use of the technique (Ex. 3.1). The contrast in register is reinforced by a contrast between strings and wind, and between unisons and full chords, and it is continued and intensified in the following bars until the entry of the chorus. The aria 'Da kam Joseph' also exploits different registers of both voice and orchestra in a dramatic and original way, vividly illustrating the image of Joseph driving away the 'raging monster' of fanaticism. The whole cantata is thoroughly characteristic of Beethoven, and Brahms's

**Ex. 3.1** WoO 87/I

comment on seeing the score for the first time in 1884 is particularly apt: 'Even if there were no name on the title page none other could be conjectured—it is Beethoven through and through!'[2]

The *Joseph* Cantata was shortly followed by a matching one (WoO 88) celebrating the elevation of his successor Leopold II as Emperor. Again the text was provided by Averdonk, and the scope and scoring are similar except that the work is slightly shorter and Beethoven adds trumpets and drums to suit the festive nature of the text. It is far less striking than the *Joseph* Cantata but again contains many original and prophetic ideas, such as the subdominant start for the aria 'Fliesse, Wonnezähre'. Leopold was elected as Emperor on 30 September 1790, with his coronation nine days later, and so the cantata was probably composed about that time. As with the *Joseph* Cantata, there is no evidence that it reached an actual performance, but one or both cantatas may have been at least tried out at some stage.

Works of this size and complexity could not have been composed without some preliminary drafting, and it is significant that the cantatas are among the first completed Beethoven works for which proper sketches survive (earlier sketch-like material consists mostly of score fragments or drafts for abandoned works). The sketches already display many features that remained characteristic of Beethoven's sketching style throughout his life, particularly their jumbled and fragmentary nature. A short sketch for the *Joseph* Cantata is jotted down on the blank back page of the autograph score of a song ('Klage', WoO 113).[3] Meanwhile the surviving sketch for the *Leopold* Cantata relates to the aria 'Fliesse, Wonnezähre', and shows a draft of nearly forty bars, followed by a group of short variants on lower staves.[4] The draft is written on two staves as if for piano, but much of the lower stave is blank, and it was not long before Beethoven was economizing on space by using a single stave for most of his sketching. Another striking feature of the draft is how different it is from the final version: the main orchestral theme is in place, but the continuation is quite different and would have required much work to turn it into the existing aria. Thus even at this early stage Beethoven must have already been indulging in extensive and elaborate sketching of the type associated mainly with his later years, although a very large proportion of these early sketches is now lost.

The rest of the sketch-leaf is, characteristically, filled not by sketches for the same movement or even the same work, but a variety of jottings which did not develop into finished works.[5] Some are pianistic in texture, usually about two to six bars in length, as in Ex. 3.2. Such jottings can be found very widely amongst Beethoven's sketches of the 1790s, and they are probably best interpreted as written-down versions of ideas that occurred to him during the course of improvisation, for each one explores a distinctive

---

[2] Cited from TF, 120.
[4] Kerman ed., *Miscellany*, ii. 89–90.
[3] Johnson, *Beethoven's Early Sketches*, i. 245–6.
[5] Ibid., ii. 227–9.

**Ex. 3.2** SV 185, f. 88v

and unusual figuration, texture or sonority independent of any context. If this interpretation is correct, then Beethoven probably spent many hours extemporizing in private, with manuscript paper close by for noting down his best or most original ideas (his interest in extemporizing was indeed noted by a number of witnesses over the next few years). The other main group of sketches found on this page is of a type already mentioned—an abandoned draft for a symphony, this time in C major: there is a lengthy but rather thin slow introduction marked 'Allegretto', followed by some ideas for an ensuing 'presto'. These sketches confirm his continuing ambitions to write a symphony, although he was clearly not yet ready to do so.

The death of Prince Nikolaus Esterházy, who had been Haydn's employer for nearly thirty years, had no immediate impact on Beethoven. But the prince's successor, Prince Anton, who had much less interest in music, promptly disbanded his orchestra, and for the first time Haydn was able to fulfil a long-held desire to travel abroad. His name was already known in Spain, France, Germany, and England, and he could be assured of a warm reception in any of these places. It was Johann Peter Salomon, a native of Bonn but now a concert manager in London, who persuaded Haydn to come to England, after visiting him in Vienna. This fortunate combination of circumstances meant that Haydn would inevitably pass through Bonn on his way to London. He arrived there on Christmas Day, a Saturday, and after Mass at the court chapel the following morning he was introduced to the Bonn musicians, some of whom then had dinner with him. Thus Beethoven and Haydn met for the first time. Their meeting was brief, however, and it is not known whether Beethoven was one of the favoured few at the dinner party. Haydn departed almost immediately to continue his journey to England, and it was not until his return visit on his way back to Vienna a year and a half later that anything significant resulted.

Beethoven's first major compositional task in 1791 was to write the music for a ballet devised by his patron Count Waldstein. This *Ritterballett* (Knight Ballet, WoO 1) was performed on 6 March (the Sunday in the Carnival season). Either through some confusion or by a deliberate piece of deception the music was reported as having been composed by Waldstein himself, for Beethoven did not indicate at the time that he was the composer. A glance at the score might lead one to believe that Waldstein had indeed written it, for it is far simpler than the two cantatas of 1790. Rhythms are straightforward and mostly in four-bar phrases, the key scheme is unadventurous, being based in and around D major throughout, and the harmony consists mainly of tonic and dominant chords. The work illustrates Beethoven's lifelong tendency to develop his compositional style not in a gradual and progressive manner but in an irregular way in which he sometimes seems to take a step sideways or even backwards before advancing in some new direction.

Here he is actually showing his awareness of the varying requirements of different genres. In all his music for dancing (and he was to write plenty more) he maintained a light and popular style, much closer to other composers than in any other genre, with strong but regular rhythms and simple harmonies. (The style occasionally infiltrated his more serious music— most notably in the finale of the *Eroica* and the fourth movement of his String Quartet, Op. 130.) The *Ritterballett* is, however, not quite as unsophisticated as it first appears. The first movement, for example, has a few irregular phrase lengths, a rather elaborate accompaniment pattern in the second violins, and a brief but unexpected excursion into D minor towards the end. The orchestration is also rich, varied, and imaginative; and, most notably, the work concludes with a lengthy Coda, which develops and resolves some of the earlier ideas. For example, a scale pattern that appears almost incidentally in the middle of the Trio section of No. 6 ('Trinklied', see Ex. 3.3a) resurfaces in the Coda, first in A major and then, with a gesture of finality and resolution, in the tonic at the very end (Ex. 3.3b).

Ex. 3.3

(a) WoO 1/VI

(b) WoO 1/VIII

Another work that can be dated to the first half of 1791 with reasonable confidence is a set of twenty-four variations on the aria 'Venni Amore' by Vincenzo Righini. The set was published around July by Schott's of Mainz, and is so prophetic of the later Beethoven style that it was for a long time thought to have been revised around 1800 for an edition published in 1802, since no copy of the original edition was known. Discovery in the 1980s of the original edition, which is essentially identical to that of 1802, has indicated that this work is actually one of the most remarkable from Beethoven's Bonn period, containing a veritable hoard of original ideas that anticipate his middle and even his late style.[6] His exploration of registral contrast has already been noted in the *Joseph* Cantata, but is now further developed in several variations, where the hands are at times up to four octaves apart (on a keyboard which was then limited to five octaves). Other particularly striking features are a very long coda, with abrupt and startling modulations to remote keys, and the idea of treating Righini's rests as if they were a motif for development. Perhaps the most astonishing variation is the penultimate one, marked 'Adagio sostenuto', in which the somewhat banal theme is utterly transformed into an entirely different world, as can be seen in the last four bars of each (Ex. 3.4a and b): the variation demonstrates how far Beethoven had progressed beyond the bounds of convention by early 1791, with exploitation of register, silence, rhythmic complexity, strange melodic lines, new harmonies, sharp dynamic contrast, and profound emotion.

Beethoven probably remained in and around Bonn during 1791 until about the end of August. At that point he set out for Mergentheim with about two dozen other members of the court orchestra, since the Elector was due to attend a grand meeting of the Teutonic Order there and wished to have some music to entertain him. The journey to Mergentheim was almost exactly the same distance as Beethoven's 1783 journey to Rotterdam, but in the opposite direction (such dualities are surprisingly common in his life and work). The musicians sailed up the Rhine and Main, and on reaching Aschaffenburg, beyond Frankfurt, Beethoven and a few other musicians visited Johann Sterkel, one of Germany's leading pianists.[7] Sterkel obligingly played to them, in a light, delicate and 'somewhat ladylike' manner very different from Beethoven's. Beethoven was then asked to take his turn. He was reluctant to do so as he always had an aversion to being put on show in front of people. Sterkel, however, managed to entice him into performing by questioning whether he could actually play his newly published Righini Variations, which Sterkel had noticed were exceedingly difficult. Stung by this remark, Beethoven promptly went to the piano. Neither man

---

[6] For a list of the main ones, see Cooper, *Creative Process*, 72.
[7] Two independent accounts of this visit survive, written by Wegeler and Simrock, and they agree in almost every detail.

Ex. 3.4  WoO 65

(a)

(b)

had his own copy of the work to hand, but Beethoven played the variations from memory as best he could, and then astonished everyone by improvising some additional ones, imitating Sterkel's peculiar manner exactly. Sterkel was full of admiration.

Beethoven's outstanding ability at extemporization also drew praise after he reached Mergentheim. Carl Junker, a minor composer, heard him there and wrote an extremely enthusiastic report, published in November 1791, about his improvising skills. Meanwhile the court orchestra, while in Mergentheim, found time to rehearse a cantata by Beethoven several times; they did not perform it at court, however, because it proved too difficult, with all the figuration 'completely unusual', as Simrock reported.[8] This was presumably either the *Joseph* Cantata or the *Leopold* Cantata.

The Elector's lengthy meeting at Mergentheim ended on 20 October, and the musicians returned to Bonn some time thereafter, beginning their new

---

[8] TF, 106.

opera season on 28 December, somewhat later than usual. Among the new works was Dittersdorf's *Das rote Käppchen*, premièred in Vienna in 1788 and now produced in Bonn in February 1792. This at once became very popular there, and its success evidently induced Beethoven to write a set of piano variations on one of its airs, 'Es war einmal ein alter Mann' (WoO 66). Though far less striking than the Righini Variations, they reveal Beethoven's humorous side. He was probably attracted to this particular air by a dramatic whole-bar rest, with pause, that Dittersdorf had inserted actually in the middle of a perfect cadence. Beethoven retains this rest in each of the thirteen variations, but frequently springs a surprise immediately after the suspense by changing register, dynamic, figuration, or even metre, with highly comical effect.

Another popular air from *Das rote Käppchen* was 'Ja, ich muss mich von ihr scheiden', and Beethoven also wrote a set of variations on this. The history of these variations, scored for piano trio and eventually published as Op. 44, was for long obscure and is still not wholly clear. When the work was published in 1804 the theme was not named, and it was assumed to be an original one by Beethoven himself (especially as it bears a superficial resemblance to some of his *Prometheus* and *Eroica* music) until the 1990s, when Sieghard Brandenburg identified it.[9] A brief sketch for the work dates from 1792, and the variations were probably completed then, shortly after the production of the opera, since their style points to a date well before 1800.[10]

During his last three years in Bonn Beethoven composed many more works, which cannot be precisely dated. Surprisingly little is piano music, but there are a short pair of movements, sometimes called a sonatina (WoO 50), that Beethoven gave to Wegeler, and two more sets of variations—a rather simple set of six for piano solo on a Swiss air (WoO 64), and a more elaborate set for piano duet on a theme by Waldstein (WoO 67). The latter work is normally described as containing eight variations, but there is actually a ninth, unnumbered variation followed by a lengthy coda; here, Beethoven startles the listener not by changing key several times as in the Righini set but by repeatedly changing the metre, concluding with a 'presto' ending which, like most of the preceding variations, demands a high level of technical skill from both players. These two sets of variations, and also the Dittersdorf set (WoO 66), were not published at the time, but copies of the three works were given to his friend Simrock, who started a music publishing business in 1793 and eventually published them all.

[9] See Weber-Bockholdt, 'Beethovens Opus 44'.

[10] Otto Jahn claimed he had seen a sketch for it in the sketchbook Grasnick 2 of 1799, but when Nottebohm examined this sketchbook the sketch could not be found (see N-II, 484). The sketchbook has several leaves missing, but those in the relevant section were already missing by 1830 and may well have been removed by Beethoven himself (see JTW, 85). Thus Jahn must have incorrectly identified some other sketch material: several sketches in the right part of the book are slightly similar to Op. 44, notably an unused one at the top of p. 64.

No piano sonatas and very few multi-movement instrumental works of any kind date from this period, making it difficult to trace any gradual evolution of Beethoven's sonata style between the works of the mid-1780s and those of the mid-1790s. The notable exception is a piano trio in E flat (WoO 38), which probably dates from 1791 (a little earlier, then, than the variations Op. 44 for the same instruments in the same key). No sources survive from his lifetime, but it was published in 1830. This is the first known Beethoven work to include a movement entitled 'Scherzo', but this appears instead of, rather than as well as, a slow movement, and it is possible that a slow movement has been lost. The first movement contains several notable features. The recapitulation begins with further development of the opening theme, so that the customary boundary between development section and recapitulation is somewhat blurred. In the exposition, the second subject veers briefly into B flat minor, but in the recapitulation it appears unexpectedly in F major; the change to F minor is then ingeniously used as a lever to shift the music back into the tonic. There is also a sizeable coda, conspicuously longer than in earlier sonata-form movements, although not nearly as substantial as those in some of the contemporary variation works.

The other important instrumental work from this period is a violin concerto in C (WoO 5). Only a fragment of the autograph score survives, containing the first 259 bars, but unlike uncompleted works it does not peter out gradually, coming instead to an abrupt halt at the end of the gathering, in the middle of the development section; this feature suggests that the rest of the movement, and probably the whole concerto, was completed at the time. This work, too, shows many original and striking features. The rising semitone at the end of the first phrase is developed symphonically as a fundamental motif for the work, creating a strong sense of integration. The opening ritornello contains several unexpected modulations, touching on A flat major at one point. Meanwhile the solo line uses several large leaps, including a particularly dramatic one of over three octaves (which is followed by a whole-bar general pause to intensify the drama). If this work continued as it begins, it was certainly a major achievement on Beethoven's part.

Many of Beethoven's compositions during his last three years in Bonn were vocal rather than instrumental. Apart from his two large-scale cantatas, he wrote several short Lieder and three arias with orchestral accompaniment. A few of the Lieder were printed in 1805 in his collection Op. 52, but most remained unpublished. The majority are unremarkable strophic settings, but a few are through-composed. Easily the most outstanding is 'Klage' (Lament), WoO 113. This is the first of several Beethoven works in a gentle E major that relate in some way to the night sky (in this case the poem is addressed to the moon). The presence of lengthy performance instructions in German ('Throughout the notes must be slurred and as much as possible held on and connected together') is a sign that Beethoven himself had great affection for the song. So, too, is the time he spent on it:

the first autograph score predates the *Joseph* Cantata of early 1790 (see above), but he then wrote out a revised score, and even made some further sketches for possible changes after he had left Bonn.[11] After a contemplative first section recalling past happiness, the music moves to E minor, with the instruction 'Here the movement becomes slower and slower'; the second half, marked 'very slow and sad' is then entirely in the minor, with some suitably anguished chromaticism, and the final chord actually has the minor third at the top, which is extremely rare in any music. This is a wonderfully profound and evocative setting, highly Romantic in conception and in many ways fifty years ahead of its time.

Of the three arias with orchestral accompaniment, two (WoO 89 and 90) are humorous German settings probably written for the singer Joseph Lux, who was noted for singing this type of music. The third, *Primo amore* (WoO 92) is quite different—a multi-sectional operatic *scena* for soprano, with a gentle opening, some accompanied recitative in the middle, and a brisk conclusion. For a long time this work was thought to date from the mid-1790s, partly because of its sophistication and partly because it was assumed Beethoven did not set Italian words until he began his studies with Salieri. But the handwriting is earlier and the paper is from Bonn, not Vienna, and so the work proves that, even before his studies with Salieri, there was little wrong with his setting of Italian. The music is closer to Mozart than most of his late Bonn works, and his confidence with standard operatic devices demonstrates how thoroughly he had absorbed the style of Italian opera from his experiences in performing in the court theatre during this period.

Haydn left England at the end of June 1792 and stopped again at Bonn the following month on his way back to Vienna. By this time Beethoven had written a substantial number of very impressive works in a variety of genres, as has been demonstrated above. There were piano works, chamber works, ballet music, songs, and choral cantatas, while *Primo amore* hinted at potential as an opera composer. Although these works have received little attention since his death, most of them contain music that is striking and individual. Indeed, the level of originality and mastery of compositional technique displayed far exceeded what might be expected from a provincial composer of only twenty-one, and indicated a powerful, serious and elevated creative spirit. Any of the works described above would certainly have impressed Haydn, and he was probably shown some of them. Wegeler specifically mentions that Haydn was struck by an unspecified cantata (most likely the *Joseph* Cantata) when he had breakfast with the court orchestra at Bad Godesberg (near Bonn) and urged Beethoven to continue his studies. Beethoven, however, had effectively outgrown Bonn. There was nobody there who could bring him further in the art of composition, and he needed a more challenging environment in which to develop his skills.

[11] See Johnson, *Beethoven's Early Sketches*, i. 255, 99.

Vienna would be ideal, for there were many fine musicians there, and music—especially chamber music—had been reaching new levels of excellence. Thus it must have been at this meeting between Haydn and Beethoven in July 1792 that agreement was reached for Beethoven to go to Vienna to study with Haydn himself.

If Beethoven needed Vienna, Haydn must surely have perceived that Vienna equally needed Beethoven. Mozart had died the previous December, and his loss was keenly felt in the city, especially by those who preferred the more elevated style of music (such as Prince Karl Lichnowsky and Baron Gottfried van Swieten, who had both patronized Mozart and were shortly to patronize Beethoven). Most of the more serious composers such as Albrechtsberger and Haydn himself were of an older generation, while the more prominent younger composers tended to be preoccupied with the lighter type of theatre music. Vienna was clearly in need of a successor to Mozart, and Haydn probably recognized Beethoven as more likely to fulfil that role than anyone he knew in Vienna itself. Thus although Beethoven's visit was meant to be a temporary one, there was always the possibility that it would be extended indefinitely, and no time limit was fixed for his return.

Preparations for the trip had been completed by the beginning of November, and some urgency was lent to Beethoven's impending departure by the political situation. France invaded the Rhineland area and captured Mainz in October, and the threat to the Electoral court in Bonn was real and pressing. The Elector left his residence for a few weeks on 22 October, and there was no longer any immediate need for Beethoven's services. It is surely significant that, only two days later, some of Beethoven's friends began writing farewell wishes in a little album that he was to take with him: the proximity of dates suggests that, but for the French invasion, he might have been obliged to remain in Bonn until the end of the opera season four months later. Altogether fourteen friends entered farewell greetings in Beethoven's album, the latest ones dated 1 November, the eve of his departure. None of the court musicians appear (perhaps they produced a separate farewell album now lost) and there are some other surprising absentees. Only two of the Breunings (including Eleonore) made entries, and the only member of the nobility was Count Waldstein. His entry, however, is by far the most interesting for its prophetic vision:

Dear Beethoven! You are now going to Vienna in fulfilment of your long frustrated wishes. Mozart's Genius is still mourning and lamenting the death of its pupil. She found a refuge in the inexhaustible Haydn, but no occupation; through him she still wishes to be united with someone else. Through uninterrupted diligence you will receive: *Mozart's spirit from Haydn's hands*.
Bonn, 29 October 1792.
Your true friend Waldstein.[12]

---

[12] All the album entries including Waldstein's are in N-II, 138–44, and more fully in Schiedermair, *Der junge Beethoven*, 229–33.

The image of Beethoven as Mozart's true successor was by now deeply entrenched in the collective Bonn psyche, including Waldstein's, and it penetrated Beethoven's own mind to the extent that in his early years in Vienna he intensified his efforts to follow Mozart, copying out several passages from Mozart's music when working on similar compositions, and writing much music that shows unmistakable Mozartean influence. Meanwhile Haydn was rightly seen by Waldstein as a refuge rather than a home for Mozart's spirit. Haydn had been a close friend of Mozart and they had shared many ideals, but Haydn had his own very different spirit and, being much older than Mozart, was not suitable as an heir to him. What Waldstein could perhaps not perceive was that Beethoven, too, had a strong and independent spirit that was so different from Mozart's that he could never thoroughly absorb it. Schubert was to come much closer to doing so.

Beethoven left Bonn at 6.00 a.m. on Friday, 2 November, taking with him various personal mementoes and a large quantity of his music, both finished scores and sketches. Many pages amongst these manuscripts can have been of little use in Vienna and greatly added to the bulk of his baggage, but his lifelong reluctance to discard such material (for which posterity must be extremely grateful) was already in evidence. He also took a small memorandum book, known as his *Jugendtagebuch*, which he continued to use for jottings after reaching Vienna. This provides fascinating details about the first part of his journey, during which he was accompanied by an unidentified companion. The journey took them up the Rhine valley to Koblenz, and thence to Montebaur and Limburg through the war zone (had they been a day later, they might not have made it). When they reached Würges, a small village on the road to Frankfurt, Beethoven and his companion went their separate ways after calculating their expenses in the notebook; these expenses included a tip for the driver 'because the fellow drove us at the risk of a cudgelling right through the Hessian army driving like the devil'.[13] The remainder of the journey to Vienna is unrecorded, and Beethoven reached his destination on or shortly before 10 November, to begin a new chapter in his life.

[13] The complete notebook is transcribed in Busch-Weise, 'Jugendtagebuch'. The original is in London, British Library, Zweig MS 14.

# 4

# The conquest of Vienna (1792–5)

During the eighteenth century Vienna had become arguably the musical capital of Europe, and certainly of the German-speaking lands. With a population of around 200,000, it had attracted a large number of musicians from elsewhere (especially Bohemia), and provided enormous opportunities and challenges for an aspiring musician such as Beethoven. Opera flourished in the two Court theatres (the Burgtheater and the Kärntnertor Theatre), and church music was of a high quality. But it was in instrumental music that Vienna particularly excelled. Many noblemen supported a private orchestra, and there were also occasional public concerts. Although most of the private orchestras, including Esterházy's, were disbanded in the 1790s (more for social than economic reasons), the noblemen continued to support musicians in various ways, sponsoring private concerts and purchasing publications.

Beethoven, having no doubt been recommended by both Waldstein and Maximilian Franz, uncle of the new emperor Franz (Emperor Leopold had died in 1792), would have been immediately welcome in such circles. His most generous supporter in his early years in Vienna was Mozart's former patron Prince Karl Lichnowsky—probably almost from Beethoven's arrival, although there is no proven contact before 1794. Lichnowsky's eagerness to assist may have been sharpened by a sense of shame that he had not done more to help during Mozart's decline. He was a distant relative of Waldstein (he had married Countess Maria Christiane Thun, daughter of the sister-in-law of Waldstein's uncle, in 1788), and he apparently filled a somewhat similar role for Beethoven in Vienna to Waldstein's in Bonn.[1]

Whatever support the nobility may have provided for Beethoven, however, he received little help with the problems of everyday life. Some of these are revealed in his *Jugendtagebuch*. He lived first in an attic flat (45 Alstergasse) in the suburb of Alsergrund, but he soon moved to the ground floor of the house (the first floor was one of Lichnowsky's residences). Immediately on arrival in the city he made a list of planned expenditure: 'wood, wig-maker, coffee . . . overcoat, boots, shoes, piano desk, seal,

---

[1] See May, 'Lichnowsky', 30–1.

wood, writing desk, piano desk [again!], dancing master . . .', and he wrote down the address of a dancing master.[2] (Dancing was a necessary social accomplishment, although Beethoven was reportedly no good at it. He may also have wished to consult a dancing master for advice about composing appropriate dances.)

These needs required considerable outlay, and the *Jugendtagebuch* gives an insight into his immediate financial problems. The main currency in Vienna was the silver florin or gulden, which was divided into 60 kreuzers. Also in use was the gold ducat, normally worth four-and-a-half florins (though its value varied at times). The cost of living in Vienna was higher than a few years earlier, and higher than in Bonn. In 1793 it was calculated that an unmarried middle-class gentleman with a fairly basic lifestyle (a description that would apply broadly to Beethoven) would require 775 florins per year, spent as follows:[3]

| accommodation | 144 fl. |
|---|---|
| heat/light | 30 |
| food | 365 |
| clothing | 170 |
| laundry | 30 |
| miscellaneous | 36 |

Beethoven's own figures for monthly expenditure around January 1793 show a comparable picture, although he spent rather less on meals and a little more on accommodation:[4]

| house rent | 14 fl. |
|---|---|
| piano [rent] | 6 fl. 40 kr. |
| heating [per day] | 12 kr. [= 6 fl./month in winter] |
| food with wine | 16 fl. 30 kr. |

He also needed to pay for clothing, tuition, admission to musical events, and other miscellaneous items such as manuscript paper. He had been promised a subsidy towards his expenses by the Elector, but noted on arrival in Vienna that he had received only 25 ducats, and commented: 'In Bonn I counted on receiving 100 ducats here, but in vain. I have to equip myself completely anew.'[5] Perhaps he intended to send this information to Maximilian Franz or some new, Viennese, patron, in an attempt to obtain further funding. By 12 December he had only 15 ducats left, and his quarterly salary of 50 florins plus another 50 that were regularly transmitted to him through his father (as agreed some years earlier), was clearly going to be woefully inadequate. Similar financial problems were to beset him repeatedly throughout his life.

---

[2] Busch–Weise, 'Jugendtagebuch', 71–2.
[3] Figures taken from Hanson, 'Incomes', 178.     [4] Busch–Weise, 'Jugendtagebuch', 74.
[5] Ibid., 72–3.

During his first year in Vienna Beethoven maintained contact with Bonn through various letters written or received, although details are scanty. No doubt he heard from his brothers that their father died on 18 December 1792, but this time he did not return. He did, however, write to the Elector in April pointing out that the 50 florins per quarter formerly paid through his father should henceforth be paid direct to him, and the Elector agreed to this. Thus Beethoven continued to receive quarterly payments of 100 florins throughout 1793. Meanwhile his friend Simrock, who had for some years run a music shop in Bonn, began publishing music. Almost his first publication was Beethoven's WoO 66, one of the three sets of variations that the composer had left with him before departure; this appeared in autumn 1793, and Simrock sent him a copy (Beethoven was displeased not to be sent more copies). Beethoven also wrote to Neefe and several other Bonn friends during the course of 1793. One of these letters, to Eleonore von Breuning,[6] refers to an 'unfortunate quarrel' that they had had shortly before he left Bonn and indicates a problem that was to remain with him throughout his life: his impulsive behaviour and his tendency to become angry too readily, resulting in regret and pleas for forgiveness. This trait is reflected in much of his music, with its sudden dissonant outbursts and rash modulations, although in his music the apparent impulsiveness is of course fully under control.

Beethoven's main purpose in visiting Vienna had been to study composition with Haydn, and he began shortly after arrival, continuing throughout 1793. Haydn's teaching was based mainly on Fux's *Gradus ad Parnassum*, and his customary method was to teach the rules of counterpoint (such as those concerning parallel fifths) before making the student work through exercises in each species of counterpoint in two voices, then each species in three voices, then in four, resulting in about 300 exercises altogether. Beethoven's copy of the rules is lost, but 245 of his exercises survive, some with corrections probably in Haydn's hand.[7] It has sometimes been assumed that such a large number of exercises was spread through most of the year. However, it has not hitherto been noted that the ink used in these exercises is absolutely and strikingly consistent, while other Beethoven manuscripts from the same year show a variety of inks, mostly of a darker shade.[8] The conclusion must be, therefore, that these exercises were written rapidly, in perhaps less than six weeks. Beethoven's numerous errors also suggest a certain hastiness in his completion of the exercises. Haydn marked a few of the errors, but he did not pedantically annotate every one;

---

[6] A-7.

[7] See Nottebohm, *Beethoven's Studien*, 21–43. The original MS is in Vienna, Gesellschaft der Musikfreunde, A75. I.

[8] See Cooper, 'Ink'. The ink in the counterpoint exercises for Haydn appears to match type C, which is found on three 'Kafka' leaves of the same paper type, but never at the beginning of the leaf.

many were probably just discussed orally, and it cannot be assumed from the unmarked ones, as many writers have done, that he took insufficient care with his pupil's work. One notable feature of the exercises is that they were based in the church modes, enabling Beethoven to become thoroughly acquainted with composing in the modal system—a sound he was to return to in some of his late works.

According to a well-known and widely believed account written by Johann Schenk in 1830, Beethoven grew dissatisfied with Haydn's teaching after about six months, and from then on Schenk secretly helped Beethoven with his counterpoint exercises, without payment; Beethoven had to write out each exercise after Schenk had corrected it, so that Haydn would think it was Beethoven's own work. There are, however, inaccuracies and inconsistencies in Schenk's account, and it cannot be reconciled with the 245 counterpoint exercises in Beethoven's hand. This manuscript can hardly be the fair copy incorporating Schenk's corrections, since it contains a large number of grammatical errors but no obvious copying errors. It could be the version presented initially to Schenk (since the annotations have not been confirmed as being in Haydn's hand); but if so, Schenk overlooked a surprisingly large number of errors, and it would be odd that Beethoven preserved this version rather than the corrected one. Coupled with numerous other inaccuracies in Schenk's account, however, these problems indicate that the entire story was probably invented by Schenk in an attempt at self-aggrandizement.[9]

In addition to counterpoint exercises, Beethoven's studies probably involved looking at scores and in some cases discussing them with Haydn, who tended to prefer this method of teaching.[10] Beethoven also studied some works by copying them out—his handwritten copy of Haydn's Quartet, Op. 20 No. 1 still survives, although it probably dates from the following year. For the rest of 1793 he was evidently composing, practising and improvising on his own, and performing at private or semi-public musical events (most often extemporizing rather than playing set pieces). He may also have done some teaching. Evidence for his private improvisations comes from numerous manuscripts that can be dated to 1793 on the basis of paper type and handwriting. Many of these show the same kind of written-down fragments that were discussed in Chapter 3: short, disconnected ideas for piano, usually with some striking texture or figuration that was worth recording for possible future use in a composition, or in an improvisation before an audience.

As well as these proto-compositions, several actual works were completed during 1793. In some cases their dates were established only in the 1970s through study of paper types and handwriting. Most popular of these works was a set of variations (WoO 40) on 'Se vuol ballare' from Mozart's *Marriage of Figaro*. This is scored for piano and violin, and

---

[9] Cf. Webster, 'Haydn and Beethoven', 10–14.     [10] Ibid., 17.

Beethoven began sketching it in Bonn before completing it in Vienna, where it proved so popular that he was, by his own account, pestered to publish it;[11] it appeared at the end of July 1793, as his Opus 1. He was actually reluctant to publish any sets of variations at that date, as he wanted to wait until he had 'some more important works', so as to make a bigger impact; but after performing it before audiences he was afraid that other composers would, as sometimes happened, 'note down on the following day many of my original ideas and proudly palm them off as their own. Now as I foresaw that such things would soon be published, I decided to forestall them.'[12]

Thus Beethoven was aware that the work displayed many original features, which had clearly made a striking impression in performance. Although the theme itself is by Mozart, there is very little figuration in the ensuing variations that bears more than a passing resemblance to his style, and much that is quite overtly Beethovenian, such as his exploitation of contrasting registers and sudden dynamic changes. One of his most characteristic passages occurs in the coda, where the right hand (and later the left) has to play a trill and a melody at the same time with different fingers (Ex. 4.1). Evidently this technique was previously unknown, and Beethoven wanted 'to embarrass those Viennese pianists', whom he perceived as rivals, by writing something they could not play properly. When he sent a dedicatory copy to Eleonore von Breuning back in Bonn, however, he urged her not to be discouraged by this difficult passage. 'For the composition is so arranged that you need only play the trill and can leave out the other notes, since these appear in the violin part as well.'[13] This combination of mischievous wit and striking originality is highly characteristic of Beethoven.

**Ex. 4.1** WoO 40

---

[11] See A-7.     [12] A-10 and A-9.

[13] A-9. The copy was evidently sent in November 1793 (see BB-11), not June 1794 as suggested in Anderson, *Letters*.

Another work that occupied him during 1793 was his Piano Concerto in B flat, eventually published as Op. 19. This had been begun and probably completed in Bonn (see Chapter 2), but evidence suggests he wrote out a new, revised score during 1793, presumably for some unrecorded private performance. Fragments of cadenza sketches dating from the same time confirm that he must have played it somewhere that year. At this stage the work had an earlier finale than the present one, but this became separated from the rest of the manuscript (which is lost) and is now known as a separate work (WoO 6). Its theme shows typical finale characteristics and bears a passing resemblance to that of the first Violin Sonata (Op. 12 No. 1), and the movement is in standard sonata-rondo form. Its most remarkable feature is its inclusion of an extended andante section in E flat, which functions as the contrasting middle section. This sounds quite alien to the rest of the movement, and it may even have been included instead of a slow movement, since the present slow movement was composed only later and no earlier one is known. Either way, however, the result is a highly unusual structure that anticipates the compound movements found in some of Beethoven's late works.

Another concerto from 1793 is one for oboe (Hess 12), but unfortunately the score is lost. All that survives is a copy of the opening bars of each of the three movements, plus some extended sketches for the slow movement, but Beethoven may well have expended more effort on this work than on any other during the year and it was almost certainly performed on some occasion at this date. Also surviving only fragmentarily is a quintet in E flat for oboe, three horns and bassoon (Hess 19), for which we have the middle portion but not the beginning or end. Another work for wind instruments written about the same time was an octet in the same key, published posthumously and eventually known as Op. 103. These two works were no doubt composed in response to Vienna's seemingly insatiable demand for wind music. *Harmoniemusik*, as it was known, had become extremely popular in the time of Mozart, who had made important contributions to it. Its typically light, elegant, and graceful style suited Mozart better than Beethoven, but he adapted to it well, and the Octet displays more of Mozart's spirit than almost any other work. Only occasionally are there hints of the Beethoven style, such as the almost obsessive development of a little semiquaver motif from the first subject, or the use of E flat minor at the start of the Menuetto.

In the autograph this Menuetto, the third movement, is followed by the first eight bars of an Andante, which have been crossed out.[14] The Octet must therefore have been designed originally with five movements, as in a number of divertimenti of the period, for it is almost inconceivable that such an Andante would be used as a finale. Beethoven then decided to

---

[14] See Johnson, *Beethoven's Early Sketches*, i. 407; Johnson suggests this movement was to be the finale of the Octet.

include just the usual four movements, and so he wrote out the Andante separately as an independent work, headed 'Rondo' (WoO 25). This is scored for the same combination of instruments, but the horns have much greater prominence here, and the very unusual sound of muted horns just before the end is a particularly lovely effect. Both the Octet and Rondo are written on Viennese paper, contradicting Thayer's assertion that it was 'improbable that Beethoven would have found either incentive or occasion soon after reaching Vienna to write pieces of this character'.[15]

In November 1793 Beethoven assembled some recently completed works to send to Maximilian Franz as evidence of his progress, and wrote a slightly apologetic letter indicating that he had spent much of the year studying music rather than composing, and expressing the hope that he would be able to send something better the following year as a result. Haydn wrote to the Elector at the same time, commenting briefly on the works being sent:

I am taking the liberty of sending to your Reverence . . . a few pieces of music—a quintet, an eight-voice 'Parthie', an oboe concerto, a set of variations for the piano and a fugue, composed by my dear pupil Beethoven who was so graciously entrusted to me. They will, I flatter myself, be graciously accepted by your Reverence as evidence of his diligence beyond the scope of his own studies. On the basis of these pieces, expert and amateur alike cannot but admit that Beethoven will in time become one of the greatest musical artists in Europe, and I shall be proud to call myself his teacher.[16]

The copies sent to the Elector do not survive, but the first four works on Haydn's list correspond exactly to the four that Beethoven is believed to have completed in Vienna that year. The quintet is almost certainly Hess 19; the eight-voice Parthie must be the Octet (the autograph of which is headed 'Parthia'); and the oboe concerto is the lost Hess 12. The set of variations for piano is more puzzling, since Beethoven's earlier sets had been written in Bonn (Simrock had copies) and no more are known before 1795; but Haydn was probably referring to the *Figaro* Variations for piano and violin. Indeed it would be surprising if this work were not sent to the Elector, since it was the only one yet published in Vienna. Moreover the printed title page describes it as variations 'pour le clavecin ou piano-forte', with the violin part 'ad lib.'.[17] Haydn's loose description of 'variations for piano' is therefore compatible with it. The one item unidentified is the fugue. This may be completely lost, but it could be one of the fugues now associated with Beethoven's studies with Albrechtsberger in 1794. Of these, the most likely candidate is the Fugue in E minor for string trio (Hess 29).

The Elector's reply, dated 23 December, must have been a shock to Haydn:

---

[15] TF, 122.          [16] TF, 144.

[17] This was, of course erroneous since the violin part is essential. Indeed, Beethoven immediately demanded that the title page be altered, and in later impressions the violin part was duly described as 'oblige'. See KH, 483–4.

The music of young Beethoven which you sent me I received with your letter. Since, however, this music, with the exception of the fugue, was composed and performed here in Bonn before he departed on his second journey to Vienna, I cannot regard it as progress made in Vienna. . . . I very much doubt that he has made any important progress in composition and in the development of his musical taste during his present stay, and I fear that, as in the case of his first journey to Vienna, he will bring back nothing but debts.[18]

If taken at face value these comments are damning, suggesting that Beethoven deceived Haydn and tried to deceive the Elector. The manuscript material for the four works in question, however, paints a very different picture. The only one of the four for which extensive sketches survive on Bonn paper is the *Figaro* Variations; but there are further substantial sketches for this on Vienna paper, indicating that the work did not reach its final version in Bonn. The other three works are unequivocally Viennese: extensive sketches for the second movement of the Concerto and the third of the Octet, and the autographs of the Octet and the Quintet, were all written on Vienna paper; the remaining manuscript sources are lost, and the only sign of any pre-Vienna activity on these works is a tiny four-bar motif from the Octet, written on a Bonn leaf but perhaps not until the autograph was being written out in Vienna.[19] Although it is conceivable that all four works had been completed in Bonn and were merely revised (though rather thoroughly) in Vienna, there is no evidence, apart from the Elector's letter, that this was the case. Moreover, if Beethoven were submitting works merely revised, why did he not include the impressive and newly revised B flat Piano Concerto? And why would he write to Simrock in August 1794, 'Have you performed my Parthie yet?',[20] if the Octet were a work already heard in Bonn before his departure? Thus the Elector or his advisers must have confused these four works with others written by Beethoven before he left Bonn, and Haydn was fully justified in sending him them as evidence of Beethoven's progress.

A further dispute with the Elector concerned finance. Haydn's letter claims that Beethoven was allotted only a hundred ducats (roughly 450 florins) for the year—a sum so insufficient that Haydn had had to lend him a further 500 florins. The Elector replied that Beethoven's allocation was 500 florins, plus his regular salary that amounted to 400 florins. If this was true, then Beethoven should have had almost enough for the year, especially if one adds on what the publisher paid him for the *Figaro* Variations (which Beethoven described as a good fee, although he would have been lucky to receive more than 40 florins). There is, however, no record of the hundred ducats being paid—only the 25 that Beethoven received on arrival, plus the

[18] TF, 145.
[19] Johnson, *Beethoven's Early Sketches*, passim.
[20] A-12.

400 florins of his regular salary. His total income (including any subsistence from other patrons), and how far it fell short of his needs, are therefore unclear; what is certain is that he did not live extravagantly, and probably needed all he borrowed from Haydn.

Thus the conventional picture of Beethoven's relationship with Haydn in 1793 needs adjusting on three counts. Haydn probably took far more care with Beethoven's exercises than would appear from the few annotations. Schenk's story of helping Beethoven secretly can for the moment be dismissed. And Beethoven did not attempt to deceive Haydn and the Elector by sending works that had been finished before he moved to Bonn. The relationship between the two great composers was therefore more friendly throughout 1793 than has been assumed. Beethoven's *Jugendtagebuch* records that he paid for them to have chocolate and coffee together in November that year, while Haydn lent him a much-needed sum of money to help with his expenses. Beethoven was not fully satisfied with Haydn's teaching, and claimed later that he had never learned anything from him. However, he saw no reason to change teacher until Haydn's departure for his second visit to England on 19 January 1794.

Haydn's departure would have been a natural moment for Beethoven to end his studies in Vienna and return to Bonn. Indeed the Elector actually suggested in his letter of 23 December: 'I am wondering therefore whether he had not better come back here in order to resume his services.'[21] Instead, however, Haydn arranged for Beethoven to continue his studies in Vienna with Johann Albrechtsberger, a noted theorist, composer, and leading disciple of the Fux tradition of learned counterpoint. In the absence of Haydn, he was the obvious choice. Maximilian Franz visited Vienna early in 1794 and presumably endorsed this new arrangement; but he terminated Beethoven's salary, with the last payment being in February, covering the first quarter of the year. Beethoven was allowed to remain 'without salary in Vienna, until recalled';[22] but the recall never came, and before the end of the year the Elector himself had been driven out of Bonn for good by the French.

Who supported Beethoven after March is unclear, but he was not left penniless. Waldstein was also in Vienna during the early part of 1794, and he may have made sure that other noblemen, in particular Lichnowsky, took over Maximilian's role thereafter, although Beethoven had no formal arrangement with Lichnowsky until 1800. Meanwhile, Beethoven's links with Bonn were further loosened around May 1794, when his brother Carl joined him in Vienna, leaving his other brother Johann as the only family member still in Bonn.

Study with Albrechtsberger was strict and methodical, and Beethoven visited him three times a week, at least initially. The teaching was based

---

[21] TF, 145.    [22] TF, 168.

mainly on Albrechtsberger's own *Anweisung zur Composition*, and proceeded from species counterpoint, through fugues for two, three, and four voices (based on a series of thirty fugue subjects provided by Albrechtsberger), on to invertible counterpoint at the octave, tenth, and twelfth.[23] It is extremely fortunate that this material survives, for it provides an invaluable window into what must have been an absolutely fascinating series of tutorials, and it reveals much about both Beethoven's ability and his difficulties. Albrechtsberger's view of him, according to Ries, was that he was 'always so stubborn and so bent on having his own way that he had had to learn many things through hard experience which he had refused earlier to accept through instruction'.[24] Certainly Beethoven's exercises, though extremely musical and well-written, confirm that he was not very systematic at grasping some of the more subtle rules of counterpoint, and there are occasional infelicities of part-writing. Albrechtsberger was quick to spot and correct these, and he was also able to suggest numerous improvements or alternatives to what Beethoven submitted. In the two-voiced fugue quoted as Ex. 4.2a,[25] Beethoven's stretto is inexact (bars 25–7); he then introduces unnecessary imitation in the lower voice in bars 28–9, resulting in a rather aimless flow to the music in these and the ensuing bars until the cadence in bar 34. Albrechtsberger's amendments (Ex. 4.2b) create exact stretto for the entire theme, followed by free counterpoint up to the cadence. He also eliminates the unsatisfactory unison in bar 26, the octave in bars 29 and 32, and the fourth in bar 32, while removing redundant bars to tighten up the phrase, and introducing an extra suspension (bar 27) to increase the momentum. Such changes demonstrate Albrechtsberger's extraordinary mastery of contrapuntal technique and reveal him as a very able teacher. Beethoven can surely have had few complaints here.

Beethoven continued his studies with Albrechtsberger for a little over a year, and nearly two hundred pages of exercises survive. It is impossible to be certain how far they affected his style in general. What they did provide for him, however, was much greater confidence in using contrapuntal devices of the kind learnt with Albrechtsberger, and more awareness of the importance of good part-writing. Albrechtsberger's attention to detail must also have reinforced Beethoven's view that a composer should not be satisfied with what is good, but constantly seek better alternatives.

Beethoven's studies with Albrechtsberger were supplemented in 1794 by thrice-weekly violin lessons with Schuppanzigh. Ignaz Schuppanzigh became the leader of a string quartet at Prince Lichnowsky's about that time, but it may have been his father who gave Beethoven tuition. We hear nothing of piano tuition at this date: perhaps Beethoven was by then so advanced on the instrument that he had little to learn from anyone in Vienna. But he continued working at the instrument on his own.

[23] See Nottebohm, *Beethoven's Studien*, 47–193, which includes a large number of examples.
[24] WR, 75.  [25] Taken from Nottebohm, *Beethoven's Studien*, 80.

**Ex. 4.2**    Fugue in D minor

(a)

(b)  The same, amended by Albrechtsberger

The intensity of all this study left him little time for composing, and the number of works completed in 1794 is even smaller than in 1793—hardly more than a few songs. This was the period, however, when he finished preparing the ground for his launch as a major Viennese composer. He was fully aware that he was nearing the end of his apprenticeship period, as is evident from a resolution jotted down in his *Jugendtagebuch* around the beginning of the year, most likely on New Year's Day itself: 'Courage. In spite of all weaknesses of the body, my spirit shall rule. You are 25 years old; this year must determine the complete man—nothing must remain undone.'[26] Here he makes himself two years older than reality, indicating

[26] Busch–Weise, 'Jugendtagebuch', 77.

continuing casualness towards his age; but far more significant are his characteristic determination to succeed, come what may, and his implied ambition to conquer the musical world of Vienna after thorough preparation, which was nearly complete. At about the same date he noted down someone else's report on him: 'Another six months in c[ounterpoint] and he can work on whatever he wants.'[27] This comment is presumably Haydn's, perhaps sent to Albrechtsberger when Beethoven changed teachers, and much more specifically concerns his musical progress. But it, too, suggests that the end of Beethoven's apprenticeship as a composer was close at hand.

The timing of major events in Beethoven's life seems as uncanny as the timing of major events within his compositions. Sometimes it was fortuitous, as when his move to Vienna closely coincided with the death of his father and the French invasion of the Rhine. On other occasions, however, Beethoven manipulated events himself; and he was certainly determined to have control of the timing of his 'arrival' as a composer. Thus he kept out of the limelight in 1794, to enable himself to make a bigger impact the next year, when he would take Vienna by storm. Not a single work was offered to a Viennese publisher in 1794, although several could have been (including some that Haydn had sent to Bonn). His only publication that year was Simrock's edition of the old piano-duet variations on Waldstein's theme (WoO 67). When he heard in June that this work was about to appear, he sent Simrock a revised version so that it would come out in 'as perfect a form as possible'. But he added, 'The fact is that I had no desire to publish any variations at present, for I wanted to wait until some more important works of mine, which are due to appear very soon, had been given to the world.'[28] This confirms that he held back deliberately so as to make a more striking impression once he had full command of contrapuntal technique and had composed some major new works. Thus in 1794, although he completed next to nothing, he began work on several major compositions (indeed, some of these may have been begun before then, while others make use of brief ideas sketched independently at an earlier date).

The works begun in earnest in 1794 and completed in 1795 include three piano trios published as Op. 1, three piano sonatas published as Op. 2, probably the String Trio, Op. 3, a new piano concerto in C (known today as No. 1), two extended songs, 'Adelaide' and 'Seufzer eines Ungeliebten' (Sighs of an Unloved One), and yet another attempt at the old Piano Concerto in B flat (No. 2), for which a new slow movement and finale were now composed. Although the new movements of the B flat Concerto were written before the C major one, and most of Op. 1 preceded most of Op. 2, the precise order of composition of all these works is far less clear than for most of his later music, and there was certainly some overlap between many of them. His intention, then, was to bring to public notice several works in

27 N-II, 566.     28 A-10.

different genres—piano solo, piano with accompaniment, strings, song, and concerto—in quick succession after polishing them all up for some months. The conquest of Vienna was to come about through a long-prepared and many-sided attack.

The first work brought before the public was a new concerto, which Beethoven performed at his Viennese public debut on Sunday 29 March 1795. The occasion was a charity concert at the Burgtheater, and the programme also included an oratorio by Antonio Cartellieri. The theatre was normally used for opera, but during Holy Week opera was not permitted and concerts could take place instead. Whether Beethoven played his Concerto in C or the one in B flat has been disputed, since extensive sketches for both can be found from the period 1794–5. But the work played was described as 'entirely new', which seems to exclude No. 2, the first movement of which was quite old and must have been known in private circles in Vienna by then.[29] Nevertheless, the extensive sketches for two new movements for the B flat Concerto, slightly earlier than those for the C major, imply a performance of it not long before this date. A possible occasion was 2 March, 'at a concert of Prince Lobkowitz, where one named Beethoven touched everybody'.[30] The Lobkowitzes were an extremely musical family, and the young Prince Franz Joseph Maximilian became one of Beethoven's leading patrons in the ensuing years. In all likelihood an orchestra was present at the concert, in which case Beethoven had an excellent opportunity to try out his partly new concerto, the slow movement of which would surely have made a deep impression.

Neither of the two concertos reached its final form in 1795, but nearly all their main features were present by then, and subsequent changes were mostly of detail. No. 2 is today regarded as conventional and relatively weak, at least compared with Beethoven's later concertos, but in 1795 it must have seemed bold and striking, with many unorthodox ideas. The first movement shows a much clearer organization of thematic material than his previous piano concerto (WoO 4 in E flat), and the opening orchestral ritornello is remarkable for its range of modulation: this section normally did not stray far from the tonic key throughout, but in this concerto there is an extended digression from B flat through various keys to F minor and then to a new theme in D flat major. The return to the tonic is followed by further development of the dotted figure of the opening motif, creating a roundedness and sense of return that is comparatively rare in opening ritornellos. Meanwhile the use of D flat major in the ritornello provides a subtle foretaste of the solo exposition, in which the music again modulates to this key for a new theme. This device of introducing remote keys that

---

[29] See Cooper, *Creative Process*, 294–5, where the arguments are set out in more detail.

[30] Landon, *Haydn*, iii. 294. The description is that of Count Zinzendorf. Landon suggests the work played may have been the *Rondo a capriccio* (Op. 129), but this is hardly a work likely to make such a great impression, and something on the scale of the B flat concerto seems far more likely.

have long-range significance was to become a feature of many of Beethoven's later works, and this concerto is one of his earliest uses of the device.

The second movement is a wonderfully profound Adagio. Beginning very simply, it makes great use of dynamic contrasts and Mozartean expressive appoggiaturas. The piano part becomes increasingly decorative, again in a Mozartean manner, but in the recapitulation the decoration is so elaborate that it far surpasses anything in Mozart's concertos. The main theme of the finale is characterized by a humorous and slightly disorientating short-long rhythm, which Beethoven strengthens by characteristic sforzandos on the second note. During the movement he plays around with this whimsical motif, sometimes making it long-short (bars 65–9), sometimes eliminating the initial short note by tying it to a preceding long (bars 126–7), and finally, in the coda, shifting the figure rhythmically (and in G major!) so that the short falls before the beat instead of on it. This ingenious but wholly audible manipulation of minute motifs is another hallmark of Beethoven's style that we see emerging in this concerto.

The C major Concerto builds on some of the ideas of No. 2, while introducing new features and possessing a rather different, more military character emphasized by its use of trumpets and drums, which were absent in its predecessor. Again the strong rhythm of the initial figure is developed extensively in the rest of the movement, indeed rather more so than in the previous concerto; and again the opening ritornello veers to a remote key (E flat), which reappears, albeit briefly, in the solo exposition (bars 175–6). Later in the exposition (bars 219–20) Beethoven hints at an even more distant key—A flat major—and this also has long-range significance, for A flat major is the key of the second movement. This remoteness between the main keys of the first two movements is counterbalanced by a close thematic relationship: in the opening theme of the second movement, stated by the piano, the right hand recalls the rhythm and shape of the first movement's second subject (originally in E flat), while the left hand, reinforced by the strings, recalls the rhythm of the first subject (see Ex. 4.3a–c). Further connections to the first movement are found in the piano part in bars 30–1, which are a close variant of the opening piano theme in the first movement (bars 107–10). Exploration of flat keys continues in the finale,

**Ex. 4.3**

(a) Op. 15/I                                (c) Op. 15/II

(b) Op. 15/I

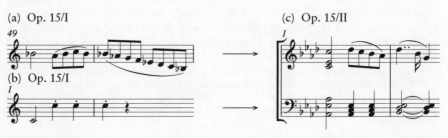

while they are counterbalanced towards the end (as in No. 2) by a remote sharp key, this time B major. Greater diversity within greater unity, and reconciliation of opposites, are concepts being added here to Beethoven's range of innovative ideas.

This profoundly original work was brought into being in circumstances far from ideal, as reported by Franz Wegeler, another Bonn native who had recently arrived in Vienna:

Only on the afternoon of the second day before the concert did he write the rondo, and then while suffering from a rather severe colic which frequently afflicted him. I relieved him with simple remedies as best I could. In the anteroom sat four copyists, to whom he handed each sheet as soon as it was ready. . . . At the first rehearsal, which took place in Beethoven's room the next day, the pianoforte was a semitone lower than the wind instruments. Beethoven immediately had these instruments and the others tune to B flat instead of A, and played his part in C sharp.[31]

This was a very hectic period for Beethoven. Having composed the finale on 27 March, rehearsed the concerto on the 28th and performed it on the 29th, he performed an improvisation at a concert the following day and an unspecified Mozart concerto the day after. He was now well and truly in the public eye, and shortly afterwards began making arrangements for the publication of his Opus 1. This was a set of piano trios, to be dedicated to his patron Prince Lichnowsky and published by subscription, with the printing done by the leading Viennese firm of Artaria & Co. (His existing Op. 1, the *Figaro* Variations, was demoted to a mere 'No. 1'.) Details of the contract are known but have not always been well understood, while some writers give incorrect figures. Close examination of the details enables us to see how important and successful a publication it was for Beethoven.

Subscriptions were invited, at a price of one ducat per copy, in a newspaper advertisement of 9 May, reprinted on the 13th and 16th, and the contract with Artaria was signed on the 19th.[32] Beethoven handed over the trios and agreed to pay Artaria an initial 212 fl. for making the plates (whether this sum was paid by Lichnowsky, or by Beethoven himself, or whether he gave Artaria other works in lieu of payment, or whether the sum was left on account to be deducted from receipts from sales, is uncertain and of little consequence). Artaria was to print at least fifty copies within six weeks, and to sell Beethoven up to 400 copies altogether, at 1 fl. each. Printing seems to have been delayed slightly, but the subscribers' copies were available for collection from Beethoven from late August, when an announcement was made to this effect on the 29th. In the end there were 123 subscribers, who between them ordered 245 copies altogether.[33] The

[31] WR, 38.

[32] See TDR, i. 504–5; Anderson, *Letters*, iii. 1417. Anderson's translation of the second paragraph, however, is incorrect.

[33] The list of subscribers was printed in the copies and is reproduced in Landon, *Beethoven*, 64–5. A less accurate list is in TDR, i. 506–8.

agreement also provided that Artaria would buy back the plates for 90 fl. and could begin selling copies abroad as soon as Beethoven received the first batch; Artaria could also sell copies in Vienna from two months after that date. Since he began doing so on 21 October, we may conclude that Beethoven received the first batch around 21 August. Beethoven's net costs were therefore 122 fl. for the making of the plates, and 245 fl. for the copies he required. These he sold at one ducat each to make 1102 fl. 30 kr., giving a total profit of 735 fl. 30 kr.—enough to cover basic living expenses for nearly a year.

The impressive list of subscribers, and the large profit he made, are indications of how successful he had been in commanding attention during his first two and a half years in Vienna: even in a city with numerous composers, he was already widely recognized as out of the ordinary. Many aristocrats appeared in the list, including several personally known to him either then or later, such as Count Browne, Count Dietrichstein, Prince Esterházy, Prince Lobkowitz, Count Razumovsky, and Baron Swieten. Prince Lichnowsky ordered no fewer than twenty copies, while other members of his family ordered several more, so that Beethoven's costs were already almost covered by these orders alone. Any further secret subsidy by the prince, which some writers suggest may have taken place, would therefore have been wholly unnecessary.

The trios had certainly been heard before publication, but probably only in a few private trials at Prince Lichnowsky's. Wegeler reports that at one such trial the cellist (Anton) Kraft suggested that the finale of No. 2 be notated in 2/4 instead of 4/4; this report is confirmed by the fact that late sketches for the movement show it still in 4/4, whereas the printed version is in 2/4 with note values halved. The trios were, however, still almost unknown when the first copies began appearing in late August. By chance, Haydn arrived back in Vienna on 20 August, just in time to see the work appear in print, and was able to attend a soirée at Lichnowsky's that introduced it to the music world. Ries reports:

Most of Vienna's artists and music lovers had been invited, above all Haydn, whose opinion was anxiously awaited by everyone. The trios were played and caused a tremendous stir. Haydn, too, said many fine things about them but advised Beethoven not to publish the third one in C minor. This astonished Beethoven, since he considered it the best, and in fact to this day it is always found to be the most pleasing, and has the greatest effect.[34]

The date of this soirée was long thought to be before Haydn's second visit to England and therefore around the end of 1793, since Haydn would have been too late to advise against publication by the time he returned. But the extant sketches for No. 3 clearly date from around late 1794 and show the work still at a fairly early stage. Thus, although there is no need to dismiss the gist of Ries's story, Haydn's advice must have been retrospective—some-

[34] WR, 74.

thing like, 'I wouldn't have published that if I were you.' Beethoven, ever suspicious of those around him, deduced that Haydn was envious and did not wish him well; in fact, Haydn had merely not expected the public to take so readily to such a serious, stormy, elevated, and difficult work. All three trios are actually serious and elevated, and should be seen as steps on the road to a full-scale symphony. Their grand, expansive manner, complex textures, extensive motivic development, and four-movement form are all more characteristic of the symphony than the piano trio of this period. Here and in several of his immediately following chamber works Beethoven was using a basically symphonic style within the sonata, as if working towards the symphony proper.[35]

Like most of his multi-work opus numbers, the trios were evidently composed in numerical order. Thus No. 1 in E flat was his first attempt at meeting the Viennese serious multi-movement genre on its own ground; and so, whatever its shortcomings (it is generally considered the weakest of the three trios), it is particularly significant in demonstrating how thoroughly he had mastered the style and was developing it along his own lines. Certain features stand out among many that would have impressed the first audiences. The richness of the texture, the elegance of the melodies, the seriousness of purpose, the dramatic power of the dynamic contrasts, and the urgency of the rhythmic momentum would all have tended to set Beethoven apart from his contemporaries, although these features were not new to his own music. More subtle are certain underlying ideas, some of which had been anticipated by Haydn while others are original. The opening motif is a rising arpeggio, reminiscent of the old 'Mannheim rocket' openings beloved of Mannheim composers of the mid-eighteenth century. Landing on a high Bb, the motif has an air of instability that generates forward propulsion. Not until the coda does Beethoven reverse the motif and use it descending; and not until the very end of the coda does he place it (ascending) above a V–I cadence so that it ends on the tonic with maximum stability. From now on, lengthy codas were to be the norm in Beethoven's sonata-form movements, and they were generally used to resolve instabilities set up earlier in the movement. Recent writers have demonstrated this procedure in many of his works, and it is illuminating to find it appearing clearly, for the first time, here in Op. 1 No. 1.

The main theme of the second movement is characterized by two repeated notes in the pattern strong–weak. In the ensuing bars Beethoven isolates this essentially unstable rhythm to draw attention to it, but he only reverses it into the stable weak–strong at the end of the movement, to create a sense of finality. The third movement is headed 'Scherzo' (a title also used in No. 2 and many of his subsequent minuet-type movements), and the joke is immediately apparent in the ambiguous opening. Is it in C minor, or

---

[35] For further discussion of these points, see especially Johnson, 'Decisive', 18, and Broyles, *Beethoven*, chapters 1–2.

perhaps F minor, or rather B flat major? It hints at all these keys in turn before settling in E flat, the key of the whole work. The finale begins by emphasizing the high B♭ from the arpeggio that began the work; this note is then used as the start of a descending arpeggio, providing a fitting answer to the 'question' that opened the work, and generating a sense of overall unity that makes the work greater than the sum of its parts. As in the two contemporary concertos, there is a lurch into a remote sharp key towards the end of the finale—this time to E major; both the key itself and its relationship to the tonic are different from the remote keys in the concertos.

Thus Beethoven's concerns in this trio included enriching textures, exploring remote key relationships, creating subtle organic connections within and between movements, resolving thematic instabilities in lengthy codas, contrasting a wide range of moods, manipulating short motifs in ingenious ways, and producing a symphonic grandeur overall. Similar concerns and subtleties can be found in the other two trios, as well as in the three piano sonatas that followed them as Op. 2. But each time the procedures are handled differently. For example, in Op. 2 No. 1, there is again a rising arpeggio for the first theme; but this time it is 'answered' not in the coda but in the second subject, which has almost the same rhythm but descends, and is legato instead of staccato. Complete resolution then comes at the very end of the whole sonata—a descending arpeggio with maximum stability covering a full four octaves. In Op. 2 No. 3 in C major the theme of the second movement is a subtle transformation of that of the first, transposed to the remote key of E major. The connection is made apparent when the slow movement modulates back to C major for a fortissimo statement of the theme (bar 53).

The three sonatas Op. 2, like all Beethoven's piano sonatas, owe little to those of Haydn and Mozart. They come closest to Muzio Clementi—a composer whom Beethoven evidently admired—in their thoroughly idiomatic use of the piano, and several authors have pointed out direct similarities between passages in their respective sonatas. Yet the differences are considerable: Beethoven's main themes tend to be more unusual and distinctive; his textures are richer and more complex; modulations are more frequent and daring; motivic development is more intensive; contrasts are sharper and more dramatic; and emotions, whether of exuberance, tenderness or anguish, are much more strongly characterized. These features enabled the sonatas to have a very great impact when they first appeared. They were probably completed about summer 1795 after quite a long period of gestation—indeed Nos. 1 and 3 incorporate short passages from a piano quartet of 1785 (WoO 36 No. 3)—and were published the following year with a dedication to Haydn. This is a further indication of the close bond of friendship between the two composers; it is significant in this respect that Beethoven never dedicated anything to either Neefe or Albrechtsberger.

In the remainder of 1795 Beethoven continued to compose prolifically. A score of the six-movement String Trio, Op. 3 was written out, although there is evidence that the work may have already existed in an earlier version.[36] Meanwhile the Wind Octet (Op. 103) was taken up and converted into a string quintet. The model for this idea was Mozart's 'Parthia' for wind octet K. 388, which had been arranged as a string quintet (K. 406) in 1788. But whereas Mozart made a transcription that is almost mechanical, even to the extent of including figuration that does not particularly suit strings, Beethoven took the opportunity to rework his Octet thoroughly. The size was greatly increased, the texture enriched with many polyphonic countermelodies, and the range of modulations expanded. The result is not an octet arranged for strings, but a string quintet worthy to be published as Op. 4. Also dating from about the same time is a sextet for two horns and string quartet, published some years later with the misleadingly high opus number 81b. In this work the horns are given a concertante role with some exceedingly virtuosic passage-work, and are often treated antiphonally either against each other or as a pair against the strings.

Alongside these larger works, Beethoven was occupied with smaller ones. His first venture into theatre music since arriving in Vienna resulted in two arias (WoO 91) for insertion into a revival of Ignaz Umlauf's *Die schöne Schusterin*. At least three sets of piano variations (WoO 68–70) and perhaps a fourth (WoO 72) were also composed in 1795, and one of them, a set of nine on a theme from Paisiello's *La Molinara* (WoO 69), was actually published as Op. 2 before the end of the year. (Like the *Figaro* Variations, it was demoted in reprints to 'No. 2'.) All four sets show considerable imagination in varying the theme, and the codas are quite interesting, but there is nothing particularly exceptional here. They were probably requested or commissioned by various pianists, as was evidently the case with WoO 70, a set of six variations on another theme from *La Molinara*. On this occasion, according to Wegeler, a lady told Beethoven she had lost a set of variations by another composer on this theme, and Beethoven promptly wrote his set overnight for her.

More significant than these sets of variations was the song 'Adelaide', to a text by Friedrich Matthisson. Beethoven derived particular pleasure from composing this song, as he told the poet when he sent him a dedicatory copy in 1800; and the numerous sketches indicate that he continued working intermittently on it for an unusually long time during 1794, 1795, and perhaps 1796. In his setting, Beethoven overrides the straightforward structure of the poem and creates a tripartite form, in which the first two parts function as the exposition and development of a sonata form, while the

[36] This evidence is based on a report by William Gardiner that he played the work in Leicester about 1794 from a set of parts newly brought from Germany by Abbé Dobbeler (TF, 166–8; Forbes suggests these were manuscript parts somehow acquired by Dobbeler in Bonn, but his ideas for how this might have happened seem unconvincing). Gardiner, however, gives several different dates for this event in different accounts, and it seems most probable that Dobbeler did not leave Germany until 1796 (the year given in one of Gardiner's accounts), after Op. 3 had been published, and that he brought printed parts to England. If so, the surviving autograph of 1795 was probably the first and only one.

third part is at a faster tempo and builds to a grand climax before dying away to nothing. The poet's idea of seeing his beloved everywhere is mirrored by an all-embracing musical setting quite different from normal Lieder of the period. Whether Beethoven had any particular beloved in mind who inspired 'Adelaide' is unknown, and his relationships with women at this date are lacking in detail. But Wegeler, who was in Vienna with Beethoven from October 1794 to early 1796, recorded: 'In Vienna Beethoven was always involved in a love affair, at least as long as I lived there, and sometimes made conquests which could have been very difficult indeed, if not impossible, for many an Adonis.'[37]

Further signs of Beethoven's interest in affairs of the heart appear in another highly original setting from about the same time: the double song 'Seufzer eines Ungeliebten' (Sighs of an Unloved One) and 'Gegenliebe' (Love Returned), two complementary poems by Gottfried Bürger. Beethoven sets them as a miniature Italianate cantata, beginning in C minor with a recitative followed by a gentle aria in E flat; after a brief transition the concluding section, 'Gegenliebe', is in C major, with a cheerful and very straightforward melody later used in his Choral Fantasia. Here, then, his newly awakened interest in remote key relationships is combined with his fascination with the C major/minor contrast to create a unique but most expressive structure.

Interest in remote key relationships is also evident in two sets of dances (WoO 7 and 8) written for the annual ball of the Gesellschaft der bildenden Künstler on 22 November. To be asked to write these dances was quite an honour, for in the previous three years they had been written by much more senior figures—Haydn, Kozeluch, and Dittersdorf respectively—but Beethoven's reputation as a composer in Vienna had grown so much in 1795 that he was now in considerable demand. Both sets of dances display a carefully planned key sequence in which the tonic triads of adjacent dances invariably have one note in common. Haydn's sets show a similarly wide range of keys, but less careful planning overall, as is apparent in the set of twelve German dances (Hob. IX.13) for the 1792 ball, where consecutive movements may be in the same key or only a tone apart:

Hob. IX.13:  D – G – F – C – A – F – D – D – G – D – A – D
WoO 7:       D – B♭ – G – E♭ – C – A – D – B♭ – G – E♭ – C – F
WoO 8:       C – A – F – B♭ – E♭ – G – C – A – F – D – G – C

WoO 8, a set of twelve German dances, includes a lengthy coda, written in the Beethovenian manner but retaining the strong rhythms of the dance.

These were essentially lightweight works—pleasant digressions from Beethoven's more serious purposes of writing music of the most elevated kind. For him the noblest and grandest instrumental genre was the symphony, and he must have been aware that his own style was peculiarly well

---

[37] WR, 43.

suited to this, since many of the most prominent features of his style—intensive motivic development, teleological drive, and continual flux—are characteristic of the symphony in its purest form. Thus it was merely a matter of time before he wrote a full-scale symphony, and he was already beginning to embark on one in C major in early 1795. He continued working intermittently on it during the rest of the year, and by about December had a draft for a complete slow introduction and first-movement exposition. He even began a full score at this stage, of which the first page survives. Completion of his first symphony, however, was to be a long and arduous process, and was not achieved for over four years, by which time the work had been so thoroughly overhauled that hardly anything remained from his early efforts. Nevertheless, it is significant that a firm intention to write a symphony in C major emerged almost before Op. 1 was completed, and signalled the direction in which he was to move in the ensuing years.

# Wider horizons (1796–8)

Having firmly established himself during 1795 as one of Vienna's leading young composers and pianists, Beethoven sought wider horizons during the ensuing period, when he visited and performed in several other major cities. The 1790s lay almost at the beginning of the era of the travelling virtuoso, but outstanding players were starting to find that, by visiting several cities and giving recitals in each, they could attract a series of large audiences and thereby earn far more than by remaining in one place. Singers had been doing this for many years (mainly to take part in opera seasons) but, with the rapid rise in instrumental music during the second half of the eighteenth century, instrumentalists began following a similar pattern. Beethoven had become almost equally noted in performance and composition, and so a concert tour, in which he could extemporize, perform his two newish concertos (still unpublished), and compose for local musicians or their patrons, formed a natural continuation of his previous activities.

The itinerary of his first and longest tour involved a northward journey to Prague, Dresden, Leipzig, and Berlin, and was clearly planned in conjunction with Lichnowsky. The prince had accompanied Mozart on a tour to precisely these four cities in 1789, and now went with Beethoven as far as Prague. Although the route was chosen largely for practical reasons, the symbolic nature of Beethoven inheriting Mozart's mantle by undertaking an identical tour should not be overlooked. Lichnowsky did not go to Prague solely for Beethoven's sake, of course. He may have had business reasons, and he was also able to visit relatives there: his wife Maria Christiane, whom he had married in 1788, was the daughter of Count Franz and Countess Maria Wilhelmine Thun, who lived in Prague (another of their three daughters, Maria Elisabeth, had married Count Razumovsky, Russian ambassador to Vienna, also in 1788). The Thuns were great patrons of music, like Lichnowsky, and had subscribed to three copies of Beethoven's Op. 1 the previous year; meanwhile another Countess Thun (née Kollowrath), who also lived in Prague and was presumably Count Franz's sister-in-law, had ordered no fewer than twenty-two copies of Op. 1—as many as Prince and Princess Lichnowsky together. Thus Beethoven could be very confident of the warm reception that he duly received in Prague. He wrote to his brother Johann (who had settled in Vienna at the end of 1795): 'My art is winning me friends and renown, and what more do I want?', and he added that he expected to make 'a good deal of money'.[1]

Beethoven and Lichnowsky probably arrived in Prague around the beginning of February (the journey normally took just over two days), and certainly before 11 February, for on or shortly before that date Beethoven gave a performance for the benefit of the Poor Institute of Prague,[2] doubtless gaining more 'friends and renown'. He followed this with another performance on 11 March (and perhaps others, too, for documentation is very sparse), but there is no indication of what music was played. Lichnowsky, meanwhile, had left Prague, but Beethoven remained there until the second half of April.

While in Prague, Beethoven composed several works for the nobility there. A set of six unpretentious German dances for violin and piano (WoO 42) was given to 'the two Countesses Thun'—presumably the two who had subscribed to Op. 1. Four short pieces for mandolin and piano (WoO 43–4) were written for Countess Josephine Clary, of which the Allegro in C (WoO 44a) is particularly delightful, with a light, delicate sound utterly unlike the usual Beethoven. A more serious and extended work was also written for Countess Clary—the *scena Ah! perfido*, which was published only some years later, without opus number (it now bears the number Op. 65). Its first known performance was in Leipzig in November 1796, by the Prague singer Josepha Dussek, but it seems probable that either she or the Countess herself (who was a singer as well as a mandolinist) would have performed it first in Prague while Beethoven was there, for otherwise she would have had difficulty obtaining the score.

The work shows Beethoven returning to the genre of voice with orchestra for the first time since leaving Bonn. It is a typical operatic *scena*, beginning with an extended recitative, followed by an extended bipartite aria (slow–fast, although the second part has several tempo changes). Mozart's influence is apparent almost throughout—far more so than in the Trios, Op. 1 or the Sonatas, Op. 2. Mozart was particularly highly esteemed in Prague, and had even written a similar *scena* himself for Josepha Dussek in 1787 ('Bella mia fiamma', K. 528). Perhaps, then, Beethoven was deliberately aping Mozart's style to please his own patrons. Only in the rather prolonged coda does Beethoven's personal voice begin to show through clearly; and the way he turns the opening motif of the second part of the aria (Ex. 5.1a) into a closing motif in the orchestral postlude (Ex. 5.1b) is also highly characteristic of him: the rising end to the motif is heard eight times in the course of the aria, but only in the postlude does the motif fall instead to the tonic to indicate finality.

---

[1] A-16.
[2] This important event is rarely noted in the Beethoven literature; see Loos, 'Beethoven in Prag', 72.

**Ex. 5.1** Op. 65

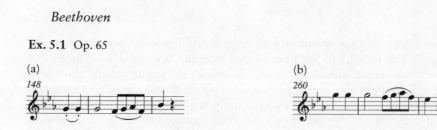

(a)
148

(b)
260

Several other works can be dated to Beethoven's period in Prague in 1796 on the basis of the paper types of their sketches or autograph score.[3] One is the Piano Sonata in G, Op. 49 No. 2. This was clearly not intended as a successor to his three big sonatas of Op. 2, for it is really just a two-movement sonatina, probably commissioned by a pianist of mediocre ability. Even after sketching it, Beethoven decided to simplify it, for the opening theme was sketched with semiquavers (Ex. 5.2a), which he eventually replaced with quaver triplets (Ex. 5.2b). He also tightened up the thematic writing in the final version, using material from the transition as a closing theme for the exposition, whereas in the sketches the figuration is not strongly thematic in either passage. The second movement uses the rhythm, but not the form, of a minuet, and again the final version shows some simplifications of figuration compared with the sketches.

**Ex. 5.2**

(a) SV 185, f. 106r

(b) Op. 49 No. 2/I

Also written in Prague was the Wind Sextet, Op. 71, which Beethoven later claimed to have written in a single night. This may be true of the original draft, but the sketches suggest a rather longer period from conception to completion. Several more works were sketched extensively without, apparently, being brought to completion. These include a piece (probably a quartet) in G for piano and wind instruments that was to conclude with a set of variations on the popular 'Ah! vous dirai-je, maman', and also three Goethe songs whose titles have become familiar today from Schubert's settings: 'Erlkönig', 'Rastlose Liebe', and 'Heidenröslein'. Meanwhile a few more sketches were made for the symphony in C begun the previous year, but without significant progress.

The next major city on the route to Berlin was Dresden. Here Beethoven stayed for about a week at the end of April, enchanting all who heard him play. These included the Elector of Saxony, who invited him to play all alone

---

[3] See Johnson, 'Prague and Berlin'.

for an hour and a half. As usual, there is no indication of what was played: most probably it was a series of extemporizations, which Beethoven preferred to prepared pieces. After Dresden, he made a slight detour to take in Leipzig (no details of this visit survive), and then went on to Berlin, where he stayed for about two or three months, again making a great impression.

As in Prague, Beethoven responded to his new surroundings by writing appropriate music, but this time much of his music written in Berlin was on a more formal level for the royal court, rather than for private patrons. The King of Prussia, Friedrich Wilhelm II, was a great lover of music in general and especially the cello, an instrument he played well. Beethoven therefore wrote two cello sonatas, in F major and G minor, which were performed at the Prussian court by the court cellist Jean-Louis Duport and himself. They may have been commissioned by the King, and were dedicated to him when published as Op. 5 the following year. Both have the rather unusual structure of a substantial slow introduction followed by a main Allegro and then a final Rondo, with no intervening slow movement—particularly surprising in view of the lyrical, expressive nature of the cello. Indeed Beethoven did at one stage sketch a slow movement in A flat for the F major sonata, reviving his recent interest in the use of remote keys for slow movements, but in the end each sonata consisted of only two movements. Most remarkable about these works, however, is that they were the first sonatas of their type, in which both piano and cello played an equally important role. Beethoven creates a great variety of textures, with the relationship between the two instruments constantly changing: each instrument in turn functions as either soloist or accompanist, or they may engage in dialogue, or both may be given lines with melodic interest simultaneously. Various earlier composers had written sonatas for cello with accompanying bass or keyboard continuo, or for piano with violin either accompanying or in a more obbligato role. But to give the cello an elaborate soloistic role alongside an active and even virtuosic piano part poses problems because of the different natures of the two instruments, and Beethoven was the first composer to solve these problems. Whether Duport himself assisted in their solution is not known, but he subsequently codified, in a cello tutor, some of the techniques required in the sonatas.

Beethoven further explored the combination of cello and piano in two other works written about the same time: Twelve Variations on 'See the Conqu'ring Hero Comes' from Handel's *Judas Maccabaeus*, and Twelve Variations on 'Ein Mädchen oder Weibchen' from *The Magic Flute*. These were published in 1797 and 1798 respectively as Nos. 5 and 6 in a gradually growing series of works to which Beethoven deliberately avoided giving an opus number (a series that had begun with the demoted *Figaro* Variations as No. 1); more recently they have become known as WoO 45 and Op. 66. The choice of a theme by Handel is significant. Beethoven was reportedly first introduced to Handel's music, shortly after moving to Vienna, by Haydn, who had been extremely impressed by it during his first visit to

England. Beethoven rapidly became a great devotee, soon holding Handel in higher esteem than any other composer. What he particularly admired in Handel was the ability to create wonderful effects out of very simple material—a skill in which Beethoven himself was to excel. He also had a chance to hear some Handel in performances organized by Baron Swieten, a noted Handel enthusiast, and these included *Judas Maccabaeus*, performed in 1794. Meanwhile, however, Friedrich Wilhelm himself was responsible for introducing Handel oratorios to Berlin. In 1795–6 the main work performed by the Berlin *Singakademie* was also *Judas Maccabaeus*,[4] and Beethoven actually attended two meetings of this body, performing extemporizations for them. Thus there was every reason why he should select, during his stay in Berlin, the most popular movement from this oratorio as the basis for a set of variations. Quite probably both sets of variations were, like the two sonatas, played in Berlin by Duport and Beethoven, although the sketchy records do not indicate this kind of information.

Another work probably completed in Berlin is the Quintet in E flat for piano and winds, Op. 16, since sketches for all three movements can be found on paper that Beethoven used there. This work seems to have functioned as a replacement for the quartet in G for piano and winds begun in Prague slightly earlier, and was probably also written at the request of some patron from either Prague or Berlin. An inscription on a sketch-leaf used in Berlin includes the draft of a letter that appears to refer to this quintet: 'I have the honour [to send] you here the quintet, and you will greatly oblige me if you regard it as an unimportant gift; the only condition I must make is that you give it to absolutely nobody else.'[5]

This type of gift was a common way for Beethoven to show his appreciation for some past favours, whether or not the work had actually been requested or commissioned. His normal practice was to delay publication of the new work, so that the recipient would have exclusive benefit of it for a certain period; but he was always very careful to emphasize that the manuscript should not be circulated, in case it fell into the wrong hands and appeared in print without his authority, depriving him of a fee for publication.

Although in only three movements, the quintet can be regarded as further preparation for a full-scale symphony, its first movement in particular having symphonic aspirations. After a grand slow introduction, inconclusive phrase endings (such as first-inversion chords) and overlapping phrases (where the final chord of one phrase also functions as the first chord of the next) generate symphonic momentum and continuity. Like his other wind music of the 1790s it shows a strong Mozartean influence. Mozart's piano-and-wind quintet (K. 452), also in E flat, has even been described as a model for Beethoven's, but how well he actually knew this work is uncertain since it was still unpublished (though probably not unknown in Vienna), and he

---

[4] Johnson, 'Prague and Berlin', 37–8.     [5] Johnson, *Beethoven's Early Sketches*, i. 364.

surely did not need a model for his own quintet. Moreover, Beethoven adopts different proportions from Mozart in his first movement, writing a characteristically long development section and coda, with the latter positively dwarfing the diminutive one by Mozart.

During his stay in Berlin Beethoven also expended much effort on the Symphony in C major that he had been sketching the previous year.[6] This was his most substantial composition to date, although it is among the least familiar. He had already drafted a complete slow introduction and exposition for the first movement while in Vienna, and had even begun a full score; he then took the sketches with him to Berlin and continued working on the symphony when not occupied with other compositions. Progress remained slow and deliberate, however, and he made very substantial changes in Berlin. Instead of continuing with his full score and sketching the rest of the movement, he went back to the beginning, making at least three more drafts for the introduction and two for the exposition on paper acquired in Berlin. The introduction drafts contain almost entirely new material, while the exposition drafts differ radically from earlier ones in some places. He could not have afforded such slow progress and so much retracing of his steps if he were trying to complete the work in a matter of weeks for a performance deadline in Berlin. Thus it must be concluded that the symphony was being composed as a result of ambition rather than commission—ambition to conquer the greatest instrumental genre of all. Although the symphony remained unfinished in this form, it was one of his most significant creations of the 1790s in terms of his development as a composer and the amount of effort expended, and it came tantalisingly close to completion.

In the later sketches the main theme of the Allegro uses a rapid scale (Ex. 5.3) which, as often noted, was eventually used in the finale of his First Symphony. The introduction at one stage began with the rising figure C–E–A–D played as a series of detached chords, but in the latest sketches these are joined together to form a scale that staggers slowly upwards (Ex. 5.4), foreshadowing but contrasting with the main Allegro theme. Shortly before

Ex. 5.3  SV 185, f. 159v

[6] For a detailed account of the chronology of this unfinished symphony, with brief comments on the music, see Johnson, *Beethoven's Early Sketches*, i. 461–9. Many of the sketches are transcribed in ibid., ii. 163–76; the remainder are in Kerman ed., *Miscellany*, ii. 166–74, 176–7. Johnson's suggestion that the work was designed for a Berlin performance and was abandoned when this did not materialize, however, is unconvincing and is rejected in the present discussion.

**Ex. 5.4**  SV 31, f. 17v

the second subject, in G, there is a sudden modulation to E flat major (a procedure already used in the C major piano concerto), with the melody again based on a rising scale; and towards the end of the exposition there is a brief excursion to A flat major, recalling a similar modulation in the introduction. Thus the exposition combines tonal variety with much motivic cohesion; but even in the latest sketches it still seems somewhat bland and diffuse in places, and in need of further work.

Sketches also survive for parts of the development and most of the coda, indicating that Beethoven may well have completed the movement (since surviving sketches often represent only a small part of the total amount of sketching done). This hypothesis is supported by the survival of an extended draft summarizing the whole of an ensuing slow movement, since Beethoven normally worked on movements in the intended order of performance. This Andante draft is in E major, like the slow movement of the C major Piano Sonata (Op. 2 No. 3) completed the previous year, thus demonstrating Beethoven's continuing interest in the relationship between these two keys (an interest that re-emerged in several later works). However, he then added an instruction to transpose the Andante to F major, and jotted down a few more sketches for this version. He also wrote an extended draft for a minuet and trio, and some brief ideas for the finale, all on paper from Berlin. Thus by the time he left Berlin he had all the main ingredients for the first three movements, needing only to polish them up and to solve the problem of what to do in the finale. These matters continued to occupy him after his return to Vienna.

Beethoven left Berlin probably in early July, returning to Vienna with a golden snuff-box full of coins, presented to him by the king. It was 'no ordinary box' either, as he boasted to Ferdinand Ries. Just as he had intended, his trip to Prague and Berlin had won him friends, renown, and 'a good deal of money'. Back in Vienna, besides preparing for publication his cello sonatas and his song 'Adelaide', and composing some new works, he now renewed the friendships made before his tour. Wegeler had returned to Bonn, and Lorenz von Breuning was to follow him in 1797, but there were others with whom Beethoven was becoming increasingly acquainted. They included Nikolaus Zmeskall (1759–1833), a minor aristocrat with whom he formed a lifelong (though not very deep) friendship, and who often helped him in practical matters such as obtaining good quills or wine.

Shortly after returning from Berlin Beethoven completed his facetiously titled *Duet with Two Obbligato Eye-glasses* (WoO 32), for viola and cello, which was evidently intended for Zmeskall (cello) and Beethoven himself: both men sometimes wore glasses.

Another important and lifelong friendship was with the piano manufacturer Johann Andreas Streicher and his wife Marie Anna (Nanette) née Stein of Augsburg, who was also from a piano-building family. In 1794 they had set up business in Vienna, together with Nanette's brother Matthäus Andreas. For a long time Beethoven preferred their pianos to all others, while in later years he often turned to Nanette Streicher for assistance with domestic matters. The friendship was firmly established by November 1796, when Beethoven embarked on another concert tour, this time heading east instead of north, to Pressburg (Bratislava) and Pest (Budapest). In Pressburg he advertised Streicher's pianos at a concert on 23 November, by playing on one sent out specially for this purpose. He wrote to Andreas Streicher four days before the performance, describing the piano as 'really excellent' and 'too good for me'! He found it 'too good' because 'it takes away my freedom to create the tone for myself', although he hoped Streicher would make all his pianos in this way.[7] What Beethoven particularly sought in pianos was a singing tone: he was better at creating this than other pianists, as descriptions of his playing indicate, but on Streicher's pianos it was very much easier to produce this kind of sound than on others.

The works Beethoven composed around this time included a short two-movement sonata for piano duet, a four-movement sonata for piano solo, and a serenade for string trio. All were published the following October (1797), as Opp. 6, 7, and 8 respectively. In addition he produced one or two songs, a set of piano variations on a dance from the ballet *Das Waldmädchen* by Paul Wranitzky (WoO 71), a short piano sonata and a piano rondo later published as Op. 49 No. 1 and Op. 51 No. 1 respectively, and further work on his Symphony in C, including a complete draft of the minuet sketched earlier and an almost complete draft of a trio section. The minuet echoes the first movement by beginning with a disjointed scale, and also by modulating suddenly to A flat major at one point. The finale, however, still remained a problem, for he had sketched numerous possible themes but not developed any of them. A further sketch apparently for the finale was made around the end of 1797,[8] but this, too, seems too slight for a conclusion in the greatest of instrumental genres. Beethoven was the first composer to appreciate the magnitude of the difficulty in creating a truly

[7] A-17.
[8] 'Kafka' Miscellany, f. 43r; see Kerman ed., *Miscellany*, ii. 194. Neither Kerman nor Johnson have linked this sketch with the symphony, but there is much evidence that it belongs with it: it is in the right key and form, has other finale characteristics, it seems to respond to some of the musical ideas in the first movement, and it is situated near another sketch referring explicitly to a symphony.

symphonic finale, once the symphony had taken on its late-Classical characteristics. The symphony, as a grand, teleological form, now demanded a strong and affirmative conclusion, whereby the forward thrust of the previous movements could culminate in a bold and sophisticated ending, while retaining something of the more popular, dance-like style associated with the finales of earlier symphonies. This 'finale problem', which confronted many later composers, faced Beethoven as early as 1796–7, and he could find no solution at this stage despite many attempts. This stumbling-block, then, was evidently the real reason why the Symphony in C, which might conveniently be labelled 'No. 0', ultimately came to nothing, being set aside and left incomplete even after so much progress.

Of the works that Beethoven did complete around early 1797, the most celebrated is undoubtedly the Piano Sonata in E flat, Op. 7. It was dedicated to the young Countess Babette von Keglevics, a very gifted piano pupil of his. Beethoven lived very near her at the time, and it is reported that he used to come for her lessons still wearing his slippers—an example of the eccentric behaviour for which he was becoming renowned. The sonata is certainly a magnificent work, described on its title page as a 'grand sonata' and published separately rather than as one in a set of three. In his six previously published piano sonatas (WoO 47 and Op. 2) the length had gradually increased each time, and Op. 7 continued this trend by being on a still larger scale, especially in the first movement.

Like each of the sonatas in Op. 2, the first movement is marked *p* at the start. On the rare occasions when Mozart begins a piano sonata with a *p* marking it signals an unusually gentle, lyrical movement; with Beethoven, however, an initial *p* is generally associated with a sense of suppressed energy and latent power, as here, where a throbbing accompaniment generates dynamism and urgency. The initial idea is a two-note motif, and two-note motifs separated by rests penetrate all four movements in some form or other to act as a binding force. At the start Beethoven makes the figure unstable, sounding strong–weak, to intensify the momentum created by the accompaniment, and he reverses it to weak–strong only at the end of the coda to indicate finality. After the first subject, the energetic drive is maintained as the music modulates to the dominant, and this key is established with a new theme (bar 41) which might be regarded as the second subject. This theme is partly based on an idea jotted down during an improvisation session some years earlier,[9] and when it concludes in a cadence (bar 59) one might expect it to be followed simply by a short closing theme to end the exposition. Instead, the size of the movement suddenly becomes apparent as a new and contrasting theme is heard. Sonata-form theory and terminology were not well developed at this date, but theorists had recognized that an exposition consisted of a series of subsections, one of which could be expected to be a prominent cantabile theme in the dominant, contrast-

[9] See Cooper, *Creative Process*, 111.

ing with the opening idea. The theme beginning in bar 59 matches that description; thus in terms of contemporaneous thought and modern terminology this must be considered the true 'second subject', for the previous theme retains the energetic character of the opening material. Hence, instead of being nearly over by bar 59, the exposition has not yet reached its halfway point. As this second subject unfolds, it suddenly lands on a 6–4 chord in C major (bar 81), and remains in this key for a while before modulating back to B flat for the rest of the exposition. C major is not forgotten: this same chord, in exactly the same register, reappears in root position as the first chord of the slow movement. Thus although Beethoven adopts a remote key for the slow movement, he ingeniously relates it to the first movement—as in Op. 2 No. 3 but by a different means.

The third movement is a minuet and trio, though titled simply 'Allegro' and 'Minore'. Originally Beethoven sketched an idea for a trio in A flat major, but he then decided on one in the bizarre key of E flat minor (a key he had already used in a piano quartet as a child), and his A flat idea was instead transferred to the trio of a later sonata (Op. 10 No. 3). The key of E flat minor is cleverly anticipated in the Minuet (bar 51), from where the music modulates briefly into C flat major, a key that was to have great significance for Beethoven in his later music. The modulation is effected by juxtaposing B flat and C flat in the bass. This same progression, notated as B flat–B natural, assumes great significance in the sonata-rondo finale (bars 62–3): it introduces the stormy middle section in C minor, where two-note figures again predominate; and it reappears near the end (bars 154–5) to herald a brief excursion to the remote key of E major. After this excursion the stormy middle section is recalled in the coda, but in the tonic key of E flat and with the two-note figures sounding peacefully over a shimmering left-hand accompaniment, to create a beautifully gentle pianissimo ending.

This sonata has been examined at some length to illustrate something of the complexity of thought with which Beethoven was now operating. The variety and originality of ideas, and the ingenuity of their interrelationships, are already well-nigh unfathomable. The whole sonata, utterly different from anything by Haydn or Mozart, comes closest to Clementi, whose piano sonatas Beethoven greatly admired. But it is much richer in texture and variety of figuration than Clementi's sonatas of a similar date, while the ideas themselves tend to be more striking and memorable. It also represents the limit in Beethoven's rapid expansion of the sonata. His subsequent sonatas were more often shorter than longer (only the 'Hammerklavier' and perhaps the 'Waldstein' are substantially longer), and he made progress in different directions instead.

During the rest of 1797 Beethoven continued composing, publishing, and occasionally performing new works. He probably also had several piano pupils, but details are sparse. On 6 April he introduced his piano-and-

71

wind quintet and an aria (probably *Ah! perfido*) to the Viennese public in a concert given by the violinist Ignaz Schuppanzigh. Meanwhile he was preparing the Wranitzky Variations (WoO 71) for publication, and they appeared later that month with a dedication to Countess Anna Margarete von Browne. Her husband, a man of Irish extraction and one of Beethoven's leading patrons, presented him with a fine horse in response. But Beethoven's inattentiveness to worldly matters is clear from Ries's account of what happened to the horse: Beethoven rode it a few times but soon forgot all about it, so that his servant was able to hire it out without him noticing. The horse and Beethoven evidently did not last long together!

It may have been during the summer of 1797 that Beethoven contracted a serious illness—typhus according to one report—for his activities at this time are completely undocumented, and his output for the year seems slightly meagre compared with 1795 and 1796. It would appear, too, that he noticed the first signs of deafness around this time. The exact date of its initial onset is far from certain, since it was a very gradual process: in June 1801 he told Wegeler that 'for the last three years my hearing has become weaker and weaker'; yet in October 1802 he wrote that he had had the condition 'for six years'. Equally uncertain is the cause of the deafness, and new theories about it continue appearing: otosclerosis, Paget's disease, some kind of nerve deafness, and sarcoidosis have all been proposed, but all pose difficulties. Whether the deafness was related to either the typhus or any of Beethoven's numerous other illnesses such as his abdominal disorders, as he himself supposed, is also disputed, while the question of whether it had any direct effects on his later compositions has led to much speculation but no firm answers (he claimed that it affected him least when composing, and was mainly a social inconvenience). What is certain is that gradually over about twenty years he was forced to reduce his performing activities, leaving more time for composition. He also withdrew from social functions for a while around 1800, in an attempt to conceal his deafness. All this lay in the future, however, and in 1797 he was probably not even prepared to admit his deafness to himself.

Beethoven's main compositions in the latter part of 1797 or early 1798 were three String Trios (Op. 9), three Piano Sonatas (Op. 10), a Clarinet Trio (Op. 11), and three Violin Sonatas (Op. 12). By now he had become so successful as a composer that most of his works were being written in response to commissions: he said himself in 1801 that he had been receiving more commissions than he could fulfil, and his brother confirmed the large number of commissions in a letter the following year. Referring to Beethoven's first thirty-four opus numbers and eighteen publications without opus, Carl stated:

These pieces were mostly commissioned by amateurs under the following agreement: he who wants a piece pays a fixed sum for its exclusive possession for a half or a whole year, or longer, and binds himself not to give the manuscript to *any-*

*body*; after this period, the composer is free to do what he wishes with the work [i.e. he can publish it].[10]

Thus the seemingly random succession of Beethoven's genres in the late 1790s was dictated largely by the preferences of various patrons. Sometimes the commissioner received the dedication when the work was finally published, but this was not automatic. The set-up meant that Beethoven's output of chamber works roughly reflected the general popularity of the various genres during this period, rather than his own personal preferences.[11] Nevertheless, the commissions he accepted were in genres that interested him; and although the commissioner chose the genre and could apparently specify if the work were to be technically easy to play, Beethoven was free to dictate the content and style of the music, and to explore musical problems and innovations of his own choice. The system also produced rich rewards. Before long he was in such demand that he could virtually name his own price for a commission (he was to receive 400 florins from Prince Lobkowitz for the six Quartets, Op. 18, in 1799–1800), and could obtain an additional fee from a publisher. The size of these fees is often unrecorded, but in the case of the three Trios, Op. 9 it was 50 ducats (225 florins). He might also receive a further present for the dedication of a work. Thus his earnings from compositions alone were now enough to support his everyday necessities, and he was still being paid something by patrons such as Prince Lichnowsky for contributions to private musical events. The system of commissioned works has important implications for chronology: it means that these works were fully completed at least six months before their date of publication, although the precise completion date is not generally known at this period since the few surviving autographs are mostly undated, unlike in later years.

The three Piano Sonatas, Op. 10 were probably begun as early as 1795, but the set took a long time to complete and was overtaken by both Op. 7 and the two Op. 49 Sonatas, with most of the sketching apparently being done in 1797. When writing a set of three works Beethoven customarily chose contrasting keys, and normally ones he had not recently used in the genre. Accordingly he chose C minor, F major, and D major for Op. 10, none of which he had previously used for a piano sonata. Having used a gradually increasing size in his previous piano sonatas, he at last reined back the expansion, especially in the first two of Op. 10, which have only three movements. The finale of No. 1 is particularly concise, with an extremely short development section and a compressed energy and intensity that foreshadow the first movement of the Fifth Symphony. The movement ends with leanings towards the subdominant that leave it sounding strangely inconclusive, with the final C major chord suggesting it might be the dominant of F rather than a true tonic. This sense is confirmed when No. 2 is played immediately afterwards, for it provides a perfect sequel to

---

[10] Alb-50.    [11] See Dorfmüller, 'Beethovens Schaffen'.

No. 1. Thus Beethoven is here exploring the concept of the hyper-work, where not only a movement but now a whole sonata is related to something outside itself, while being fully self-contained. He could not, of course, repeat the same trick between No. 2 and No. 3, but instead he foreshadowed the D major tonic of No. 3 by using this key prominently in both the first and last movements of No. 2. The three sonatas therefore form a triptych, thoroughly contrasted in character yet integrated by subtle interrelationships, with No. 3 forming a satisfying culmination by being the longest and most sophisticated in the set.

The String Trios, Op. 9, though not among Beethoven's most striking works, show several characteristic features. The first, in G, has a slow movement in E major which is effectively in 9/8 time (though notated as 3/4 with triplets); this combination of key and metre creates a very ethereal, otherworldly effect similar to several slow movements by Beethoven in this key. The second trio is a very gentle work, and his first to begin with a *pp* marking, an opening gambit that appears increasingly often in his subsequent compositions. The final trio is much more impassioned, and provides a further exploration of the relationship between C minor and C major that fascinated Beethoven so much.

The Clarinet Trio, Op. 11, written shortly after the String Trios, can be dated fairly precisely, since its finale is a set of variations on the aria 'Pria ch'io l'impegno' from the opera *L'amor marinaro* by Joseph Weigl, which was first performed on 15 October 1797. The Trio was published twelve months later, with a dedication to Countess Thun (Prince Lichnowsky's mother-in-law), having probably been completed early in 1798. It is the only one of Beethoven's multi-movement instrumental works that contains a set of variations on a theme by another composer. Although incorporating extraneous music into sonatas and similar works was quite common at the time, it was something Beethoven preferred to avoid, and he wished later that he had written a different finale, wholly his own, according to Carl Czerny. The work has sometimes been criticized for having an insufficiently idiomatic clarinet part, since this has no great agility and the chalumeau register is almost completely avoided. It seems, however, that from the outset Beethoven's intention was to write a trio that could be played by either clarinet or violin, for this is how the work was eventually published. Thus he wrote a part that was not particularly idiomatic for either instrument but which suited both. Only in one place does the violin version differ significantly from the clarinet one (first movement, bars 216–17, where the latter has some characteristic arpeggios before descending below the compass of the violin).

After completing the trio Beethoven immediately set about writing the three Violin Sonatas, Op. 12, and one was apparently ready in time for a concert on 29 March 1798, when he performed a violin sonata with Schuppanzigh. During the early Classical period, most of the musical material in violin sonatas was given to the keyboard instrument (harpsichord or piano), while the violin part was of relatively little interest and could in some cases be omitted altogether. This tradition explains why the Op. 12 sonatas were published as 'for harpsichord or fortepiano, with a violin', but such a designation was no longer appropriate. The violin is given a prominent role throughout the three sonatas, just as the cello had been in Op. 5; and the keyboard part, with all its sforzandos, crescendos, and diminuendos, could not be played satisfactorily on a harpsichord (harpsichords were anyway by now almost obsolete in Vienna). Unlike Beethoven's early piano sonatas in four movements and his early cello sonatas in two, these three violin sonatas uniformly follow the traditional three-movement pattern fast–slow–fast (rondo). Although relatively unadventurous in structure, however, the sonatas display a great range of textures, as Beethoven seems to explore every possible relationship between the two instruments.

In October 1798 Beethoven visited Prague again.[12] This time he played in two public concerts and at least one private one, as reported by Wenzel Tomaschek many years later. In the first concert Beethoven performed his C major concerto, two movements from his Sonata, Op. 2 No. 2, and an improvisation. Tomaschek was so overwhelmed that he did not touch his piano for several days afterwards. At the second concert Beethoven played his B flat concerto, which Tomaschek claimed had just been composed in Prague. Later writers have deemed this impossible, but Beethoven did revise each of its movements at this time and wrote out a new autograph score—thus the surviving score does indeed date from 1798.

By 5 November Beethoven was back in Vienna, where an Adagio of his was performed by Schuppanzigh. This work is thought to be the Romance in F for Violin and Orchestra, which was eventually published in 1805 as Op. 50; its autograph score has the same physical characteristics as that of the Op. 19 concerto, and was therefore probably written out about the same time.[13] Like the concerto, however, it may be a revision of a Bonn work. Indeed, it could well be the missing slow movement of the fragmentary Violin Concerto in C (WoO 5), for they have identical instrumentation of a type largely abandoned in Vienna (flute, two oboes, two bassoons, two horns, and strings). More significant still, the first two bars of the Romance (a common title for slow movements of violin concertos) can be seen as a varied transformation of the first solo theme of the concerto (Ex. 5.5), a procedure often found in Beethoven's slow movements. Thus the Romance has the right title, key, speed, scoring, and theme for the missing slow movement.

In terms of compositional craft, the period 1796–8 was one of consolidation for Beethoven. Having made his major impact in Vienna in 1795, he branched out into several related genres, writing works in which he continued gradually developing his own idiosyncratic brand of the high Classical

---

[12] The month has been deduced by Hans-Werner Küthen in *NA*, III/2, *Kritischer Bericht*, 32–3.
[13] Ibid.

**Ex. 5.5**

(a) WoO 5 (transp.)

(b) Op. 50

style. Each work showed him to be a master of the conventional idiom, while being far from conventional in detail. Apart from *Ah! perfido* his vocal works during this period consisted of only a few short and insignificant songs, as he concentrated, whether by choice or by request, on mastering most of the main types of instrumental music. The period was completed by the preparation of Opp. 9–12 for publication, and all four had appeared in print by January 1799. Consolidation was also achieved by the reworking of the Second Piano Concerto, while his newly-established mastery of composition was beginning to become widely known through his travels to Prague, Berlin, Budapest, and elsewhere. His wider European vision was reflected, too, in his first (and only) original song with English text, 'La Tiranna' (Ah grief to think, WoO 125), composed around the end of 1798.

With the gradual encroachment of his deafness, however, concert trips were to become increasingly unattractive, and he virtually abandoned them after 1798. Meanwhile his period of consolidation was shortly to give way to one of further innovation and exploration. A striking new piano concerto in C minor had already been conceived, although it was to lie dormant for some time; and an equally striking piano sonata in the same key (the *Pathétique*) was gradually evolving. The question of the symphony was still to be solved; and Beethoven at last felt ready to tackle the string quartet, for he began sketching the first of a projected set of six during summer 1798. One important step he took at this stage, perhaps in preparation for the set of quartets, was to begin using actual manuscript books for his sketches, instead of loose leaves that were liable to become jumbled or mislaid (since his notoriously untidy habits were already impinging on his compositional activities). The first of these sketchbooks, now known as Grasnick 1, has a regular structure that indicates it was sewn together before use, and its forty-eight leaves lasted him from mid-1798 to early 1799. It includes the earliest sketches for his set of quartets, and some sketches for the Prague revision of his Second Piano Concerto, plus much else. Not all his sketching was thenceforth done in books, for he continued to use loose leaves sporadically; but the sketchbooks greatly enhanced his ability to think on paper on a much larger and more complex scale, and may also have partly compensated for his growing deafness in later years. They provided the springboard for his rapid compositional advances of the next few years.

# 6

# First quartets and First Symphony (1799–1800)

Beethoven's compositional development in the last two years of the eighteenth century was dominated by his first achievements in what he regarded as the two noblest and most elevated forms of instrumental music—the string quartet and the symphony. These two genres had been raised to pre-eminence by Haydn above all. Ever since his Op. 33 Quartets, published in 1781 and 'written in an entirely new and special way' according to Haydn himself, the string quartet had been the most sophisticated type of chamber music, and its emphasis on interplay between the four instruments was sometimes likened to a conversation. Meanwhile the symphony, as mentioned earlier, had become a grand, public display of compositional craft in which motivic development and continuity on a large scale were prime elements. Thus a serious composer such as Beethoven could not approach either genre without due preparation if he hoped to succeed at the highest artistic level rather than produce mere works of entertainment. Here it was a question of inheriting Haydn's spirit more than Mozart's (although the situation is complicated by the fact that Mozart's later quartets and symphonies were partly inspired by Haydn's example). All Beethoven's major instrumental works of the earlier 1790s can be seen as part of that preparation; so too can his contrapuntal exercises for string quartet (Hess 30–1) written under Albrechtsberger's tutelage, and his symphony sketches of 1795–7. By mid-1800 both genres had finally been mastered, with the six quartets of Op. 18 and the First Symphony, although actual publication of the works was at least a year later. Beethoven once reportedly stated that he had never learned anything from Haydn; but these works demonstrate that he had certainly learned an enormous amount from Haydn's music.

The Quartets, Op. 18 were begun in summer 1798, and the sketchbooks show that the first of them (No. 3) was virtually complete by the end of that year. At the beginning of 1799, however, there was a digression before Beethoven started on the second (No. 1). A new opera, *Falstaff*, by the Vienna court composer Antonio Salieri, was produced on 3 January, and Beethoven immediately began composing a set of variations on a duet from it ('La stessa, la stessissima', WoO 73). This was completed very rapidly, for it was published by Artaria & Co. less than two months later, and may have been commissioned by them. There was, however, some personal connection between Beethoven and Salieri that may have led to these variations being composed, and they could have been begun even before the première of the opera.

Precisely when the two men came into close contact is uncertain. It was long believed that Beethoven began taking lessons in Italian vocal composition from Salieri shortly after arriving in Vienna, and continued until 1803; but it now seems that the period was much shorter, for all the known exercises, many of which are not very advanced, are written on paper of 1800 or later. It is significant, however, that Beethoven's Violin Sonatas, Op. 12, were published around the beginning of 1799 with a dedication to Salieri. Such an honour was bestowed by Beethoven on no other professional composer except Haydn (who received the Sonatas, Op. 2),[1] and so Salieri must have earned it in some way. It seems likely, therefore, that Beethoven sought Salieri's advice about Italian music in late 1798, and the association gradually turned into more formal instruction in the next few years. Certainly Beethoven felt indebted to Salieri more than once in 1799, for he wrote to his friend Zmeskall that year asking him urgently to obtain some copies of a work from Artaria, because, as he said, 'I must give a copy to Salieri today'.[2]

About this time Beethoven also came into contact with several notable musicians who visited Vienna. One was Joseph Wölffl, a pianist and composer whose playing surpassed Beethoven's in clarity and precision, albeit not in expressiveness and profundity. On occasion they invited comparison by playing in alternation at the same event, and both attracted a substantial following. They greatly respected each other's abilities, and Wölffl dedicated a set of piano sonatas to Beethoven shortly before leaving Vienna in 1799. Another pianist to visit Vienna was Johann Baptist Cramer, a German based in London. He arrived in September that year and remained until the following spring, becoming closely acquainted with Beethoven. Like Wölffl, he surpassed Beethoven in clarity and accuracy, but he also played with great expressiveness; according to Ries, Beethoven preferred him to all other pianists. Beethoven also admired Cramer as a composer, and occasionally thereafter imitated Cramer's style in his own compositions. A third visiting musician was the virtuoso double-bass player Domenico Dragonetti, who was in Vienna for a few weeks in spring 1799. He is reported to have achieved the very difficult feat of playing Beethoven's Cello Sonata, Op. 5 No. 2, on the double bass, accompanied by the delighted composer.

After finishing the Salieri Variations around January 1799, Beethoven resumed work on his quartets, sketching Nos. 1 and 2 during the ensuing

---

[1] The only other significant composer to whom Beethoven ever dedicated a major work was his pupil Archduke Rudolph; but he was only an amateur composer, more important as a patron.

[2] A-35.

months. Progress on these, however, was interrupted by another visitor, the widowed Countess Anna Brunsvik, who lived on an estate in Hungary with her five children. She was a great music-lover and had subscribed to Beethoven's Trios, Op. 1, in 1795. In early May 1799 she visited Vienna with her two eldest daughters, Therese (1775–1861) and Josephine (1779–1821), both accomplished pianists, and determined that they should have some lessons from Beethoven, as Therese relates in her extensive memoirs. The three of them, armed with their copy of his Op. 1, visited his home, which was then a third-floor apartment in St Petersplatz, and were welcomed most warmly.

Beethoven 'had an extraordinary aversion to teaching' in general, according to Wegeler; but, as his co-author Ries reminds us, he 'very much enjoyed looking at women; lovely, youthful faces particularly pleased him'.[3] On this occasion the charms of Therese and Josephine rapidly overcame his aversion to teaching, and he proceeded to teach them every day of their short stay in Vienna; the nominal hour allowed for each lesson was often extended to four or five hours, and he 'never grew weary of holding down and bending my fingers, which I had been taught to lift high and hold straight', as Therese records.[4] This last comment is exceedingly interesting, for it reveals an advantage Beethoven had gained over rival pianists: he had evolved a new technique, using bent fingers, which enabled him to gain more power and control, and a smoother, more singing legato, than the traditional way of playing. While in Vienna, the Brunsviks also met Count Josef Deym (1752–1804), as did Beethoven.

The immediate results of these meetings were threefold: Beethoven wrote some pieces for musical clock (WoO 33) for Count Deym, who owned a musical-instrument museum; he also wrote a set of variations for piano duet on a newly composed song, 'Ich denke dein', which he presented to the two Brunsvik sisters on 23 May at the end of their visit; and Josephine married Count Deym the following month, after which she lived in Vienna away from her family (Therese never married). The marriage was unhappy for Josephine, partly because Count Deym was nearly thirty years her senior, and she also missed her family and the Hungarian countryside. She remained faithful, however, and the couple had four children before the count's death in 1804. Meanwhile Beethoven became a regular visitor, giving her piano lessons and playing at soirées, and providing her with much affection and comfort. They fell more deeply in love after the count's death, as will be discussed later, and their relationship has generated intense speculation in recent years.

A friendship also developed in 1798–9 between Beethoven and Karl Amenda, who had arrived in Vienna from Courland. A theologian by training, and an excellent violinist, he became Beethoven's closest friend during early 1799. He returned home later that year, but shortly beforehand

---

[3] WR, 24 and 104.     [4] TF, 235.

Beethoven presented him with a set of parts for his recently completed String Quartet in F, Op. 18 No. 1, and wrote on the first violin part:

Dear Amenda: Take this quartet as a small memorial of our friendship, and whenever you play it recall the days we spent together and the sincere affection felt for you then and which always will be felt by

Your warm and true friend

Ludwig van Beethoven

Vienna, 25 June 1799.[5]

Thus this quartet, the second of Op. 18 to be written, had been completed before this date, and in fact Beethoven was on to the third, if not the fourth, by now. A well-known anecdote about the F major Quartet was told by Amenda. After hearing Beethoven play its slow movement, Amenda commented that it seemed to evoke the parting of two lovers. This delighted Beethoven, who added that he had been thinking of the tomb scene in (Shakespeare's) *Romeo and Juliet*. This rather surprising admission is one of very few cases where an abstract instrumental work by Beethoven has specific external associations. Indeed, one might be tempted to doubt Amenda's testimony, but it is corroborated by some equally unusual jottings in French amongst the sketches for the movement: 'il prend le tombeau'; 'desespoir'; 'il se tue'; 'les derniers soupirs' (he takes [i.e. enters] the tomb—despair—he kills himself—the last sighs).[6] Normally any words found amongst Beethoven's sketches for abstract instrumental works are purely musical ones, such as names of keys, tempo marks, or indications of form. Here, however, is a clear sign that he had some poetic idea in mind. According to his pupil Carl Czerny, and others, he actually did so quite often, but the examples Czerny gives are not confirmed by any relevant comments amongst the sketches, and the references in these quartet sketches remain an isolated case.

Amenda is often said to have been tutor to the children of Prince Franz Joseph von Lobkowitz (1772–1816). There is no evidence for this in the extensive Lobkowitz archives. Nevertheless, it was for the prince that the Op. 18 Quartets were written. He had established a private orchestra at his palace in 1796—a practice that had become unfashionable in the 1790s—and soon became one of Beethoven's most enthusiastic admirers and patrons. It was he who commissioned the set of Quartets, Op. 18 from Beethoven, as has recently become apparent from documents in the Lobkowitz archives. He ordered payment of 200 florins for the first three quartets on 7 October 1799, and Beethoven received the money a week later.[7] Meanwhile Beethoven's sketchbook indicates that he proceeded to the fourth Quartet (Op. 18 No. 5) immediately after completing the first three. The last three, however, were also interrupted by other works, and it

---

[5] TF, 224; BB-42.
[6] The sketches are in SV 46, pp. 8–9: see Virneisel ed., *Skizzenbuch*.
[7] Brandenburg, 'Streichquartette', 275.

was another twelve months before he received similar payment from Lobkowitz for these, on 18 October 1800. Moreover, the first three underwent substantial revision during that year, as will be seen.

During the last few months of 1799 Beethoven concentrated mainly on composing his Septet, Op. 20, and his Variations on 'Kind, willst du ruhig schlafen' (WoO 75), and seeing into print the latter work, another set of variations (WoO 76), and three piano sonatas composed earlier—the *Pathétique* (Op. 13) and the two Sonatas, Op. 14, in E and G major. The *Pathétique* and WoO 76 were announced by the firm Hoffmeister as available on 18 December, while the Op. 14 Sonatas and WoO 75 were announced by Mollo three days later.

Of these works, the *Pathétique* Sonata is the earliest composition by Beethoven that is really popular today, and also his first work with a very well-known tune: the theme of the slow movement has been transformed into numerous versions ranging from Anglican chant to pop song. The sonata fully deserves its acclaim. It surpasses any of his previous compositions, in strength of character, depth of emotion, level of originality, range of sonorities, and ingenuity of motivic and tonal manipulation, anticipating in many ways his style of the next decade. Its origin, however, is shrouded in mystery. Since it was published in December 1799, it should be represented in one of the two sketchbooks covering the period from summer 1798 to summer 1799. Yet there is no sign of it in either. The most likely explanation is that it was composed in the first half of 1798, with publication delayed either at the request of the original commissioner (assuming there was one) or by some hold-up with the printers. Yet, as with Op. 14 No. 2, there are no significant sketches from this period either, whereas Op. 14 No. 1 is very fully represented. Alternatively the *Pathétique* could have been composed during the period of the two sketchbooks but outside them; or it could have been completed rather quickly immediately after the second one had been filled, since a sketchbook thought to have been used in late 1799 and early 1800, which would have contained sketches for the Septet and First Symphony, is lost.

The few sketches that do survive merely deepen the mystery. The earliest seems to be a casual jotting of 1796 that was later incorporated into the slow introduction.[8] The next two are more puzzling: they appear amongst sketches for the String Trios, Op. 9, and have figuration more suitable for strings than piano, but they show the end of the finale[9]—a section not usually sketched until a work is at least well under way. The finale theme appears in A flat major within a C minor context, exactly as in the final version of the *Pathétique*, although in other respects these sketches differ greatly from the final version. Was Beethoven planning to use this theme, and this ending, in the C minor string trio? And, since the A flat version of the finale theme recalls the slow movement of the *Pathétique*, as several

[8] 'Kafka' Miscellany, f. 48r, staves 9–10; see Kerman ed., *Miscellany*, ii. 200.
[9] See N-II, 42–3.

observers have pointed out, was this slow movement already sketched too?

Subsequent sketches are equally puzzling. There is an outline of part of a sonata movement in C minor, dating from about early 1798, that shows many similarities to the first movement of the *Pathétique*;[10] but it is so different in melodic detail that most scholars have failed to connect it to the sonata. Finally, any suggestion that the sonata was finished in 1798 is dispelled by a short fragment of autograph score written on a paper type not used by Beethoven before 1799, for it shows the opening still not in its final version (Ex. 6.1).[11] The problems of the genesis of the sonata have been compounded by confusion about its publication, since there are two Viennese editions, issued by Eder and Hoffmeister. Hoffmeister's was announced on 18 December, and Eder's was thought to be somewhat earlier, thus restricting the possible dates for completion of the sonata; but Eder's is now known to be based on Hoffmeister's, and so the sonata could have been completed at any time up to October 1799.

**Ex. 6.1** SV 61, p. 49

The sonata is one of Beethoven's few instrumental works with an authentic descriptive title. This places it in the category of 'characteristic' sonata, similar to but distinct from the programmatic sonata. In a 'characteristic' work or movement, as was recognized in the eighteenth century, a specific mood is expressly evoked, without any actual narrative. Carl Friedrich Cramer explained in 1786 that in ordinary sonatas 'several different characters are presented mixed up together', whereas in a characteristic work 'only one definite character is expressed throughout the piece'.[12] In the *Pathétique*, Beethoven combines standard sonata procedures with the intense expression of pathos from every angle and by every conceivable means.

The choice of key is extremely significant. C minor was widely accepted as a 'pathetic' key in the late eighteenth century, and was also rapidly

[10] See Kerman ed., *Miscellany*, ii. 156; Cooper, *Creative Process*, 67–8.

[11] Mikulicz ed., *Notierungsbuch*, 45.

[12] Carl Friedrich Cramer, *Magazin der Musik*, ii (1786), 1308–10; cited from Kirby, 'Pastoral Symphony', 610.

becoming a personal emblem for Beethoven. He had used it in Bonn in his first published composition—the Dressler Variations—and in his first known draft for a symphony, as well as in his greatest Bonn work, the *Joseph* Cantata. It reappeared in Vienna in the most successful of his Trios, Op. 1—the one Haydn had recommended withholding from publication—and again in the String Trio, Op. 9 No. 3, and the Piano Sonata, Op. 10 No. 1. Considering that Beethoven preferred to vary the keys of successive works in the same genre, it is surprising that he should return to C minor so quickly; the fact that he did so further singles out this key as being particularly personal for him. It is unlikely that any single event (such as the death of his close friend Lorenz von Breuning in 1798) prompted the sonata, but Beethoven had already experienced intense suffering on several occasions, and was thus able to combine personal feeling with standard musico-rhetorical devices, including a suitable choice of key.

The intensity of the work is evident in the very first chord, which firmly establishes the mood of pathos. Its key, its register (entirely in the bass clef except for the top note), its texture (thick and heavy, utilizing a low E♭ for added weight), its dramatic dynamic mark (*fp*), and its ponderous length (more than three whole seconds), are all carefully judged and combined to maximize the sense of an anguished groan. The remainder of the slow introduction, incorporating sharp contrasts of dynamic and register, harsh dissonances, chromaticism, and a mixture of very long notes, very short ones, and dramatic rests, reinforces the initial mood, and by its intensity of expression transcends all previous attempts at evoking pathos.

After this powerful Grave comes a highly agitated Allegro, only to be interrupted by reminiscences of the introduction. Beethoven had used a similar idea in one of his very earliest sonatas (WoO 47 No. 2), but in the *Pathétique* the device is handled in a much more complex and sophisticated way. Part of the Grave is also recalled in the development section of the Allegro itself, at the new tempo, thereby fusing the two parts of the movement into one. In the final reprise of the Grave, at the start of the coda, the ponderous chords are replaced by dramatic silences. Since rests had already formed part of the Grave theme, these new silences are in themselves thematic developments. Beethoven was perhaps the first composer to manipulate rests as if they were notes rather than just gaps between notes, and he returned to this procedure in several later works.

The start of the second movement (Adagio, in A flat) is striking both in texture and register: the right hand plays simultaneously a cantabile melody and an oscillating accompaniment—a highly unusual combination at the time, although it has been widely imitated since; meanwhile the pitch of the melody is unusually low, located mainly in the tenor register to produce an unusually rich sonority, and starting on that same middle C that had begun and ended the first movement. The movement is in simple rondo form with a short coda, and the gentle oscillations in the accompaniment give way to throbbing repeated notes in the first episode, which begins in the relative minor. The second episode begins in the tonic minor before modulating to the subdominant of its relative major—a fearsome F flat major, which Beethoven for practical reasons notated as E major. Here the throbbing is faster—in triplets, which persist to the end of the movement, invading the accompaniment to the main theme and generating a sense of increasing agitation.

The finale resumes the C minor tonality, and contributes much to the unity of the sonata by relating to both the previous movements. The original despairing mood returns, and the main theme begins with a motif from the second subject of the first movement (bar 55), before introducing echoes of the Adagio theme, in the form of pairs of falling fifths (Ex. 6.2a). These echoes are developed in the second episode, and the connection with the Adagio becomes still more palpable in the coda (bars 202–4: Ex. 6.2b). Here part of the finale theme is heard in the same key and register as the opening of the slow movement; but whereas the Adagio melody had proceeded 3–2–5, resisting the expected fall to the tonic, this time the melody retains the shape of the finale theme—essentially 3–2–1, dropping to the tonic as if in pathetic resignation, and implicitly absorbing the Adagio into the underlying emotion of the whole sonata.

**Ex. 6.2** Op. 13/III

(a)

(b)

The two other piano sonatas (Op. 14) published in the same month as the *Pathétique* are less strikingly original, but show many characteristic features. The first, for which extensive sketches survive from early to mid-1798 (not 1795, as was once believed), is in E major. Curiously, in all Beethoven's multi-movement works in which E is the keynote, every movement is in E major or minor, a pattern first encountered in this sonata. Here the middle movement is in E minor and, as in the F major Sonata, Op. 10 No. 2, Beethoven cleverly gives it the function of both slow movement and minuet, it being a slowish Allegretto in minuet-and-trio form. The second sonata is unusual in having a finale headed 'Scherzo'. It is not a scherzo and trio, for it is in sonata-rondo form, but it is full of Beethovenian wit and humour, with a main theme that is rhythmically extremely disorientating (Ex. 6.3).

**Ex. 6.3**  Op. 14 No. 2/III

The final work composed in 1799 was the Septet in E flat (Op. 20), for which nearly all the sketches are lost. The scoring for clarinet, horn, bassoon, violin, viola, cello, and double bass is extremely unusual, if not unprecedented, but whether it was Beethoven's choice or that of whoever commissioned the work is uncertain. This is his only chamber work to include the double bass, but his recent encounter with Dragonetti did not tempt him to give this instrument any solo material here: mostly it just doubles the cello or provides a harmonic bass when the cello has thematic material. Essentially the Septet is in the light and elegant divertimento style, but this is blended with a seriousness of purpose typical of Beethoven. There are six movements—an echo of the traditional divertimento—but the structure is original and skilfully planned. There are two contrasting slow movements in the middle, a profound Adagio and an Andante in variation form. These are interspersed with two different minuet-type movements: a moderately paced Tempo di Menuetto and a rapid Scherzo. The first and last movements each have a slow introduction, so that altogether there are eight tempos, neatly alternating slow and fast throughout. The theme of the Tempo di Menuetto (though not its working-out) was borrowed from the still unpublished Piano Sonata, Op. 49 No. 2. Beethoven did not normally make such borrowings except where the earlier work was to remain unpublished (as with the borrowings from WoO 36 in Op. 2), and so it seems probable that in 1799 he had no intention of ever publishing the sonata.[13] The six movements seem disparate and self-contained, as in a divertimento, yet they are all (except perhaps the Scherzo) related by themes that outline or decorate a falling and rising semitone, resulting in greater coherence than might be expected.

The Septet was first performed on 20 December 1799: a little-known letter written by Josephine Deym the next day states that her brother Franz had attended music played by Schuppanzigh, 'and was transported by it, especially by a septet composed by Beethoven, which must have been the *non plus ultra*, as much for the performance as for the composition'.[14] The work received its first public performance the following April, when it was announced as dedicated to no less a figure than Empress Maria Theresia, and it rapidly became very popular.

Almost immediately after completing the Septet, Beethoven returned to his long-neglected Symphony in C major, determined now to bring it to a rapid completion. One of his main problems with the symphony in 1796–7—perhaps the chief stumbling-block—had been the finale (see Chapter 5 above), which needed to have sufficient weight to round off the symphony, while retaining the traditional element of tunefulness. Now, around the end of 1799 (the exact date is uncertain, for no sketches survive from this period), he found the solution: of the ideas sketched already, he must have concluded that by far the best for a finale theme was the one he had already used up in the first movement! Thus he felt obliged to transfer this theme from the first movement to the last, and compose the rest from scratch. With this stroke of genius he overcame the impasse, and his work on the First Symphony then progressed with extraordinary rapidity.

The transfer of this theme from first movement to finale had two further repercussions. Firstly, the finale acquired something of the weightiness customarily associated with the opening movement, thus providing an important step in a shift in symphonic writing towards a more end-orientated structure (a shift that reached its apogee in the Ninth Symphony). Secondly, the rest of the Symphony had to be constructed around a pre-existing finale theme, in contrast to Beethoven's normal procedure of starting with ideas for the first movement. Thus the rising scale at the start of the finale theme had to be subtly prepared in the preceding movements, in such a way that it seemed a natural outgrowth and culmination of them.

The preparation for this scale is extensive. The first hint (unless one counts the two-note opening figure as a fragment of scale) is a seemingly insignificant scale in the strings in the last bar of the slow introduction, accompanying some wind chords. It is followed by the main theme of the first movement, which also duly rises an octave, but more as arpeggio than scale. In the second movement, most of the scales are short and descending, based on the dotted figure in bar 3. In the coda, however, this dotted figure

[13] See Cooper, *Creative Process*, 68–9.
[14] The letter is cited, in the original French, in Johnson, *Beethoven's Early Sketches*, i. 388, and elsewhere.

is extended into a complete scale (bars 184–6); and when this is repeated (bars 188–90: Ex. 6.4) it is accompanied by the flute playing a rising scale as a countermelody, ingeniously pointing towards the scale that forms the main theme of the third movement. This theme in turn is at exactly the same register as the scale at the start of the finale, although it uses slightly different accidentals and continues beyond a single-octave compass. Thus the rising scale in the finale theme, though built up slowly in the first instance, truly seems to grow from ideas heard earlier.

The other striking motif in this symphony, developed even more than the scale idea, is the two-note opening figure. As most commentators have noticed, this figure is astonishing for beginning out of key, on an unstable dominant 7th of F major. Still more astonishing, however, is the huge variety of ways in which this rising semitone is manipulated and exploited throughout the symphony. Moreover, towards the end the motif is increasingly often reversed, either melodically as a falling semitone or rhythmically as a weak–strong motion—in both cases giving it greater stability.

By placing the opening figure first in F, then in C, then in G in the first four bars, without actually using a simple C major chord at all, Beethoven circumscribes the tonic key, emphasizing it even more strongly than he would by using a plain tonic chord. Also striking about this opening are the carefully marked dynamics, and especially the highly original orchestration: the wind instruments bear the main weight, accompanied only by light, pizzicato strings until the G major chord is reached. Beethoven was signalling a new approach to orchestration in symphonies, where wind and strings were equal partners, as they are throughout this symphony. So shocking was this approach that the reviewer of the first performance could not accept it, claiming that 'the wind instruments were used too much, so that it was more wind-band music than full orchestral music'.[15] This criticism made no impact on Beethoven, who continued exploiting wind instruments extensively in all his symphonies. Indeed his highly imaginative and original uses of the orchestra, which go far beyond Mozart and Haydn, are one of the greatest yet least celebrated achievements in his symphonies. In many other aspects, however, he simply carried on from the point Haydn had reached in his 'London' Symphonies, using a similar length and structure, and the same types of motivic play and thematic development that Haydn had perfected.

Beethoven probably wrote the symphony during the winter of 1799–1800 in the hope of obtaining a date for a benefit concert the following spring at the Burgtheater or the Kärntnertor Theatre (other possible venues were less suitable for various reasons). Such dates were allocated by the court theatre director Baron Peter von Braun, but were very difficult for a composer to obtain, for the theatres were generally reserved for opera except during Holy Week; Beethoven had not managed to obtain one in previous years.

---

[15] TF, 255.

**Ex. 6.4** Op. 21/II

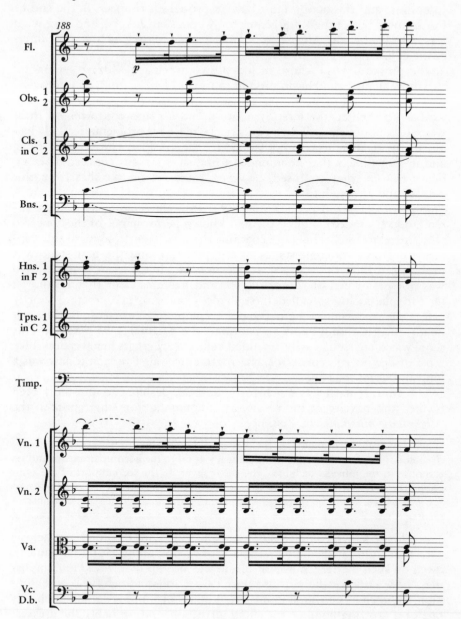

However, he had just dedicated his Sonatas, Op. 14 to the Baron's wife Josephine, and this action must have improved his chances. In the end he was granted use of the Burgtheater for Wednesday 2 April, and gave what was described in the *Allgemeine musikalische Zeitung* as 'the most interesting concert in a long time'.

The programme he chose included an unspecified Mozart symphony, two movements from Haydn's recent oratorio *The Creation*, an improvisation on the piano by Beethoven himself, and three of his most impressive works—the Septet, the First Symphony, and a piano concerto. All three were still unpublished. Which concerto he played is problematical. He had already worked on his C minor Concerto (the so-called Third) by this time, and it seems likely that he intended to finish it for this concert. The evidence is somewhat confused, however: there are no sketches from this period, and although this concerto appears to be dated 1800 on the autograph score, closer inspection suggests that the final figure is a badly written (and very faded) '3'; and the first known performance of the concerto was indeed in 1803. The score contains three different colours of ink, representing three different stages of composition, and the first stage was probably in 1800, but even this is questionable. In the event, this concerto was not performed on 2 April 1800, and it seems clear that Beethoven instead played his so-called First Piano Concerto, in C major. Shortly before the performance he wrote out a completely new score of this, evidently incorporating many revisions to the original 1795 version. This score was then itself heavily amended before reaching its final version. Like most of Beethoven's concertos, its progress from first version to last was a long and hazardous one.

The concert itself left much to be desired, despite the unusually high quality and novelty of the music, as is apparent from the report in the *Allgemeine musikalische Zeitung*:

When they were accompanying, the players did not bother to pay any attention to the soloist. As a result there was no delicacy at all in the accompaniments and no response to the musical feeling of the solo player. In the second part of the symphony they became so lax that despite all efforts on the part of the conductor no fire whatsoever could be obtained from them, particularly from the wind instruments.[16]

Beethoven's own comments on the concert are not recorded, but he was surely far from satisfied after such lack of co-operation. He had no time to dwell on such matters, however, for he was promptly involved in composing a new work for the virtuoso horn player Johann Stich (who was commonly known as Giovanni Punto, the Italian form of his name). Stich was one of a growing band of travelling virtuosos, and probably the greatest horn player of his day. Thus his arrival in Vienna prompted Beethoven to write his Horn Sonata, which they performed together on 18 April, just

---

[16] TF, 255.

over two weeks after Beethoven's benefit concert. Since Beethoven had been rushing to try and finish his symphony, and must also have been occupied with the practical arrangements for his benefit concert, he would have had no opportunity to write the Horn Sonata until afterwards, and so he must have written it very rapidly. This is duly confirmed by Ries:

Beethoven almost always postponed the composition of the majority of his works due by a certain date until the very last moment. He had, for instance, promised Ponto [Punto], the famous horn player, that he would compose a sonata (Opus 17) for piano and horn and would play it with him at a concert given by Ponto. The concert with the sonata was announced, but the sonata was not yet started. On the day before the performance Beethoven began the work and had it ready for the concert.[17]

Since Ries was not in Vienna at the time, Beethoven's rapidity in writing the sonata may have been exaggerated. The work was, however, clearly written very quickly, and is quite short, with no full slow movement but just a seventeen-bar slow section preceding the finale. In other respects the speed of composition is not evident from the music itself: Beethoven shows great sensitivity to the capabilities of the natural horn, exploiting open and stopped notes in a thoroughly idiomatic way (an effect largely lost on the modern valve horn).

Another travelling virtuoso appeared in Vienna about the same time as Stich—the pianist Daniel Steibelt. Again Ries relates what happened: both men performed a work of theirs at a musical gathering at the house of Count Moritz von Fries, with Beethoven playing his Clarinet Trio. A week later there was another meeting, and after Steibelt had performed one of his quintets he played a carefully prepared 'improvisation' on the very theme (by Weigl) that Beethoven had used in his Clarinet Trio. Ries continues:

This outraged Beethoven's admirers as well as Beethoven himself. It was now his turn to improvise at the piano. He seated himself in his usual, I might say unmannerly, fashion at the instrument, almost as if he had been pushed. He had picked up the cello part of Steibelt's quintet on his way to the piano, and placing it upside down on the music rack (intentionally?), he hammered out a theme from the first few bars with one finger. Insulted and irritated as he was, he improvised in such a manner that Steibelt left the room before Beethoven had finished, never wanted to meet him again, and even made it a condition that Beethoven not be invited when his own company was desired.[18]

Beethoven's skill in improvisation had long been admired. He could create great effects out of the most insignificant motifs, as his compositions of this period demonstrate, and he could continue developing a theme indefinitely. Thus when he was incensed as on this occasion, any theme, even an upside-down motif from a cello part, could fire his imagination and enable him to astonish his listeners, while developing the theme in such a way as to ridicule it—so effectively that Steibelt felt both humiliated and

[17] WR, 71.     [18] Ibid.

outclassed. Beethoven did not always show much sensitivity to others' feelings; but when, as here, his own reputation was being called into question, he disregarded such niceties, and would have considered any civility towards Steibelt hypocritical. It is easy to see how he made so many enemies, despite his underlying good intentions.

Before long, he had reportedly fallen out with Stich, too. The two men went to Budapest, where they again played the Horn Sonata on 7 May, and they should have continued on to Vereb for a further performance; but owing to a quarrel Stich went there alone, with Beethoven remaining in Budapest until July. There he was within easy reach of the country estate of the Brunsviks at Martonvásár, and probably visited them several times.

During the summer, his main activity was the completion of the set of six string quartets, which had been interrupted for several months. No. 5 had been worked out the previous year, and No. 4 was probably sketched mainly in the sketchbook presumed lost that must have contained sketches for the Septet and First Symphony (and probably also the Third Piano Concerto). This left just No. 6. The sketchbook from summer 1800 (aut. 19e) is rather fragmentary, but it does contain sketches for all the movements of this Quartet. These sketches are followed, surprisingly, by some for Nos. 1 and 2, which had already been completed the previous year. The explanation for these further sketches is found in a letter Beethoven wrote in 1801 to Amenda, to whom he had earlier given a copy of No. 1: 'Do not hand on your quartet to anybody, for I have greatly altered it, since only now do I know how to write quartets properly, as you will see when you receive them.'[19] It is these alterations that are represented in the 1800 sketchbook, and comparison of the final version of No. 1 with the version sent to Amenda reveals that Beethoven had indeed learnt much about quartet writing during the course of work on Op. 18. Most of the changes are to the texture, which becomes smoother and more linear; motifs are made to stand out more clearly, while fussy accompanimental figures such as oscillating patterns are eliminated. Also, melodic lines are sometimes given added decoration in the form of appoggiaturas, sections tend to be more closely linked together, and occasionally whole bars are eliminated to produce a tighter construction. Revisions of other aspects of the music such as dynamics, harmony, and use of repeats can also be found, although structurally there are no great changes.[20]

No early version survives for No. 2 in G, but the sketches show clearly that this, too, was revised during summer 1800. Here some of the changes were evidently even more substantial than in No. 1, and included significant structural alterations to the second movement: in the 1799 sketches this

---

[19] A-53.
[20] Detailed studies have been made of the differences in the first three movements: Levy, *Choices* (first movement); Weill, 'Two Versions' (second movement); Smyth, 'Scherzo' (third movement).

movement appears as a continuous Adagio, but the following year an Allegro section was inserted in the middle, creating a very unusual form. The finale, too, was thoroughly overhauled, with parts of the development and coda being almost completely rewritten.[21] Since No. 3 had been composed before Nos. 1 and 2, this, too, was surely also revised, but no sketches for such a revision are known. They may have been made in the same missing sketchbook that contained No. 4 and the First Symphony.

Beethoven received 200 florins from Prince Lobkowitz for the last three quartets on 18 October 1800, and had probably presented the manuscript to him a few days earlier. At the same time he probably also handed over a manuscript of the revised version of the first three quartets, in exchange for the earlier copy; the latter was presumably discarded, since it is the later version that survives in the Lobkowitz archives. Publication of the quartets was delayed, no doubt because of the customary agreement that Lobkowitz should have exclusive rights for a period, which may have been as long as a year in this case: Nos. 1–3 did not appear until June 1801, and Nos. 4–6 until October, twelve months after Lobkowitz had received them. At some point before publication, Beethoven changed the order, for reasons that are unclear. The D major, the first to be written, was moved to No. 3, while the fourth and fifth quartets were interchanged. He also continued making minor compositional adjustments even after the music had been sent to the printers.

All six quartets demonstrate that Beethoven had fully absorbed the idiom as used by Mozart and Haydn. No other composer had matched their sophistication, and Beethoven probably saw himself as their true heir in this genre, as in the symphony. Indeed he had copied out two of Mozart's quartets (K. 387 and 464) during preparations for his own set, and Op. 18 No. 5 is in some ways modelled directly on K. 464. The most striking feature about the first movement of No. 1 is the intensity with which the opening idea is developed—it appears over a hundred times in the course of the movement (and even more often in the first version). The second movement is, unusually, in 9/8, and is dominated largely by melodic writing in the first violin. The dynamic level is soft or very soft almost throughout, and dies away to a very rare *ppp* just before the recapitulation. The few *forte* passages, which mostly occur in combination with an agitated demisemiquaver figure, consequently stand out in sharper relief, reaching a great climax on a very widely spaced diminished 7th chord in the coda. This chord corresponds with the sketch marked 'il se tue' in Beethoven's programmatic background to the movement. The fragmented sighing figures associated with 'les derniers soupirs' in the sketches, however, are not found in the final version.

Beethoven fills the high-speed Scherzo with witticisms of many kinds. The main theme is a rhythmically altered inversion of the opening

---

[21] See Brandenburg, 'First Version'.

turn-figure of the first movement, but it is chromatically distorted and rapidly disrupts the tonality in a rather ludicrous way. Some abrupt stops and starts contribute further to the humorous effect. Then after the first eight bars have been repeated, the music suddenly plunges into A flat, with a clear melodic echo of a passage in the same key in the first-movement transition (bar 41). In the Trio, a series of comic octave leaps on C are suddenly interrupted by a new theme (again based on a turn-figure) in the remote key of D flat—a key that recurs in the finale. Thus Beethoven's fondness for long-distance tonal relationships is once again in evidence in this quartet. The main theme of the finale is based on yet another type of turn-figure, and this is reused almost as obsessively as that in the first movement, providing yet another ingenious way of unifying the quartet as a whole.

Of the other five quartets, No. 2 is notable for the unusual structure of the slow movement already mentioned; Beethoven takes the closing figure of an initial Adagio section in C and develops it at a rapid pace in a central Allegro before returning to the initial tempo. In No. 3 he contrasts the D major of the first movement with B flat major in the second; but again the remote key has been prepared in advance, this time by being used as the tonal goal in the development section of the first movement. The theme is also related to a passage in C major near the end of the exposition of the first movement; this passage duly appears in F in the recapitulation, and E flat in the coda, so that the appearance of B flat for a related theme at the start of the slow movement is made to seem inevitable rather than incongruous.

In a set of six quartets, one was traditionally in a minor key—in this case No. 4—and Beethoven yet again chose C minor, as if in a deliberate attempt to associate himself with that key in public consciousness. The mood of the first movement is again *pathétique*, and somewhat disturbing. Some commentators have indeed been sufficiently disturbed to describe the movement as weak and even crude, and to allege that the quartet was written somewhat earlier (for which there is no evidence). Beethoven seems here to have been deliberately writing music that is uncomfortable, as in the heavy alternation of tonic and dominant chords in bars 13–16, and in the jarring C♯ that heralds the development (he often used the note C♯ as a disruptive element on later occasions); perhaps his intention was to heighten the contrast with the other quartets. The mood of the first movement is not upheld later, however. The 'slow' movement is a whimsical Scherzo in C major that affects to be fugal but actually pokes fun at the learned style, with much subtle interplay based on the repeated-note opening bar. In the third movement, a Menuetto, the Trio section is in A flat major, and is followed by a speeded-up reprise of the Minuet, while in the finale the two main episodes use the keys of the Trio and Scherzo respectively, providing yet another example of tonal integration. The finale then ends with a Prestissimo section in which the main theme appears at a faster tempo, to match the similar effect in the Menuetto. No. 5 in A is the most conventional in the set, although the Menuetto is placed second and a set of variations, with extended coda, forms the third movement (as in Mozart's K. 464). Its elegant and orthodox nature, in which everything seems to fall delightfully into place, forms an excellent counterweight to the preceding quartet.

In No. 6 in B flat, the Scherzo makes great play with rhythmic ambiguity, using off-beat sforzandos, ties across the barline, and starting halfway through the second beat. Thus there is the double uncertainty of where the barline falls, and whether the bars divide into 3/4 or 6/8. Nothing here, however, prepares for the extraordinary movement that follows—the most remarkable one in the whole set. It is an additional slow movement, entitled 'La Malinconia' (Melancholy) and directed to be played 'with the greatest delicacy'. Although Beethoven was prone to bouts of melancholy, the movement should not be regarded as in any way subjective but as a musical portrayal of a state of mind, similar to the *Pathétique*. Once again he uses every means at his disposal, stretching the bounds of convention to breaking point. An initial sense of immobility gradually gives way to tortured chromaticism, where the music turns to increasingly remote keys without finding any repose. Harsh dynamic contrasts and obsessive use of turns in a slow and ponderous progression of chords contribute further to the overall portrayal, which is one of the most vivid illustrations of a mental state in the whole of music history. The mood is rapidly dispelled in the lively finale, but reappears in the middle of the movement like an echo from the past. Beethoven returned to this highly successful procedure in certain later works, notably the Fifth Symphony and the Sonata Op. 110.

After his return from Budapest in July 1800, Beethoven spent most of the year composing a Piano Sonata in B flat (Op. 22), two Violin Sonatas (Opp. 23 and 24), and another set of Piano Variations (WoO 77). The Variations are notable as his first independent set based on an original theme, and he deliberately limited their technical difficulties. They were even described as 'very easy' when published that December, although this is a slight exaggeration. For the piano sonata he reverted to a four-movement structure. By his own standards the work is strikingly conventional, at least superficially, but it has many of his characteristic thumbprints.

The two violin sonatas were originally written and published as a single opus, but became separated as early as 1802. Nevertheless, they make an excellently contrasting pair: Op. 23 in A minor is stormy and dramatic, whereas Op. 24 is wonderfully lyrical and relaxed, so that it later acquired the nickname 'Spring' Sonata. They were dedicated to, and probably written for, Count Fries. In these sonatas Beethoven continued exploring new paths while ostensibly keeping to tradition. The second movement of Op. 23, for example, is in sonata form but lacks the customary continuity and thrust. The first subject is a four-square, lyrical theme in binary form, implying a set of variations to follow. Instead of variations, however, there is a contrasting fugato that functions as transition, then a self-contained second subject in the dominant, and a closing theme to conclude the exposition. This sectionalism anticipates that of the finale, which, unusually for Beethoven, emerges as ABACADA rather than the customary sonata-rondo. All the sections except the third episode are quite short (this third episode provides a lyrical interlude in F major, subtly pointing towards the following sonata in mood and key). Beethoven then brings back references to all three episodes in an extended coda, before a final varied statement of the A section, resulting in a highly novel realization of a form that was in danger of becoming stale.

In the 'Spring' Sonata the emphasis is on melody in all four movements, and the main themes are again related in various subtle ways. The opening melody, however, is as striking for its originality as for its gracefulness (Ex. 6.5). The mixture of long and short notes makes the line utterly unpredictable; there is a surprisingly wide tessitura; and concluding the first phrase on an unstable chord II is a highly unusual procedure that lends both ambiguity and forward thrust to what might have become too regular. The oddest movement in the sonata, however, is the short Scherzo—the first time Beethoven had used such a movement in a violin sonata. Again he plays with the idea of rhythmic ambiguity, which is heightened by a lack of synchronization between the instruments for much of the time, with the violin disconcertingly echoing the piano just one beat later!

**Ex. 6.5**  Op. 24/I

Before the end of the year Beethoven had sold several works to the publisher Tranquillo Mollo. Mollo had been a partner in the Artaria firm, but had set up independently in 1798 and published Beethoven's Clarinet Trio and the two Sonatas, Op. 14. Now he was granted the 'First' Piano Concerto, the piano-and-wind Quintet, the Horn Sonata and the six Quartets, all of which appeared in 1801, as Opp. 15–18 respectively. Mollo also acquired the two violin sonatas. Meanwhile the composer and publisher Franz Anton Hoffmeister, who had published the *Pathétique* in Vienna and at one time also had associations with Artaria, moved to

Leipzig and wrote to Beethoven from there asking what works he might purchase. Beethoven replied on 15 December, offering four works (Opp. 19–22), but negotiations continued into the following year.

Beethoven remained active as a performer in private circles during 1800, although few details are known. As already noted, he competed with Steibelt at the house of Count Fries, and almost certainly continued performing for Prince Lichnowsky, who granted him an annuity of 600 florins at about this time; the intention was that this would be paid yearly until Beethoven secured a permanent post, and it appears to have lasted until at least 1806. Prince Lobkowitz, having bought the quartets, must also have enjoyed Beethoven's talents at some of the numerous musical events he held. One reference to a musical event in which Beethoven participated comes in a letter written by Josephine Deym to her sisters on 10 December:

Beethoven played the sonata with cello [probably the Horn Sonata, which he arranged for cello]; I played the first of Beethoven's three violin sonatas [Op. 12], accompanied by Schuppanzigh, who, as always, played divinely; then there was a quartet [of players], and Beethoven, who was an angel, gave his new quartets, which are still not printed, and which are composed *non plus ultra*.[22]

Thus Beethoven ended the year with publishers competing for his works, patrons competing for his performances, personal admirers like Josephine, and an income more secure than at any time since 1794. Still he was giving no hint, in public or in private, about the dark shadow of deafness that was growing increasingly menacing within him.

---

[22] Cited from Brandenburg, 'Streichquartette', 288; the original is in French.

# 7

# Hope and despair (1801–2)

The start of the nineteenth century saw Beethoven embarking on a new symphony, in D major. He was evidently well pleased with the success of his benefit concert the previous April, and no doubt hoped to repeat the success in the coming April. His sketchbook for this period (Landsberg 7) reveals that he worked intensively on the first movement at this stage, more or less finishing it in outline, and he also jotted down a few possible ideas for later movements. Work on the symphony was, however, suddenly set aside in favour of an entirely new project, a ballet entitled *Die Geschöpfe des Prometheus* (The Creatures of Prometheus). There must have been some commission, and some guarantee of performance that spring, for Beethoven to set aside his symphony, but details are unfortunately lacking.

Ballet had a long-established tradition in Vienna, where Gluck had made an important contribution in the 1760s, and it gained a new lease of life and popularity there in the 1790s. Composers of these new ballets included Haibel, Süssmayr, Weigl, and Paul Wranitzky, and Beethoven had composed sets of piano variations on themes from two of them (by Haibel and Wranitzky, WoO 68 and 71) during 1795–7. Beethoven was still virtually unknown as a stage composer in Vienna in 1800, for his only ballet music, the *Ritterballett*, had been written in Bonn, and his only contribution to the Vienna stage in the 1790s was two arias (WoO 91) written about 1795 for insertion in the singspiel *Die schöne Schusterin* by Ignaz Umlauf. Thus the choice of Beethoven for the new ballet is a sign of the impact he had made as an instrumental composer by 1800. The ballet master in charge of the choreography was Salvatore Viganò, an Italian who had arrived in Vienna a few years earlier and had already achieved great success there.

The première of *Prometheus* took place in the Burgtheater, scene of Beethoven's benefit concert of the previous year, on Saturday 28 March, the last day before the theatres closed for Holy Week. Beethoven had to work fast to complete the music on schedule, for it was his longest work yet written (over 2000 bars in full score), and there was clearly no time to finish his symphony as well at that stage. Indeed there is evidence that the ballet was to have been performed a week earlier; if so, the delay may well have been due to the music not being ready (his *Leonore* and *Egmont* music were also not completed by the intended date).

The subject is loosely based on Greek mythology, and it cannot be fully recovered since the original text and choreography are lost. There survive a brief description in a theatre announcement, an account of the work in a later biography of Viganò that partly disagrees and is probably not wholly accurate,[1] and some clues in the music and Beethoven's sketchbook. The outline is clear enough, however. After being pursued in a storm, Prometheus creates two statues and brings them to life as man and woman, making them 'susceptible to all the passions of human life'. In Act 2, he leads them to Parnassus, where they are instructed and acquainted with the arts—specifically music, theatre, and dance—by various characters from classical antiquity.[2] Ballets of the period were customarily labelled as belonging to a particular type such as comic, heroic, or tragi-pantomimic (like the categories of play mentioned in Shakespeare's *Hamlet*). *Prometheus* was described as 'heroic allegorical', with the allegory explained thus: 'It portrays an exalted spirit, who found the people of his time in a state of ignorance, and refined them through knowledge and art and brought them enlightenment.' Thus the subject was essentially about the civilizing influence of art; and however quaint it may seem to some today, it was bound to have a powerful appeal to Beethoven, who strongly believed in the ability of art to uplift and ennoble mankind. The element of creation was equally strong (the title might indeed be better translated as 'The Creations of Prometheus'): Beethoven was able to reflect on the nature of artistic creation, and the work could be perceived as his response to Haydn's oratorio *The Creation* (the two composers are said to have compared their respective works in these terms on one occasion). Also attracting him was the idea of the suffering hero, and *Prometheus* was first in a series of works in which he portrayed heroism more or less explicitly.

The music consists of a well-known Overture (apparently composed last), an Introduction, and sixteen separate numbers. Some of these are quite short—notably No. 11, which is only eight bars—and several end with an imperfect cadence to lead on to the next number. Thus the action must have been fairly continuous. The Overture in C major is somewhat modelled on the first movement of Beethoven's First Symphony of the previous year, and even begins with a similar dominant 7th chord in the 'wrong' key. After a slow introduction it is lively and energetic throughout, with some unexpected modulations to flat keys providing just a hint of what might follow. The Overture runs straight into the first item in the ballet—the Introduction, where a tremulous A flat chord suddenly burst in, heralding a storm, which gradually subsides towards the end.

Of the ensuing numbers, several are particularly striking. In No. 1 the two statues are vividly portrayed by stiff, disjointed chords marked 'Poco

[1] TDR, ii. 219–31.
[2] The characters named in the playbill are Bacchus, Pan, Terpsichore, Thalia, Melpomene, Apollo, Amphion, Arion, and Orpheus. The biography also names Mars and Euterpe, but these are probably erroneous insertions into a half-remembered plot.

adagio', which are then brought to life in two allegro sections. No. 5 includes some stunning orchestration, with three solo wind instruments (flute, clarinet, and bassoon) accompanied by harp and pizzicato strings—Beethoven's only use of the harp in any work. Imaginative and uncharacteristic orchestration continues in the second part of this number with a prominent cello solo, and then in No. 14 Beethoven writes a solo for the basset horn. No. 9, meanwhile, depicts profound tragedy, clearly Melpomene's movement: it begins in E flat major, but soon moves to E flat minor for a prominent and highly expressive oboe solo over tremolando strings, and the movement ends with another example of Beethoven's characteristic C minor mood—an anguished Allegro molto depicting the death of Prometheus and the lament of his children, according to the sketches. C minor is duly followed by C major in No. 10, for a lovely 'Pastorale', a shepherd dance in which Prometheus is evidently restored to life. No. 12 is marked 'Solo di Gioja' in one early score: the playbill tells us that Ferdinand Gioja took the part of Bacchus, who performed a heroic dance, which must therefore be this number.[3] It contains all of Beethoven's commonest rhetorical devices for expressing heroic joy, including the key of C major and a march-like theme based on a rising triad, providing a foretaste of the finale of the Fifth Symphony.

The Finale (No. 16) provides a magnificent climax to the work. Its main theme (Ex. 7.1) is so archetypal in some ways that several alleged models for it have been found, amongst the works of Clementi and others. Its harmonic structure is indeed very basic, and can be fitted more or less successfully under many other sixteen-bar melodies. Yet if the theme is based on anything, it is on music heard earlier in the ballet: the cello solo in No. 5 contains a varied 6/8 version of the first quarter of the theme, while its third quarter recalls the passage in No. 1 where the first statue is brought to life. Thus the Finale provides a unifying as well as a climactic element for the ballet as a whole; and its main theme appears four times (plus repeats) in a rondo structure, so that by the end it is indelibly impressed on the listener.

Although the first review of the performance described Beethoven's music as 'too learned for a ballet and written with too little consideration for dancing',[4] the work was a great success. It is not actually excessively learned—certainly not compared with his chamber music and symphonies of the period. Like his *Ritterballett*, it exploits for the most part strong and direct rhythms suited to dancing, and possesses a wonderful range of moods and characters, with some highly original ideas in every movement, so that it deserves to be far better known. Its early success is evident from its being performed fourteen times in 1801 and nine times the following

---

[3] See N-II, 246, and TDR, ii. 219. It is sometimes claimed that No. 8 is the heroic dance (see Kinderman, *Beethoven*, 88), but this is more military than heroic, though it does have some slight motivic connections to the first movement of the *Eroica* Symphony.

[4] TDR, ii. 237.

**Ex. 7.1**  Op. 43/XVI

Ex. 7.1 *cont.*

year; all the musical cognoscenti in Vienna therefore had ample opportunity to hear it. Beethoven rapidly made a piano arrangement of the entire ballet, and this was rushed into print by Artaria, appearing less than three months after the premiere.

While composing *Prometheus*, Beethoven occasionally had other distractions. It was probably at this date that he first met the composer and pianist Carl Czerny (1791–1857). Czerny was introduced by their common friend the violinist Wenzel Krumpholz, and in 1842 he wrote a detailed account of this initial encounter:

I was about ten years old when Krumpholz took me to see Beethoven. . . . It was a winter's day when my father, Krumpholz and I took our way from Leopoldstadt (where we were still living) to Vienna proper, to a street called *der tiefe Graben*, and climbed endless flights to the fifth and sixth storey, where a rather untidy looking servant announced us to Beethoven and then admitted us. The room presented a most disorderly appearance; papers and articles of clothing were scattered about everywhere, some trunks, bare walls, hardly a chair, save the wobbly one at the Walter piano (then the best). . . . His beard—he had not been shaved for several days—made the lower part of his already brown face still darker. I also noticed with that visual quickness peculiar to children that he had cotton which seemed to have been steeped in a yellowish liquid, in his ears. At that time, however, he did not give the least evidence of deafness. I was at once told to play something, and since I did not dare begin with one of his own compositions, played Mozart's great C major Concerto, the one beginning with chords [K. 503]. Beethoven soon gave me his attention, drew near my chair, and in those passages where I had only accompanying passages played the orchestral melody with me, using his left hand. His hands were overgrown with hair and his fingers, especially at the ends, were very broad. The satisfaction he expressed gave me the courage to play his *Sonate pathétique*, which had just appeared, and finally his *Adelaide*, which my father sang in his very passable tenor. When he had ended Beethoven turned to him and said: 'The boy has talent. I will teach him myself and accept him as my pupil. Send him to me several times a week. First of all, however, get him a copy of Emanuel Bach's book on the true art of piano playing, for he must bring it with him the next time he comes.'[5]

The account is interesting for several reasons, and some of its details are corroborated by other evidence. Beethoven was living in *Tiefer Graben* from about January 1800 to the spring of 1801, and so the meeting could have taken place in either winter; but early 1801 is most likely, since Czerny was by then 'about ten' (his birthday was in February). True, the *Pathétique* had been published in December 1799, but viewed from the perspective of 1842 it could reasonably be said that it 'had just appeared' when Czerny visited Beethoven. Beethoven was living on the third floor, but there would normally be two flights of stairs for each storey, and so Czerny's reference to the 'sixth storey' indicates that he counted individual flights of stairs.

[5] TF, 227–8.

Czerny's evidence about Beethoven's ears is especially significant. The deafness had not yet become apparent to others, but some must have been aware, like Czerny, that Beethoven was having some kind of ear trouble. It seems that the problem became considerably worse during 1801–2 (perhaps partly because of the various treatments), for it was during that period that Beethoven felt obliged to withdraw from society.

The description of Beethoven's personal appearance and the great disorder of his surroundings seems reliable, for it matches many other descriptions (which mostly refer to later periods). Czerny also reveals that Beethoven had a fairly basic standard of living, not untypical of the average unmarried middle-class gentleman of that period. The cost of living of such a person was calculated as 775 florins per year in 1793, as has been seen, but by 1804 it had risen to 967 florins;[6] thus in 1801 it would have been about 900 florins. This provides some indication of Beethoven's earnings in these years; but he was also able to afford a servant, as well as manuscript paper and occasional books.

Also noteworthy is Beethoven's preference for C. P. E. Bach's keyboard treatise *Versuch über die wahre Art das Clavier zu spielen*, which had appeared as long ago as 1753. He had probably used this himself while studying with Neefe, since little else was then available. By 1800 there were a few alternatives, notably Daniel Gottlob Türk's *Clavierschule* (1789), but Beethoven continued to prefer Bach's treatise, and still did so in 1809 when preparing teaching material for Archduke Rudolph. Beethoven's willingness to instruct Czerny, even 'several times a week', indicates that his general distaste for teaching was not as wholehearted as some reports suggest, and that he was prepared to make an exception for a boy of such amazing talent; but one can easily imagine his impatience with any pupils who lacked ability.

Also occupying Beethoven's attention during the composition of *Prometheus* were his dealings with Hoffmeister, the publisher who had recently moved from Vienna to Leipzig. In January Beethoven renewed his offer of the four works Opp. 19–22, in a letter dated '15 January (or thereabouts)'[7] (he was never very good with dates!). He proposed 20 ducats each for the Septet, the First Symphony and the Piano Sonata, Op. 22, and 10 ducats for the so-called Second Piano Concerto. He explained that the first three works were all the same price because sonatas sell better, even though symphonies should be worth more; and the concerto was an early work, not one of his best (the best one at that stage was actually the still unfinished C minor Concerto). It is perhaps significant that the prices were quoted in gold ducats. Beethoven was finding conversion into florins difficult, 'because I really am a poor businessman and mathematician'. He went on in his letter to make a Utopian proposal that there should be a market for art, where the artist would 'bring his works and take what he needed'.

---

[6] Hanson, 'Incomes', 178.     [7] A-44.

What Beethoven really needed, of course, was a secretary who could organize the commercial side of his composing activities and leave him more time for actual composing. This need was partially fulfilled in later years by a number of different men, but in 1801 he was still having to do the work himself.

Despite Hoffmeister's acceptance of Beethoven's offer, the works had still not been sent by mid-April and Hoffmeister was becoming impatient. The problem was that not all the works were quite in a publishable state, and Beethoven had been too busy with *Prometheus* to attend to the matter (he was also unwell for a time). The Concerto in particular was deficient, for he had never actually written out the piano part in full, having performed it from memory (probably with improvised variants each time). He now wrote it out for the first time in April 1801, and to save time sent it to Hoffmeister in his own 'not very legible handwriting', as he explained in a letter of 22 April.[8] He apparently sent all four works that month, urging prompt publication, but Hoffmeister proved even more dilatory than Beethoven and none was published before December, when the concerto and symphony appeared.

Another problem with the Concerto was that when Beethoven looked through his full score (which had been written out in 1798) he noticed several passages in the first movement that were still unsatisfactory; he now amended them, using a distinctive grey ink. To transfer all these amendments to the set of parts being sent to Hoffmeister, however, would have taken considerable time (as was the custom, the work was to be published in parts, not score, and so Hoffmeister needed a correct set). Beethoven therefore compromised his artistic goals and sent off the parts unaltered, to save time. His conscience excused him on the grounds that he had already told Hoffmeister that the concerto was not one of his best works, and was being sold at half-price. As a result, the version published by Hoffmeister and customarily performed today is not the latest and best one.[9]

On the same day that Beethoven wrote to Hoffmeister, he also wrote to Breitkopf & Härtel in Leipzig, who like Hoffmeister had enquired whether he had any suitable works for publication. He had to disappoint them on this occasion, since all his latest works had already been allocated, but the firm later became one of his main publishers. They were also the publishers of the *Allgemeine musikalische Zeitung*, a journal that had reviewed several of his works, often unfavourably. Thus he took the opportunity to warn them that the concerto to be published by Hoffmeister was 'one of my first concertos, and consequently not one of my best compositions'. He hoped to forestall further unfavourable criticism, for he had found earlier

---

[8] A-47.
[9] A few of the changes were not written out and are lost, but there are fourteen passages where the amendments could be incorporated either as they stand or with minor editorial amendments: see Block, 'Gray Areas'; Cooper, *Creative Process*, 297–303.

reviews of his music 'very mortifying' until he realized that the reviewers really knew little about music.[10]

After *Prometheus* had been completed, Beethoven's next major project was some piano sonatas: Op. 26 in A flat, Op. 27 Nos. 1 and 2 (E flat and C sharp minor), and Op. 28 in D. Completion of the Second Symphony could safely be left until the following spring since there would be no opportunity for a benefit concert before then. The sketchbook for summer 1801 (the Sauer Sketchbook) survives only in fragments, making it hard to chart his precise progress on these sonatas, but he probably composed them in numerical order, working on all of them at some stage during the summer. Op. 26 was begun before *Prometheus*, and its first sketch is headed 'Sonate pour M.—' (Landsberg 7, p. 56), indicating it was commissioned by someone unidentified (the M. may simply stand for 'Monsieur'). This initial sketch indicates a first movement consisting of variations, then a minuet or march, and finally a movement in 2/4 with running semiquavers. Thus the sonata was to have an unusual structure, somewhat reminiscent of Mozart's A major sonata (K. 331). Eventually Beethoven decided on a minuet (or rather a scherzo) as well as a march, before a 2/4 finale that is said by Czerny to imitate the style of J. B. Cramer, who had visited Vienna in 1799.

The most original movement is the third, a profound funeral march in A flat minor (a key already used for the third variation in the first movement). Headed 'Funeral march on the death of a hero', it shows that Beethoven had been captivated by the idea of expressing heroism in music, and needed more than just a couple of movements in a heroic ballet to explore the concept. The return of war heroes from the campaign against Napoleon may have intensified his interest, for he had taken part in a charity concert in aid of the war wounded in January 1801. Structurally the movement is very simple: a ternary form (major–minor–major) with a short coda, but there are extraordinary innovations in melodic writing and texture. The main theme begins with a repeated note played no fewer than thirty-four times, challenging all conventional definitions of the word 'melody', although the shifting harmonies provide a kind of countermelody. The music then modulates to the relative major (C flat), before plunging into the minor mode of this key, notated as B minor rather than an absurd C flat minor. An enharmonic diminished 7th eventually brings the music back to the tonic for a brief reprise. Here the melody, which had till now been relatively quiet and low-pitched, rises rapidly to a high-pitched fortissimo climax. This contrast in dynamic and register is then used as a prime ingredient of the middle section (Ex. 7.2); but the most striking feature here is the recurring combination of tremolando and crescendo. Beethoven may have derived the idea of tremolandos from Daniel Steibelt, whose use of them at the famous

---

[10] A-48.

Ex. 7.2  Op. 26/III

contest between him and Beethoven the previous year was said to have been
entirely new. But Beethoven's use of the device is surely far more artistic, for
he develops it thematically (a common feature of his style is to develop thematically an idea that appears to be purely ornamental). The rapid
repeated notes inherent in a tremolando also recall the repeated notes of the
first section, while the pedal is used to intensify the sound, which by hinting at drum rolls subtly conveys the mood of a grand military or state
funeral. In this highly compressed middle section of only eight bars,
Beethoven's uses of register, theme, sonority, and musical rhetoric are combined with utmost ingenuity.

In his next two sonatas, Op. 27, Beethoven moved even further from the
conventional sonata pattern—so far, in fact, that he labelled each of them
'Sonata quasi una Fantasia'. The first is based on the conventional four-
movement structure, but the movements are to be played without a break,
and the first movement inserts an Allegro in C between two Andante sections in E flat. The third movement, an expressive Adagio, is somewhat
short, and part of it reappears just before the end of the finale—a device
reminiscent of the recall of 'La Malinconia' in the finale of the Quartet, Op.
18 No. 6.

The second of the two sonatas is the so-called 'Moonlight', although this
nickname, coined after Beethoven's death, is scarcely appropriate. The
popularity of the first movement can easily distract from its remarkable
originality. It was rare but not unprecedented to begin a sonata with a slow

movement; the sonority and texture, however, were highly novel for a sonata. The movement resembles a Romantic cavatina, with its emphasis on an aria-like melody, accompanied by patterned figuration, all swathed in a misty background caused by the absence of dampers throughout (it is marked 'sempre pianissimo senza sordino'). The beginning has surprisingly much in common with the 'Funeral March' in the Sonata, Op. 26: dotted rhythms, repeated notes on the dominant, a melodic descent to a cadence in the relative major, and immediate substitution of the minor mode of this key. Again there is the feeling of profound tragedy, intensified at times (as in Op. 26) by the use of the flattened supertonic. The second movement provides a sharp contrast of mood, but its cheerful nature might be taken to imply past rather than present happiness, and it is only a brief interlude before the angry and agitated finale. Here the triplets of the first movement are expanded into surging arpeggios that cover almost the whole keyboard, in a sonata-form movement that carries the main weight of the work. Beethoven's persistent desire to create unity, continuity, and forward thrust throughout a whole work finds a new manner of realization in this sonata.

The next sonata, Op. 28, provides a complete contrast. It is lengthy, relaxed, totally unheroic, and pastoral in mood, especially in the first and last movements; indeed it acquired the nickname 'Pastoral' not long after publication. Beethoven's ability to produce four such different sonatas so quickly is remarkable, and never again did he write so many piano sonatas in such a short space of time.

Beethoven briefly interrupted work on these sonatas during the summer to write two very long and deeply moving letters to close friends whom he had not seen for some time—Wegeler in Bonn and Amenda in Courland.[11] The letter to Wegeler is dated 29 June, but it is so long (over 1,500 words) that Beethoven may not have finished it until a day or two later; he then wrote along similar lines to Amenda, in a letter dated 1 July. Of central concern in both letters is his hearing problem, which he asks the recipients to keep secret. He mentions the misery and unhappiness it is causing, the social isolation that has resulted, and how it has become worse in recent months despite attempts at treatment. To Wegeler, a doctor, he describes in detail symptoms of tinnitus (humming in the ears) and the difficulty of hearing soft voices or high notes. He reports that his deafness is a great professional handicap; yet to Amenda he claims it affects him least when playing and composing, and is more a social disadvantage. He seems to have been particularly anxious about the reactions of other musicians: 'If my enemies, of whom I have a fair number, were to hear about it, what would they say?' He hints to Wegeler that some of his friends were in fact already aware of the problem; but presumably they did not gossip about it. He also mentions abdominal complaints, which he believed were related to his

---

[11]  A-51 and A-53.

deafness, but which had recently been responding to treatment. There is in both letters a lament that nothing could apparently be done, and he was left to follow the path of resignation.

Intermingled with the complaints, however, are a confidence, determination and hope to overcome the difficulties, and indications of a highly successful career. To Amenda he writes: 'I am convinced that my luck will not fail me—at the moment I feel equal to anything.' He tells Wegeler that six or seven publishers are competing for his works (letters to Hoffmeister and Breitkopf & Härtel, already mentioned, seem to bear this out); that he is receiving more commissions than he can fulfil (which suggests that all four piano sonatas of that summer were commissioned); and that with publishers 'I state my price and they pay', which is certainly what had happened in the case of Hoffmeister with Opp. 19–22. Later in the letter he describes his total absorption in composition: 'I live entirely in my music; and hardly have I completed one composition when I have already begun another. At my present rate of composing, I often produce three or four works at the same time.' Thus both letters convey a sense of struggle between confidence and resignation, between hope and despair. His innate strength of character and his determination demanded that he 'bid defiance to my fate', yet he regretted that he would not achieve 'all that my talent and my strength have commanded me to do'.

The rest of the two letters is concerned mainly with personal relationships—both to the recipients, to whom he expresses warm friendship, and between himself and others. He reveals to Amenda that close acquaintances like Zmeskall and Schuppanzigh can never be his true friends, and rather shockingly says, 'I value them merely for what they do for me'. But he praises Prince Lichnowsky for his beneficence; and one true friend had recently arrived in Vienna, Stephan von Breuning, whom Beethoven was now seeing almost every day. Another friend, the young Ferdinand Ries, son of Beethoven's old violin teacher Franz Ries in Bonn, was also expected, and duly reached Vienna in October. Thereafter he received piano lessons from Beethoven for four years, and in return provided him with much practical help. Many of Ries's reminiscences about Beethoven published in 1838 derive from this period.

Beethoven wrote another letter to Wegeler on 16 November.[12] Some of the sentiments are the same as before, but the emphasis is more on hope than despair. The change, as he explains,

has been brought about by a dear charming girl who loves me and whom I love. After two years I am again enjoying a few blissful moments; and for the first time I feel that—marriage might bring me happiness. Unfortunately she is not of my class—and at the moment—I certainly could not marry—I must still bustle about a good deal.

---

[12] A-54.

Thus his social isolation had also meant two years of sexual isolation, which is revealed to have been one of the main causes of his despair during the summer. (His last known beloved before this date was Magdalena Willmann, to whom, according to her niece, he had proposed marriage some time around 1795; but his comment to Wegeler that 'for the first time' he was thinking of marriage in 1801 suggests that the claim of Magdalena's niece may be incorrect.) The new beloved in 1801 was Countess Giulietta Guicciardi (1784–1856), who had probably met Beethoven through her cousin Josephine Deym or other members of the Brunsvik family. Beethoven began giving her piano lessons (unpaid) around 1801, and dedicated his 'Moonlight' Sonata to her. She was certainly not 'of his class', however, and eventually married one Count Gallenberg in 1803. An interesting sidelight on her relationship with Beethoven is cast by a conversation of 4 February 1823.[13] Writing in French, so that he could be neither overheard nor understood by others around him (except Anton Schindler, to whom the comments were addressed), Beethoven stated:

I was loved by her, and more than her husband ever was. Yet he was more her lover than I. . . . She was born Guicciardi. She was already his wife before [they emigrated] to Italy—and she sought me weeping, but I rejected her. . . . If I had wished to give the strength of my life to that life, what would have remained for the nobler, the better?

This last sentence, written in German, reinforces Beethoven's comment to Wegeler in 1801 that he still had to 'bustle about' and therefore could not marry. At that time, as he said, he was living entirely in his art, which afforded him the greatest delight. Marriage was perceived as an unwanted distraction that would undermine the 'nobler' side of life, rather than being noble in itself. He clearly felt that a solitary life was essential if he was to achieve his highest artistic aims. Thus, on the rare occasions when a woman was prepared to give herself to him, as may have been the case here, he held back and found reasons for rejecting her.[14] He was already, in effect, wedded to music.

None of Beethoven's personal struggles of 1801 are evident in the music written that summer. After finishing his four piano sonatas, his next major composition was a String Quintet in C commissioned by Count Fries, probably written in late summer and published in 1802 as Op. 29. Its most important innovation is the key of the second subject in the first movement. Beethoven had explored remote key-relationships in several earlier works, and had sometimes placed part of the second group in an unexpected key (the dominant minor in Op. 2 No. 3; the minor of the relative major in the *Pathétique*); but the main part of the second group had always been writ-

[13] BKh, ii. 365–6.
[14] It has been suggested, however, that Giulietta did not love Beethoven as deeply as he imagined; see Tyson, 'Guicciardi', 13.

ten in the dominant or the relative major. Now, for the first time, he tried a different approach: the lyrical second subject is in A major, and the exposition closes in A minor. This innovation was so successful that before long he was using the mediant or submediant for the second subject nearly as often as the dominant. On this first occasion, however, there had to be some exceptional musical justification for using A major in such a conspicuous position. The explanation comes in the finale. This is essentially in sonata form, but just before the recapitulation Beethoven inserts a minuet-style passage in a completely different metre from the surrounding material. This wholly unexpected insertion is in A major, and so the second subject of the first movement provides a long-range pointer to a startling irregularity. Meanwhile the minuet-style passage duly returns in the coda, but in C major, to resolve the sense of disruption caused earlier.

Several other works are thought to date from around the latter part of 1801, but a dearth of sketches means this cannot always be verified. They include the Serenade for Flute, Violin, and Viola (Op. 25), the Romance in G for violin and orchestra (Op. 40), the Variations on 'Bei Männern' from *The Magic Flute*, for cello and piano (WoO 46), some unaccompanied Italian partsongs (WoO 99), and a collection of contredanses (WoO 14).

The partsongs were written as exercises under the instruction of Salieri, who annotated some of them. Most were formerly thought to date from the 1790s, but study of their paper indicates a date of around 1801. They were probably composed intermittently almost throughout the year, and the earliest ones may date from 1800. In several cases the same text has been set more than once, and sometimes there are even two slightly different versions of the same setting. The Serenade, Op. 25, was also long believed to have been written in the 1790s, but the single known sketch is contemporary with some of the partsongs for Salieri, indicating a date of 1801. Since Beethoven generally tried to number his works in chronological order, it was most likely written shortly before the Sonatas, Opp. 26–8. It is a light and tuneful work, as befits its scoring, and consists of seven movements written in the popular divertimento style. No sketches are known for either the 'Bei Männern' Variations or the Romance. The variations appeared in 1802 (the edition is actually dated 1 January, although it was not advertised until April); the Romance, which like its predecessor in F is in varied rondo form, may not have been composed until early 1802, but there is no sign of it in the sketchbooks of that period, where one might expect to find it.

The other work put together at the end of 1801 was a collection of Twelve Contredanses WoO 14, the last of Beethoven's big orchestral sets of dances. The best-known of the twelve is No. 7, for it is based on the main theme of the finale of *Prometheus*, a theme that reappears in the *Eroica* Symphony. Many writers have claimed that the contredanse represents the original version of the theme and predates *Prometheus*. This error illustrates the importance of examining the sources properly rather than relying solely on internal criteria. The sketches for *Prometheus* show the theme being created as an integral part of the ballet, and it appears in a slightly primitive form in one sketch (Landsberg 7, p. 139). This would not have happened if the contredanse had existed already, and so the ballet must have come first. This conclusion is confirmed by the autograph score of WoO 14 No. 7.[15] It is found as the third of a set of four contredanses written for a Monsieur de Friederich (whom Beethoven facetiously named 'Liederlich'— slovenly or lewd—in the manuscript). The other three pieces in the set (WoO 14 Nos. 10, 9, and 2) were not sketched until late 1801 in the Kessler Sketchbook (SV 263, ff. 9r–10r), a full six months after the première of the ballet, and so this must be when Beethoven adapted the *Prometheus* theme as a contredanse.

In order to assemble a set of twelve contredanses for publication, Beethoven placed these four alongside a pair (Nos. 5 and 1) written slightly earlier, a group of three (Nos. 3, 4, and 6) written about 1795, and a copyist's score of Nos. 8, 4, and 12. Most of the dances bore numberings that reflected their position in their original groups (thus the first four were numbered 1–4), and so he now renumbered all of them, using a red crayon or *Rötel*, an implement he started relying on for late alterations to manuscripts. Some dances were renumbered more than once, but he eventually ended up with their present numbering (and with the second copy of No. 4 disregarded). Since there were only eleven dances represented, he adapted another part of the *Prometheus* finale to create No. 11. The set of twelve dances was then sent to Mollo, who published them the following April.

During the winter of 1801–2 Beethoven resumed work on his Second Symphony, in anticipation of a benefit concert in the forthcoming Holy Week (11–17 April). Most of the sketches for the two middle movements are lost and must have been made on loose leaves, but the finale is fairly fully represented in the Kessler Sketchbook, which was in use from late 1801 to mid-1802. One intriguing sketch in the book, headed 'andante sinfonia' (f. 8v), is evidently for the slow movement, and contains ideas that were developed in two different ways in the two middle movements. The family relationship between these three themes becomes very apparent when they are all placed in the same key (Ex. 7.3 a–c). The kinship highlights the kind of thematic unity Beethoven was striving for in many of his works, and indeed the main themes of the two outer movements also belong within this family of themes, both rising from tonic to dominant and back.

The symphony was apparently more or less complete by February, although some touching up, including an extension of the coda of the finale, doubtless went on in the following months. On a grander scale than its predecessor, it was perhaps the longest symphony to have been written at that date, although it was soon to be overshadowed by No. 3, the *Eroica*. It is in some ways thoroughly conventional, continuing along the path set

---

[15] Description in Klein, *Autographe*, 162.

Ex. 7.3    (a) SV 263, f. 8v    (b) Op. 36/II (transp.)    (c) Op. 36/III, Trio (transp.)

by Haydn, but it is full of original ideas, with great motivic and formal sophistication, especially in the finale. As in the *Pathétique*, Beethoven uses a motif from the slow introduction (in this case the opening repeated-note figure) during the main Allegro of the first movement (e.g. bars 96–101). This in itself requires no great ingenuity; the difficulty is to integrate the motif into the Allegro so thoroughly that it is hardly noticed, which is what he achieves so successfully.

After he had finished sketching the symphony, Beethoven turned his attention to a couple of shorter works: a full-scale Italian terzet for soprano, tenor, bass, and orchestra (*Tremate, empi, tremate*, Op. 116), written as a continuation of his studies with Salieri; and a triple concerto in D major (called a concertante in the sketches), for piano trio and orchestra. The first of these was apparently not performed until 1814 and not published until 1826 (hence its high opus number). The concerto fared even less well, being abandoned shortly after Beethoven began writing out the first movement in score. It was presumably intended for his expected benefit concert in April; but he already had a piano concerto (in C minor) that needed finishing, or at least polishing up, and so it is curious that he should embark on another concerto at this stage—especially one in the same key as the symphony.

In the end the benefit concert was cancelled by the theatre director, as is clear from a letter to Breitkopf & Härtel dated 22 April, the week after the concert should have happened. By now, Beethoven's longstanding need for a secretary to assist with his business affairs had been supplied by his brother Carl, who found time between his duties as a civil servant to assist Beethoven in many ways from early 1802 for the next four years. It was he who wrote to Breitkopf on 22 April: 'My brother would have written to you himself, but he is now not in the mood for anything, because the theatre director Baron von Braun, who is clearly an ignorant, rude man, did not allow him the theatre for a benefit concert and gave it over to other, utterly mediocre artists.'[16] It is tempting to believe that the triple concerto was abandoned when the benefit concert was cancelled, but in fact it was probably set aside some weeks earlier. On 28 March, when the concert was apparently still expected, Carl had offered Breitkopf the Quintet Op. 29 and also 'a grand symphony and a piano concerto', which were to be available in three to four weeks. The concerto must have been the one in C minor, and so it seems that Beethoven was planning by this stage to perform this work rather than the triple concerto. Earlier abandonment of the latter also seems indicated by the chronology of the sketchbook, where the concerto is followed by the three Violin Sonatas, Op. 30. Carl offered these to Breitkopf on 22 April, and so unless he made the offer well in advance of their completion (seemingly not his normal practice), they must have been begun, and the concerto abandoned, at least several weeks earlier, probably February or early March.

One work that appears to date from early 1802 but is not represented in the sketchbooks is a set of six songs with texts by Christian Gellert. A copyist's score of the songs is dated 8 March 1802,[17] earlier than they were once thought to have been written. The texts were religious—an unusual choice for Beethoven—but he had been thinking about them since at least 1798, when he jotted down a few sketches for the third poem, 'Vom Tode'— sketches that were not eventually used. In the first five songs only the first stanza is set, with the implication that the remaining stanzas are to be sung to the same music. The last song, however, is through-composed, with a first, sorrowful section in A minor followed by a longer, optimistic section in A major, thematically related to the first. Throughout all six songs, Beethoven shows great sensitivity to the rhythm and meaning of the words, even though there is little scope for pictorialism. Most striking is the contrast between the third and fourth songs: 'Vom Tode' is set pianissimo in F sharp minor, a solemn and serious reflection on death, with several anguished discords and mostly low register; 'Die Ehre Gottes aus der Natur', on the other hand, is in C major, mostly loud, and grand in effect. It concerns nature's praise of God, and concludes with the image of the sun as a hero, to which Beethoven responds with massive and characteristically heroic chords.

The three aforementioned Violin Sonatas, Op. 30, were composed in a concentrated burst of energy during the spring. Ries relates that the finale of the 'Kreutzer' Sonata, Op. 47, was originally composed as the finale of Op. 30 No. 1 but was substituted by the present finale 'because the other movement was too brilliant for this sonata'.[18] This improbable story is fully confirmed by the sketches, which show the 'Kreutzer' finale amongst the sketches for Op. 30 No. 1, with the present finale not sketched until the set was nearly finished. As usual, one sonata (No. 2) is in the minor, and again C minor was chosen, with a particularly striking theme for the stormy finale.

[16] Alb-38.    [17] JTW, 117.    [18] WR, 72.

Beethoven's activities during the spring also involved further dealings with publishers, including a new firm formed by Joseph von Sonnleithner and Josef Schreyvogel, pretentiously named the *Bureau d'Arts et d'Industrie* (later also known as the *Bureau des Arts et d'Industrie* or the *Kunst- und Industrie-Comptoir*). The first Beethoven work they published, in May 1802, was his string-quartet arrangement of his Piano Sonata, Op. 14 No. 1. In general he did not favour such arrangements, but made this one because of a particularly earnest request from someone, and it works rather better as a string quartet than would most of his sonatas. The arrangement involved transposing the piece from E to F, to enable the bottom string on the cello to function as a dominant at times.

Many of Beethoven's business dealings were by now being organized by Carl, who showed himself increasingly enterprising in his attempts to earn money for the two of them. He had begun by dramatically increasing the price of Beethoven's works. Beethoven had sold his First Symphony and Septet for 20 ducats apiece, but Carl demanded—and obtained—38 ducats for the String Quintet, and dared to ask Breitkopf for 130 ducats for the three Violin Sonatas, Op. 30. They may not have agreed to this, for the sonatas were bought by the Bureau for an unknown price, but it was surely not much less than 130 ducats.

Carl's next plan, observing the popularity of arrangements, was to offer Breitkopf a supply of such works, arranged by someone else but checked and if necessary amended by Beethoven himself. Such works could then be advertised as arranged by the composer, who would earn a significant amount for relatively little work. Without such a scheme, publishers would simply make their own arrangements, for which Beethoven would receive nothing since there was no copyright protection. Breitkopf, however, rejected Carl's offer, much to Beethoven's satisfaction: 'As to the works to be arranged I am heartily delighted that you have refused them. The *unnatural mania*, now so prevalent, for transferring even *pianoforte compositions* to stringed instruments, instruments which in all respects are so utterly different from one another, should really cease.'[19] His view was that only the composer, or at least someone equally able, was capable of arranging works satisfactorily, and indeed his arrangement of the E major sonata does include several ingenious pieces of motivic reworking. Carl's plan, however, was soon taken up by other publishers, and during the next few years several of Beethoven's works appeared in arrangements made by Ferdinand Ries and others.

Carl's third money-spinning idea was to publish numerous early works that had still not appeared, using Beethoven's great popularity as a selling-point. Thus from 1803 a spate of such works suddenly appeared, seemingly through Carl's involvement in Beethoven's activities. Ries reports: 'All his little compositions and many things he never wanted published, since he

[19] A-59.

did not consider them worthy of his name, were secretly brought out by his brothers. Thus songs he had composed in Bonn years before his departure for Vienna became known only after he had achieved a high reputation.'[20]

In April 1802 Beethoven retired to the quiet of the countryside on the advice of his doctor (Johann Schmidt), in a final effort to combat his encroaching deafness. He chose the village of Heiligenstadt, two miles north of the city, and remained there until October, making only occasional visits to Vienna. By his own account he was less active than usual, and he had time to pause for reflection. The effects of this were partly detrimental and partly beneficial (his life and work seem filled with such dualities). His isolation led to brooding on his deafness, which showed no signs of improvement, and he became increasingly suicidal, his anguish leading ultimately to the outpourings of his famous Heiligenstadt Testament in October. His first ideas for new compositions at Heiligenstadt, however, were extremely original even by his standards: two sets of variations (Opp. 34 and 35) worked out in an entirely new manner. As he later told Breitkopf & Härtel: 'Usually I have to wait for other people to tell me when I have new ideas, because I never know this myself. But this time—I myself can assure you that in both these works the manner is quite new for me.'[21]

When he came to publish the two sets, he even wanted a preface announcing their novelty placed at the beginning of the edition. This was no mere frivolity, as some have suggested, for they are fundamentally different both from each other and from any previous set of variations. He first sketched some variations on the finale theme from *Prometheus*, then jotted down a new idea for a set of variations in F, with 'every variation in a different metre' (Kessler Sketchbook, f. 88v). These will be discussed presently. Work on the two sets, however, was interrupted by a communication from the Swiss firm of Nägeli in Zurich, requesting three new sonatas for their series *Répertoire des Clavecinistes*. Carl proposed a fee of 100 ducats, which was accepted, and Beethoven set to work at once, completing all three sonatas (Op. 31) in Heiligenstadt. Carl then wanted to sell them to a Leipzig publisher (presumably for a higher fee), but Beethoven refused to dishonour his agreement with Nägeli and gave them to Ries to send there at once.[22]

All three sonatas abound in interesting ideas, but the one that has attracted most attention is the second, in D minor. Often known as the 'Tempest' Sonata, on account of an anecdote by Schindler once widely believed, it is certainly tempestuous, at least in the first movement, which never once settles properly in a major key despite the promise of the opening A major chord. Beethoven originally planned to begin with a bold D minor arpeggio theme, but he replaced this with a single mysterious chord played arpeggiando. It was the first time he had begun a sonata with a dominant chord, and the effect is many-sided: it creates uncertainty about

---

[20] WR, 112.     [21] A-62.     [22] WR, 76.

key, instability through its first-inversion position, and ambiguity about whether it is a slow introduction or the main theme itself (or both simultaneously). It is a tremendously forward-looking gesture: a similar ambiguity occurs at the start of the Ninth Symphony, also in D minor, while the Fifth Symphony resembles the sonata in that it begins with a short motif that seems merely introductory but proves to contain the main thematic material. In the sonata, the slow chord is used in alternation with a descending allegro motif, and this duality provides the principal theme of the movement (the treatment of the arpeggiando chord is another example of Beethoven developing thematically an idea that seems purely ornamental). The first emphatic D minor chord appears in bar 21, suggesting that this is the true first subject, but it proves to initiate the transition to the dominant. The second subject is equally ambiguous, for some see it as beginning in bar 41, while others see this passage as so similar to first-group material that they regard bar 55 as the start of the proper second subject, which is then developed in the rest of the exposition. Debates on which is the right interpretation are futile: Beethoven has ingeniously contrived that the movement can be perceived in more than one way. The most remarkable feature in the movement, however, is the start of the recapitulation (bar 143). Here the arpeggiando chord, which carries with it a traditional association with recitative, is followed immediately by some actual recitative, while the chord itself is sustained by the pedal to create an eerie, cavernous and wholly unprecedented effect, which is heard twice (Beethoven generally repeats his most striking effects, as do many great composers).

The second movement, in B flat major, is in many ways a complete contrast, peaceful and stable, and never once settling in a minor key. Yet it does have connections to the first, for it begins with an arpeggiando chord, and expands the idea of arpeggios into cascades of broken chords in the recapitulation. It also, like the first movement, uses the turn figure both as a decoration (bar 10) and a melodic shape (bars 18–19). The finale makes further use of arpeggios, employing them as a main accompaniment figure throughout. Like the first movement, it has a strong emphasis on minor keys (the second group is once again in A minor), but it does have a brief flirtation with the key of the second movement (bars 234–41), to provide integration; and its descending D minor arpeggio at the very end provides the perfect long-term 'answer' to the A major 'question' that began the sonata: everything in between can be perceived as in some sense parenthetical to this fundamental progression.

As soon as he had finished the sonatas, Beethoven returned to his two sets of variations, completing the F major set and then the *Prometheus* one in quick succession. When he and Carl wrote to Breitkopf on 18 October they described the sets as containing eight and thirty variations respectively. In the score they appear to contain only six and fifteen, which has led some writers to conclude that they were still far from finished when the letters were written; but, as Beethoven explained in a later letter, the total depends on the method of counting, for each set contains irregularities. A closer study of the music shows that Carl's claim, echoed by Beethoven's letter, that the variations 'can be counted' as eight and thirty, is justifiable. See Table 7.1 for the structure of the first set.

TABLE 7.1

|   |        |    |     |         |                      |
|---|--------|----|-----|---------|----------------------|
|   | Theme  | F  | 2/4 | 22 bars | Adagio               |
| 1 | Var. 1 | D  | 2/4 | 22 bars | [Adagio]             |
| 2 | Var. 2 | B♭ | 6/8 | 22 bars | Allegro, ma non troppo |
| 3 | Var. 3 | G  | 4/4 | 22 bars | Allegretto           |
| 4 | Var. 4 | E♭ | 3/4 | 22 bars | Tempo di Menuetto    |
| 5 | Var. 5 | c  | 2/4 | 22 bars | Marcia: Allegretto   |
|   | link   |    | 2/4 | 6 bars  |                      |
| 6 | Var. 6 | F  | 6/8 | 22 bars | Allegretto           |
| 7 | 'Coda' | F  | 6/8 | 17 bars | [Allegretto]         |
| 8 | (Var.) | F  | 2/4 | 22 bars | Adagio molto         |
|   | (coda) | F  | 2/4 | 3 bars  |                      |

The structure of Op. 35 is more complex:

TABLE 7.2

|       |                 |                           |
|-------|-----------------|---------------------------|
|       | Basso del Tema  | 1+16 bars                 |
| 1     | a due           | 16 bars                   |
| 2     | a tre           | 16 bars                   |
| 3     | a quattro       | 16 bars                   |
| 4     | Tema            | 16 bars                   |
| 5–9   | Vars. 1–5       | 16 bars each              |
| 10    | Var. 6 (in c)   | 24 bars (2nd repeat varied) |
| 11–17 | Vars. 7–13      | 16 bars each              |
| 18–19 | Var. 14 (minore) | 32 bars (double variation) |
| 20–1  | Var. 15 (Largo) | 32 bars (double variation) |
| 22    | 'Coda'          | 8 bars                    |
| 23–6  | Finale alla Fuga | 132 bars                 |
| 27–30 | Andante con moto | 64 bars (2 double variations) |
|       | (coda)          | 9 bars                    |

Thus in Op. 34 there are eight main sections after the theme, and the total is fully equivalent to eight variations, while in Op. 35 there are the equivalent of at least thirty variations in terms of overall length. Hence both sets were probably virtually complete by 18 October. Far more significant, however, is the extraordinary originality of the structures shown above. In Op. 34, Beethoven combined his original idea of using a different metre in each successive variation with the notion of using a sharply contrasting key too. To prevent the whole work falling apart, he had to use some unifying factor, and this was the opening phrase, which recurs several times in each variation and is often left more or less intact. Thus in Var. 1, the original tempo and metre are retained and so the theme is decorated; but in Vars. 2, 4, and 5, where both key and tempo are new, the initial melodic outline is left unvaried. In Var. 3 there is limited melodic decoration, but this is counterbalanced by the resumption of the duple metre of the theme (though notated as 4/4, not 2/4). In Var. 6 the start of the theme is again left intact since there is a different rhythm. The 'Coda' includes some motivic development, while the final, unnumbered variation brings the work full circle by resuming the initial metre and tempo, facilitating some highly florid decoration.

The sudden changes of key and metre in successive variations enable Beethoven to explore the device of thematic transformation—one of the three basic ways (along with decoration and development) in which a theme can be manipulated. The device was far from new, having been used in pairs of dances in the sixteenth century and in more extended form in variation suites of the early seventeenth century, where several dances in various rhythms were based on the same thematic material. But Beethoven's approach is different, foreshadowing that of the Romantics, for he uses a single theme in several different metres and keys which utterly transform not just its rhythm but its character: this can become a lively gallop (Var. 2), a graceful dance (Var. 4) or a lugubrious funeral march (Var. 5) while retaining an unchanged melodic shape. He also combines transformation with decoration in Vars. 1 and 3, and some later parts of the other variations, so that the music is continually fluctuating between the two principles. Beethoven was to exploit thematic transformation in several later works, but never again so thoroughly and systematically as here.

The *Prometheus* Variations (as Beethoven wanted them called) show an equally extraordinary structure, although some of its features have become familiar through the finale of the *Eroica* Symphony, which is based on the same theme. After an opening chord, Beethoven begins with just the bass line of the theme. This would be strange enough with an ordinary bass line, but here the third quarter consists entirely of rests and repeated notes, which scarcely seems like music at all! This bass line is followed by three variations in which one, two, then three other parts are added as counterpoint, respectively above, around, and below the original bass. Only then does the well-known tune (and it was already well-known in Vienna by 1802) appear. Thus the stiff, unharmonized bass line seems gradually brought to life during four variations—an echo of the *Prometheus* ballet in which the statues were brought to life. In the ensuing variations it is the theme, not the bass line, that provides the thematic basis, but the bass takes over in the 'finale', where its first four notes form the subject of an elaborate fugue, which leads to further variations of the tune to round off the work. Apart from their length, complexity, and high level of originality,

119

both sets of variations possess a range of character and emotions more characteristic of a sonata than variations, and as a result Beethoven decided to give them opus numbers, which he had not done for any of his previous sets.

It seems that it was while Beethoven was finalizing the variations that he wrote what has become his most famous literary document, the so-called Heiligenstadt Testament, which he dated 6 October 1802. It is addressed to his brothers, although blank spaces are left for Johann's name (and also, originally, for Carl's), and was designed 'to be read and executed after my death'. Parts of it, however, are addressed in effect to his friends, to the world at large, or to God. Its exact function is therefore somewhat ambiguous. But no one reading it can fail to be moved by its depth of emotion and despair, which had evidently been building up during Beethoven's time at Heiligenstadt, and which now, as he was about to leave the village with his last hope of cure gone, found an outlet. The Testament begins:

O you men who think or say I am hostile, peevish, or misanthropic, how greatly you wrong me. You do not know the secret cause which makes me seem so to you. From childhood on, my heart and soul were full of the tender feeling of goodwill, and I was always inclined to accomplish great deeds. But just think, for six years now I have had an incurable condition, made worse by incompetent doctors, from year to year deceived with hopes of getting better, finally forced to face the prospect of a lasting infirmity (whose cure will perhaps take years or even be impossible). Though born with a fiery, lively temperament, susceptible to the diversions of society, I soon had to withdraw myself, to spend my life alone. And if I wished at times to ignore all this, oh how harshly was I pushed back by the doubly sad experience of my bad hearing; and yet it was impossible for me to say to people, 'Speak louder, shout, for I am deaf.' Ah, how could I possibly admit weakness of the *one sense* which should be more perfect in me than in others, a sense which I once possessed in the greatest perfection, a perfection such as few in my profession have or ever have had.

Oh I cannot do it; so forgive me if you see me draw back when I would gladly have mingled with you. My misfortune is doubly painful to me as I am bound to be misunderstood; for me there can be no relaxation in human company, no refined conversations, no mutual outpourings. I must live quite alone, like an outcast; I can enter society practically only as much as real necessity demands. If I approach people a burning anxiety comes over me, in that I fear being placed in danger of my condition being noticed.[23]

Thus Beethoven paints a vivid picture of the personal and social life he was leading during the composition of such works as the Second Symphony, the Violin Sonatas, Op. 30, the Piano Sonatas, Op. 31, and the two new sets of variations. He goes on to describe an occasion when someone standing near him heard a distant flute while he heard nothing. The person may have been Ries, who reports that on one occasion (perhaps the same one),

---

[23] The original is in the Staats- und Universitätsbibliothek, Hamburg. The translation given here is from Cooper, *Compendium*, 170, where the document is given in full.

I called his attention to a shepherd in the forest who was playing most pleasantly on a flute cut from lilac wood. For half an hour Beethoven could not hear anything at all and became extremely quiet and gloomy, even though I repeatedly assured him that I did not hear anything any longer either (which was, however, not the case).[24]

Beethoven states that such incidents 'brought me almost to despair', and that he had contemplated suicide, being held back only by his art. Instead of suicide, however, he chose patience and endurance. He had arrived at Heiligenstadt full of hope, but bade farewell to the village on 10 October (in a postscript to the Testament) with his hope abandoned. His final paragraph is a prayer for a day of pure joy, which he feared he would never again experience.

Beethoven's decision to reject suicide, and overcome his feelings of despair by writing them down here, can be seen as marking a turning point in his life. Never again did he record such deep despair and self-pity. He carefully preserved the Testament for the rest of his life (it was discovered and published shortly after his death), and it is a symbol of his determination to overcome his fate rather than succumb to it. The period of mourning for being bereaved of his fine hearing had come to an end, and the writing of the Testament functioned as a kind of ceremonial burial. He returned to Vienna with his spirit revived, and ready to break new ground in the development of his art.

[24] WR, 86–7.

# 8

# After Heiligenstadt (1802–3)

'Heiligenstadt, 10 October 1802, thus I take leave of thee—and indeed sadly.' This is how, in a postscript to his Testament, Beethoven bade farewell to the village of his hopes and ultimate despair. He returned to Vienna, probably that day, and promptly threw himself into his work—a common means of overcoming grief. Only eight days later he wrote enthusiastically to Breitkopf & Härtel about his two new sets of variations (Opp. 34 and 35), and about how 'nearly all foreign publishers are continually writing to me for compositions'.[1] The return from Heiligenstadt also marked a new beginning, and from this moment there is a distinctive change in the nature of his output. Of course, all his major works show novel features, and his two new sets of variations exhibit more innovations than most. Beethoven had also already been consciously exploring new directions, according to Czerny, who reports that between the composition of the Sonata, Op. 28, and the three of Op. 31 Beethoven said: 'I am not very well satisfied with the work I have thus far done. From this day on I shall take a new way.'[2] Nevertheless, the works written immediately after Heiligenstadt can be seen as more profoundly innovative, pointing in new directions and moving much further away from the legacy of Haydn and Mozart. The first works conceived after Heiligenstadt are extremely important in this respect: the oratorio *Christus am Oelberge* (Christ on the Mount of Olives) and the *Eroica* Symphony, both of which had deep personal significance, as will be seen. The new attitude is also reflected in a letter dated 23 November 1802 from Carl to the publisher Johann André, who like other publishers had applied to Beethoven for new compositions:

If you should want three pianoforte sonatas, I could provide them for no less than 900 florins, all according to Vienna standard, and you could not have these all at once, but one every five or six weeks, because my brother does not trouble himself much with such trifles any longer and composes only oratorios, operas etc.[3]

---

[1] A-62.
[2] Sonneck, *Impressions*, 31; here Czerny dates the conversation *c.* 1800, but in *Proper Performance*, 13, he dates it *c.* 1803.
[3] Alb-49; BB-113.

This last comment may seem absurdly pompous, but it doubtless reflects Beethoven's own desire to move away from sonatas to more elevated types of composition, and the reference to 'oratorios, operas etc.' is not as inaccurate as might first appear. He had been finishing an operatic duet, 'Nei giorni tuoi felici' (WoO 93), as the culmination of his studies with Salieri and with the intention of moving on to a full-length opera (he had been greatly impressed by the French operas by Cherubini introduced to Vienna earlier that year). And evidently he was already planning the new oratorio which he began sketching that winter. He was therefore reluctant to write yet more sonatas, which may be one reason why Carl demanded a still higher price than before (equivalent to about 160 ducats in 1803, whereas the three Sonatas, Op. 31 had been sold for only 100 ducats). When Beethoven did eventually return to sonatas in 1803, he was to produce works of strikingly new grandeur and power—the 'Kreutzer' and the 'Waldstein'. Thus his new direction after Heiligenstadt is reflected both in new genres (oratorio and opera) and a major advance in his instrumental style as reflected in the *Eroica* and these two next sonatas. To suggest that his 'second period' began in 1802, with the two new sets of variations or the works that immediately followed, is an oversimplification, and the idea is now frequently challenged. But it is undeniable that there was in a short space of time a dramatic change in his style, both in terms of new genres and new approaches to old ones, and the notion that this change marks in broad terms the beginning of the second great period of his *œuvre* is likely to survive.

As indicated by Beethoven's sketchbook (the Wielhorsky), the first work conceived after returning from Heiligenstadt was (with the possible exception of *Nei giorni*) the oratorio *Christus*. This work was highly significant in terms of his spiritual development, for it embodies many of the same emotions of terror, isolation, struggle, fear of death, love of mankind, desire for goodness, and ultimate triumph that were apparent in his letters to Wegeler and Amenda, and in the Heiligenstadt Testament. It appears that, on returning from Heiligenstadt, Beethoven sought a subject to match his personal feelings, identified Christ's suffering on the Mount of Olives as somewhat analogous to his own, and decided, without any external commission, to write an oratorio on this. The subject matter is unusual in concentrating entirely on Christ's agony in the Garden of Gethsemane and his eventual arrest, stopping short of his subsequent trial and crucifixion. Thus the oratorio seems to be Beethoven's concrete realization of his view, expressed in the Heiligenstadt Testament, that sufferers can take comfort by reading of the sufferings of others. He quickly found a local librettist, Franz Xaver Huber, and they worked closely together on the libretto. Comparison between this and Beethoven's own writings of the preceding months—notably the Heiligenstadt Testament itself—reveals an astonishing number of parallels, apparently confirming that Beethoven made a major contribution to the text.[4]

---

[4] See Cooper, 'Beethoven's Oratorio'.

Beethoven's progress with his new works was abruptly halted in November by a tiresome legal matter. He had sold his Quintet, Op. 29, to Breitkopf, but before they had time to publish it Count Fries, who had commissioned the work and therefore owned a manuscript of it, apparently gave this to Artaria in Vienna for publication, having been told by them that the work was already in print. When Beethoven heard about the deceit he was furious with the 'archscoundrel Artaria', who eventually undertook not to publish the work until Breitkopf's edition had been available in Vienna for fourteen days. Beethoven and his brother Carl spent an enormous amount of energy trying to reassure Breitkopf and resolve the problem, which was compounded by the fact that Beethoven had at some stage corrected the proofs for Artaria and therefore had had a hand in their edition. The matter dragged on into the following year and even later before being resolved.

Around the beginning of 1803 Beethoven was appointed as composer at the Theater an der Wien, the main independent theatre in Vienna, where the directorate, led by Emanuel Schikaneder (librettist of *The Magic Flute*) wanted him to write an opera. The immediate advantages were that he was able to take rooms at the theatre, along with his brother Carl, and to plan for a benefit concert there. In 1802, when he had hoped for such a concert at one of the Imperial theatres, Baron Braun had allocated the theatre to other artists, but the Theater an der Wien could be relied on to support its own composers, and Beethoven duly staged his concert on Tuesday 5 April 1803.

Unlike in his 1800 concert, all the works were his own: the First and Second Symphonies, the Third Piano Concerto, and *Christus*. All of these except the First Symphony were receiving their first performance. Other works were intended too, but the programme proved long enough without them. The whole day was in fact extremely long for Beethoven. Ries found him in bed at 5 a.m. writing out trombone parts for the oratorio—perhaps a last-minute addition—and relates what happened later. The rehearsal began at 8 a.m. and continued until 2.30, by which time everyone was exhausted. Their spirits were restored by a lunch of cold meat and wine, which had been arranged by Prince Lichnowsky, and afterwards the oratorio was tried again. The concert began at 6 p.m., and must have lasted about three hours.

The Second Symphony had been completed a year earlier (see Chapter 7), but the concerto and oratorio were only just finished in time. Indeed the piano part of the concerto was still not fully written out, according to an amusing recollection from Ignaz Seyfried, who like Beethoven was working at the Theater an der Wien:

In the playing of the concerto movements he asked me to turn the pages for him; but—heaven help me!—that was easier said than done. I saw almost nothing but empty leaves; at the most on one page or the other a few Egyptian hieroglyphs wholly unintelligible to me scribbled down to serve as clues for him; for he played nearly all of the solo part from memory, since, as was so often the case, he had not had time to put it all down on paper. He gave me a secret glance whenever he was at the end of one of the invisible passages and my scarcely concealable anxiety not to miss the decisive moment amused him greatly and he laughed heartily at the jovial supper which we ate afterwards.[5]

Beethoven had actually begun the concerto several years earlier: the first sketches—almost the only ones to survive—date from 1796 and already show some of the main thematic gestures of the first movement; but the work had been set aside repeatedly, and lack of subsequent sketches makes it impossible to trace progress adequately. It may have been sketched mainly in 1800, but the final stages were probably reached only a few days before the concert. Its similarity to Mozart's C minor Piano Concerto (K. 491)— especially in the opening bars—has often been noted, and most writers have assumed that Mozart's work had a profound influence on Beethoven's. Yet it is doubtful whether Beethoven actually knew Mozart's concerto when he was first sketching his own. K. 491 remained unpublished until about August 1800, by which time Beethoven had undoubtedly made substantial progress with his own work, and the anecdote that he heard Mozart's at a concert while with Cramer in 1799 is highly unreliable.[6] More probably Beethoven conceived his concerto independently. Indeed he might not have made parts of it so similar to K. 491 had he known it.

The concerto is Beethoven's only one in a minor key, and yet again he chose C minor. The orchestral exposition, as in virtually all his previous concertos (but unlike Mozart's), spends much time away from the home key, before returning to it towards the end. The initial unison phrase for the strings is full of possibilities for development, which are exploited in the rest of the movement, and the end of the phrase, alternating C and G, suggests timpani; the timpani eventually do take over this motif, just after the cadenza. This thematic use of the timpani is one of the most original ideas in the concerto, and it is remarkable that it was also one of the earliest ideas, for the motif is found among the 1796 sketches, with the words: 'In the concerto in C minor, timpani at the cadenza.'[7]

The second movement is noteworthy for being in E major—evoking a completely different world from C minor. Beethoven highlights the remoteness of the relationship by concluding the movement with a prominent G♯, and then beginning the finale with the motif G–A♭. This second note seems far removed from the earlier G♯, even though it is exactly the same pitch! The two seemingly incompatible keys are eventually brought into accord towards the end of the finale (bars 253 ff.), in typical Beethoven fashion, where he modulates from C minor to E major, using the A♭/G♯ as a pivot

---

[5] TF, 329–30.

[6] The anecdote (see TF, 209) was related only many years later by Cramer's widow, who was not present at the concert, and the identity of the concerto was not a central part of the story.

[7] Kerman ed., *Miscellany*, ii. 58.

note. After returning to C minor he has still one further surprise: the coda is in C major (an echo of his Dressler Variations), with the main theme transformed in 6/8; and the link is made by the same Ab/G♯ heard at the beginning of the movement, this time reinterpreted as a chromatic neighbour-note to the following A. The concerto still belongs stylistically in his first period, but shows many features that point to later developments, such as thematic use of the timpani, and extremely remote key relationships.

The other new work performed at the concert in April 1803 was *Christus*. It is Beethoven's only true oratorio, and probably would not have been composed without the precedents set by Haydn's two late oratorios (*The Creation* and *The Seasons*), although it is much shorter than these, lasting only about an hour. In its 1803 version it was shorter still, for it lacked the great central chorus 'O Heil euch', which was added for the revival in 1804, when a few other small changes were also made.[8] Its structure is divided into six numbers, but this is not entirely evident in performance since some of these fall into several sections, while Nos. 4 and 5 follow their predecessors almost without a break. Although the text is German, much of the music is very Italian in style, reflecting Beethoven's extensive study with Salieri in the preceding years.

The work begins with an orchestral introduction in E flat minor, a key that surely struck appropriate terror into the average orchestral player of the day. After moving through several other keys it leads to the perhaps inevitable C minor, for the first recitative and aria, in which Christ sings of his terror and anguish, concluding with the words 'Nimm den Leidenskelch von mir' (Take the cup of suffering from me)—a sentiment that Beethoven surely shared as he contemplated his deafness. This was one of the passages most extensively sketched, and it was revised in 1804 as he strove for utmost intensity in the expression of the text. The following number is a recitative and aria for the Seraph. In 1803 the aria consisted of a short Larghetto followed by a longer Allegro, but in 1804 Beethoven extended the movement, gradually increasing the tension until it builds up to one of the greatest climaxes in his entire output: during the Allegro in this version the chorus enters at the start of the recapitulation, and then in the coda the Seraph launches into coloratura runs, which give way to an Allegro molto as the trombones enter. This continues to build up until a ferocious diminished 7th is repeated without resolution for over nine bars, and with the whole chorus and every instrument in the orchestra marked *fff*, at the words 'Verdammung ist ihr Loos!' (Damnation is their lot). The effect is astonishing, especially as Beethoven hardly ever goes beyond *ff* in any of his music. This passage of unprecedented power immediately gives way to a wonderfully sublime coda addressed to those who remain true in faith, hope, and love.

[8] See Tyson, '1803 Version'.

The duet in No. 3, in which Christ accepts the burden of suffering, is equally moving, and is enriched by some beautiful Mozartean chromaticism. The ensuing numbers contain most of the action, as Christ and his disciples are hunted and eventually caught by a chorus of soldiers, and Peter is told to calm his anger and love his enemies. Finally there is a chorus of joy and praise for the world's redemption. Predictably, Beethoven uses C major, thus placing it as far as possible from the E flat minor of the opening, and symbolizing the progress from darkness to light. The work as a whole was recognized in the nineteenth century as exceptionally fine (George Thomson of Edinburgh wrote to Beethoven in 1819 that it would 'suffice on its own to make you immortal'[9]), and its more recent neglect is curious.

The reviews of the concert were somewhat conflicting in their assessment of the works themselves, and say little about the standard of performance, which must have been uneven, given the length, difficulty and unfamiliarity of the works. The performance was a great financial success, however, for Beethoven made 1800 florins from the event—more than he could expect to earn in an entire year—having been allowed to treble the normal ticket prices. His music was clearly much in demand from Vienna's connoisseurs.

In the weeks after the concert Beethoven faced more problems from publishers. Breitkopf had complained that there were not as many variations in Opp. 34 and 35 as had been promised, and so Beethoven had to point out that the variations could not be numbered in the normal way because of the unusual structure of the works (in later correspondence, however, his brother referred to the sets as containing 7 and 24 variations respectively). Meanwhile Nägeli brought out the first two sonatas of Op. 31 that same month, without having sent Beethoven a proof for correction. Ries reports that, when the sonatas arrived, Beethoven was busy and asked him to play them through. Beethoven became increasingly agitated about the numerous misprints, and finally 'jumped up in a rage' on hearing four whole bars that were not meant to be in the first movement of No. 1 (Ex. 8.1). Perhaps Nägeli composed these bars in a misguided attempt to balance the phrase structure. More probably, Beethoven's manuscript was unclear at this

**Ex. 8.1** Op. 31 No. 1/I, between bars 298 and 299

---

[9] Alb-265; BB-1357.

point—the sketches show some indecision in this section and do not contain the final version, with or without the four spurious bars. It seems likely, then, that Beethoven wrote these bars before cancelling them, and that Nägeli misread the manuscript. Whatever the reason for all the misprints, Beethoven through his brother instructed the *Allgemeine musikalische Zeitung* to announce that the new sonatas contained many errors, although no such announcement was published. Meanwhile Ries was told to make a list of the errors (about eighty) and send them with the sonatas to Simrock in Bonn so that a correct edition could appear.[10] Simrock's edition duly appeared later that year, labelled unconvincingly 'Editiou [!] tres Correcte' and with nearly all the misprints rectified. How many Beethoven and Ries overlooked, however, is uncertain: in bar 19 of No. 1, for example, the second chord in the right hand in both editions has a C, which is possible but does not match other similar bars. Modern editors have assumed this to be a misreading for a D, which may or may not be the case.

During April 1803 the virtuoso violinist George Bridgetower arrived in Vienna, and it was for him that Beethoven completed his Violin Sonata, Op. 47, known as the 'Kreutzer' Sonata after its eventual dedicatee. As noted in Chapter 7, the finale was already in existence, having been intended for Op. 30 No. 1 but replaced there. Thus Beethoven had the unusual task of writing the first two movements to go with a pre-existing finale. Indeed he might have done this even without the arrival of Bridgetower: Ries reports that 'a large part of the first Allegro was ready at an early stage',[11] and the sketches confirm this, some of them even appearing earlier in the sketchbook than the last ones for *Christus*. The slow movement, however, was barely finished in time for the first performance, which Bridgetower and Beethoven gave on 24 May.

From the pre-existing finale Beethoven first extracted a few of its features for the first two movements. The development section of the finale seems to begin in A minor, while its 'tonal goal' is F major. Thus he placed the first movement in A minor and the slow movement in F major, to create overall tonal coherence; as in so many of his works, not only the main key but important subsidiary keys reappear during the course of the work. The A minor Allegro and A major finale—a curious combination—are preceded by a grand slow introduction that begins in A major but moves to A minor after four bars. These first four bars, however, are particularly striking, since they consist of chords played by unaccompanied violin, using multiple stops—one of the most original beginnings to any Beethoven sonata, and made still more remarkable by the change to A minor for the rest of the movement. The slow introduction is linked to the Allegro by the motif E–F, which is derived from the appoggiatura in bar 4 and becomes the head-motif of the Allegro after several repetitions at the end of the introduction.

---

[10] WR, 77–9.    [11] WR, 72.

In the slow movement, a set of variations, the Allegro motif is reversed as F–E, beginning a rich and glorious melody on which the variations are based. The work as a whole exudes tremendous power and grandeur. Beethoven advertised its imposing character by describing it on the printed title page as 'written in a very concertante style, like a concerto', and the first two movements seem to suit the brilliant finale far better than do those of Op. 30 No. 1. He had made a wise substitution.

By about the end of May Beethoven was beginning to collaborate with Schikaneder on a new opera, but it was some time before the first sketches appeared. Meanwhile he started several new works, including the song 'Der Wachtelschlag' (The Quail Call) and two sets of variations. The latter were probably commissioned by some anglophile, since they are based on two patriotic British songs: 'God save the King' and 'Rule Britannia' (WoO 78–9). The variations on 'God save the King' are relatively conventional in their use of melodic decoration, before a march-like rhythmic transformation of the theme towards the end. The 'Rule Britannia' set, however, is much more innovative. Here Thomas Arne's melody disappears altogether in most of the variations, which retain only an approximation to the harmonic outline of the original. The minor-key variation (Var. 4) is in the relative minor rather than the usual tonic minor, although the melody at last becomes clear again here; and in the coda the little run from bar 2 of the theme is whimsically developed through various keys and chromatic distortions before returning to the tonic.

While Beethoven was putting the finishing touches to the second of his two sets of British variations he was, ironically, embarking on the *Eroica* Symphony—a work intended for Britain's arch-enemy, Napoleon Bonaparte. Although Beethoven was certainly no political activist, he was well aware of the political situation developing in Europe, and had made a somewhat cynical reference to Napoleon's concordat with the Pope in a letter the previous year. As a strong opponent of all forms of tyranny, he greatly admired the British constitution, but he also admired Napoleon as the champion of the poor, and the man who would overthrow the old oppression. *Liberté* and *fraternité* (though perhaps not *égalité*) were ideals close to his heart throughout his life.

At what stage the idea of Napoleon became associated with the forthcoming symphony is unknown. The sketches provide no clue, and Schindler's tale that the idea was suggested to Beethoven by Napoleon's General Bernadotte when in Vienna in 1798 is clearly without foundation. But Beethoven may have been aware of references to Napoleon as a latter-day Prometheus figure, and his own *Prometheus* music played an integral part in the formation of the symphony from the outset. The earliest sketches for the symphony date from around October 1802, either shortly before or shortly after the Heiligenstadt Testament. Immediately after the last sketches for the *Prometheus* Variations, Beethoven sketched on the next page-opening a plan for a great new symphony in E flat (Wielhorsky

Sketchbook, pp. 44–5). The details are very different from the *Eroica*: there is a slow introduction; the second movement is an Adagio in C major; the third movement is a 'Menuetto serioso', followed by a Trio in G minor; and the themes are unrecognizable. Yet some melodic fragments resemble ideas in the *Eroica*, and the similarity grows stronger during the detailed sketching on the second page. Most strikingly, there is no sketch for a finale, and it must be assumed that Beethoven had already decided to incorporate the theme from *Prometheus* that he had just used for the variations sketched on the previous pages. Other ideas in the set of sketches also point towards the *Eroica*. The slow introduction is based on a triadic theme, as in the first subject of the *Eroica*; and the first attempt at a main Allegro theme is clearly derived from the bass-line that plays such an important part in the *Prometheus* Variations and again in the *Eroica* finale. Furthermore, the subsidiary keys of C major and G minor, though not eventually used for main movements, do play an important role in the final version. Thus Beethoven's initial idea was a grand and heroic Promethean symphony, whether or not Napoleon was involved.

The plan lay dormant for several months while other works were written, but Beethoven revived it about June 1803, sketching the work very intensively during the summer. It was finished quite quickly, for Ries informed Simrock on 22 October that Beethoven had recently played it to him (on the piano), and that a full performance would make Heaven and Earth tremble.[12] The main theme reached its final form almost at once, complete with the dissonant C♯ that generates so much uncertainty and has such long-range effects, although the two initial tonic chords were a later addition. Another early idea was the theme in the remote key of E minor in the middle of the development section. Beethoven had been trying out increasingly remote keys as the tonal goals of his developments in the preceding years, and E minor after E flat major was the furthest yet. Much has been made of the fact that there is a new theme at this point in the development, but such a feature is not unprecedented; moreover the E minor theme is distantly related to the main theme (as indeed are almost all the numerous themes in this movement). What is so astonishing here, however, is the complete contrast of character that Beethoven achieves through a combination of remote key, unusual instrumentation, and change of register, coupled with an extraordinarily prolonged build-up to this point.

Throughout the movement, in fact, the proportions between the sections are unusual, even though the sonata-form structure is regular in outline, and Beethoven's sketches show much effort to obtain proportions that satisfied him. The modulation to the dominant in the exposition comes quite early (bars 42–4), and is followed by a series of themes and motifs in B flat, leading to a cadence that seems to herald the end of the exposition (bar 83). Had it done so, the innocent ear would suspect nothing amiss (the music

---

[12] Alb-71; BB-165.

could have jumped from bar 82 to bar 144 without destroying the sonata form). Yet only here does a prominent new theme begin: this point is not the end of the exposition but only halfway through. Thus Beethoven adopts the same ploy as in his Grand Sonata in E flat, Op. 7, where an early modulation to B flat leads to a theme and a cadence, followed by the true second subject (see pp. 70–1). In the *Eroica*, however, unlike the sonata, he repeats the ploy in the development, which is again twice as long as expected: when the recapitulation is due, according to normal proportions, the E minor theme appears instead, again only halfway through. Thus Beethoven cleverly makes the proportions of the development match those of the exposition. To reach E minor, the development moves through various keys before settling in F minor for the start of a fugato (bar 236). From here the music repeatedly moves sharpwards round the circle of fifths, creating a sense of heroic uphill struggle, culminating in harsh discords and a dramatic single-beat rest (bar 280: see Ex. 8.2), before the development's only direct reference to the second subject, which is reharmonized as a strongly dissonant dominant minor 9th. This passage forms the pivotal point in the development, with maximum disruption in harmony, rhythm, melody, texture, and key—the opposite pole to the smooth, harmonious, four-bar main theme.

The rest of the movement contains many more surprises, including the famous premature entry of the second horn just before the recapitulation, a sudden excursion to F major shortly afterwards (with the dissonant C♯ used as a pivot note in the modulation), and an extremely long coda to resolve the earlier instabilities and bring the disparate ideas into an overall unity. The extraordinary level of originality and ingenuity in the movement has generated an enormous amount of literature, yet much still remains to be said about its composition and structure.

The second movement is a funeral march in C minor; but the rising tonic triad that played such an important part in the melodic contours of the first movement reappears in the second in a central section in C major. It seems odd to have a funeral march so early in a heroic symphony, especially when the hero Napoleon was still alive and overrunning half of Europe. Thus the symphony is clearly not simply a portrait of Napoleon or anyone else. Beethoven perceived true heroes as immortal, and indeed had a strong interest in the concept of immortality, which repeatedly surfaces in his letters.[13] To represent immortality in the symphony, he therefore placed the funeral march second, after a lifelong struggle and ultimate triumph in the first movement; this enabled the third movement apparently to symbolize resurrection (though it is simply headed 'Scherzo'), and the fourth to represent the hero taking his place among the immortals. This scheme would account for the use of the *Prometheus* theme in the finale. The theme was

---

[13] For example, in November 1803 he wrote to the painter Alexander Macco: 'Continue to paint—and I shall continue to write notes; and thus we shall live—for ever?—yes, perhaps, for ever.' (A-85)

**Ex. 8.2** Op. 55/I

132

already very well known to his potential audiences, as was its association with Prometheus (the association would have been still stronger if Breitkopf had not neglected, despite Beethoven's request, to refer to *Prometheus* on the title page of the Variations, Op. 35, which appeared in August 1803). Indeed the finale of the *Eroica* appears to reflect the plot of the *Prometheus* ballet quite closely. Like the ballet, it begins with a storm, followed by an unharmonized, statuesque version of the bass-line, which is gradually brought to life by various counterpoints and eventually the main melody, as in Op. 35 (again recalling the statues brought to life in the ballet). In the rest of *Prometheus* the statues are introduced to various arts on Parnassus; likewise in the remainder of the symphony Beethoven introduces a range of musical arts—variation, fugue, march, development—in a form so complex that it cannot be readily labelled. The *Eroica* was to undergo several changes before its eventual publication in October 1806, including an important change of dedication, to be discussed later, but all its main musical features seem to have been in place by the end of summer 1803. Although clearly in the symphonic tradition of Haydn and Mozart, it far exceeds any previous symphony in length, complexity, and grandeur of conception, while its originality and its intriguing extramusical associations provide endless scope for reflection. The true hero of the work is Beethoven himself.

Besides writing such a long and complex symphony that summer, Beethoven amazingly also found time to write a few lesser works. These include three Marches for piano duet, Op. 45. Ries had once improvised a march for a gathering at Count Browne's, and an old countess, believing the march to be by Beethoven, 'went into ecstasies over it'. Ries did not disillusion her, and the next day, when Beethoven himself appeared, Ries was asked to play the march again—much to his embarrassment, especially as it 'turned out much worse' this time. Beethoven 'then received from everyone the most extravagant praise for his genius, to which he listened in utter confusion and anger, until at last he dissolved into roaring laughter.'[14] This incident illustrates both Beethoven's readiness to appreciate a good joke, and the intensity with which his devotees now admired his music, so that his mere name sufficed to convince them of its quality, even if the work were in reality an improvisation by Ries. The outcome, however, was that Browne immediately commissioned the three Marches, Op. 45, from Beethoven, and sketches for them appear amidst those for the *Eroica* in Landsberg 6. Recalling the problems Fries had caused over the publication of the String Quintet, Op. 29, by giving a score to Artaria, Beethoven heard a rumour that the same had happened with the first two marches of Op. 45; he anxiously wrote to Ries asking him to investigate,[15] but fortunately the rumour proved groundless. Beethoven also interrupted work on the *Eroica*

[14] WR, 79–80.
[15] A-61. Ries dates this letter as 1802 (see BB-96); if he is correct, the first two marches must have been first drafted then, and only the third composed entirely in 1803.

that summer to write a song, 'Das Glück der Freundschaft', which was sketched shortly after the marches and appeared in print as early as October. Whether this poem, about the joys of friendship, had any special significance for Beethoven at this date is unknown, but as with many of his songs the subject matter often recurs in his writings.

After sketching the *Eroica*, Beethoven's next major project was Schikaneder's opera, *Vestas Feuer* (The Vestal Flame), which Beethoven claimed occupied him for six months, although his main creative work on it was clearly far shorter—probably about September to December 1803. Unlike with *Christus*, he seems to have had no hand in the libretto, for he later complained that he had 'been told neither the scheme nor anything else whatever'; and he even failed to persuade Schikaneder, who was 'so infatuated with his own opinion', to have the libretto corrected and improved by someone else. He considered the text unbearable in places: 'Just picture to yourself a Roman subject . . . and language and verses like those of our local apple-women.'[16] The language is indeed pretty banal, but the sentiments of forgiveness and true love expressed by the characters appealed to him, and he managed to rise above the text. He completed one scene of 275 bars altogether, in slightly less than full score, and it consists of several contrasting but linked sections in different keys and metres. There are some fine touches, such as a harsh dissonance and sudden shift of key at the words 'Ach, er hasst mich' (Oh, he hates me), and the last section is an ecstatic trio in G major, 'Nie war ich so froh wie heute' (Never was I so happy as today), in which the soprano's triadic theme surges up to a high B. This section was later adapted as 'O namenlose Freude' (O nameless joy) in *Fidelio*.

Beethoven's exasperation with Schikaneder and *Vestas Feuer* finally reached breaking point by about December, and he abandoned the work. While casting around for a new libretto, he wrote a piano sonata in C major, known as the 'Waldstein' (Op. 53). Count Waldstein, Beethoven's old friend from Bonn, had moved to Vienna in the 1790s but did not thereafter associate much with him. Whether Waldstein commissioned the sonata or merely helped Beethoven in some way shortly before the work was dedicated to him in 1805 is not known, but Beethoven's reasons for making dedications were usually short-term rather than long-term; thus it is doubtful whether the dedication was an expression of thanks for Waldstein's earlier assistance in Bonn.

One impetus for the Sonata was perhaps the arrival of a new piano, which had been sent to Beethoven by the manufacturers Erard, of Paris, on 6 August 1803 as a mark of their esteem (its date of arrival is unknown). This piano possessed a larger compass than Beethoven's earlier pianos, extending up to $c''''$ instead of only $f'''$. The 'Waldstein' is his first sonata to

---

[16] A-87a.

make use of notes beyond $f'''$, yet it does so only tentatively: for much of the first movement, $f'''$ remains the highest note, and the music never strays beyond $a'''$. Thus the influence of the Erard on this sonata may have been exaggerated by some writers.

Just as the *Eroica* marks a major advance in symphonic writing, so does the 'Waldstein' in sonata writing. Despite its great power, it is remarkable how much of the sonata is marked *pp*, generating a sense of latent energy which often bursts out explosively. Contrasts of register figure prominently. The first subject begins deep in the bass clef, with tenor *e* the highest note of the first chord; by contrast the second subject is in a high register, with the lowest note of its first chord a whole octave above that initial tenor *e*. The finale also explores some unusual textures: at the start, the left hand plays both bass and melody in turn, while the right hand fills in semiquaver figuration in the middle—a texture Beethoven had first explored in Var. 8 of the *Prometheus* Variations. The sound is enhanced by use of the sustaining pedal, which prolongs the bass notes while creating a slightly blurred effect above. The movement ends with a prestissimo coda of formidable technical difficulty, including glissando octaves for each hand in turn (bars 465–74).

Much of the dynamism of the first movement results from the home key of C major never being strongly established at the start: the music seems frantic to move away from the tonic as fast as possible and has modulated to G major by bar 3. Although it is brought back to C major by bar 14, it moves away again just as quickly, and goes further afield than usual, with the second subject appearing in E major (thereby drawing out the implications of that initial tenor *e*). Another noteworthy feature is a new relationship between C major and C minor. There are strong suggestions of C minor within the first subject and again during the development, and this mixture of modes is matched by the second group, which utilizes both E minor and E major. The finale, too, employs C minor briefly during the first subject and at greater length during the second episode. Thus instead of his customary progression from C minor to C major, Beethoven emphasizes the major throughout but repeatedly allows it to be coloured by hints of the darker minor mode.

Between the outer movements Beethoven composed a lengthy and leisurely Andante. One of his friends, however, suggested the sonata was too long, according to Ries, and Beethoven soon reached the same conclusion. Thus he replaced the Andante with a very brief but profound Adagio molto, treating this as an introduction to the finale and labelling it 'Introduzione'. The Andante was then published separately as an *Andante favori* (WoO 57). The Introduzione, only 28 bars long, is a model of compression. In places highly chromatic, it relates to the first movement in numerous subtle ways, such as the opening chord progressions, which in both cases contain a bass line that descends chromatically over a perfect 4th. Although beginning on F, the Introduzione rapidly moves to an E major chord and then E minor, providing further echoes of the first movement, and it ends with a reference to the C major/minor relationship.

Another movement perhaps intended for the 'Waldstein' is the Bagatelle in C, WoO 56, whose opening theme has similar contours to that of the 'Waldstein'. At any rate, it was sketched immediately after the finale of the sonata, and has the form and metre of a minuet and trio. It could have been intended as a replacement for the Andante, creating a three-movement structure similar to Op. 14 No. 1, but its brevity suggests it was to have been an additional movement between the Andante and the finale, creating a short diversion as in the 'Spring' Sonata. Beethoven soon abandoned any notion of including it, however, and it lay unpublished until after his death. By the time he sketched it, his search for a suitable opera libretto was over. The first sketches for what became known as *Leonore* or *Fidelio* appear on the same pages as those for the bagatelle, and they mark the beginning of a new phase in his life and work.

# 9

# L'amour conjugal (1804–6)

I have finally broken with Schikaneder, whose empire has really been entirely eclipsed by the light of the brilliant and attractive French operas. . . . I have quickly had an old French libretto adapted and am now beginning to work on it.

These comments by Beethoven, in a letter to Friedrich Rochlitz dated 4 January 1804,[1] are the earliest indication of his decision to compose *Leonore*, later known as *Fidelio*. Rochlitz had sent Beethoven the first act of a libretto he had written, but Beethoven rejected it, claiming the public was prejudiced against subjects with magic, though the prejudice was more Beethoven's than the public's. He preferred grand, heroic topics, and on various occasions expressed distaste for the subjects of most of Mozart's major operas. French operas, however, were a different matter. Several by Luigi Cherubini, the leading opera composer in Paris at the time, had been introduced to Vienna in 1802, some by Schikaneder at the Theater an der Wien, others by Baron Braun at the Court Theatre. Although performed in German in heavily adapted versions, they had made a great impact, as Beethoven indicates in his letter, and he himself became an enthusiastic admirer of Cherubini, as well as of French librettos. Thus he naturally turned to France for a subject after breaking with Schikaneder and his lamentable *Vestas Feuer*.

The one that attracted him was *Léonore, ou l'amour conjugal* (Leonore, or Conjugal Love), a text by Jean-Nicolas Bouilly that had been set by the French composer Pierre Gaveaux in 1798. It tells of one Florestan who has been imprisoned for political reasons and is rescued by his wife Leonore from the evil Pizarro, after she has disguised herself as the young man Fidelio and gained employment at the gaol. The heroic last-minute rescue is typical of many French operas of the time, but this was only one of several features that appealed to Beethoven. Another was Leonore's bold opposition to tyranny, for Beethoven had developed strongly anti-tyrannical views while still in Bonn. He was also able to sympathize readily with Florestan, whose extreme suffering and isolation in the dungeon recalled Beethoven's own, caused by his deafness. He had already explored the concept of suffering in *Christus am Oelberge*, but here was another

---

[1] A-87a.

opportunity. Finally, the devoted *amour conjugal* of Leonore reflected Beethoven's ideal woman: he longed for marital bliss and the undying love of a woman, and his feelings must have intensified while composing this opera as he fell in love with Countess Josephine Deym (née Brunsvik).

The translation and adaptation of Bouilly's libretto was by Joseph Sonnleithner, one of the co-founders of the *Bureau des Arts et d'Industrie*, but Beethoven probably collaborated. Particularly striking is the change in the second half of Florestan's recitative at the start of his dungeon scene. Bouilly's and Sonnleithner's versions read respectively:

> N'est-il donc point, grand dieu, de terme à ma souffrance?
> Dois-je finir mes jours dans ces indignes fers?[2]

(Great God, is there then no end to my suffering? Must I finish my days in these unworthy chains?)

> O schwere Prüfung! Doch gerecht ist Gottes Wille!
> Ich murre nicht—Das Mass der Leiden steht bey dir!

(O hard trial! Yet God's will is righteous. I do not grumble—the measure of sufferings stands with Thee.)

Whereas in Bouilly's text Florestan merely seeks the end of his suffering, expressing sentiments not very different from the ensuing aria that laments his fate, the German adaptation is rich and profound, with powerful resonances from Beethoven's Heiligenstadt Testament, his letters to Wegeler and Amenda, and the libretto of *Christus am Oelberge*. To regard the sufferings as a 'trial', and perhaps a necessary part of God's plan; the patient submission to God's will; and the willingness to accept whatever measure of suffering was ordained; all would be unlikely ideas in French opera of the period, and they seem to provide a window into Beethoven's very private religious world. They are consistent with his religious comments in earlier and later writings, which indicate a firm belief in an omnipotent and just Father, and they suggest that Beethoven identified himself so closely with Florestan that he drafted the outline for this part of the text.

Sketching for the opera began as soon as the first part of the libretto was ready, and Beethoven proceeded through the various numbers roughly in order, though with a certain amount of digression to earlier or later ones. The original plan was to have the opera ready by Easter, but this soon became an unrealistic target. Progress was slow and painstaking, and he was also having ideas for other works. Amongst the first sketches for *Leonore* are very early ones for three major works that were not completed for several years and had to wait until 1808 for their public première: the Fifth and Sixth Symphonies, and the Fourth Piano Concerto. Also jotted down at this period were early ideas for two works that were produced somewhat quicker: a Piano Sonata in F (Op. 54) and a Triple Concerto in C (Op. 56) to replace the one in D abandoned in 1802. Indeed the concerto

---

[2] See Lühning, 'Florestans Kerker', 172–3.

was mentioned in a letter from Carl dated 14 October 1803, although there is no other evidence that it had even been begun at this date. Perhaps Beethoven turned to these works while awaiting later sections of the libretto of *Leonore*, for as late as about March 1804 he was still requesting Sonnleithner to finish the text 'so that I can press on with my work and so that the opera can be produced in June at the latest'.[3] It was evidently in March, too, that he made the revisions to *Christus am Oelberge* noted in the previous chapter; this revised version was performed at a concert on 27 March that also included Beethoven's Second Symphony, fresh from the press of the *Bureau*.

Further delays in *Leonore* arose through a change of management at the theatre. Baron Braun, already in charge of the two court theatres (the Burgtheater and the Kärntnertor), now bought the Theater an der Wien too, on 11 February 1804. Schikaneder was promptly dismissed, and Beethoven had to change rooms to a 'wretched hole' where his servant had to sleep in the kitchen. Beethoven was keen to leave as soon as possible, and before long had moved to the *Rothes Haus* in the suburbs, where his friend Breuning was living. With his contract at the theatre terminated, Beethoven proceeded much more slowly with *Leonore*, turning his attention to the F major Piano Sonata and the Triple Concerto, which were probably both finished that spring.

These two works, though written so soon after the pathbreaking *Eroica* and 'Waldstein', are among Beethoven's least popular sonatas and concertos. Most of his greatest works are imbued with a very strong character, unusually energetic or thrusting rhythms, and striking melodies. These two, however, for all their excellence, lack an abundance of such features, and without them clever motivic manipulation alone is insufficient to capture the imagination of many music-lovers. Neither work has any really fast movements, despite some fast passages, and so both seem rather tame and laid-back. Meanwhile the one really slow movement, the Largo of the Triple Concerto, lacks great profundity (by Beethoven's standards) and is less than fully developed, consisting of a theme, a single variation, and a 13-bar transition to the Finale.

Both works, however, are highly original. Op. 54 is best viewed as the valley between the mountains of the 'Waldstein' and the 'Appassionata', and is Beethoven's first big piano sonata in only two movements (the two-movement sonatas of Op. 49 are scarcely more than sonatinas, which he did not even publish initially). The moderately paced first movement is marked 'Tempo di Menuetto'—a minuet in rhythm, but not in form or style. The form resembles a simple rondo with coda, but the refrains are increasingly decorated, while the two episodes use the same material as each other and are very unequal in length—45 bars and 12 bars respectively. Two main rhythms are set up in opposition: dotted rhythms in the main theme and

---

[3] A-88.

triplets in the episodes, with the two combined and reconciled in the coda. The second movement, an Allegretto, uses incessant semiquaver motion throughout (apart from two strategically placed trills). It is in a modified sonata form, with no distinctive second subject, and the exposition is extremely short, barely 20 bars, followed by an enormous development section, then further development after a reprise of the main theme. Thus the proportions of the movement are bizarre, with Beethoven deliberately flouting convention; but they are none the less very finely judged, for the reprise of the main theme appears precisely where one might expect, about three-fifths of the way through, and close to the point of the Golden Section.[4]

In the Triple Concerto in C it is the scoring for piano, violin, cello, and orchestra that is so unusual. It recalls the concerto grosso of the early eighteenth century, but there is no exact precedent for Beethoven's concertino group, and he himself pointed out to Breitkopf & Härtel that such a concerto was surely something new. Sometimes the soloists are treated as a group, but often one or other has solo passages, and in each movement it is the cello, perhaps surprisingly, that initiates the first solo section. For the finale Beethoven turned once again to a dance rhythm—this time the polacca, a triple-time dance in which the second beat is often stressed—and there is an Allegro coda in which the theme is rhythmically transformed. Unexpectedly, however, the polacca returns at the very end.

By the time the Triple Concerto was completed, the *Eroica* had probably been written out in full score, and it was certainly ready by May 1804. A copyist's score was also made, so that instrumental parts could be prepared for a trial run. On 20 May, however, Napoleon, to whom the symphony was to be dedicated, proclaimed himself Emperor. Ries brought Beethoven the news, as he relates in a famous anecdote:

I myself, as well as many of his close friends, had seen this symphony, already copied in full score, lying on his table. At the very top of the title page stood the word 'Buonaparte' and at the very bottom 'Luigi van Beethoven', but not a word more. Whether and with what the intervening space was to be filled I do not know. I was the first to tell him the news that Bonaparte had declared himself emperor, whereupon he flew into a rage and shouted: 'So he too is nothing more than an ordinary man. Now he also will trample all human rights underfoot, and only pander to his own ambition; he will place himself above everyone else and become a tyrant!' Beethoven went to the table, took hold of the title page at the top, ripped it all the way through, and flung it on the floor. The first page was written anew and only then did the symphony receive the title *Sinfonia eroica*.[5]

---

[4] The Golden Section, which has been widely used in music since at least as early as the thirteenth century, is the point where the proportion of the smaller section to the larger section of the movement is equal to the proportion of the larger section to the whole (B: A = A: A+B).

[5] WR, 68.

Ries's account illustrates two particularly prominent characteristics of Beethoven—his irascibility and his hatred of tyranny—as well as his acute political judgement. What Ries saw must have been the autograph score, which has since disappeared. The copyist's score, however, still survives in the Gesellschaft der Musikfreunde, Vienna, and it bore a slightly different title: 'Sinfonia grande / intitolata Buonaparte / del Sigr / Louis van Beethoven.' This, too, was evidently attacked while Beethoven was still in a rage, for the word 'Buonaparte' has been deleted so violently that there is a hole in the paper! The rest of the page now includes instructions for copying out the parts, and other annotations. Most significantly, however, the words 'written on Bonaparte' can be found in German in Beethoven's hand, in faded pencil immediately beneath his own name. Often, once his initial anger had cooled, he was willing to forgive and make amends. So too, this time; and when he offered the symphony to Breitkopf & Härtel that August, he stated that the title of the symphony was really *Bonaparte*. Only at a late stage did he substitute the name *Sinfonia Eroica* (Heroic Symphony), which is not found on the copyist's score but only in the first printed edition.

At one time Beethoven had considered dedicating the symphony, which he considered his greatest work thus far, to Napoleon, but Prince Lobkowitz offered 400 ducats (a huge sum) for exclusive use of the work for six months, and also apparently a separate sum for the dedication, and so it was he who received it: Beethoven's decision to change the dedication was not a political but a financial one, unlike the change of title. Lobkowitz also enjoyed the first performances of the symphony, which was played privately in his palace several times. The earliest record of these performances is an invoice dated 9 June 1804, which refers to two 'rehearsals' of the *Eroica* (presumably trial runs) that had just taken place. A concerto was also played on these two occasions, and there is evidence indicating that this was Beethoven's newly completed Triple Concerto.[6] Thus both works were completed and performed earlier than once thought. Ries reports that he was present at the first rehearsal, and that the *Eroica* 'went appallingly'. The horn, however, entered correctly at its famous premature entry at the start of the recapitulation (bar 394), where it creates a discord with the violins; Ries thought this was a mistake too, and Beethoven was a long time forgiving him for saying it sounded terrible![7] During the performances of the *Eroica* at Lobkowitz's palace Beethoven made many minor adjustments to the music, which are reflected in alterations to the manuscript score. He also tried the first movement several times both with and without the repeat of the exposition before concluding that it was preferable to include it (paradoxically, the movement seems excessively long without it). The repeat was finally confirmed in a letter from Carl to Breitkopf dated 12 February 1805: 'My brother thought at first, before he had heard the

---

[6] See Volek and Macek, 'Beethoven's Rehearsals', 78–9.    [7] WR, 69.

symphony, that it would be too long if the first part of the first movement were repeated, but after several performances it was found disadvantageous if the first part were not repeated.'[8]

A month after the first trial of the *Eroica* Beethoven's anger boiled over again, this time in a dispute with Breuning about the accommodation they were sharing. Beethoven jumped up in a rage during a meal, knocking over his chair, and went off to stay in Baden. From there he wrote to Ries: 'If I happen to be irritated at a time when I am more liable to fly into a temper than usual, then I also erupt more violently than anyone else.' Beethoven was particularly angry that Breuning had maligned him to Ries and the caretaker, for he regarded such behaviour as utterly base. As always, he demanded from both himself and others that same nobility of intent that permeates his music, and he considered that he himself had acted nobly; thus Breuning was 'not worthy of my friendship', and could not have a friendly relationship with him again.[9] Yet by autumn, after a chance meeting, all animosity between him and Breuning was set aside. He gave Breuning a miniature portrait of himself, adding: 'To whom could I give it indeed with a warmer heart than to you, faithful, good and noble Steffen— Forgive me if I hurt you.'[10] This was not the last breach, or the last reconciliation, between them.

While at Baden Beethoven was relatively inactive, by his own account. The opera was nearly at a standstill, and there were no other pressing commissions. Soon afterwards he moved to Oberdöbling, and returned to the city centre in October. Before doing so, however, he wrote to Breitkopf & Härtel on 26 August offering six new works: *Christus am Oelberge*, the *Eroica*, the Triple Concerto, and three piano sonatas. Concerning the last, he wrote: 'Should you like to have one of these with an accompaniment, I would also agree to this too.'[11] The first two were of course the 'Waldstein' and Op. 54, and since it was not Beethoven's practice to compose *ad libitum* accompaniments for sonatas already written, the clear implication is that the third sonata was not yet composed. It was probably begun shortly afterwards, however, for Ries claims that the finale of a new sonata—the 'Appassionata'—was conceived while Beethoven was still in Oberdöbling, which must indicate the period around September 1804 since Beethoven did not stay there again for many years. This date also concurs with references to the sonata in letters written to Breitkopf by Beethoven and his brother in the ensuing months. The date seems to be contradicted by the sketchbook (Mendelssohn 15), since sketches for the song 'An die Hoffnung', probably written in November–December, appear on pages 151–7, while the main sketches for the 'Appassionata' (almost entirely for the first movement) appear further on (pages 182 and 187–98); but there is evidence that these pages were not filled in consecutive order. Brief ideas for *Leonore* were inserted on numerous pages early on, with the gaps beneath them and on

---

[8] Alb-98; BB-212.    [9] A-94, A-93.    [10] A-98.    [11] A-96.

adjacent pages being filled up later, both by more *Leonore* sketches and sketches for other works, in a rather unsystematic way. Thus sketches for both 'An die Hoffnung' and the sonata appear on pages already partly filled by ideas for *Leonore*.

Ries's reference to the 'Appassionata' is significant not just for the date it implies but still more for its revelation about how the finale was conceived. The sketches in Mendelssohn 15 show detailed work on the first movement, culminating in drafts that are close to the final version; but the finale is shown only in a very primitive state, with even the main theme quite different. The new main theme was conceived during a walk near Oberdöbling, as Ries reports:

We went so far astray that we didn't get back to Döbling, where Beethoven lived, until nearly eight o'clock. The entire way he had hummed, or sometimes even howled, to himself—up and down, up and down, without singing any definite notes. When I asked what this was, he replied: 'A theme for the last Allegro of the sonata has occurred to me' (in F minor, Opus 57). When we entered the room he rushed to the piano without taking off his hat. I took a seat in the corner and he soon forgot all about me. He stormed on for at least an hour with the new finale of this sonata, which is so beautiful. Finally he got up, was surprised to see me still there, and said: 'I cannot give you a lesson today. I still have work to do.'[12]

Sometimes Beethoven laboured long over creating his themes. On other occasions, as here, they just 'occurred' to him, after he had already sketched several other possibilities; the labour lay then in refining and developing the new one. Often his best ideas came when he was on long walks, usually solitary ones; but on this occasion he had a companion, although he seems to have paid little attention to him. In later years Beethoven used to carry around manuscript paper—even whole manuscript books—but in 1804 he apparently had none with him, and humming and howling had to suffice. Ries could not discern any notes, but the theme is actually one of Beethoven's least singable, consisting of runs of semiquaver figuration, and only a very able singer would have been able to hum it in such a way that 'definite notes' could be heard.

Once back at his lodgings Beethoven worked away at the finale by extemporizing on the piano. His hearing was still sufficiently good to make this viable, and he apparently often composed in this manner at this stage of his life. Innumerable variants could be tried out, much quicker than on paper, and new ideas were likely to emerge during the extemporization. While at the piano he became totally oblivious of his surroundings, entirely immersed in creating beautiful sounds. Even normally he had a propensity for absent-mindedness, but this intensified during a burst of creative energy, when he seemed to operate in a different world—the world of the spirit and the empire of the mind (as it was variously described in his day)—where mundane matters like piano lessons and meals could be ignored, and his

[12] WR, 87.

spirit could roam freely, storming up and down the piano in search of new ideas.

According to Beethoven's own account, the 'Appassionata' was finished by about the end of 1804, and Czerny states that Beethoven considered it his greatest sonata before the 'Hammerklavier'. It possesses, especially in the first movement, all those features that were notably absent in the previous sonata and the Triple Concerto: strong character and intense emotion, powerful and concentrated rhythmic cells, and wonderful lyricism. The descending F minor triad at the start, which falls to what was then the lowest note on the piano, is profoundly tragic, as if drawn from Florestan's dungeon scene, which Beethoven had just been sketching and which is in the same key. The rhythm of this motif permeates much of the movement, as does another rhythm—three quavers and a crotchet, first heard in bar 10 (Ex. 9.1)—and the two rhythms between them provide the movement with tremendous energy and drive. Lyricism is prominent mainly in the second subject (Ex. 9.2), which is surely one of the finest melodies he wrote. Surprisingly, however, the early sketches show an exposition in which this theme is entirely absent, with bar 34 effectively followed by bar 51, a theme in A flat minor. Only after much sketching did Beethoven insert bars 35 ff.,

**Ex. 9.1**  Op. 57/I

**Ex. 9.2**  Op. 57/I

144

to produce two main themes in the second group—one in the major and one in the minor. Even so, to end the exposition in the minor form of the relative major was a new departure, intensifying the tragic character of the movement.

Many other innovations and subtleties can be found in the movement. For example, to integrate the added second subject Beethoven made it motivically related to the first subject, although its character is very different. As the two themes are developed, their relationship becomes increasingly plain, until at the end of the coda they are virtually fused together into a single melodic line. As so often, Beethoven's coda provides a reconciliation of opposites, and the movement finishes with the same motif with which it had begun. Another interesting facet of the movement is his manipulation of individual pitches and degrees of the scale. The interplay between C and Db, often supported by F minor and G flat major triads respectively, is one of the primary foundations of the movement, and indeed the whole sonata. Sometimes the two notes occupy corresponding positions in consecutive phrases: thus the opening phrase begins on C and the second on Db. Sometimes they are juxtaposed in a single motif, as in Ex. 9.1 above; the two notes are even superimposed in bars 235–6, where this same motif occurs with the specific instruction 'sempre Ped.' to create a blurred effect. The eventual release of the pedal in bar 237, enabling the motif to be heard once again with crystal clarity, is one of the most striking moments in the entire sonata.

The second movement is in D flat major, and when Db and C are heard consecutively (bars 7–8), it is as part of a peaceful, almost static melody. The movement consists of a set of increasingly decorative and energetic variations, but barely a hint of a modulation until the mysterious diminished-7th chord in the penultimate bar, which then leads into the finale without a break. The finale resumes the mood of the first movement, with again much development of the C–Db relationship. The movement is in sonata form, but with two significant formal innovations: a repeat is marked for just the second part of the movement (development and recapitulation); and the coda begins with a section in a closed binary form marked 'Presto' and suggesting some wild dance. The main finale theme then returns at this new speed, and the movement concludes with descending F minor arpeggios, matching the first movement.

By the time Beethoven had finished sketching the 'Appassionata', the situation at the Theater an der Wien had changed again. Schikaneder was reinstated, and the idea of performing *Leonore* was revived. The sonata was apparently left not quite ready to send to a publisher, and remained so for a long time, while Beethoven resumed working on his opera. He was certainly doing so by 24 November, when Carl reported that Beethoven could not readily check the pieces intended for Breitkopf because he was so busy with the opera. Beethoven then concentrated mainly on *Leonore* for nearly a year, making slow but steady progress.

During the autumn he became increasingly friendly with Josephine Deym, whose husband had died in January 1804. She and her sister Charlotte visited Beethoven in June when he was staying in Hetzendorf and they were in nearby Hietzing, and by mid-November he was giving her regular piano lessons, as he had done before her marriage in 1799. Before long their friendship was deepening into love, and Charlotte began to suspect something, writing to her brother Franz on 21 December: 'Beethoven is with us almost daily, gives lessons to Pipschen [Josephine]—vous m'entendez, mon coeur!'[13] Prince Lichnowsky also suspected an intimate friendship was developing, for when he was at Beethoven's one day he saw a newly composed song, 'An die Hoffnung', evidently with some kind of inscription to Josephine. After Beethoven had presented it to her, most likely on 1 January (the customary day for making gifts), she sent it to her sister Therese Brunsvik, but with a request to tell nobody she had the score, even if she performed it. Therese was thrilled, and wrote to Charlotte: 'Beethoven's song is divinely beautiful. I thank Pepi a thousandfold that she had the kind thoughtfulness to send me it.' Shortly afterwards (20 January) she wrote, referring to the same song: 'Your song, dearest, is my treasure since I received it. After two days I knew it by heart. When I sang it, it created a furore, but no-one gets to see the score.'[14] The song is indeed one of Beethoven's loveliest—a setting in E flat major of a poem by Tiedge addressed to Hope, who comforts the sufferer by reminding him that an angel in Heaven counts his tears. The sketches show that Beethoven worked hard to create a melody that blends lyricism with very precise observation of verbal rhythm and intense expression of the words, with a strikingly effective modulation to C major in the middle of each verse. One can sense that he wrote this song *con amore* (as he would have put it).

The first explicit indication of Beethoven's love for Josephine comes in a letter written early in 1805 (one of a series of thirteen letters from him to her that aroused great interest when first published in 1957). After mentioning that Lichnowsky had suspicions about them because of the song but was too discreet to spread gossip and was thoroughly in favour of their association, Beethoven continues:

Oh, beloved J, it is no desire for the opposite sex that draws me to you, no, it is just you, your whole self with all your individual qualities—this has bound my regard—all my feelings—all my emotional power to you—When I came to you— it was with the firm resolve not to let a single spark of love be kindled in me. But you have conquered me. . . .

Long—of long duration—may our love become—it is so noble—so firmly founded on mutual regard and friendship—even the great similarity in so many things, in thought and feeling—Oh you let me hope [NB] that your heart will long—beat for me—Mine can only—cease—to beat for you—when—it no longer beats at all—Beloved J . . .[15]

---

[13] TF, 359.  [14] Goldschmidt, *Unsterbliche Geliebte*, 194.
[15] A-110. See also A-112, an incomplete copy of a letter of possibly even earlier date, where Beethoven expresses similar sentiments and refers to Josephine as his 'only beloved'.

Josephine's drafts of her replies indicate that the love was indeed mutual:

A feeling that lies deep in my soul and is incapable of expression made me love you; even before I knew you your music made me enthusiastic for you—the goodness of your character, affection increased it.[16]

There was, however, an impediment to their love, hinted at in Therese's letter to Charlotte:

But tell me, Pepi and Beethoven, what shall become of it? She should be on her guard! I believe you were referring to her when you underlined the specific words: 'Her heart must have the strength to say No,' a sad duty, if not the saddest of all!![17]

And Josephine did have the strength to say No, while indicating the strength of her love:

This favour which you have granted me, the pleasure of your company, would have been the finest ornament of my life if you had been able to love me less sensuously—that I cannot satisfy this sensuous love—does this make you angry with me—I would have to break holy bonds were I to listen to your desire—Believe me—that it is I through the fulfilment of my duty who suffer the most—and that my actions have certainly been dictated by noble motives.[18]

What was this 'duty', what these 'noble motives'? They were based in the laws and customs of the time, which made it exceedingly difficult for a noblewoman to marry a commoner, especially if she had children. During her short marriage (less than five years) Josephine had conceived four children, all of whom had survived. Were she to marry Beethoven, she would lose her title and, far worse, the guardianship of her children, whose future would be unsure and unsafe, since Beethoven would not have been granted the guardianship.[19]

Josephine's reference to Beethoven's desire for 'sensuous love' is ambiguous, for it could denote anything from caressing to full-scale marriage. But caressing, or even extra-marital sex (which the two apparently rejected anyway as immoral), would not have endangered her children. Thus Beethoven must have made some kind of marriage proposal to her—the only thing that would have meant her sacrificing the 'holy bonds' with her children. She felt this to be too high a price, and she was therefore forced to reject his proposal, even though her action was bound to cause extreme anguish for both of them. Thus they contented themselves with a non-sensuous love, permeated with a mixture of joy and sadness that are very evident in his later letters to her, which continued until at least 1807. Ironically, it was her concern for her children that eventually led to her unhappy second marriage, in 1810, for she saw in Baron Christoph von Stackelberg a man who could support her children should she herself die.[20]

---

[16] Alb-100; BB-265. Albrecht suggests early 1805; Brandenburg about two years later. See also Alb-99 (BB-215), where Josephine again expresses her love.

[17] TF, 377.   [18] Alb-100.   [19] Tellenbach, 'Psychoanalysis', 125.

[20] Goldschmidt, *Unsterbliche Geliebte*, 168.

A final poignant postscript to the relationships appeared in Therese's diary many years later, in 1846:

Beethoven! It seems like a dream that he was the friend, the intimate of our house—a stupendous spirit! Why did not my sister J., as the widow Deym, accept him as her husband? She would have been happier than she was with St[ackelberg]. Maternal love caused her to forego her own happiness.[21]

These comments confirm the above scenario, and Therese's awareness of it: there clearly was a marriage proposal (perhaps not a formal one); it was made before Josephine married Stackelberg; and she rejected it and 'her own happiness' for the sake of her children. Although most discussions of Beethoven's marriage plans have centred on alleged proposals to Magdalena Willmann (*c.* 1795) and to Therese Malfatti (1810), in both cases the evidence is only second-hand. With Josephine, however, it seems compelling, since it is based on what she herself wrote at the time, and is corroborated by her sister, whose recollections can generally be trusted. That the proposal was made and rejected while Beethoven was deeply involved with the composition of an opera subtitled *Conjugal Love* only adds further irony.

*Leonore* remained Beethoven's main musical preoccupation almost throughout 1805, but he did have a few significant distractions. In February the *Eroica* received a semi-public performance, along with his First Symphony; its public première, which he conducted, finally took place at the Theater an der Wien on 7 April. The reactions of the audience at these two performances are admirably summarized by one critic:

Some assert that it is just this symphony which is his masterpiece, that this is the true style for high-class music, and that if it does not please now, it is because the public is not cultured enough. . . . Another faction denies that the work has any artistic value and professes to see in it an untamed striving for singularity which had failed, however, to achieve in any of its parts beauty or true sublimity and power. . . . The third party, a very small one, stands midway between the others— it admits that the symphony contains many beauties, but concedes that the connection is often disrupted entirely, and that the inordinate length . . .wearies even the cognoscenti, and is unendurable to the mere music-lover.[22]

Thus the *Eroica* set the pattern for numerous major new works for the next century and a half, by Wagner, Stravinsky, Webern, and others. While some members of the audience were able to perceive that it pointed forward to the music of the future, the more conservative ones were left utterly bewildered, unable to appreciate any coherence or unity.

Beethoven continued to attend musical soirées from time to time. At one of them at Prince Lobkowitz's in 1805, Ignaz Pleyel, a former pupil of Haydn and now a prominent composer in Paris, was present, and

[21] Landon, *Beethoven*, 195.     [22] TF, 376.

Beethoven astonished the audience with a wonderful extemporization on some arbitrarily chosen and insignificant notes from the second-violin part of one of Pleyel's quartets. This recalls an earlier occasion when he extemporized on an inverted cello part by Steibelt; but Pleyel, unlike Steibelt, reacted to Beethoven's display with great enthusiasm. Another composer from Paris who visited Vienna that year was Cherubini, whom Beethoven first met at a musical soirée at Sonnleithner's in July.

A different sort of distraction from *Leonore* concerned the works sold to Breitkopf the previous year (three piano sonatas, the *Eroica*, the Triple Concerto, and *Christus*). It became clear that the firm were not prepared to pay Beethoven as much for them as he had expected, and he angrily demanded his scores back. Breitkopf, too, had by June grown tired of waiting for the Triple Concerto and the 'Appassionata', which had still not been sent, and consequently returned the remaining scores.[23] All were eventually published locally by the *Bureau* (as Opp. 53–7), except the oratorio, which he failed to sell and ultimately had to give to Breitkopf without fee some years later.

By September, *Leonore* was almost ready for production, and the première was fixed for 15 October. The work had filled the equivalent of over three sketchbooks (the *Eroica*, by contrast, occupies about half a sketchbook), and had taken Beethoven far longer to compose than anything previously. It might have taken even longer but for some borrowings from earlier works. The duet 'O namenlose Freude' was adapted from the abandoned *Vestas Feuer*, while the beginning of the final act, where Florestan is alone in the dungeon, shows such a similar conception to the opening of the *Joseph* Cantata of 1790 that some regard it as virtually a quotation. A still more direct borrowing from the cantata, however, comes near the end of the opera: the aria 'Da stiegen die Menschen ans Licht' (Then men rose to the light) from the cantata was adapted to a new text as part of the finale, though it is far more elaborate and well developed here. The last item to be composed was, as usual, the overture, which at this stage was the one now known as *Leonore* No. 2. Another number written or at least revised only at a very late stage was Leonore's aria. This was originally to have been a two-strophe aria entitled 'O brich noch nicht', which may even have been sung at the first performance, as is indicated by the 1805 word-book; but Beethoven evidently became dissatisfied with the text and demanded a new one. Sonnleithner reworked it as four lines of recitative, followed by the aria 'Komm, Hoffnung'.[24] Was it Beethoven who, remembering Josephine, proposed including the word 'Hoffnung'? The suggestion seems far from improbable.

As preparations for the première took shape, the censor intervened and banned the work on 30 September, but the ban was rescinded after a petition and some minor changes to the text. Nevertheless, the opera had to be

---

[23] Alb-104; BB-226.    [24] N-II, 447–52.

postponed for five weeks, mainly because of unprecedented difficulties in the music and Beethoven's continuing desire to make changes. It was eventually performed, under the title *Fidelio, oder Die eheliche Liebe*, on 20 November. Meanwhile, however, the French army had advanced on Vienna, entering the city a week before the première. Most of the aristocracy, many of whom were Beethoven's supporters and might have been expected to attend his new opera, had left Vienna, and the first three performances (20–2 November) were played before a nearly empty theatre. Financially and musically they were a disaster, and Beethoven began to consider revising the work almost at once. Despite its two subsequent revisions, however, nearly all its essential features were in place in the 1805 version, and in the right circumstances with sufficiently well-trained performers it could have made a much greater impact, as has been demonstrated by successful modern performances.

The foundation of the work is a grand tonal design which, though not planned at the outset or rigorously followed, provides the basis for much of the music's symbolism. C major, the 'natural' key and the key of rejoicing, is the basis for the final scene and effectively the key of the whole opera. The aria for Leonore, who sings in heroic and elevated tones about the star of hope, is in E major (four sharps), while that of Florestan, who lies chained in the deepest dungeon, counterbalances by being in four flats. This scheme is summarized in the 1805 Overture, which is in C major but quotes Florestan's aria in A flat in the slow introduction and later moves to E major for the second subject. The wicked Pizarro's music is centred on D minor/major, while the chorus of prisoners is set in B flat (two flats, halfway to Florestan's four). G major tends to be used for suggesting expectant release from captivity, appearing in 'O namenlose Freude' after Leonore has revealed her identity to Florestan, and in several other significant places.

The separate numbers are connected not by recitative but by spoken dialogue, following the tradition of the French *opéra comique* and the Cherubini operas that had recently been introduced to Vienna. But there is relatively little dialogue—less than in the singspiel tradition—and most of the action takes place during the musical numbers. The overall atmosphere is one of initial innocence gradually giving way to increasing darkness and horror until the dramatic turning point when Leonore finally reveals her identity. Thus at the beginning Marzelline's aria 'O wär' ich schon mit dir vereint' (O were I already united with you) and her ensuing duet with Jaquino, whose love for her is not being returned, seem to belong in the everyday world of *opera buffa* rather than high drama. Leonore's entry adds greater profundity, in a quartet constructed as a canon or round—a clever use of the device to indicate the very different emotions of the four characters. But the entire first act in this three-act version is relatively light.

The march-like Introduction to Act II (WoO 2b, formerly thought to belong to a different work) sees Pizarro enter, but the music subtly hints at his dubious character, with disconcertingly abrupt modulations. His ensuing aria is marked by highly chromatic writing, with numerous awkward, angular melodic lines and fierce discords to emphasize his evil nature. Leonore's aria, however, which follows shortly afterwards, seems the embodiment of nobility and heroic virtue, with a florid style that owes something to the *opera seria* tradition. The orchestration is particularly striking, with three prominent horn parts, as in the *Eroica*, lending an inner strength to the character of the music. The multi-sectional structure of the finale that follows, in which almost all the characters appear, is derived from the *opera buffa* tradition, where such finales had been the norm for half a century; but here any sense of the comic has long since been dispelled by the previous numbers. Beethoven movingly evokes the sensations of the prisoners as they gradually grope their way towards the warm sunlight and contrast it with their grave-like dungeon.

Florestan is seen for the first time at the start of the final act. The music of the prelude is extraordinarily vivid, with Beethoven operating on several different levels at once, pictorial and emotional. Tremolandos evoke a sense of fear, anguish, and shivering cold; dissonances express both horror and pain, while sharp contrasts of register, especially at the opening, suggest an alternation of groans and cries, as well as both the depth of the despair and the depth of the dungeon. Most remarkable is the use of the timpani, which are tuned a diminished 5th apart, the traditional interval of evil; they greatly heighten the sense of tension and anguish, with hints of an anxiously beating heart. In profundity of expression, originality of means, and complexity of texture, Beethoven far surpasses the original Gaveaux setting of this scene, as well as settings by other contemporary composers (the subject was also used for operas by Simon Mayr and Ferdinand Paer).[25] After a short recitative, Florestan's aria in A flat begins with the notes C–B♭–A♭; this motif implies a sense of complete resignation, but it also relates to the overall tonal scheme of the opera—a progression from the natural, everyday key of C through the prisoners' key of B flat to Florestan's own A flat. This ingenious technique of relating local events to the whole work was often used by Beethoven; a similar example had occurred in *Christus*, where the central duet of Christ's resignation to suffering is once again in A flat, and his theme begins with the notes E♭–C–A♭, which relate to the opening in E flat minor, his aria in C minor, and the duet itself in A flat.

After Pizarro has entered to murder Florestan, the drama builds rapidly to its climax, reached when Leonore reveals her identity with the words 'Tödt' erst sein Weib!' (First kill his wife!): see Ex. 9.3. Here Beethoven uses one of his most astonishing, and least-known, discords (it was suppressed in the later versions): a dominant 7th of A flat major—the dungeon key— is distorted by Leonore's high B being natural instead of flat; her note is thus associated with the liberating keys of E major and G major, and creates an extraordinary whole-tone chord. It might be assumed that

---

[25] See Lühning, 'Florestans Kerker', 171–9, for a detailed comparison.

**Ex. 9.3** *Leonore*/XVI

Beethoven simply forgot to insert the flat sign, but this is missing from all the relevant accompanying instruments too, and the sketches confirm his intentions with a natural before the B. Moments later, as Pizarro moves to attack Leonore, she produces a pistol, and with perfect dramatic timing an off-stage trumpet call is heard, signalling the arrival of the minister Don Fernando, of which we had been forewarned. The opera finally ends in C major—the natural key, the tonal pivot of the work, and Beethoven's customary key of triumph of light over darkness—with a chorus of rejoicing in which a couplet from Schiller's 'An die Freude' has been adapted:

> Wer ein solches Weib errungen,
> Stimm' in unsern Jubel ein.
> (Whoever has gained such a wife, let him join in our rejoicing.)

Although Beethoven's opera was founded on the French tradition, it incorporates several Italian features, with so many new ideas that it is really *sui generis*. Beethoven rose above the facile dramatic conventions and style of so many of his contemporaries to create almost a new type of opera, and its enormous technical demands contribute much to the unique effect. Nevertheless, he was well aware that the work was far from perfect, and his friends agreed. The main problem was the dramatic pacing, which was too slow. His propensity for writing long-drawn-out movements, which served him well in instrumental music, militated against him in a stage drama. Accordingly, he and Stephan von Breuning set about revising the libretto (mainly in the first act), while Beethoven systematically reviewed the entire score, changing whatever he thought necessary, in preparation for a revival in spring 1806. Most of the changes were fairly minor, and nearly all the features described above were retained except the three-act structure (the first two acts were now combined, with the Introduction to Act II replaced by a new march). He told Sonnleithner that 'to make the opera move more

TABLE 9.1. *Leonore* in 1805 and 1806 versions

|  | 1805 | 1806 |
| --- | --- | --- |
| Overture | 530 bars | 638 bars |
| 'O wär ich schon' | 97 | 97 |
| 'Jetzt, Schätzen, jetzt' | 234 | 220 |
| 'Ein Mann ist bald genommen' | 106 | 67 |
| 'Mir ist so wunderbar' | 52 | 52 |
| 'Hat man nicht auch Gold' | 91 | 0 (omitted) |
| 'Gut, Söhnchen, gut' | 232 | 211 |
| Introduction/March | 40 | 38 |
| 'Ha, welch ein Augenblick' | 122 | 117 |
| 'Jetzt, Alter' | 181 | 181 |
| 'Um in die Ehe' | 98 | 80 |
| 'Ach, brich noch nicht' | 188 | 174 |
| 'O welche Lust' | 667 | 544 |
| 'Gott, welch Dunkel' | 129 | 110 |
| 'Nur hurtig fort' | 122 | 104 |
| 'Euch werde Lohn' | 190 | 148 |
| 'Er sterbe' | 207 | 207 |
| 'Ich kann mich' | 289 | 184 |
| 'Zur Rache' | 487 | 330 |

swiftly I have shortened everything as much as possible'.[26] The reductions are shown in Table 9.1.

Altogether, then, over 500 bars were removed from the vocal numbers for the 1806 production, as well as Rocco's entire aria 'Hat man nicht auch Gold', resulting in a much tighter, more compact dramatic structure. Much of the overture was condensed, too, although it ended up longer altogether. The revised overture, known as *Leonore* No. 3, is based on the same material as its predecessor, but the slow introduction, exposition, and development section are each shortened, and so the trumpet calls at the end of the development begin at bar 272 instead of bar 392. In the 1805 version they are followed soon after by a presto coda, but in the revision there is a proper recapitulation before the coda, resulting in a much better musical structure, as well as an extremely powerful—almost too powerful—piece of drama.

Among other changes for the 1806 version of the opera, one in the grave-digging duet 'Nur hurtig fort' stands out. Beethoven had had the highly original idea of giving the main orchestral motif to the double basses to emphasize the subterranean gloom. He probably found them insufficiently

[26] A-128.

penetrative on their own, however, and so in 1806 they were doubled by a contrabassoon,[27] which greatly enhances the eerie effect.

The revised version was finally performed on 29 March and 10 April. According to Thayer and others, the theatre directors announced the work as *Fidelio*, as in 1805 and against Beethoven's wishes. Yet Breuning actually states the reverse, reporting on 2 June that Beethoven 'could not get the announcements printed under the altered title *Fidelio*. . . . Contrary to word and promise, the first title *Leonore* appeared on the posters.'[28] Josef Röckel, who took over the part of Florestan in 1806, concurs with this version of events. Moreover, Sonnleithner had referred to the work as *Fidelio* in his petition to the censor in October 1805. Thus the situation regarding Beethoven's preferred title is far less clear than is sometimes assumed.

Breuning and Röckel both state that there were three performances in 1806, but only two are known. Either way, however, Beethoven lost out financially from so few performances, for he was being paid a percentage of receipts. Moreover, the standard of performance was abysmal, with no attention paid to the dynamics. Deeply despondent, he wrote: 'All desire to compose anything more ceases completely if I have to hear it like that!'[29] He did not cease composing, but instead turned once again to instrumental music. His relationship with the theatre, like his relationship with Josephine, had proved an unhappy one.

[27] *SGA*, xi, p. XL. In this edition the contrabassoon part is misleadingly inserted into the 1805 version for technical reasons, as explained in the commentary.
[28] Alb-116 (not in BB).          [29] A-130.

# 10

# A cluster of masterpieces (1806–8)

Beethoven remained deeply depressed for some time after the performances of his opera. The dispute over its title, the paucity of the receipts (which left him convinced he had been swindled), and the inevitably poor standards of performance, all took their toll. Another probable cause of distress was his brother Carl's increasing interest in one Johanna Reiss, daughter of an upholsterer. The couple married on 25 May 1806, some months after she had become pregnant, and she gave birth to Beethoven's only nephew, Karl, on 4 September. Documentation concerning Beethoven's attitude to the relationship is lacking, but we may surmise that he was strongly opposed to it. First, it meant that Carl would cease to be of much assistance in Beethoven's business dealings, since this was not considered a task for married men and Beethoven always in later life used a bachelor. But far more importantly, anything that disrupted the family unity and drew the brothers apart tended to meet his opposition. He would also have been appalled by the immoral nature of the couple's early relationship and, being a generally perceptive judge of character, he surely became quickly aware of serious flaws in Johanna. He could also have contrasted the couple's base, sensual lust, and rapid marriage, with his own exalted but unhappy relationship with Josephine Deym, where a union of souls had remained unfulfilled.

None of this, however, came to the surface; nor did Beethoven allow it to impinge on his composing. Instead he embarked in 1806 on a remarkable cluster of masterpieces that still form some of the cornerstones of the orchestral and chamber-music repertory. The year was particularly productive: apart from the *Fidelio* revisions, he composed two concertos, the Fourth Symphony, the three 'Razumovsky' Quartets and the Thirty-two Piano Variations in C minor (WoO 80)—almost one major work per month in the latter part of the year. No proper sketchbook appears to have been used during this time, with Beethoven resorting instead to loose leaves, large numbers of which have been lost; thus the precise chronology of these works is difficult to establish. The first to be written, however, was the Fourth Piano Concerto. This had been conceived early in 1804, for a concept sketch, containing just the first five bars, survives among the earliest sketches for *Leonore*; but the work was apparently not sketched in detail until after the completion of the opera. It was then resumed and completed after the opera had been revised in 1806, although it did not reach its published form until somewhat later. A score of some sort, however, was ready by 5 July 1806, for Beethoven wrote to Breitkopf & Härtel that day that his brother was about to travel to Leipzig bringing, amongst other things, a score of 'a new piano concerto'.[1] The visit did not eventually take place, but the essential elements of the concerto were evidently fixed by that time, for later sketches are associated with relatively minor details.

Beethoven's initial sketch for the concerto in early 1804 is already very close to the final version of these five bars, and it is remarkable how many ideas in the rest of the concerto are generated by this opening phrase (Ex. 10.1). Its gentle, lyrical nature sets the mood for the whole work, which does not use trumpets and timpani until the finale; meanwhile the five-bar phrase, expanded from the customary four bars, points to a new breadth of expression that has been freed from the grandeur of the *Eroica*. The five-bar phrase structure, with an isolated first note that seems introductory, reappears in the main theme of the second movement, and again in the third movement (though here it is notated as ten short bars), creating an unusually strong bond between the movements. The prominence of the note B is taken up in bar 6 with an unexpected B major chord (which reappears in bar 6 of the second movement, though in an E minor context); similarly the A minor chord in bar 3 anticipates the one in bar 29, where the second main thematic idea of the movement first appears. In addition, the four-note rhythmic figure in bars 1–2 is taken up and treated as one of the main motifs of the movement, reminding us of several other Beethoven works from this period where a similar four-note rhythm is used—notably the Fifth Symphony.

**Ex. 10.1** Op. 58/I

Most remarkable of all, however, is the use of the solo piano at the start, for all previous piano concertos (at least, all that Beethoven is likely to have known) begin with the orchestra, and normally with an extended tutti before the entrance of the soloist. It is as if Beethoven has deliberately set up an unconventional opening, before using the rest of the movement to

---

[1] A-132.

justify the unorthodoxy. The purpose of giving the opening to the piano proves to be that it heralds a new and closer relationship between piano and orchestra, with greater continuity between the standard sections. For example, in his previous concertos the opening ritornello ended with a very solid cadence and caesura before the soloist entered; here, however, the orchestra continues developing material beyond the cadence (bar 68) and the structural close of the ritornello (bar 72), with the piano entry seeming to grow out of the orchestral extension in bar 74. A similar sense of continuity and homogeneity occurs at the end of the solo exposition. The convention here was to have a big cadence, probably decorated by trills, followed by an emphatic central ritornello affirming the new tonic (see bars 235–7 of his C major piano concerto, for example). Here, however, the central ritornello (bars 170–92, corresponding to bars 50–72 of the opening ritornello) begins with four bars played softly by the piano with light orchestral accompaniment, starting on a dominant 7th instead of the new tonic.

The changed relationship between piano and orchestra is taken up as a principal issue in the second movement, which like the first begins with an isolated note introducing a five-bar phrase. Here the orchestra plays angry unison motifs that alternate with gently pleading phrases from the piano and are eventually pacified by them, dying away to a peaceful close. The structural similarity to the scene between Orpheus and the Furies in Gluck's *Orfeo ed Euridice* is unmistakable, and has led some writers to conclude that the movement is programmatic. The slow movement of the Quartet, Op. 18 No. 1, had a hidden programme, and Czerny states that some other movements did too, claiming that the finale of the Piano Sonata, Op. 31 No. 2, was sparked off by the sound of a galloping horse. Yet there is no firm evidence linking the concerto movement to the Orpheus myth. The myth itself is archetypal and symbolic—wildness tamed through culture and art, demons overcome by the power of music. Such myths are widespread: Beethoven's *Prometheus* ballet embodies related concepts, as does the Biblical narrative of Saul's anger being assuaged by David's harp. Thus it is preferable to regard the concerto movement as reflecting all these stories and the universal idea of art overcoming barbarism, music dissolving hostility, and gentleness pacifying anger, rather than restricting interpretation to a single legend. Universal representations of this kind reappear in several of Beethoven's works, and have prompted much needless programmatic speculation.

Almost before he had finished detailed work on the concerto, Beethoven turned his attention to a set of three string quartets that had been commissioned by Count Andreas Razumovsky, the Russian Ambassador. Razumovsky had lived in Vienna for some years and had married Countess Elisabeth Thun, sister of Princess Lichnowsky, in 1788. He was therefore closely connected with Beethoven's circle, and was a great music-lover, as well as an accomplished violinist who sometimes took part in quartet playing. When he commissioned three quartets from Beethoven, it was agreed that each should include a Russian theme (the explicit incorporation of folksongs into sonata-type works was common at that time, though it is not found elsewhere in Beethoven's output). To obtain the themes, Beethoven drew on a collection of Russian folksongs published by Ivan Prach in 1790, borrowing two melodies and transposing them to keys that suited him;[2] one was used in the finale of the first quartet and the other in the trio section of No. 2. In No. 3 he used no borrowed material but instead composed a slow, Russian-style dance for the second movement. He began writing out the first quartet as early as 26 May, and probably completed it the following month.

While still at work on the second quartet, in late summer, Beethoven travelled with Prince Lichnowsky to stay at his castle at Grätz in Silesia, near the town of Troppau (now Opava, near the Czech-Polish border), some 140 miles north-east of Vienna. This was only about thirty miles from the castle of Count Franz von Oppersdorff, by Oberglogau (Glogowek), and Lichnowsky and Beethoven took the opportunity to visit the count. It may have been on this occasion that Oppersdorff commissioned the Fourth Symphony from Beethoven. At any rate, the Razumovsky quartets were set aside while the new symphony was composed, and it was completed very quickly (its earliest mention is in Beethoven's letter to Breitkopf & Härtel dated 3 September). Oppersdorff paid Beethoven 500 florins for six months' exclusive use, and may have received a score as early as November, although the fee was not paid until the following February.

After the enormous size of the *Eroica* it was inevitable that Beethoven's next symphony would be on a smaller scale, but the Fourth is still very substantial and contains many innovations within its traditional four-movement structure. One of the most notable is new approaches to the links between sections—an issue already explored recently in the Fourth Piano Concerto. The slow introduction merges into the main Allegro without any clear break, and the actual change of time signature is notated four bars before the arrival of the main theme; then at the repeat of the exposition, what sounds like the end of the slow introduction is incorporated into the lead-back, further blurring the structural outlines. At the recapitulation there is still more ambiguity: after a striking enharmonic change, in which the timpani play a prominent role, the main theme arrives without the four-bar preparation found in the exposition, implying retrospectively that these four bars are not a true part of the exposition.

The raised profile given to the timpani in the first movement is continued in the second. Here a prominent accompanying motif first heard in bar 1 in the second violins and later played by the entire orchestra (bar 9) is eventually given just to the timpani (bars 64 and 102). Integrating the timpani into

---

[2] Originally they were in G minor and A major: see N-II, 90.

the thematic design—an idea already introduced in the C minor piano con-certo—became of increasing interest for Beethoven from now on.

Count Oppersdorff was clearly delighted with the new symphony for he later commissioned another (No. 5); but meanwhile Beethoven resumed work on the quartets, and also at last finished work on the long delayed 'Appassionata' Sonata. Its autograph score was evidently completed while he was in Grätz, and it is marked by some prominent water stains that are explained by a curious incident. One day in October he had been asked to play the piano for some visitors at Grätz, but he had long disliked being put on show in this manner. On this occasion he became so angry that he promptly left and hurried back to Vienna. During the long journey (about three days) he encountered a violent storm, and the water penetrated his trunk, damaging the 'Appassionata' manuscript. It also evidently damaged the first two movements of the second 'Razumovsky' quartet and some sketches for the later movements (which suggests that the last two move-ments, and the third quartet, had still not been written out).[3] On reaching home, he was reportedly still so angry that he smashed the bust of Prince Lichnowsky that he had previously kept on display. Yet, as usual, the anger subsided and before long there was a reconciliation between the two men, though they never seem to have been quite so close thereafter. His anger did not affect him too deeply, for on arrival in Vienna he laughingly showed the still wet manuscript of the 'Appassionata' to Count Razumovsky's librarian Paul Bigot. Bigot's wife Marie was an accomplished pianist, and she imme-diately sight-read the sonata from the wet manuscript (according to an account written by Bigot much later). She then begged Beethoven to give her the manuscript after the work had been printed. He duly obliged, and she kept it with her when she later moved to Paris, where it still resides today.

Once back in Vienna, Beethoven resumed and rapidly completed the remaining two string quartets, and by February all three had been tried out in performance. The new expansiveness already found in his recent sym-phonies, concertos, sonatas, and the opera is applied to chamber music in these quartets, which are strikingly long. No. 1 in F major is particularly imposing. Its starting-point was the theme of the finale, as in the First and Third Symphonies and the 'Kreutzer' Sonata. In this case it was the bor-rowed Russian folksong, which is played by the cello at the start of the finale. This sound is foreshadowed at the very beginning of the work, by the same instrument playing in the same register and with some of the same notes (Ex. 10.2). The texture here, with a cello melody beneath throbbing second violin and viola, is identical to the main theme of the *Eroica*; in the quartet, however, the accompanying instruments play an implied 6–4 chord, so that although a tonic chord is present in outline, there is a sense of instability that provides great forward thrust. This thrust is combined

---

[3] See Tyson, 'Razumovsky', 128–30.

*Beethoven*

**Ex. 10.2** Op. 59, No. 1/I

160

with a spaciousness generated by an extraordinarily slow harmonic pace: in the first eighteen bars there is only one change of harmony (from tonic to dominant in bar 7), while the cello's long melodic line, taken over by the first violin in bar 9, does not reach a conclusion until bar 19; the melody ends with the four notes from bar 1 played three octaves higher and four times as slowly, providing a further indication of the gigantic size of what is to follow. The instability of the opening phrase is not fully resolved until the coda, where it is heard in the first violin above stable tonic harmony at a great climax (bar 348). When the autograph score was first written out, Beethoven intended a repeat of the development and recapitulation (as in the finale of the 'Appassionata'). This would have meant an already long movement being even more gigantic, with the great climax delayed almost unbearably; but he cancelled the repeat at a very late stage.

The second movement is one of the most witty and whimsical that Beethoven ever wrote. Again the cello leads, but its 'theme' consists of a single note, unaccompanied, repeated in a distinctive rhythm. This has amused many performers, but the way the theme is developed is equally hilarious. The humour involves sudden dynamic contrasts, absurd effects, double meanings, and the clever manipulation of keys, registers, motifs, textures, and rests. The third movement, by contrast, is profoundly tragic, in F minor. Amongst the sketches, Beethoven wrote: 'A weeping willow or acacia tree onto the grave of my brother.'[4] This might provide a clue to the meaning of the movement, or it may in some way reflect his attitude to his brother Carl, whose marriage took place about the time these sketches were written (the autograph of the quartet was begun the day after the wedding); but its real significance is obscure and his brother did not die until 1815. The movement closes with a trill on C with D♮; this cunningly provides the first two notes of the Russian theme of the finale, where the mood again changes very sharply.

The other two quartets are equally original in their way, although No. 3 is superficially more traditional, with a stately minuet for its third movement. No. 2 in E minor has a glorious slow movement in E major, marked to be played 'with much feeling'. According to Czerny, Beethoven conceived this movement when contemplating a starry sky, and certainly several other pieces referring explicitly to stars are in the same key (e.g. Leonore's aria 'Komm, Hoffnung'). The finale of this quartet begins in C major, and in the rest of the movement there is a continual battle between this key and E minor. A similar battle between C major and G major had appeared in the finale of the recently completed piano concerto, but in the quartet the battle has a surprising outcome: the quartet finishes in E minor, but C major wins the war, being the key of No. 3. Thus Op. 59 can be seen as a complete cycle, in which C major is approached from first the flat and then the sharp side, with hints of the final key evident even in the first note of No. 1.

---

[4] N-II, 83. The page in question is Vienna, Gesellschaft der Musikfreunde, A 36, p. 44 (cf. Tyson, 'Razumovsky', 120).

C major is not reached without a struggle, however, for No. 3 begins on the most tonally ambiguous chord—a diminished 7th—before meandering slowly through several uncertain keys in a highly chromatic introduction. When the main Allegro is finally reached, the first two notes are E and F, recalling the keys of the two previous quartets. It is tempting to regard such link-ups as accidental, but they occur so often in Beethoven's music that they can hardly be the result of pure chance.

By the time Beethoven had finished the 'Razumovsky' quartets, he had gained a new self-confidence. Within the four years since the Heiligenstadt Testament he had fully mapped out the new path on which he embarked in 1802, having written new types of composition in all the genres he evidently considered most important—opera, oratorio, symphony, concerto, string quartet, and piano sonata—and having established himself incontestably at the forefront of new music. Recognition was coming from as far away as London and Edinburgh, and he determined to continue on his set path. On 1 November he told George Thomson of Edinburgh (who had asked him for compositions) that he would never lower himself from 'that elevation and originality of style which . . . characterises my works so advantageously'.[5] And the admiration his new works had received meant that his deafness was no longer a cause of anxiety. Amongst the sketches for the finale of the third 'Razumovsky' Quartet he wrote: 'In the same way that you rush into the whirlpool of society, so it is possible to write operas despite all social hindrances—let your deafness be no more a secret—even in art.'[6]

Far from resting on his laurels, however, Beethoven continued composing with great energy, and before the end of 1806 had produced another masterpiece—the Violin Concerto in D (Op. 61). In a letter to Breitkopf, dated 18 November 1806, there is no mention of this work, which implies it was barely begun; yet it was performed on 23 December, having been completed, according to Czerny, about two days before the performance. It was composed for Franz Clement, leader of the orchestra at the Theater an der Wien and a friend of Beethoven's (who wrote at the head of the autograph, 'par Clemenza pour Clement'). It was perhaps Beethoven's way of thanking him for his efforts in *Leonore*. Like most Beethoven concertos, the Violin Concerto did not reach its final form until some time after the première. The version represented by the original ink in the autograph score was the one played by Clement, but various alterations were added the following year in a different ink (see below).[7] Again, however, these later changes were matters of detail rather than of fundamental conception.

In the first movement the opening idea combines two features that Beethoven had been exploring recently: integration of the timpani into the thematic design, as in the slow movement of the Fourth Symphony; and a

[5] A-136.　　　　　　　　　　　　　[6] N-II, 89.
[7] The autograph score, which has been published in facsimile (Graz, 1979), contains several unusual features discussed by various writers; see especially Kojima, 'Solovioline-Fassungen'.

main motif based entirely on repetitions of a single note, as in the Allegretto of the first 'Razumovsky'. In the concerto, however, the motif is even more elemental—and hence susceptible to extensive development—consisting of four unaccompanied crotchets played by the timpani (followed by a fifth crotchet that overlaps with the start of an oboe melody). The device is extraordinarily original, despite its ancestry, and despite works by earlier composers that also begin with unaccompanied timpani (such as Bach's *Christmas Oratorio* and Haydn's 'Drum Roll' Symphony); and the way Beethoven develops the motif is even more remarkable. The four drum-strokes on D in bar 1 are answered by four more on A in bar 5, and are then developed as an extension to the main theme (bar 10, on a disconcerting D♯), and as an integral part of each of the other five main thematic ideas in the opening ritornello (bars 18, 28, 43, 65, and 77). In each of the six themes apart from the one in bar 65, alternation of tonic and dominant harmony figures prominently, providing ample scope for incorporation of the opening motif. In bar 18, for example, the repeated notes are semiquavers in the accompaniment; in bar 65, however, they appear once again as crotchets, as part of a melody for the violins. The harmonic relationship between the other themes is unusually close, and the two at bars 43 and 77 can actually fit together simultaneously in perfect harmony, as Fritz Kreisler demonstrated in his well-known cadenza for the concerto.

Close thematic integration was a common procedure in symphonic writing, but was uncharacteristic of the traditional concerto, where the custom was to have a series of different ideas in the opening ritornello, which were then developed in the remainder of the movement. In this work, however, by relating all the main themes of the first movement to the opening motif, Beethoven created a sense of symphonic breadth, cohesion, and motivic development within the concerto genre. At times, indeed, the movement sounds more like part of a grand symphony, with its unhurried speed ('Allegro ma non troppo') and continuous development. Yet structurally it still bears all the hallmarks of the traditional concerto form, with its combination of ritornello and sonata-form procedures. The only substantial irregularity is the central ritornello, which modulates (from A to C major) like the start of a symphonic development section, instead of establishing the dominant key like a typical concerto ritornello.

The second movement is a set of variations followed by an extended coda that runs into the finale without a break. This practice of running together the last two movements had by now become practically the norm with Beethoven, and it reflects his increasing desire for continuity and cohesion within a work. The finale is in sonata-rondo form, but as in the Fourth Piano Concerto one reprise of the A section in the traditional ABACABA form is omitted: that time the third statement was omitted; this time it is the final one, so that the reprise of the B section runs straight into an extended coda at bar 260. Beethoven was becoming increasingly sensitive to the danger of sonata-rondo form sounding repetitious, and used it relatively rarely in his later works; even where it does appear it is usually modified in some way, as here.

Around the end of 1806 Beethoven composed a set of Piano Variations in C minor (WoO 80). Its precise position within the chronology of his works is unclear: all we know is that it was sketched alongside part of the finale of the third 'Razumovsky', and that its publication was announced on 20 April 1807. Thus it was composed immediately around the time of the Violin Concerto, and it heralded a year in which virtually all his completed works were in C major or C minor. He evidently did not regard it as a major work, for he published it without dedication or opus number, merely giving it a plain number (No. 36), like most of his earlier sets of variations. Yet it is another highly original work. The theme is only eight bars long, creating a compressed intensity that foreshadows the Fifth Symphony, but its brevity is compensated by an unusually large number of variations—thirty-two in all—and an extended coda. In the variations, it is the harmonic outline of the theme, rather than its melodic shape, that tends to be preserved, suggesting a chaconne rather than a set of variations, and indeed the theme uses the traditional chaconne rhythm and metre. But Beethoven maintains a delicate balance between harmony and melody, and in some variations, such as Var. 15, the outline of the melody is more clearly discernible than the original harmonic progressions. Metre and tempo remain unchanged throughout—another echo of the chaconne—and many of the variations run smoothly into the following ones, creating a very strong sense of powerful, monolithic unity.

Something of the emotional intensity and pathos of the set of variations reappeared in Beethoven's next work, the overture to Heinrich Collin's play *Coriolan*. Again little is known about the origin of the work—no sketches survive and the reason why it was composed is uncertain. The play dates from 1802, but it was revived in Vienna for a single performance on 24 April 1807. Since Beethoven would have been unlikely to write a dramatic overture without the incentive of a performance in the theatre, the overture was probably composed for this occasion (despite Thayer's assertion to the contrary). If so, however, it was completed surprisingly long in advance, for it was ready by the beginning of March, and was heard that month in two private concerts organized by Prince Lichnowsky and Prince Lobkowitz (these were before select audiences, and so would not have detracted from the public première at the theatre the following month).

The *Coriolan* Overture confirms a sudden turn away from the more lyrical style that prevailed in most of the 1806 works, back to the heroic gestures of the preceding years and forward towards the dramatic fire of the Fifth Symphony. One of the overture's most striking features is the new relationship between slow introduction and main Allegro. The opening idea, which recalls the beginning of the *Joseph* Cantata and of the dungeon scene in *Fidelio*, is heard as seven very slow beats, with the eighth beat marking the start of the main Allegro theme. Thus there is already a rhythmic overlap between the end of the slow introduction and the ensuing music. But the true nature of the slow introduction becomes apparent to the listener only later, when it is developed as an integral part of the Allegro, and what had been heard as slow notes is now heard as prolongations within a fast tempo. The 'slow introduction' proves to be an illusion! The concept of integrating a slow-moving opening passage with the ensuing Allegro had already been tentatively explored in the Piano Sonata, Op. 31 No. 2, and in the Fourth Symphony (where the same motif is heard both before and after the change in tempo); but in the *Coriolan* Overture it is developed in an extraordinary new way. The introduction and the following quaver theme are totally unified within a very powerful first subject.

It is significant that the *Coriolan* Overture was composed when Beethoven had already begun sketching a new overture for his opera—the so-called *Leonore* No. 1.[8] He had apparently sensed by now that the two previous overtures revealed too much of the narrative by including the denouement—the trumpet calls—thus making the ensuing opera dramatically redundant. At any rate, *Leonore* No. 1, though still containing a quotation of Florestan's theme, suggests little of the drama to follow, like the earlier *Prometheus* Overture. With *Coriolan*, Beethoven took a middle road. Since what follows here is a play rather than an opera or ballet, it was possible to embody the whole drama in the overture, without creating the sense of duplication that arises when *Leonore* Nos. 2 or 3 are used with the opera. Accordingly, strong rhetorical gestures are used throughout the *Coriolan* Overture to stress the moods rather than the narrative of the drama, starting with the initial outbursts of anger that recur intermittently during the course of the overture. Also discernible are a prevailing sense of foreboding and despair, the gently lyrical pleading of the second subject, and ultimate death, represented at the end by melodic disintegration and eventual annihilation. Overall, the overture owes something to the dramatic style of Cherubini and the French school, but this is fused with the Viennese symphonic style in a highly original and successful creation.

Like the *Coriolan* Overture, the Fourth Symphony and the Fourth Piano Concerto received their premières in private performances in March 1807, alongside his first three symphonies and excerpts from *Leonore*. Beethoven was, however, distracted that month by more worldly matters. He had become a close friend of the Bigots, and on 4 March he invited Marie Bigot for a drive in the country, with her young daughter but without her husband (who was otherwise occupied). The Bigots considered this improper and she declined the invitation. Beethoven felt hurt and refused to accept there was any impropriety, since he had no amorous intentions but just regarded them as very dear friends with whom he could be entirely open. He wrote two long letters to them, explaining his feelings and providing a fascinating glimpse of several aspects of his attitudes to life:

[8] See Tyson, 'First Leonore', for a detailed account of the dating of this overture.

It is one of my chief principles never to be in any other relationship than friendship with the wife of another man. For I should not wish by forming any other relationship to fill my heart with distrust of that woman who some day will perhaps share my fate—and thus by my own action to destroy the loveliest and purest relationship. . . . I am extremely natural with all my friends and I hate any kind of constraint. . . . Never, never will you find me dishonourable. From childhood on I have learnt to love virtue—and everything beautiful and good.[9]

From what is known from other sources, this is a fairly accurate self-portrait. He had evidently been taught by his mother to love virtue and goodness, and he was a man of high moral principles who always aimed to behave honourably (even if he occasionally fell short of his ideals). The unspoken assumption seems to be that, to be regarded as a great man and great artist, his personal life had to be beyond reproach. His desire for eventual marriage also resurfaces here, as well as his high respect for the marital state, and his unwillingness ever to become emotionally involved with a married woman. He had by this time become so fond of the Bigots that he expressed a desire to live with them permanently, but this had no sexual connotations. Meanwhile his statement that friends should be able to speak their minds, even if it might cause offence, is entirely characteristic of him; it was an attitude that helped to cement some friendships but destroy others. With the Bigots, the friendship remained strong until they moved to Paris in 1809.

In early April 1807 the London-based composer, pianist, piano-maker, and publisher Muzio Clementi arrived in Vienna on his way to Rome. Beethoven was a great admirer of Clementi's piano sonatas, and his own early sonatas follow Clementi's more closely than any other composer's; but he had been wary of associating with him during Clementi's previous visits in 1802 and 1804, and no proper contact had been made. This time, however, the ice was broken and they rapidly agreed a publication contract. This was dated 20 April and witnessed by Baron Ignaz von Gleichenstein (who about this time took over Carl's former role as Beethoven's secretary): Clementi was to receive the British publication rights to Beethoven's five latest large-scale works: the Fourth Piano Concerto, the 'Razumovsky' Quartets, the Fourth Symphony, the Violin Concerto and *Coriolan* (Opp. 58–62). Clementi also asked for the Violin Concerto to be arranged as a piano concerto, which Beethoven agreed to prepare and send to London as soon as possible. For these six works, Clementi agreed to pay £200 (approximately 2000 Viennese florins, although the value of the florin was becoming increasingly unstable). Beethoven was also able to sell the continental publishing rights for these works locally, and they went to the *Bureau des Arts et d'Industrie*, who by this time had published (or were about to publish) his previous five major instrumental works, Opp. 53–7.

<hr />

[9] A-139; see also A-138.

Both parties were delighted with the contract: Clementi described it as a 'very good bargain', while Beethoven called it a 'really satisfactory arrangement'.[10] Three works—the piano concerto, the symphony, and the overture—were despatched by courier almost immediately, on 22 April. A set of parts for the quartets, however, was not available at the time, and had to be sent on later, while the Violin Concerto was kept back so that Beethoven could prepare a piano version. The contract also stipulated that he should compose, at his convenience, three piano sonatas, or two sonatas and a fantasia, for £60. Two years later this was fulfilled, and Clementi received Opp. 77–9, which he duly published. He also eventually published the 'Razumovsky' Quartets and the Violin Concerto (in both versions), but surprisingly, he never published any of the three works sent by courier. The courier was travelling to London via Russia, and the precious manuscripts were probably lost in transit.

Beethoven seems to have embarked on the piano version of the concerto almost at once, deferring work on a mass that had been commissioned by Haydn's patron Prince Nikolaus Esterházy. The need for a piano part also gave an opportunity for Beethoven to revise the solo violin part, which had been composed somewhat hastily. Thus he worked on the two together, producing not so much a violin concerto and piano arrangement as a concerto for either piano or violin, where some of the violin figuration may have been influenced by his work on the piano part. Sketches and drafts for both parts are liberally scattered in the blank staves at the foot of the autograph score and even in the middle of the score itself, and are easily distinguishable since they are in pencil or lighter ink than the main score written six months earlier.[11] The two solo parts had been written out and sent to the Viennese publisher by August, and the work was published the following year. By a touching coincidence, Beethoven's old friend Stephan von Breuning, a talented violinist, married Julie, an excellent pianist and daughter of Beethoven's former doctor Gerhard von Vering, in April 1808. Thus Beethoven was able to give them a particularly suitable wedding present: the violin version of the concerto was dedicated to Stephan and the piano version to Julie.

Having dealt with the material for Clementi, Beethoven spent most of the summer in Baden and then Heiligenstadt composing the Mass in C for Prince Esterházy. The prince habitually commissioned a new mass each year, to be performed on his wife Maria's name-day (8 September) or the first Sunday thereafter. Haydn had composed his six late masses for this purpose, and Hummel had also contributed, but it was logical for Esterházy to turn next to Beethoven. Extensive sketches survive in a

---

[10] TF, 418–19; letters to Clementi's partner William Collard and Beethoven's friend Franz Brunsvik respectively.

[11] See the facsimile edition. The drafts at the foot of the score were formerly thought to represent a complete second version, but they are too fragmentary and sketchy in places (see Kojima, 'Solovioline-Fassungen').

home-made sketchbook devoted almost exclusively to the Mass in C; they seem to indicate that the Credo was the last movement composed but that, as usual, the remaining movements were sketched in the right order (with some overlap between them). Beethoven had hoped to have the Mass ready before the end of July, but he was delayed by the work for Clementi and by a head illness, exacerbated by toothache. The Mass was eventually completed about a month later.

Beethoven composed it with some apprehension—not so much because it was his first church work (apart from some unpublished accompaniments for the *Lamentations of Jeremiah*, *c.* 1791) but because he was aware of inevitable comparisons with Haydn. Accordingly he deliberately set the text in a manner in which it had rarely been treated (as he later told his publisher); and although he copied two short sections of Haydn's 'Creation' Mass (1801) into his sketchbook while working on the Mass in C, the work as a whole is quite unlike any of Haydn's, despite superficial similarities. It contains several bizarre ideas, such as beginning the entire work with a bar for unaccompanied chorus basses (recalling the unaccompanied timpani opening of the Violin Concerto); and the opening instrumental figure in the Credo is said by Czerny to have been based on a village musician's bungled attempt at an arpeggio. Among the most innovative features is the wide range of keys. This is signalled as early as the 'Christe', which is in E major, like the second subject of the 'Waldstein' Sonata and both of the *Leonore* overtures thus far completed. Key contrast is continued with a 'Qui tollis' in F minor, 'Et incarnatus' in E flat major, Sanctus in A major, Benedictus in F major (followed by a return to the Osanna in A), and Agnus Dei in C minor. The return of the opening music at the end of the 'Dona nobis pacem' is also striking, although there were precedents for this.

In 1807 Princess Esterházy's name-day fell on a Tuesday, and so the performance was scheduled for the following Sunday, 13 September. Beethoven travelled to Eisenstadt on 10 September to rehearse the work, and remained there until the 16th. As usual, preparations for the performance seem to have been somewhat casual, for at the rehearsal on the Saturday four of the five contraltos were absent. The performance itself was far from successful, and Prince Esterházy wrote a few days later: 'Beethoven's mass is unbearably ridiculous and detestable, and I am not convinced that it can ever be performed properly. I am angry and mortified.'[12] Schindler's claim that Beethoven left Eisenstadt in a rage on the day of the performance, however, is clearly incorrect.

Back in Vienna, Beethoven exchanged a few more brief letters with Countess Josephine Deym and perhaps saw her a few times, as he had done earlier in the summer. He indicated that she was still his 'only beloved', while she promised to take a 'deep interest' in him for the rest of her life.[13] Nevertheless, they seem to have agreed that it would be better not to see

---

[12] Landon, *Beethoven*, 219.
[13] A-151; Alb-127. The latter may not have been written until 1809: see BB-403.

each other, and there is no confirmed association between them after this date.

Beethoven now resumed and completed the new overture for *Leonore* that he had been sketching intermittently. Plans had been made for a performance of the opera in Prague, and it was for this that the new overture was made ready.[14] Beethoven wrote out the autograph score (now lost); his copyist, as was usual, made a fair copy that Beethoven then annotated; and a set of orchestral parts was prepared. The projected performance, however, did not materialize, and Beethoven completely suppressed the new overture: unlike other orchestral works not immediately published, it was never tried out in private or offered to publishers (as far as is known), and it did not emerge until after his death. When the rest of the opera was published in vocal score in 1810, it was *Leonore* No. 3, not the new No. 1, that was published with it. Perhaps Beethoven decided, shortly after completing it, that his efforts to reduce the dramatic power of the overture had gone too far. Early sketches had exhibited extended passages in C minor, but these ideas became absorbed into *Coriolan* or abandoned altogether, leaving a somewhat emasculated movement in which the intrusion of the theme of Florestan's aria seems out of place. Whatever the reason for its abandonment, however, it was by this time extremely unusual for Beethoven simply to lay aside a movement already completed.

No such problems affected the other major work finished at about the same time—the celebrated Symphony No. 5 in C minor. As mentioned above, this had been begun in early 1804 but laid aside during the composition of *Leonore*; then, when Count Oppersdorff commissioned a new symphony, Beethoven quickly wrote one in B flat rather than complete the one in C minor. Oppersdorff, however, had now commissioned another one, again for 500 florins, and had even paid a deposit of 200 florins in June 1807, by which time sketching for No. 5 had been resumed and was probably well under way. Work on it continued after the Mass in C had been written, and it was virtually finished by about the end of the year.

The lengthy gestation of the symphony is perhaps related to its extraordinary originality: works that Beethoven contemplated for several years, such as the Fifth and Ninth symphonies, tend to contain more profound innovations than those written rapidly, like the Fourth and Eighth, although there are exceptions on both sides. The earliest known sketches (Landsberg 6, pp. 155–6) are for the third movement, and they already show the four-note motif from bars 19–20 that (with different accentuation) was to play such a prominent role in the first movement and indeed the whole symphony; a Trio in C major with running bass quavers is also represented.[15] The following pages show the opening section of the first movement—also surprisingly close to the final version, albeit somewhat abridged as was often the case with early sketches for a work. Thus the

---

[14] Tyson, 'First Leonore', 296.     [15] Nottebohm, *Skizzenbuch 1803*, 70.

fundamental idea of a highly charged, motivically concentrated first movement was present from the outset, but the overall shape of the work took longer to achieve. Another group of sketches, about mid-1804, shows the second-movement theme marked 'Andante quasi Menuetto', with a 'quasi Trio' marking for the theme at bar 22. The finale, however, was at this stage to be a 6/8 movement in C minor, utterly different from what eventually emerged.

The mood of pathos and agitation implicit in the early sketches for the first movement is developed to an extraordinary degree in the final version. Although containing echoes of Haydn's 'Sturm und Drang' style, the atmosphere is reinforced by grand rhetorical gestures more characteristic of French rescue opera. Equally remarkable is the intensity of motivic development, with the initial four-note motif generating almost all that follows, including the second subject, which is closely related. During the development section, the second subject becomes pared down to two chords (bars 196 ff.) and eventually just one (bars 210 ff.). This point marks the ultimate in the thematic fragmentation process that characterizes so many development sections, for although only a single chord remains, it is still unmistakably motivic and continues to be developed. At this point, too, comes the ultimate in tonal digression, as the music moves into F sharp minor—as far as possible from the home key, thus providing the culmination of a tendency for increasingly remote tonal goals that had been a mark of many of Beethoven's recent sonata-form movements (E minor in the *Eroica* in E flat, and C sharp minor in the G major Piano Concerto, had provided notable landmarks along the route). Rarely had any work, by Beethoven or his predecessors, embodied such sustained emotional intensity throughout the movement, or such extreme motivic concentration and integration; and never before had these two features appeared together to this extent.

The extreme integration of the first movement demanded matching integration for the symphony as a whole—both motivic and emotional. Motivically the integration was achieved mainly through manipulation of the initial four-note motif in different guises in each of the remaining movements. In terms of rhetoric, unity was achieved through the construction of a kind of narrative, in which C major gradually increases in prominence in each movement until it ultimately overwhelms C minor. Particularly crucial in this process is the transition from the C minor third movement (too serious to be called a scherzo, though it often is) to the C major march of the finale. This transition, like many others, required a disproportionate amount of sketching. Initially no transition seems to have been planned, but the finale would have seemed too disconnected without some kind of link. Beethoven's customary desire for integration, and for increased weight on the finale as the culmination of all that had gone before, necessitated some link, as in several recent works (Opp. 53, 56, 57, 59 No. 3, and 61). Such a link would confirm the sense of progress from darkness to light, tragedy to joy, struggle to victory,[16] and in his sketching Beethoven strove to make the link as smooth as possible. The broad sweep and continuity characteristic of the symphony genre were now no longer confined to single movements but embraced the entire work, and were reinforced by the unexpected reprise of part of the third movement within the finale.

In a letter datable to March 1808, Beethoven told Oppersdorff that the symphony had been 'ready for a long time', and he continues: 'The last movement of the symphony is with three trombones and piccolo—though not three timpani, but will make more noise than six timpani, and indeed better noise.'[17] This comment, besides announcing that trombones were to be introduced to symphonic writing for the first time, shows that Beethoven (and perhaps Oppersdorff too) was still occupied with the role of the timpani, after his innovations for them in several recent works; he was wanting to move away from their traditional use as primarily noise generators and explore new avenues. Accordingly in the second movement, in A flat, the timpani are tuned to C and G instead of the tonic and dominant, so that they can both strengthen the modulations to C major as part of the grand rhetorical plan, and also harmonize with tonic and dominant chords during the passages in A flat. The timpani also play a very important role in the transition to the finale, where they take over the main motif, pianissimo, against a background of held chords. The sustained hush at this point makes the contrast at the beginning of the finale all the more striking, with the fortissimo reinforced by the trombones and piccolo to create, in Beethoven's phrase, 'more noise than six timpani'.

Beethoven's letter to Oppersdorff promised that a score would be sent almost at once, in exchange for the remaining 300 florins; the letter implies, however, that the count was still entitled to refuse the work instead of paying 300 florins, and a receipt dated 29 March 1808 indicates that he paid 150 florins as a further instalment without receiving the score. He had still not received it by November, when Beethoven explained that he had had to sell the score to 'someone else',[18] but he promised that Oppersdorff would still receive a score. He had a second copy made, for use at a forthcoming concert (see below), and there is every likelihood that this went to Oppersdorff after the concert, in exchange for the remaining 150 florins, although there is no record of this transaction. The person who received the first copy was Gottfried Härtel, of the publishers Breitkopf & Härtel, who were by now back in favour with Beethoven and published all his major works from Op. 67 (the Fifth Symphony) to Op. 86 (the Mass in C) during 1809–12.

A change in management at the two court theatres during 1807 induced Beethoven to apply for a permanent position as an opera composer. The details of his proposal, in which he pledged to write one grand opera and

---

[16] Schindler's claim that the opening motif represented Fate knocking at the door, besides being manifestly spurious, is wholly inadequate as a rhetorical interpretation of the work.

[17] A-166.  [18] A-178.

one or more smaller works each year, in exchange for 2,400 florins and certain other benefits, are perhaps of less interest than the fact that he felt dissatisfied by his hand-to-mouth existence; and the freedom and renown he was by then enjoying as a freelance composer were accompanied by both considerable insecurity and meagre remuneration from patrons and publishers. He clearly saw opera as one of the highest genres, where he could most fully develop his talents in a challenging context that he had still not completely explored. The petition was unsuccessful, but our perception of him as primarily a composer of instrumental music might have been very different if his request had been granted. Even without the theatre position, his interest in opera persisted during 1808, with plans to collaborate with Collin on either *Macbeth* or *Bradamante*; but neither came to fruition.

Instead, Beethoven continued mainly with familiar instrumental genres. During the winter of 1807–8 he composed the Cello Sonata in A, Op. 69, which he dedicated to his friend Baron Gleichenstein, no doubt in gratitude for all the practical assistance that the baron had been giving him. Gleichenstein was a cellist himself, and so the sonata may originally have been commissioned by him. Unusually, the second movement is a Scherzo in the tonic minor, which is followed by an Adagio that breaks off after only eighteen bars and leads straight into the finale.

A lesser project completed early in 1808 was four settings of Goethe's poem 'Sehnsucht' ('Nur wer die Sehnsucht kennt'). Why four settings of a single text? Perhaps Beethoven recalled a project of the previous year, when the poet Giuseppe Carpani invited him and no fewer than forty-five other composers to set to music his poem 'In questa tomba oscura'; some composers produced more than one setting, resulting in sixty-three settings altogether (Beethoven's single attempt is WoO 133). Thus the idea of producing multiple settings of a single text was fresh in his mind, and he may have set 'Sehnsucht' as an experiment in different approaches to a single text. His own curious explanation, however, written on the autograph score, is perfectly plausible: 'Nb: I did not have enough time to produce a good one, so here are several attempts.' This seemingly paradoxical remark reflects the way in which he often composed vocal melodies. As is evident in several sketchbooks, he commonly approached text setting by sketching several or even many alternative melodies in quick succession. From these he would derive the best one and gradually mould it into its best shape, perhaps incorporating one or two elements from the discarded alternatives.[19] As in other works, each melody for 'Sehnsucht' has great intrinsic beauty and expressiveness, and for once he decided to work them all into complete settings (the first three are so short that this was not difficult), instead of just concentrating on the more elaborate final one. The first three are indeed little more than amplified sketches—short, strophic settings of only eleven bars each. The fourth, however, composed slightly later and perhaps

[19] See Cooper, *Creative Process*, 133–9, 223–4.

after the inscription, is richer and more profound (Ex. 10.3). It is through-composed, with close portrayal of individual words, a reprise of the opening, and a highly poignant A♭ four bars from the end, substituted for the expected A♮ and recalling earlier uses of the note in the central section in E flat major.

The inscription on the autograph must have been intended for Joseph Ludwig Stoll and Leo von Seckendorf, who had just begun editing a new

**Ex. 10.3** WoO 134 No. 4

## Beethoven

Ex. 10.3 cont.

journal entitled *Prometheus*, and wanted a song from Beethoven as a musical supplement (an increasingly common practice with journals at this time). The manuscript was sent to them about late February, for it bears a censor's approval dated 3 March, and the first setting duly appeared in the May issue (not until 1810 did all four settings appear together, in an edition issued by the *Bureau des Arts et d'Industrie*). Later in 1808 Beethoven sent Seckendorf another song, 'Andenken' (WoO 136), for *Prometheus*, but the journal ceased publication after 21 September without including this song.[20]

About the time the settings of 'Sehnsucht' were composed, Beethoven began a major new project—the *Pastoral* Symphony in F major. Every summer since at least 1799 he had spent an extended period in the country, usually in some nearby village such as Baden to the south or Heiligenstadt to the north of Vienna, and he once wrote: 'No one can love the country as much as I do.'[21] Ideas for a pastoral composition of some sort to express his fondness for the country had been sketched as early as 1803, but he now brought them together for a new symphony.

He was no doubt aware of a long tradition of pastoral music, stretching back at least to the late seventeenth century, if not to the Ancient Greeks. The distinctive features of the classical pastoral style had crystallized in the early eighteenth century, and were exploited by numerous composers, often in the context of Christmas music. They commonly included gentle moods, homophonic texture, prominent use of woodwind instruments, drone basses (in imitation of bagpipes) or very simple harmonies, major keys (most often G or F), lyrical or dance-like melodies in mainly conjunct motion, often in compound metre, and sometimes actual rural sounds such as imitation birdsong or horn-calls. Beethoven used most of these features plus several new ones. He was, however, faced with two main problems in writing a symphony in the pastoral style: the first was to prevent the music degenerating into mere scene-painting or story-telling; the second was to combine the pastoral style, leisurely and undramatic, with the thrust and dynamism of the symphonic style.

To combat the first problem, Beethoven kept reminding himself about the nature of the work with little comments amongst the sketches:

Sinfonia Caracteristica—or recollections of country life
It is left to the listener to discover the situations himself
All tone painting in instrumental music loses its value if pushed too far

Such comments, which are extremely unusual amongst his sketches, highlight his concerns about pictorial music, and these persisted right through to the final version, where the work was eventually entitled: 'Pastoral Symphony, or recollection of country life. More expression of feeling than painting'.[22] Even in the published version, the first movement retained a

---

[20] *NA*, XII/1, *Kritischer Bericht*, 35–7.    [21] A-258.    [22] N-II, 378; A-204.

title that stressed emotion rather than imagery: 'Awakening of cheerful feelings on arrival in the country.' Beethoven's titles for the remaining movements are more explicitly pictorial: 'Scene by the Brook'; 'Merry Gathering of Country People'; 'Thunder, Storm' (an interpolated movement between the customary scherzo and finale); and 'Shepherds' Song: Glad Feelings with Thanks to the Godhead after the Storm'. Nevertheless, he concentrated for the most part on feelings associated with the scenes, rather than direct pictorialism, and he reminded himself, in another little note among the sketches, that such titles should be superfluous: 'Even someone who maintains only an idea of country life can think for himself what the author intends, without many titles.'[23]

The second problem, the apparent incompatibility of pastoral and symphonic styles, was at its most acute in the first movement, but Beethoven managed to fuse the two styles together in a wholly convincing and original way. As in the Fifth Symphony, the movement is based on a small number of distinctive motifs, but these are subjected to far more repetition than normal development, creating an unusually static character in which often the only changes are in dynamic level or instrumentation. Almost at the start, he evokes what he used to call an 'unbuttoned' mood, introducing a blatant pair of consecutive 5ths (bars 11–12) to suggest informality. Even in the development section the customary sense of forward thrust is largely lacking, with remote keys juxtaposed rather than used as the basis for tonal progression. The pastoral mood is also enhanced both by many traditional pastoral features (for example, the movement remains almost entirely in major keys) and by unusual emphasis on the subdominant—the key that most effectively relaxes tension. Particularly notable is the passage immediately before the recapitulation. At this point Beethoven often did something extraordinary (the discordant horn entry in the *Eroica*, and the reintroduction of third-movement material in the finale of the Fifth Symphony, are notable examples) and he increasingly tried to avoid a conventional dominant preparation for the return of the main theme. Thus in the *Pastoral* Symphony he used a subdominant preparation—four bars of B flat harmony (bars 275–8)—instead of the usual dominant.

Despite these unusual features, however, the symphonic genre remains firmly in evidence, both in the first movement and in the rest of the symphony. The second movement, like the first, is in standard sonata form, and its only specifically non-symphonic feature is the introduction of bird-calls in a kind of woodwind cadenza near the end (though even these are motivically derived). To prevent any doubt about this passage, Beethoven instructed the copyist to insert the names of the relevant birds—nightingale, quail, and cuckoo—into the score and parts. These bird-calls have been the subject of much misunderstanding, partly through Schindler, who claimed that Beethoven had heard the actual birds during a walk at

---

[23] N-II, 375.

1. Beethoven's grandfather, also called Ludwig (or Louis) van Beethoven. Beethoven had this oil painting by Leopold Radoux sent to him from Bonn in 1801, and preserved it carefully. The music in the portrait is a passage from Pergolesi's *La serva padrona* (I am grateful to Jos van der Zanden for this information).

2. Title-page of the corrected copy of the *Eroica* Symphony. The phrase 'intitolata Buonaparte' has been deleted so heavily (presumably by Beethoven) that there is a hole in the paper. The page also includes instructions from Beethoven to a copyist, and Beethoven used this score during performances of the Symphony.

3. Beethoven depicted in oil (1804–5) by Joseph Willibrord Mähler. The painting is full of subtle symbolism: note particularly the classical temple in the background, the lyre in Beethoven's hand, and the cloud formation that suggests he leads from darkness to light.

4. Countess Josephine Deym (née Brunsvik, later Baroness Stackelberg). Unsigned pencil miniature. Josephine was Beethoven's beloved in 1804–5, during the period when he was composing *Leonore*.

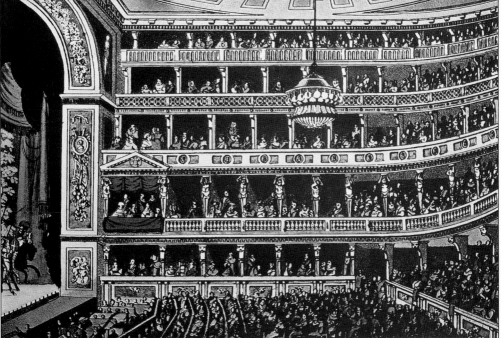

5. Theater an der Wien. Anonymous engraving. It was in this building that Beethoven's two great concerts of 1803 and 1808 took place, which included the premières of his Second, Fifth, and Sixth Symponies and several other works. Here, too, were heard the premières of *Leonore* (1805) and the Violin Concerto (1806), and the first public performance of the *Eroica* (1805).

6. Bronze bust of Beethoven by Franz Klein, based on a life mask of his face taken in 1812, and therefore a fairly accurate representation of his facial features

7. Unsigned ivory miniature found after Beethoven's death along with his letter to his Immortal Beloved, and probably a depiction of her. The portrait was formerly identified as Therese Brunsvik or Marie Erdödy, but is now believed to be of Antonie Brentano.

8. Oil painting of Beethoven by Josef Carl Stieler. Although dated 1819 on the back, the portrait was actually painted in 1820 and was commissioned by Franz Brentano. In Beethoven's conversation books are several references to the portrait sessions, and in April Stieler asked about the key of the then unfinished *Missa solemnis*, in order to insert it in the painting. He shows the key as 'D#'—an old-fashioned abbreviation for D major.

9. Archduke Rudolph of Austria, Beethoven's patron and sole composition pupil. Oil painting by Johann Baptist Lampi, c.1825.

10. Beethoven's nephew Karl as a young man in cadet's uniform. Karl joined the army in January 1827, and never saw Beethoven again

11. A page from a sketchbook of 1822 (Artaria 201, p.111). The top four staves are for *Die Weihe des Hauses*, the next four contain unused material, and the rest includes one of the earliest sketches that show the 'Freude' theme from the Ninth Symphony in its final form. After an early version of the second-movement theme (stave 12) Beethoven wrote: 'very fugal. The symphony in 4 movements or the second movement in 2/4 as in the sonata in A♭; this [3rd?] could be in 6/8 major and the 4th movement...'; then, having run out of space, he used a cross-reference sign ('100') and added the 'finale' theme on stave 10. Thus the 'Freude' theme was written before either of the middle two movements was properly begun.

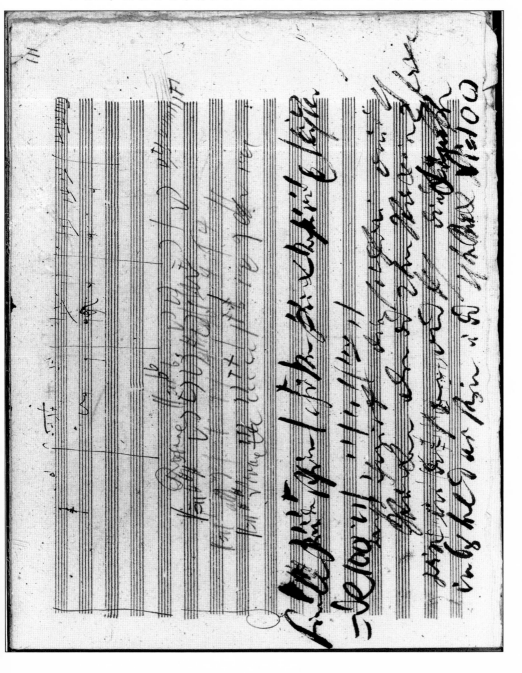

12. Beethoven's funeral procession, 29 March 1827. Watercolour by Franz Stöber. About 20,000 people are reported to have attended as his body was moved to the cemetery. In the background of the picture can be seen the Schwarzspanierhaus, where he had lived for the last two and a half years. His apartment was on the top floor—the fifth to ninth windows to the right of the church attached to the building.

Heiligenstadt, and partly through an early and widely quoted review that suggested the birds were introduced as a joke.[24] The birds are not random ones that Beethoven happened to hear but were chosen for their symbolic significance. The nightingale is surrounded by a whole aura of symbolism, including love and sweetness of tone. The cuckoo, likewise, is renowned as the harbinger of summer, while the quail has religious overtones of divine providence (based on the story in the book of Exodus). Beethoven had written a song about the quail-call ('Der Wachtelschlag', WoO 129) in 1803, in which the bird was portrayed as worshipping God; and, perhaps influenced by Christian Sturm's popular book *Betrachtungen über die Werke Gottes im Reiche der Natur* (Reflections on the Work of God in the Realm of Nature), he perceived all nature as capable of praising God. He once wrote: 'It seems as if in the country every tree said to me "Holy! Holy!" '[25] Thus the bird-calls in the symphony can be seen as an expression of Nature's praise of God, just as the finale represents man's (the shepherds'), and the birds chosen are poetic, archetypal, and symbolic. Schindler's suggestion that they were real birds that Beethoven had heard is as implausible as it is superficial; moreover, this part of the symphony was evidently composed in spring 1808 while Beethoven was still in Vienna, before he moved to Heiligenstadt in the summer.

The one movement that disturbs the rural calm is the fourth movement— the Storm. This was necessary to provide emotional contrast with the rest of the work, and Beethoven cleverly builds up the tension and energy in the previous movement so that the storm seems an almost inevitable outcome. And what a storm! Storm music, like pastoral music, had a long tradition and well established conventions (chiefly in the field of opera); but Beethoven transcends these with music of unprecedented power. Tonally the movement is almost completely unstable, with numerous diminished 7ths and constantly shifting chromatic harmony, while rhythmically it never settles into a standard pattern of phrase lengths for long. As the storm reaches its height, previously silent instruments are added—a shrill piccolo and then two trombones—which reinforce the power of the storm. It then gradually subsides, and the initial 'rain' motif is eventually transformed into a rainbow-like phrase in C major for the woodwind instruments, heralding the *ranz des vaches* (an Alpine herding call) that marks the start of the finale. In terms of both poetic idea and its means of realization, the *Pastoral* Symphony was one of Beethoven's most original, inspired, and influential works.

The symphony was evidently completed about August 1808, and Beethoven immediately turned his attention to two piano trios (Op. 70). When he offered the symphony to Breitkopf & Härtel about 8 July, he

---

[24] The review is quoted, for example, in Jones, *Pastoral Symphony*, 46. Schindler also claimed that Beethoven incorporated a goldfinch into the movement, but his whole account is thoroughly implausible (see Cooper, 'Schindler').

[25] TF, 501.

indicated his next work might be two piano sonatas or another symphony; but a few weeks later, in his response to their reply, he indicated he had decided on two trios 'since such trios are rather scarce', or a symphony.[26] The first trio was well under way by the time the contract for sale of these works was signed on 14 September, but the second had barely been begun, for where Härtel left blank spaces for Beethoven to insert the keys of the works, only the key of No. 1 in D was filled in. No. 2 was, however, completed by about October, according to Beethoven's own testimony. It was finished in the apartment of Countess Marie Erdödy, where Beethoven moved after his summer stay in the country (he had previously been living mainly in the house of Baron Pasqualati on the Mölkerbastei—now a Beethoven memorial house). The Countess was separated from her husband, and lived on Krugerstrasse with her three young children, Marie, Friederike, and August. How long she had known Beethoven is uncertain (there is no firm connection between them before this date) but they now became very close friends, although there is no evidence of any amorous or sexual relationship between them.

Several other people entered Beethoven's life about this time. One was Archduke Rudolph, youngest brother of the Emperor and destined to play a major role in Beethoven's life for the next dozen years. The earliest recorded connection is Beethoven's dedication to Rudolph of the Fourth Piano Concerto, which was published in August 1808.[27] Meanwhile Ries returned to Vienna from his travels on 27 August and remained until the following year. Another visitor to Vienna was the composer Johann Friedrich Reichardt, who arrived from Kassel on 24 November and remained for a few months. The importance of his visit derives from his detailed account of it, with several references to Beethoven, published as early as 1810 in *Vertraute Briefe* (Intimate Letters). Beethoven invited Reichardt to dinner at the home of Countess Erdödy (whom Reichardt described as Beethoven's 'landlady') on 5 December, and extemporized for the assembled company for about an hour, so movingly that Reichardt 'shed the hottest tears about ten times, and finally could find no words to express my inmost delight'. Five days later Reichardt was invited back, this time to hear the first of Beethoven's new piano trios. Then on 31 December he heard both trios, again at the same venue. He described the first as having great power and originality. It is also particularly notable for the shimmering tremolandos in its D minor slow movement, which have earned the work the nickname 'The Ghost'. In No. 2 in E flat, which is in four movements, Reichardt was particularly charmed by the lyrical third movement, which he described as

---

[26] A-169.

[27] Tyson has suggested that a list naming Rudolph as the dedicatee was probably written out in summer 1807 (Tyson, 'Razumovsky', 134). But as it refers to the dedicatee of the piano version of the Violin Concerto as 'Madame de Breuning', and she was not married until April 1808, the list cannot have been prepared much before then.

'the loveliest and most graceful I have ever heard; it exalts and melts my soul whenever I think of it'.[28]

One other event described in detail by Reichardt was Beethoven's long-delayed benefit concert of 22 December 1808. Beethoven had been involved in several public or private performances of his music during the course of the year, and his symphonies were gradually gaining in popularity, but he felt entitled to a benefit concert and had indeed been promised one several times by the authorities without result. Now he was granted use of the Theater an der Wien on a freezing cold Thursday evening, for a concert that began at 6.30 p.m., lasted about four hours, and consisted entirely of his own music. As Reichardt put it, it is possible to have too much of a good thing. The programme was as follows:

| *Part I* | *Part II* |
|---|---|
| *Pastoral* Symphony | Fifth Symphony |
| *Ah! perfido* (Op. 65) | Sanctus from the Mass in C |
| Gloria from the Mass in C | Piano Fantasia (extemporized) |
| Fourth Piano Concerto | Choral Fantasia, Op. 80 |

Only two of these works had been published, the concert aria *Ah! perfido* and the Fourth Piano Concerto, and the latter was receiving its public première. So, too, were the two movements from the Mass in C (which had to be advertised as hymns with Latin text in the church style, to circumvent restrictions on performing church music in the theatre). The two symphonies were previously unheard, as was the Choral Fantasia. This final work was written at great speed specially for the concert, and was not polished up for publication until the following year. It fulfils its purpose admirably, for it combines all the disparate forces used earlier in the concert—piano, orchestra, solo voices, and choir. It also provides a reminiscence of the Fifth Symphony heard earlier, by progressing from C minor to C major, but it adds a new dimension to the sense of growth, by gradually increasing its forces from solo piano to tutti, and by evolving from a seemingly formless, improvisatory opening (actually improvised at the concert) to a highly ordered series of variations on a very regular theme (which was borrowed from Beethoven's unpublished song 'Gegenliebe' of 1794–5). The text, reportedly written by Christoph Kuffner, celebrates the power of words and music to bring peace and joy: 'Night and storms become Light.' As a model of progress from darkness to light, and evolution from primordial chaos to artistic order, it is unsurpassed, and its overall plan provided an excellent starting-point for the finale of the Ninth Symphony years later.

The performance of the Choral Fantasia did not go smoothly. The several reports of the occasion differ in detail, but all agree that, through insufficient rehearsal, one place went so badly wrong that the performers had to start again. The other works, however, succeeded without major mishap, and the concerto included a surprise. As Czerny reports, Beethoven

[28] All the relevant passages in Reichardt's account are in TDR, iii. 184–9.

performed this very mischievously, inserting in the decorative passages many more notes than were in the printed edition. The manuscript score that Beethoven evidently used for directing the performance still survives (the middle movement is missing), and in over a hundred bars there are minute, sketchy annotations of variants in Beethoven's handwriting. These were probably made in preparation for this performance, and they demonstrate how he was never fully satisfied with even his greatest works. Over a year after preparing the work for publication, he saw many places for minor adjustment, and this revised version is more virtuosic, sophisticated, sparkling, and original than the standard one.[29] Beethoven also made slight adjustments to the Fifth and Sixth Symphonies 'during the performance', as he put it (presumably he meant, during the rehearsals), since he had never heard them before, and later sent a list to Breitkopf & Härtel for incorporation into their edition. The financial rewards of the concert are not known, but in terms of its content this was the most remarkable concert of his entire career.

[29] See Cooper, 'Beethoven's Revisions', which includes a transcription of the changes. Hans-Werner Küthen has suggested that Beethoven made them earlier for an arrangement of the work for piano and string quintet to be performed at Prince Lobkowitz's palace (see *NA*, III/3, *Kritischer Bericht*, 6–7); but the evidence connecting the elaborations with this chamber version is flawed, and the theory is highly improbable: see the present writer's letter in *BJo*, xiv/1 (1999), 45–6.

# 11

# Financial security? (1809–10)

Towards the end of 1808 Napoleon's brother Jerome, who had been appointed 'King of Westphalia', sent an invitation to Beethoven to become his Kapellmeister at Kassel, for an annual salary of 600 ducats. The offer was tempting, for Beethoven had long wished for a permanent appointment to relieve him from the uncertainties of his hand-to-mouth existence (Prince Lichnowsky having long since withdrawn his support). The proposed duties were not onerous, and Kassel was only about two days' journey from his beloved Bonn. Moreover, he believed he had numerous private enemies in Vienna, and complained that the music scene there was becoming steadily worse, with kapellmeisters who could hardly read a score. Thus in January 1809 he accepted the offer, and began making plans to move from Vienna.[1]

He had more supporters in Vienna than he realized, however, and some of them soon rallied on hearing of his impending departure, putting together a rival offer designed to keep him living in the city. The plan was set in motion by Gleichenstein and Marie Erdödy, who found three sponsors willing to contribute to a lifetime annuity of 4000 florins: Archduke Rudolph (1500 fl.), Prince Lobkowitz (700 fl.) and Prince Kinsky (1800 fl.). Of these three, Lobkowitz had long been one of Beethoven's most generous patrons, while Rudolph, though new to the scene and just turned twenty-one, was rapidly becoming the most ardent of all his followers. Ferdinand Kinsky, however, was a more surprising choice, for he had virtually no previous connection with Beethoven (though he was a second cousin of Lichnowsky). More likely candidates would have been Razumovsky, the Brunsviks, or Lichnowsky himself; how Kinsky came to be involved—especially with such a large grant—is unclear.

An agreement between Beethoven and his three sponsors was drawn up in February, and was ratified on 1 March. The sponsors, recognizing 'that only one who is as free from care as possible can devote himself to a single department of activity and create works of magnitude which are exalted and which ennoble art', agreed to give Beethoven the annual sum so that the necessities of life would not 'cause him embarrassment or clog his

---

[1] A-192.

powerful genius'.[2] Thus Beethoven was expected to continue composing as before, but there was no requirement for particular numbers or types of work, as might be expected in normal contracts. The other condition was that he should continue to reside in Vienna 'or in a city in one of the other hereditary countries of His Austrian Imperial Majesty'. He decided that Vienna's attractions outweighed any drawbacks, and remained a resident for the rest of his life, receiving a salary that should at last have meant financial security. This hope proved illusory: although 4000 fl. was in theory worth more than Kassel's 600 ducats, inflation had already brought its real value below that sum and was shortly to reduce it still further.

Nevertheless, with a regular income, Beethoven at last considered marriage a realistic possibility, and wrote to Gleichenstein towards the middle of March:

Now you can help me look for a wife. If you find a beautiful girl in F[reiburg] where you are at present, who would perhaps now and then grant a sigh to my harmonies, please form the connection in advance—but she must not be like Elise Bürger [who had left her poet husband Gottfried Bürger after only two years]. She must, however, be beautiful, for I cannot love anything that is not beautiful—or else I should have to love myself.[3]

Here Beethoven sketches his picture of the ideal wife. Her background was unimportant, but she had to be beautiful and faithful, and fond of his music. It is particularly notable that he stresses his love of beauty, for this was also a major concern in composition, despite all his bizarre ideas that so perplexed his more conservative listeners.

No suitable woman could be found for the moment, however, and shortly after he had signed his annuity contract he had a fierce quarrel with Marie Erdödy concerning some payments to a servant. He wrote angrily: 'What more can you still want? You have now got a servant for the master. What a replacement!!!! What a fine exchange!!!!' He soon attempted to make peace with her: 'I have acted wrongly, it is true—Forgive me.'[4] It was some years, however, before they became close friends again.

During these upheavals in the first three months of 1809, Beethoven was largely preoccupied with another major work—the Fifth Piano Concerto, known in English-speaking countries as the 'Emperor'. His C major/minor phase had by now given way to an E flat phase, and four works were written in this key in quick succession: the Piano Trio, Op. 70 No. 2 of late 1808, and the 'Emperor', the piano sonata known as 'Les Adieux', and the 'Harp' Quartet, all from 1809.

The writing of the piano concerto may well have been prompted by Archduke Rudolph, a keen and able pianist who received the dedications of both it and its predecessor in G major. Its grand, majestic first movement, which gave rise to the work's nickname, shows several innovations, especially in the role of the piano. In the previous piano concerto

<hr />

²  TF, 457.       ³  A-202.       ⁴  Alb-136; A-207.

Beethoven had broken with tradition by allowing the soloist to initiate the opening orchestral ritornello before falling silent. This idea was extended in the 'Emperor', where the opening consists of three grand orchestral chords each followed by elaborate decorations from the soloist; only after this curtain-raiser is the main theme heard, with the soloist once again falling silent for the rest of the ritornello. Yet this opening is in no way extraneous to the main movement, for the same three chords return (with different piano decorations) at the start of the recapitulation. With so much bravura figuration in these prominent places, Beethoven considered a full-scale cadenza unnecessary, and instead wrote out just a short one, more motivic than decorative, that is fully integrated into the movement. This was the first time (with the obvious exception of the Triple Concerto) that he had provided a written-out cadenza instead of leaving it to be improvised, but it set the pattern for all the major concertos for the rest of the century.

The main theme of the first movement is decorated by a turn, but this figure is then developed symphonically, reappearing well over a hundred times during the movement and providing one of the finest examples of Beethoven's habit of treating a seemingly decorative figure as a main motif for development. The transition is remarkable for modulating rapidly to the remote key of C flat major, with the second subject then appearing in the minor (bars 151–8, notated enharmonically as B minor) before reverting to the major in a passage of extreme delicacy. Here the clarinet plays an outline of the theme, decorated by the piano (bars 159–66), before the full orchestra suddenly bursts in in B flat major with a march-like transformation of the theme (bars 166–74). This whole passage has long-range implications that are among the most striking in Beethoven's entire output. The key of C flat major (notated as B major) reappears for the slow movement, and the connection is reinforced by the similarity of thematic material. In his slow movements, Beethoven most often made the main theme a distant cousin of that of the first movement, as in his Fourth Piano Concerto. In the 'Emperor', however, the link is clearly from the second subject. The clarinet outline, the march-like transformation, and the slow movement's main theme all begin on the mediant, move to a dominant chord at the end of the first phrase, and move from dominant to supertonic in the second phrase (see Ex. 11.1 a–c). Thus despite their very different characters and rhythms, all have broadly similar contours.

The other notable feature about the clarinet outline and the march-like transformation is that the harmonies are in bold primary colours, consisting entirely of tonic and dominant chords. This feature is avoided in the slow movement, where Beethoven incorporates considerable harmonic variety; but it is revived in the finale, where the main theme, despite some extraordinary rhythmic irregularity, is once again accompanied by a bass line consisting entirely of tonics and dominants (providing much opportunity for the timpani). Thus yet another new route to overall cohesion is

**Ex. 11.1**

(a) Op. 73/I, bars 159-66, clarinet 'outline' (sounding pitch)

(b) Op. 73/I, bars 166-74, main melody

(c) Op. 73/II, bars 1-4, violin 1

found and, like the Violin Concerto, the work as a whole has many features more characteristic of the symphony genre than the concerto.

The 'Emperor' may have received a trial run at some private venue in 1809, but no performances are recorded before 1811, long after the work had been published. This was largely due to the political situation at the time. Beethoven's letters in March already refer to the threat of war, which was eventually declared on 9 April. Before long, Vienna was under direct threat from Napoleon's army, and the Viennese aristocracy prepared for evacuation. Among those leaving was Archduke Rudolph, who was by now such a close friend that Beethoven decided to mark his departure with a suitable composition. This was a sonata movement entitled *Das Lebewohl* (The Farewell), and to clarify his intentions Beethoven actually wrote the syllables 'Le-be wohl' above the first three notes of the movement. In his sketchbook he drafted the inscription: 'The Departure—on 4 May, dedicated and written from the heart [to] His Imperial Highness', and there is a similar inscription on the autograph score. This score was evidently presented to Rudolph just before his departure, and is still preserved with other material of his at the Gesellschaft der Musikfreunde in Vienna. Beethoven may have planned from the outset to add two more movements—*Abwesenheit* and *Das Wiedersehn* ('Absence' and 'The Return')—but these were not composed till some months later. The sonata as a whole is significant as the only one with specific autobiographical connections; but, like the *Pastoral* Symphony, it cannot be described as programmatic. Each movement merely evokes a mood, using mainly traditional rhetorical devices, and develops the musical material in a purely abstract way.

The war took its course, and the French reached Vienna within a week of Rudolph's departure. On the night of 11–12 May the city suffered heavy bombardment, during which, Ries tells us, Beethoven took refuge in his brother Carl's cellar, covering his head with a pillow to protect his weak ears. Vienna was occupied next day, and its citizens suffered great hardships, even after the armistice of 12 July. Prices were rising, additional levies were being made, there were shortages, and Beethoven had still not received the first instalment of Kinsky's share of his salary. He wrote to Breitkopf & Härtel on 26 July:

We have lately been suffering misery in a most concentrated form. Let me tell you that since 4 May I have produced little coherent work—practically just a fragment here and there. The whole course of events has for me affected both body and soul. . . . What a destructive, disorderly life is here around me, nothing but drums, cannons, and human misery in every form.[5]

Beethoven had been unable to move to the country as he normally did, and an account by Baron de Trémont, who visited him during the French occupation and reported with delight on his skill at extemporization, confirms the extreme disorderliness of his rooms, which was due partly to Beethoven's lack of a servant on the day in question:

Picture to yourself the dirtiest, most disorderly place imaginable—blotches of moisture covered the ceiling; an oldish grand piano, on which the dust disputed the place with various pieces of printed and manuscript music; under the piano (I do not exaggerate) an unemptied chamber pot; beside it, a small walnut table accustomed to the frequent overturning of the secretary placed upon it; a quantity of pens encrusted with ink, compared with which the proverbial tavern-pens would shine; then more music. The chairs, mostly cane-seated, were covered with plates bearing the remains of last night's supper, and with clothing etc.[6]

Several other writers have reported on the general untidiness of Beethoven's rooms, but Trémont seems to have found them in a worse state than usual.

Beethoven's sketchbook (Landsberg 5) confirms that his productivity, extremely impressive in the previous three years, had suffered too. After intensive work on the 'Emperor' and *Das Lebewohl*, the sketchbook shows

[5] A-220.    [6] Sonneck, *Impressions*, 70.

(pp. 46–69) odd little jottings for the period in question—ideas for piano pieces, an overture, a Sanctus, quartets, two symphonies, and Lieder.[7] Most of these ideas came to nothing, although the overture was developed as the 'Namensfeier' Overture some years later. Concentrated work obviously proved very difficult at this time, and this pattern of sketching odd jottings was to become increasingly prevalent during the next decade.

One positive activity during these months, however, was the preparation of teaching material in composition for Archduke Rudolph. Hitherto, Beethoven had always refused to teach composition to anybody, and had sent Ries to Albrechtsberger. Now, however, perhaps moved by the recent deaths of both his own counterpoint teachers, Albrechtsberger and Haydn (in March and May respectively), he was prepared to make an exception for Rudolph, and began assembling material from composition treatises by Fux, Kirnberger, Albrechtsberger, and others, in anticipation of the archduke's return. It was probably during this summer, too, that he composed cadenzas for each of his first four piano concertos (No. 5 did not need one) and the piano version of the Violin Concerto, as well as two for Mozart's D minor Piano Concerto (K. 466). These were presumably also intended for Rudolph, although at least one of the Mozart ones was evidently given to Ries shortly before his departure that summer.

Beethoven's long letter to Breitkopf & Härtel in July indicates a desire to obtain a collection of scores by Mozart, Haydn, J. S. Bach, and C. P. E. Bach, which he asked the firm to supply. These were to be used for private study and in performances at friends' houses, or at little singing parties that he had initiated before the war and now hoped to resume. In addition, the letter thanks the firm for sending the tragedies of Euripides, while other letters from that summer ask the firm for editions of poetry by Goethe, Schiller, Wieland, Homer, and Ossian. It seems, then, that he was spending more time than formerly in study and general reading. This may have been because, with the security offered by his annuity, he no longer felt quite the same pressure to compose to support himself. Another reason may have been the disruption to society caused by the war. The absence of so many friends limited social intercourse and opportunities for music-making, and reading great literature afforded an alternative leisure occupation.

Beethoven's former level of productivity returned about August, and he rapidly completed a new string quartet—the 'Harp' (Op. 74), so called because of the unusual and striking pizzicato effects in the first movement. He told Breitkopf & Härtel that he was composing more than one quartet, but Op. 74 had no immediate successor. Instead he returned to his Choral Fantasia to compose a proper introduction. At its première the previous December, he had improvised the introduction on the piano, but something more permanent was needed for publication. The published version is,

---

[7] Transcribed in Brenneis ed., *Skizzenbuch*.

therefore, perhaps the nearest thing we have to a written-down improvisation from him, and it is clearly contrived to sound improvisatory in character. It must be stressed, however, that in actual extemporization he could just as easily create a regular form such as sonata form or variations, and was not restricted to the rhapsodic style that begins the Choral Fantasia.

Beethoven next produced a short set of Piano Variations (Op. 76), followed by a fantasia and two sonatas for piano (Opp. 77–9), probably prompted by Clementi, who had commissioned these three works in 1807 and was now back in Vienna. The Fantasia and the Sonata in F sharp (Op. 78) were evidently completed in October, with Op. 79 partially overlapping in time. The remaining two movements of the sonata for Archduke Rudolph were also composed about this time, in anticipation of his return.

Of the three works for Clementi, by far the most original is the Fantasia, a seemingly chaotic work that begins in G minor but ends in the remote key of B major. The fantasia genre, as developed by Mozart and others, consisted of a series of sharply contrasting sections, with limited thematic connections between some of them. Beethoven, following his customary habit of stretching the bounds of convention, attempted to make the contrasts as extreme as possible, using sudden changes of mood and key reminiscent of accompanied recitative at its most dramatic. But, lest contrast should itself become the unifying element, the second half of the work consists mainly of a theme and seven variations in which there is not a single proper modulation and barely even a note out of key. Some of the textures and procedures in these variations are very forward-looking, anticipating those in the variation movements in his late piano sonatas.

In this Fantasia Beethoven appears to be demonstrating that a great work does not have to have thematic, structural, or even tonal unity—a notion that might seem heretical to some analysts. Nevertheless, the work possesses enough underlying cohesion to prevent it from falling apart. The main keys encountered during its course contrast sharply:

G minor (bars 1–3)
B flat major (bars 15–28)
D minor (bars 39–78)
B minor (bars 90–156)
B major (bars 157–221, 228–45)

Yet the key structure is cunningly designed so that, as in his early sets of dances (WoO 7 and 8), one tonic triad and the next always have a note in common. Beethoven also gradually increases the length of the sections containing tonal stability, with the final one in B major actually returning after a brief digression. Thus there is a sense of gradual progress from instability to stability. There is also some motivic cohesion, the two main motifs being a rapid descending scale and (usually three) repeated notes. The scale is initially highly disruptive, yet it is eventually incorporated inconspicuously into the final variation, so that when it reappears in the coda it seems far less threatening and eventually brings the work to a very emphatic close.

Meanwhile the repeated notes seem merely incidental when they first appear in the B flat section, but they are more prominent in some of the ensuing link passages, and re-emerge as the main motif in the theme on which the variations are built. The Fantasia is one of Beethoven's most original, challenging, and forward-looking piano works, with a Romantic wildness that easily obscures its ingeniously crafted design.

During the latter part of 1809 Beethoven also composed a number of songs. This sudden spate, in which more songs were completed than in the entire previous six years, suggests that he may have resumed the singing parties that had been abandoned during the war. Five of the songs (including one duet) were to Italian texts, but the majority were German Lieder, mainly settings of poems by Christian Ludwig Reissig. Reissig was an army captain who had been wounded in the war, but he now persuaded several composers to set his verses to music, and Beethoven, feeling sympathy for him, agreed to do so.

The chronology of these Reissig settings, as with several other works of 1809, is not entirely clear, but the first one appears to have been completed in early August, for on 8 August Beethoven wrote to Breitkopf & Härtel that he had just sent them a sextet and two German Lieder. The sextet, an early work, was published by them as Op. 71, while one of the Lieder was 'Andenken' (WoO 136), which had been intended the previous year for the ill-fated journal *Prometheus*. The other Lied must have been one of the Reissig settings, and was probably 'Der Jüngling in der Fremde' (WoO 138). This short, strophic composition, however, was originally a setting of a different poem by Reissig, 'Lied aus der Ferne', as is clear from the autograph score, and it was probably this text that was sent to Breitkopf & Härtel. He then made a new, much more elaborate and through-composed setting of the same words (WoO 137), and his brother Carl sent this to Breitkopf & Härtel at the end of January, with a brief note that arrived on 5 February 1810.[8] Beethoven's own letter of 4 February 1810 confirms that his brother had recently sent them 'Gesang in der Ferne',[9] and the term 'Gesang' is significant, for it denotes a more elaborate setting than a 'Lied'.[10] WoO 137 was initially headed 'Lied', but this was then changed to 'Gesang' in the autograph score,[11] whereas WoO 138 was clearly not a 'Gesang'. Breitkopf & Härtel published WoO 137 almost immediately, and 'Andenken' (WoO 136) shortly afterwards, but never published WoO 138—probably because it was a simpler setting of the same text as WoO 137.

While working on his new songs, which included three more by Reissig, Beethoven also resurrected and revised a few older ones, notably his

[8] This date was recorded by the firm (see BB-422). Some scholars have suggested 1804–5 for the date of the note (see Albrecht ed., *Letters*, i. 153, and TDR, ii. 626), but this is impossible, for the only song sent at that time was sent by Beethoven, not Carl, and as part of a larger package: see A-108.

[9] A-245.　　　　　　　　　　　　　　　　[10] See Lühning, 'Gattungen', 195.

[11] See NA, XII/1, *Kritischer Bericht*, 39–42, for more details about these sources. The editor, Helga Lühning, comes to a similar conclusion about the chronology of WoO 138 and 137.

'Flohlied' of 1793 and 'Neue Liebe, neues Leben'. These he added to the new ones to produce a collection of twelve, which he offered to Breitkopf & Härtel on 4 February along with all the major instrumental works he had completed during 1809: the concerto, the string quartet, the Choral Fantasia, the piano variations, the piano fantasia and the three piano sonatas. All these works were also promised to Clementi, apparently through verbal agreement while Clementi was still in Vienna, so that both firms could publish the works simultaneously—thus enhancing the deal for Beethoven without loss to the firms. With minor modifications, these plans materialized during the course of 1810–11, and the works appeared as Opp. 73–82.

Meanwhile Beethoven had embarked on a project that was to occupy him much during the next ten years—composing settings of mainly British folk-songs. The Scotsman George Thomson had for some years been publishing volumes of Scottish and Welsh folksongs in settings by Pleyel, Kozeluch, and Haydn. Determined to make his collection better than rival publica-tions, Thomson had applied to some of the best composers in Europe, and had asked them not merely for accompaniments but introductions and postludes too, and for accompaniments not just for piano but with optional violin and cello. The three composers had supplied many settings, but all had by 1809 ceased for various reasons, and Thomson turned to Beethoven, whom he had first contacted in 1803. In September 1809 Thomson sent him forty-three melodies—mainly Welsh and Irish, with two Scottish ones—for making into settings like those of Pleyel, Kozeluch, and Haydn. He also asked Beethoven for three quintets and three piano sonatas, offering £60 or 120 ducats for the six works. Since Clementi had offered the same amount for only three piano works, Beethoven refused to write these instrumental compositions unless Thomson doubled his offer. The folksong settings, however, provided a new challenge, which Beethoven was prepared to accept. He had already made a start by the time he replied to Thomson on 23 November, and he hoped then to have the whole group of forty-three finished within about a week. Delays caused by an illness in December and various other commitments, however, prevented him from finishing the set for some months, and it probably took him longer than he had anticipated to create settings that fully satisfied his high standards. As he said in the letter to Thomson, in an important statement of his artistic ideals: 'You are dealing with a true artist who likes to be paid honourably, but who likes glory and also the glory of art even more—and who is never content with himself and tries always to go further and make yet greater progress in his art.'[12]

This aim to go further and make greater progress is as apparent in his folksong settings as in any of his larger works, for they in many ways far surpass any previous settings. This is evident right from the very first of the

---

[12] A-229.

forty-three settings in the first batch—a setting of the Welsh tune 'Merch Megan' (Ex. 11.2). In a conventional introduction by one of his predecessors, there was most often a statement of the first phrase of the song, followed by some unrelated answering phrase leading to a perfect cadence. Kozeluch nearly always adopts this pattern, while Pleyel and Haydn normally quote the opening of the song melody before digressing with new material. Beethoven, by contrast, almost always adopts a more motivic approach reminiscent of his symphonic writing, developing some small motif that is usually, as here, taken from the song, and often using irregular phrase structures. 'Merch Megan' also illustrates his tendency to generate much more energetic accompaniment figurations than was normal, both in the introduction and during the vocal section and postlude. The string parts, which had previously just filled out the harmony and reinforced the bass, were given a variety of roles in Beethoven's settings, such as motivic development (bars 1–4) or antiphonal effects (bars 5–6, 9–11). The introduction sometimes, as here, ends with a perfect cadence, but the music always flows on immediately with some kind of run, rather than coming to a complete halt; the same applies at the end of the vocal section. Even more significant, at the end of the postlude Beethoven almost always writes some kind of link to the beginning of the next verse. After the final verse there is then a supplementary section of postlude to bring the piece to conclusion. Thus, in contrast to all previous settings, which were continually being halted by a series of perfect cadences, Beethoven's customarily flow continuously from beginning to end without a break. The sense of forward thrust and momentum that has so often been noted in his instrumental works is equally evident in the folksong settings, providing a sense of unity and cohesion that was lacking in all earlier settings. In his harmonies, too, he was often unconventional, particularly favouring drone basses to suggest a rustic context, although this is not very evident in 'Merch Megan'.

In his letter to Thomson of November 1809, Beethoven protested that setting folksongs was not an activity that gave an artist great pleasure; but he seems to have found the task more rewarding than he initially expected. When he finally sent the first batch in July 1810 he told Thomson he had composed most of them *con amore*, and that he wanted to show his esteem for the British people by cultivating their national songs. Thomson had by this time acceded to Beethoven's demand for £120 (or 240 ducats) for three quintets and three piano sonatas; yet Beethoven never wrote any of these works, whereas he continued religiously to provide settings for every little folksong melody that Thomson sent. Thus he had apparently come to regard the provision of fine settings for these time-honoured melodies as one of his most important occupations.

One reason Beethoven gave for not accepting Thomson's original offer of £60 for the six instrumental works was the rapidly rising cost of living: 'We are living here in a time when everything costs a terribly high price, since

**Ex. 11.2** WoO 155 No. 11

one pays three times as much as before.'[13] Rampant inflation had set in, brought about by the government printing money to pay for the war. Such inflation was little understood since there were no immediate historical precedents to alert people to the dangers, although Beethoven knew that the war was to blame. Prices had indeed risen threefold within a few years, and were to continue rising for a few more years before inflation was brought under control. He complained to Breitkopf & Härtel about the problem in several letters in 1810, telling them on 6 June: 'My 4000 florins, on which I can no longer live (and, moreover, Kinsky has not yet paid me a farthing, although his contribution is guaranteed), are not worth even a thousand florins in assimilated coinage.'[14] He is referring here to the falling value of paper money. His salary of 4000 florins was payable in banknotes, which were meant to be equivalent to the same amount in silver currency, known as 'assimilated coinage' (Conventionsmünze, or CM). This was fairly stable in value, but even when his salary agreement was first drawn up, the 4000 florins were worth less than 2000 fl. CM, and were now worth less than a thousand, as he says. His annual cost of living, as far as we can tell, was somewhat over 1000 fl. CM, which explains why he says he could no longer live on his salary, especially as Kinsky had still not paid his agreed contribution. In August he gave some examples of prices: 30 fl. (banknotes) for a pair of boots, and 160–70 fl. for a coat[15]—high prices indeed for someone on a salary of 4000 fl. His expected financial security, which was intended by his sponsors to enable him to 'create works of magnitude', had vanished within a year of the contract being signed! This misfortune is no doubt one reason why he suddenly offered Breitkopf & Härtel such a large number of works (Opp. 73–82) in February 1810, and why he was prepared to haggle for so long about the price.

Despite the high prices of goods, Beethoven made some curious purchases that spring. He asked Zmeskall on 18 April to buy him a looking-glass to replace one that was broken. He gave Gleichenstein 300 florins (and 50 more a few days later) to buy some cotton for shirts and 'at least half a dozen neckcloths' which Beethoven wanted, and he sent 300 florins to Joseph Lind, a leading tailor; then on 2 May he wrote to Wegeler in Koblenz with an urgent request for his (Beethoven's) baptismal certificate, offering to pay all expenses including, if necessary, a return journey from Koblenz to Bonn.[16] The attempts to smarten his appearance suggest he had fallen in love once more, and a note to Zmeskall about 19 April confirms this: 'Do you not remember the situation I am in, just as Hercules once was with Queen Omphale??? . . . never have I felt so deeply as now the strength or the weakness of human nature.'[17] (Hercules was not in love with Queen Omphale but became her slave; but Beethoven obviously saw the two conditions as synonymous.)

---

[13] A-229.    [14] A-261.    [15] A-272.
[16] A-251, A-252, A-253, A-256.    [17] A-259 (misdated as May 1810: see BB-430).

The girl in question must have been Therese Malfatti, since Beethoven had no known close association with any other woman that spring. Gleichenstein, fulfilling Beethoven's request of the previous year to find him a wife, had acted as go-between, and Beethoven did indeed consider marriage for a time—hence the need for his baptismal certificate, which Wegeler duly sent. Beethoven presented Therese with a copy of an unidentified sonata, and in April he wrote the popular *Für Elise* for her. It was not published during his lifetime, but the autograph score was found years later among her papers and was published by Ludwig Nohl in 1867, although the manuscript has since disappeared. It bore the inscription 'Für Elise am 27. April zur Erinnerung von L. v. Bthvn' ('For Elise on 27 April as a memento from L. v. Beethoven'). The absence of the year has caused some uncertainty. The earliest sketch for the work is from 1808. A longer draft is undated (its paper-type was used by Beethoven from 1808 to 1810); but Beethoven was not familiar with Therese until 1810, as far as is known, and the manuscript containing the draft was clearly being used in 1810 since it contains ideas for two other works composed that spring. Thus it seems that the presentation to Therese must have been made in April that year.

The identity of 'Elise' has caused even more problems. Max Unger's suggestion in the 1920s that Nohl had simply misread the name 'Therese' has been widely believed, but it is impossible. 'Therese' and 'Elise' look quite different in Beethoven's handwriting, and Nohl insisted that the autograph did not say 'Therese', although he felt it should have done since it came from among Therese Malfatti's papers and nobody in the family was called Elise.[18] The explanation for the puzzle must be that Beethoven used 'Elise' as a kind of pet name for Therese. He was fond of using modifications of people's names: a Monsieur de Friederich he had called Liederlich in 1801, and in later years he was to call Peter Simrock 'Überrock' (overcoat), and Anton Diabelli 'Diabolus' (devil), for example. Moreover, he had good reason for not putting Therese's actual name on the manuscript, and for omitting the year. He had suffered considerable embarrassment with his previous beloved when Lichnowsky had spotted Josephine's name on 'An die Hoffnung' in 1805, although fortunately the prince had been discreet about his observation. Thus Beethoven would have wanted to avoid a repetition, by disguising the identity of the woman and substituting some name similar to Therese; 'Elise' was ideal, since it sounded suitably poetic (it is sometimes used as the name of the beloved in songs, e.g. Beethoven's 'Schilderung eines Mädchens'). The melody and accompaniment of *Für Elise* evoke an appropriate mood of intense longing (the first song in Schumann's *Dichterliebe*, which also portrays intense longing, employs strikingly similar figuration, although Schumann could not possibly have known *Für Elise*); and the limited technical difficulty of the piece, which has made it very popular for learners, probably reflects Therese's abilities on the piano.

[18] The problem has been re-examined in Van der Zanden, *Beethoven*, 64–75.

Beethoven's plans for marriage did not materialize. The reasons are not entirely clear, but it seems that Therese's family, though happy to welcome Beethoven as a musician, did not want him as a relative. Gleichenstein probably brought him the news after visiting the Malfattis in the country at Walkersdorf, prompting the following response from Beethoven; it lacks any specific detail but certainly fits this scenario:

Your news plunged me again from the heights of ecstasy down into the depths. And why did you add that you would let me know when there would be music again? Am I then nothing but a music-maker for you or the others? At least, your remark can be interpreted thus. So only in my own heart can I again find a support, for there is none from outside; no, friendship and similar feelings have nothing but wounds for me. So be it then, for you, poor B[eethoven], there is no happiness from outside; you must create everything for yourself inside you, only in the world of ideals can you find friends.[19]

In about August, Breuning wrote to Wegeler confirming that Beethoven's marriage plans had collapsed and that he therefore no longer felt such an urge to thank Wegeler for the baptismal certificate (this letter, incidentally, is the only known explicit reference at the time to a marriage plan that spring). Where Beethoven failed, however, Gleichenstein succeeded, for he became engaged to Therese's younger sister Anna later that year and married her the following May. After this they lived mainly in Freiburg, and his role as Beethoven's secretary was taken over by a young clerk named Franz Oliva.

While Beethoven was contemplating marriage he was also becoming friendly with some members of the Brentano family. Franz Brentano had married Antonie von Birkenstock in 1798 and they had lived in Frankfurt for a time before returning to her native Vienna in 1809 just before her father died. They then continued to live in the Birkenstock house while sorting out her father's large collection of books, antiquities, scientific specimens, and *objets d'art*. Also living there in 1810 was Franz's half-sister Bettina, a friend of Goethe. Like Franz and Antonie, she became closely acquainted with Beethoven about 1810; indeed she might seem a more plausible candidate than Therese Malfatti for his marriage proposal that spring, but the evidence does not support this. Her accounts of their relationship are unfortunately extremely unreliable, but she had a genuine fondness and admiration for him and his music—especially some of his recent settings of Goethe's poetry. She moved to Berlin later that year and married the poet Achim von Arnim the following March. Meanwhile Antonie, often ill and still lamenting the death of her father, drew great comfort from Beethoven's extemporizations for her, and their friendship continued to develop during the next two years.

---

[19] A-254; BB-445. This letter evidently dates from after Beethoven's 2 May letter to Wegeler, but before his cool but friendly letter to Therese written around the end of May (A-258; date from notes to BB-442).

Beethoven's main composition during spring 1810 was the Overture and Incidental Music to Goethe's *Egmont*. The theatre directors, no doubt sensitive to the political situation, decided to produce two dramas about resistance to foreign occupation—*Egmont* and Schiller's *Wilhelm Tell*. New music was commissioned for both; according to Czerny, Beethoven would have preferred *Tell*, but this was allocated to Gyrowetz. Beethoven set to work on *Egmont* early in 1810, in preparation for a première in May, and probably began with the two songs for Clärchen. He had already made several sketches for a setting with piano of her second song, 'Freudvoll und leidvoll', amongst his group of Lieder settings of 1809, and so he readily took up this text again, although the final version with orchestra has almost nothing in common with the early sketches with piano and was designed to take into account the singing abilities of Antonie Adamberger, the actress playing Clärchen.

The play certainly had enormous attraction for Beethoven. His long-standing admiration for Goethe had been increasing recently, as is reflected by several Goethe songs written around that time, and it was no doubt fuelled by his new friendship with Bettina Brentano. The subject matter, too, was very close to his heart. Count Egmont was a leader of the Dutch people in the sixteenth century, when the Netherlands was ruled by Spain through a regent, Margaret of Parma. Her reluctance to be too repressive leads to her replacement by the Duke of Alba, who ruthlessly crushes all opposition. Egmont is arrested on a trumped-up charge, his beloved Clärchen attempts in vain to rally support for him, and he is finally executed, but not before predicting ultimate freedom for his people (a prediction duly fulfilled in real life). Thus, as with *Leonore* in 1805, subjects dear to Beethoven throughout his life—resistance to tyranny, hopes for freedom, and intense personal love—were particularly apposite during the writing of the work, as he endured both the effects of the French occupation and the pains of unfulfilled love. The Incidental Music consists of nine movements:

1. Song, 'Die Trommel gerühret'
2. Entr'acte I
3. Entr'acte II
4. Song, 'Freudvoll und leidvoll'
5. Entr'acte III
6. Entr'acte IV
7. Music for Clärchen's death
8. Melodrama, 'Süsser Schlaf' (speech with music)
9. Victory Symphony

After setting the songs, Beethoven next worked mainly on the last act, and his music accompanying Egmont's vision at the end of the melodrama is particularly effective. In the vision Freedom appears, in the form of Clärchen, and reveals that Egmont's death will lead to freedom for his country and a crown of glory for himself. An off-stage drum-roll suddenly interrupts, Egmont awakes and the apparition vanishes. All this narrative is portrayed vividly and in great detail in Beethoven's music.

He then turned to the entr'actes, where the traditional procedure was to reflect the preceding action in the first part of each, and anticipate the following act in the second part. This pattern is clearest in the bipartite Entr'acte I, where the second part strikingly represents the turmoil of Act II. The second entr'acte is a single movement, part of which reappears in the Entr'acte IV. The third entr'acte begins by reflecting the preceding action, with echoes of Clärchen's song, before continuing with a march. This gradually increases from *pp* to *ff*, unmistakably representing the coming of Alba's troops, and the movement closes with an abrupt change from C major to C minor, from military precision to tense anxiety, setting the scene for a populace grown suddenly fearful. Thus Beethoven adapts tradition to the immediate dramatic situation, even portraying an event that Goethe omits—the approach of the army. Another notable feature of the entr'actes stems from his desire for continuity, which had already found new means of expression in the folksong settings he was still composing. Three of the four entr'actes end with the music hanging in mid-air, to propel the audience into the ensuing act. This unusual procedure greatly enhances dramatic continuity, but it creates difficulties for concert performance. Breitkopf & Härtel drew attention to the problem as soon as they received the score from Beethoven, pointing out that his procedure would make the music difficult to sell. Beethoven eventually offered to compose concert endings where necessary, and suggested, tongue in cheek, that some proof-reader from their music journal might alternatively do the job instead, 'for they haven't a clue about it';[20] but by then the firm had arranged for other composers to insert suitable endings, and published the work with these. Either way, concert performance is not wholly satisfactory.

The one number regularly performed in the concert hall is the magnificent Overture in F minor, completed last, as usual. Though cast in traditional form, with a slow introduction followed by a sonata-form Allegro, it embodies all the main elements of the play: the heavy hand of the oppressors, the tenderness of Clärchen, the despair of the people (descending motifs and main theme), the death of Egmont (a whole-bar rest with pause), the ensuing lamentation (four slow, solemn chords), and ultimate victory. For the latter, Beethoven simply transplanted the Victory Symphony in F major from the incidental music, to form an extended appendix to the Allegro. These diverse ideas were integrated partly through extensive sketching of the transitions between the sections, and partly by ingenious motivic interconnections. For example, the main motif of the second part of the slow introduction, a rising step and falling tetrachord, reappears in a speeded-up version at the transition to the main Allegro, and

[20] A-345.

again to herald the recapitulation. It then appears in inversion at the start of the triumphant F major conclusion, symbolizing that the old order has been literally turned upside down. Throughout the overture the emotional level, whether in despair or triumph, is typically intense, generating an overwhelming sense of dramatic power.

Working with characteristic thoroughness, Beethoven was unable to complete his *Egmont* music in time for the first performance of the new production on 24 May, and it was not heard until 15 June. Immediately after this, he returned to his folksong settings to add some final details. By this time Thomson had sent him ten more melodies, all Irish, and so Beethoven set these as a second group, making fifty-three settings altogether. He then arranged for three copies to be made, and sent these on 17 July (date of his letter to Thomson) by three different routes, hoping that at least one would beat Napoleon's blockade, although none did for a very long time. Much to his surprise, however, the ten works he had offered to Clementi (Opp. 73–82) did beat the blockade, and began appearing in London from late August onwards, even before Breitkopf & Härtel's editions. But the blockade was sufficiently effective to discourage any continental publisher from obtaining Clementi's edition and producing a pirated edition, which had been a major worry for the Leipzig firm.

Beethoven spent the latter part of the summer in Baden, writing a new string quartet—Op. 95 in F minor. The date on the autograph score, October 1810, fits well with the fact that the main sketches follow immediately those for *Egmont*, but this date was probably inserted retrospectively since the paper of the autograph appears to belong to about 1814. The chronology of the sketches is also not straightforward. The main batch in Landsberg 11 appears to date from about July–September 1810, but others are found in the next sketchbook, now dismembered, suggesting that 'Beethoven appears to have continued to work on the quartet in 1811'.[21] However, the known sketches in this later book clearly predate some in Landsberg 11, indicating an overlap between consecutive sketchbooks that is almost unique. Thus the quartet probably was completed around October 1810, even if a fresh score was written out a few years later (as happened also with the Piano Trio, Op. 97 and the Violin Sonata, Op. 96).

The quartet was not offered for publication until later still. This may be because, as Beethoven stated, it was 'written for a small circle of connoisseurs and is never to be performed in public'.[22] Yet this statement was not made until after the work had appeared in print, and it seems to refer more to the character of the quartet than any prohibition on public performance. This character is announced in the title 'Quartett serioso' that is found in the autograph score (though not in the first edition) and the work possesses an extraordinary compressed intensity that would surely have bewildered

---

[21] JTW, 198. The relevant sketch leaves in the dismembered book are now in New York and Stockholm, SV 390 and 373.
[22] A-664.

the public in 1810. The key is F minor, and the overall mood is of extreme anguish. The first movement is characterized by sudden short and angry outbursts, with much emphasis on G♭, as in the 'Appassionata' Sonata, and on dominant minor 9ths—one of Beethoven's favourite chords in such movements. With a mere 151 bars and no repeats, the movement lasts little over three minutes (going by his own metronome marking), yet it manages to give the impression of being condensed rather than small-scale, with numerous modulations and changes of texture and dynamic. The second movement begins gently, but is disconcertingly set in D major rather than the more probable D flat, allowing the note G♭ to be heard in a new context as F♯; and before long it is engaged in tortuous chromaticism reminiscent of the kind used in the 'Malinconia' movement in Op. 18 No. 6. Beethoven frequently linked the last two movements together at this period, but here he unusually links the middle two movements. The link is provided by an enharmonic diminished 7th, which supplies both the last, soft chord of the slow movement and the angry opening of the ensuing Allegro, where the key and mood of the first movement are resumed. After further emphasis on the note G♭, the Trio section is mainly in D major, like the second movement, providing a sense of unity in dissociation that was to become a hallmark of Beethoven's late style.

The agitated finale, again highly condensed, maintains the general mood of anguish until a coda in F major, which is a complete contrast to everything that has gone before. The link is provided, inevitably, by the note F♯, which was already present at an early stage in the sketching, and this is followed by light, fluttery sounds and rising scales with a 'molto leggieramente' marking. Much uncertainty has surrounded the interpretation of this section. Is it a joke? Is it ironic? Even a mistake? Perhaps it is best viewed as a complement to the *Egmont* Overture, which also has a coda in F major after an intense F minor movement. The chronological proximity of the two works is striking—they represent Beethoven's F minor phase that briefly succeeded those in C and E flat of the preceding three years. In both works, the coda evokes a tremendous sense of liberation from everything preceding it, with the first violin soaring to a high *c''''*. In the quartet this free-as-a-bird sensation is enhanced by the fluttering accompaniment. Just as the 'Dona nobis' in Beethoven's *Missa solemnis* is a 'prayer for inner and outer peace', so the codas of the quartet movement and the *Egmont* Overture can be seen respectively as inner and outer liberation: inner liberation from mental anguish and external liberation from political oppression. The key-relationship also contains echoes of the *Pastoral* Symphony, where the shepherds are liberated in F major from the terrors of a storm in F minor. Once again, he has found a new means of deploying an earlier idea.

While writing this quartet, Beethoven was still finalizing his negotiations with Breitkopf & Härtel over the sale of Opp. 73–84. After sending the first batch, Opp. 74–9, in early July, he forgot precisely which songs were in Op.

75, and so the second batch, which should have included three more songs, contained only the concerto, the Choral Fantasia, and *Egmont*. When he was finally informed which songs the firm had received, he realized he did not have three others suitable, and so he promptly wrote three new ones, which became Op. 83. Having been immersed in *Egmont* for half the year, he not surprisingly chose three Goethe poems. In the first, Beethoven may have been attracted by the paradoxical title 'Wonne der Wehmuth' (Bliss of Melancholy—another example of unity in dissociation)—and his through-composed setting of this short text contains particularly detailed word-setting, with the poetry mirrored by the music in every conceivable way. The three songs were the last works he completed in 1810. They were sent to Breitkopf & Härtel at the beginning of 1811, appearing in print later that year, and they marked the end of his business dealings with the Leipzig firm. They also brought to an end the most intensive phase of song composition in his life.

# Immortal Beloved (1811–12)

The start of a new decade saw Beethoven, now settled in Baron Pasqualati's house, working on a new piano trio in B flat. The autograph score of this work is dated 3 March 1811 at the beginning, and 'Finished on 26 March 1811' at the end. Although the manuscript itself appears to be a fair copy dating from about 1814, the dates seem to reflect accurately the period in which the work was first written out, for Beethoven referred to it as new in letters to Archduke Rudolph dating from the end of March 1811. The next month he tried, through his friend Oliva, to sell it to Breitkopf & Härtel, but for some reason the sale did not materialize and the work was laid aside, along with the Op. 95 Quartet. Not until 1816 did it appear in print as Op. 97, with a dedication to Archduke Rudolph.

Like most of Beethoven's piano trios, the 'Archduke' Trio is constructed on a grand, four-movement scale, and it is yet another work containing ingenious long-range tonal connections. For example, in the first movement the second subject is unexpectedly in G major, and the end of the recapitulation is marked by a surprising G major chord within a B flat context (bar 265). The corresponding point at the end of the exposition has a dominant 7th of E flat—a chord that reappears at the start of the finale. The main theme of the sublime slow movement, unusually placed third, is reminiscent of the twenty-third Righini Variation and the slow movement of the Sonata, Op. 2 No. 2: all are profound, slow themes in D major, in 3/4 time, beginning on the same F♯. The theme is followed by four variations with increasingly elaborate decoration, and a fifth that merges into the coda. The closing motif of this coda, utterly peaceful and gentle, is then suddenly transformed into a humorous little figure that forms the main theme of the finale.

The most original movement, however, is surely the Scherzo, and more particularly the Trio section. This begins with a cello solo that lacks clear pulse or key, with a chromaticism bordering on atonality (Ex. 12.1). The theme is then treated as a strange, eerie fugato in B flat minor, but three times the fugato is interrupted by a bold, waltz-like tune, first in D flat, then E, and finally in B flat. Beethoven's humour here goes far beyond that of the preceding Scherzo, which is merely comical by comparison, to produce a kind of grotesque farce that sounds almost insane. Both the form and style of the section are quite unprecedented.

**Ex. 12.1**  Op. 97/II

125

While Beethoven was writing out the score of the 'Archduke' Trio, the financial crisis facing the country finally came to a head. The paper florin had
been depreciating for some years, but there had been hopes that it would
eventually regain its former value. Now, however, on 15 March it was officially devalued fivefold, with the new florins known as redemption bonds.
Beethoven's annuity of 4000 fl. therefore became 800 fl. in the new Viennese
Currency (Wiener Währung, or WW). He believed that the full value of his
annuity ought to be restored, but this did not happen. Rudolph agreed at
once and began paying Beethoven at the rate of 1500 fl. WW a year, but
Kinsky (who had finally begun paying his share, including arrears, on 31
July 1810) calculated his portion at the old rate divided by five, i.e. 360 fl. a
year. The government then decreed (13 September) that contracts such as
Beethoven's should be partially revalued, entitling him to his original sum
divided not by 5 but by 2.48; but Kinsky responded by halting payments
altogether after the end of August.[1] As for Lobkowitz, he experienced
financial difficulties about this time, and until 1815 was able to pay
Beethoven nothing at all, although he agreed in principle to revalue his
share to the full amount of 700 fl. Beethoven expended considerable effort
in the next few years in an attempt to obtain satisfaction from these two
sponsors.

In April 1811, taking advantage of an intended visit to Weimar by Franz
Oliva, Beethoven wrote to Goethe for the first time. He mentioned their
mutual friend Bettina Brentano, and expressed the greatest admiration for
Goethe's writings. He also promised Goethe a copy of the music for
*Egmont* (which he asked Breitkopf & Härtel to send direct). Goethe even-
tually replied from his holiday address in Karlsbad, expressing the hope
that they could meet, and that he would try to have *Egmont* performed in
Weimar with Beethoven's music (which he did in 1814).[2]

During 1811 Breitkopf & Härtel issued most of the remaining works that
Beethoven had sold to them, but the publications gave him almost as much
irritation as satisfaction. Some works were printed without him seeing the
proofs, and with many mistakes, some quite serious: the piano arrangement of the *Egmont* Overture even had a whole bar missing. Sometimes a
proof was sent, but no second proof to confirm that the mistakes had been

---

[1] TF, 523. Thayer suggests that Kinsky probably paid Beethoven at the revalued rate of
725.8 fl. from September, but Beethoven's letter of 12 February 1813 (TF, 553; A-404) makes
it clear that this had not been done.

[2] A-303; Alb-155.

corrected; and with the 'Emperor' Concerto, although proofs were sent, the firm then issued copies for sale without waiting for the corrections. 'Mistakes—mistakes—you yourself are a unique mistake,' he wrote to them in exasperation. 'All the same I do esteem you very highly. As you know, it is the custom with human beings to esteem one another for not having made even greater mistakes.'[3] He could be magnanimous even when angry! There were other problems too. Some of the page turns were unnecessarily awkward for players. The Op. 82 songs, intended for Princess Kinsky, appeared without a dedication. In contrast the Choral Fantasia, for which Beethoven omitted to send the name of a dedicatee, appeared with a dedication to the King of Bavaria. 'If you intended by so doing to pave the way for an honourable present to me, well then, I am prepared to thank you for it. But, if not, such a dedication does not suit me at all.'[4] Dedications were normally made in return for past favours, although this letter makes it clear that they were sometimes also made in the hope of future recompense. With the *Lebewohl* Sonata, Beethoven agreed that the title could be published in French as well as German, but he objected on seeing 'Lebewohl' translated as 'Les Adieux', which was much less personal. Unfortunately the latter name has stuck. He had also wanted the date '4 May 1809' (the date of Rudolph's departure from Vienna) included in the title, but it was omitted.[5] Meanwhile in *Christus am Oelberge* the publishers changed the words in No. 4, replacing 'Schlag links den Weg nur ein. Er muss ganz nahe sein,' by 'Entfliehen kann er nicht, sein wartet das Gericht,' which makes the musical expression wholly inappropriate at this point. Beethoven was displeased, too, that the firm published so many bad reviews of his works in their *Allgemeine musikalische Zeitung*, yet favourable reviews of 'the most contemptible bunglers'. His growing reputation as a quarrelsome individual was largely due to his having so much justifiable cause for complaint.

Another setback during spring 1811 was his poor health. He had a headache for over a fortnight in March and a violent fever in April. By June he had decided, on the advice of his doctor (Giovanni Malfatti, uncle of Therese), to spend two months in Teplitz (Teplice). The spa towns of northern Bohemia, notably Teplitz and Karlsbad (Karlovy Vary), were popular holiday resorts for the rich and the cultured of both Germany and Austria, and their waters were renowned for their medicinal properties. Normally Beethoven spent the summer months in a village near Vienna, and he had not travelled as far as Teplitz—some four days' journey—since his trip to Grätz in 1806. After several postponements he eventually left about the end of July, arriving on 4 August and staying until 18 September.

---

[3] A-306.          [4] A-325.

[5] Anderson (*Letters*, p. 338) suggests this remark was intended ironically, but it was clearly sincere: this very special date is in his sketches and the autograph score, and he demanded that in future all his headings should be retained exactly.

While at Teplitz, Beethoven composed two one-act singspiels, *Die Ruinen von Athen* (The Ruins of Athens) and *König Stephan* (King Stephen) for the celebratory opening of a new theatre in Pest (Budapest). This, at any rate, is what he appears to claim in his letter of 9 October:

Just as I was getting into my carriage to drive to Teplitz I received a parcel from Buda with the request to compose something for the opening of the new theatre at Pest. Well, after spending three weeks at Teplitz I felt fairly well. So, although my doctor had forbidden me to work, I sat down to do something for those moustachios who are genuinely fond of me; and on 13 September I sent off my parcel to them in the belief that the performance was to take place on 1 October.[6]

The suggestion, however, that Beethoven only began work on these two compositions three weeks after arriving in Teplitz, i.e. 25 August, and was able to send them off on 13 September, is wholly implausible, even though widely accepted. Both are scored for chorus and full orchestra, and their combined length is well over 2,000 bars. Even working at his fastest, Beethoven could surely not compose so much music in three or even six weeks. He did not cut corners when writing these works, for there are extensive sketches in his normal manner, often with several drafts per section. Indeed he may even have extended his sketching process at this time, for his first known pocket sketchbook contains sketches for *Die Ruinen von Athen*. Such sketchbooks, which became plentiful during his final ten years, were evidently used out of doors and are written almost entirely in pencil; they supplement the desk sketchbooks which continued to be used simultaneously and whose contents overlap, but they are of much smaller dimensions. Apart from the sketches in this pocket sketchbook, substantial numbers of ink sketches survive elsewhere for both *Die Ruinen von Athen* and *König Stephan*. Thus nothing in the sketches indicates that these works were written at great speed. The music for *Egmont* is less in quantity than for either of these works, yet, far from being composed in three weeks, it was actually finished three weeks late. With the 'Archduke' Trio, roughly the same length as one of these works but with far fewer instruments, the autograph score alone took three weeks to write out. And the next major works, the Seventh and Eighth Symphonies, took about seven and six months respectively to compose. Thus one might expect the two singspiels to take at least five or six months. Moreover, Beethoven did not spend the whole time at Teplitz working; he was writing letters, taking the warm baths, and meeting people, such as the writers Karl August Varnhagen (who left an interesting account of their meeting), Christoph Tiedge, and Elise von der Recke, plus the singer Amalie Sebald. Furthermore, if Beethoven did not begin the singspiels till August, what was he composing from April to July? The sketchbooks show nothing between the 'Archduke' Trio and *König Stephan*. He spent some of this time checking proofs for

---

[6] A-325. The packet may not have been sent until Monday 16 September: see BB-523 and BB-525.

Breitkopf & Härtel; he had to arrange for a fresh copy of his fifty-three folksong settings to be written out and checked, since none of the first three copies had reached Edinburgh; and he was unwell some of the time. Nevertheless, there is an uncomfortable gap in his productivity, if the accepted chronology is followed. Thus all the evidence indicates that at least one of the singspiels must have been begun before he left for Teplitz. Once it is accepted that even a few notes were written in Vienna, his story is undermined, and it becomes likely that much of the music for Pest was composed during the spring and early summer. His claim is probably not completely untrue, but the 'parcel' he received just before departure must have been the final instalment of the texts to be set, rather than two entire librettos.

The works sent to Pest on or about 13 September were designed as the first and third items in a triple bill, with the middle item a spoken drama. Beethoven's contribution is often described as 'incidental music', but only by those who have not studied it properly. Unlike the incidental music to *Egmont*, which consists mainly of entr'actes and a couple of short songs, *König Stephan* and *Die Ruinen von Athen* consist mainly of musical numbers, which are no more 'incidental' than those of, say, *The Magic Flute*. The texts were written by August Kotzebue, a colourful and widely travelled character who was eventually assassinated in 1819 on suspicion of being a Russian spy. The two works, on patriotic subjects, were carefully tailored to the precise needs of the Pest theatre, but they suited it so well that they have made little impact in any other context.

*König Stephan*, the opening work, was composed first. The quality of Beethoven's music for it has often been questioned, but the text is so lacking in drama, tension and opportunities for characterization that no music could have brought it to life. King Stephen proclaims the greatness of Hungary, forgives his enemy, receives his bride, and is crowned as the mists disperse to reveal the city of Pest. Beethoven uses his characteristic C minor/major contrast to portray the darkness of the past and the light of the present; and in the melodramas (which are used in certain places instead of recitative) the music is carefully judged to match the spoken dialogue. In the final chorus he writes a demandingly high part for the sopranos, as in the finale of the Ninth Symphony; but he was sensitive to the needs of the Hungarian audience, and music that was intellectually or emotionally demanding would have been quite out of place here.

*Die Ruinen von Athen*, the final work for the triple bill, has slightly more dramatic and musical interest. Mercury and Minerva appear in Athens and are horrified to see that a city once the centre of culture has been overrun by barbarous Turks. The scene gives Beethoven an opportunity to write a wonderfully wild chorus of Dervishes, with strange chromatic intervals and frenetic rhythms. There follows a Turkish march, for which he borrowed the theme from his Variations, Op. 76—probably to save time (he initially made a few sketches for a new march before abandoning them).

Mercury and Minerva flee from Athens and land by the Danube, where they are delighted to find a temple of culture in Pest (where else?). The muses of comedy and tragedy, Thalia and Melpomene, are honoured by a high priest, a Sarastro-like figure who sings a profoundly expressive aria ('Will unser Genius') accompanied by four concertante horns. This marks the musical highpoint of the work, although the dramatic climax comes immediately after, when a portrait of the Emperor suddenly appears between the altars to Thalia and Melpomene.

Although the opening ceremony in Pest was planned for 1 October, it suffered a lengthy postponement and Beethoven's works were not heard until 9 February the following year. They met an enthusiastic reception and were repeated on the two following days. *Die Ruinen von Athen* was also revived some years later in Vienna under the title *Die Weihe des Hauses*, with the words suitably modified (see Chapter 17).

Beethoven left Teplitz much revived, and apparently made a brief visit to Lichnowsky's castle at Grätz before returning home. He now planned to write an opera, if a suitable text could be found, and started on his Seventh Symphony. The only work he completed before the end of the year, however, was the song 'An die Geliebte' (To the Beloved). There are several different versions of this, though all quite similar, and the chronology is not entirely clear. Autograph scores survive for two versions; both are dated December 1811, but the later one appears to have been written out in 1814 and dated retrospectively. Another version, similar to but not identical with the earlier one, was published in 1826, while a fourth version can be retrieved from drafts in Beethoven's sketchbook.[7] These sketches are found immediately below and after the last known sketches for *Die Ruinen von Athen*, suggesting they were made in September rather than December 1811, and raising the question of why Beethoven laid them aside for three months when they show a version in some ways more advanced than the earlier of the two autographs. A September date would also cause difficulties in that the poem by Joseph Stoll was unpublished and must have been obtained by Beethoven through personal contact; yet Stoll is not known to have been in Teplitz that summer. A possible explanation is that the sketches were made in December, but were jotted down in the last available blank spaces before the sketches for the Seventh Symphony, so as not to become entangled with these.

An equally pressing question is why Beethoven wrote the song. He resumed his little singing parties about the end of the year, but there may have been a deeper significance in choosing this particular poem. The accompaniment in the earlier autograph was scored, unusually, for piano or guitar, which suggests the song may have been composed for Antonie Brentano, an expert guitarist who was by now very close to Beethoven. If

[7] The four versions are published in *NA*, XII/1, nos. 86, 55, 54, and 106 respectively.

this scenario, first suggested by Maynard Solomon, is accepted, Beethoven may actually have approached Stoll for a poem on this subject; it is significant that, amongst the sketches, he noted that he would like a second stanza. An inscription at the head of the autograph is also highly suggestive: '2 March 1812, requested by me from the author', apparently in Antonie's handwriting.[8] The romantic idea that Beethoven composed this song to express his love for her cannot be confirmed, however. Apart from the possibility that the song was conceived in Teplitz, when Antonie was nowhere near, one must note that there is no inscription to her from Beethoven, as there had been with 'An die Hoffnung' for Josephine Deym and *Für Elise* for Therese Malfatti (was he now being ultra-cautious?): Antonie had to beg the score off him. The song may not even have any immediate personal significance; as Beethoven wrote the following February: 'The artist must often be able to assume all humours,' and therefore would not necessarily reveal his true feelings on any particular occasion. Thus the song may be just an idealized portrayal of romantic love.

Among the people Beethoven had met at Teplitz was Joseph von Varena, a music-lover from Graz in Styria. Varena followed up this meeting with a letter to Beethoven in Vienna requesting scores to perform at charity concerts in Graz. Beethoven was delighted to co-operate, for one of his greatest pleasures throughout his life was to use his art to help the needy. He promptly sent his newly published oratorio *Christus am Oelberge*, the Choral Fantasia and the *Egmont* Overture. He even corrected the text in the oratorio where the publishers had made an unauthorized alteration. Shortly afterwards he sent the overtures of the two works for Pest, and a chorus from *Die Ruinen von Athen*, even though all these were still unpublished. He refused payment for any of this work, although he eventually accepted some delicacies made by the nuns in Graz; and he continued supporting Varena's efforts for some time.

During the winter of 1811–12, when he was again plagued by poor health, Beethoven completed nine more Irish folksong settings for Thomson, which he despatched in February, but his main work was on the Seventh Symphony, the autograph score of which is dated 13 April 1812. Each of his symphonies possesses a markedly distinctive character and inhabits an entirely different sound world. In the Seventh, the most fundamental element is the energetic, repetitive rhythmic patterns found in every movement, justifying Wagner's description of the work as the 'apotheosis of the dance'. The second movement, with its constant alternation of dactyls and spondees throughout several repetitions of the main theme (a theme originally conceived in the context of the third 'Razumovsky' Quartet), makes a particularly powerful rhythmic impact, although a more lyrical countermelody is almost as prominent.

---

[8] Solomon, *Beethoven*, 175. The identity of the hand is questioned in *NA*, XII/1, *Kritischer Bericht*, 90.

Another feature contributing to the distinctive sound of this symphony is the horns: since the symphony is in A major, the horns are crooked in A, giving them an unusually high register that Beethoven exploits to the full. Also prominent is the use of drone basses—perhaps an offshoot of his work on the Irish folksongs, where this type of harmony was common. In the first movement, almost the entire first subject is harmonized by a pedal A; this procedure, coupled with the prominent horns and galloping rhythms, give the movement an open-air quality that can also be detected in the finale. The repeated notes that characterize the second-movement theme are transformed into repeated As in the bass to accompany the central theme in A major (bars 101 ff.). The trio section of the third movement has drones almost throughout; and in the finale the main theme is accompanied by repeated Es. Thus the four movements are bound together by harmonic as well as rhythmic similarities.

Tonally the symphony is also very distinctive and unified. The slow introduction, which is so extended that it almost becomes a movement in itself, makes two extended excursions from A major, to C and F, and both keys play important roles later on. C major is the main key in the development section, where F major also appears briefly. The second movement is in A minor, but its central section in A major contains a very striking modulation into C, from where the music works back to A minor. The third movement, a scherzo in all but name, is actually in F major, though with a first section that rapidly modulates to A as a reminder of the key of the symphony as a whole. Then in the finale the keys of C and F are once again prominent in the development section. Indeed, the repeated emphasis on these two keys seems to provide a pointer to Beethoven's next symphony, which is in F and was begun immediately after the Seventh. The Eighth, however, was not completed until October, after an eventful summer.

During this period Beethoven was once again deeply in love, this time with a woman who has become known to posterity as his Immortal Beloved. We learn of her from a letter he wrote on 6–7 July in which he at one point addresses her by this phrase. Yet so discreet was he about the whole affair that the letter provides almost the only firm evidence that he was in love at all at that time. And the letter was probably never sent to the woman, for it was found amongst his possessions after his death (though she could have returned it to him) and furthermore there is absolutely no sign it went through the post—no postal marks or remnant of sealing wax such as one would expect on a letter of that period. As with *Für Elise*, Beethoven was careful to omit both the year (he writes '6 July, morning') and the name of the intended recipient, who is addressed at the head simply as 'My angel, my all, my self'. Not until the twentieth century was the year finally established as 1812, and the identity of the woman is still being debated. Maynard Solomon appeared to have demonstrated conclusively in 1972 that she was Antonie Brentano, but some observers have remained convinced she was Josephine Deym or even, implausibly, Marie Erdödy. Let us therefore re-examine the events, the claims and the counterclaims.[9]

Because of his uncertain health Beethoven again decided to spend the summer in Teplitz. The Brentanos, meanwhile, had almost finished sorting out the Birkenstock estate and were planning to move back to Frankfurt. Neither Antonie nor her husband Franz was in the best of health, and they too decided to spend the summer in northern Bohemia, but in Karlsbad, some sixty miles from Teplitz. On 26 June Beethoven completed a delightful little one-movement Piano Trio (WoO 39), with a relatively easy piano part, and presented it to the Brentanos' eldest surviving daughter, Maximiliane, who was ten. Three days later, probably on Monday 29 June, Beethoven set off on the three-day journey to Prague, where he remained from 1 to 4 July (two days and three nights). While there he attempted to reach agreement with Prince Kinsky about his annuity, but was given only an interim payment of 60 ducats with a promise of more to follow. The Brentanos arrived in Prague on 3 July and probably left the following day, heading west to Karlsbad while Beethoven headed north-west to Teplitz.

As for Josephine, she had married Baron Stackelberg in 1810 and had already borne him two children to add to her four by her previous marriage. On 14 June 1812 he wrote that they were planning to visit his native Estonia that summer, but these plans did not materialize. Their marriage was already on the verge of break-up by this time (he finally left her the following March), but unfortunately there is in the diary of Josephine's sister Therese a gap between 9 June and 6 August, and so Josephine's precise whereabouts in early July cannot be confirmed. There is also conflicting evidence as to whether she and Stackelberg were still living together at this time. However, around the middle of July she wrote from Vienna to her brother Franz concerning some business matters, as is indicated by his reply dated 25 July, and the implications are that she had not been away.

Because of wet weather Beethoven's journey to Teplitz was prolonged and he did not arrive until 4 a.m. on Sunday 5 July. He made a temporary registration of arrival (it could not be confirmed until the Tuesday), and the next morning (Monday) he began the famous letter, in which, unlike in his letters of 1805–7 to Josephine, and other letters to women, he uses the intimate *du*, rather than the more formal *Sie*, for 'you':[10]

My angel, my all, my self.—Only a few words today, and indeed with pencil— (with yours) only tomorrow is my lodging firmly fixed, what a worthless waste of

[9] Solomon's hypothesis is presented in his *Beethoven*, chapter 15. The Josephine hypothesis is presented in greatest depth in Tellenbach, *Beethoven* (summarized in English in her 'Beethoven and the Countess'). Solomon provides further evidence against Josephine in 'Recherche de Josephine Deym'. The Marie Erdödy hypothesis has been advanced by Gail Altman, but has been shown to be impossible; see Cooper, 'Beethoven's Immortal Beloved'.

[10] Beahrs, 'Translation', provides what is described as a 'literal translation' of the letter. The one given here attempts to improve on minor details (e.g. 'endure' rather than 'exist' for 'bestehn'). 'Unsterbliche Geliebte' is sometimes translated as 'eternally beloved', which is less literal (and would normally be 'ewig Geliebte' in German).

time on such—why this deep grief, where necessity speaks—can our love endure other than through sacrifices, through not requiring everything. Can you alter it, that you are not completely mine, I not completely yours. Oh God look into beautiful nature and calm your soul over the inevitable—love demands everything and quite rightly, so it is *for me with you, for you with me*—only you forget so easily that I must live *for myself and for you*, were we wholly united, you would feel this painfulness just as little as I.

Beethoven then describes his terrible journey from Prague before continuing:

We shall surely see each other soon, even today I cannot convey to you my observations which I made during these few days about my life. Were our hearts always close by each other, I would surely make none such. Oh there are moments when I find that speech is still nothing at all—cheer up—remain my faithful only treasure, my all, as I for you. The rest the gods must send, what must be and shall be for us. Your faithful Ludwig.

That evening he added a postscript indicating that he had not sent the letter because the post to 'K' went early on Mondays and Thursdays only, and that she would therefore probably not hear from him until Saturday. He also added further expressions of love:

Wherever I am, you are with me, I talk with myself and with you, arrange that I can live with you. . . . However you love me, I love you even more deeply—yet never hide yourself from me. . . . So near! so far! is not our love a true heaven-edifice, but also as firm, like the firmament of heaven.

Next morning he added a second postscript, in which he wrote:

I can live either only wholly with you or not at all, yes I have decided to wander about in the distance, until I can fly into your arms, and can call myself entirely at home with you, can send my soul surrounded by you into the realm of the spirits. Yes unfortunately it must be—you will compose yourself all the more, since you know my faithfulness to you, never can another possess my heart, never—never. . . .

He then heard that the post went every day during the summer (he had apparently misread the schedule, which looked somewhat misleading), and so he quickly terminated the letter, with a few more expressions of love and desire to live together. Why he did not post it is unclear; most likely his anxiety that the letter would fall into the wrong hands overcame his desire to communicate with his beloved, and perhaps he sent instead a letter that revealed less.

Beethoven did, however, take much trouble to mask the identity of the woman. Karlsbad is referred to as 'K', and there is no mention of a husband or children; the only hint that she is married is his request that she, not he, should arrange for him to live with her, and even this remark may be meant figuratively, like the one preceding it. He also does not mention any meeting in Prague, although there must have been one since he describes his journey only from there to Teplitz. Thus it took scholars many years to deduce that K must be Karlsbad, and that the woman must have been in Prague in early July then in Karlsbad by about the 6th. Registers of arrivals and departures were kept, in both places (as well as Teplitz), and these indicate that Antonie Brentano was in both places at exactly the right times, as Solomon has shown. Much of Solomon's other evidence is open to question or reinterpretation (such as the song allegedly written for Antonie), but the main evidence is irrefutable.

Josephine, however, appears to have remained in Vienna, and there is no record of her being in either Prague or Karlsbad that year (though there is for 1811). Thus to propose her as the Immortal Beloved, one must postulate that she made an unplanned visit to Prague, for no obvious reason; that she travelled incognito, so that her arrival there was not recorded; that she then travelled on to Karlsbad, somehow evading the police register of guests (or possibly she told Beethoven she was travelling there but did not do so); that she returned to Vienna incognito; that she arrived back in time to deal with some business with her brother by about the middle of the month, even though a return journey to Karlsbad would take over a week and would not be worth making at all unless she stayed there several days; and that she did all this without Therese making any reference to this extended trip in any of her subsequent notes, memoirs or letters. Such an improbable sequence of events, for which there is absolutely no direct evidence, would be hard to accept even if no other candidate had been proposed.

Ultimately, the identity of the Immortal Beloved is at present a matter of faith rather than proof, and some may continue to support claims for Josephine no matter how strong the opposing evidence. Solomon's case for Antonie, however, seems even more secure now than when it first appeared, for it has withstood vigorous attack by several writers. Moreover, while the external criteria greatly favour Antonie, internal ones are almost as persuasive if the letter is interpreted correctly. Beethoven made several references to hopes of living with the woman. This did not necessarily have the sexual connotations that one might assume today. He had lived with Marie Erdödy in 1809 without any suspicion of a sexual relationship; and he had once told the Bigots that he would like to live with them for ever. Thus his initial proposal to Antonie (assuming she is the woman) is that she should arrange space for him in the Brentano household—whether in Frankfurt or Vienna is left unsaid. In the third part of the letter, however, he decides he can live 'only wholly' with her, or not at all: in other words, he will not join the Brentano household but will 'wander in the distance' until he can actually make a home with her ('ganz heimathlich' are his words). The implication is that marriage was being prevented by some barrier that might one day disappear. The explanation would be that Franz, five years older than Beethoven, might die first, leaving Antonie and Beethoven free to marry (in the event, Franz outlived Beethoven).

None of this scenario would fit with Josephine. She and Beethoven had considered the issues in 1805, and she could not marry him then because of her children. Nothing had changed in 1812, except that she was now remarried with two more children, creating a further impediment to union with him. Thus any hopes of making a home with her would be futile. The letter also seems designed to address a new situation, the implications of which required consideration. With Josephine there could be no new situation markedly different from that of 1805. With Antonie, however, there clearly was one: she had grown intensely fond of Beethoven, whom she came to consider 'as a human being greater than as an artist';[11] yet when they parted in Prague there was no certainty they would ever meet again. The Brentanos were about to move to Frankfurt—perhaps even before Beethoven returned to Vienna after his summer break. The pain of permanent parting was likely to provoke a desperate reaction from one or both parties—even perhaps a declaration of previously concealed love, as appears to have happened. Hence Beethoven's attempt at reassurance: 'We shall surely see each other soon . . . cheer up.' They did indeed see each other soon, for Beethoven moved to Karlsbad later in July—but it was on the advice of his doctor (Jakob Staudenheim, perhaps encouraged by Beethoven himself) and was not specifically pre-planned. With Josephine none of this would apply. They had not been seeing each other during 1812, as far as is known; and there was no fear of a permanent separation, for Beethoven would have been able to visit her frequently once back in Vienna.

Much more will doubtless be said about the meaning of the letter and its psychological implications; but the identity of the Immortal Beloved is now as well established as many of the other 'facts' in Beethoven's life. Throughout the episode, Beethoven's noble sentiments and high moral standards shine through. Once more, he had been unable to help falling in love, and this time the woman felt equally strongly. Yet his rule never to interfere with another man's wife can be discerned, even though some of his expressions are ambiguous and open to misinterpretation. After indicating his desire to live in her home, he realizes the dangers and difficulties of such a situation, and decides to live permanently apart. But he also resolves never to marry another woman: 'Never can another possess my heart, never—never.' The preservation of the letter, once he had decided not to send it, became a symbol and reminder of his love and fidelity, and in later life he kept it hidden with his most precious possessions in a secret drawer.

By chance, both Antonie and Josephine gave birth to a child about nine months later: Karl Josef Brentano (born 8 March 1813) and Minona Stackelberg (born 8 April). Some have speculated, without tangible evidence, that Beethoven was the father of one or other child (nobody has yet suggested both children!). Attempts to prove or disprove his paternity now are futile without recourse to genetic tests; but as far as is known both

---

[11] Solomon, *Beethoven*, 182.

women remained faithful within marriage. Minona may have been conceived after Stackelberg had left Josephine, but it was more probably just before; and Antonie, a devout Christian, seems an unlikely person to break her marriage vows after giving birth to five children.

The morality of both Josephine and Antonie stands in marked contrast to that of the women favoured by Beethoven's brothers. Carl had married Johanna in 1806 when she was already about five months pregnant, and in 1811 she had been convicted of the theft of some pearls, for which she was sentenced to a year's imprisonment, reduced on appeal to a month in police custody. Meanwhile the other brother, Johann, who had been very successful as a pharmacist since moving to Linz, was now in 1812 living immorally with one Therese Obermayer, who already had an illegitimate daughter, Amalie Waldmann (born 1807), from an earlier relationship. Beethoven resolved to visit them in Linz.

From Teplitz, where he had at last met Goethe, he moved to Karlsbad in late July, occupying the same guesthouse as the Brentanos, and had ample opportunity to communicate to Antonie his latest feelings while (technically) living with her. He gave a charity concert on 6 August before moving on with the Brentanos to Franzensbad. Later he moved back (without them) to Karlsbad and eventually Teplitz, complaining that his doctor was leading him round in circles. There he fell ill with a gastric complaint, which delayed his departure for several days, but he finally left for his brother's house in Linz on 29 September,[12] arriving at the beginning of October (he had been there 'for a few days' when his arrival was announced locally on 5 October).

It appears that the principal purpose of Beethoven's visit was to bring to an end Johann's relationship with Therese Obermayer. When Johann refused to comply, Beethoven appealed to the bishop, the authorities, and the police to have Therese removed. Johann's only option was to marry her, on 8 November; he claimed in later years that Beethoven had driven him into marriage by his interfering actions. It is easy to condemn Beethoven, as Thayer does, for assuming an authority over his brother to which he was not entitled. It is also tempting to speculate, like Solomon, that his actions were psychologically driven by a reaction to his own relationship with the Immortal Beloved. It is more illuminating, however, to view the matter from Beethoven's angle. Since his teens he had felt responsible for the well-being of his brothers, as the effective head of the household, and had induced them to join him in Vienna. Some vestiges of that responsibility still remained in his mind, and his lasting concern for Carl was shortly to become apparent. He always expected those he loved to uphold his own high moral standards, and was mortified whenever they did not. He had already seen Carl marry a woman who had turned out utterly unworthy— mismanaging money and eventually stealing (for which crime she tried to

---

[12] BB-448, note 1.

blame others).[13] Now he saw his other brother in danger from a woman equally unworthy, and the zeal with which he addressed the problem stemmed from the noblest of motives, despite showing extraordinary lack of sensitivity. In his life, as in his music, Beethoven strove for the highest ideals, and the energy which he devoted to attempts at improving those such as Johann who were falling short is matched only by the energy he expended in the creation of great works of art through intensive and extensive sketching.

Some of that creative energy was put to good use even while he was staying with Johann, for it was there that he finished his Eighth Symphony in October. This is indicated on the autograph score, although he made some modifications at a later date, including a much extended coda to the first movement (bars 333 ff.). The Eighth Symphony seemingly began in the early sketches as a piano concerto, but he was already planning to write two new symphonies to follow the Seventh, and there are many ideas for possible symphonies in the sketchbook, in a variety of keys. Before long, the pianistic runs found amongst the early sketches for the Eighth Symphony had disappeared, and a symphony was emerging.

The most outstanding characteristic of the Eighth is perhaps its wit and humour, and in this feature, as well as its conciseness, it is closer to Haydn than to Beethoven's other symphonies. It is none the less highly original, and much of its subtle humour can be overlooked by the uninitiated. For example, in a conventional first movement the music generally moves to the dominant of the dominant in preparation for the second subject; here Beethoven ridicules convention by moving in the opposite direction, to the subdominant of the subdominant (bars 24–32), where the music appears to become stuck, with no obvious escape route (Ex. 12.2). Then by a sleight of hand, in which the dominant 7th of E flat is treated as an implied augmented 6th, Beethoven leads the music into D major, where a bassoon seems to poke fun at the strings. Humorous devices are plentiful throughout the symphony, and include octave displacements (covering a full five octaves near the end of the finale), and improbable continuations and interruptions, such as the sudden unison fortissimos in the second movement (an Allegretto scherzando that replaces the usual slow movement). This movement, the wittiest of all, also includes a five-note scale played five times (bars 36–9 and 69–72), cutting across the duple rhythm of the underlying pulse and further dislocated rhythmically by syncopated slurring. In its overall structure and character the symphony follows the Piano Sonata, Op. 31 No. 3, but in the symphonic world it is quite unprecedented.

The other work written in Linz was composed at the request of the cathedral Kapellmeister Franz Xaver Glöggl. Glöggl had a set of old trombones, and asked Beethoven to write for these a type of funeral music known there as an *equale*. Beethoven responded with three such pieces (WoO 30), each

---

[13] Tellenbach, 'Psychoanalysis', 89.

**Ex. 12.2** Op. 93/I

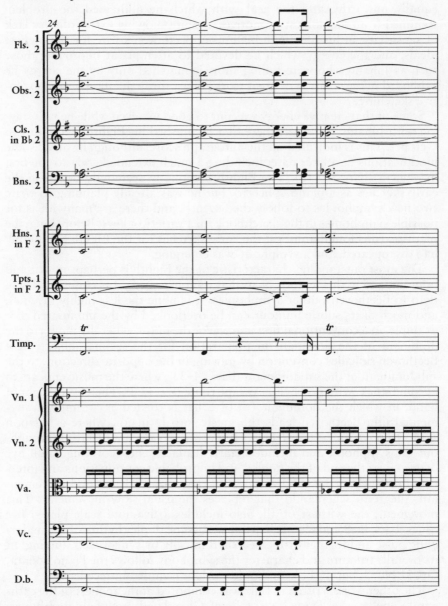

Ex. 12.2 *cont.*

scored for four trombones, and presented the music to Glöggl on All Souls' Day (2 November), when it was presumably performed in the cathedral. (The first and third of these short, solemn pieces were later adapted with text by Ignaz Seyfried for use at Beethoven's own funeral.)

Beethoven's return to the Pasqualati house in Vienna passed unnoticed, and he again became susceptible to bouts of depression: 'Since Sunday I have been ailing, although mentally, it is true, more than physically,' he wrote to Rudolph in December or January.[14] He had much cause for despondency. The Brentanos had left for Frankfurt, depriving him of one of his closest friendships (he continued to correspond with them for years); and his hopes of marriage to his beloved were effectively at an end. The violent dispute with Johann and its unfortunate consequences were still fresh in his memory. His other brother, Carl, fell ill about this time and began needing financial support from Beethoven. Meanwhile Prince Kinsky, who had promised to pay all Beethoven's arrears at the revalued rate of 1800 fl. WW, had died in early November as a result of a riding accident, without fulfilling his pledge. Another problem was that some of Beethoven's compositions were meeting with disapproval: he received two letters from Thomson, dated 5 August and 30 October, saying that the parcels of folksong settings had finally arrived and that they were 'worthy of the greatest applause', but that nine of them—six from the first fifty-three and three from the latest batch—would need revising or rewriting, because either the piano parts were too difficult or the introductions were insufficiently melodious. 'In this country there is not one pianist in a hundred who could make the two hands go well together in the first ritornello,' wrote Thomson, concerning a passage in 'To the Blackbird' (Hess 206) where the right hand has semiquavers while the left has triplet quavers.[15] The prospect of having to redo so many settings was repugnant to Beethoven, who was not accustomed to revising his works at the whim of those who commissioned them.

Characteristically, Beethoven did not give in to despondency but energetically strove to overcome his problems. He wrote to Princess Kinsky, after a respectful delay, presenting his case at some length and emphasizing the fairness of his claim. Instead of revising his folksong settings (which he considered an unsatisfactory approach since each small change would affect the whole and might require further changes), he set about producing nine entirely new settings of the melodies in question. In addition, he threw himself into work on a new violin sonata, later published as Op. 96, once again using activity as a means of overcoming despair. The sonata may have been begun earlier, but fresh impetus for its completion was provided in December by the arrival in Vienna of the noted French violinist Pierre Rode. Beethoven did not hurry to complete the sonata because, as he told Rudolph, he was busy with other works (presumably the folksong settings),

---

[14] A-394.    [15] Cooper, *Folksong Settings*, 16.

and the finale in particular was delayed: 'In our finales we like to have fairly noisy rushing passages, but this does not suit R[ode]'s taste, and hampered me somewhat. However, everything ought to go off well on Tuesday.'[16]

'Tuesday' was 29 December, when the Sonata received its première at Lobkowitz's palace, played by Rode and Archduke Rudolph. The finale consists of a set of variations on a gentle theme marked 'poco allegretto'. Variation 5 is a slow, expressive one, and is followed by an Allegro section in which four more rather irregular variations can be discerned. Here there are a few noisy passages of the type that Rode was said not to like, but there is less sense of brilliance than in many of Beethoven's concluding sections. The performance was repeated on 7 January, and the sonata probably received some minor revisions thereafter.

The remaining way in which Beethoven tackled his despondency was by starting a kind of diary or *Tagebuch*, which he continued using until 1818. It was more a memorandum book for odd jottings than a proper diary, and it eventually contained all manner of notes, including quotations from literature, comments about practical, musical, or philosophical matters, personal prayers, and advice to himself. The document disappeared shortly after his death, but fortunately a copy had by then been made by Anton Gräffer, which appears to be reasonably reliable. The first entry is headed '1812' and was probably made late that year, after Beethoven's return from Linz, judging by its anguished contents and the fact that the third entry is dated as late as 13 May 1813. The first entry is a reflection on his personal situation and his intended response to it:

Submission, deepest submission to your fate, only this can [give] you the sacrifices — — — for this matter of service. O hard struggle!—Do everything that still has to be done to plan what is needed for the long journey. You must — — find everything that your dearest wish grants, yet you must bend it to your will.—Maintain an absolutely steady attitude.

You must not be a *human being, not for yourself, only for others*; for you there is no longer any happiness except within yourself, in your art.—O God! give me strength to conquer myself, nothing at all must fetter me to life.—In this manner with A everything goes to ruin — — — — — — — — —[17]

The reference to submission to fate echoes sentiments expressed by Beethoven during his deafness crisis, while his expectation of finding happiness only in his art recalls his words to Gleichenstein after his rejection by Therese Malfatti. His desire for self-sacrifice and the service of others, and for strength to conquer his weaknesses, is also entirely characteristic: whereas he had told his beloved he must live for himself and her, now he would live only for others. The long journey he mentions may indicate a

---

[16] A-392.

[17] See Solomon, 'Tagebuch', 212. Solomon's article includes the whole Tagebuch in German and English, with commentary. Single dashes between sentences are characteristic of Beethoven's style, but multiple dashes, reproduced here from Gräffer's copy, are not and may represent words or passages in Beethoven's original that he could not read.

symbolic journey through life, but he did have ideas of travelling far afield at that time, although nothing definite had been planned. The reference to 'A' is particularly intriguing, since it probably denotes Antonie, as his Immortal Beloved; but yet again, as in the letter to her, the sentence is left deliberately unspecific and open to many possible interpretations. Clearly Beethoven was going through an emotional crisis at this point; but for the moment, at least, he was determined to continue his struggle, and not to let the many setbacks hinder his art.

# 13

# The political phase (1813–15)

Beethoven took a lifelong interest in politics. He was not politically active in the conventional sense, but a number of his best-known compositions have political overtones, including the *Eroica* Symphony, *Fidelio*, and the *Egmont* Overture. These three, however, could be regarded as isolated instances; the only time he composed a series of politically-inspired works was during the period 1813–15, and they are among his least celebrated works today. The reason for the rapid burst of such works lay in the changing situation in Europe. For a decade or more the continent had been dominated by Napoleon, who had brought much glory to France but much misery to the people of Vienna and elsewhere. Thus when Napoleon's attack on Russia in summer 1812 was succeeded by an ignominious retreat in October–December in which he lost most of his army, there was a general sense of optimism in Austria. International politics became everybody's concern. With so many friends amongst the aristocracy, Beethoven inevitably became involved in the general rejoicing that followed Napoleon's subsequent defeats and eventual overthrow in 1814.

At the beginning of 1813 the first tangible benefits of Napoleon's retreat from Moscow were already being felt. Beethoven noted in a letter to Thomson in February that the postal routes were now completely open, so that a letter from London would reach Vienna in a mere thirty days. He had indeed recently received two new melodies from Thomson, which were sent from Edinburgh on 21 December 1812 but probably arrived by the end of January. Since composing his first sixty-two settings he had already received a further nineteen Irish melodies from Thomson up to the end of 1812, and during the period December–February he set all of these. For the last one, 'When far from the Home', he actually composed two settings, inviting Thomson to publish whichever he preferred; and despite his annoyance at being asked to amend nine of his previous sixty-two, he produced entirely new settings for all nine. It seems that these twenty-nine settings—the nine replacements plus the other nineteen and the alternative for 'When far from the Home'—were already completed when the two latest melodies arrived. One was Welsh and one Irish (they were later printed as 'When Mortals all' and 'Judy, Lovely, Matchless Creature') and they particularly pleased Beethoven, especially the Irish one, which was based on a rather unusual scale pattern that provided an interesting challenge for harmonization. Thomson had written it out in A flat major with the direction 'Amoroso', but Beethoven felt the key did not suit this term and transposed the melody into B flat. He is known to have been very sensitive to the characters of different keys, but this is almost the only instance where he made a specific and reliably documented comment on the subject.

Beethoven had not been sent the words for any of the folksong melodies, despite his vigorous demands for them. Thomson now explained, however, that in most cases the words were still in the heads of the poets, for he commissioned poems separately and married them to the settings at a later stage. This might seem a strange procedure today, but the texts of Scottish and other folksongs were often being replaced or revised, so that few tunes had a fixed and immutable text. Beethoven applauded Thomson's approach, for it meant that the poet could perhaps to some extent adapt his verses to the settings.

When he had completed the thirty-one settings, Beethoven may have returned to his Violin Sonata, Op. 96. Its surviving autograph score, like those of Op. 95 and 97, was written out around 1814 with a retrospective dating, which in this case is, curiously, 'February 1812 or 13'. Since the sonata was completed just before Rode's performance on 29 December 1812, the written date is puzzling, but perhaps Beethoven made some small revisions after he had finished dealing with the folksong settings, and then dated the original score 'February 1812', making the common mistake of writing the previous year's date. After copying this date in 1814 he would have remembered that the work was not so old, and added 'or 13'. Whatever the explanation, the manuscript provides a good example of how unreliable his dates can be.

In March 1813 Beethoven composed a short 'Triumph-Marsch' (WoO 2a) for use in Christoph Kuffner's tragedy *Tarpeja*,[1] and on 3 May he completed a new song, 'Der Gesang der Nachtigall', with a text by one of his favourite poets, Johann Gottfried Herder. The rest of his composing activity during spring and early summer, however, is uncertain. Clearly nothing was completed at this stage, and many sketches from this year have apparently gone missing; but it was probably during this spring and summer that he made extensive sketches for a short choral work, *Meeresstille und glückliche Fahrt* (Calm Sea and Prosperous Voyage, Op. 112). The earliest known sketches for this are on a page (SV 252, f. 1r) bearing the date '3 March 1813', and there are numerous sketches for it on the following pages of this now dismembered sketchbook. The work consists of a setting of two poems by Goethe—the first describing a ship becalmed and the second a successful wind-assisted voyage to land. It was perhaps natural that, after finally meeting Goethe in Teplitz in 1812 and spending time with him every day,

---

[1] The 'Introduction to Act II' (WoO 2b) formerly thought to belong to *Tarpeja* was apparently written for *Leonore* (1805): see *NA*, IX/7, 222.

Beethoven should take an early opportunity to set more of his poetry, and he was particularly attracted by the contrast in these two poems (exploitation of direct contrast was to play an increasingly prominent role in his later music). It seems, however, that Beethoven himself became becalmed during the course of composing the work, and he did not bring it successfully to land until 1815.

The reasons for Beethoven's apparent inactivity in composition at this period are difficult to discern. Successive writers, attempting an explanation, have built up an image of him undergoing a mental crisis near to breakdown, largely on account of the loss of his Immortal Beloved. In this image, his creativity 'came to a full stop' after the Violin Sonata of December 1812;[2] he supposedly began making use of prostitutes; he went around dirty and untidy, indulging in repulsive habits, contemplated suicide, and was finally rescued from his sorry state during the summer by Nanette and Johann Streicher, the piano makers. There is little basis for this moving but fanciful scenario. As we have seen, his creativity did not cease at the end of 1812 and did not diminish before March at the earliest, recovering after a gap of no more than a few months. It would be difficult to explain why the creative gap occurred at this stage if it were a reaction to separation from his Immortal Beloved, although this was certainly one factor still much in his mind, as is evident from his *Tagebuch*:

13 May 1813. To forgo what could be a great deed and to stay like this—what a difference from an unstudied life which I so often pictured to myself—O terrible circumstances, which do not suppress my feeling for domesticity, but whose execution O God, God look down upon the unhappy B., do not let it last thus any longer.[3]

One can only speculate about what great deed Beethoven had in mind, though it may well have involved travel; and the causes of his unhappiness are left unspecified. His domestic circumstances, however, were far from ideal, quite apart from the lack of a wife, for he was still unable to find a satisfactory servant and enlisted Zmeskall's help several times for this purpose.

Beethoven's untidy appearance was not confined to 1813, but became a regular feature of his life. His repulsive habits at table, which were observed by the artist Blasius Höfel in 1814, no doubt resulted from his general eccentricity and insensitivity towards others' feelings. By all accounts, he preferred to behave naturally rather than observe all the decorum and etiquette demanded by society. The suggestion that the Streichers began to care for him during that summer, however, comes from the extremely untrustworthy Schindler, as does the report that Beethoven planned to starve himself to death (which Schindler placed in 1803 but Solomon proposed moving to 1813). There is no evidence that the Streichers were

---

[2] Solomon, *Beethoven*, 219.     [3] Solomon, 'Tagebuch', 214. Note the faulty syntax.

involved with Beethoven at a domestic level at this time, although Nanette was some years later.

As for the prostitutes, this hypothesis was advanced by Editha and Richard Sterba in 1954, in a book (*Beethoven and his Nephew*) that patently set out to denigrate Beethoven's reputation. These authors interpreted various references to 'fortresses' in Beethoven's letters to Zmeskall as a code-word for prostitutes: 'Be zealous in defending the fortresses of the Empire which, as you know, have long since not been virgins and have already received many a shot' (28 February 1813); 'I need not warn you any more to take care not to be wounded near certain fortresses. Why, everywhere there is profound peace!!!!!' (5 September 1816).[4] The Sterbas' hypothesis has been far too readily and widely accepted; there are many possible interpretations for these cryptic remarks, and theirs does pose severe problems. If Beethoven is using metaphor, why does he refer to virgins (*Jungfern*) so directly, and why does he make such a platitudinous remark that the fortresses are not virgins? Why should Zmeskall avoid only 'certain' fortresses, and how might he be 'wounded near' them? He would surely not be described by Beethoven as 'Proprietor, Governor, Pasha of various rotten fortresses'[5] unless he actually ran a brothel, for which there is no evidence. Bearing in mind his occupation as a secretary in the Hungarian chancellery, it would be easier to interpret fortresses as minor government officials, some of whom were under his supervision and some of whom were corrupt (were not pure 'virgins' or were 'rotten'). Alternatively, the fortresses could denote the mines that Zmeskall is known to have owned; some of these might well have been shot at or disused during the war, hence 'rotten'. Government officials could be described as being 'of the Empire', and so could mines if they were fortified for military purposes (which is likely in 1813), but the phrase seems inappropriate for prostitutes.

Even if prostitutes were the subject in question, the suggestion that Beethoven used them is based on a faulty translation of one of his letters. A correct translation reads: 'I thank you heartily, my dear Z, for your discussions with me. Concerning the fortresses, I would think that you had my view that I do not wish to stop in swampy districts.'[6] Perhaps Beethoven, despite his shortage of cash, does not wish to become bogged down in some dubious financial scheme operated by Zmeskall's colleagues, or to visit Zmeskall's mines; but whatever the nature of the fortresses, he clearly wishes to avoid them. There is, in fact, no real evidence that he visited prostitutes at this or any other time; allegations that he contracted syphilis at some stage are similarly unfounded.

---

[4] A-407, A-653.  [5] A-562.

[6] A-715. Anderson's translation is freer than here but essentially correct. The faulty translation is discussed, along with several other doubtful references to sexual activity, in Tellenbach, 'Psychoanalysis', 90–1. Solomon's evidence, assembled in *Beethoven*, 220–1 and 262, for Beethoven's alleged use of prostitutes is at best ambivalent.

Although the received image of Beethoven in 1813 is therefore far from accurate, he was nevertheless in considerable emotional turmoil: 'So many unfortunate incidents occurring one after the other have really driven me into an almost disordered state' he wrote to the Archduke on 27 May.[7] Some may take this statement as an indication of Beethoven's paternity of either Antonie's or Josephine's new baby, but it is nothing of the sort. Several new problems had arisen in 1813. He made enormous efforts to obtain the arrears due from the Kinsky estate and Prince Lobkowitz, writing several long letters and enlisting the help of Zmeskall, Pasqualati, and Archduke Rudolph, but without success. Indeed, he indicated in letters to Varena and Rudolph in July that his efforts to obtain what was due had prevented him both from composing and from attending to their needs for his assistance. Since he had published almost nothing for over a year, he had earned little from publishers, and the cost of living was still rising. To make matters worse, Carl's health deteriorated so much that he seemed likely to die; he even signed a declaration on 12 April that, should he do so, Beethoven should be appointed guardian of his son Karl. Meanwhile Beethoven had to spend all he had on providing for Carl and his family. He reported his circumstances to be the most unfavourable ever, and that he had no money left. It may be surprising that he made no attempt to publish his latest compositions at this time, or write some new, readily marketable ones rather quickly, but it seems he simply had too many other distractions. Yet despite his depleted resources, when the nuns of Graz sent him 100 florins for the scores he was providing for Varena he refused the gift, and after using some of the money to defray copying costs, he returned the rest. Though he was poor, he knew there were others poorer.

A final blow came in April. He hoped to use his two new symphonies and perhaps some numbers from his two recent singspiels for a benefit concert that month. All suitable venues were refused, however. Lobkowitz, in charge of the theatres, proposed some date after 15 May, but by then many among the potential audience would be out of town and a benefit concert would no longer be worth while. Beethoven therefore abandoned the idea, and with it any hopes of a substantial windfall from a successful performance. Moreover, if he could not gain from performances of his latest two symphonies, there was little point in writing a third at this stage, as had been intended. No sonatas or chamber works were being commissioned from him, Thomson having withdrawn his request for sonatas that incorporated folk melodies. Thomson was still asking for six English songs, for which he sent the verses in September, but these probably did not appeal greatly to Beethoven and he made no known attempt to compose settings. Instead he made tentative attempts at setting various German texts—the two by Goethe and Herder already mentioned, plus Count Paul Haugwitz's 'Resignation' and a second attempt at Tiedge's 'An die Hoffnung'.

---

[7] A-426.

Preliminary sketches for both these last two can be found in the 'Meeresstille' Sketchbook, but neither was completed till later.

Beethoven was finally roused from his compositional torpor by a decisive military event. On 21 June the Duke of Wellington won a crushing victory over the French in Iberia at the Battle of Vittoria (Vitoria), and by October had driven them back across the Pyrenees. The battle was seen as a turning-point, and when news of it reached Vienna in July there was great jubilation. Soon Austria, which had been officially neutral since 1809, joined Russia, Prussia, Sweden, and Britain in the war, and Napoleon was finally defeated in October at the Battle of Leipzig.

Living in Vienna at that time was the brilliant inventor Johann Maelzel. Among his inventions was a kind of mechanical orchestra of wind and percussion instruments known as a 'panharmonicon', far surpassing the musical clocks for which Beethoven had once composed. Now in 1813 Maelzel invented a chronometer for accurately measuring tempo, and enlisted the help of various composers, including Beethoven, to promote it. Beethoven was duly impressed, for as recently as July 1812 he had lamented to Breitkopf & Härtel that he had been unable to indicate the tempo properly in the Gloria of his Mass in C, and that such things had to be left to chance. His support for the invention was announced in a Viennese newspaper on 13 October, and he also indicated his enthusiasm privately to Zmeskall around that time.

Meanwhile Maelzel had begun designing some machines to assist Beethoven's weak hearing, although they proved largely ineffective. To encourage him, Beethoven composed a work for the panharmonicon, celebrating the Battle of Vittoria—a 328-bar Victory Symphony in D major.[8] This consists of a march-like movement that is twice interrupted by passages that quote 'God save the King', leaving no doubt who the victors were. There is then a final fugato, which begins with running semiquavers that are set in counterpoint against 'God save the King' in quavers. The whole movement is highly unusual in construction and exhibits Beethoven's renowned skill in developing small motifs at considerable length.

Beethoven then decided to compose a descriptive movement portraying the battle itself, and also, prompted by Maelzel, to arrange the Victory Symphony for full orchestra. The battle movement was therefore also designed for orchestra, to precede the newly orchestrated Victory Symphony, and the work as a whole was entitled *Wellingtons Sieg, oder die Schlacht bei Vittoria* (Wellington's Victory, or the Battle of Vittoria, commonly known as the 'Battle Symphony', though Beethoven regarded it more as an overture than a symphony). Maelzel contributed a few trumpet signals for this movement, but the evidence from the manuscript sources

[8] *SGA*, iv. 71–97.

supports Beethoven's claim that the original initiative for both movements was his, not Maelzel's.[9]

Battle music had a long tradition, stretching back to the sixteenth century, but by 1813 the genre had become debased, although plenty of battle pieces were still being composed and some were very popular. Beethoven had previously held aloof from such genres, but *Wellingtons Sieg* gave him an opportunity to express his patriotism and to show his affection for the British, while tackling the fresh musical challenge provided by a popular genre. This first movement is surely the mother of all battle music, as it portrays the course of the battle with extraordinary vividness. The British are represented by the key of E flat major and the theme 'Rule Britannia', which is heard in a simple harmonized version, immediately after the opening trumpet calls. The French are then heard in C major with their theme; Beethoven avoided the 'Marseillaise' as it had ambiguous associations in Vienna at the time,[10] and opted instead for the French tune 'Malbrouk s'en va-t-en guerre' (which unfortunately is today associated with the words 'For he's a jolly good fellow'). The French and British keys are set against each other, and the battle itself is suitably wild. Supplementing the orchestra at this point are cannons, with the French and British ones clearly distinguished in the score. At first there is some regularity in the cannon shots, but they are soon made to sound remarkably random and unpredictable, occurring on any beat of the bar and with varying gaps between them. For a time, both sets of cannons are heard frequently, but during the 'Storm-March' the French ones are gradually silenced. The outcome of the battle is further indicated by tonality: the key of the 'Storm-March' rises by semitones from A flat to B major, but then instead of moving a further semitone into the French key of C, the music suddenly modulates to the British key, E flat.

The quality of *Wellingtons Sieg* has been much debated. The work is often regarded as the nadir of Beethoven's compositional achievement, although it has also been described as a masterpiece. A case could be made for either viewpoint, but to compare it qualitatively with the rest of his orchestral output is futile: it is different in kind, designed to be entertaining rather than serious and sophisticated. Beethoven responded supremely well to the challenge of writing a programmatic work in an overtly vulgar style. The degree of realism he achieves, particularly with the cannons, far surpasses any previous attempts, as does the musical complexity in terms of keys, motivic development and tonal organization; but these features are combined with many of the traditional features of battle music—march-like rhythms, trumpets and drums, and victory celebrations. As with the folksong settings, Beethoven takes a time-honoured genre and raises it to a new level in a highly imaginative and original composition.

[9] See Küthen, 'Neue Aspekte'. There is no certainty, however, that Maelzel did not contribute other ideas for the work too, or even the initial conception.
[10] Röder, 'Beethovens Sieg', 247.

*Wellingtons Sieg* received its première on 8 December at a grand charity concert in aid of war victims, organized by Maelzel and given at the University Hall. The Seventh Symphony also received its first public hearing at this event. Several outstanding musicians gave their services, including the composer Louis Spohr (1784–1859), who in his autobiography left an amusing if exaggerated account of Beethoven's conducting at the event:

Whenever a *sforzando* occurred, he tore his arms, which he had previously crossed upon his breast, asunder with great vehemence. At a *piano*, he bent himself down; the softer he wanted it, the lower he bent. If a *crescendo* then entered, he raised himself gradually again, and at the entry of the *forte* sprang up high. To increase the *forte* yet more, he sometimes joined in with a shout without realizing.[11]

Spohr actually places in 1814 his first experience of Beethoven's conducting, after the revival of *Fidelio* and at the Redoutensaal, but he certainly participated when Beethoven conducted on 8 December 1813. Although the rest of his account of Beethoven's conducting may be equally unreliable in detail, the overall impression is probably not far wrong, and Beethoven's gestures doubtlessly looked comical and eccentric. They were, however, designed to draw out maximum expression from the orchestra, and were in some ways far ahead of their time.

The concert was an enormous success and was repeated four days later, producing combined net receipts of 4006 florins. Particularly admired were *Wellingtons Sieg* and the slow movement of the Seventh Symphony, while the patriotic sentiments unleashed by the defeat of Napoleon could only add to the joy of the occasion. Beethoven was now at last permitted to hold his own benefit concert, which took place at the Redoutensaal on 2 January 1814. *Wellingtons Sieg* was performed yet again, by popular request, and the last three numbers from *Die Ruinen von Athen* were at last introduced to the Viennese public. Beethoven's popularity soared to unprecedented heights, especially amongst those who had found his music too learned and difficult but could readily grasp the direct appeal of *Wellingtons Sieg*. He publicly thanked the participants, through an announcement in the newspaper, the *Wiener Zeitung*, and he was granted another benefit concert on 27 February. The celebrated battle piece was heard again, along with the Seventh Symphony and the première of the Eighth. Also included in the programme was a vocal trio, *Tremate, empi, tremate* (Op. 116), which had been written in 1802 as part of Beethoven's studies with Salieri, but had never previously been performed.

Maelzel played no part in these two benefit concerts. Even before *Wellingtons Sieg* had been completed, he quarrelled violently with Beethoven, who was angry that Maelzel had announced the work as his property and had advertised the charity concerts without mentioning the composer. The two men also could not agree over Maelzel's plan to take the work to London, and Beethoven would not give him the score. Maelzel

---

[11] TF, 565; Sonneck, *Impressions*, 97.

therefore obtained a copy of the instrumental parts by stealth, and took the work to Munich, performing it there on 16 and 17 March. Beethoven attempted to take legal action for this blatant infringement of his rights, but after a protracted dispute they agreed to settle their differences.

Some biographers have regarded Beethoven's behaviour as unjust (Thayer called it one of the few blots on his character). He should certainly have made it more clear that, when he first gave Maelzel the score of the Victory Symphony, he was not conferring any rights beyond permission to process the work for the panharmonicon. Maelzel evidently did not appreciate, or chose to ignore, Beethoven's wish to retain performing rights and the work as a whole. Maelzel must also have felt entitled to a reward for his efforts to assist Beethoven's hearing, and for contributing at least a few ideas for *Wellingtons Sieg*, yet he had gained nothing—not even a share in Beethoven's benefit concert. Beethoven could therefore be accused of insensitivity and lack of generosity towards him. Nevertheless, Beethoven was clearly more sinned against than sinning. Maelzel was certainly never entitled to describe the work as his, nor to perform it without Beethoven's permission, nor to make a copy of it by some underhand method. Such unethical behaviour was precisely the kind of thing most likely to arouse Beethoven's ire.

*Wellingtons Sieg* was the first in a series of politically-inspired works. When Napoleon's overthrow became certain, the playwright Georg Friedrich Treitschke wrote a one-act singspiel *Die gute Nachricht* (The Good News), the music for which was written by several composers. Beethoven's contribution was the final chorus, 'Germania', and the work was performed on 11 April. The political situation, coupled with Beethoven's new-found popularity, was probably also behind a request by the court theatre directors to revive *Fidelio*. Beethoven agreed, but only on condition that he could make extensive revisions. Treitschke was asked to rework the libretto, thus becoming the fourth author to have a share in it, and did a masterly job in intensifying and elaborating the drama and improving the dramatic pace. Beethoven wrote to him in April: 'Had you not taken so much trouble with it and revised everything so advantageously, for which I shall ever be grateful to you, I would hardly be able to bring myself to it. You have thereby salvaged a good few remnants from a ship that was stranded.'[12]

Many of the revisions call for comment. Treitschke reversed the first two musical numbers, placing Marzelline's aria second, so that the work begins on an everyday level and her desire for Fidelio becomes apparent only gradually. Two whole numbers—'Ein Mann ist bald genommen' and 'Um in die Ehe'—and also the Adagio section of Leonore's aria 'Komm, Hoffnung' were removed, since they held up the dramatic flow; the final portion of her aria, 'Ich folg dem innern Triebe', must also for musical reasons have been

---

[12] A-479.

reduced to its present length at this stage, with its opening tonal digression (to the words 'O du für den') excised. The end of Act I had been dramatically weak, with Pizarro storming in merely to tell Rocco to hurry up. Treitschke rewrote this entire passage, so that Pizarro's anger is aroused by the prisoners having been allowed out of their cells; Rocco has to fumble for an excuse (eventually remembering that it is the king's name-day, which he claims allows them to be let out), and he is ordered to send them back at once. Thus the act now ends with the prisoners returning to their cells, as a foretaste of Florestan's dungeon at the start of Act II. Beethoven took full advantage by writing a memorable closing section ('Leb' wohl, du warmes Sonnenlicht'), which leans towards the subdominant and gradually descends in a mood of regret and resignation to a peaceful conclusion.

In Act II, the ecstatic duet for Leonore and Florestan, 'O namenlose Freude', had been sung only after Rocco had seized Leonore's pistol and left them defenceless in the cell—an improbable sequence that had already come in for criticism. Treitschke instead had Rocco give the couple a gesture of support that convinces Leonore they will be released, so that their ensuing duet follows naturally. Treitschke also moved the last scene, where Florestan is finally released, from the dungeon to the courtyard, thereby creating a neatly rounded overall structure of great universal mythic power: light – darkness – light; life – death – resurrection – ascension.

Treitschke's most noteworthy change, however, is perhaps in Florestan's aria. The combined efforts of Bouilly, Sonnleithner, and Breuning had produced a bipartite structure in which Florestan first laments his plight and then merely recalls happier days, leaving little scope for dramatic and musical impact. In 1841 Treitschke wrote a vivid account describing how the problem was overcome—an account that itself betrays his keen sense of drama:

Beethoven for his part wanted to distinguish poor Florestan with an aria, but I offered the objection that it would be impossible to allow a man nearly dead with hunger to sing bravura. We wrote one thing and another; at last, in his opinion, I hit the nail on the head. I wrote words which describe the last blazing up of life before its extinction. . . .

What I now relate will live forever in my memory. Beethoven came to me about seven o' clock in the evening. After we had discussed other things, he asked how matters stood with the aria. It was just finished; I handed it to him. He read, ran up and down the room, muttered, growled, as was his habit instead of singing—and tore open the piano. My wife had often vainly begged him to play; today he placed the text in front of him and began wonderful improvisations, which unfortunately no magic could hold fast. Out of them he seemed to conjure the motif of the aria. The hours passed, but Beethoven improvised on. Supper, which he had intended to share with us, was served, but he did not let himself be disturbed. It was late when he embraced me, and declining the meal, he hurried home. The next day the admirable composition was finished.[13]

[13] TF, 572–3.

This account is one of very few that reveal the intimate connection for Beethoven between improvisation and composition, and it portrays him in the white heat of inspiration, when mundane matters such as supper had to be ignored. The sketches confirm that this new second part of Florestan's aria, 'Und spür' ich nicht linde, sanft säuselnde Luft' (And do I not sense soft, gently rustling air), was indeed composed very quickly at a late stage, after the sketches for the revision of the Act II finale. In this section, Florestan has a vision of a Leonore-like angel leading him to freedom in Heaven (a scene bearing clear echoes of Egmont's vision, which Beethoven had set four years earlier). Beethoven uses a solo oboe to penetrate Florestan's darkness, and places tremendous emphasis on the word 'Freiheit' (freedom), in an exceedingly high-pitched conclusion.

In addition to making large-scale changes, Beethoven went through the entire score of the opera, as in 1806, making numerous adjustments. The revisions were begun even before his February concert, which he regarded as a tiresome interruption necessitated only by his lack of resources; but most were done during March–May. The première of the new version was fixed for 23 May, and the last item composed beforehand was a new over-ture, which unlike the previous three was written in E major, partly so that it could lead smoothly into the new No. 1 in A (which had been inter-changed with No. 2 in C minor/major). Unfortunately the new overture was not ready in time, and after a hasty attempt to patch up the 1805 over-ture (the so-called *Leonore* No. 2), Beethoven substituted a different one— probably that from *Die Ruinen von Athen*.[14] The new overture was finally heard three days later, on 26 May.

In this revised form *Fidelio* was so successful that it was repeated several times in the coming weeks, and Beethoven was at length granted a benefit performance on 18 July. For this occasion he reintroduced Rocco's aria and the Adagio section of Leonore's 'Komm, Hoffnung', both significantly revised, and also wrote a new recitative, 'Abscheulicher!', to precede the lat-ter. These changes finally ended the opera's lengthy gestation. Soon it was being sent to other cities, and a vocal score arranged by Ignaz Moscheles was published by Artaria as early as August 1814—Beethoven's first sub-stantial publication since the termination of his dealings with Breitkopf & Härtel in 1812.

One remarkable feature of the final version is the perfect proportions between the two acts, whose relative lengths are almost precisely those of the Golden Section: Act II compared to Act I closely matches Act I to the whole work, and if it is measured by bar numbers, for example, only three bars would need to be added to Act II for the figures to be exact—three in a total of over 3,000. Beethoven, who could not even multiply, let alone cal-culate long division and decimals, recognized that the proportions were wrong in the first two versions of the opera, with the first part far too long,

---

[14] Tyson, 'Yet another', 201–2.

and in May 1814 it was too short; but in this final version he instinctively sensed that the proportions at last had a harmonious relationship (mathematical precision is not necessary in such cases).

Another notable aspect of the final version is its tonal scheme. In the earlier versions, the large-scale descent from C to B flat (prisoners' chorus) to A flat on arrival in the lowest dungeon had been encapsulated in the first three notes of Florestan's aria. Now, however, although the implied overall tonality was still C major, the opera began with an E major overture, creating a different large-scale progression: E–(C)–A flat. Thus Beethoven now ingeniously summarized this in a local event, in a revision to Florestan's recitative, where he created a striking modulation from E major, through C to A flat major, on the single word *Leiden* (sufferings: see Ex. 13.1). The macrocosmic is thereby once again encapsulated in the microcosmic, and Florestan's *Leiden* become the kernel of the whole opera.

**Ex. 13.1** Op. 72/XI

With the defeat of France and the exile of Napoleon to Elba, the political scene turned relatively quiet during the summer of 1814, as plans were made for a grand congress to be held in Vienna to discuss the shape of postwar Europe. Beethoven, too, turned away from political works to write a series of highly personal compositions for individual friends. In May he composed an *Abschiedsgesang* (WoO 102) for the farewell party of one Leopold Weiss. Next month he produced a little Italian cantata, *Un lieto brindisi* (WoO 103), for the nameday of his doctor Giovanni Malfatti (24 June). After this he wrote an *Elegischer Gesang* (Elegiac Song), Op. 118, to commemorate the third anniversary of the death of Baron Pasqualati's wife on 5 August, when the work was presumably performed privately.

All three works remain little known. Their brevity makes them difficult to fit into ordinary concert programmes, as does their unusual scoring: three male voices; four voices (including two tenors) and piano; and four-part choir (or soloists) and string quartet. These odd scorings may have been designed purely to fit the demands of the occasions, but they also suggest something more profound. Beethoven was continually seeking fresh challenges. *Wellingtons Sieg*, with its necessarily vulgar style, had provided one such challenge, and now here was another type. It is noteworthy that he composed more of these short occasional pieces at this time than during any other period in his life, as he strove to stretch the bounds of music in new directions. The combination of string quartet and four voices for the gentle and moving *Elegischer Gesang*, which in the autograph score is actually dedicated to Pasqualati's 'transfigured wife', is particularly original and uplifting. These works could be regarded as a stylistic cul-de-sac, for they do not point the way forward to his final period to any great extent; but this was a period when all avenues were being explored, before the explosion of his late style.

During the summer Beethoven also wrote a new piano sonata in E minor (Op. 90). It was his first for five years, and the genre seems to have held less attraction for him than it had done a decade earlier. Although the work exhibits no startling novelties, it offers a new solution for a two-movement structure: an energetic first movement and a more lyrical finale—approximately the reverse of the pattern in Op. 78. The contrast is heightened by a change from E minor to E major, and the overall approach is more Romantic than in earlier sonatas. Both movements are headed by a lengthy instruction in German instead of the customary Italian tempo mark (Beethoven was to show a marked preference for German terminology from now on), and the instructions indicate expression rather than just tempo: the first movement calls for 'feeling and expression throughout' and the second for a very cantabile touch. This second movement displays an unhurried, song-like quality that is more characteristic of Schubert than Beethoven. Another feature placing this sonata closer to Schubert and the early Romantics than to typical late Beethoven is its almost complete lack of counterpoint. Nearly all the thematic material in both movements is in the right hand; where the left does temporarily take over in the first movement (bars 113–29), the texture is a tenor melody with figuration for the right hand. A similar texture appears briefly in the finale (bars 229–33 and 237–45), one of a number of subtle relationships between the two movements. Others include the emphasis on the third of the scale in the main themes, resulting in direct contrast between the G of the first movement and the G♯ of the second; the use of C major as the tonal goal (the passage of tonal stability furthest from the tonic) in both movements; and self-contained opening sections leading to firm perfect cadences (bars 24 and 32 respectively)—such closure is common in a sonata-rondo finale, but rare in a sonata-form first movement. The autograph score is dated 16 August 1814; after its completion Beethoven turned once again to political works, in anticipation of the Congress of Vienna.

Emperor Franz invited numerous heads of state to the congress at his own expense, and they began arriving in September. Much entertainment was provided for their periods of leisure, including firework displays, parades, plays, balls, and grand musical performances. Patriotic fervour and euphoria were felt everywhere in Vienna, and many composers contributed new works, especially battle music, dance music, and works of greeting. Beethoven remained somewhat on the fringes of the main festivities, but nearly all his compositions during the next six months or more can be related to his political and social surroundings. They are listed here in approximately chronological order, although there was some overlap:

| | |
|---|---|
| WoO 95 | *Chor auf die verbündeten Fürsten* (Chorus on the Allied Princes) |
| Op. 115 | 'Namensfeier' (Nameday) Overture |
| Op. 136 | Cantata, *Der glorreiche Augenblick* (The Glorious Moment) |
| Op. 89 | Polonaise |
| WoO 143 | Song, 'Des Kriegers Abschied' (The Soldier's Departure) |
| WoO 96 | Incidental music for *Leonore Prohaska* |
| WoO 97 | Chorus for singspiel *Die Ehrenpforten* (The Triumphal Arches) |

Feelings of patriotism can be very intense; but where works of art express a triumphalist patriotism, they often lose their force if transferred to another time and place. Thus Beethoven's patriotism, though sincerely felt, can no longer touch us today and may even generate feelings of embarrassment. Many of the works on the above list, like *Wellingtons Sieg* and his two singspiels for Pest written in earlier years, can never achieve their full impact outside the context for which they were created, and are unlikely to appeal to modern audiences. Yet they are not necessarily any less carefully crafted, or indeed any less original, than his symphonies and sonatas. It is all too easy to regard them as being in a debased style that William Kinderman calls 'kitsch',[15] and a pale imitation of Beethoven's heroic music of the previous decade: bombastic music without any real feeling. But to dismiss them thus is to misunderstand Beethoven's intentions. This was a time for celebrations, not profound meditation, and Beethoven designed the music to suit perfectly its context. Although modern performers avoid such works, Kinderman rightly states that scholarly neglect of them is unjustified.

Not all of the works listed above have equally strong political overtones. The most ostentatiously patriotic is surely *Der glorreiche Augenblick*, a massive cantata of over a thousand bars. Its text, by the surgeon Alois Weissenbach, has no great literary merit, seeming overblown and faintly ridiculous today, but the cantata was effective within its context. Beethoven worked on it with great diligence, making large numbers of sketches as usual, and it was performed on 29 November in a highly successful benefit concert, which was repeated three days later and again on Christmas Day.

---

[15] Kinderman, *Beethoven*, 169–80.

The Overture in C major, later published as Op. 115, is an entirely different sort of work, and was originally conceived without any patriotic intentions. Its earliest known sketches date from 1809, at which time it was in E flat major, like most of Beethoven's main works that year, and was described as an 'Overture for any occasion, or for concert use'. He then set it aside, but began writing out a score in 1811, still in E flat major. This, too, was abandoned, with the largely empty score being used for sketches for *König Stephan* and *Die Ruinen von Athen*. The following year he considered incorporating part of Schiller's famous poem 'An die Freude' (Ode to Joy) to form a choral overture in C; this idea also came to nothing, although it provides an interesting anticipation of the Ninth Symphony. Finally the overture was worked out in detail in 1814, evidently for use as a celebratory piece during the Congress. It was already firmly associated in Beethoven's mind with expressions of joy, as is clear from the reference to Schiller's poem in the sketches; and when the autograph score was written out it was headed '1 October 1814, eve of our Emperor's nameday'. It seems likely, therefore, that Beethoven intended it at that time to be performed as part of the nameday celebrations, and indeed it has become known as the 'Nameday' Overture. It was not ready in time, however, and was still being refined several months later, for a few brief sketches date from about March 1815. The first performance was not until the following December. Such a lengthy period of gestation was unusual for Beethoven, and suggests he may have had misgivings about its overall conception. It has also proved one of his less popular orchestral works. Nevertheless, it exhibits his customary skill in motivic manipulation, with a two-note falling figure heard in the first bar of both the slow introduction and the main Allegro being developed in all kinds of ingenious ways, even to the extent of generating the second subject.

The Polonaise, Op. 89, composed in December 1814, is even less overtly political, for it is simply a short piano piece. Polonaises had recently become a popular genre, and it is reported that Beethoven, on the advice of a friend, decided to compose one for the Empress of Russia, who was in Vienna at the time. Presumably he felt that Poland was sufficiently close to Russia for a Polish dance to make an impact. The empress was pleased with the work and the dedication to her, and rewarded Beethoven with 50 ducats. He was also paid 100 ducats for the earlier dedication to the Russian Emperor of the Violin Sonatas, Op. 30, for which he had previously received nothing. The Polonaise was published almost immediately, in March 1815, and was advertised as Beethoven's first original polonaise for piano, to emphasize its novelty. It was to remain his only composition of this type.

The last of the works Beethoven wrote for the main Congress of Vienna period was the incidental music to the tragedy *Leonore Prohaska* by Friedrich Duncker, who was in Vienna with King Friedrich Wilhelm III of Prussia. The music, written in early 1815, consists of three short numbers plus an orchestrated version of the funeral march from the Piano Sonata, Op. 26, transposed to B minor.

A final postscript to Beethoven's political phase was added after Napoleon's escape from Elba and subsequent defeat at Waterloo. To celebrate the event, Treitschke wrote another short singspiel, entitled *Die Ehrenpforten*, and Beethoven was again invited to contribute the closing chorus, with the appropriate words 'Es ist vollbracht' (It is accomplished). The work was first performed on 15 July 1815. By this time, however, Beethoven's artistic preoccupations lay elsewhere.

# 14

# Declining productivity (1815–17)

Beethoven's fortunes and popularity had improved considerably during the Congress of Vienna. His genius had been recognized by several heads of state, who had attended *Fidelio* or his benefit concerts in autumn 1814; he had been rewarded by the Empress of Russia, and he performed at a grand concert in her honour on 25 January 1815. At last, too, the Kinsky affair was settled: by an agreement dated 18 January 1815, the heirs of the Kinsky estate consented to pay Beethoven's annuity at the rate of 1200 fl. WW. Although this was less than the 1800 fl. to which he felt entitled, it was more than the 726 fl. he was due legally, and seemed a reasonable compromise. Full arrears—a total of 2479 fl.—were also paid at the new rate on 26 March, the anniversary of his first ever public performance. Shortly after this, Prince Lobkowitz agreed to pay his share of the annuity at the full rate of 700 fl., and Beethoven received arrears of over 1000 fl. from him in August. From this time until his death, he received regular payments amounting to 3400 fl. per year from his three sponsors (1500 from Rudolph, 1200 from Kinsky, and 700 from Lobkowitz). The combination of the arrears payments, the revalued annuity, income from the benefit performances of 1814, and the sale of many folksong settings meant that Beethoven was now at last on a sound financial footing.

He also now had a collection of unpublished works to offer to publishers. He did not revive his association with Breitkopf & Härtel, however, but turned to a relatively new local publisher, Sigmund Anton Steiner. When Beethoven's funds had been exhausted in 1813, Steiner had lent 1500 fl. to help support Carl and his family, but instead of using his new wealth to refund Steiner in 1815, Beethoven gave him some compositions. The full list of what Steiner acquired at that time appears in a document dated 29 April 1815:

*Fidelio*, full score
*Der glorreiche Augenblick*, full score
String Quartet (Op. 95)
Vocal trio (*Tremate*, Op. 116)
*Wellingtons Sieg*
Symphony No. 7

236

Symphony No. 8
Piano Trio (Op. 97)
Violin Sonata (Op. 96)
Three overtures (*Die Ruinen von Athen, König Stephan*, 'Namensfeier')
Twelve 'English Songs'[1]

Steiner thus became Beethoven's principal publisher until the 1820s, although several works on the list did not appear for some years. Steiner was assisted by Tobias Haslinger, who eventually succeeded him as manager; they became good friends of Beethoven, who often visited Steiner's music shop in the Paternostergasse to browse through the music and meet other musicians. As a result of these visits, Steiner was sometimes able to amend the plates he had used for printing Beethoven's works, so that later impressions are often more accurate than the initial one, even though at first sight they seem identical.[2]

In his dealings with Steiner and Haslinger, Beethoven began at an early stage to use military terminology in a humorous way. He dubbed himself the 'Generalissimo', Steiner the 'Lieutenant General' and Haslinger the 'Adjutant'. Sometimes the metaphor was extended, with ducats being 'armed men', and Steiner 'taking the field' with new Beethoven compositions. The atmosphere of war had been so prevalent in Europe for so long that such metaphors seemed entirely natural. Moreover, Beethoven seems to have regarded himself as in some ways the musical equivalent of Napoleon. He had once remarked about Napoleon, according to Krumpholz: 'It's a pity that I do not understand the art of war as well as I do the art of music: I would conquer him!'[3] As two of the most celebrated leaders of the day, they do indeed have something in common; and just as Napoleon's army had overrun much of Europe, so Beethoven's music was doing likewise.

Unlike Napoleon's army, however, Beethoven's music had succeeded in crossing the English Channel, and was already becoming popular in London when in 1814 he sent a score of *Wellingtons Sieg* to the Prince Regent (later George IV), to whom the work was dedicated. He was angered and disappointed that the prince sent no reward or acknowledgement in return, but the prince did pass the score on to Sir George Smart, who conducted the work in London on 10 February 1815, where it was an enormous success. When Beethoven heard the news he contacted Smart asking him to find an English publisher for his latest compositions. The works on the list sent to Smart included all those bought by Steiner except

---

[1] Anderson, *Letters*, iii. 1423. The 'English songs' were evidently twelve selected from the 29 Irish folksong settings printed by Thomson (along with a Haydn setting) in 1814. Thomson sent a copy of this volume to Beethoven, who examined it carefully before returning a list of errata, which Thomson corrected before the official date of publication in March 1815. Steiner, however, never printed the twelve Beethoven gave him, partly because of delays in translating the texts into German.

[2] Tyson, 'Steiner'.          [3] TF, 403.

the vocal ones. Eventually one publisher, Robert Birchall, agreed to take four of the works—the Violin Sonata, the 'Archduke' Trio, and the piano arrangements of *Wellingtons Sieg* and the Seventh Symphony—for a total of £65.

The enormous boosts to Beethoven's income should have made him begin to feel prosperous at last. Alas, he did not see it that way. Taxes had been raised, and he told Thomson he had had to pay nearly £60 in 1814. The rise in taxes was probably to offset inflation, which continued apace and affected him directly:

The bad paper money of our State has once already been depreciated to a fifth of its value. Whereupon I was then treated according to the scale. After a prolonged struggle I have obtained, although at a considerable loss, the full value. But now we are so placed that the paper money has been depreciated again far below a fifth of its value; and I am faced with the prospect of seeing my income being reduced to *nothing* for the second time, and without my being able to hope for any compensation.[4]

As we have seen, his original 4000 florins were actually worth little over 1600 fl. CM when his annuity was begun, and was by law revalued to this sum at the time of the fivefold devaluation in 1811; but his sponsors had now agreed to pay him over twice this amount. Thus he should have had adequate funds, but further inflation meant that his annuity of 3400 fl. WW was worth much less than it would have been in 1811. Its value in 1815 is hard to calculate precisely, since it was constantly changing and different methods of calculation yield different figures; but by the time the silver florin was reintroduced in 1818, his 3400 fl. WW had depreciated by 60% to 1360 fl. CM.

Another drain on Beethoven's resources was the care of his brother Carl, still unwell with tuberculosis. Beethoven spared no expense to make life easier for Carl and his family: 'It is not worth while to let anyone suffer for the sake of a few wretched florins.'[5] By November 1815 Beethoven estimated he had spent 10,000 fl. WW—equivalent to nearly three years' salary at its revalued rate. One must regard such a figure with circumspection, since his arithmetic was habitually poor and he was prone to exaggerate his financial difficulties. Nevertheless, he clearly contributed a great deal to Carl's welfare during this period, and it is understandable that he felt unable to repay a loan from the Brentanos at this time.

In a letter to Amenda in April 1815 Beethoven lamented that he was living almost entirely alone, practically cut off from everybody he loved. This, too, was an exaggeration, for his beloved Carl was close by, and some other quite good friends were around—Zmeskall, Steiner, Rudolph. But those with whom he could communicate on the deepest level were absent or in some way alienated from him: Franz and Antonie Brentano were in Frankfurt, while Bettina was in Berlin; Amenda himself was in Latvia with

[4] A-544.    [5] A-555.

a wife and five children; the Wegelers were in Koblenz; Stephan von
Breuning had never been close after their quarrel; and Beethoven had
resolved to keep away from Josephine. Tiedge, Varnhagen, and Amalie
Sebald, close friends whom he had met in Teplitz, were all far from Vienna.
Lack of a wife and family left a void in his life, as he hinted in his letter to
Amenda. He resolved to 'share a meal every day with someone, such as
musicians, where one can discuss this and that,'[6] but this could not allevi-
ate his more profound loneliness and despondency. Some consolation,
however, came with his reconciliation with Marie Erdödy, probably in
February 1815. He noted in his *Tagebuch* that he had received thirty-four
bottles (of wine) from her, and soon he was visiting her at her estate in
Jedlesee, about five miles north of central Vienna. Beethoven was delighted
to renew the friendship, and became very fond of her three children Marie,
Friederike, and August, known affectionately as Mimi, Fritzi, and Gusti.
The countess employed a resident music teacher for them, Joseph Brauchle,
who was joined about this time by the cellist Joseph Linke.

The names of Brauchle and Linke are intertwined in a curious little
canon written by Beethoven (WoO 167) presumably that year (Ex. 14.1).
Notated as a single melodic line, the piece resolves into four parts as individual voices enter at two-bar intervals. Beethoven had studied canon as
part of his training with Albrechtsberger years earlier, but only in later life
did he develop the habit of composing short canonic exercises as presentation pieces—sometimes humorous, sometimes serious, sometimes both.
Some are extremely short; others are more extended, such as *Kurz ist der
Schmerz* (Grief is short), presented as a farewell gift to Spohr in March
1815. There are a few isolated examples from earlier years (discounting the
spurious *Ta ta ta*, one of Schindler's more imaginative inventions and supposedly the basis for the second movement of the Eighth Symphony), but
from 1815 onwards Beethoven tended to write several each year. Works as
slight as *Brauchle, Linke* may not have much significance in themselves;

**Ex. 14.1** WoO 167

nevertheless, the canons forced Beethoven to focus on contrapuntal part-writing and voice manipulation as a central issue. He was certainly contemplating the nature of canons at this time, as is indicated by a little memorandum in his *Tagebuch* from early 1815: 'The best opening phrases in canons are built on harmony.'[7] And the polyphonic thinking that he was nurturing in these small canons can perhaps be seen as a foretaste of the great contrapuntal movements of his final period, where every note has a melodic and thematic as well as harmonic significance.

Imitative writing even began to infiltrate Beethoven's folksong settings. One melody in the batch of fifteen that he was setting in early 1815 (Group VI) had an opening phrase built entirely around a D major chord. In his setting, later published with the words 'Dim, dim is my Eye', he created imitation between the voice and the bass line, perhaps recalling (or prompting) the remark about canons built on harmony. Another noteworthy, though slight, piece of counterpoint in this batch of folksong settings appears in the final one, 'O swiftly glides'. Here, however, the stimulus for imitation came from Thomson, who wrote: 'Mr Beethoven will be good enough to harmonize the second repetition of this air for three voices: and if he can do so with a little imitation in a very simple form, this would be very agreeable.'[8] Beethoven's response, some light imitation at the start of the refrain, was the only true piece of counterpoint for the voices in any of his folksong settings. The setting, which was completed in May 1815 and sent with the rest of the batch the following month, pleased Thomson, for he asked for further use of imitation in Beethoven's next batch, towards the end of 1815. Beethoven, however, responded only with some voice exchange in a duet setting ('Sunshine'); and as the verses Thomson chose for this song were designed for a solo voice, the second voice, and the voice exchange, were suppressed on publication.

Beethoven's other main composing activity during the first part of 1815 was work on a new piano concerto, in D major (Hess 15). Extensive sketches for this survive in his two desk sketchbooks of the period (Mendelssohn 6 and Scheide), and further sketches appear in his first substantial pocket sketchbook (Mendelssohn 1; its only known predecessor is the very small one of 1811 mentioned in an earlier chapter). He even began writing out a full score, but this peters out in the middle of the solo exposition, and the work was left unfinished.[9] The surviving material clearly indicates, however, that he did not always wait until sketching was more or less completed before beginning the autograph score; many others of his autographs may therefore have been begun at a much earlier stage than is generally assumed. As in his two previous piano concertos, Beethoven introduces the soloist unusually early. In this case, however, the piano enters with a cadenza-like passage only after the orchestra has played the opening theme—a new procedure. It

---

[7] T-37.     [8] Cooper, *Folksong Settings*, 166–7, 139.
[9] See Cook, 'Unfinished'.

then remains silent for the remainder of the orchestral ritornello. The sketches give no clear indication of anything else very remarkable or unconventional in the rest of the movement, beyond an uncommonly symphonic approach such as is also found in his Violin Concerto. Indeed, the ideas and their working out seem almost too conventional at times, with little sign of progress from his previous three concertos.

Why was the concerto abandoned? Unlike some composers, Beethoven very rarely developed his ideas so far without bringing a work to completion. He possibly had reservations about its whole conception and its lack of innovation, or about specific features; but such musical problems generally served as a spur and a challenge to be overcome, and so it seems unlikely that he would have admitted defeat so easily. He may have simply set the concerto aside while he attended to another work, but this would not explain why he did not return to it later. Most likely, practical considerations intervened. No benefit concert was being planned (the last mention of one was in December 1814, whereas the concerto was not abandoned until about May 1815), and so there was no immediate incentive to finish the work. Beethoven himself was finding it increasingly difficult to play in public because of his deafness (one of his last recorded appearances was in January 1815, playing the accompaniment for his song 'Adelaide'). More significantly still, Archduke Rudolph, for whom the concerto may well have been intended, had at just about this time developed rheumatism that severely impeded his piano playing.[10] Thus there was little prospect of his ever recovering sufficiently to perform the concerto in public at some future concert. This was surely a major disincentive to completion of the work; and Beethoven never attempted another concerto. As a result of the work's abandonment, 1815 became the first year since the 1790s when Beethoven did not complete a large-scale work with orchestra, and it marked the start of a conspicuous decline in productivity that was not reversed until 1818.

The decline was gradual, however. Immediately after the sketches for the concerto appear some for the song 'Das Geheimnis' (The Secret, WoO 145), one of Beethoven's least-known but loveliest Lieder, which like many of his later songs is in varied strophic form. These sketches are in turn followed in the Scheide Sketchbook by several pages devoted to the Cello Sonata, Op. 102 No. 2—mainly the finale. The absence of substantial sketches for the first two movements, and for Op. 102 No. 1, suggests that Beethoven mislaid the sketchbook for a time and sketched these movements elsewhere; the contemporary pocket sketchbook is almost equally lacking in sketches for the missing movements, although it, too, has plenty for the finale of No. 2. Most likely, his final departure during the spring from Baron Pasqualati's house, where he had spent the best part of the previous

---

[10] Kagan, *Archduke Rudolph*, 5. Kagan indicates 1814 as the year when the rheumatism crippled him (no source is given); but the process was probably gradual, and he may have entertained hopes of recovery until well into 1815.

ten years, resulted in the temporary disappearance of many of his papers including the sketchbook. 'All my affairs are still in such confusion,' he wrote to Brauchle,[11] not long after the move.

The two cello sonatas were probably written at the request of Countess Erdödy, who would have wanted them for her cellist Linke and herself to play at Jedlesee. She showed much kindness to Beethoven after they renewed their friendship, and he was doubtless delighted to be able to compose something for her in return. The autograph of No. 1 in C major is headed '1815 towards the end of July', and No. 2 in D major is dated the beginning of the following month. The scores may have been completed a few weeks later, and sketching was certainly begun earlier, but these dates indicate the approximate period of composition.

The C major sonata is qualitatively different from any previous Beethoven sonata, or indeed any of his earlier compositions. That it belongs among his late works has been recognized ever since the days of Czerny, who wrote:

[It] belongs to the last period of Beethoven's career, in which he no longer embellished his ideas by the ordinary effects of the pianoforte, (as passages and the like,) but ordered the construction of the work in its simple grandeur; so that the player must the more endeavour to impart to each thought, as well as to each note, its full significance.[12]

It is indeed a clear harbinger of the style that was to pervade his music for the remainder of his life, possessing qualities that have been described in other late works as abstract, transcendent, or timeless. Here Beethoven turns away from the Romantic style of his Piano Sonata, Op. 90, into a new inner world of heightened sophistication—true musicians' music. It is remarkable how suddenly so many features of his late style emerge here, and if one had to identify the first work in this late style (a dangerously simplistic approach), it would surely be this innovative and prophetic sonata.

These broad impressions are confirmed by a closer look at the music. Most important is perhaps a new sense of polyphony that so often pervades the texture: not strict fugal writing in this case, but a texture where the lower parts have far greater motivic interest than in previous sonatas, with an obbligato style that owes something to the textures of Bach. This feature is evident as early as the third bar, where, after a striking opening for unaccompanied cello, part of its theme reappears in the bass of the piano part, with a countermelody above. Even where figuration is decorative rather than motivic, there is a new sophistication evident, with the figuration often employing novel and irregular patterns, as in the following extract from the Adagio section (Ex. 14.2); and the figuration is soon being treated like a motif, being passed from piano left-hand to the alto part (bar 4) and eventually the soprano (bar 5). The harmonic direction may also be

---

[11] A-539.     [12] Czerny, *Proper Performance*, 79/89.

*Declining productivity (1815–17)*

**Ex. 14.2**  Op. 102 No. 1/II

243

clouded, and there is increased use of irregular 6–4 chords, as is also illustrated in Ex. 14.2 (bar 5, second crotchet).

Another notable innovation is the overall structure of this sonata. Like Beethoven's three previous cello sonatas, it has no proper slow movement, but this time both of the main allegros are preceded by slow introductions, marked Andante and Adagio respectively. More remarkably still, material from the opening Andante is recalled between the central Adagio and the second Allegro. This new idea was to reappear in Beethoven's next piano sonata (Op. 101), and again in the Ninth Symphony (where all three earlier movements are recalled near the start of the finale). The resulting structure of the sonata, with increased fragmentation within movements, is counterbalanced by a greater sense of continuity between each section.

As in many other late works, Beethoven also explores here the concept of direct contrast between diametrically opposed ideas. The slow introduction in C major begins with a theme descending stepwise from tonic to dominant and then back again; the ensuing Allegro is unexpectedly in the relative minor, and its main theme ascends stepwise from tonic to dominant and back, providing a direct tonal and melodic contrast with the introduction. Sometimes Beethoven liked to reconcile the two opposing ideas at a later stage, and here he does so very neatly. In the second Allegro, the key is that of the opening Andante, but the binary rhythm and the rising and falling shape of the main theme recall the first Allegro. Thus the opposing ideas presented in the first movement are in a sense fused together in the finale, with an unusually high level of motivic sophistication that is common in Beethoven's late works. Not all features associated with his late period are evident in this sonata, but it certainly contains a surprisingly large number.

The new style was continued in the ensuing D major sonata. Here at last there is a full-scale slow movement for cello and piano, and it contains some highly intricate decoration—once again with strange and irregular patterns of figuration. This movement leads without a break into the finale, where Beethoven's growing interest in polyphony at last manifests itself in a fully-fledged fugue. Writing a fugue for the medium of cello and piano provides an enormous challenge, since there is one odd timbre in the middle of an otherwise uniform sonority, but the contrapuntal texture is here maintained more or less throughout—unlike in earlier pseudo-fugues such as the finale of the third 'Razumovsky' Quartet.

The other sizeable work completed in 1815 was Beethoven's short cantata *Meeresstille und glückliche Fahrt*, which had evidently been begun a couple of years earlier. It was probably finished during the autumn, and was first performed at a charity concert on Christmas Day that also included the première of the 'Namensfeier' Overture and an unseasonal performance of *Christus am Oelberge*. *Meeresstille*, it will be remembered, is a setting of a pair of poems by Goethe, and the direct contrast between the stasis of the first and the thrust of the second had attracted Beethoven, as he later informed Goethe. The first movement, the calm sea, is much the more original, and although it lacks the polyphonic style of Beethoven's late period it contains many features that anticipate later works—especially the *Missa solemnis* and the Ninth Symphony. In particular, he sought to intensify every image in the poem by the most vivid means possible, notably in the phrase 'in der ungeheuern Weite' ('in the monstrous expanse'), which he sketched at least thirty-seven times![13] He finally achieved a sense of vastness that almost defies description (Ex. 14.3): the close spacing at the start of the phrase suddenly changes to extremely wide spacing, with huge leaps in opposite directions for soprano and bass, and an extraordinarily long held chord on 'Weite', so that the vast expanse is illustrated in two different dimensions.

**Ex. 14.3** Op. 112 (voice parts)

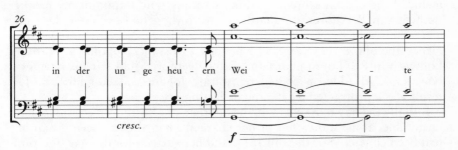

During the summer Beethoven appeared mostly cheerful, according to the English musician Charles Neate, who stayed near him in Baden for several weeks and purchased his three latest overtures for performance in London by the Philharmonic Society. In the autumn, however, his underlying gloom deepened. By about the end of September Marie Erdödy, one of his few close companions, had left Vienna with her three children and two musicians (she had long since separated from her husband), to take up residence on her estate in Croatia. Meanwhile his brother Carl's illness was worsening. Despite these setbacks, Beethoven remained determined to accomplish great deeds, as is indicated by entries in his *Tagebuch*. He considered ways of self-improvement: through travel; through acquiring portraits of great composers; through study and learning; and through contemplation of the Godhead. It was probably during the autumn that he copied down lengthy passages from Gottfried Herder, Zacharias Werner, and translations of Indian writings and of the orientalist William Jones, all tending to emphasize virtues such as wisdom, fidelity, endurance, and self-sacrifice. He wrote to Marie Erdödy about obtaining 'joy through suffering', and some of the

---

[13] Cooper, *Creative Process*, 230–8.

extracts in his *Tagebuch* express similar sentiments on the necessity of suffering:

Do you want to taste honey without suffering bee-stings? Do you desire the wreaths of victory without the danger of battle?

In adversity do not despair of seeing that day which will bring you joy for sorrow, and pleasure for grief.

Without tears fathers cannot instil virtue in their children, nor teachers the beneficial services of learning.[14]

Beethoven's spiritual and philosophical outlook had changed little from his early years, and was now being reinforced from a variety of new sources.

He was to need all his reserves of inner strength. Carl finally died of tuberculosis on Wednesday, 15 November, leaving a widow (Johanna) and their nine-year-old son Karl. The day before, Carl had written a will, which included the crucial sentence, 'Along with my wife I appoint my brother Ludwig van Beethoven co-guardian.' According to Beethoven, he came across this will by chance, and objected to Johanna being co-guardian. Hence the above sentence was amended to read: 'I appoint my brother Ludwig van Beethoven guardian.' After Beethoven had left his brother's, however, Carl added a codicil reinstating Johanna as co-guardian. The result was a protracted legal struggle lasting five years.

Initially the boy remained with his mother, but Beethoven considered her unsuitable. Some indication of her character has already been given. She had been convicted of theft in 1811, and her sexual morals were questionable: Karl had been conceived several months before her marriage, and in 1820 she was to give birth to an illegitimate daughter (who was, ironically, named Ludovica, the feminine of Ludwig); she then claimed alimony from one Johann Hofbauer, although the real father was a Hungarian named Raicz. She was also financially incompetent, but evidently had no scruples about misleading her creditors.[15] Beethoven was sufficiently aware of her faults to conclude that, whatever qualities of love and affection she might bring as a mother, she was unfit to be a co-guardian and was likely to be a bad influence on Karl. Once convinced of this, he put as much energy and determination into attempts at excluding her from the guardianship as he put into composition and all his other activities, for he saw Karl's education as a sacred duty that had been bestowed on him. Some of his subsequent comments about Johanna's evil nature may have been exaggerated as a result of his desire to put his case, but his references to her as 'Queen of the Night', after the character in *The Magic Flute*, certainly had some basis, and several other people referred to her behaviour unflatteringly.

---

[14] T-56, T-58, T-67. The first two are from Herder, the third from an unknown source (or written by Beethoven himself).

[15] Tellenbach, 'Psychoanalysis', 89–90; Wolf, *Neffenkonflikt*, 149.

Beethoven put his case concerning Karl's guardianship to the *Landrecht* on 28 November, and several meetings were held before a verdict was reached. He prepared several written documents, and amongst much verbiage and rhetoric, including sexist comments that women were incapable of supervising an older boy's education—comments that now seem strange but were probably normal at the time, when guardianship was seen essentially as a male duty—his case rested on two firm supports. First, he claimed that the codicil to Carl's will was added unwillingly under pressure from Johanna, and that the codicil was then taken from the building by the lawyer; when Beethoven returned, Carl urged him and Carl's nurse Anna Wildmann to retrieve the codicil quickly so that it could be withdrawn, but unfortunately the lawyer could not be found until too late. There is no reason to doubt the essence of this story, although Carl's precise intentions, when he was so near to death, are unclear.

The second basis of Beethoven's claim was the guardianship laws then in force. Guardians were expected to be of upright character and impeccable morals, and a criminal conviction was taken as proof of unsuitability. Thus, while it might have been difficult to prove his case on the grounds of Johanna's sexual attitudes and financial ineptitude, however well known these were, her conviction for theft was legally sufficient for her exclusion. Beethoven succeeded in persuading the *Landrecht* that what was legally correct was also right, proper, and in the boy's own interests, whatever Carl's intentions had been in the questionable codicil, and they ruled in his favour on 9 January 1816. Karl was removed from his mother on 2 February, and placed in a boarding school run by Cajetan Giannatasio del Rio. Johanna doubtless felt the loss acutely, especially as it came so soon after the loss of her husband. At least, however, she knew Karl was not completely gone but was on a kind of neutral ground; and she made strenuous efforts to visit him at the school, although Beethoven soon attempted to limit these visits because of the harmful effects they appeared to have on Karl.

The change in Beethoven's life through his adoption of Karl undoubtedly had a profound psychological effect on him. How profound the effect was is unclear, but at the very least it meant a reorientation of his priorities. Karl, rather than the Immortal Beloved or any other woman, became the focus of his love, and Karl's upbringing became his most important task, rivalling even composition itself. His love for the Immortal Beloved did not cease, but it became more spiritual, exalted, and distant; meanwhile any notion of bringing a wife into his new domestic situation was rejected—his Beloved was unavailable anyway. As he contemplated these thoughts, he resolved to compose some songs on the subject of distant love.

First came a setting of Reissig's poem 'Sehnsucht', in which the lover lies awake yearning for his absent beloved. Sketches for this song appear shortly after some for two canons dated 24 January 1816, and so the song was probably composed in February. The proximity with significant events in

Beethoven's personal life is striking, but the situation in the song did not match his exactly, and he seems to have cast around for something still more apposite. Poems about a distant beloved were common, and he had already set nearly a dozen, but in virtually all of these, including 'Sehnsucht', there is either some doubt about whether the love is mutual, or else there is an anticipation of reunion. Beethoven evidently wanted something depicting an absent beloved who would not return, and he may have actually proposed this subject to a local poet, Alois Jeitteles. At any rate, he obtained from Jeitteles a set of poems that were unknown and unpublished (unlike Reissig's 'Sehnsucht'), on the subject of distant love. Thus there are striking parallels with the creation of *Christus am Oelberge* in 1802–3: a personal crisis (isolation through deafness, or separation from a beloved), a resolve to overcome it, leading to a composition in which the crisis is represented indirectly in a newly written text by a local author—on isolation in suffering (Huber) or separated lovers (Jeitteles).

What Jeitteles produced was a series of six poems (possibly only five, with the middle one split in two by Beethoven) entitled *An die ferne Geliebte* (To the Distant Beloved). In Beethoven's autograph, dated April 1816, it is actually *An die entfernte Geliebte*—the word 'entfernte' implying one who has become distant, as was the case with his own beloved. In the first song the poet contemplates the distance between him and his beloved. In the second, he imagines where she is and longs to be there. The third and fourth songs portray natural go-betweens: the wind, the brook, the birds. Next come thoughts of happy domesticity for all creatures except the poet and his beloved. Finally he resolves to reach her heart through his songs; this idea also appears at the end of the first song—perhaps transplanted there by Beethoven himself.[16] That the love is reciprocated is made abundantly clear, and yet there is no hint of reunion: the whole essence of the text is the contemplation of love that will remain apart. The series of poems possesses a satisfying unity and continuity, which Beethoven exploited to create virtually an entirely new genre, the song cycle. Although various adumbrations can be found, including his own song pair 'Seufzer eines Ungeliebten' and 'Gegenliebe' (WoO 118), there is no direct precursor that could be regarded as a model.

Each of the first five songs, like the preceding 'Sehnsucht', is in varied strophic form, so that a folk-like repetition of the tune is enhanced in each verse by subtle variants in either voice or piano that mirror individual words or ideas in the text. Particularly striking in this respect is the middle stanza of the second song, where calm is depicted by the voice singing entirely on a monotone, while the piano carries the tune. Each song has a distinctive tempo and melody, yet the set is completely continuous, with a piano interlude smoothly linking each song to the next. This use of hybrid structures that lie somewhere between completely independent movements

---

[16]  See Kerman, 'An die ferne Geliebte', 126.

and merely subsidiary sections is a common feature in Beethoven's late period, and has already been seen in the Cello Sonata, Op. 102 No. 1. The last song is in the same key (E flat) as the first, and in its final stanza the melody of the first reappears, to be developed in an extended coda. This recall, another device found in various guises in many of Beethoven's late works, heightens the sense of cyclic unity in the work, and was to influence many of his successors. Another important 'late' characteristic in the cycle is the combination of the artless and the sophisticated. Each song has a simple, folk-like melody that sounds entirely spontaneous (although the melodies were in reality carefully crafted). The overall tonal structure of the cycle, however, shows great ingenuity, especially in the use of subdominant relationships. For example, the second song is in G major but its middle stanza is in C; this relationship matches that of the cycle as a whole, for the middle two songs are set in the overall subdominant, A flat. Some of Beethoven's earlier songs had been criticized as over-elaborate; here, however, he produces seemingly simple songs while creating a complex overall structure.

Whether Beethoven reflected on his own distant beloved while composing the song cycle is unclear, and on publication in October it was dedicated unrevealingly to Prince Lobkowitz. Like *Christus am Oelberge*, however, it does seem to have provided a vent for his emotions, and he could subsequently be more open about his beloved. In a letter to Ries written on 8 May, the month after the cycle was composed, he refers (with surely feigned casualness) to what had been a closely guarded secret: 'All best greetings to your wife. Unfortunately I have none. I found only one [woman], whom I shall surely never possess; but I am not a woman-hater on that account.'[17]

Not long after, about 12 September, he made a further revelation, telling Giannatasio that he had met a woman five years earlier with whom he longed to be united (the 'five years' is another pointer to Antonie Brentano, whom Beethoven had met about five–actually six—years earlier). The conversation was noted in an entry in the diary of Giannatasio's daughter Fanny, who recorded that Beethoven added, 'I have not yet been able to get it out of my mind'.[18] Further references apparently to Antonie (or Toni, as she was often known) appear about this time in Beethoven's *Tagebuch*: 'Nevertheless be as good as possible towards T; her devotion deserves never to be forgotten—although unfortunately advantageous consequences could never arise for you.' This was written about October, and a little earlier he had noted: 'With regard to T. there is nothing else but to leave it to God, never to go where one could do wrong out of weakness . . .' The identity of this 'T' cannot be confirmed; but these jottings seem to indicate that he was indeed unable to get his love for Toni out of his mind.

[17] A-632.
[18] TDR, iv. 534. Fanny also published essentially the same story many years later: see TF, 646.

Apart from his song cycle, Beethoven's main compositions in the first part of 1816 were some more folksong settings. George Thomson, not content with Scottish, Irish, and Welsh collections, now planned to produce a volume of continental folksongs. After applying unsuccessfully to contacts in Berlin and Madrid to send him local specimens, he wrote to Beethoven, in a letter dated 1 January 1816, asking him to find two or three airs from each of Germany, Poland, Russia, Tyrol, Venice, and Spain (he also sent a Ukrainian one that he had managed to obtain, along with five more Scottish melodies). It was a tall order: there were few collections of continental songs available, and none containing songs from such a wide range of countries. Nevertheless, Beethoven enthusiastically began gathering what was required, and fulfilled the commission almost precisely, collecting songs from all the countries specified. 'I think a folksong hunt is better than a manhunt of the heroes who are so highly praised,' he wrote later.[19] By the beginning of May he had assembled and provided settings for no fewer than eighteen melodies, which he sent to Thomson along with settings of the other six he had received. The eighteen came from a variety of sources, including operas and other stage works, issues of the *Allgemeine musikalische Zeitung*, and the Russian folksong collection that he had already used for the 'Razumovsky' Quartets; in some cases his source is unknown and the song may even have been communicated orally. Thus this is a remarkable collection for its date—the first truly international one of its kind. In some of the eighteen, he took over existing accompaniments virtually as they stood, so that his own contribution is little more than the introduction, postlude, and optional string parts. Other settings, however, are more original, like his settings of British melodies. A full list gives a clearer indication of the range of his sources, and the energy with which he must have collected his material (see Table 14.1[20]).

After despatching these two latest batches of folksongs on 2 May, Beethoven concentrated on two new works, a piano trio in F minor and a piano sonata in A major. Extensive sketches for both can be found in the Scheide Sketchbook. The new piano trio was being written out of affection for Marie Erdödy's three children, as he told her in a letter of 13 May. Even before he had posted the letter, however, he heard the tragic news that her son Gusti had died suddenly, and Beethoven promptly wrote another letter expressing his deeply-felt condolences. The indications are that the boy's tutor Brauchle had struck him on the head, causing a fatal injury, but nothing was proved. While Beethoven continued working on this new trio, he recalled a work drafted years earlier (perhaps in 1803) for the same medium: a set of variations on Wenzel Müller's theme 'Ich bin der Schneider Kakadu'. He now wrote out a fair copy of this, adding some revisions,[21] and

---

[19] A-1013.    [20] Based largely on Dorfmüller, 'Volksliederjagd'.
[21] The paper dates from 1816, and the piano compass used points to a late date. See Edelmann, 'Wenzel Müllers Lied', 94–100.

TABLE 14.1. Sources of Beethoven's 1816 collection of folksongs

| | |
|---|---|
| 1–3 | Three Russian songs (WoO 158/1/13–15) from Ivan Prach's *Collection of Russian Folksongs* |
| 4 | Tyrolean song (WoO 158/1/4), music by Franz Xaver Tost, from the play *Der Lügner* |
| 5–7 | Three Spanish songs (WoO 158/1/19–21), provenance unknown |
| 8 | Venetian song (WoO 157/12), provenance unknown |
| 9 | Portuguese/Spanish song (WoO 158/1/11) published in the *Allgemeine musikalische Zeitung* (*AmZ*) in 1799 |
| 10 | Portuguese song (WoO 158/1/12), provenance unknown |
| 11–12 | Two arias from Wenzel Müller's singspiel *Das neue Sonntagskind* (1794) |
| 13 | German, pseudo-Swiss song (WoO 158/1/18), music by Johann Friedrich Reichardt, published in the *AmZ* in 1811 |
| 14 | Venetian song (WoO 158/1/23), provenance unknown |
| 15–16 | Two Tyrolean songs (WoO 158/1/5–6) from a set of three by Friedrich Satzenhoven |
| 17–18 | Two Polish songs (WoO 158/9–10), provenance unknown |

offered it to Breitkopf & Härtel on 19 July, but without result (it was later published by Steiner).

Another interruption to work on the F minor piano trio and the A major sonata was a March for military band (WoO 24). Dated 3 June 1816 in the autograph, this is the longest and most impressive of all his military marches; despite its large forces, which include eight trumpets, six horns, and a serpent, it was apparently written fairly rapidly. Soon afterwards Beethoven received another commission from Thomson for folksong settings, further delaying progress on his two main projects, especially as he was once again asked to find airs from specific countries—Sweden, Denmark, Sicily, and Calabria (a task in which he was only partially successful). 'Finish the sonata and the trio,' he wrote in his *Tagebuch*,[22] evidently impatient at his slow progress. Practical matters also reduced his productivity: after investing 10,000 fl. WW from his recent earnings, apparently as a planned legacy for Karl, he had to arrange for Karl to have a hernia operation, which took place on 18 September; he also began making plans to take Karl home from boarding school and have him taught privately; and in September he received a visit from Peter Simrock, son of his old friend Nikolaus from Bonn. During the visit Peter acquired for his father's firm the publication rights for Beethoven's two new cello sonatas.

On 14–15 October Beethoven fell ill; he remained in bed for at least a week and stayed indoors for some time after that. By November, however,

---

[22] T-91.

he was well enough to finish the much delayed Piano Sonata in A (Op. 101) begun about six months earlier, which bears the date 'November 1816' at the head of the autograph score. It was published by Steiner three months later, in a series entitled *Museum für Klaviermusik* (Museum for Piano Music). This series was designed to include 'only musical products of recognized value, compositions that are particularly distinguished by aesthetically pure design (*Tonsatz*) developed with art, charm and clarity,' as was stated on the original title page. Unlike all the ephemeral music being produced by Viennese salon composers of the day, Steiner and Beethoven intended this work, and others in the series, to stand out as possessing lasting value. The notion of composing works for posterity, to be preserved like museum-pieces, seems never to have been far from Beethoven's thoughts.

The sonata displays an elevated, somewhat esoteric style typical of Beethoven's final period, continuing the pattern set by the cello sonatas the previous year, with its polyphonic textures and unusual structure. Indeed it follows the C major cello sonata quite closely in having a short Adagio section, followed by a reminiscence of the opening movement, immediately before the finale proper. In other respects, however, Op. 101 has no obvious precursors. The opening movement has the textures of a Bach prelude at the start and in several other passages, and begins on the dominant (like Op. 31 No. 2), producing a sense of tonal ambiguity that is only gradually resolved. Indeed the first strong tonic chord in root position does not appear until near the end of the recapitulation! Although the movement is in a fairly regular sonata form, it is on a minute scale—only 102 bars and no repeats—so that the main weight of the whole sonata is placed on the finale, as in so many of Beethoven's later works.

The second movement is, unusually, a march with trio, rather than a minuet or scherzo; then comes the brief Adagio that functions more as an introduction to the final Allegro than a movement in its own right. The Allegro is even more polyphonic and Bachian than the first movement, and includes an elaborate fugato in the development section. For a long time this fugato seems almost like a real fugue, with rigorously maintained four-part polyphony, but its tonal scheme is highly unorthodox: the 'fugue theme' is stated in A minor, but the answering voice, which should be in E minor, appears in C major, and the other two voices enter in D minor and A minor respectively. The incessant polyphony in the rest of the development section creates the impression of a titanic struggle against almost insuperable difficulties; victory, in the form of a long-awaited return to the major and the start of the recapitulation, is achieved only after the addition of unprecedented power in the form of a bottom E—a note that piano makers had only recently made available (Ex. 14.4). To avoid any ambiguity, Beethoven adds the words 'Contra E' at this point (originally he proposed inserting the names of all the left-hand notes here); it seems as much a shout of triumph as a warning to pianists unfamiliar with such a low note. This low E accompanies a double augmentation of the main theme in its lowest regis-

Ex. 14.4   Op. 101/IV

Contra E

ter, creating a thunderous discord that marks a thrilling climax to all the preceding counterpoint.

The technical difficulties of the movement are part of its underlying aesthetic, as Beethoven revealed in a half-humorous letter to Steiner, in which he proposed calling the work 'The Difficult-to-play Sonata' (a phrase adapted from a review of his Seventh Symphony), and added: 'For what is difficult is also beautiful, good, great etc. Hence everyone will realize that this is the most lavish praise that can be given, since what is difficult makes one sweat.'[23] In this sonata, too, he finally adopted German terminology, referring to the piano as the 'Hammerklavier' as well as using German tempo marks (which had also appeared in Op. 90). The sonata was dedicated to Dorothea Ertmann, a former pupil and formidable pianist, who was also a noted Bach enthusiast—hence a particularly suitable dedicatee.

The piano trio in F minor fared less well. Despite being offered to a publisher on 1 October, it remained unfinished, with no further sketching. Indeed, during the twelve months after the sonata Op. 101 was completed, Beethoven composed remarkably little. This uncharacteristic hiatus has been noted by many writers, who have offered various possible explanations. It could, for instance, have resulted from the repressive regime of Clemens von Metternich, which tended to inhibit cultural development with heavy censorship; other suggestions are that Beethoven had domestic problems with servants, that he was struggling with Johanna over Karl's guardianship, that he had to attend to Karl's personal needs, or that the

[23] A-749.

absence of friends such as Marie Erdödy, the illness of Antonie Brentano's youngest son Karl Josef, or the misfortunes of Josephine caused such depression that he felt unable to compose. None of these factors, however, can have affected his composing more than marginally. The guardianship struggle had entered a quiescent phase, while Karl remained at Giannatasio's boarding school throughout the period, needing no more attention from Beethoven than in any other year after Carl's death. And if Beethoven's productivity had been susceptible to the effects of either the political situation or the personal misfortunes of himself or his close friends, few periods in his life would have escaped unscathed. Much the most plausible explanation for his sharp decline in productivity during 1817 is the one provided consistently and unequivocally by Beethoven himself:

On October 15th I succumbed to an inflammatory fever, from the after effects of which I am still suffering, and my art also.
(Letter to Kanka, late March 1817)

Since my illness I have been able to compose only extremely little.
(Letter to Neate, 19 April 1817)

Owing to my illness, since I can compose very little, my earnings are meagre.
(Letter to Marie Erdödy, 19 June 1817)

If my health is completely restored, so that I can again earn more money . . .
(Letter to Giannatasio, 1 November 1817)[24]

Thus Beethoven asserted that the 'inflammatory fever' contracted in mid-October was responsible for his lack of substantial works up to November 1817. The illness may not have been life-threatening, but its after-effects were clearly long-lasting, leaving him weak and debilitated for many months. Several types of viral infection can have this effect, and there may have been other complicating factors during the year, for his health fluctuated considerably. Emotional suffering may have played a part too, but he tended to combat this with activity rather than inertia. Whatever the root cause of his illness, he had to stay in bed or at least indoors for long periods. Almost as frustrating for him as the illness itself were the numerous remedies prescribed by his doctors:

From April 15th until May 4th I had to take six powders daily and six bowls of tea. . . . After that I had to take another kind of powder, also six times daily; and I had to rub myself three times a day with a volatile ointment. Then I had to come here [Heiligenstadt] where I am taking baths. Since yesterday I have been taking another medicine, namely, a tincture, of which I have to swallow 12 spoonfuls daily.[25]

Much of what little energy he had was thus being devoted to futile efforts to overcome an illness that was unlikely to respond to such treatment.

[24] A-771, A-778, A-783, A-834.    [25] A-783.

The after-effects of the fever also set back Beethoven's plans to bring Karl to his own home. In his *Tagebuch* he reflected how much better it is when children live at home rather than in an institution, but that he could not contemplate bringing Karl home just yet. The boy continued to be educated at Giannatasio's boarding school throughout 1817, and it was agreed in May that his mother should make regular payments from her pension towards his education.[26] She was allowed to see him occasionally, but this arrangement proved unsatisfactory after her visit on 10 August. A few days after the visit, Beethoven told Giannatasio that he had tried to treat her more tolerantly in the hope that she would reform her ways; but she had evidently responded by spreading malicious gossip about Beethoven to Giannatasio and Karl, just as she had earlier said unkind things about Giannatasio to Beethoven. He therefore decided she should be allowed to see Karl only twice a year from then on,[27] and indeed it was more than six months before her next visit.

Some writers have suggested that Beethoven developed an all-consuming possessive instinct for Karl, and a hatred for Johanna.[28] The evidence does not support either of these views. His love for Karl was so deep that he was prepared to make enormous sacrifices; but his 'possessive instinct' did not override Karl's own needs, and Beethoven recognized that Karl was better situated at Giannatasio's than at his own house, at least for the time being. Later he even wanted to send Karl to an institute many miles away—which clearly demonstrates that he did not allow his own desire for possession to take priority over Karl's development. His supposed hatred for Johanna is also a fallacy. He saw the bad example she was setting, but he insisted that Karl should always honour her, without imitating her example. Shortly before her visit in August 1817 he showed notable sensitivity to her feelings: 'It might hurt Karl's mother to have to visit her child at the house of a stranger; and in any case it is a less charitable arrangement than I should like.'[29] In private prayers jotted in his *Tagebuch* early in 1818 he wrote:

And Thou Almighty seest into my heart, knowest that I have set aside my own welfare for my dear Karl's sake, bless my work, bless the widow [Johanna]. . . . Thou seest my innermost heart and knowest how it pains me to have to make someone [presumably Johanna] suffer through my good works for my dear Karl!!![30]

These are not the words or actions of someone filled with hatred. Nor are Freudian explanations of a love–hate relationship between Beethoven and Johanna, in which he alternated rapidly and frequently between animosity and conciliation, a satisfactory account of his behaviour towards her. He had been placed in an invidious position, having to associate so closely with someone whose character was so far from ideal, but he attempted to

---

[26] Anderson, *Letters*, iii. 1366–7.  [27] A-800.

[28] See, for example, Elliot Forbes, in TF, 698; his account is based on Sterba, *Nephew*, which has been discredited as a balanced account of Beethoven's relationship with Karl.

[29] A-793.  [30] T-159, T-160.

behave magnanimously towards her in general. The exception was when Karl's interests were involved, for Beethoven rightly saw these as paramount. If they conflicted with his own interests, he would make sacrifices; if they conflicted with Johanna's desires, he would oppose her by every means possible, including separating her from Karl for lengthy periods. His apparent aggression towards her, far from being 'a denial of his desire for her',[31] derived solely from her wrongdoing and from his fear that she would have a bad moral influence on Karl. No doubt his actions will continue to be criticized by those who do not share, or even understand, his high ideals. His behaviour, however, was not due to pathological fantasies about his relationships with Johanna and Karl, but can be seen—like his music—as a reflection of his lofty ambitions, his high moral principles, and ultimately, his underlying religious beliefs and devotion to God. Whether his actions were indeed always in Karl's best interests can be contested, but that he intended them to be cannot be doubted.

During his long illness of 1816–17 Beethoven turned to Nanette Streicher for help with domestic matters. He had known her and her husband Johann, piano manufacturers, since the 1790s, but it seems to have been only from about the start of 1817 that she became involved in his everyday affairs. From this date onwards he wrote numerous letters to her about his (and her) health, his problems with servants, his lodgings, arrangements with his nephew, and even his laundry, and they frequently visited each other. He also wrote to her rather than her husband in July 1817 when he wanted Johann Streicher to adapt a piano to be as loud as possible. His hearing became perceptibly weaker during his illness (perhaps because of it), and he was now prepared to hire a new piano specially adapted for his needs, since his other pianos were no longer adequate.

Apart from Nanette, Beethoven still had few true friends in Vienna, and believed he was being treated badly by most people around him. 'True friendship can only be founded on the connection of similar natures,' he wrote in his *Tagebuch* in April or May.[32] One solution would have been to travel, and his letters and *Tagebuch* indicate that at this time he frequently contemplated a journey, with several destinations being considered. Around March he wrote: 'There is no other way to save yourself except to leave here, only through this can you again lift yourself to the heights of your art, whereas here you are submerged in vulgarity.'[33] Nothing came of these intentions, however. He had too many ties in Vienna—not least his nephew—and probably had insufficient energy to make the necessary arrangements for a long journey.

Beethoven apparently spent much of this period of relative inactivity reading and meditating. Some clues to his reading material are found in his *Tagebuch*, where he copied down proverbs and short excerpts from Kant, Schiller, Pliny, and Ovid, while he also noted a few prayers and what appear

---

[31] Solomon, *Beethoven*, 236.    [32] T-127.    [33] T-119.

to be private thoughts of his own. One of them, 'Sensual gratification without a spiritual union is and remains bestial,' has sometimes been taken as evidence that he was visiting prostitutes and writing from recent personal experience; but it could equally indicate his determination to keep clear of such a lifestyle, just as another comment, 'Tranquillity and freedom are the greatest treasures,' does not indicate he was experiencing such blessings at that time. Religious thoughts began to infiltrate his letters. He wrote to Nanette in July, 'Today happens to be Sunday, and if I am to read you out something more from the Gospel, then "Love one another" etc.' And at some point in his life, perhaps around this period, he copied out three sayings derived (via Schiller's *Die Sendung Moses*) from ancient Egypt, on the nature of the Godhead:

I am that which is.
I am all, what is, what was, what will be; no mortal has uplifted my veil.
He is One and of himself, and to this One all things owe their being.[34]

These sayings seem to sum up Beethoven's perception of God, and according to Schindler Beethoven had this copy framed in glass and kept on his writing desk.

Beethoven's meagre output during the twelve months after completion of Op. 101 began with two Lieder (WoO 147–8). The first, 'Ruf vom Berge', is a simple strophic setting of a reworking by Treitschke of a folksong published many years earlier by Gottfried Herder. Like *An die ferne Geliebte*, the text concerns an inaccessible distant beloved, and again Beethoven must have obtained it direct from the author, since Treitschke's version first appeared in 1817 along with Beethoven's music. The implication must be that Beethoven was still thinking of his own far-off beloved. The setting is very short (a mere twenty-one short bars), a sign of his limited energy, and is perhaps closer than any of his other Lieder to the style of his folksong settings, with a prelude that hints at the melody, and an extended postlude after the final stanza. 'Ruf vom Berge' was written in December 1816, and was closely followed by 'So oder so', printed in February 1817 shortly after being composed. The text here is more philosophical, but the setting is scarcely any more substantial.

Beethoven had prepared eleven more folksong settings (Groups X-XI) for Thomson in September 1816, but they were not quite ready for despatch when he fell ill in October. They were still sitting in his room when Thomson informed him that plans for a volume of continental songs had been abandoned because of difficulties in translation, and that only two of the eleven were therefore needed. Unwilling to forgo a fee for work already done, Beethoven sent all eleven in the usual way. Before they had arrived, however, Thomson sent a further ten Scottish melodies, along with a letter dated 24 January, and offered 50 ducats for settings of these ten plus the two

---

[34] TF, 481–2.

that were still wanted from the previous batch (not knowing that these were already on their way). Beethoven was thus faced with a problem: how to send twelve settings and obtain the 50 ducats (two more than the normal rate) with only ten new melodies. He solved it in a most unexpected and original way: 'You spoke to me before of a Danish and a Sicilian song, which I could not then find despite all my efforts; I have now succeeded in obtaining them and here they are instead of the two Scottish ones'.[35] Regarding the language, he presumably thought that the Sicilian song would not cause difficulty since it had a Latin text ('O Sanctissima'), and he hoped the Danish one would also be acceptable 'in view of the affinity of the English language with Danish'! These two settings were sent to Thomson along with the other ten (Group XII) on 26 February; neither was published by Thomson, although he expressed admiration for the Sicilian one, which does indeed have a most evocative setting.

After completing these twelve songs Beethoven composed practically nothing more until 3 May. That day, to commemorate the sudden death of his friend Wenzel Krumpholz the previous day, he jotted down a twelve-bar setting, for three male voices, of the Song of the Monks from Schiller's *Wilhelm Tell*. The text evidently meant much to him, for he had copied it into his *Tagebuch* a few months earlier. His next completed work, not produced until August, was an arrangement for string quintet of his Piano Trio, Op. 1 No. 3. This was written in rather curious circumstances. A certain Herr Kaufmann brought to Beethoven his own rather literal arrangement of the trio. Beethoven had it copied out, despite ridiculing it as a '3-part quintet', and then made substantial revisions to the part-writing. He did, however, allow some of Kaufmann's more imaginative details to stand and even built on them in places.[36] Thus the work, eventually published by Artaria as Op. 104, was clearly not entirely his own, but more on a par with piano arrangements by Ries and others that had been undertaken under Beethoven's supervision and published as his in earlier years. He composed nothing more until towards the end of the year, when he completed a short Fugue for string quintet (Op. 137), an even shorter movement (of recent discovery) for string quartet, and the song 'Resignation'. He had worked intermittently on the song since about 1813, and it seems to embody something of his deeply depressed state of mind.

Thus it appears that, during his long period of debility, he was capable of short bursts of activity: there are plenty of letters (mostly quite brief) from this period; folksong settings, where the basic material was already present, could be managed, as could arrangements or short pieces; he was also able to spend time and effort working out metronome marks (using a newly refined version of Maelzel's invention) for his eight symphonies and the Septet (the figures were published by Steiner towards the end of the year); but the prolonged effort required for a sizeable work was evidently beyond

---

[35] A-757, dated 15 Feb. 1817.    [36] See Tyson, 'Authors of Op. 104'.

him throughout 1817, and the paucity of compositions provides some indication of the enormous and sustained energy he customarily put into each act of creation. Only when his health had recovered sufficiently could he return to original works of great substance.

His difficulties are illustrated by his attempts at a new symphony. On 9 June Ries wrote to Beethoven on behalf of the Philharmonic Society of London, inviting him to visit the city the following January, and to bring two new symphonies for use during the Society's next season, which was to run from February to June. Beethoven's reply of 9 July accepted the invitation, promised to have two new symphonies ready, and stated that he was 'beginning at once to work on composing these symphonies'.[37] Although he proposed certain conditions which the Philharmonic Society did not accept, it seems that he eventually agreed to go. The fee offered for the two symphonies and his presence for the season was 300 guineas, roughly twice his annual salary of 3400 fl. WW (which about that time became fixed at the rate of 5:2 in relation to the newly re-established *Conventionsmünze*, yielding 1360 fl. CM). Such an incentive, coupled with his long-expressed desire to travel, should have been sufficient inducement to begin intensive work on at least one new symphony.

Signs of this intention can indeed be found in his sketches. The Scheide Sketchbook of 1815–16, like the Petter Sketchbook of 1811–12, had included numerous little jottings—some even marked as symphony sketches—that provided a fund of ideas for possible future use. One of these ideas was indeed later taken up as the theme of the second movement of the Ninth Symphony, but in the Scheide Sketchbook there is no clear indication that this was to be its function. Shortly after the agreement with the Philharmonic Society, however, come the first definite signs that Beethoven was now planning a new symphony in D minor. Losses of sketch material from the second half of 1817 make it difficult to see much pattern,[38] but he certainly made very little progress at this stage. Sketches from early 1818 show that he had hardly advanced beyond the opening of the first movement, and could not possibly have had even one symphony ready much before the end of the Philharmonic Society's season. Such lack of progress was probably one reason why he did not make the journey. It confirms that, whatever were the underlying causes, the lack of the energy required for composing a major work remained with Beethoven right to the end of 1817.

[37] A-786.  [38] See Brandenburg, 'Neunten Symphonie', 98–100.

# 15

# Gigantism (1818–20)

During 1817 Beethoven's hearing had worsened, and by early 1818 it had degenerated so much that he began using conversation books—little notebooks in which friends and visitors wrote down their side of conversations, with Beethoven generally responding verbally. He also soon began using these books for occasional memoranda and even musical sketches. The earliest such book known dates from February to March 1818, although no more survive from that year. Similar one-sided conversations were sometimes jotted down on odd scraps of paper or a slate that could be wiped clean afterwards. On better days, too, he could often still manage with an ear trumpet. Thus the notebooks—even those that survive—do not give anything like a full record of his conversations; and without his responses (except rarely), the information they provide is tantalizingly incomplete. Nevertheless, they reveal an enormous amount about his everyday life in his last few years, especially when read in conjunction with other documents.[1]

Despite Beethoven's increasing deafness, by the beginning of 1818 the worst phase of his general debility was over. He was at last able to bring Karl home to live with him, and the boy moved out of Giannatasio's school on 24 January. Thereafter he was instructed by a personal tutor, while Beethoven himself spent two and a half hours a day teaching him music.[2] A new servant known as Peppi was appointed, with the help of Nanette Streicher, and she proved to be a good cook, albeit not entirely satisfactory in other ways. Beethoven's compositional energies were also gradually returning, and he began intensive work on a new piano sonata in B flat, the earliest sketches for which probably date from December 1817. This was the famous 'Hammerklavier', a nickname that seems more appropriate for this sonata than for its gentler predecessor Op. 101, which had also used the word 'Hammerklavier' for piano on its title page.

Amongst the sketches for the first movement is an idea for a choral work for Archduke Rudolph, using the text 'Vivat Rudolphus' and a melody

---

[1] A painstakingly thorough edition of the conversation books is in BKh. It must be mentioned here that, after Beethoven's death, Schindler appropriated the conversation books and proceeded to insert numerous fictitious conversations. These misled many later writers including Thayer, and the forgery was not discovered until the 1970s (see BKh, esp. vol. 7).

[2] Anderson, *Letters*, iii. 1368.

resembling that of the 'Hammerklavier'. This choral work was soon abandoned, but the concept of writing a work specifically for Rudolph was transferred to the sonata itself, which from an early stage was intended for Rudolph's nameday (17 April), as Beethoven himself stated. The first two movements were indeed ready by then, with the remaining two being worked out during the summer at Mödling. The sonata is the first manifestation of a new feature in Beethoven's late style—one which may be termed gigantism. Just as, in 1803, he had begun composing on an enlarged scale after the crisis at Heiligenstadt, with works such as the *Eroica* and the 'Waldstein' Sonata, so now in 1818 the scale was enlarged again, resulting in a series of works of unprecedented proportions—the 'Hammerklavier', the Ninth Symphony, the Diabelli Variations and the *Missa solemnis*—all begun within quite a short space of time. Beethoven's prolonged lay-off from composition, his enhanced awareness of the greatness of the created universe and its Creator, and a repetition of his 1803 desire to extend the scope of his own creations, may be suggested as possible causes for this new approach, in which his thoughts operated on an expanded plane, not just in terms of length of composition but in several other dimensions. Thus the 'Hammerklavier' was designed to be grander, more elaborate and more imposing than any previous sonata, bar none; Czerny reports that Beethoven actually told him, while the work was in progress, 'I am writing a sonata now which is going to be my greatest'.[3] Its unprecedented length is combined with such features as extraordinary power and complexity, and a vast tonal range in which practically every key-signature from six flats to six sharps is used.

The power of the sonata is evident right from the start, where the first three sounds combine to form a gigantic *fortissimo* chord spanning over four octaves, followed by a suggestion of the rhythm 'Vivat vivat Rudolphus' (Ex. 15.1). The initial left-hand leap—two octaves plus major 3rd—has thematic significance for all four movements. Nevertheless, it is the concept of chains of falling 3rds that provides much of the underlying melodic and harmonic structure of each movement, helping to bind the

Ex. 15.1 Op. 106/I

---

[3] Czerny, *Proper Performance*, 10.

work into a unified whole. Descending 3rds even provide much of the tonal architecture of the work: the second subject, for example, is in G major, a 3rd below the tonic, rather than in F, and the key of the slow movement is a major 3rd below the original tonic, though it is notated as F sharp minor. The second movement, a scherzo, is relatively brief, but the ensuing slow movement is Beethoven's longest—a huge sonata form with extended coda. It is also one of his most highly emotional, marked 'Appassionato e con molto sentimento', and its deeply anguished lyricism derives from the same world as the Cavatina in the String Quartet, Op. 130. The first subject is in a regular sixteen-bar structure, with the second half then repeated and extended before being broken off by a sudden rest (bar 27). The transition, unusually, is equally lyrical, consisting of an almost operatic, Italianate melody with some highly ornate decoration. The second subject is in D (another example of a descending 3rd), and contains dialogue for the right hand between registers a full four octaves apart, while the left hand plays a quiet accompaniment in the middle. During the first theme there is much emphasis on the chord of G major, the flattened supertonic, which greatly intensifies the mood of profound tragedy; the second subject eventually reappears in this key in an extended coda, before the music returns to F sharp, with fragments of both the transition theme and the first subject.

The finale begins with a slow introduction in which metre is temporarily abandoned, evoking a sense of timelessness. Beethoven instructs the performer to count in semiquavers, but much of the introduction is written without bar-lines, so that the enormous first 'bar' lasts for thirty-five semiquavers (excluding pauses), and the second is even longer. The main movement, following the example of Beethoven's last cello sonata, is a fugue, but 'with some licences', including not beginning the fugue theme itself until the sixth bar of the Allegro risoluto. The theme starts with a large leap, reminiscent of that at the start of the sonata, and is enormously long, generating a massive fugue that incorporates traditional contrapuntal devices including augmentation (bars 84 ff.), retrograde (bars 143 ff.) and inversion (bars 198 ff.). In none of these variants does the theme flow as naturally as in its original form, and the sense of conflict is thus heightened—particularly in the augmentation, where because of the triple metre the accentuation is distorted, and in the retrograde, where the runs have a disconcerting tendency to halt on weak semiquavers, resulting in further rhythmic disruption. At bar 240 a new theme in contrasting style is introduced; this is then combined in counterpoint with the original fugue theme, following the example of some of Bach's fugues. It is the main theme, however, that predominates towards the end—especially its trill, which is developed as an important motif during much of the movement (one of many examples where Beethoven uses an ornamental device motivically), and is eventually stretched into enormous trills lasting several bars (bars 359–70). In every way, this work is a giant among sonatas.

Shortly before the sonata was finished, Beethoven received an appropriately magnificent piano, sent by Thomas Broadwood of London in recognition of his outstanding ability, and bearing the autographs of several musicians living in London, including Ries and Johann Baptist Cramer. Beethoven was informed in January that the instrument was on its way, and the news may even have induced him to concentrate on the 'Hammerklavier' rather than his projected symphony during the ensuing months. He wrote thanking Broadwood on 3 February, and although the piano was delayed at Trieste, it eventually reached him in Mödling in late spring. For the rest of his life he greatly treasured the instrument, perhaps even preferring it to the Streicher pianos that he had always admired so much.

The imposing character of the 'Hammerklavier' Sonata may reflect not only the grandeur of the new piano but also the strength of the friendship that had developed between Beethoven and Archduke Rudolph. Beethoven often expressed rather sycophantically his desire to be of service to the Archduke, and his pleasure at being in his company. On the other hand he tended to be much less complimentary in his references to Rudolph in letters to other people, and so it is difficult to assess his true feelings about their friendship. It could never be on entirely equal terms, a proper 'union of souls', since the relationship was based on the inequalities of both teacher/pupil and artist/patron, with an age gap of over seventeen years; nor was it in all senses a 'connection of similar natures' such as Beethoven believed necessary for true friendship—Beethoven's irascible nature contrasted strongly with Rudolph's distinctly gentle character. It seems clear, however, that Beethoven had a profound affection for him, and their moral and religious outlooks were broadly similar.

Rudolph did not make any entries in Beethoven's conversation books. This may have been because his soft voice was unusually clear; more probably, however, it was because their meetings almost always took place at the Archduke's palace, where more elegant facilities than scrappy notebooks would have been available for written conversation. Rudolph occasionally provided Beethoven with financial help beyond the regular annuity, and appears to have paid extra for his composition lessons.[4] But he may at times have asked for money in return. Beethoven wrote in March 1818: 'Through my unfortunate connection with this Archduke I have been brought almost to beggary. I can't see people starve. I must help them.'[5] The implication is that Rudolph had induced Beethoven to make substantial contributions to help the needy.

Connections between the two men were further strengthened in early 1818, when Beethoven composed a four-bar theme entitled 'O Hoffnung' (WoO 200) and set Rudolph the task of composing some variations on it. Rudolph responded by composing during the year a set of forty variations,

---

[4] Kagan, *Archduke Rudolph*, 18.    [5] A-895.

more than in any of Beethoven's sets (although the theme was very short). The variations are preceded by an extended introduction in the tonic minor, an idea probably derived from Beethoven's 'Kakadu' Variations, completed two years earlier but still unpublished; and the last five variations are much more extended ones in which the theme is greatly developed, culminating in a grand fugal coda of nearly a hundred bars. Beethoven looked through Rudolph's composition as if it were one of his own, making numerous amendments. Rudolph then wrote out a second version incorporating these amendments, and again Beethoven examined the score in great detail, with many further suggestions, which were also adopted by Rudolph.[6] The final result, published as Rudolph's work in 1819, owes much to Beethoven's teaching and example, as might be expected, even in passages he left untouched. The partwriting is less skilled and the methods of variation not so imaginative as in Beethoven's own compositions, but the work is a remarkable fusion of ideas by the two composers, and Beethoven described it as a masterpiece. He surely recalled it many times when writing his own next sets of variations.

In contrast to his work on the 'Hammerklavier', Beethoven made little headway with his two new symphonies during early 1818, and must have abandoned the idea of a visit to England that winter long before he wrote to Ries on 5 March telling him of the decision: 'Please inform the Philharmonic Society that my poor health has prevented me from undertaking the journey. But I hope perhaps to make a complete recovery in the spring and then later in the year to avail myself of the offer the Society has made to me . . .'[7] Some sketches for the Ninth Symphony are found amongst those for the 'Hammerklavier' in about February–March, but Beethoven was evidently finding it as difficult to make progress as he had done with his First Symphony in 1795–6 and the Fifth in 1804–5. This suggests that he may once again have been planning something radically new; but these early sketches reveal little about the proposed scale of the work. Some inkling that the new gigantism was intended to spread beyond the limits of the 'Hammerklavier' can, however, be gained from among his jottings. In January or February he noted in his *Tagebuch* a plan: 'To write a national song on the Leipzig October and perform this every year. N.B. each nation with its own march and the *Te deum laudamus*.'[8] The 'Leipzig October' refers to the defeat of Napoleon at the Battle of Leipzig in 1813. Beethoven was thus planning a grand celebratory work embracing many nations, containing echoes of his *Wellingtons Sieg* but incorporating a religious dimension in the form of the Te Deum. The Te Deum in its German form ('Herr Gott dich loben wir') resurfaced in another idea sketched

---

[6] Kagan, *Archduke Rudolph*, 76–108. Susan Kagan has edited the work in Archduke Rudolph of Austria, *Forty Variations on a Theme by Beethoven* . . . (Recent Researches in the Music of the Nineteenth and Early Twentieth Centuries, xxi, Madison, 1992).
[7] A-895.  [8] T-153.

about two months later, when it was merged with his projected symphonies:

Adagio Cantique — Pious Song in a symphony in the old modes, either on it own or as an introduction to a fugue — Herr Gott dich loben wir, alleluja. Perhaps the whole second symphony characterized in this way, where then the voices enter in the last movement or already in the Adagio. The orchestral violins etc. in the last movement are increased tenfold. Or the Adagio is repeated in some way in the last movement, where first the voices enter one by one — In the Adagio text Greek myth, ecclesiastical canticle — in the Allegro festival of Bacchus.[9]

There is an extraordinary pool of ideas here, some of them incompatible. Two concepts, however, stand out as particularly significant in the present context. One is the all-embracing nature of the work, with texts incorporating Greek myth, Bacchanalian feast and pious Christian canticle. The other is the huge overall scale implied, with the symphony being enlarged by massed voices and a tenfold increase in the strings. This sketch is therefore the first indication that an enlarged scale of thought had become an integral part of Beethoven's creativity and not just confined to a single sonata. At this stage the Ninth Symphony was still intended to have an instrumental finale, and these ideas were for the Tenth Symphony; but they were eventually thrown into the melting-pot from which the Ninth was fashioned, and several features of its finale are foreshadowed here, including the use of voices and the all-embracing nature of the text. Another noteworthy feature of the above sketch is the reference to the old modes. Beethoven was now seeking an expansion of the entire tonal system of twenty-four keys by reviving the church modes, which he had not used since his studies with Albrechtsberger. In preparation for their revival he wrote out two of them—white-note scales based on A and D—on the inside covers of his conversation book of February–March 1818, adding a bass line to create two-part harmony. Before long, modal elements were infiltrating his compositions, as will be seen.

No sketchbooks of either type survive between August 1818, when Beethoven was finishing off the 'Hammerklavier', and the following April. During the first part of this period, however, he was preoccupied with composing eight more folksong settings and twelve sets of variations for George Thomson. Thomson had by now published two volumes of Irish settings by Beethoven, one of Welsh and one of Scottish, but sales were poor. He therefore proposed in June 1818 that, as there were many flautists in Edinburgh, the twenty-five Scottish settings published, plus the eight new ones, should have their violin part arranged for flute *ad lib.*, and that Beethoven compose twelve sets of variations, for piano and optional flute, on folksongs he had set previously. Such a request might not have pleased Beethoven, since he

---

[9] Bonn, Beethoven-Archiv, BSk 8/56; for dating, see Brandenburg, 'Neunten Symphonie', 103.

had in earlier years expressed distaste for both optional accompaniments and music for flute. Nevertheless, he dutifully fulfilled both these requests, also accepting Thomson's suggestion that most of the variations should be on British themes but that two or three should be Tyrolean. He worked fairly intensively on this material during the next few months, and despatched the eight settings and twelve sets of variations on 18 November. In choosing the British melodies he seems to have been guided by personal preference, for his previous settings are scattered throughout both his own manuscripts and the volumes Thomson had published; four are taken from the Scottish volume, one from the Welsh, and four from the two Irish volumes. Beethoven also selected one British melody that he had not previously set: 'Of Noble Race was Shinkin'. This was an old song, sometimes attributed to Purcell, but where Beethoven obtained it is unknown. The last two in the set are Tyrolean themes that he had sent to Thomson in 1816. A full list of the twelve is as follows (Table 15.1).

TABLE 15.1. Twelve Sets of Variations, 1818

|  | Name | Opus/No. | No. in Thomson Coll. |
| --- | --- | --- | --- |
| 1 | O thou art the Lad | 107/9 | Scottish, 3 |
| 2 | The Highland Watch | 107/10 | Scottish, 5 |
| 3 | Bonny Laddie | 107/2 | Scottish, 7 |
| 4 | O Mary at thy Window be | 107/8 | Scottish, 19 |
| 5 | The Cottage Maid | 105/1 | Welsh, 3 |
| 6 | Of Noble Race | 105/2 | — |
| 7 | Sad and Luckless | 105/4 | Irish, ii.3 |
| 8 | Put Round the Bright Wine | 105/5 | Irish, ii.13 |
| 9 | The Pulse of an Irishman | 107/4 | Irish, ii.17 |
| 10 | English Bulls | 105/6 | Irish, i.12 |
| 11 | I bin a Tyroler bua | 107/1 | — |
| 12 | A Madel, ja a Madel | 107/5 | — |

Each piece consists of an original harmonization followed by three, four or five variations. There is usually a short coda, and sometimes also a brief linking passage before the final variation. The flute part is cunningly contrived so that when it is performed it sounds absolutely essential, but when it is omitted the texture still seems complete. The characteristics of Beethoven's late style appear only intermittently rather than consistently. There is an enormous range and variety of figuration patterns, some conventional and some highly unusual, and there is a richly ornate adagio variation in 'The Highland Watch'. Polyphonic writing comes to the fore occasionally, notably in the coda of 'The Cottage Maid', which begins with a fugato in G minor before reverting to G major. A change of mode is also sometimes adopted for a whole variation; the most striking example of this is in 'I bin a Tyroler bua' in E flat major, where there is a variation in E minor instead of E flat minor. Vestiges of the 'Hammerklavier' Sonata appear in the coda of 'Sad and Luckless' (now known by its later title, 'The Last Rose of Summer'), where there is an extraordinary chain of seven descending thirds in the bass, taking the music from E flat to C flat, followed by a neat shift back to the tonic. Although individually each set of variations seems rather slight compared with some of Beethoven's others, together they form a very large and impressive compendium of variation techniques, some of which seem to foreshadow ideas in the Diabelli Variations.

Despite Beethoven's efforts to keep the music technically simple, Thomson found Nos. 2, 4, and 11 too difficult and unsuited to the Scottish lady amateurs who were his intended market, and asked for three replacements in early 1819. Beethoven responded with two sets (Op. 107 Nos. 6 and 7) on tunes from his earlier folksong settings, and one set (Op. 105 No. 3) on an Austrian tune, 'A Schüsserl und a Reindl' (a tune related to the well-known 'Gaudeamus igitur'). These pleased Thomson greatly, but he had meanwhile decided that No. 12 in the original set was also too difficult, and so he asked Beethoven for yet another one (Op. 107 No. 3). In the end he published nine sets before abandoning the project. Beethoven then reorganized the sixteen sets into two groups, and had them published as Op. 105 and Op. 107 by Artaria and Simrock respectively.

Throughout this period Beethoven was beset by pressing personal problems, although his composing remained relatively unaffected. Johanna had become increasingly frustrated by the severe limits Beethoven had imposed on her meetings with Karl, and took to bribing his servants and meeting Karl in secret, as Beethoven reveals in a letter written in June 1818. At that time Karl was receiving tuition, along with several other boys, from the local priest in Mödling, Johann Baptist Fröhlich, but he left after a month. Fröhlich used to discipline his pupils by making them 'lie down on a bench like soldiers, and the toughest of them had to act as corporal and thrash the culprits with a cane,' according to Beethoven.[10] Beethoven refused to allow Karl to be treated thus, with the result that the boy became unruly and impossible for Fröhlich to handle. Whether Beethoven could be blamed for Karl's misbehaviour is debatable, but Johanna used this excuse to try and remove Karl from Beethoven's guardianship. Aided by a relative named Jakob Hotschevar, she took the case to what seemed the appropriate court, the *Landrecht*, but her petition was rejected on 18 September. She then tried to have the boy placed in a public school—the Royal Imperial Convict—but the *Landrecht* rejected this proposal on 3 October (Beethoven opposed the scheme on the grounds that there would be insufficient personal supervision). Karl therefore remained with Beethoven until, on 3 December, he ran away to his mother. The reason he gave was that she had promised to send

---

[10] Anderson, *Letters*, iii. 1406.

him to a public school, and he thought he would not make good progress being taught privately. There may have been other reasons, such as Beethoven's overbearing nature, his deafness (which prevented normal conversation), and perhaps a desire to see his mother more often; but Johanna was not directly involved in inducing Karl to run away, and she co-operated with the police when Beethoven called on them to bring Karl back.

Nevertheless, the boy's action had far-reaching consequences for the history of music. Johanna made a third legal application for him, and on 11 December the *Landrecht* held a fresh hearing concerning Karl's future, interviewing all three Beethovens involved. Documents supporting Johanna were also submitted by Hotschevar and Fröhlich. From the court records much can be learnt about Beethoven's everyday relationship with Karl at that time. Karl reported that Beethoven treated him well in general; punishments were frequent but only when deserved, and Beethoven had only once ill-treated him. Hotschevar, however, alleged that Beethoven was careless about Karl's clothing, and that when Karl had run away he showed symptoms of frostbite, an accusation that Beethoven denied. Karl sometimes used to make derogatory remarks about his mother to Beethoven in order to please him, a practice that horrified Fröhlich, who considered it a breach of the Fourth Commandment (to honour one's parents), and as evidence that Beethoven was morally unfit. Yet Beethoven had given Karl much moral and religious advice and instruction, said prayers with him twice a day, and had instructed him to honour his mother. However, Beethoven came to believe that this principle was difficult or impossible to observe in her case, and probably regarded many of Karl's comments as merely stating plain fact rather than dishonouring her: Karl's description of Johanna as a 'ravenmother' (a word formed by analogy with 'ravenfather', which denoted an unnatural father) was also used of her by both Fanny Giannatasio and Beethoven himself.

The main result of the hearing hinged on Beethoven's accidental revelation that the 'van' in his name, unlike the 'von' in similar Austrian names, did not indicate he was of noble birth. The case was therefore transferred from the *Landrecht*, which dealt with the nobility, to the *Magistrat*, the Viennese magistracy that dealt with the lower classes. Beethoven was deeply wounded by this 'disastrous' decision; although he had not claimed to be of noble birth, he believed he was noble in character, and that his exceptional ability and high principles raised him above the common herd; he had friends among the aristocracy, and they had treated him as an equal. 'Since I have raised my nephew into a higher category, neither he nor I belong with the M[agistrat], for only innkeepers, cobblers and tailors come under that kind of guardianship.'[11]

Beethoven's anxieties were well-founded. The *Magistrat* viewed sympathetically Johanna's claim that his deafness and generally poor health made

---

[11] A-979.

him unsuitable for guardianship, and they ruled in her favour on 11 January 1819. The court itself assumed chief guardianship, since neither Beethoven nor Johanna was now deemed suitable, although Beethoven continued to function as guardian for the next few weeks. Meanwhile Karl, who had been temporarily back at Giannatasio's institute, stayed briefly with his mother before returning to Beethoven again, and began being educated as a day pupil at an institute run by Johann Kudlich. Beethoven was satisfied with this arrangement, but because of these complications he remained preoccupied with Karl's welfare throughout 1819. Karl's actions therefore indirectly caused Beethoven's plans to travel to London, postponed from the previous winter, to be deferred again. Beethoven wrote to Ries on 30 January:

At the moment it is impossible for me to come to London, because I am involved in so many kinds of affairs. But God will assist me to go to L next winter for certain; and I shall bring the new symphonies with me. I am expecting to receive very soon the text of a new oratorio which I am composing for the music club here; and no doubt this work will serve us in L as well.[12]

These comments, besides referring obliquely to Beethoven's problems with Karl, also shed some small light on his composing activities in the winter of 1818–19, a period from which no sketchbooks survive. What was he working on between the despatch of the material for Edinburgh, on 18 November, and the receipt of letters from Thomson in January, requesting three new sets of variations and a setting of 'O Charlie is my Darling'? And between February, when this material was completed, and April, when he received his next commission from Thomson? These questions have not previously been asked, at least not in this form. The only known work from this period is the Wedding Song, 'Auf, Freunde, singt dem Gott' (WoO 105), a 44-bar piece for voices and piano, written to celebrate the wedding of Anna Giannatasio (Fanny's sister) and Leopold Schmerling on 6 February. It is unlikely that these months were another of Beethoven's dormant phases like that of 1817. The letter to Ries suggests he was probably concentrating on more sketches for the Ninth Symphony, perhaps with one or two early ideas for a Tenth. As for the 'new oratorio', this was *Der Sieg des Kreuzes* (The Victory of the Cross), which had been commissioned by the Gesellschaft der Musikfreunde. The text was being prepared by Beethoven's friend Carl Joseph Bernard, who had provided the text for the *Chor auf die verbündeten Fürsten* in 1815, and Beethoven received an advance payment of 400 fl. WW for the work in June 1819. It was never written, however.

Beethoven also spent time checking the Quintet, Op. 104, and the 'Hammerklavier' Sonata during winter 1818–19. After sending Ries a copy of both works for publication in London, he supplied extensive correction lists for them in March. Then in a letter dated 16 April he provided

---

[12] A-935.

metronome marks for the sonata, and also the first bar of the slow movement, which he said was 'still to be inserted'.[13] This bar (Ex. 15.2), which introduces a two-note motif heard later in the movement, makes a remarkable difference to the overall effect, as Ries himself observed; it provides an ingenious transition between the preceding Scherzo and the remote key of the slow movement, and it also relates to the opening of the first movement, second movement, and final fugue theme in that all begin with some form of rising 3rd. It seems extraordinary that such an important feature was added at such a late stage, and it illustrates once again how Beethoven was always liable to find improvements in works already long completed.

**Ex. 15.2**  Op. 106/III

Two new projects did emerge during the dark phase of early 1819, both of gigantic proportions: the Diabelli Variations and the Mass in D, known as the *Missa solemnis*. Their precise dates of origin are unknown, but both were under way by the beginning of Beethoven's next known sketchbook, the 'Wittgenstein'. This starts with sketches for the last set of folksong variations (Op. 107 No. 3), composed between 16 April and 25 May, and immediately afterwards are several pages devoted to the Diabelli Variations, although these are clearly not the earliest sketches for this work.[14]

The idea for the Variations originated with the composer Anton Diabelli, who after working for Steiner for a time had set up his own publishing firm with Pietro Cappi. He invited all the major composers in Vienna to compose a variation on a waltz he had written, as a monument to the country's musical talent. Some of the invitations may not have been sent immediately, for several composers did not contribute until 1823 or 1824, but the earliest dated variation is by Beethoven's former pupil Carl Czerny, whose manuscript is dated 7 May 1819. Czerny seems to have been closely involved in the project, for it was he who provided a massive coda when the collaborative collection was finally published in 1824. Thus Diabelli's initial invitation was probably circulated not long before 7 May 1819, a date that would concur well with the sketches in the Wittgenstein Sketchbook.

---

[13] A-940. Despite its apparent date, the letter was probably not written until June. See BB-1309.

[14] Two earlier leaves of sketches survive in Paris, Ms 58B (see Kinderman, *Diabelli*, 9–12); others, perhaps in a pocket sketchbook, are lost.

Beethoven had disliked collaborative ventures ever since his song 'In questa tomba oscura' had been published in this format in 1808, and so he rejected the idea of composing just a single variation. A small group of variations would have been equally unappealing, since he had just produced over a dozen such sets for Thomson. Thus from the start he planned a large set of variations (contrary to Schindler's account), roughly on the scale of Archduke Rudolph's. Perhaps he did not wish to be outdone by his pupil; but certainly a large set posed new and interesting compositional problems. An early idea to include a grand Introduction like that in Rudolph's set was soon abandoned, but Beethoven decided that his Diabelli Variations should culminate, like his *Prometheus* Variations and Rudolph's set, in a grand fugue, followed by some kind of epilogue or finale. By about June 1819, he had produced a nearly complete draft of the work, comprising twenty-three variations and lacking only the detailed working-out of the final section.[15] Since he had written almost fifty variations for Thomson during a four-month period, July–November 1818 (plus several more since then), the twenty-three new ones probably occupied him for no more than a couple of months.

Once the draft was written, the Diabelli Variations were set aside in favour of detailed work on the *Missa solemnis*. From the outset, Beethoven intended this work for the enthronement of Archduke Rudolph as Archbishop of Olmütz. The previous archbishop died on 20 January 1819, and Rudolph, who already had the right of succession, was officially appointed on 4 June, with the ceremony scheduled for the following March. Beethoven, however, did not wait for the official announcement, for on 3 March 1819 he wrote to Rudolph: 'The day on which a High Mass composed by me is performed at the ceremonies for Your Imperial Highness will be the most glorious day of my life.'[16] Thus his preliminary work on the *Missa solemnis*, which included writing out the entire Latin text with German translation and annotations, probably began in February, well before the first conversation-book reference from early April, which was once thought to indicate approximately the start of the project.[17] Indeed Beethoven had been contemplating a work for the Church the previous year, for one of his last *Tagebuch* entries reads: 'In order to write true church music go through all the ecclesiastical chants of the monks etc. Also look there for the verses in the most correct translations and most perfect prosody of all Christian-Catholic psalms and hymns in general.'[18]

[15] The complete draft has since become split into several sections, three of which survive in different locations while a fourth is lost. For details, see Kinderman, *Diabelli*, 12–17.

[16] A-948; for dating of this letter, see BB-1292.

[17] BKh, i. 42; see Winter, 'Riddles', 222–4; Drabkin, *Missa solemnis*, 11–15. The lack of mention of the Mass—in contrast to *Der Sieg des Kreuzes*—in Beethoven's letter to Ries of 30 January suggests it had not been conceived at that stage.

[18] T-168.

On the other hand Beethoven could not have made much progress on the Mass in February–April before turning to Op. 107 No. 3 and the Diabelli Variations; for the batch of Kyrie sketches in the Wittgenstein Sketchbook, immediately after the Diabelli sketches and therefore dating from about June, while showing recognizable material for the 'Kyrie eleison', contains extremely primitive sketches for the 'Christe' in which only the key—not even the metre—has been established (Ex. 15.3). Surprisingly, however, there are virtually no further sketches for this movement. Some writers have conjectured that Beethoven simply did not make many, but it seems inconceivable that he would have created such a sizeable, original and sophisticated movement without very extensive sketches; to do so would have run counter to all his normal procedures. Most likely the remaining Kyrie sketches were made mainly in pocket books now lost. The few in 'Wittgenstein' are followed by many pages devoted to the Gloria, and the Mass then remained his principal compositional preoccupation for the rest of the year.

**Ex. 15.3**  SV 154, p.16

The *Missa solemnis* is the most conspicuous sign of a subtle change in Beethoven's religious outlook, which became more overtly Christian and less deistic during 1818–19, perhaps through the influence of Archduke Rudolph. He was now contemplating the problem of writing 'true church music', and proposing to study 'Christian-Catholic psalms'. He was planning an oratorio on Christ's crucifixion. He was making passing references to Christianity in his letters—references that, though almost insignificant, are symptoms of the change. To Steiner: 'Though I am a good Christian, one Friday in the week is enough for me.' And to Rudolph, when urging him to publish his Variations: 'Let the order of Apollo (or, more Christian, St. Cecilia) be made public.'[19] Previously he had always referred to Greek and Roman gods, rather than Christian saints. He was also determined to give Karl a Christian upbringing, as he indicated to the *Magistrat* on 1 February 1819: 'I have found an excellent cleric who gives him special instruction about his duties as a Christian and a man. For only on such a foundation can true human beings be raised.'[20] And when one day in 1819 Karl visited his mother instead of going to confession, Beethoven insisted on accompanying him to confession personally when he found out. In early 1820 he wrote, concerning his capacity for endurance, 'Socrates and Jesus were

[19] A-906 (Aug. 1818) and A-963 (Aug. 1819).     [20] Anderson, *Letters*, iii. 1374.

models for me'.[21] He had, of course, always been basically religious, but specific Christian comments such as these were far more common in his last nine years than they had been earlier.

Another sign of Beethoven's religious outlook emerged with a new plan for Karl's education. He decided that, despite Kudlich's efforts, the boy would fare best if he were sent to a Catholic institution at Landshut, near Munich, and placed under the care of Johann Michael Sailer, a renowned professor of theology and future bishop. An approach was made in February 1819 through Antonie Brentano, a friend of Sailer, and Sailer evidently accepted the proposal. The plan met with approval from many sources, including Carl Joseph Bernard, the councillor Matthias von Tuscher (who became Karl's official guardian on 26 March), the Abbot of St Michael (a very holy man known as Father Ignatius), and Archduke Rudolph. Had it succeeded, Karl would have received an excellent Christian education, under the supervision of a man whom Beethoven greatly admired; Johanna would no longer have been able to exert a corrupting influence on him; Beethoven would have been spared the everyday domestic cares associated with Karl's upbringing, leaving him free to concentrate on composition; and he would have been able to fulfil his promise to visit London, no doubt calling at Landshut on the way. Unfortunately, Johanna objected to the plan, apparently for selfish reasons, and the *Magistrat* proposed instead that Karl go to some institute in Austria rather than Bavaria. Nowhere suitable could be found, but a passport allowing him to go to Landshut was refused.

Meanwhile there had been further developments at home. Johanna ceased contributing to Karl's upkeep after January, so that the whole financial burden fell on Beethoven. Then in March, when Karl had misbehaved on one occasion, Beethoven pulled him roughly off his chair, causing slight injury in a spot that had been sensitive ever since Karl's hernia operation of 1816. The injury was very minor, and the doctor confirmed no harm had been done, but Karl went to Johanna's for a short time before becoming a boarder at Kudlich's institute. Tuscher was appointed guardian about this time, with Beethoven's approval (Beethoven apparently hoped to reduce Johanna's animosity towards him by this move). While Karl was at Kudlich's, Johanna had intermittent access to him, and she allegedly persuaded him to fail his Easter examinations so that he would not be eligible to go to Landshut. As a result, he had to repeat a year of his schooling, much to Beethoven's distress.

Karl was allowed out of Kudlich's from time to time, and on 30 May he was permitted to visit Johanna to celebrate her nameday. After eating and drinking too much, he stayed the night before walking back to school the next morning feeling quite ill. Beethoven blamed the illness on Johanna's overindulging Karl; she apparently claimed, implausibly, that Karl had

---

[21] BKh, i. 211.

never properly recovered from the injury Beethoven had inflicted in March. In any case, the boy returned to her home and remained in bed for three weeks, while Beethoven tried to have him readmitted to Giannatasio's. This proved unsuccessful, and on 22 June Karl was admitted instead to a boarding school run by Joseph Blöchlinger, where he remained until 1823.

In July, Tuscher resigned the guardianship of Karl, and Beethoven resumed it unofficially until the court could make a fresh appointment. On 17 September they decided to accept Tuscher's resignation, but instead of reinstating Beethoven they appointed Johanna, along with a municipal trustee named Leopold Nussböck. This was too much for Beethoven. Immediately on return to Vienna from his summer lodgings in Mödling, he set about writing a petition to the *Magistrat* to return the guardianship to him. This petition, however, was rejected on 4 November, as was a subsequent one on 20 December. Beethoven then turned to the Court of Appeal, making enormous efforts to promote his case when he should have been concentrating exclusively on finishing the Mass for Rudolph's enthronement in March. He began by sending the Court a petition dated 7 January 1820, giving three reasons why he ought to be reinstated: he had been nominated as guardian by the boy's father, and confirmed by the *Landrecht*, who had excluded Johanna; neither Johanna nor Nussböck could satisfactorily supervise Karl's higher education since they were not themselves well educated; and he himself was prepared to pay whatever was necessary to support Karl's education. The *Magistrat*'s far from impartial countersubmission to the Appeal Court alleged that Beethoven was unfit for guardianship because of his deafness and his hatred of Johanna, that her crime of 1811 was no longer a bar, and that allegations of her bad influence had not been definitely proven. In a later statement they also claimed that Beethoven's plan to send Karl to Landshut was done merely out of malice towards Johanna, and not for Karl's benefit. The *Magistrat*, however, were clearly 'not suited to unusual cases', as Karl Peters shrewdly observed,[22] and the partiality of this supposedly neutral body is clear from the following points, which suggest that Beethoven was entirely justified in taking the matter to the Appeal Court:

(i) Beethoven was now proposing a co-guardian to overcome the deafness problem;

(ii) He had no hatred of Johanna, as we have seen, but he could not tolerate her undermining Karl's moral and spiritual development;

(iii) Her crime of 1811 was still a legal bar, and was symptomatic of a generally immoral character, as was her pregnancy with an illegitimate child during the appeal process;

(iv) Several of Beethoven's friends and acquaintances were unanimous in their condemnation of her;[23]

---

[22] BKh, i. 271 (*c*.25 Feb.).

[23] Bernard: 'You must struggle with his mother and her intrigues.' Tuscher(?): 'All communication with the mother must be made impossible.' Oliva: 'He should be able to be

(v) The *Magistrat*'s opinion about Karl's proposed move to Landshut contrasts sharply with that of others; Father Ignatius said, according to Bernard: 'If I thought for 100 years, I could not imagine anything better than to send the boy to Prof. Sailer.'[24]

While Beethoven was preparing a more detailed account of his case, he happened to read in a local journal, the *Wiener Zeitschrift*, an article by a professor of astronomy. He was particularly struck by the final sentence, which cited Kant: 'There are two things which raise man above himself and lead to eternal, ever-increasing admiration: the moral law within us, and the starry sky above us.' He noted in his conversation book: ' "The moral law within us, and the starry sky above us" Kant!!!'[25] The words are actually a somewhat loose paraphrase of Kant's original text, and commentators used to assume that Beethoven, who like most educated people was acquainted with Kant's writings, had jotted down a half-remembered phrase studied during his youth. The discovery of the article, however, indicates he had a much more immediate source. Nevertheless, the quotation has more than passing significance, for it encapsulates much of Beethoven's deepest philosophical and moral belief. The 'starry sky', which he loved to contemplate, embodies the laws of nature that direct the universe, while the 'moral law' directs man's personal life. The macrocosmic is set beside the microcosmic, in a duality that is reflected in several of Beethoven's late works, where dualities of various kinds are prominent. Kant's idea, however, was not original but is nearly 3,000 years old, appearing in Psalm 19, which contemplates the cosmos in its first section and moral law in its second. This psalm had a significant influence on Enlightenment texts: parts are paraphrased in 'The heavens are telling' from Haydn's *Creation* and in Beethoven's song 'Die Ehre Gottes' (The Praise of God by Nature, Op. 48 No. 4), while its image of the sun running joyfully across the heavens 'like a hero' is clearly echoed in Schiller's 'An die Freude', soon to be incorporated into Beethoven's Ninth Symphony.

Kant's vision of the starry sky remained with Beethoven during the next few weeks, as he composed the song 'Abendlied unterm gestirnten Himmel' (Evening Song under the Starry Sky), WoO 150. Here the soul, by contemplating the stars, leaves earthly cares behind, where 'false fortune rewards the evil', and sets its hopes on the Judge enthroned in the stars: 'Soon at God's throne I shall reap a glorious reward for my sufferings.' It is extraordinary how closely the text mirrors Beethoven's personal situation at the

completely separated from the mother's influence.' Blöchlinger: 'She is simply a scoundrel, I am sufficiently convinced of this.' Josef Köferle: 'Her looks and her speech (though enticingly pleasant to the child) are poison.' See BKh, i. 39, 40, 44; ii. 152, 189. Even Hotschevar, who supported her, later refused guardianship of her illegitimate daughter Ludovika because of Johanna's poor lifestyle: see Tellenbach, 'Psychoanalysis', 89.

24 BKh, i. 72.
25 BKh, i. 235 and 473. The passage appeared in the *Wiener Zeitschrift* dated 1 February, and Beethoven copied it out the following day.

time, as he witnessed his immoral sister-in-law gaining a false reward, while he himself hoped for a judgement that would be inspired by the heavenly Judge, as well as ultimate reward in Paradise. Nothing is known of the poet, Heinrich Goeble, but Beethoven evidently obtained the text from a small manuscript collection lent to him about 11 February by Johann Schickh, editor of the *Wiener Zeitschrift*.[26] Beethoven had promised Schickh a contribution for his journal, but had been unable to find a suitable text until he came across Goeble's. Its echoes of his own feelings must have struck him forcefully, and his setting is certainly one of his most poignant. Though essentially a strophic song with four stanzas, every nuance of the text is reflected by subtle modifications to the vocal line, while the piano provides a continuous commentary that greatly intensifies the meaning of the words and the ideas behind them.

The song was completed on 4 March, by which time Beethoven had produced a gigantic Memorandum,[27] the longest prose document he ever wrote, to support his case in the Appeal Court. The original draft, dated 18 February 1820, was forty-eight pages long; had it been read out in court it would have lasted almost as long as a performance of the entire *Missa solemnis*! He was assisted in its preparation by his friend Johann Baptist Bach, a lawyer, who had advised him in January 'to proceed as moderately as possible in all things so that it does not appear as if there were malice'.[28] The Memorandum is divided into several sections, like the movements of some grand symphony. The first outlines the case against Johanna; the second describes in detail the deficiencies in the *Magistrat* in their function as chief guardian; the next three summarize Karl's progress, Beethoven's financial support for him, and the financial support available from Carl's estate and Johanna; the document ends with a short conclusion, followed, as in so many of his compositions, by an extended coda in the form of a Supplementary Statement tying up some loose ends. A few of the allegations are unfounded, such as the claim that Johanna's crime of 1811 brought about Carl's illness that led to his death; but there is sufficient material to make a strong case, and the document is written with great conviction. Beethoven clearly believed everything he wrote, and in the final paragraph he appeals to the Almighty to be his witness.

Help was also sought from all who might be able to influence the members of the Appeal Court. Meanwhile on 30 March Beethoven's 'Abendlied' appeared in the *Wiener Zeitschrift*,[29] perfect timing for a work that surely elicited for him the sympathy of any waverers. A ruling in his favour was finally made on 8 April. He and his friend Karl Peters, a court councillor and tutor to the children of Ferdinand Lobkowitz, were appointed guardians; Johanna was excluded. Whether this decision was justifiable

---

[26] BKh, i. 256–7.    [27] See Anderson, *Letters*, iii. 1388–1408.

[28] TF, 753; BKh, i. 188.

[29] Though dated 28 March, the song evidently did not appear until two days later. See BKh, i. 506.

will remain contentious, for it touches on a profound moral dilemma: when should a child be forcibly removed from its parents? It is generally agreed, now as then, that this should be done only in extreme cases, where the child is seriously at risk. Beethoven and his supporters clearly believed that this was an extreme case, as did the *Landrecht* and the Appeal Court. In a comparable case today this view would be less likely to prevail, since Johanna had not been violent. Moral demands were stricter in those days, however, as is evident from the guardianship laws; and it is significant that nobody was prepared to say that Johanna was really of good character, that Beethoven's allegations were unfounded, or that she had reformed since her criminal conviction. Her case rested on three points: she was the mother, Carl had nominated her as guardian, and Beethoven suffered from deafness and ill health. The *Magistrat* were clearly far from neutral, though whether they had supported her out of sympathy, through friendship (they had dined with her several times) or through bribery (she had, after all, bribed Beethoven's servants) is unclear. In such circumstances the final decision, upheld after an appeal to the Emperor, seems reasonable within its context.

Beethoven, for his part, had remained absolutely unswerving throughout. He had failed, certainly, to empathize fully with Johanna or Karl, probably making little attempt to soothe their feelings through gentle persuasion, but the nobility of his aims for Karl and the soundness of his underlying principles are palpable. And any accusations of hypocrisy are unsustainable. His friend Franz Janschikh had asked him, about 10 February: 'Where were you going about 7 o' clock today by the Haarmarkt hunting for girls?' And a few days later Bernard wrote in a conversation book: 'Peters says that his cloak was pulled from him by Frau Janschikh like Joseph's was by Potiphar's wife. Also that you have slept with Frau Janschikh,' and Peters adds: 'I am witness.'[30] But these remarks need not be taken at face value: Beethoven's visit to the Haarmarkt was clearly not to hunt for girls but to see Tuscher, since he had noted down Tuscher's address (682 Haarmarkt) just four pages earlier in the conversation book; meanwhile Bernard's comment may simply be a teasingly suggestive way of saying that Beethoven had slept at Frau Janschikh's house. Thus there is no clear evidence of immorality on his part during this period, nor of any fundamental ill-will towards Johanna. He had given her many chances to reform, and had tried to treat her kindly in the hope that she would; but Karl's welfare was paramount for him. It took precedence over her rights as a mother, if Karl was in danger of being corrupted by her; it superseded Beethoven's own desire to have Karl with him, so that he was prepared to send him to the best school available, wherever it was; his own personal comforts could be sacrificed to give whatever financial support was necessary (and he was eventually left very short of funds); and, most remarkably, he was even prepared to set aside his devotion to his Art, in order to bring

[30] BKh, i. 254, 262. Potiphar's wife falsely accused Joseph of sexual impropriety.

about a satisfactory outcome for Karl. The Mass, composed for one of his closest and most admirable friends, lay only half finished by the day of Rudolph's enthronement in Olmütz on 9 March. The day which Beethoven had predicted would be 'the most glorious of my life' never happened. Recognizing his sacrifices, he noted in his Memorandum of 18 February a quotation from Janus Anysius: 'Lite abstine, nam vincens, multum amiseris.' (Abstain from litigation, for even if you win, you will have lost much.)[31] He had indeed lost much; but the titanic struggle, generated by his intense love for Karl, was essential in his view, and he was overjoyed at the final outcome.

[31] Anderson, *Letters*, iii. 1389.

# 16

# Completion of the Mass (1820–2)

Once Beethoven had realized that his Mass would not be ready in time for Archduke Rudolph's enthronement as Archbishop of Olmütz on 9 March 1820, he began turning his attention to other compositions. The Mass remained his primary long-term project, in preference to the Diabelli Variations or the two symphonies for London, but it was no longer a priority and was not even mentioned directly in correspondence between him and the archduke during March and April. Meanwhile he wrote several shorter works of more immediate need during 1820.

First of these were his last two folksong settings for Thomson, composed in January–February. By now Thomson was becoming increasingly disillusioned with Beethoven's settings, which were proving too elevated and recherché for the intended market, and he commissioned no more from him. 'I have no expectation of ever receiving any benefit from what Beethoven has done for me. He composes for posterity,' wrote Thomson in 1821.[1] Next among the short works was the song 'Abendlied' discussed in the previous chapter. This was followed by a couple of very brief folksong settings (Hess 133–4) which Beethoven jotted down in a letter to Simrock on 18 March, during negotiations for the sale of the sets of variations Op. 107 and the *Missa solemnis*.

Another distraction from the Mass came from Beethoven's friend Friedrich Starke. About 6 February Bernard wrote in a conversation book that Starke wanted a little piece of music from Beethoven, and some brief biographical details, for a piano tutor that he was publishing (to which several other leading composers were contributing). This innocuous request had far-reaching repercussions that indirectly affected Beethoven's next piano sonata and two sets of bagatelles. The 'little piece' was duly written a month or two later, for Franz Oliva, who was by now acting as Beethoven's unpaid secretary, asked him on 19 April: 'Are you giving that to Starke as a single piece?'[2] Meanwhile, however, Beethoven had had a request from the publisher Adolf Schlesinger of Berlin for some new sonatas. Before he had indicated whether he was accepting this commission, Oliva proposed an

[1] Cooper, *Folksong Settings*, 43.
[2] BKh, ii. 72. The date is determined by an earlier and a later conversation, both of which took place that day (see ibid., notes 195 and 205).

idea for giving the composition of these sonatas a flying start: 'And use the little new piece for a sonata for Schlesinger perhaps.'[3] Beethoven evidently took up Oliva's suggestion, for his sketchbooks reveal that the first movement of his next sonata, Op. 109 in E major, was written separately in March–April, before Schlesinger's commission, and must have been the 'little piece' intended for Starke. He then resumed the Mass, more or less completing the Credo by June. By this time he had reached agreement with Schlesinger on the fee for three sonatas (90 ducats, agreed on 31 May), and so he began work on the rest of Op. 109, probably shortly after 9 June.[4]

The origins of the first movement of Op. 109 as a separate contribution for a piano tutor may partly explain its very unusual structure, although this is no more original than several of his other first movements. Its most striking feature is its fantasia-like alternation between vivace and adagio sections, with three flowing vivaces interspersed with two adagios that differ from them not only in tempo but in almost every other way: a contrast between 2/4 and 3/4, dynamism and stasis, regular and irregular rhythm—suggesting images of action set against thought, dance against oratory, Martha against Mary, time against timelessness. Yet this contrast, perhaps designed to provide learners with a double challenge within a single piece, takes place within a more or less conventional sonata form: the first adagio, in the dominant, functions as the second group in the exposition, and reappears in modified form in the tonic in the recapitulation. The adagios, however, also function as interruptions to what would be a continuous movement in *perpetuum mobile* style. The structure has even been described as 'parenthetical',[5] although this is inexact: with a true parenthesis, the material on either side could be joined without any change in register or dislocation of metre, but this does not happen here, as can be seen in Ex. 16.1. This shows the end of the first vivace section, a harmonic summary of the intervening adagio, and the start of the second vivace section; although the right hand resumes in bar 16 where it had left off in bar 8, there is a disjunction in register for the left hand, and also a metrical disjunction through the extra half-bar at 'Tempo I'. Moreover the structure of the vivace sections joined together would not be properly balanced, whereas it should be if the adagios were truly parenthetical.

Nevertheless, the structure of the movement is more complex than just a plain sonata form with a second subject in contrasting metre. The first subject is unusually short in proportion to the rest of the movement, and the second group is not announced by the usual strong cadence and affirmation of the new tonic. Both these features had already appeared in the first movement of the Sonata, Op. 101, another highly original structure; but combining them with adagio interruptions creates an even more abnormal design for Op. 109. This technique of re-using original ideas in a new way

---

[3] BKh, ii. 87. See Meredith, 'Op. 109', and Marston, *Op. 109*, 15–31, for fuller accounts of the origins of this piece.

[4] See Marston, *Op. 109*, 36.    [5] Kinderman, *Beethoven*, 219–20.

**Ex. 16.1** Op. 109/I

is very characteristic of Beethoven, who often made artistic progress by a series of small, cumulative steps. In Op. 109, then, the second group enters not merely in a different metre but with a disruptive diminished 7th replacing the expected B major chord, which is postponed to bar 15. The most disorientating note in Ex. 16.1, however, is not in bar 9 but the E♯ in bar 12, for it contradicts all the surrounding tonality, whereas an E natural would have been easy to explain as part of a transitional chord between C sharp minor and G sharp minor. Thus the whole of this adagio section can be viewed on several different levels, and its quality of continual disruption of metre, register, tonality, dynamic level, rhythm, and texture sets up a diametric opposition to the smooth continuum of the vivace. Such bipolarity is a common feature in late Beethoven, although it is rarely as prominent as here.

For the remaining two movements Beethoven expanded the element of contrast: the second movement is a Prestissimo in E minor and the third a set of variations on a slow, saraband-like theme. These two movements were apparently composed quite quickly, for on 28 June Beethoven told Schlesinger that the sonata was 'ready'. His initial composing draft may indeed have been ready (more or less) by this date, but he then spent a long time revising it; and in a letter the following year he mentioned that the sonata had been drafted more fully than usual, which confirms that there was some kind of preliminary composing score now lost. Various other factors also delayed the despatch of the sonata, so that when he next wrote to Schlesinger on 20 September the sonata was still only 'almost completely ready except for correction',[6] and was not sent until some time after that.

The delay was due partly to minor matters. Archduke Rudolph returned to Vienna during the summer and Beethoven resumed lessons with him. Beethoven also spent some time negotiating the possible sale of the *Missa solemnis*, believing this to be nearly ready. The principal delay, however, was caused by the preparation of a set of Scottish folksongs (Op. 108) that Beethoven had also agreed to sell to Schlesinger. George Thomson had published these twenty-five settings (along with five sent earlier by Haydn) in 1818, and Beethoven now succeeded in selling the continental rights for his twenty-five to Schlesinger. In June he arranged for them to be copied from Thomson's edition, but on checking the copy he became increasingly dissatisfied. The first problem was that the songs were in a far from ideal order, and so he spent much time and energy rearranging them into the best possible sequence, maximizing contrast between successive songs. This activity is reflected in two groups of sketches,[7] each of which shows various attempts at numbering and renumbering the songs. For example, 'The Maid of Isla', which had been ninth in Thomson's volume, was numbered 11, then 5, then 13, and then 16, before being placed at No. 12 in the manuscript for Schlesinger (who published it as No. 4). The second problem was the musical text, which had been slightly modified and abridged by Thomson. Instead of restoring the original version, Beethoven now went through the entire manuscript copy, making numerous minor improvements and adjustments, which he entered neatly (by his standards!) into the manuscript. He was further held up by a few days of ill health, and by difficulties in obtaining the services of someone able to copy out the English texts of the songs; thus the manuscript was not finally sent until towards the end of September. Only after this did Beethoven resume work on polishing up the Sonata, Op. 109, which may not have been sent until early 1821.

After dealing with Opp. 108 and 109, Beethoven remembered his promise to Starke, who had been deprived of the piece intended for him (Op. 109, first movement). To replace it, Beethoven composed five short bagatelles (Op. 119 Nos. 7–11), whose combined length of 102 bars roughly equals that of the movement displaced. Their exact date of composition is puzzling: the autograph score is dated 1 January 1821, yet the sketches appear immediately after the last ones for Op. 109, which are still some way off the final version. If, as might be expected, the bagatelle sketches were made only a few days before 1 January, and the sonata was still not fully sketched only a few days before that, the situation would be incompatible with Beethoven's repeated statements that the sonata was virtually ready during

---

[6] A-1033.        [7] Paris, Bibliothèque Nationale, Ms 65; Bonn, Beethoven-Archiv, NE 43.

the summer. The explanation must lie in the date '1 January', which indicates something absolutely different from 2 January: New Year's Day was
the traditional day for exchange of gifts, and in several known instances
Beethoven gave or received something that day. The bagatelles are clearly
another example. It seems that he characteristically refused to accept any
payment from his friend Starke for them; meanwhile Starke refused to
accept something so valuable without payment—thus the solution was for
Beethoven to present the bagatelles as a New Year gift (Starke presumably
reciprocated in some way). Hence the bagatelles could have been sketched
at any time in the second half of 1820. Apparent confirmation that they
were composed at least before mid-October comes from a recently deci-
phered inscription on p. 6 of the pocket sketchbook BH 109.[8] The inscription, which refers to Beethoven's imminent move from his summer lodgings
in Mödling to his winter residence in Vienna on 26 October, postdates the
bagatelle sketches, but probably not by very long, and it seems most likely
that he sketched the bagatelles as soon as he had finished dealing with the
folksongs for Schlesinger, towards the end of September.

The bagatelles formed the last of Beethoven's small projects before he
resumed intensive work on the *Missa solemnis*. Despite assuring Schlesinger
in September that he was proceeding to the remaining two piano sonatas
'without delay',[9] the sketchbooks show only occasional ideas for new
sonatas, and intensive work on the Benedictus and Agnus Dei of the Mass.
Beethoven clearly believed that this work was almost finished, for he repeatedly promised it to Simrock during the summer, indicating it would be sent
within a month or two. The same message was conveyed to others. In a conversation-book entry of about 20 August, Franz Gebauer enquired: 'Is the
Mass ready?' The reply must have been fairly positive, for Gebauer
responded: 'May I come and have a look at it sometime?' Beethoven probably said something about a possible performance of it, for Gebauer then
mentioned that he was going to resume his concert series in October.[10] By
November Beethoven was suggesting that the only hold-up was in obtaining
a German translation for the Mass. The sketchbooks, however, reveal that
he was being absurdly over-optimistic, or deliberately misleading, in his
estimation of the work's completion date. The Benedictus remained in a
primitive state until at least October, and the Agnus Dei was taken up later
still. It was clearly unrealistic for Beethoven to expect to complete so much
music within a month; although he had occasionally done so in the past (the
Violin Concerto is a notable example), the Mass movements were more
complex and likely to take longer. The Agnus Dei probably also expanded
beyond the length originally envisaged, for the 'Dona nobis' section is of
huge dimensions. There are few chronological reference points in the

---

[8] William Kinderman's reading of the inscription is noted in Meredith, 'Conference
Report', 33.
[9] BB-1410: 'ohne Aufschub'; not 'uninterruptedly' as in A-1033.      [10] BKh, ii. 219.

sketches of this period, and it is not impossible that a full score was completed in outline by the end of 1820;[11] but the detailed filling in and revision of this score, which ended up with large numbers of alterations, clearly dragged on into 1821 and beyond.

Indeed, progress on the Mass soon came almost to a complete halt, as did all Beethoven's composing. During the nine months after writing the bagatelles for Starke, he finished just one work, a short piano piece (WoO 61) written for Ferdinand Piringer and dated 18 February 1821. Its twenty-seven bars could easily have been produced in a single morning. There are a few sketches of possible ideas for a second sonata for Schlesinger, but Op. 110 in A flat did not begin to take shape until the second half of 1821, and was not completed before December. The only known composition between WoO 61 and the sonata is a canon on Tobias Haslinger's name (*O Tobias*, WoO 182). Beethoven claimed that this piece occurred to him on 9 September in a dream that he promptly forgot but remembered a day later, when he added a third voice to his original two-part canon. The sketches suggest a slightly longer period of gestation, but such a work could not have taken much time. He quoted the canon again in a letter to Piringer on 6 November, when he commented: 'Here is what you asked for. . . . You can see from this that for eight months now I have received[?] nothing.'[12] The word used for 'receive'—*empfangen*—can, however, also mean to conceive a child. Thus the letter should surely be interpreted as a response to an enquiry about what works Beethoven had written since presenting Piringer with WoO 61: he had produced no brain-children during the eight months since 18 February, apart from one insignificant canon.

A similarly bleak picture emerges about his daily life in 1821. No conversation books survive from between mid-September 1820 and the end of May 1822, and so his activities during that time are largely undocumented. His friend Oliva, who had dominated the conversation books of 1820, departed for St Petersburg that December, leaving Beethoven with no similarly close assistant until Schindler took over the role some two years later. Beethoven's letters are almost as sparse as his conversation books for a period: few survive from 1821, and only four from the first half of the year, whereas in most of his later years one would find at least twenty to forty from a similar timespan. The correspondence that does survive from this period is concerned mainly with further negotiations over the *Missa solemnis*, and matters associated with Schlesinger's publication of Opp. 108 and 109.

---

[11] The relevant sketchbooks (Grasnick 5, parts of Artaria 180, and the beginning of Artaria 197) are probably slightly earlier than proposed in both JTW and Drabkin, 'Agnus', in view of Kinderman's above-mentioned dating of part of BH 109.

[12] A-1058. See also BB-1444, confirming Piringer as recipient; the editor here implies that Beethoven's comment about receiving nothing may refer to a failure by Kinsky to pay Beethoven's annuity, but receipts survive indicating Beethoven received all due payments that year (see Albrecht, *Letters*, ii. 197).

This almost complete cessation of activity in 1821 was evidently due to poor health, as in 1817, but this time the illness was more than just a general tiredness and debility. The first reference is a statement in the *Allgemeine musikalische Zeitung* of 10 January 1821: 'Herr von Beethofen was sick with a rheumatic fever. All friends of true music and all admirers of his muse feared for him. But now he is on the road to recovery and is working actively.'[13] The report conveys the seriousness of the illness, but the prognosis proved optimistic. On 7 March Beethoven wrote: 'For six weeks I have been laid up with a violent attack of rheumatism.' And on 14 March he attempted an explanation, not only for his own inactivity but that of others: 'I was confined to bed for six weeks, during which time I was not allowed to attend to anything. . . . The same happened to the translator [of the Mass] and to everyone I know around me. This strange and terrible winter here . . . is to blame for it.'[14] Among those who were ill that winter was Josephine, Baroness Stackelberg; no longer in contact with Beethoven, and deserted by her husband, she died on 31 March, in her early forties.

Beethoven recovered, but only gradually. His health remained precarious during the spring, and during the summer he suffered from a prolonged and extremely unpleasant attack of jaundice till the end of August, which prevented him resuming composition. 'In general, I don't work when I'm sick,' he told Gerhard Breuning some years later (if Breuning's recollections are reliable). 'I have to be in the right state for it. Many times I haven't been able to compose for long periods of time; but it always comes back sooner or later.'[15] Clearly 1821 included one of the longest of those 'long periods', and definite illness rather than just the wrong 'state' was to blame on this occasion.

During this fallow period Beethoven did manage to struggle through to the end of the *Missa solemnis*, and there are reasons to believe he completed a preliminary score at this time. The sketches (in Artaria 197 and associated pocket sketchbooks) show extensive work on the 'Agnus' and 'Dona' sections, including a (foreshortened) version of the very end of the work.[16] In the next section of Artaria 197 (pp. 64 ff.) Beethoven turned to detailed work on the next sonata for Schlesinger (Op. 110), and he would have been unlikely to do this just before reaching the end of the score of the Mass. Moreover, his letters after this period refer to the Mass in slightly different terms. Whereas earlier letters had promised that the work would be sent 'next month', or once the translation had been completed, his letter of 12 November 1821 to Franz Brentano implies that a copy now existed: 'The Mass could certainly have been sent earlier, except that it must be minutely looked over, for publishers abroad are not very capable with my manuscripts . . . and such a copy for printing must be checked note for note.'[17] Another reference to a copy occurs in a letter of 19 May 1822, when

[13] TF, 775–6.    [14] A-1050, A-1051.    [15] Breuning, *Memories*, 97.
[16] Drabkin, 'Agnus', esp. 138, 155–6.    [17] A-1059.

Beethoven indicates that Archduke Rudolph had had a copy for some time and had returned it only three days earlier. It is also significant that in each of Beethoven's last three sonatas, which were contemporary with the Mass, at least one movement had to be written out again after the score had been completed, because there were so many alterations. Thus it seems highly probable that he completed a score of the Mass during 1821 before revising it the following year. Whether this score was practically completed before his eight-month illness (January–August), or was worked on intermittently during that period, has not yet been confirmed, but it makes little difference in practice.

Some of Beethoven's early sketches for Op. 110 are found near those for his Tobias Haslinger canon of early September, and so the sonata must have been begun by this date. He had still not fully recovered, and as late as 12 November he wrote to Franz Brentano that he had been constantly ill since the previous year. He added, however, that at last his health had shown real improvement, and that he could again begin to live for his art, after about two years of almost constant interruption by illness and worldly cares (an apparent reference to his struggle for his nephew). His music manuscripts confirm that his composing did now return to something like its normal rate, and he was able to finish Op. 110 before the end of the year. The autograph score is dated 25 December 1821—apparently the completion date—and he received payment for the sonata from Schlesinger's agent on 11 January 1822.[18] As with the *Missa solemnis*, he made extensive revisions in the score, and the finale became so messy that he eventually wrote out a fair copy, which needed little further alteration before publication.

The Sonata in A flat is a highly unusual structure. A gentle first movement in sonata form is followed by an Allegro Molto and Trio in 2/4 time. This movement might be called a march, but it is most unlike a normal one, and far too fast, while it is far too serious for its common appellation as a scherzo. Like the so-called scherzos of the Fifth Symphony and the Quartet, Op. 95, it is simply a fast middle movement in minuet-and-trio form that is neither a minuet nor a scherzo. What follows is even more unusual: a recitative-like section, a slow 'Arioso dolente', a quick fugal section, a reprise of the Arioso, and a resumption of the fugue. This cunning structure can be perceived equally as one movement or two: either a slow movement, followed by a finale in which the preceding movement is recalled (as in the Sonata, Op. 27 No. 1 and the Fifth Symphony); or a single movement in five sections in which arioso and fugue alternate. It has even been treated as a recitative followed by a finale of four sections,[19] but this requires the finale to begin halfway through a bar. Beethoven's autograph implies a single movement, which is how most modern writers view it, but Schlesinger's original edition sets it out as two separate movements: an Adagio and a Fuga. Either way, there is a contrasting duality like that of the first move-

---

[18] Alb-283.     [19] Tovey, *Companion*, 264.

ment of Op. 109, and to argue the case for one or other view is to miss the point. This is one of several late works in which Beethoven creates a hybrid, where a unit is too short or incomplete to be regarded as a separate movement, but too independent to be seen as a mere section of some larger movement. (Other examples include the opening unit of the Cello Sonata, Op. 102 No. 1, the third and sixth units of the Quartet, Op. 131, and the penultimate unit, 'più allegro', of the Quartet, Op. 132.)

The sonata is unified in a number of ways—most notably, perhaps, in its thematic organization. The main themes of all four movements (if we regard them as four) begin with a phrase covering a range of a sixth (see Ex. 16.2a–d). Moreover, the first and fourth have similar contours reaching up to the sixth of the scale (F), while the Arioso theme begins with a direct transformation of the opening of the second movement, both descending gradually from the dominant. The note F, which forms the peak of the first phrase of the sonata, plays a prominent role in the rest of the work. It forms the climax of the opening paragraph in bar 11, where it is marked *sf*; it is the first note of the second subject when the latter finally appears in the tonic key (bar 79); and in the closing theme of the movement, which consists of a series of rising scales each covering, once again, the range of a sixth, the peak is another sforzando F in the recapitulation (bar 90).[20] There are several other places in the movement where F is prominent, and most of these Fs are supported by subdominant harmony, which helps to heighten the sense of gentleness and loveliness that characterizes the movement. F then becomes the tonic for the second movement, and another high sforzando F begins the Trio section. The third movement, too, begins with F at the top, and the Fugue theme also peaks on F.

**Ex. 16.2** Op. 110, main themes

<hr />

[20] The theme of the second movement should be heard as an inversion of these rising scales; too much has been made of its chance resemblance to a folksong set by Beethoven in 1820, with which it surely has no intended connection. The same applies to a motif (bars 17–20) allegedly derived from another folksong: this motif is also related to the thematic structure of the sonata. It was not Beethoven's habit to borrow themes in this manner, and many of the supposed borrowings can be refuted by reference to his sketches.

The prominence given to F and to scales rising up to it gives the note G a special, elusive character since it is repeatedly omitted from these patterns. Thus when yet another rising pattern (first movement, bars 108–10), after reaching the F, goes beyond it to G and A♭, there is a wondrous sense of achievement and fulfilment. A similar procedure appears twice in the finale, just before the arioso interruption and just before the end (bars 102 and 201), where the music again bursts through the F barrier in gestures of triumph.

The tonal scheme of the sonata is equally fascinating. In the first movement the development section strays much less far than usual, just passing through the local keys of F minor, D flat major and B flat minor (another example of Beethoven's predilection at this time for falling 3rds) before returning to the tonic. After such a limited tonal range, the sudden excursion into E major (the key of the previous sonata) during the recapitulation is totally unexpected, and seems to open up a whole new sound world. A matching gesture is required for the finale, but what key can be used that has an equally startling effect? The unlikely, and therefore obvious, answer is the key of G—that elusive note that had been avoided in the first-movement and fugue themes. Accordingly, the Arioso reappears not in its original key but transposed down a semitone to G minor; and the fugue resumes in the totally foreign key of G major before working round through C minor to the tonic. Here we find extraordinary contrapuntal ingenuity, with the fugue theme inverted, augmented, and diminished, and with parts of it combined in two or more voices at once. Augmentation and especially diminution are not normally possible in a triple-time fugue such as this, since the accentuation becomes distorted, but Beethoven seems to battle with the laws of music to find ways of forcing the notes to fit into his overall scheme. Through this sense of struggle, the 'exhausted, lamenting' mood of the G minor Arioso gradually dissolves into a triumphant, fortissimo conclusion.

During the composition of Op. 110 Beethoven was already contemplating its successor. One idea was a sonata in B flat, whose main theme eventually emerged in the String Quartet, Op. 130 in that key; another idea was a C minor sonata beginning with a 6/8 movement; an idea initially sketched for the third movement of such a sonata, however, was eventually adopted as the main theme of the first, still in C minor, and a C major Adagio consisting of a theme and variations was devised as the second and final movement.[21] Once again, then, Beethoven sets up a direct contrast—between stormy and gentle, fast and slow, C minor and C major; even, according to some, between Earth and Heaven. His choice of keys also balances those of the two previous sonatas to create a trilogy whose main keys are the same as those in *Fidelio*. Though published with separate opus numbers, the three sonatas form a set as coherent as any of his previous groups of three

[21] N-II, 466–7.

works, and they contain many subtle links: for example, just as Op. 110 moves to E major (the key of Op. 109) during the first movement, Op. 111 includes a second subject in A flat (the key of Op. 110).

The main sketches for the sonata immediately follow those for Op. 110, and the autograph score of the first movement is dated 13 January 1822. This presumably indicates when the score was begun rather than its completion date, since Op. 110 was completed less than three weeks earlier. As with the finale of Op. 110, the composing score of the new sonata became so messy that Beethoven wrote out a fair copy, this time for both movements; and after sending a version to Schlesinger in mid-February he found he needed to send a revised copy of the finale, with a request that the earlier one be destroyed, although it was probably the earlier one that was eventually used by the printer.[22] As with Op. 110, printing of the sonata was done in Paris through Schlesinger's son Moritz, who had set up a branch of his father's firm there. Beethoven also later sent manuscripts of both sonatas to Ries in London, where they were published in 1823 by Clementi.

Op. 111 begins with a dramatic downward leap of a diminished 7th, followed by a full diminished 7th chord. Such an idea was not completely unprecedented—the third 'Razumovsky' Quartet also begins with a diminished 7th chord, while the Fantasia, Op. 77 begins with descending scales outlining the same chord; nevertheless it was unusual for Beethoven to begin with such ambiguous tonality, and the power of the opening gesture admirably sets the mood for what follows. The slow introduction leads without a break into a stormy Allegro, in which the main theme includes a striking diminished 4th. Melodic disjunction thus plays a key role in this movement, and it reaches the *non plus ultra* during the second subject group (bars 32–4; see Ex. 16.3), where what sounds as a single melodic line includes leaps of over four octaves (the leaps are even larger in the recapitulation, but less angular). Beethoven, following the lead of Mozart and Handel, had long been developing large melodic leaps, in works such as *Fidelio* and *Meeresstille*, and he had even sketched a leap of two octaves for

**Ex. 16.3** Op. 111/I

22 See Timbrell, 'Op. 111', 207–10, and BB-1458 of 20 February (not in Anderson, *Letters*, or Albrecht, *Letters*).

the words 'Et resurrexit' in the *Missa solemnis*. The piano, however, provided far more scope than any singer, and he was by now increasingly exploring the outer limits of the enlarged keyboard.

Despite all its dramatic power, expressive ritenutos, and ingenious invertible counterpoint, the first movement is perhaps surprisingly conventional, echoing the mood of several other C minor works. Indeed, Czerny even believed it to have been composed at some earlier date. The second movement, by contrast, possesses an extraordinary visionary quality, transcending all previous piano music and even challenging the limits of the notational system in which it was written. Conventional notation, unlike medieval notation, is designed primarily for binary subdivisions of each note value, and copes much less well with ternary divisions, which require numerous triplet signs and/or dotted notes. In these variations Beethoven explored some of the possibilities of ternary division (possibilities that had lain neglected since the fifteenth century), creating notational peculiarities that bewildered some of his contemporaries.

The 'Arietta' theme is deceptively simple, with a cantabile melody whose opening C–G–D–G recalls that of the Diabelli Variations; unlike Diabelli's theme, however, the broad outline of the first phrase is C . . . E . . . B, a subtle reference to the C–E♭–B of the first-movement theme. The Arietta consists of two conventionally repeated pairs of four-bar phrases, although these are run together to create an almost seamless continuity that is typical of late Beethoven. The metre, however, is an unusual 9/16, providing a hint of the ternary divisions to follow. The theme is followed by four variations which, following age-old tradition, use increasingly short note values, so that bars in successive variations are typically divided into 9, 12, 24, and 27 notes. The fourth variation is a double one (the repeats being written out and varied differently), and it is followed by an extended developmental interlude before the final variation (bars 130–46), which omits the repeats, and a substantial coda. Thus the structure, theme – four variations – link – final variation – coda, resembles that of several of the variation sets written for Thomson (Opp. 105 and 107).

In its metrical scheme, however, the movement is highly innovative. The rhythm of the opening figure, quaver–semiquaver, is developed obsessively in Variation 1, and reappears twice as fast (with note values halved) in Variation 2, then twice as fast again (note values quartered) in Variation 3. To accommodate these subdivisions within the underlying three-beat pulse, Beethoven resorts to peculiar time signatures of 6/16 and 12/32. These are not strictly correct by modern rules, since the former implies two groups of three semiquavers and the latter four groups of three demisemiquavers, but these conventions were not established in Beethoven's day. His notation is anyway perfectly comprehensible, and no modern time signature is capable of indicating a bar consisting of three beats each of which divides into four sub-beats which in turn divide into three. More confusing is his omission of triplet signs and dots, so that in Variation 2 some semiquavers are longer than others (depending on whether or not they are followed by a demisemiquaver—an unintentional revival of a medieval convention formerly applied to breves and semibreves). A similar situation arises in Variation 3. From Variation 4 onwards each beat divides into nine, and so the correct time signature would be 27/32, but Beethoven uses 9/16 with implied triplet signs. Thus the Theme and Variation 1 contain bars of $3 \times 3$; in Variation 2 it is $3 \times 2 \times 3$; in Variation 3 it is $3 \times 2 \times 2 \times 3$; and from Variation 4 it is $3 \times 3 \times 3$. It is remarkable that such strange mathematical puzzles could come from a composer who was, as he admitted himself, so bad at arithmetic.

In Variation 3 the incessant, fast lilting rhythms, combined with chords struck fractionally before the beat, create an extraordinarily forward-looking, jazz-like effect. The fourth variation is even more remarkable, with shimmering sounds in a low register alternating every eight bars with extremely high, delicate twinkling. Huge contrasts of register continue in the remainder of the movement, and sound particularly striking on a piano of Beethoven's period, where differences in tone between high and low notes were much greater than on a modern piano. During the coda, trills figure prominently, and the movement ends with the opening figure inverted to form a closing gesture in typical Beethoven manner. When Moritz Schlesinger received Op. 111 he enquired tentatively whether there might not be a third movement, accidentally forgotten by the copyist. Superficially this seems a plausible supposition, since sonatas usually had three movements, with a quick finale after an Adagio. Yet surely nobody who heard this sonata could possibly imagine anything to follow this enormous, unfathomable and uplifting movement.

While working on his last two sonatas Beethoven must have thought frequently about the *Missa solemnis*; and he returned to it—specifically the 'Dona'—immediately after completing Op. 111. He was still not fully well, and complained in May of having had gout on the chest for four months, but he could do at least some work. It was probably at this stage, around April–June 1822, that this section was expanded to its present length; he also made minor adjustments to the other movements during these and the ensuing months, as is evident from the sketchbook Artaria 201, and arranged for a fresh copy of the Mass to be written out. Although a few slight alterations were made later still, it seems to have reached virtually its final form by summer 1822.

Beethoven repeatedly referred to the *Missa solemnis* as his greatest work, and with considerable justification. In both its emotional depth and its musical and intellectual ingenuity it is unsurpassed. The depth of his religious feelings during its period of composition is very evident, as was seen earlier, and in the autograph score these feelings find immediate expression in the inscription at its head: 'From the heart — may it return — to the heart.' Beethoven stated later: 'My chief aim when I was composing this grand Mass was to awaken and permanently instil religious feelings as much in the singers as in the listeners.'[23] He attempted to realize his intentions by careful attention to every word of the text; after writing it out with a translation and annotations to ensure he understood it thoroughly, he brought out its full meaning by using exceptionally vivid portrayal of each image, as he had done, for example, in his cantata *Meeresstille*.

A good example of this musical imagery is provided in the very first word, 'Kyrie' (Lord). The Lord as omnipotent, eternal creator is portrayed by a massive orchestral D major chord, repeated twice, from which the rest of the work seems to flow; and the gesture is heard again a few bars later with the addition of the choir (Ex. 16.4). This chord provides one of several symbols for the Deity in the Mass (God is clearly too vast a concept to be comprehended by a single symbol). The word 'Kyrie' in this context, however, denotes not only the Almighty but also the individual human voice addressing Him with the phrase 'Lord, have mercy'. Accordingly, the massive chords portraying the Lord are alternated with solo voices—tenor, then soprano, then alto—representing individual suppliants begging for mercy. Thus Beethoven, while being absolutely direct in his imagery, ingeniously operates on more than one level simultaneously.

**Ex. 16.4**  Op. 123/I

The beginning of the Gloria, with the words 'Gloria in excelsis Deo, et in terra pax . . .' (Glory to God in the highest, and on Earth peace), contains further opportunities for vivid word-painting. Placing the words 'excelsis Deo' on high notes is obvious, but insufficient for Beethoven; the glory

---

[23] A-1307.

must also be heard to rise up to God, and so rising phrases are heard over and over again, sung by each voice in turn. By contrast, the phrase 'Et in terra pax' is introduced by the basses, almost at the bottom of their register to portray the lowly Earth, and on a single pitch to denote the stillness of peace. A turn to the subdominant at the end of this passage reinforces the message, for the subdominant always has the effect of reducing tension.

The long text of the Credo presents many further images and ideas susceptible to obvious musical portrayal. For words such as 'omnipotentem' and 'descendit' Beethoven strains the bounds of what is musically possible: 'omnipotentem' must seem more powerful, the descent in 'descendit' further and steeper, than anything ever heard before, in order to drive home the message. For 'Et incarnatus est' ordinary tonal relationships are suspended, replaced by quasi-modal melodic lines and harmonic progressions not directed to a clear keynote, as if from another world. The Holy Spirit, likened to a dove in the Bible, then appears in the form of unmistakable bird-calls on the flute. Many other musical images representing aspects of the text appear in the remainder of the Credo, and no great musical insight is needed to perceive them—especially as they often appear in an extreme form.

For Beethoven, unlike Bach, the Sanctus ('Holy, holy, holy') demanded hushed and reverent devotion rather than triumphant celebration, and the tremolandos at the end of this section symbolize the trembling awe of those in the presence of God. The Sanctus and Benedictus are linked by a Praeludium, since it was common for the Consecration, where the bread and wine are transformed by the entry of the Divine presence, to take place at this moment in the Mass, often accompanied by organ improvisation. The Praeludium fulfils the function of this improvisation, and the Divine presence is represented by a solo violin, which enters at a high pitch at the end of the Praeludium and remains throughout the Benedictus.[24]

Some of Beethoven's most original portrayals, however, are found in the 'Dona nobis pacem' section, with the concept of 'peace' explored from all angles. The main character of the section, with its lilting rhythms, 6/8 metre, and imitation bird-calls (bars 100–6), is clearly pastoral, as several commentators have suggested; that Beethoven was consciously evoking the pastoral idiom is confirmed by his comment 'pacem pastoralisch' amongst the sketches.[25] Peace is broken during the movement by two interpolations. The first (bars 164–89) is military in character, with martial rhythms played by trumpets and drums, and the word 'war' itself appears more than once amongst the relevant sketches.[26] The second interpolation (bars 266 ff.) consists of a violent fugato for orchestra alone, and its 'presto' marking contrasts with the gentle allegretto vivace of the main part of the 'Dona'. A clue to this apparently puzzling passage is Beethoven's inscription at the

---

[24] See Kirkendale, 'New Roads', for a fuller explanation of this and several of the other pictorial devices mentioned above.
[25] Artaria 180; see Drabkin, 'Agnus', 137.     [26] Drabkin, 'Agnus', 137.

head of the 'Dona': 'Prayer for inner and outer peace'. Whereas the first interpolation portrayed war as the threat to outer peace, this second one portrays inner turmoil as the threat to emotional and mental peace. Beethoven's earliest idea for this fugato was an entirely extraneous theme in a foreign key (C major), while a later sketch shows the main 'Dona' theme simply speeded up.[27] The first idea fails since the disturbance is not from within, while the second fails since the theme is not greatly altered. Eventually he based the orchestral fugato on a horribly distorted version of the 'Dona' theme, as if the mind were being attacked internally. Thus he again sets the text by working on several different levels, portraying peace as lack of violence, as cheerful mood, and as Arcadian idyll, as well as relief from either war or mental anguish (both of which he had experienced so much in real life).

Some of Beethoven's means of expression in the Mass are therefore quite subtle; but many are extremely plain and direct. They convey something of the strength of emotion in the music's conception, and are designed to be intelligible to the most uninitiated listener. Indeed such blatant forms of word-painting might lead to charges of naivety, were it not for the extraordinary musical sophistication infusing the entire work. Beethoven binds it into a thoroughly unified whole through various technical means, despite the variety of individual images.

The key scheme is based firmly around D major throughout, with certain subsidiary keys also playing an important role. As in several of Beethoven's late works, these keys do not include the dominant, and the absence of any extended passages in A major is one of the most striking features about the overall tonality. Instead, the first section of the Kyrie moves through A major to F sharp major and eventually B minor for the start of the 'Christe'. This last key had already been signalled at the opening of the Kyrie, where a B minor chord is the first sound after the initial D major sonority; and that same B minor chord reappears at the start of the Agnus Dei (which, following tradition, begins away from the main tonic). In contrast to the weak dominant, much emphasis is placed on the subdominant—both the overall subdominant and local subdominants. The third section of the Kyrie has an extended passage in G major (bars 152–66), and the Gloria utilizes this key several times, with strong C major chords appearing daringly close to the end of the movement; indeed, since these C naturals are never cancelled again by C sharps, it could be argued that the Gloria actually ends in G with an imperfect cadence, rather than a plagal cadence in D. The 'Pleni' section ends inconclusively on a G major chord, and G major finally asserts itself fully in the Praeludium and Benedictus, before appearing more briefly in the Agnus Dei. Another key with long-range effect is B flat, the main key of the Credo (although this begins on the subdominant of B flat) and also of the 'Gratias' section of the Gloria. Its reappearance at the end of each of

[27] Drabkin, 'Agnus', 147, 155.

the two interpolations in the 'Dona' surely has symbolic significance: it recalls the concept of belief expressed in the Credo, and this enables inner and outer peace to be restored by the 'Lamb of God' to whom frantic appeals are made.

Each movement is also unified in its form. Some are based loosely on various kinds of modified sonata form, suitably adapted to the text. In particular there is a clear sense of recapitulation after tonal digression, in the Kyrie (bar 128), the Benedictus (bar 167, where the recapitulation begins in the subdominant, C major), and the 'Dona' (bar 212, which also quickly veers to the subdominant). In the movements with long texts, unity is aided by recall of the opening motif. In the Gloria the initial idea reappears in the coda (bars 525 ff.), after the last 'Amen', providing a frame for the movement. In the Credo the opening motif, to the words 'Credo, credo', appears three times—once for each person of the Trinity (bars 5–11, 37–42, 267 ff.)—and is developed extensively the third time in a symphonic manner.

There is no prominent main theme underlying the whole work, but the movements have the same kind of affinity with each other as do those of Beethoven's symphonies. It is also possible to see more subtle connections: a distinctive motif in bars 3–6—a rising 4th followed by stepwise descent, which has been described as a germinal figure for the work—reappears in various guises in later movements, including the main theme of 'in gloria Dei patris' in the second movement. Another subtle relationship appears in the endings of the five movements. The first four all end on a weak beat or half-bar, hinting that more is to follow; only in the Agnus Dei does the final chord begin on the first beat of the bar.

The Mass shows many retrospective features, and is firmly rooted in the Austrian Mass tradition. Yet the handling of these features is so original that the overall effect is entirely new and unrepeatable. Inevitably the work shows superficial similarities to many works of earlier times, but there are no specific allusions. One phrase in the 'Dona' is alleged to have been borrowed from the 'Hallelujah Chorus' from Handel's *Messiah*, but the sketches show that, like Beethoven's other supposed borrowings, the similarity was fortuitous, since the passage 'was conceived entirely from thematic material presented earlier and was *not* originally intended as a quotation from another work'.[28]

The effort Beethoven put into composing the work is reflected in the vast number and complexity of the sketches, which are still far from thoroughly studied. It is also evident from the work's musical complexity. This reaches its apogee in the two great fugues at the close of the Gloria and Credo, with their intricate polyphonic writing and ingenious technical devices. Beethoven clearly devoted more time and energy to this work than to any other (with the possible exception of *Fidelio* in its various versions), and it

---

[28] Ibid., 148.

was this devotion, coupled with the grandeur of the overall conception, with its eternal truths and time-honoured text, that enabled him to say with such confidence that this was his greatest work. It is therefore understandable that he spent so long on detailed adjustments after the last note had been written, and was so reluctant to part with his brain-child. The manuscript was checked, revised, checked again, and changes were still being made towards the end of 1822, if not later. Rudolph finally received his presentation copy, three years late, on 19 March 1823, and publication of the work was to wait even longer.

The *Missa solemnis* provides some indication of Beethoven's artistic goals, but he also articulated them more explicitly in a number of letters, including several written around this period. He stressed that his main aim was to master the art of music; he was and always had been thoroughly devoted to his Muses, finding in them the happiness of his life. He did not compose for the purpose of earning money, and preferred to accept only what was necessary to live on, concentrating rather on furthering the cause of art. He would have liked to write only the most elevated types of work—symphonies, operas, oratorios, quartets, and ideally the music for Goethe's *Faust*. However, financial need, exacerbated by the requirement to provide for Karl's education, forced him to consider other genres. One cause for the delays in the Mass in 1821 was the need to finish what he called some 'potboilers' to keep himself alive. The only works being composed when he made this comment were his last two piano sonatas—perhaps the most remarkable potboilers ever written! Even when, as then, he was composing for a specific commission, he would not compromise his style, and considered only how to make the best of the work in question.

One venture that promised both to advance the cause of art and relieve Beethoven's financial embarrassment, which was by now quite acute, was the proposed publication of his collected works. He had considered this idea for some years, but in 1820–2 he mentioned it to several publishers in an effort to get it started. The plan was to reissue works already published, making minor, 'unimportant' changes as necessary; to include one new work in each genre that was published; and to complete the entire enterprise within two years, for a fee of 10,000 fl. CM. Such an ambitious plan proved unrealistic—indeed, something approaching the complete publication of all his works was not achieved until 1971 with the final volume of Willy Hess's Supplement to the old *Gesamtausgabe*. It seems that his publishers were not greatly interested in reprinting existing works, and there would have been some tricky negotiations in cases where works had recently been sold to other publishers, although copyright provision was still in its infancy.

Another means advancing the cause of art—ultimately a more successful one—was to return to the Ninth Symphony, which had lain dormant since early 1820. 'What might the Philharmonic Society [of London] offer me as an honorarium for a grand symphony?' wrote Beethoven to Ries on 6 July 1822.[29] He was still considering a visit to London early the following year, for the society's next season, and bringing one or possibly two new symphonies. Before even receiving a reply from Ries, he was jotting down a few sketches for them, and completion of the Ninth, almost as great a task as completion of the Mass, was to be his primary occupation over the next two years.

[29] A-1084.

# 17

# Completion of the Ninth (1822–4)

When Beethoven finished his last phase of intensive sketching for the *Missa solemnis* in spring 1822, he did not immediately return to the Diabelli Variations or the Ninth Symphony, both of which he had earlier set aside. Instead he began rounding up various works still unpublished. He had received requests from several publishers begging him for compositions, including Artaria, Diabelli, Steiner, the Schlesingers, Carl Friedrich Peters of Leipzig (who wrote to him on 18 May), and Antonio Pacini of Paris (who wrote on 22 June). Beethoven had an urgent need to sell some works, for by summer 1822 he owed money to Steiner, Artaria, Brentano, and his brother Johann, but he had nothing new apart from the Mass. He therefore drew up some price lists (along with Haslinger) for works that were either dug out from the past or might be written in the future. The lists could be used either in responding to publishers or in connection with his plans for a collected edition. Besides the obvious items, some surprises were included: otherwise unknown songs (for example 'Ich wiege dich in meinem Arm'), and genres that he never wrote, such as a Graduale, Requiem, and *opera seria*.[1]

Johann, who had acquired an estate at Gneixendorf near Krems in 1819, arrived in Vienna in late spring, and began to be involved in Beethoven's business dealings, perhaps in an effort to help him reduce his debts. Indeed Johann may have assisted in drawing up the lists and suggesting prices. If so, he was continuing their brother Carl's work of 1802–5, helping Beethoven to sell old works and obtain the best prices for new ones. The Mass had long since been promised to Simrock for the equivalent of 900 fl. CM, but in late 1821 Beethoven offered it to Adolf Schlesinger, eventually agreeing a price equivalent to 975 fl. Now, in early June 1822, Johann proposed that Beethoven offer it to Peters for 1000 fl.; Beethoven apparently expressed unease, but Johann replied, 'That's business'.[2] He had clearly lost none of the commercial skills that had enabled him to make a sizeable fortune. Beethoven duly wrote to Peters on 5 June offering the Mass at the new price, along with several other works, some not yet written.

Shortly afterwards, Johann told Beethoven that Rossini, who was in Vienna for a few months, greatly desired to meet him. The meeting duly

---

[1] Alb-288.    [2] BKh, ii. 263.

took place, but as neither Beethoven nor Rossini was fluent in the other's language, there was little communication. There was something of a craze for Rossini in Vienna at the time, but Beethoven never rated him as highly as Mozart, Haydn, or even Cherubini. Johann observed that Rossini had become quite rich through writing operas, and suggested that Beethoven might do the same.[3] Beethoven did indeed often consider a new opera during the next few years, but it never materialized.

Beethoven spent much of the summer at Oberdöbling, just outside Vienna, while Johann returned to Gneixendorf. Although there had been frequent quarrels, the bond of affection between the two brothers remained strong, and they corresponded frequently during the next few months. Beethoven sometimes teased Johann in his letters with such overblown phrases as 'high and mighty landowner' or 'owner of all the Danube islands near Krems, director of the entire Austrian pharmacy'.[4] Johann, for his part, often described himself as 'Landowner' in his business letters, and a widely circulated anecdote relates that, when Beethoven once received such a communication, he wittily replied as 'Brainowner'. Since he frequently mentioned his need to live by his mind and by his pen, the story is highly plausible.

During the summer at Oberdöbling, Beethoven's main activity seems to have been sorting out material to send to Peters, who, in response to the list of works available, agreed to buy the Mass, three Lieder with piano accompaniment, a few bagatelles, and four marches for military band.[5] Beethoven rather rashly promised to send all this by 15 August, the date he planned to move to Baden for medical reasons, but preparing the shorter works proved irksome: several were not quite complete, while others, some of which dated right back to the 1790s, needed substantial revisions to improve their quality and update their style. He had also not decided precisely which works to send from his collection.

Instead of moving to Baden on the 15th, Beethoven extended his stay in Oberdöbling so that he could continue visiting Rudolph in Vienna for frequent composition lessons. These visits occupied so much time that the material for Peters was still not ready when he finally arrived in Baden at the beginning of September. Shortly after arrival he was greeted by Carl Friedrich Hensler, the manager of the newly rebuilt Josephstadt Theatre in the suburbs of Vienna. Hensler planned to reopen the theatre with a production of Beethoven's *Die Ruinen von Athen*, but it required adaptation, and a change of title to *Die Weihe des Hauses* (The Consecration of the House), to suit its new context. Hensler succeeded in persuading Beethoven to make the necessary musical alterations, which included a new chorus ('Wo sich die Pulse', WoO 98) and a new overture (Op. 124). These movements and the other changes were completed with astonishing speed,

---

[3] BKh, ii. 269–70.    [4] A-1087, A-1103.

[5] Alb-290, Alb-294; fuller versions in BB-1469, BB-1475.

despite the lengthy baths Beethoven was taking for health reasons (apparently an hour and a half a day), and the première took place on 3 October.

The Overture is Handelian in character, with a slow introduction followed by a fugal Allegro. Some have suggested echoes of Handel's *Messiah*, but the chains of descending suspensions set against dactylic figuration are more strongly reminiscent of the overture and the final chorus of *Alexander's Feast*, which Beethoven also knew. By now he admired Handel above all other composers, as several independent witnesses confirm. He had long been familiar with some of Handel's music, and as recently as 1820 had contemplated writing some orchestral variations on the 'Dead March' from *Saul*, but the Overture to *Die Weihe des Hauses* is perhaps the work most directly inspired by Handel's example. Nevertheless, many of its similarities to Handel are superficial, and most of it is unmistakably Beethovenian.

Beethoven directed the première of *Die Weihe des Hauses* on 3 October and the performances on the following three days. It seems to have been at this time that he became closely acquainted with Schindler, who led the violins for these performances and was soon fulfilling the secretarial role vacated by Oliva in 1820. In later years Schindler made out that he had known Beethoven far longer, but the first documented connection between them dates from this month, and Schindler's first genuine entries in the extant conversation books were written the following month.

During October Beethoven apparently continued preparing the music for Peters, and he gathered no fewer than twelve bagatelles into a little portfolio. Each of them was evidently revised during this period—in some cases quite substantially—but he had difficulty making a final choice from such a disparate group, which included a rough draft for *Für Elise* (the fair copy having long since been given away), abandoned ideas for sonata movements and ballroom dances, and miscellaneous fragments jotted down in 1793. Meanwhile he had decided that some of the marches needed trio sections, and these may have been composed at this stage. He was also, however, beginning to think of larger projects, and about this time he made several sketches for his two planned symphonies and the Diabelli Variations (mainly in the sketchbook Artaria 201, pp. 116–25), as well as jotting down an idea for an overture on the theme B–A–C–H. In the Ninth Symphony only the first movement had been partly sketched, but now ideas appear for the others: for the second Beethoven planned a scherzo-like movement using a fugue theme from an abandoned string quintet (Hess 40) of 1817, although the theme was to be modified before being finally adopted; the Adagio was undecided, and he was also considering a 2/4 presto, either instead of the proposed second movement or between the Adagio and the Finale; most significant, however, are the Finale sketches, which show for the first time his decision to write a choral movement using Schiller's 'An die Freude' (Ode to Joy). Some early sketches for a Tenth Symphony (never to be completed) appear a few pages later in the sketchbook and on a separate bifolio. These show a curious first movement (or first two movements) combining an Andante in E flat with an Allegro in C minor, and one sketch shows a synopsis of what might follow: a movement in G minor, a fugue in B flat major, and a minuet-like finale in E flat that incorporates a reprise of part of the opening Andante.[6] The theme of this projected finale, however, was shortly afterwards plundered for a new work in honour of Hensler, which Beethoven entitled *Gratulations-Menuett* (WoO 3). This brief orchestral work was performed at a short concert for Hensler on 3 November, the eve of his name-day, although Beethoven was apparently not present since he was attending a performance of *Fidelio* elsewhere.

Beethoven was still making minor changes to his Mass, notably for the word 'judicare' in the Credo, which he sketched repeatedly during the autumn. His main achievement in the latter part of November, however, was finally to assemble a set of six bagatelles for Peters (now known as Op. 119 Nos. 1–6). He had made great efforts to produce a coherent set from his heterogeneous collection, but the problem of finding a satisfactory final piece proved insuperable, and so he composed one specially. The six are remarkably well balanced and contrasted in terms of keys, tempos, and time signatures, and he cleverly used a mixture of three different metres, and both fast and slow tempos, in the concluding piece as a summing up of the set.[7] The set had still not been put together when he wrote to Peters on 22 November, but the autograph score is dated November 1822; thus it was probably written out just before the end of the month.

During November Beethoven was sent two letters that were to have a profound effect on his creative output for the next two years. One was from Ries, who in response to Beethoven's enquiry of 6 July (see page 297) had asked the Philharmonic Society to commission a new symphony. Ries now informed Beethoven that the Society would offer £50 (about 500 fl. CM) for the manuscript of a new symphony, which would have to remain unpublished for 18 months. Beethoven gladly accepted the offer, and expressed the intention of visiting London in spring 1824. The Ninth Symphony, which was still in its early stages of composition, now became his prime concern, although he had to finish off a few other items before beginning intensive work on it. The second letter was from Prince Nikolas Galitzin (or Golitsin) of St Petersburg, asking Beethoven to name his price for up to three string quartets. Galitzin had lived in Vienna during his childhood in 1804–6, and had since become a great admirer of Beethoven's music, as well as a keen cellist. His request was remarkably consonant with Beethoven's own intentions, for a projected string quartet was among the works he had offered to Peters during the summer, and so Beethoven readily agreed, for a fee of 50 ducats (225 fl. CM) per quartet. Three quartets were therefore

---

[6] See Brandenburg, 'Neunten Symphonie', 111–12.
[7] See Cooper, *Creative Process*, 271–5.

placed behind the Ninth Symphony in the lengthening queue of projected works that was forming in Beethoven's mind. He probably already had some ideas for the first new quartet, but no sketches for it survive from before 1824.

The *Missa solemnis* had still not been sent to a publisher, and the lengthy saga of its sale does Beethoven little credit. He had promised it to Simrock, Peters, and Schlesinger, although by June he had decided to exclude Schlesinger for having played a 'Jewish trick' (Beethoven had apparently lost 12–13 fl. through the payment method used for the last two piano sonatas).[8] Simrock and Peters, however, were daily expecting the Mass to arrive, Simrock having agreed to the higher price of 1000 fl. Artaria and Diabelli had also been offered it. To satisfy demand, Beethoven therefore decided to write a second (and later a third) new mass, which joined his lengthening mental queue. He then used this as an excuse for not sending anyone a mass in the meantime. In November he described the Mass in D as long since finished, but the other new mass was 'not yet', and his sketchbooks suggest it was not even begun (indeed it never was, as far as is known, apart from two or three brief sketches).

While prevaricating with publishers, Beethoven hit on a new plan: to postpone printing the Mass for some years, and instead offer a manuscript copy for 50 ducats to all the leading courts of Europe, and to anyone else who might subscribe. First mention of the scheme is in a letter of 27 December 1822 from Johann to Pacini, and in the ensuing months Beethoven, assisted by Schindler, Johann, and others, sent out numerous invitations to potential subscribers, as well as more personal letters to contacts who might influence the response, such as Goethe, Zelter, and Cherubini. Eventually ten copies were sold in this manner, and although copying costs were substantial, the income generated helped ease Beethoven's financial crisis. The crisis had indeed become so acute by early 1823 that he had to sell one of his eight bank shares to avoid being sued by Steiner and the tailor Joseph Lind; he had been on the brink of selling a share for some time, and had been closely watching share prices since 1820 (as is clear from the conversation books). The remaining seven shares, however, were set aside as a legacy for Karl, and were mentioned in a letter of 6 March 1823 nominating him as heir to all Beethoven's property.

At last, on Saturday 8 February, Beethoven sent off a parcel to Peters; three pieces were still missing, but these were sent a week later (though they missed the post and had to wait until the 21st). The material included the six bagatelles (Op. 119 Nos. 1–6), four marches, which Beethoven described as three tattoos and a march (WoO 18–20, 24), and three songs ('Opferlied', 'Bundeslied', and 'Der Kuss'). All the bagatelles were old pieces (*c.*1794–1802) newly revised, except the last one. The marches dated from *c.*1809–16, although the trios for the first three were new. Of the songs,

---

[8] A-1083, A-1095.

'Opferlied' was an extensively revised and elaborated version of one (WoO 126) drafted in 1794–5, revised in 1801–2, and published in 1808. The new version was scored for three soloists, four-part choir, and small orchestra, and received its first performance in Pressburg (Bratislava) on 23 December 1822; Beethoven now sent it along with a piano arrangement of the accompaniment. 'Bundeslied', likewise scored for an unusual combination of voices and instruments (or piano), was probably also of early origin, although the main evidence for this is actually misleading. The song is sketched on a leaf (Vienna A 64) dating from *c.*1795–6, but the 'Bundeslied' sketches were actually added only much later.[9] Since one of the other sketches on the leaf is yet another idea for 'judicare' (hitherto unidentified), the 'Bundeslied' sketch was probably added about the same time, in late 1822. Beethoven presumably had the leaf at hand at that date because it contained the melodic line of another song[10] that he was thinking of completing for Peters. 'Der Kuss' was based on sketches made in 1798, and had just a piano accompaniment.

Peters was greatly disappointed when the material arrived, and expressed his objections in a letter of 4 March. First, he complained that instead of four military marches he had received three tattoos and one march. The fine distinction between tattoo and march is not evident to most observers; indeed two of the tattoos had been entitled 'march' when they were first composed, and Beethoven had pointed out to Peters that all three could be used as marches. The main musical distinction apparently concerns length—each is much shorter than the fourth march (WoO 24). Peters evidently felt there was no ready market for this type of composition, and refused to accept them, despite having agreed to do so. He similarly refused the three songs, complaining that two had orchestral accompaniment and sections with chorus (although Beethoven had also supplied piano accompaniments, and the chorus voices could be omitted); and the third, 'Der Kuss', was according to Peters (following Beethoven's title) only an ariette instead of a proper through-composed Lied (it was, however, through-composed, and similar in scope to many existing Lieder). As for the bagatelles, Peters rightly guessed that these, like the marches, had been written much earlier, and stated that he had had difficulty convincing anyone that they were indeed by Beethoven; he added that they were too short (though he had not previously specified any definite length) and too easy, and that he would not publish them.

Poor Beethoven! He had several times been asked for works similar in style to his earlier ones, and to make them easy to play; Peters himself had stressed three times in a single letter that he wanted music that was 'not too difficult'.[11] Yet now Beethoven was being criticized for supplying music that was too easy and old-fashioned. He can rightly be blamed for having

---

[9] Johnson, *Beethoven's Early Sketches*, i. 136.
[10] 'Minnelied', text by Johann Voss: see N-II, 574.     [11] Alb-295.

misled publishers during this period, indicating that works such as Op. 109, the Mass, and the music for Peters were ready when they still needed attention; but the publishers often treated him equally badly. He had supplied Peters with what had been agreed, despite Peters's protestations to the contrary: four marches (three of which could be called tattoos), some bagatelles, and three songs with piano accompaniment (and with no extra charge for orchestral versions for two of them); yet Peters had made excuses for not publishing any of them. Worse was to follow. As was his custom, Beethoven had sent the bagatelles to Ries in London, so that they could be published there about the same time as in Leipzig, for an additional fee; and as the five bagatelles given earlier to Starke, though by now printed, were unlikely to be known in London, he enclosed these too. Ries sold all eleven to Clementi, who made no complaints that they were too easy or uncharacteristic of Beethoven but published them as *Trifles for the Piano Forte*. This edition was soon afterwards pirated by Moritz Schlesinger in Paris, and thence by Sauer & Leidesdorf in Vienna.[12] Thus Beethoven was deprived of any fee for the continental rights for the bagatelles sent to Peters—a double blow, since he had agreed with Johann that this fee would go towards repayment of a loan from him. His magnanimous response was to write a replacement set for Johann, as will be seen later, and to continue offering other works to Peters, though ultimately without success. And the very same day that he received Peters's critical letter, 19 March 1823, he at last gave Rudolph his presentation copy of the *Missa solemnis*.

Before moving on to the Ninth Symphony, Beethoven had one other project to complete: the Diabelli Variations. This work had been left unfinished in 1819, and by late 1822 Diabelli was becoming impatient for it. Beethoven made a few tentative sketches at this stage, and promised to deliver the work shortly, proposing a fee of 40 ducats if it were 'worked out on as large a scale as is planned', or for a smaller fee if it were not.[13] Since he had earlier offered it to Peters for only 30 ducats, he was clearly planning now to expand the set beyond the original twenty-three variations, while allowing for the possibility of not doing so and charging less than 40 ducats. He evidently intended the work all along for Diabelli, despite offering it to other publishers.

Beethoven resumed intensive work on the Diabelli Variations probably in February 1823. One of the original twenty-three (the twentieth) was removed and the order of the remainder was retained, while eleven new ones were added: Nos. 1–2, 15, 23–6, 28–9, 31, and 33.[14] Thus the basic shape remained unaltered, but with a few additional insertions; and the final section, as in so many of his compositions, was substantially extended at a late stage. The new variations were completed surprisingly quickly, considering that Rudolph was in Vienna from 25 February for about four

[12] Tyson, *Authentic English*, 114–15.    [13] A-1105.    [14] Kinderman, *Diabelli*, 15.

weeks and Beethoven had to give him a lesson every day for up to three hours: 'For with such lessons one is scarcely able to think next day, much less compose.'[15] During April Beethoven also found time to compose a short choral piece (WoO 106) for the birthday of his patron Prince Ferdinand Lobkowitz, and a canon (WoO 184) to greet his old friend the violinist Schuppanzigh on his return from Russia. Despite these delays, a copy of the Diabelli Variations that was destined for Ries was ready by 30 April 1823, and Diabelli probably received his copy at about the same time.

From the outset the basic plan of the work, though incorporating several traditional features, showed important innovations. Almost every variation has its own tempo mark, different from the preceding variation, and although the majority are in 3/4 time like Diabelli's waltz, towards the end of the set an increasing number use other time signatures. The main precedent for such frequent contrasts was Beethoven's set in F major, Op. 34. There, however, successive variations were in different keys as well as contrasting metres, whereas here all but Var. 32 (in E flat) are in C major or C minor, creating a much more monolithic effect. Another significant innovation is that in every variation Beethoven takes one or more motifs from Diabelli's theme—such as the initial turn figure or the ensuing repeated notes—modifies each in some way and then develops it intensively throughout the variation.[16] Although these motifs are taken from Diabelli's melodic line rather than the accompanying figuration, the overall contours of this melodic line are virtually ignored in most of the variations, which build instead on the harmonic outline that underpins the theme. In this respect the set resembles the Variations on 'Rule, Britannia' and the Thirty-two Variations in C minor (WoO 80), both of which are at times more harmonic than melodic variations. Beethoven may have felt by 1823, however, that he had moved too far from Diabelli's melody, for in several of the added variations—notably Vars. 1, 2, 15, 25, and 33—the melodic shape of the theme is recalled directly.

The overall structure embodies many different substructures, which overlap and interact with each other. It can be seen as four or five large segments (perhaps preceded by an introduction), like the movements of some grand symphony; or as a series of contrasting miniatures each of which throws a different light on the theme; or as a succession of groups of four variations (reminiscent of the groups of three in Bach's 'Goldberg' Variations), in which the speed tends either to increase or decrease within each group; or as a number of prominent 'pillars' around which the other variations are grouped; or as a single, monumental structure whose content increases gradually in complexity during the course of the work, up to a climax in the fugal Variation 32.

Within this overall structure, however it is perceived, Beethoven ranges over the whole gamut of human emotion, perhaps covering a wider

---

[15] A-1167; Rudolph's arrival date is given in BKh, iii. 439.
[16] See Münster, *Diabelli*, for the fullest account of this procedure.

spectrum than in any other work. There are humorous variations, such as Vars. 13 and 15, where he seems almost to poke fun at Diabelli's theme. In Var. 22 he quotes the aria 'Notte e giorno faticar' from Mozart's *Don Giovanni,* having noticed the similarity of its opening phrase to Diabelli's (the quotation, like Beethoven's other deliberate quotations such as the Russian themes in the 'Razumovsky' Quartets and Weigl's theme in the Clarinet Trio, Op. 11, is clearly marked in the score, unlike various alleged ones that commentators claim to have found). In contrast to the whimsical variations many are very serious, including three consecutive ones in C minor (Vars. 29–31). The last of these is an elaborate and highly decorative aria in 9/8, building on the tradition of having a slow, profound variation immediately before the final one (or, in this case, the final two). Still more profound, however, is Var. 20, in slow 6/4 time and consisting mainly of dotted minims (Ex. 17.1). Its low register, hymn-like block chords, and strange harmonic progressions seem to suggest some cavernous catacombs, where all sense of time and momentum is suspended.

**Ex. 17.1** Op. 120, Var. 20

The intricate double fugue (Var. 32) provides the crowning glory of the work, but the concluding 'Tempo di Minuetto' (Var. 33) and the ensuing coda supply a wonderfully ethereal epilogue. The general trajectory of Diabelli's theme had been to rise gradually from *c″* to *d″* early on, but with *e″* held back until well into the second part of the waltz theme; after this the melodic line rises quickly to end on a high *c‴*. This overall shape is therefore embodied in Beethoven's work as a whole, in that the final variation and coda are levitated into celestial regions far above the sorrows, the struggles, and earthy humour that preceded them.

After receiving the work, Diabelli published it remarkably quickly, in June (so quickly that a copy of the edition arrived in London before Ries had time to sell the work to a London publisher, and so Beethoven received no fee from England). Sets of variations were traditionally regarded as a less serious genre than sonatas and symphonies, but the Diabelli Variations were clearly an exception and were announced as such:

We present here to the world Variations of no ordinary type, but a great and important masterpiece worthy to be ranked with the imperishable creations of the old Classics . . . more interesting from the fact that it is elicited from a theme which no one would otherwise have supposed capable of a working-out of that character. . . . All these variations . . . will entitle the work to a place beside Sebastian Bach's masterpiece in the same form.[17]

Diabelli's point that the work is based on a theme that did not appear to have potential for greatness is well made. Beethoven had already demonstrated, in both improvisations and compositions, exceptional ability at creating great art out of next to nothing, and the Diabelli Variations are perhaps the supreme example of this skill. The reference to Bach's 'Goldberg' Variations is also particularly interesting. There is no evidence that Beethoven owned a copy of these, and how well he knew them is unclear; but Diabelli's announcement indicates that Beethoven must have known of their existence, and it is perhaps significant that both sets employ an unusually wide variety of tempos and metres in different variations. Thus Beethoven may have been making a conscious attempt to emulate one of Bach's greatest keyboard compositions. He fully succeeded, for no other set of variations can be ranked alongside these two immense works.

After despatching the Diabelli Variations to the publishers, Beethoven began intensive work on the Ninth Symphony, a task that occupied him for the rest of the year. The main features of the first movement had already been established over several years, and further sketching soon brought it to completion. For the second movement, his earlier idea of writing a 2/4 presto (like the one in Op. 110) was ingeniously combined with the plan to write a scherzo-like fugato in 3/4: the fugato was developed as the main part of the movement, while the trio section was sketched in 2/4 before being renotated in 2/2 with fewer barlines.[18] This mixing of metres, hitherto almost unprecedented in his symphonies, provides one of a number of subtle hints of what is to follow, as does the key of D major used for the trio section (the original 2/4 presto sketches had been in D minor).

The main work on the second movement had been completed by late July, when Beethoven moved on to the third. One idea for this was a slow minuet theme in A or D major; another was to transpose, from E flat to B flat, the theme previously intended for the Tenth Symphony, and perhaps also transpose the C minor theme from this work to D minor for use somewhere in the Ninth.[19] The C/D minor theme was soon abandoned, while the E flat theme was so fundamentally modified that little of its original shape (which resembled the slow movement of the *Pathétique* Sonata) was retained except the rhythm of the first bar and the melodic outline of the third (see Ex. 17.2a and b). This theme was then used as the basis for a short set of variations, but one which incorporated an entirely new concept: interspersed between the theme and the two variations were episodes in D

---

[17] Tovey, *Essays: Chamber Music*, 124.    [18] N-II, 173.
[19] N-II, 174–7; Marston, 'Anti-organicism'; Cook, *Symphony No. 9*, 11–12.

**Ex. 17.2**

(a) SV 14, p. 125

(b) Op. 125/III

and G based on the minuet theme that Beethoven had just sketched. The result somewhat resembled Haydn's double-variation procedure (as exemplified in his 'Drum roll' Symphony), but it incorporated both metrical and tonal contrast, recalling that of the second movement while foreshadowing the keys and metrical variety of the finale.

During the composition of the first three movements of the Ninth, which took until about September 1823, Beethoven was beset by the usual range of personal and musical concerns. Among the admirers who visited him that year, perhaps the most notable was an eleven-year-old boy—Franz Liszt. Liszt, a child genius like Beethoven, had moved to Vienna in 1821 and was currently having piano lessons from Beethoven's former pupil Carl Czerny. Liszt invited Beethoven to attend his forthcoming piano recital on 13 April, and years later he claimed that Beethoven had done so, and had kissed him afterwards as a mark of approval. There is conflicting evidence, however, about whether Beethoven did in fact attend (and several of Schindler's conversation entries on the subject, quoted by Thayer, are spurious).

While sketching the Ninth Symphony, Beethoven had other compositional plans in mind. The main one was a new opera, with Franz Grillparzer as librettist. Beethoven heard, about April, that Grillparzer had drafted a libretto entitled *Melusine* for him, and the poet also offered the alternative subject of *Drahomira*. In mid-May Grillparzer visited Beethoven, and some of their discussion of the matter is recorded in a conversation book. Years later Grillparzer left an account of the meeting: his recollection of the conversation itself shows little congruence with the conversation-book record, but his report of a highly disordered room rings true. Another of Beethoven's plans, which was discussed in March with Hermann von Hermannsthal,[20] was to revise *Die Ruinen von Athen* yet again; the idea was probably still with him some months later, when he asked his brother to return his manuscript of the work as he was compos-

---

[20] Not Grillparzer, as stated in TF, 845: see BKh, iii. 114.

ing something similar,[21] although this could denote the Ninth Symphony, which was his main preoccupation at the time.

Beethoven was unable to work on either of the Grillparzer operas during summer 1823, and even had great difficulty working on the Ninth Symphony. In April he had contracted an eye infection, which was made worse by the city air. Thus on 17 May, shortly after the meeting with Grillparzer, he moved to the village of Hetzendorf, while his city lodgings were occupied by Schindler. Beethoven's doctor (Dr Smetana) forbade him to read or write for three weeks in May while the infection was at its worst. The advice was not followed rigidly, but progress on the Ninth Symphony was clearly impeded for several weeks, and his eyes did not fully recover until the following year.

Meanwhile during June his brother Johann also fell ill and was bedridden for a time. Johann was staying with his wife's brother, Leopold Obermayer, next door to where Schindler was occupying Beethoven's Vienna lodgings, but Beethoven was in Hetzendorf, prevented by his eye trouble from paying a visit. Schindler eventually informed Beethoven of what went on during Johann's illness. Johann's wife Therese had found a lover, brought him to meet Johann, and then dressed up and went out driving with the lover on several occasions. Neither she nor her sixteen-year-old daughter, Amalie Waldmann, attended to Johann, who was left in the care of servants and a private nurse, and she evidently slept with her lover at least three times, aided and abetted by Amalie, who kept watch. Beethoven's misgivings about Johann's marriage to Therese in 1812 had finally proved correct ('You see how right I was to hold you back from this . . .', he wrote to Johann in a draft letter in early July).[22]

Soon Schindler himself was being condemned by Beethoven. The exact reasons are unclear, but Beethoven had evidently found him unreliable and deceitful, qualities that Schindler showed so spectacularly in later years when he wrote a deliberately misleading biography of Beethoven. Beethoven also blamed him for the loss of any fee for an intended English edition of the Diabelli Variations. 'I avoid as far as possible that low-minded, contemptible fellow'; 'his evil character, predisposed to intriguing, demands that he be treated seriously'; 'I have never met a more wretched person on God's earth, an arch-scoundrel whom I have given the sack': these are some of the comments Beethoven made about him during the late summer. Even then, however, Beethoven was prepared to be magnanimous, telling Karl not to gossip about Schindler, for 'is he not sufficiently punished, that he is *thus*'.[23] And although Schindler made no entries in the next few extant conversation books, by November he was back in Beethoven's circle. Karl, meanwhile, left Blöchlinger's school in late August, after four reasonably successful years, and resumed living with Beethoven, who had

[21] A-1231.  [22] Alb-326–8.
[23] A-1231 (to Johann), A-1233 (to Karl), A-1237 (to Ries).

moved to Baden on 13 August. This was a relatively unproblematical period in Beethoven's relationship with his nephew, and Karl continued living with him when they moved back to Vienna, with Karl enrolling at the University in October.

During the last few weeks in Baden, Beethoven received several noteworthy visitors. From England came Johann Reinhold Schultz,[24] who during a stay in Vienna went out to Baden on 28 September with two of Beethoven's friends, Haslinger and Joseph Blahetka. The following year he wrote a fascinating account of his visit, mentioning that Beethoven's hearing was not as bad as he had expected: if one spoke loudly and slowly, Beethoven could generally understand. Certainly the conversation book for that day records no entries by Schultz, and only a few by Haslinger and Blahetka; it was evidently one of Beethoven's better days. Many of Schultz's observations are corroborated by other reports, and they confirm that he was a reliable and perceptive witness. He learnt that Beethoven was writing the opera *Melusine* to Grillparzer's text; that praising Beethoven's early works, especially the Septet, was a sure way to make him angry; that he admired Handel above all other composers; that his favourite ancient writers were Homer and Plutarch; and his favourite German poets were Schiller and Goethe. During dinner, Beethoven is reported to have said, 'Man is little above other animals if his chief pleasure is confined to the dinner-table'. Beethoven evidently regarded mental and spiritual food as far more important than *haute cuisine*, and, as recorded elsewhere, he was apt to forget meal-times if his mind was on composition.

Beethoven showed no great enthusiasm for the music of Weber on that occasion, but only a week later Weber himself, along with his pupil Julius Benedict, and Beethoven's friends Haslinger and Piringer, made the journey out to Baden, and Beethoven received him very warmly. No conversation book survives for this day, but Weber later recalled:

He embraced me most heartily at least six or seven times and finally exclaimed enthusiastically: 'Indeed, you're a devil of a fellow!—a good fellow!' We spent the afternoon very merrily and contentedly. This rough, repellant man actually paid court to me, served me at table as if I had been his lady. . . . How saddening is his deafness! Everything must be written down for him.[25]

During both visits there were suggestions that Beethoven should visit England. Schultz noted Beethoven's enduring fondness for the British nation, and urged him, through Karl, to make the long-awaited trip; but despite Beethoven's ailing finances and the promise of rich rewards, his inclination to do so was waning, and he decided that sending a new symphony would have to suffice. Completion of the Ninth had been delayed several times during the summer, by illness and other distractions, and he wrote to Karl on 16 August that he was only that day beginning properly to

---

[24] Not Edward Schulz as stated by Thayer and others: see Tyson, 'Stages', 2.
[25] TF, 872.

serve his muses. On 5 September he indicated the work would be ready in fourteen days at most, and his letter to Ries that day allegedly states that the score had already been copied. Its rather ambiguous wording, however, merely claims that the score 'is being completed by the copyist one of these days' ('ist dieser täge vom Kopisten vollendet').[26] Beethoven was obviously trying once again to give the impression that the work was further advanced than it actually was, and the sketchbooks imply that he was only barely starting intensive work on the finale at that stage. Nevertheless, he may have recalled that his Choral Fantasia was written extremely quickly in 1808, and he had now decided to model the new finale somewhat on this earlier work—hence his optimistic completion date. In both works there is an extended instrumental introduction, followed by entry of solo and chorus voices, in a complex form based loosely on a set of variations on a simple, folk-like melody.

Beethoven had considered making a setting of Schiller's 'An die Freude' in the early 1790s, and may have actually done one about ten years later, although if he did, it has disappeared. Then in 1812 he had contemplated using sections of the poem in what became the 'Namensfeier' Overture, but abandoned the idea. Now, at last, he combined his long desire to set the poem with his plan of 1818 to compose a choral finale for a symphony. As in 1812, he decided not to use the whole of the rather long poem, but only its most elevated passages, treating it as a celebration of pure joy, which can bring all people together (in the famous line 'Alle Menschen werden Brüder') and can be experienced by everything from a worm to a cherub. Mention of the cherub directs attention heavenwards, first to the sky ('Froh wie seine Sonnen fliegen durch des Himmels prächt'gen Plan') and finally to the loving Father who dwells above the stars, whom Beethoven worshipped and revered so deeply.

Turning these fragmentary passages into a symphonic finale was a Herculean task, and although Beethoven retained a vision of what he wanted, the labour of working out every detail took several months. Creating the kind of theme that could be sung by 'all people' was the first problem. Although the first four lines of the eight-line theme seem to have come easily, the fifth and sixth posed a difficulty, with Beethoven undecided whether to modulate to the dominant or the relative minor.[27] Eventually he obtained the best of both worlds by modulating first to the relative minor and then the dominant, perhaps following the model of Handel's 'See the Conqu'ring Hero Comes', which he knew so well.

Working out small-scale thematic details was complemented by the task of creating a grand overall form. Free variation form, with interludes and extended coda, was the ground-plan, as in the finale of the *Eroica*, and Schiller's eight-line stanzas lent themselves well to variation treatment. Schiller had also, however, created four-line 'choruses' in a different metre,

<hr />

[26] A-1237; BB-1740.      [27] See Winter, 'Sketches', 183–95.

and Beethoven extracted two of these ('Seid umschlungen' and 'Ihr stürzt nieder') for a contrasting middle section in 3/2 beginning in G major (bars 594–654 of the final version). The theme of this was then combined with the main 'Freude' theme in a complex double fugue that can be regarded as a final variation. Beethoven also decided to introduce traditional 'Turkish' style (use of triangle, cymbals, and bass drum in a march) as representative of the non-Western world, to incorporate the whole of humanity. Consequently he extracted another of Schiller's 'chorus' sections ('Froh wie seiner Sonnen fliegen') to provide a core for two variations in 6/8 in the contrasting key of B flat major, followed by an extended development passage. Thus the main part of the finale, from the entrance of the voices, combines variation form with elements of other recognizable musical structures: sonata form (including a development in remote keys, followed by recapitulation of the main 'Freude' theme at bar 543); rondo form (a broad key-scheme of D–B flat–D–G/g–D); symphonic structure (a 'first movement' in D, 'scherzo' in B flat, 'slow movement' in 3/2 in G/g, and fugal 'finale'); and hints of other forms such as concerto form and continuous development (since each section leads on to the next without a proper resting point, just as in most of his folksong settings).[28] Yet at the heart of this vast and bewilderingly complex edifice, which can be perceived in so many different ways, lies a single, elementary theme, with stepwise motion and regular beat, uniting it all. As in the *Missa solemnis*, Beethoven's other mighty choral masterpiece from the 1820s, his bipolar approach blends the simple and direct with the complex and sophisticated, so that it can be appreciated on an enormous range of different levels.

Creating this grand choral movement, however, was relatively easy. The real difficulty lay in making such a movement seem relevant to the three preceding instrumental movements, for there was a danger of leaving a huge artistic chasm between the two parts. Beethoven tackled this almost insoluble problem from several angles, so that ultimately the finale would seem not an unrelated cantata tacked on to the end of an instrumental work, but the inevitable outcome of what had gone before. One way of addressing the disjunction between instrumental and choral movements was to make increasing disjunction itself a feature of the work. In the first movement there is merely the usual contrast between first and second groups of a standard sonata form. In the second, however, the Trio section is in a different key, mood, and metre from the main D minor Presto, while in the third there are two different themes that did not originally belong together. In this way Beethoven subtly prepares for both the internal contrasts within the finale and its dissimilarity to the first three movements.

The main key of the finale, D major, is also foreshadowed somewhere in each of the first three movements (a procedure already used in the Fifth), while its chief subsidiary keys, B flat and G, are likewise anticipated (for

---

[28] See Webster, 'Form', for a variety of views of the form of this movement.

example, in the second subject of the first movement, and the main key and second episode of the third). Moreover, the first three movements contain subliminal hints of the actual 'Freude' theme. Such an elemental theme is of course bound to contain motifs (such as three- or four-note scales) heard earlier, but its clearest thematic anticipations are unmistakable[29] and were created only after the 'Freude' theme had been conceived. From the first movement, a phrase developed just before the main second subject must be singled out—especially its appearance in D major in the recapitulation (bars 341–2: see Ex. 17.3a)—and the sketches confirm the phrase was a late idea,[30] planted, one must conclude, as a foretaste of 'Freude'. In the second movement, the outline of the 'Freude' tune is disguised by being placed in the third–fifth bars of the Trio theme, but it is still clearly visible (Ex. 17.3b). The third movement is marked 'cantabile' ('in singing style')—another hint at the vocal finale—at the start, but Beethoven also used this word to highlight two phrases in the coda: the countermelody for flute and oboe at bars 127–8 and the violin melody at bar 139 (Ex. 17.3c). These are the only passages in the

**Ex. 17.3**

(a)  Op. 125/I, bars 341-2, horn (sounding pitch)

(b)  Op. 125/II, bars 413-17, oboe

(c)  Op. 125/III, bars 127-8 (oboe) and 139 (violin)

(d)  Op. 125/IV, bars 92-5, bass strings

[29] See Solomon, 'Ninth Symphony', 14–17.
[30] See Kallick, *Advanced Sketches*, 84–92, where the relevant sketches are transcribed, though Kallick does not mention the 'Freude' connection.

entire movement specifically labelled 'cantabile', and they clearly outline the first and second phrases of the 'Freude' melody; this is therefore well prepared by the time it first appears in the finale (bar 92: see Ex. 17.3d).

Thus many important features of the finale are already foreshadowed in the previous three movements, and to cement the two parts of the symphony together still more firmly Beethoven created a lengthy introduction to the finale, so that the transition to voices was as smooth as possible. This introduction demanded matching ones for each of the other three movements, and it is noteworthy that this is the only Beethoven symphony where every movement begins with some kind of introduction. These introductions are of the most diverse types. The first movement begins with the remarkable sound of a shimmering bare 5th on A, which sounds introductory but proves to be an integral part of the movement. In the second, a motivic fragment, followed by a sudden rest, is developed for eight bars before being extended into the main theme (more surprisingly, the rest itself is treated as a motif for later development!). And in the third, there is a brief preamble for woodwind before the violin melody.

The introduction to the finale is far more substantial, as it needs to forge links with the preceding movements. It begins in D minor for orchestra alone, thereby retaining the main key and texture. Then the cellos and double-basses play some recitative—a cunning halfway point between instrumental and vocal music—alternating with recalls of each of the first three movements, thus creating specific links with them. An early idea was for each of these movements to be rejected in turn with explicit words: 'O no, not this, something else [more] pleasing is what I demand'; 'Not this either, it is no better, just somewhat more cheerful'; 'Nor this, it is too tender'. Then was to follow a fragment of the 'Freude' melody, and the comment, 'This is it, ha, it is now found'.[31] The idea of rejecting the earlier movements, as a means of preparing the ground for an entirely new type of finale, was sound enough, but it was here expressed far too prosaically. Thus Beethoven eventually transformed it into the version familiar today. The instruments alone reject, by implication, each of the first three movements and announce the 'Freude' theme, followed by two variations. The scheme is then repeated, but without specific recall of the earlier movements, and with the baritone solo proclaiming, 'O friends, not these tones, but let us sing more pleasing and joyful ones'—a neat and unspecific summary of Beethoven's initial ideas for a vocal recitative. The lengthy preparations are thereby completed, and the symphony's trend towards an increasingly vocal style reaches fulfilment, with the voices singing Schiller's words as a natural continuation of all the preceding music. The finale thus became the climax for the whole work; and Beethoven had found yet another solution to the 'finale problem' that had originally emerged with his first symphony (see Chapters 5 and 6).

[31] N-II, 190–1.

Beethoven worked out the details of this finale during the winter of 1823–4—a fairly quiet time domestically, when he could work without serious interruption. The symphony was ready by about February, but he had become so disillusioned with Viennese musical taste that he let it be known that he was contemplating a première in Berlin instead. This news prompted a lengthy petition signed by no fewer than thirty of his admirers including Streicher, Fries, Czerny, Moritz Lichnowsky, Zmeskall, the poet Kuffner, and the publishers Steiner, Artaria & Co., and Diabelli. These men, who regarded Rossini's music as shallow and foreign, knew that it was nearly ten years since Beethoven had last given a public concert of his works, and that he now had a new mass and symphony awaiting performance. In their petition, written on behalf of 'everyone whose bosom is animated by a sense of the divine in music', they urged:

Do not withhold any longer from the popular enjoyment, do not keep any longer from the oppressed sense of that which is great and perfect, the performance of the latest masterworks of your hand. . . . Do not disappoint the general expectations any longer! . . .[32]

Beethoven evidently received the petition on 26 February, and he acceded to their request. Preparations were soon in hand for the concert, and are documented in great detail in the conversation books. The date initially proposed was some time in late March, in the Theater an der Wien, venue of the premières of Beethoven's Second Symphony and *Leonore*. Count Palffy, the theatre director, agreed to provide singers and instrumentalists, but the orchestral leader there was Franz Clement, and Beethoven wanted Schuppanzigh. Other venues were therefore considered, and other dates. Beethoven applied to the Imperial Royal High Steward's Office to hold the concert in the Redoutensaal on 7 April, but was told that the decision rested not with them but Domenico Barbaja. Barbaja, however, was temporarily in Naples, and his deputy, the ballet dancer Louis Duport, offered Beethoven only the Small Redoutensaal instead the Large. For most of April, the venue, date, time, and seating prices remained unsettled. So did the names of some of the performers. Two outstanding young singers—Henriette Sontag (soprano) and Caroline Unger (contralto)—had visited Beethoven in March and persuaded him to give them solo parts, but as late as mid-April Katharina Wranitzky was being suggested as a soprano. Franz Jäger was proposed for tenor, but he declined, claiming the part was too low for him,[33] and eventually Anton Haitzinger was chosen instead. The bass was to have been Joseph Preisinger, but he was replaced by Joseph Seipelt about two days before the concert (because his part was too high, according to Schindler).

Schindler was heavily involved in the organization of the event, and at last, on Sunday 2 May, he wrote in Beethoven's conversation book: 'Thus the agreed conclusion with your consent is therefore for Friday [7 May]—

---

[32] Alb-344.    [33] BKh, vi. 35–7.

tomorrow rehearsal with the solo singers, Tuesday full, Wednesday small, Thursday general rehearsal.'[34] The two girls still did not know their parts at all, while Haitzinger received his from Jäger only that day. Various other mishaps occurred during the rehearsal period, but Schindler devoted enormous energy to helping with the arrangements. Beethoven was far too deaf to direct the concert, and his role was to set the tempos for each movement, leaving the detailed direction to Michael Umlauf, assisted by Schuppanzigh as leader. An enlarged orchestra was needed, consisting of twelve each of first and second violins, ten violas and twelve cellos or double basses, with doubled wind instruments and a large chorus. Some of the extra singers and instrumentalists required were supplied from the leading amateurs of the Gesellschaft der Musikfreunde.

The venue was the Kärntnertor Theatre (where the final version of *Fidelio* had first been heard almost exactly ten years earlier). The programme, a typical mixture of vocal and instrumental items, was announced the day before the concert:

GRAND MUSICAL CONCERT
by
HERR L. VAN BEETHOVEN
which will take place
tomorrow, 7 May 1824
in the R[oyal] I[mperial] Court Theatre beside the Kärntnertor

---

The musical pieces to be performed are the latest works of Herr
Ludwig van Beethoven.

First. Grand Overture.
Second. Three Grand Hymns, with solo and chorus voices.
Third. Grand Symphony, with solo and chorus voices entering in the finale on Schiller's song, To Joy. [etc.][35]

As with Beethoven's Mass in C at the concert in 1808, the censor did not permit the *Missa solemnis* to be advertised as a Mass but merely as a series of hymns. To perform the complete work would have taken too long, and so the Gloria and Sanctus were omitted, leaving just the Kyrie, Credo, and Agnus Dei. The 'grand overture' was that for *Die Weihe des Hauses*, the only item already heard in Vienna. (The Mass was not, however, receiving its première, for Galitzin, having bought a manuscript copy, had performed it in St Petersburg a month earlier.)

The theatre was packed for the occasion (apart from the royal box, which remained empty), and despite the small number of rehearsals and the difficulty of the music, the reception was wildly enthusiastic, as several reports indicate. Schindler wrote in Beethoven's conversation book after the event:

---

[34] BKh, vi. 117.     [35] TF, 907–8; facsimile in BKh, vi, opposite p. 96.

Never in my life did I hear such frenetic and yet cordial applause.

—

Once the second movement of the symphony was completely interrupted by applause.

—

And there was a demand for a repetition.

—

The reception was more than imperial—for the people burst out in a storm four times.

—

At the end there were cries of 'Vivat'.[36]

At one point, probably after the second movement of the symphony, Beethoven stood turning pages, oblivious to the applause until Caroline Unger tugged him by the sleeve to draw his attention and he turned to acknowledge it. Even without deafness, his behaviour might have been the same, since he was often absent-minded and inattentive to his surroundings. On this occasion, if the incident did indeed happen after the second movement, his mind would have been fully occupied with the music and with the forthcoming Adagio.

The enthusiasm of the audience was partly for the efforts of the performers struggling with such difficult music, and for Beethoven having put on, after a ten-year absence, a concert that many must have sensed was an historic occasion. Nevertheless, there was much genuine appreciation of the music itself. The anonymous review in the *Allgemeine musikalische Zeitung* stated that Beethoven's 'inexhaustible genius had shown us a new world, revealing the magical secrets of a holy art that we had never before heard or imagined!'[37] One of the most perceptive responses was that of Czerny, who was amazed by the incredible energy of the Ninth Symphony:

Beethoven . . . in the most striking manner astonished everyone who feared that after ten years of deafness only dry, abstract, unimaginative works could be produced. His new symphony for the most part breathes such a fresh, lively, indeed youthful spirit; so much power, innovation and beauty as ever [came] from the head of this original man, although he certainly sometimes led the old wigs to shake their heads.[38]

Despite the great musical and popular success of the event, it was financially a near-disaster. Beethoven had been led to expect handsome profits such as he had gained from similar events in earlier years, but the enormous copying costs and various other charges left only a very small surplus. Although he had recently received the promised £50 from the Philharmonic Society of London for a manuscript copy of the Ninth Symphony, his finances were still precarious; suspicious as ever of those around him, he became convinced that he had been cheated at the box-office. Efforts were

---

[36] TF, 909; BKh, vi. 160–1.    [37] Cited from Cook, *Symphony No. 9*, 23.
[38] TDR, v. 97.

made to persuade him that this could not have happened, but he remained angry and gloomy, with Schindler bearing the brunt of the blame.

From the outset a repeat of the concert had been planned. Beethoven's friend Johann Schickh recommended waiting until the next year, but his view went unheeded and the repetition was initially scheduled for 14 May; it was then postponed to 21 May and ultimately to Sunday 23 May, at 12.30 p.m., in the Large Redoutensaal, which Caroline Unger persuaded Beethoven was a better venue than the Kärntnertor Theatre. To attract a larger audience, the programme was modified slightly: the Credo and Agnus Dei from the Mass were replaced by Beethoven's vocal trio *Tremate, empi*, written in 1802 and performed in 1814 but still unpublished, and by the aria 'Di tanti palpiti' from Rossini's *Tancredi*, which left Beethoven open to the charge, 'See, he has to get Rossini to help'.[39] The change of programme did not have the desired effect, and the concert took place before a house less than half full, making a substantial loss for Duport, who had borne the risks and guaranteed Beethoven 500 fl. CM. As Karl explained next day: 'It was not full because, first, many people have already gone into the country. Also, many were shocked at the high price of the galleries [2 fl. CM], which were consequently quite empty. One group did not go because it was known that *you* were not getting the takings. One group stayed away because the Rossini aria disgusted them, as it did me too.'[40] Karl also pointed out that the Rossini aria had been announced on the poster without the composer's name, implying that it was one of Beethoven's latest compositions! Plans for a possible third performance, perhaps the following autumn after the aristocracy had returned to the city, were considered briefly, but they were soon abandoned, and the concert on 23 May 1824 proved to be Beethoven's last. Although he still had several new large-scale works in mind—the Grillparzer opera (*Melusine*), an oratorio commissioned by the Gesellschaft der Musikfreunde (*Der Sieg des Kreuzes*, The Victory of the Cross, to a text by his friend Bernard), a Tenth Symphony, an overture on B–A–C–H, and a mass for the Emperor—he turned to less grandiose ventures, and in particular the world of the string quartet.

---

[39] BKh, vi. 215.    [40] BKh, vi. 227–8.

# 18

# End of an era (1824–7)

Shortly after Beethoven's second large concert of May 1824 he withdrew to the country, and spent most of the summer in Baden. Here he tried to catch up on some of the compositions postponed because of the concerts. The three quartets promised to Galitzin were now planned as his next major task, but first he had to deal with repaying his debt to Johann. They had agreed that, instead of cash, Beethoven would give Johann works being sold to publishers, the six bagatelles and three songs already offered unsuccessfully to Peters, plus the Overture to *Die Weihe des Hauses*; but as the bagatelles (Op. 119 Nos. 1–6) had been pirated by Moritz Schlesinger from the English edition and published in Paris at the end of 1823 (see Chapter 17), Beethoven felt obliged to compose a similar set for Johann. This set (which eventually appeared as Op. 126) is first mentioned in a letter of 25 February 1824 to Heinrich Probst of Leipzig, the latest publisher to write to Beethoven asking for new compositions. Beethoven offered the overture and the three songs, plus 'six bagatelles for piano solo, which however are longer than those previously published by me'.[1] This must refer to a planned new set, rather than the set rejected by Peters or a selection of six more from the portfolio of bagatelles assembled in 1822. The first sketches for the new bagatelles follow in the sketchbook (Vienna A 50) almost immediately after the last sketches for the Ninth Symphony, separated only by a page of ideas for the embryonic Tenth Symphony. On 4 May, three days before the première of the Ninth, Karl commented, 'The bagatelles are really fine,'[2] but he was probably referring to the new Viennese edition of Op. 119 (pirated from Schlesinger's), rather than Op. 126. Composition of this set was evidently begun in earnest only after the two May concerts, and finished in early June.

The new set was in some aspects modelled on that rejected by Peters (Op. 119 Nos. 1–6). From the outset, it was conceived as a 'cycle of bagatelles' (as noted in Beethoven's sketchbook), an idea that had emerged only during preparation of the set intended for Peters. The key sequence, though different from that set, was equally carefully prepared, while the time signatures in both sets are almost identical; and again the final piece sums up

---

[1] A-1266.    [2] Bkh, vi. 137.

the set by using contrasting time signatures. Despite the similarities, however, Beethoven had clearly heeded Peters's criticisms of Op. 119 Nos. 1–6—that they were too short, too easy, and obviously not new. The pieces in Op. 126 were therefore longer (as had been decided even before they were composed), more difficult, and fully in his late style (though quite different from the Romantic style that was appearing in short piano pieces by Schubert and others). The first one, for example, begins by combining a lyrical, cantabile theme with strict three-part polyphony; and the opening four-bar phrase is answered in the bass while the treble plays a descant. Then in the reprise the roles are reversed, with the first four bars played in the bass and the answer in the treble, thereby displaying characteristic emphasis on lyricism, antiphonal partwriting, and contrasts of register. There is also a typically large number of irregular 6–4 chords, and some remarkable manipulation of note values in the middle section, where time itself seems to become compressed by some outside force, even though the pulse remains constant. The remaining five bagatelles are equally original in different ways, and show Beethoven was just as capable at excelling in small forms as in large ones. These bagatelles probably provided a welcome relief after the enormous labour of composing and performing the Ninth Symphony, but he clearly gave them all his customary care and attention, and did not merely dash them off hurriedly to placate Johann.

The price Beethoven asked Probst for the six bagatelles was only 30 ducats, much less than the eight ducats apiece he had asked from Peters. For the three songs he again proposed 24 ducats, while the overture was priced at 50 ducats. Probst rounded the total down to 100 ducats (or 450 fl. CM), and Beethoven agreed to this in March, well before the bagatelles were completed. Meanwhile he was making renewed efforts to sell the *Missa solemnis* and the Ninth Symphony, priced at 1000 and 600 fl. CM respectively. They were offered to Moritz Schlesinger in February, Probst on 10 March, and Schott's Sons, of Mainz, on the same day. Schott's were planning to publish a music journal entitled *Caecilia* (which ultimately proved very successful), and had written to Beethoven asking for a contribution, plus any new works that they might publish. Beethoven declined to write an article for the journal, since he felt 'a greater innate calling to reveal myself to the world through my compositions';[3] but he offered them the Mass and the Symphony at the usual price, plus a new quartet (not yet begun) for 50 ducats. The offer was accepted, and Schott's, who were at least the seventh publisher to be offered the Mass, eventually received it, and the symphony, in January 1825.

Much of the intervening period, summer and autumn 1824, Beethoven spent composing the first quartet for Galitzin (Op. 127 in E flat) and checking the scores of the two great choral works for Schott's. Since his chief copyist, Schlemmer, had died in August 1823, he had had to use less skilled

---

[3] A-1270.

men who often had difficulty with his handwriting, and so he had to go through both the scores for Schott's several times to satisfy himself they were correct. During this period he also had the usual domestic concerns—in particular, Karl's welfare. Karl was becoming bored with his studies at the university, and eventually told Beethoven on 20 June that he wanted to join the army. Beethoven naturally objected, but the seeds of Karl's future career had been sown, and the conversation could be regarded as the start of a new phase in Beethoven's relationship with Karl. The first phase, dominated by the guardianship dispute (1815–20), had been followed by a quiescent phase in which no serious disputes are recorded. The new phase was essentially one of adolescent conflict, as Karl became increasingly determined to escape Beethoven's overbearing demands and restrictions. Such conflicts between adolescents and parents are extremely common; and when, as apparently here, there are attempts to mould the adolescent into an idealized image, then guilt and fear of possible failure intensify the psychological pressures, sometimes with disastrous consequences.[4] Karl's quest for independence developed slowly, however, and for the present he continued at the university.

While in the countryside that summer, Beethoven lived on his own with an illiterate servant, and sometimes inevitably felt lonely. Schindler had been sacked again, and Beethoven relied increasingly on Karl (who regularly visited) for practical assistance. There were few other visitors, the most significant being the London harp-maker Johann Stumpff, who arrived in Vienna in late September and met Beethoven several times in the next few weeks. He later wrote a detailed account of his visit, describing some of his conversations with Beethoven (which do not appear in the conversation books). One conversation was about other composers, and Beethoven, while expressing admiration for Mozart and Bach, declared once again that he regarded Handel as the greatest. Stumpff asked if Beethoven owned Handel's works, but Beethoven mentioned only *Messiah* and *Alexander's Feast*, whereupon Stumpff resolved secretly to supply him with a full set if such could be found. Just over two years later he succeeded, sending Samuel Arnold's forty-volume edition of all Handel's major works.

Beethoven's health was still uncertain, and he was ill in bed for several days after returning to Vienna in early November. His work was also delayed during late November and December, when he had to give Rudolph a two-hour lesson each day, which he found quite exhausting. In addition there were disputes with Johann, whom Beethoven began describing as his Cain-brother. A central issue was that Beethoven had still not paid his debt. He had not sent the works promised to Probst, for he had agreed to supply piano-solo and piano-duet arrangements of the Overture, and these had to be prepared by Czerny. Moreover, Beethoven had decided to revise—yet

---

[4] See Wolf, *Neffenkonflikt*, esp. pp. 149–63, for a fuller discussion of the psychological aspects of this 'puberty conflict'.

again—two of the three songs, 'Opferlied' and 'Bundeslied', and finally finished doing so only about December. Meanwhile Johann, noting that all
the works for Probst were technically his property, felt that they had been
sold too cheaply at 100 ducats, and decided they should be offered to
Schott's for 130 ducats. Obtaining an agreement between the two brothers
and a publisher, each with different interests, inevitably took time; but
eventually, in February 1825, Schott's received all the works for 130 ducats:
'Opferlied' (Op. 121);[5] 'Bundeslied' (Op. 122); 'Der Kuss' (Op. 128); the
Overture *Die Weihe des Hauses* (Op. 124) and Czerny's arrangements of it;
and the Bagatelles (Op. 126). Probst received merely an apologetic letter
from Beethoven, explaining that he had tried unsuccessfully to persuade
Johann not to undermine the previous agreement, and offering one or two
string quartets (not yet written) to compensate. Probst, however, had by
now lost interest in obtaining anything from him.

Although Beethoven's output during the last six months of 1824 comprised
little more than a single quartet, the numerous business negotiations and
other distractions left him feeling as overwhelmed with work as usual. Yet
despite these preoccupations, his poetic vision remained undimmed. To
Nägeli he wrote on 9 September:

Only in my divine art do I find the supports which give me the power to sacrifice
the best part of my life to the heavenly Muses. From childhood my greatest happiness and pleasure have been to be able to do something for others.[6]

And a few days later to Schott's:

Before my departure to the Elysian fields I must leave behind what the Spirit
inspires and bids me complete. Why, it seems to me as if I have written scarcely any
notes. I wish you every success in your efforts for art, for it is only art and knowledge that intimate to us and let us hope for a higher life.[7]

Beethoven's devotion to art and knowledge, his sense of compulsion to
compose, his remarkable modesty ('scarcely any notes'!), and his desire to
help others, are recurring themes throughout his life.

His vision was next realized in the Quartet in E flat, Op. 127, which took
far longer to compose than expected, not just because of other distractions
but because of his limitless aspirations and a new method of composing.
Although it was planned in 1823 or earlier, Beethoven had barely even
decided its key by May 1824, for one sketch from this period suggests 'F
minor quartet', with an Adagio in C and an Allegretto in D.[8] Once the
bagatelles were completed, however, detailed work on the new quartet was
soon under way, and in an attempt to obtain what he later described as a
new kind of partwriting, he began making frequent use of sketching in

---

[5] Now known as Op. 121b, to distinguish it from the 'Kakadu' Variations, which Steiner
had published as Op. 121.

[6] A-1306.          [7] A-1308.          [8] Brandenburg, 'Op. 127', 235.

open score on four staves, instead of merely on one or two as before. Although he had occasionally made such score sketches in earlier years, only in his late quartets did this become a standard procedure. The score sketches did not supplant other types of sketching, but ran parallel with them. Thus there were now three modes of sketching: using pencil in pocket sketchbooks (or single leaves) generally filled outdoors; using desk sketchbooks indoors, mainly written in ink; and using loose folios or bifolios of manuscript paper for score sketches. Often two or three of the four staves of a score sketch were left blank, but the extra space available, which could if desired be filled with countermelodies or dialogue between instruments, facilitated the creation of works far more contrapuntally conceived than his earlier quartets. Haydn in his quartets had pointed the way for this type of texture, by distributing important motifs to all four instruments, but Beethoven now developed the idea much further, where all four parts continually have their own individual interest, whether they all have similar or quite different figuration at any one point. One might expect the score sketches to have functioned as an intermediate stage between ordinary sketches and autograph score, but some belong to a very early stage of composition of individual movements, whereas some of the normal sketches were jotted down when Beethoven was already occupied with writing out the autograph.

As well as new types of texture, Beethoven also contemplated structural innovations for Op. 127, such as having six movements instead of the usual four; and even when the first movement was nearly finished, he was sketching a fast second movement entitled 'la gaieté' before the slow movement.[9] The first movement has a tender, lyrical quality with much emphasis on the sixth of the scale, as in the Sonata in A flat, Op. 110; and having felt there that a slow movement would not follow successfully without an intervening Allegro molto, he initially had a similar idea for Op. 127, before reverting ultimately to the standard four-movement form, with slow movement second. Innovative structure was held in reserve for later quartets.

Within the seemingly regular structure of sonata-form Allegro, variation-form Adagio, Scherzando and Trio, and sonata-form Finale, however, there are plenty of formal irregularities and innovations. The Maestoso introduction, where the first violin stresses E flat then G and ultimately C, recurs twice during the development section, appropriately in the keys of G and C. It contains an alternation of short and longer notes (though rhythmically dislocated), and rises over a range of a sixth; both these features reappear in the themes of the second and third movements. The note C itself, which forms the melodic climax of the Maestoso and the bridge to the ensuing Allegro, and was to have been the keynote for 'la gaieté', finally achieves predominance in the coda to the Finale, where the music suddenly switches to C major before returning to the tonic; meanwhile the A flat

⁹ N-II, 218–20; Brandenburg, 'Op. 127', 273–4.

chord supporting that initial C foreshadows the key of the slow movement. Thus the first six bars, though seemingly a contrast to what follows, actually prepare for the whole of the rest of the quartet, through their melody and harmony. They also prepare for it rhythmically: their strange, dislocated accents introduce the concept of metric disruption, which becomes a unifying feature of the quartet as a whole, since, for the first time in a four-movement work, Beethoven introduces a change of metre in every movement. This combination of dissociation and integration is one of the most important characteristics of his late style.

Variation form, used in the second movement, is also prominent in his late style, but it is treated with great diversity. Here the theme is in 12/8, which gives it unusual breadth and expansiveness, even though it just consists basically of two four-bar phrases each immediately repeated. The first two variations are of the decorative variety, but with a profusion of ornamental figures and motivic fragments that generate some of the most elaborate and intricate textures that had ever been seen in quartet writing. In the third variation, however, Beethoven adopts the model of his Piano Variations, Op. 34, transforming the theme by means of a remote key (E major) and new rhythm to create an entirely different character—one of profound stillness and contemplation similar to that of other meditative slow movements in E major, such as the slow movement of the second 'Razumovsky' Quartet. The key of E was originally planned to reappear in an Adagio at the beginning of the Finale, but instead it returns just briefly in the final coda.

The precise date of composition of each movement is uncertain, but by 17 December 1824 there remained, according to Beethoven, only a 'slight addition' to be made to the finale. The première was then planned for 23 January 1825 in Schuppanzigh's quartet series, and was actually announced three days beforehand. Yet when the day came, the new quartet had to be substituted by Op. 95. It seems that Beethoven was becoming increasingly self-critical, and reluctant to release a work until he was fully satisfied (which, of course, he never was, as he aimed for that unattainable goal of absolute perfection).

A further disruption occurred because Beethoven had also offered the quartet to the cellist Joseph Linke, who wanted to have the honour of staging the première, but it was eventually agreed that Schuppanzigh should give it on 6 March, with Karl Holz (second violin), Franz Weiss (viola) and Linke (cello). All four players then signed an agreement written out by Karl:

Each one is herewith given his part and is bound by oath and indeed pledged on his honour to do his best, to distinguish himself and to vie each with the other in excellence.

Each one who takes part in the affair in question is to sign this sheet.
Schuppanzigh             Beethoven
Weiss

Linke, the great master's accursed cello
Holz, the last, but only with this signature[10]

The performance was far from fully successful. Schuppanzigh as leader bore the brunt of the blame, but all four players had difficulties, some of which were mentioned in the conversation books in the ensuing weeks. There were inevitably some copying errors that only gradually came to light, for Beethoven had been unable to find an adequate replacement for Schlemmer. The irregular figurations and numerous leger lines for the first violin were bound to cause problems, even when correctly copied; and another notational difficulty occurred in the finale, where Beethoven had confusingly used the alto clef for the cello at one point. Another setback arose at the concert, when one of Schuppanzigh's strings broke and he had no spare violin handy. The biggest difficulty, however, was that of ensemble. The metrically disruptive opening, followed by numerous changes of metre during the work, needed much more rehearsal time than normal, and the performance was inevitably ragged in places. Karl mentioned that 'things were not properly together', while Schuppanzigh himself stated that, although no passages were too difficult for him, 'the ensemble is difficult'.[11] An added hazard in the first performance was a 'meno vivace' near the end of the finale (probably at bar 281 rather than, as is usually assumed, at the beginning of the coda, where there is also a change of tempo); but Beethoven excised this before publication.

Schuppanzigh also stated that 'the originality makes it difficult, which one cannot grasp at first sight'.[12] The work did indeed display great originality at many levels, creating a conceptual difficulty for the performers which was intensified by the changes of metre, making it harder to grasp the overall design. Schuppanzigh took about a year to understand the Adagio, and from a single violin part it would indeed be difficult to perceive that the movement was a set of variations (which were not numbered), based on a theme with a prelude and postlude like Beethoven's folksong settings, and that there was an interlude before a final half-variation (bars 109–17) and coda, creating an overall structure akin to some of the folksong variations of Opp. 105 and 107. With no clear concept of the shape of the movement, Schuppanzigh would have found it difficult to create the right sense of purpose and direction in performance.

Some people, however, including Schuppanzigh, appreciated the extraordinary quality of the work, and Beethoven soon decided on a second performance, with Joseph Böhm as leader. The other three players remained the same, and the work was tried out on 18 March, followed by two successive performances in a single evening on 23 March—an idea evidently

---

[10] TF, 940; BB-1940. Schindler acquired the document later and added 'Schindler secretarius' to give the impression that he was involved.
[11] BKh, vii. 177, 201.     [12] BKh, vii. 198.

suggested by Holz. The work gradually gained acceptance, and several more performances followed later that year.

During early 1825 Beethoven was once again contemplating a visit to London. This time he was invited by Charles Neate, Ries having moved to Bad Godesberg, near Bonn, the previous autumn. As in earlier years, Beethoven was willing to go, but demanded 100 guineas more than the Philharmonic Society were prepared to pay. He had received so many assurances of making a fortune in London that, had he really wanted to go, he would surely have been willing to take the risk without any fee at all; but his habitual dislike of long journeys remained, and he always found impediments to going. Eventually, interest from the Philharmonic Society dwindled after they mounted a rather disastrous performance of the Ninth Symphony on 21 March, and the plan was abandoned.

Ries, however, continued his efforts to promote Beethoven's music, and began planning a performance of the Ninth Symphony at the forthcoming Lower Rhine Music Festival in Aachen. Having established that Schott's would not be printing the work in time, he wrote to Beethoven requesting the score and parts. Beethoven duly sent what he had available, but needed part of the work copying out again. The task was entrusted to Ferdinand Wolanek, who made so many mistakes that Beethoven soon became angry. Wolanek then returned what he had copied, excusing himself thus:

I remain grateful for the honour you have done me by employing me; as for the other disagreeable behaviour towards me, I can regard it smilingly as just a fit of temper to be accepted: in the ideal world of tones so many dissonances prevail—should they not also in the real world?

I am comforted only by the firm conviction that the same fate as mine would have befallen Mozart and Haydn, those celebrated artists, had they been employed by you as copyists.

I ask only that you do not confuse me with those common copyists who consider themselves fortunate to be able to maintain their existence by being treated like slaves. . . .

Beethoven, enraged, crossed out the entire letter and wrote across it in large letters: 'Stupid, conceited, asinine churl'; then at the bottom: 'So I must yet compliment such a scoundrel, who steals money from people! Instead I'll pull his asinine ears.' Turning over, he continued, 'Bungling scribbler! Stupid churl! Correct your mistakes made through ignorance, arrogance, conceit and stupidity—this would be better than wanting to teach me, which is just as if the *sow* wanted to teach *Minerva*.' In the margins he added: 'It was decided yesterday and even before then to have you write no more for me;' and, 'Do Mozart and Haydn the honour of not mentioning them.'[13] Such vehemence in the face of arrogance and incompetence was highly characteristic of Beethoven.

---

[13] Alb-399.

He continued to lament the dearth of good copyists in a letter to Ries some days later, when he sent him a carefully corrected copy of 'Opferlied' to replace an inaccurate one sent earlier. 'Here you have a sample from the wretched copyists I have had since Schlemmer's death—one can scarcely rely on a single note.'[14] Several other unpublished works were also sent, but arrived too late to be of use, and Ries performed only the Ninth Symphony (abridged through lack of rehearsal time) and *Christus am Oelberge*. The Symphony was performed by about 400 people, and was greatly admired, especially by Ries himself.

Beethoven, meanwhile, had begun a new quartet (Op. 132), the second for Prince Galitzin. As early as January 1825 it was known amongst his friends that the quartet was to be in A minor, and Linke had understood that it would have a concertante cello part.[15] This was not so, but the cello does begin on its own and has a prominent motif during the first subject. Like Op. 127, the quartet has a slow introduction, and the opening is dominated by a curious angular motif based on a reordering of the last four notes of the harmonic minor scale (marked *x* in Ex. 18.1). Various versions of this figure went through Beethoven's mind during this period, and it was to play a prominent role in his next two quartets. A melodic line based on similar contours had already been sketched, in E flat and marked 'Thema' (aut. 11/2, f. 27r), apparently as a possible theme for the finale of Op. 127. And there is an even earlier appearance of a different ordering of the four-note figure *x* amongst sketches for the slow movement of Op. 127 (aut. 11/2, f. 5v).[16] (Schindler identified this sketch as intended for a four-hand sonata commissioned by Diabelli, but the sketch almost certainly relates to a

**Ex. 18.1** Op. 132/I

14 A-1358.    15 BKh, vii. 90.
16 See Kinderman, *Beethoven*, 296 (Ex. 99(a)).

*minore* section in the slow movement of Op. 127, and eventually evolved into bars 99–101. As for the sonata, Beethoven agreed to write it but never did so; and, remembering that Diabelli had just published a collection of fifty variations by fifty other composers on his famous waltz, alongside Beethoven's own Diabelli Variations, he facetiously proposed that the members of this 'army of composers' be invited to contribute a bar each to the desired sonata![17])

The allegro section of the first movement of Op. 132 begins with new material, but motif $x$ from the introduction reappears in various guises to haunt the allegro—another means of combining integration with dissociation. The second movement opens with the same G#–A that began the first, but it is a lively, scherzo-like movement in A major, with a Trio section dominated by drone basses. Yet, hidden in the middle of the Trio is a version of an Allemande (WoO 81) that Beethoven had placed in his portfolio of bagatelles for possible publication in 1822. Thus he was deliberately incorporating extraneous material and building a Trio around it, in yet another approach to integrating diversified ideas into a unified whole.

Beethoven had more or less completed the first two movements of Op. 132 by April 1825, at which time Karl decided to abandon his university studies and enrol for a course in business at the polytechnic (where he remained for over a year). Meanwhile Beethoven became seriously ill with an intestinal inflammation. After unsuccessfully sending for his usual doctor, Jakob Staudenheim, he turned to Dr Anton Braunhofer on 18 April. Braunhofer prescribed little medicine but a strict diet—no wine, coffee, or spices, and various other restrictions—and predicted Beethoven would recover completely if he kept to it. The treatment was successful and Beethoven was able to move to Baden on 7 May to recuperate. A few days later he wrote to Braunhofer saying he felt a little stronger, and sent him an appropriate four-part canon, 'Doktor sperrt das Tor dem Tod' ('Doctor bars the door to death', WoO 189).

A more substantial musical result of the illness was the third movement of Op. 132, which was composed during May and June. A few sketches were made in his conversation book, where he drafted a possible title at the end of May: 'Hymn of thanks from a sick man to God on his recovery—feeling of new strength and reawakened feeling'.[18] The title of the movement was eventually modified to: 'Sacred song of thanks from a convalescent to the Godhead, in the Lydian Mode'. The movement is in double-variation form, with the main theme consisting of a chorale in the Lydian Mode—F major but with B naturals—creating an antique, religious flavour. Beethoven had already used quasi-modal harmony at 'Et incarnatus' in the *Missa solemnis*, but his growing interest in the old church style now reached the point where he was able to construct a whole movement using strictly modal harmony. The theme is treated as in a chorale prelude,

[17] Alb-392.     [18] BKh, vii. 291.

with each phrase preceded by a brief introduction, and in the two variations that follow there is increasingly elaborate counterpoint while the melody shines through as a Renaissance-style cantus firmus. Although Beethoven modelled this music more on contemporary organ improvisation practice than on genuine sixteenth-century examples,[19] the atmosphere of timeless piety is unmistakable. Alternating with the theme and two variations are two livelier, dance-like sections in D major marked 'feeling new strength'. These function as a complete contrast in style, and this contrast becomes the unifying factor of the movement: the dissociation is the integration, while the specific connection between the two styles lies outside the music itself—the interweaving of thanksgiving and physical recuperation.

For the fourth movement, Beethoven was at first undecided whether to use a March or an 'Alla danza tedesca', and evidently composed both, in A major. He finally chose the March, which is followed by a brief, recitative-like passage before the finale. These twenty-two bars could be regarded as a separate movement, and indeed they were by Beethoven, who referred to the quartet as possessing six movements. Thus, as in the Sonata, Op. 110, there is deliberate ambiguity about whether short sections should be viewed as a single, compound movement. The finale itself, like the second movement, incorporates borrowed material, for part of the main theme was originally sketched in D minor as a possible instrumental finale for the Ninth Symphony. Thus, although the quartet possesses very strong overall coherence, the kind of unity in which everything grows from a single opening germ clearly does not exist here.

Once Op. 132 was finished, in June, Beethoven pressed straight on with the third quartet for Galitzin (Op. 130 in B flat), largely undistracted. He rarely went into Vienna from Baden that summer, and apart from Karl's regular Sunday visits there were few callers: the minor composer Carl August Reichardt in early June; Schindler about a week later, in an effort to renew his acquaintance with Beethoven, and later Czerny (who came with Karl); in July, two visits from Johann and several from Holz, who now began a close association with Beethoven; and on 3 August the Dutchman Samson Moses de Boer,[20] who was presented with an untexted canon (WoO 35). Beethoven soon found Holz to be an interesting and cultured companion, who could quote Schiller from memory and make pertinent comments about Goethe and Shakespeare, as well as providing useful practical assistance such as arranging for the copying of the parts for Op. 127. Holz meanwhile felt honoured to be of service to such a great man, and the friendship blossomed quickly. After one visit by Holz and Karl, when Beethoven clearly enjoyed himself, he wrote how depressed and sad he felt

---

[19] See Brandenburg, 'Historical Background'.
[20] Not the painter Otto de Boer, as Thayer suggested; see Van der Zanden, *Beethoven*, 128–40, for details about de Boer.

afterwards, alone with a housekeeper whom he regarded as an 'old witch'.[21]

The isolation, however, enabled Beethoven to devote himself to creativity with rare intensity. The last three movements of Op. 132 had been written quite quickly, in May and June, and by early July he had sketched the first two movements of Op. 130 and was thinking about the third. Thus he optimistically wrote to Galitzin, about 6 July, that this quartet was nearly finished. As in the previous two, the first movement contains a slow introduction that is recalled several times, but one of its most unusual features is the key of the second subject—G flat in the exposition, and D flat (followed by B flat) in the recapitulation. These remote keys provide a hint that some of the later movements will be in keys more far-flung than usual. The first movement has a spacious breadth, but the second—a Presto in B flat minor with contrasting Trio in the major—is extremely condensed, almost to the point of absurdity, with most of the sections consisting of just two four-bar phrases.

Beethoven's sketches reveal that when he completed these two movements he had very little idea what would follow. The key and nature of the third movement had not been fixed, although it would have to be some kind of slow movement; nothing concrete had been decided about the finale; and it was also unclear how many movements there would be altogether. The quartet was thus being created as a kind of narrative, rather than a canvas where the overall outline is clear from the start. The later movements could be moulded to suit the earlier ones, but the earlier ones were in no way fashioned as preparation for what follows—unlike, for example, the 'Kreutzer' Sonata, the *Eroica*, and the Ninth Symphony. And, however inevitable the ending may seem, it was in fact totally unpredictable. The same may apply to some of Beethoven's other works (though there are rarely sufficient sketches to demonstrate this), but from an early stage this quartet's 'narrative' means of composition was stronger than usual. This in turn was probably a factor in the unique situation that eventually emerged with the finale.

Beethoven was already starting on the third movement around 6 July, for early ideas appear on the same page as a draft of the letter written to Galitzin about that time (De Roda Sketchbook, f. 24v). Shortly after this, he decided on a lyrical, aria-like movement in D flat, but he rapidly became bogged down in it, trying various metres but rarely proceeding beyond the first few bars. These ideas fill several pages of the De Roda Sketchbook and most of a pocket sketchbook (Egerton 2795, ff. 6–16); and one of the latest (on Egerton 2795, f. 15r) appears in very similar form in a conversation book[22] several pages after de Boer's entries of 3 August. Thus the mental impasse represented by these numerous sketches for an aria-like movement in D flat must have lasted almost a month.

---

[21] BKh, viii. 34–5, 38; A-1414, A-1408.     [22] BKh, viii. 39.

At last, towards the middle of August, the impasse was broken. A quite different movement in D flat was quickly sketched, much livelier than what had been planned. Marked 'poco scherzoso', it begins apparently in B flat minor, continuing from where the previous movement left off, and quoting the first two notes of the first movement, before the main theme is presented by the viola. The themes are decorated by the kind of elaborate, complex accompaniments found in the slow movement of Op. 127, but Beethoven's extensive use of staccatos and soft dynamic levels makes the movement seem light and airy, despite the richness of the decorations.

Beethoven seems at first to have contemplated moving straight from this movement to the finale, but eventually he decided to include two extra movements to make six—as he informed his nephew and Holz in letters of 24 August, three days after he had last seen them. The six-movement structure consisted of six real, self-sufficient movements (unlike the 'fifth' of Op. 132); it recalled the eighteenth-century divertimento genre, which customarily used more than four movements and had already been explored in Beethoven's Serenade, Op. 8 and Septet, Op. 20. Often in such works the extra movements were dances, and Beethoven had a ready-made dance to hand—the 'Alla danza tedesca' discarded from Op. 132. This was in A major, a most unsuitable key, but he now transposed it to G, a key he often exploited in works in B flat (for example, the 'Archduke' Trio). While light and airy like the previous movement, the Tedesca provides a sharp contrast, both in its diametrically opposite key-signature and its heavy emphasis on dance rhythms, with four-bar phrases employed almost incessantly.

For the fifth movement, Beethoven revived the D flat aria-like theme that had proved so troublesome in July. Having now used D flat for the new third movement, he decided to transpose his original ideas to E flat, while the metre was at last established as 3/4. The theme was quickly extended into a broad, expansive melodic line, and the movement was entitled 'Cavatina'—a type of slow, expressive, operatic aria.[23] The name is extremely appropriate, for the first violin acts as a solo singer throughout, even keeping entirely within the range of a mezzo-soprano, while the other three instruments play a relatively simple, unobtrusive accompaniment. In no other quartet movement does Beethoven maintain a single texture so consistently. The melody, though seemingly simple, was so skilfully crafted and thoroughly sketched that it is actually highly original and almost entirely unpredictable, with subtle irregularities of phrase structure that neatly contrast with the rigidity of the preceding dance rhythms. Its broad, carefully arched lines seem filled with intense longing, and the mood is intensified in an extraordinary middle section in the deeply profound key of C flat major. Here the melody is marked 'beklemmt' (anguished and oppressed), and it is interspersed with little rests or sighs, as if the singer is

---

[23] The direct connection between the early D flat ideas and the Cavatina, questioned in Marston, 'Beethoven's Sketches', 237–8, is clearly illustrated in De Roda, 'Quaderno', 612–21.

gasping for breath, in a rhythm quite unrelated to the triplets underneath (Ex. 18.2). Quasi-vocal style, so prevalent in Beethoven's late instrumental music, finds its culmination in this extraordinarily beautiful movement. According to Holz, it cost Beethoven tears in its writing, and nothing he had written had so moved him—merely thinking of the movement later on made Beethoven weep.[24] Holz was a generally reliable witness, and his report is partially confirmed by the problems in the early sketches for this movement.

**Ex. 18.2**  Op. 130/V

When Beethoven wrote on 24 August that the quartet was to have six movements, he predicted it would be finished in ten or twelve days—a reasonable forecast if the finale were to be of standard length, for not much more than this time-span had been needed for the previous finale (Op. 132), and also for the third movement of Op. 130, despite its elaborate figuration. By now he had sketched at least a dozen possible finale themes, but none was evidently very weighty in character, although the earliest one suggested

[24] TF, 975.

some kind of fugato or 'Fuga' during the course of the movement.[25] His latest idea was to begin the finale with a theme in running semiquavers.
Searching for further ideas, he returned to the angular E flat 'Thema' originally considered for the finale of Op. 127 and later partially adapted for
the start of Op. 132. He now transposed this eighteen-note theme to B flat
and then shortened it to just eight notes (Ex. 18.3),[26] before incorporating
it into the finale of Op. 130. It first appears in the sketches as a subsidiary
idea or countermelody, but as Beethoven came to develop it he discovered
so many possibilities that he made it the main theme and began turning the
movement, seemingly almost by accident, into a gigantic *Grosse Fuge*
(great fugue)—perhaps as a monument to Bach, whose inspiration was
very much in his mind at the time (he had been contemplating an overture
based on the theme B–A–C–H since 1823, and had made several sketches
for it). Thus instead of the twelve days originally envisaged, the movement
took about four months to complete.

**Ex. 18.3** SV 28/2, f. 26v

While these ideas were starting to take shape, Beethoven received a visit
from the Danish composer Friedrich Kuhlau. When Kuhlau had arrived in
Vienna in late July Beethoven had apparently known nothing of him, for he
had to be informed by Czerny in August that Kuhlau was a 'Danish
kapellmeister. He has written an opera *Die Räuberburg*, which has been
very successful there.'[27] Kuhlau visited Beethoven in Baden on 2 September
along with Haslinger, Holz, Piringer, and others, and after a long walk in
the beautiful Helenenthal, where Beethoven enjoyed the challenge of the
hills as much as he enjoyed the challenge of reaching musical heights, they
sat down for a very merry dinner party with much champagne. After touching on the problems of the censorship (which now covered even compositions without text, on the grounds that the titles might be subversive), the
conversation turned to musical matters and making puns. Kuhlau then
wrote in Beethoven's conversation book a musical puzzle representing
Bach's name; Beethoven responded by sketching a canon that used the
B–A–C–H motif to the words 'Kühl nicht lau' ('cool, not lukewarm'). The
canon, though prompted by Kuhlau's puzzle, has a broader background of
both the planned B–A–C–H overture and the Bach-inspired *Grosse Fuge*,
whose theme bears a certain kinship to the B–A–C–H motif since both

---

[25] See Cooper, *Creative Process*, 209–12.
[26] Aut. 11/2, f. 26v. See N-II, 550, and Stadlen, 'Possibilities', 111–13.
[27] BKh, viii. 50.

consist of pairs of semitones.[28] The next day Beethoven sent Kuhlau a polished version of his canon (WoO 191), but admitted that the champagne had gone to his head and he could not remember what he had written the previous evening; despite his penchant for alcohol, he rarely became as intoxicated as on that occasion.

The day after, Sunday, 4 September, the publisher Moritz Schlesinger came to Baden with Karl. Beethoven, always glad of the company of such a cultured man, welcomed him warmly. Schlesinger had heard from his father Adolf, the Berlin publisher, that Beethoven was asking 80 ducats each for two new quartets, and despite the high price Moritz Schlesinger was prepared to buy them both. He revealed that he actually wanted three quartets (Op. 132, the still unfinished Op. 130, and one yet to be written) and also three quintets, as the first stages of a complete edition of Beethoven's works. This request did not match Beethoven's plans for new works, but Schlesinger assured him that his quartets were as much masterpieces as an oratorio and would live as long, adding: 'If you write quartets and quintets you gain for your nephew more money than with any other great works.' It was a cunning and persuasive remark: Schlesinger had observed that Beethoven had no desire for riches but felt a great need to provide for his nephew and would therefore readily respond to this suggestion. Schlesinger continued: 'He who lives with the wolves must howl with them, and the world is these days a den of wolves,' implying that the world wanted these works, would pay for them, and had to be fed with them. He stressed the point again a little later, saying that if Beethoven were to write still more works in this genre they would be highly welcomed by himself and the public alike.[29]

Public demand for quartets was indeed rising rapidly, and other publishers had expressed interest in Beethoven's latest two, including Steiner, Mathias Artaria (who had set up a firm in Vienna independent of the original Artaria & Co.), and Peters, although Peters later withdrew. Schott's, who had taken Op. 127 for 50 ducats, were also shortly to ask for another one, and were prepared to pay the new rate of 80 ducats. Thus demand for Beethoven quartets greatly outstripped what he could supply. 'Quartets are now in demand from all sides, and it really seems that our age is advancing,' noted Beethoven a few months later.[30] Schlesinger's request proved decisive, and before long Beethoven was contemplating two new quartets to follow the three for Galitzin. It is often assumed that, after the Ninth Symphony, Beethoven turned his back on the public, withdrawing into a private world to write string quartets purely for his own satisfaction. Nothing could be further from the truth. Although his late quartets were supposedly sparked off by a request from Galitzin and sustained by his own love of the genre, it was public demand, filtered through a number of pub-

---

[28] Cf. Platen, 'Über Bach', which, however, somewhat strains the idea of thematic relationships.

[29] BKh, viii. 102–6.                    [30] A-1481.

lishers, that fuelled this unprecedented burst of activity in a single genre. Beethoven had been asked for quartets by both Schlesinger and Peters even before Galitzin's commission had arrived; and Schott's and probably Steiner had also joined the chase before a note of Op. 127 was written. These and other publishers then sustained Beethoven's activities in the genre with offers of high rewards unmatched, as Schlesinger confirmed, in other types of music such as operas, oratorios, or symphonies, all of which were being planned by Beethoven. (He had, it is true, received 600 fl. from Schott's for the Ninth Symphony—more than the 360 fl. now being offered for a quartet—but in proportion to the work involved the rate was lower.) Public demand for quartets at this date marks the final stage in a gradual change in society during Beethoven's lifetime. In the 1790s most of his chamber music was written for individual patrons, with publication being of secondary importance; but by the mid-1820s the situation was closer to that of today, with publication being his main source of additional income. Only in Russia, where society had changed less, was an individual such as Prince Galitzin still prepared to commission chamber music from him.

Schlesinger left Baden confident that he had obtained the rights for Opp. 132 and 130, and three days later he heard the first trial run of the former, in a room at his inn in Vienna. Beethoven was not there, but Holz told him the next day that they had been charmed by the music. The quartet was played again—twice—at the same venue on 9 September and again on Sunday, 11 September, before slightly larger audiences that included Beethoven and also the Englishman Sir George Smart, who wrote a brief description of the events. A dinner party followed the Sunday performance, after which Beethoven enchanted everyone present by extemporizing on the piano—a rare event in his later years. Conversation with him was, as usual, written down, but he could still hear a little if one spoke in his left ear, according to Smart. Five days later Smart went out to Baden, where like others before him he unsuccessfully attempted to persuade Beethoven to visit England. Before he departed he was presented with a four-bar canon, *Ars longa vita brevis* (Art is long, life is short, WoO 192).

Beethoven returned from Baden to Vienna in mid-October, taking up residence in the Schwarzspanierhaus, in a spacious second-floor apartment that became his final home. It was very close to Stephan von Breuning's home, and before long they had renewed their friendship after several years' separation. Breuning's son Gerhard, just twelve at the time, also came to know Beethoven well, and many years later wrote a vivid and detailed account of his memories of the composer.[31]

By the time Beethoven returned to Vienna the *Grosse Fuge* was well advanced and he began contemplating his next work. One possibility was still a B–A–C–H overture, and he made a few more sketches for this,

[31] See Breuning, *Memories* (originally published in German in 1874).

noting beside them: 'This overture with the new symphony thus we have a concert in the Kärntnertor Theatre'.[32] The 'new symphony' is represented more extensively on adjacent pages, and was the projected Tenth already sketched briefly in 1822 and 1824. The new sketches, like those of 1822, show a slow, gentle section in E flat major followed by a stormy Allegro in C minor, exactly matching Holz's later description of what he had heard Beethoven play on the piano as the first movement of the projected symphony. The Andante then returns in modified form at the end of the movement.[33] The theme of the Andante section had already been adapted for the slow movement of the Ninth Symphony, but the modifications were so fundamental that only the third bar remained unchanged (cf. Ex. 17.2 above). Thus when Beethoven returned to the Tenth Symphony in 1824 and 1825 he revived the original theme but changed the third bar so that instead of rising it falls to the lower tonic (Ex. 18.4); hence a single thematic idea was to generate themes for two different symphonies!

**Ex. 18.4** SV 26/1, f. 1v

Altogether there are about 250 bars of sketches for the first movement of the symphony, plus various ideas for possible later movements; and although no single sketch for the movement exceeds about twenty bars, together they form a coherent picture of it. The two versions of the third bar of the Andante form one of the primary motivic ingredients. The earlier G–B♭–E♭, ascending as if towards heaven, was replaced by a descent to earth, G–F–E♭ (these two patterns tend to be used by Beethoven with connotations of aspiration and resignation respectively—for example, in Florestan's aria in *Fidelio*); and one or both of these motifs is present in some guise in almost all the sketches for both the Andante and the Allegro. Moreover, both motifs appear in their most stable form in sketches apparently intended for the end of the movement, providing the kind of thematic resolution so common in Beethoven's codas. Also very characteristic is the direct contrast of two opposing ideas; but here the contrast infuses not just the motivic content but also the overall structure, with its opposition of gentle major and stormy minor. Such an opposition also occurs in his final piano sonata (Op. 111), which has been likened to a contrast between heaven and earth. It seems that Beethoven envisaged a similar concept for his Tenth Symphony, but with the bipolar structure (Andante and Allegro) matched by the bipolar motivic pair (rising 6th and falling 3rd) through

---

[32] N-II, 12.

[33] See Cooper, 'Newly Identified', for a fuller summary of the contents of these 1825 sketches.

their joint extramusical implications of heaven and earth. Although such an explicit interpretation must be treated with caution, even for Op. 111 and still more with these incomplete sketches, it receives strong support from a comment beside one of them: 'Come, come, take me away to the transfiguration' (i.e. to heavenly life).[34] Whatever the explanation, the sketches reveal the work as highly characteristic of Beethoven's style while utterly different from any of his other symphonies, and they show him developing old ideas in new ways.

Instead of persisting with the symphony, Beethoven quickly returned to the finale of the Quartet, Op. 130, which was completed about December. The work was finally sold not to Schlesinger but to Mathias Artaria, who paid Beethoven his 80 ducats on 9 January 1826. Thus Beethoven still owed Schlesinger the second quartet promised him, and had already begun a new one (Op. 131) by mid-December. The key chosen was C sharp minor—a key he had more than once considered using for part of Op. 130—and the work occupied him for most of the first half of 1826. Meanwhile the first performance of Op. 130 was finally given by Schuppanzigh's quartet on 21 March. The first five movements were well received—especially the second, fourth, and fifth (the three most straightforward)—but the finale, a massive fugue of 741 bars, was inevitably found bewildering; for Beethoven, following his principle that difficulty and greatness are closely connected, seems to have set out to make the movement extremely taxing both to perform and to comprehend. It begins out of key, in G major (recalling the fourth movement and simultaneously taking up the final note of the Cavatina melody), with a short 'Overtura' that changes character several times. The main eight-note fugue theme dominates this section but undergoes repeated transformations; it is also joined by a fragment of the running semiquaver theme that was originally to have begun the movement, and which is taken up later. After this 'Overtura', the main 'Fuga' can be divided into three sections that correspond to the three movements of a sonata—an Allegro, a slower movement, and a lively concluding one in 6/8; thus, as in the finale of the Ninth Symphony, Beethoven suggests the structure of an entire work within a single multi-sectional movement, again blurring the distinction between a movement and a section. All three sections, however, are unified by the single fugue theme that is present most of the time, and further cohesion is provided during the third section by recalls of material from the first two.

In the first large section, the fugue theme is accompanied first by incessant repetitions of a dotted rhythm, which is combined with large leaps to provide a daunting, forbidding sound; later the dotted rhythms give way to repeated triplet quavers and then repeated dactyls (quaver plus two semiquavers), which accompany various developments of the fugue theme. Throughout this section, the combination of continuous rhythmic

---

[34] See Brandenburg, 'Neunten Symphonie', 110; Cooper, 'Subthematicism'.

repetitions, dense textures, angular melodic lines, and incessantly loud dynamic level, creates a monolithic jaggedness that intensifies the music's apparent impenetrability. The second section, pianissimo almost throughout, where the running semiquaver idea is developed alongside a smoother version of the fugue theme, provides much-needed relief, in the key of G flat major (like the second subject in the first movement); the section concludes with slow written-out trills in B flat minor leading to B flat major. In the third and longest section, there is greater variety of dynamic levels, keys (including an extended passage in A flat), note lengths, and textures, so that the recalls of the first two sections seem in no way out of place. Meanwhile contrapuntal devices such as stretto, augmentation, and inversion increase in complexity, counterbalanced by passages of greater textural simplicity such as one- or two-part writing or grand unisons, and trills become a prominent feature that is extensively developed. The overall effect is therefore of extremely disparate elements being united into a single coherent movement. Beethoven's highly characteristic combination of dissociation and integration, which had permeated the whole quartet, with its wide range of keys and sharply delineated movements, reaches an extreme form in the *Grosse Fuge*.

While some in the audience at the first performance were tempted to reject the *Grosse Fuge* as the confused ramblings of a madman, the more discerning connoisseurs must have sensed that extended study of the movement would reveal it as another masterpiece. This view was evidently communicated to Mathias Artaria, who told Beethoven on 11 April, perhaps with some exaggeration:

There are already many requests for the Fugue arranged for piano four hands—would you allow me to publish it thus?

—

Score—parts—the Fugue arranged by you for four hands to publish simultaneously.[35]

Artaria had probably heard that Schott's were about to issue a four-hand arrangement (by Christian Rummel) of Op. 127 to aid exploration of it, and hoped to do even better himself by obtaining Beethoven's own arrangement of the *Grosse Fuge*. Beethoven, however, was unwilling to do such routine labour, and so it was agreed to ask Anton Halm, who had played the piano part of the 'Archduke' Trio at the concert that had included the première of Op. 130. Halm produced the arrangement within a fortnight, but Beethoven was dissatisfied with it, mainly, it seems, because Halm distributed certain motifs between the two players to make them more easily playable, but in the process the gestures lost some of their shape. Eventually Beethoven made his own arrangement, but felt obliged to sell it to Artaria for only 12 ducats rather than the 25 or more that he thought it worth, since

---

[35] BKh, ix. 184–5.

the publisher had already paid Halm for his arrangement, which would no longer be publishable.

Long before Beethoven arranged the fugue, however, he had completed his C sharp minor quartet, generally regarded as his greatest, or at least first among equals. Beethoven himself evidently shared this view. Certainly it is the most concentrated and thoroughly integrated of his late quartets, despite its odd collection of what look like seven movements. In reality there are only five full ones, for the third of the seven is a brief, eleven-bar link to the extended set of variations that follows; and the sixth, which is not much longer, runs straight into the Finale. Thus in Op. 131 Beethoven again obscures the standard distinction between an independent movement and a section, writing two sections that might or might not be regarded as movements. The distinction is further blurred by the quartet as a whole, which might almost be regarded as one gigantic movement that explores various keys but does not reaffirm the initial tonic until its final seventh section. Indeed its key structure more resembles that of a single movement than a typical multi-movement work: c sharp–D–b–A–E–g sharp–c sharp.

This new type of quartet required a new method of composing, and Beethoven's approach is strikingly different from that in the previous quartet, where there was relatively little long-range planning. This time he repeatedly considered the quartet's overall shape, in a series of synopses summarizing its design.[36] In these sketches he exhibits especial interest in the tonal structure, and in continuity between the movements, revealing that from the outset he planned a more unified work than its immediate predecessors. This did not mean that he selected the precise nature of the later movements any more promptly. In the first overview the opening fugal movement is followed by a series of ideas of which only the variation movement that forms the great central core of the work survived to the final version; and his plans for the finale changed as often as in the previous quartet in B flat, while the eventual finale was first conceived as a penultimate movement in F sharp minor. Nevertheless, the procedure helped Beethoven achieve his goal of creating a work that was structurally, tonally, and motivically more integrated than usual.

Structural integration was achieved through special attention to continuity between successive movements, so that each movement seems to grow naturally out of the end of its predecessor. The tonal integration arose from emphasis on a particular combination of subsidiary keys. C sharp minor has the characteristic of inviting tonal exploration on its flat side, so as to reduce rather than increase the number of accidentals, and Beethoven had done this in his previous big C sharp minor work, the 'Moonlight' Sonata, where much of the first movement and some of the last is on the flat side of the tonic. The key evoked a similar response in the quartet. Particularly noteworthy is the use of D major for the second movement: this relates to

[36] See Winter, *Compositional Origins*, 113–34.

a prominent D natural in bar 6 of the first movement (an ultra-serious, a-cappella fugue that provides another example of vocal style in his late quartets, like the 'Heiliger Dankgesang' in Op. 132 and the Cavatina in Op. 130). Beethoven had difficulty composing a suitable 'answer' to his fugue subject, since a strictly correct one would have given an unsatisfactory augmented 4th; eventually he decided on an answer in the subdominant instead of the usual dominant, thereby generating the prominent D♮ which, though composed at a relatively late stage (apparently after the key of the second movement had been fixed), has such great tonal significance. The note then reappears so strongly at the end of the movement that one could argue that the movement is not really in C sharp minor but the Phrygian Mode (the mode with a flattened second). Beethoven's interest in the old modes having been aroused in several late works, it was almost inevitable that he would eventually allude to the Phrygian, which is perhaps the most distinctive of them. As in the 'Moonlight' Sonata, the finale is the only movement in sonata form. Its second subject is in E major, the key of the fifth movement, but in the recapitulation the theme returns in D rather than A; and the movement ends with such heavy emphasis on the subdominant that, like the first movement, it possesses a Phrygian quality. Many other tonal relationships occur in the quartet as a whole, since Beethoven, as in so many works, chose to use only a restricted range of subsidiary keys that recur in several places.

There are also some remarkable motivic interconnections, especially between the first and last movements. The opening fugue theme (Ex. 18.5a) falls into two parts—an opening four-note group and a flow of crotchets. The finale then begins with a snappy gesture in which, apart from two incidental quavers, the same four-note group appears, but in a different order, C♯–G♯–A–B♯. Later, as if to emphasize the connection, Beethoven introduces the same four notes in bars 21–3 in yet another order (C♯–B♯–A–G♯) at the start of a subsidiary theme (Ex. 18.5b); and lest anyone should overlook the resemblance, this theme is given precisely the same rhythm as the theme of the first movement. Most often when relating movements he used similar melodic contours with different rhythms; here, however, he uses the same rhythm but a new melodic shape. Yet it was not completely new, for the sixth movement had begun with a strikingly similar line (Ex. 18.5c). And a blend of all these variants can be found in a theme originally devised for a supplementary eighth movement (Ex. 18.5d), when all the intense anguish and tragedy implied in the earlier movements yields to complete calm in the peaceful key of D flat major, in a movement headed 'sweet song of rest' in one sketch.[37] This theme, which was later used for the next quartet, begins with six notes from the end of the fugue theme (Ex. 18.5a), but it is also almost literally a major-key version of Ex. 18.5b, and therefore relates also to Ex. 18.5c. Thus it would have formed a natural resolution for

[37] Klein, *Autographe*, 84.

Ex. 18.5

(a) Op. 131/I                               (b) Op. 131/VII

(c) Op. 131/VI                              (d) SV 24, p. 99

the preceding material. Eventually, however, Beethoven decided that resolution and rest were inappropriate in this highly agitated work, and he
made it end precariously on an unstable C sharp major chord, leaning
towards the subdominant.

Schlesinger and Artaria both hoped to purchase Op. 131, but for various
reasons Beethoven sold it to Schott's (who seem to have been his favourite
publisher, perhaps because they belonged to his beloved Rhine country).
He told them on 20 May 1826 that it was already finished, and he may well
have reached the end of the score by then. But the work underwent the usual
protracted revisions, and continued susceptible to alteration for two or
three months while Schott's organized payment and Beethoven rechecked
the manuscript. Schott's asked that it be an 'original quartet': Beethoven
was stung by this request and so, with typical wit, he wrote on the copy that
the work was 'zusammengestohlen aus Verschiedenem diesem und jenem'
('rustled together from various odds and ends'). Only in his letter a week
later did he reveal the joke—which was of course particularly pertinent for
such an integrated and innovative quartet.

As he had still not fulfilled his promise to Schlesinger, Beethoven began
work on yet another quartet (Op. 135 in F) as soon as he had finished Op.
131. The earliest explicit reference is in a conversation book of about 7 July,
when Holz writes: 'That would then be the third in F.'[38] By now Op. 127
had been published, and there was evidently considerable demand for it
amongst eager amateurs, demonstrating that the publishers' marketing
instincts had been sound. The new quartet progressed rapidly during July,
as Beethoven decided it would be on a smaller scale than its immediate predecessors. It is also retrospective in several other ways, notably its light,
carefree character and the witty motivic interplay throughout the first
movement. Having recently drawn inspiration from the old modes and a-
cappella style in the 'Heiliger Dankgesang' of Op. 132 and the fugue of Op.
131, Beethoven now looked to the late eighteenth century and the world of

[38] BKh, x. 26.

Haydn. Nevertheless, there are still some unmistakable Beethoven hallmarks: the opening ornamental figure, played by viola and avoiding the tonic chord, is a typical Beethoven innovation; and the ornament characteristically becomes a main motif for development during the movement. The third movement, in D flat, was probably written particularly fast. Not only is it quite short—a mere fifty-four bars with relatively simple figuration—but its theme had been composed earlier, since it was originally planned as the extra eighth movement of Op. 131. Its middle section is in C sharp minor, providing dark hints of the preceding quartet, but otherwise the movement fulfils its previous designation as a 'sweet song of rest'.

While Beethoven was working on these movements and wondering about a possible finale, a dispute arose with one Ignaz Dembscher, who wanted Op. 130 performed at his house but had not attended Schuppanzigh's première in March. Beethoven demanded, through Holz, that Dembscher exonerate himself by sending Schuppanzigh the subscription price. Dembscher replied, according to Holz, by asking 'whether it must be'. Beethoven, evidently intrigued by the quasi-philosophical nature of such a question, responded by composing the canon 'Es muss sein' ('It must be! yes yes yes yes! Out with your wallet', WoO 196).[39] This canon, completed at the very end of July, gave Beethoven the perfect theme for the finale of his quartet. Half-humorous, half-philosophical, it provided an ideal conclusion for a witty but profound quartet. Beethoven preceded the finale theme with a slow introduction, in which the 'Es muss sein' motif is inverted and in F minor to denote the question 'Muss es sein?', and headed the entire movement 'Der schwer gefasste Entschluss' (The Difficult Decision). Although the concept stemmed from a specific situation in his life, it embodies a universal experience, like several of his other works (such as *Christus am Oelberge* and *An die ferne Geliebte*). Indeed, the movement could be regarded as providing a summing up not just of the quartet but of Beethoven's entire career, which had been replete with difficult decisions, both within his compositions and in everyday life. Even the decision to use this theme for the finale was hard to take—especially after the vacillations over the two previous finales. Schlesinger reports that Beethoven wrote (when he finally sent the quartet) that the work had given him much trouble and that he could not bring himself to compose the finale, hence its curious heading. Whatever its implications, the portentous title hints that there is far more to this movement than first meets the eye, and it is full of the kinds of motivic, tonal, metrical and structural subtlety that had appeared in so many of Beethoven's earlier works.

While Beethoven was at work on this quartet, matters with Karl finally reached a crisis. Karl had become increasingly frustrated by Beethoven's attitude, which though complex and idiosyncratic was in some ways typi-

---

[39] TF, 976; see also BKh, x. 63, 70. Schindler's alternative explanation for the origin of the canon is clearly fabricated.

cal of many over-solicitous parents. Beethoven would frequently ask Karl to help with practical matters such as writing to publishers, copying parts, or making purchases; he alternated rapidly between fierce criticism and deep affection, as he strove to ensure Karl stayed on the straight and narrow; some of the criticism was undeserved and there were frequent rows. Beethoven demanded that Karl visit him more often, and wanted him to account for every kreuzer and every hour of the day; he sent Holz to check on Karl, and to challenge him to billiards in order to ascertain whether Karl spent too much time at play; he disapproved of Karl's close friend Joseph Niemetz (whom Karl had known since their days together at Blöchlinger's Institute), and tried to discourage the association. The fact that Beethoven's attitude was soundly motivated and not directly reprehensible probably just made things seem worse for Karl, who felt imprisoned by his situation, psychologically tormented by Beethoven, and fearful that he could not live up to the standards demanded. There was also the looming threat of examinations. Karl had evaded these at the University by transferring to the Polytechnic at an opportune moment, but he was now about to face some, and the possibility of failure. Although he was confident of passing and denied they were the cause of his worry, they probably affected at least the timing of his actions.

In some ways it was a classic adolescent crisis, in which suicide seemed the only way of escape from an increasingly intolerable situation. By 3 August Karl had bought a pistol, intent on shooting himself. But Mathias Schlemmer, Karl's landlord, somehow heard of the plan and removed the pistol that day. Karl, however, was not to be thwarted. He sold his watch and bought two new pistols on the Saturday (5 August), then instead of returning to his lodgings went out to Baden, and next morning in the Helenenthal, fired twice at his head. The first bullet missed, and the second only injured him, leaving a bad wound. He was discovered there and taken back to his mother's in Vienna. As in many suicide attempts, Karl did not really wish to die. Otherwise he would surely not have aimed so carelessly—twice—nor would he have revealed his intentions the previous week. In two minds, he played a kind of Russian roulette, aiming the pistol near enough his head to risk death, and leaving himself in the hands of fate, which decreed he should live. Beethoven, who had remained in Vienna that summer, was greatly agitated by Karl's disappearance, and eventually found him at Johanna's. The next day Karl was removed to hospital by the police (suicide was regarded as a crime) and given further treatment there, where he gradually recovered. He also received some religious instruction, which was required after suicide attempts. For a month he refused to see Beethoven, who was unable to discover Karl's motives for the suicide attempt. When Karl did eventually make his next entries in Beethoven's conversation book, it was to confirm his determination to join the military, and Beethoven was forced to agree.

By all accounts Beethoven was completely devastated by the events, but they had surprisingly little effect on his composing, apart from setting him back several days while he dealt with the practical repercussions. Holz was his main companion during the crisis, and did much to help him through it. In the second half of August Beethoven finally made his own piano-duet arrangement of the *Grosse Fuge*, having been dissatisfied with Halm's. Such work required less concentration than original composition, and may therefore have been more suitable at this stage if his mind was still preoccupied with Karl. The new version was sent to Artaria through Holz, and Beethoven was duly paid his 12 ducats on 5 September.

At this stage the *Grosse Fuge* was still the finale of the B flat quartet, and had been engraved as such by Artaria. The proofs had even been checked several times. Yet both Beethoven and the publisher felt uneasy about it: however well it absorbed and resolved ideas from earlier in the quartet, it must have seemed somewhat inappropriate. Usually Beethoven's multi-movement works have some unity of character or idea, however diverse the movements might seem superficially. Yet here the second, third and fourth movements are totally out of keeping with the massive fugue, in both scale and style; unlike the earlier movements of the Ninth Symphony, they provide not the least hint of the finale, as is confirmed by the sketches, which show they were composed before Beethoven decided what sort of finale to write.[40] Meanwhile the sketches for the fugue itself imply that the movement grew to a much greater size than first intended, as Beethoven discovered unsuspected possibilities in the theme.

Various incidents now helped to prise the fugue apart from the rest of the work. It alone had been arranged for piano for separate publication, first by Halm and now by Beethoven (who showed less enthusiasm for arranging the other movements when this was suggested); and it was the only movement for which Artaria requested rehearsal letters, which were duly inserted for the first edition. Thus when Holz, according to his own account, was asked by Artaria to take on the seemingly impossible task of persuading Beethoven to write a substitute finale and publish the *Grosse Fuge* separately, he succeeded quite quickly.[41] The actual conversation is not recorded, but some of Holz's written comments are relevant: 'You could have easily made two quartets out of the B flat quartet' (*c.* 5 September); and about a week later, 'Artaria is delighted that you so embraced his proposal; he will gain very much thereby; the two works separately will be more sought after.'[42] Beethoven made the new finale his top priority, to be written immediately after Op. 135. Naturally he expected to

---

[40] Klaus Kropfinger concluded that Beethoven intended from the outset something akin to the *Grosse Fuge* (see Kropfinger, 'Das gespaltene Werk', 315), but intermediate sketches seem to contradict this suggestion; even if Beethoven did at first consider some kind of fugue, he clearly did not envisage the overwhelming movement that eventually resulted. Also, when the larger aesthetic context is considered, although the movement forms a suitable companion to the preceding Cavatina and perhaps the first movement, it is surely disproportionate to the quartet as a whole, both in scale and difficulty.

[41] His own recollections of the incident are in Solomon, *Beethoven*, 324.

[42] BKh, x. 185, 197.

be paid extra for the new movement, but the decision to write it must have been made on aesthetic grounds: he would never have compromised his artistic integrity for the sake of a few ducats; nor would he have composed a simpler movement merely because of perceived technical difficulties, or to placate a few friends. Although the *Grosse Fuge* is widely preferred as the finale today, Beethoven clearly intended the new finale to replace it, and the *Grosse Fuge* to be performed as a separate work.

Karl finally left hospital on 25 September, but needed to recuperate before joining the army. Beethoven, too, needed some time away, since he had not taken his usual break from Vienna that summer. For some years his brother Johann had proposed that Beethoven visit his Gneixendorf estate, and Beethoven now agreed, thinking it would be a good place for Karl's recuperation. Because of its distance, Beethoven had much to clear up before departure, and he suggested postponing the visit; but Johann insisted that the weather would soon deteriorate, and they agreed to set off on 28 September.

One essential matter before they left concerned the Ninth Symphony, which Beethoven had decided to dedicate to the King of Prussia, Friedrich Wilhelm III. Permission had been obtained, a manuscript copy had been prepared, and Samuel Spiker, the Prussian librarian, who happened to be in Vienna at the time, had agreed to take the score back to Berlin. Only the metronome marks needed to be worked out and inserted. This was a task Beethoven found irksome (Schott's had repeatedly asked him, without success, for metronome marks for the works he had sent them), but the day before leaving for Gneixendorf he finally tackled it. He hurriedly sat down with the metronome and called out the figures to Karl, who wrote them in the conversation book. The figures were then copied into the score for Berlin, and were also sent the next month to Schott's, who printed them separately in *Caecilia* before incorporating them into their edition of the work. All went well for the most part, but there were a few mishaps—three in particular—which have blighted performances ever since. For the Trio section, Karl noted 116 for minims; but this seems extraordinarily slow, especially as the previous section is also 116 and there has been an accelerando. Yet 116 per semibreve seems too fast (although the tail of the minim became so worn in Schott's edition that the note has sometimes been read as a semibreve). Perhaps the most likely explanation is that Beethoven called out '160' rather indistinctly, and Karl misheard (the two figures sound very similar in German). Indeed, many performers have since adopted a speed close to minim = 160. A second problem arose at the start of the Finale, noted as '66' in the conversation book, the Berlin manuscript, and the letter to Schott's. Unfortunately, when Schott's published the numbers in *Caecilia*, the printer placed the first '6' upside down, giving 96. This number was then copied unthinkingly into their edition, and even into a letter Beethoven later sent to London. A third mishap occurred at the

Turkish march (finale, bar 331). Here Karl wrote '84' but omitted the note value. He later guessed a dotted crotchet, but Beethoven almost certainly intended a dotted minim—twice as fast.[43] Most of his metronome marks seem quite reliable, but these three mistakes illustrate some of the problems liable to arise.

The Beethovens left for Gneixendorf on 28 September, and arrived the following day. The scenery pleased Beethoven, reminding him of his native Rhineland district (which he still hoped to revisit), and Johann provided well for him and Karl. Krems was only half an hour's drive away, and most things could be purchased there (on arrival Beethoven jotted down a shopping list, which included wax candles, cotton, pencil, ordinary writing paper, and the inevitable blotting paper). Beethoven took advantage of the fine weather and country air at Gneixendorf to resume his customary habit of composing outside, sometimes humming or waving his arms, to the bewilderment and amusement of the inhabitants. The F major quartet was finished by 13 October, according to his letter to Haslinger, but he could not find a copyist locally and eventually wrote out the parts himself. They were finally taken into Vienna, for despatch to Schlesinger and collection of the fee, by Johann around 30 October.

As soon as Op. 135 was finished, Beethoven turned to the new finale for Op. 130, sketching several possible themes before deciding on one. Like the *Grosse Fuge*, this finale takes up some of the tonal ideas of the earlier movements: it begins by using the G from the previous two movements, and it also has an extended section in A flat in the middle; but it is much lighter in texture, and its smaller scale and optimistic character—much closer to that of most of his earlier ideas for possible finale themes than the awe-inspiring *Grosse Fuge*—suit the quartet as a whole. Like Op. 135, it seems at times to recall the eighteenth century, leading back to normality after the extraordinary profundity of the Cavatina. Yet it is of considerable size and contains many subtleties typical of Beethoven's finales. Its start in C minor recalls the first complete chord of the entire quartet, and the subdominant key emerges soon after (bars 25–30), within the main theme. Thus Beethoven here goes one stage further than in the finales of the Fourth Piano Concerto and 'Archduke' Trio, where there are continual struggles to overcome the subdominant, for this time two keys threaten to undermine the stability of the tonic. The discursive tonality of the main theme also serves as a reflection of the wide-ranging keys of the previous movements, and demands an extended coda to resolve its tonal uncertainty.

The movement was written fairly quickly in October–November, and a copy sent to Artaria (through Haslinger) on 22 November. Without a break Beethoven then started composing a string quintet in C—his last major compositional undertaking. It was probably intended for Diabelli, who had requested a quintet some time earlier, but Schlesinger also wanted one (or

---

[43] See Del Mar, *Symphony No. 9: Critical Commentary*, 56–7.

rather, three), and might have eventually acquired it. Beethoven completed a score of the first movement, though perhaps only a score sketch rather than a final draft, and had started sketching a second movement before his final illness overcame him. The score of the first movement was purchased after Beethoven's death by Diabelli, but he published only two arrangements (WoO 62), for piano solo and piano duet, before apparently discarding the original. Once again the movement is retrospective in character, consisting of a short polonaise in closed binary form. This is quite unlike the start of most of his chamber works; the closest precedents are two serenades, Opp. 8 and 25, which also begin with a short, binary-form movement. Thus Beethoven was apparently seeking yet another route for moving forward through looking backward, as in so many of his late works.

As November drew to a close, it became clear that Beethoven and Karl would have to return to Vienna, despite Johann's suggestion that Beethoven stay in Gneixendorf semi-permanently at a cheap rate (40 fl. CM per month for 'everything', which presumably included board, lodging, and servants). They had already stayed far longer than originally planned, and the situation, though seemingly idyllic, was far from ideal. There were frequent disputes between Beethoven and either Karl, Johann, or his wife Therese— most often Karl, who felt psychologically more able to withstand Beethoven after the suicide attempt. Karl had also taken advantage of his extended holiday, having recovered from his wound, and was becoming increasingly idle. Beethoven, meanwhile, was far from well, and one of his own doctors in Vienna would be preferable to an untried one from Krems. They finally left on Friday 1 December, and spent that night in a freezing inn, where Beethoven suffered a feverish chill and other unpleasant symptoms.

They arrived back at the Schwarzspanierhaus next day and promptly sent for a doctor. Beethoven also sent for Holz, with a letter containing the canon *Wir irren allesamt* (WoO 198), which proved to be his last completed composition. Neither of his two usual doctors, Braunhofer and Staudenheim, was able to come, and a third, Dominik Vivenot, was himself sick. Holz finally obtained the services of Professor Andreas Wawruch, who came on 5 December. Beethoven was very weak and sick, suffering from a serious attack of pneumonia, but with skilled treatment he began to recover over the next few days. On 7 December, though still in bed, he managed to write a long letter to Wegeler (replying to one written nearly a year earlier!); and two days later, at last able to get up and walk about, he wrote to Schott's and perhaps made a few more sketches for his quintet. Respite was only temporary, however, for the next day he suffered what Wawruch called a *Brechdurchfall* (illness with diarrhoea), apparently triggered by one of his characteristic rages. Jaundice and dropsy set in, and he never recovered.

His friends and Karl gave what support they could, while Karl made preparations to join the regiment of Baron Joseph von Stutterheim (who eventually received the dedication of Op. 131 for his assistance to Karl).

Holz, having married, could come less often, but Schindler became a frequent visitor, as did Stephan von Breuning and his son Gerhard. On 14 December, the forty-volume collection of Handel's works sent by Stumpff arrived, and Beethoven was overjoyed. Much of his limited energy was soon being spent poring enthusiastically over the volumes. Meanwhile his body had swollen so much that, on 20 December, an operation was performed to drain the accumulated fluid. Karl finally left on 2 January 1827 to join his regiment in Iglau, and the next day Beethoven wrote a will leaving all his property to Karl, who was never to see his uncle again (some years after Beethoven's death, Karl left the army, married, and fathered five children, some of whose descendants are alive today). Beethoven's former doctor Malfatti was now called to assist, and his suggestion of iced punch brought temporary relief; but Beethoven had to undergo three more abdominal operations in early 1827, and showed no real sign of recovery. Thanking Stumpff profusely for the gift of the Handel scores, he indicated that he now faced poverty as he was too ill to compose. The news was passed to the Philharmonic Society, who resolved to send him £100 to provide for his comforts. Beethoven also asked Schott's to send him some fine Rhine or Moselle wine, which was generally unobtainable in Vienna.

The gifts duly arrived. Beethoven dictated a letter to Moscheles in London on 18 March thanking the Philharmonic Society for their generosity and offering to compose for them either a new symphony 'which lies already sketched in my desk' or a new overture.[44] Five days later he wrote for the last time, adding a codicil to his will, on the advice of Breuning, who was anxious lest Karl squander Beethoven's entire assets: the codicil provided that Karl could not touch the capital but only the proceeds. It contained several misspellings that Beethoven had no energy to correct: 'My nephew Karl shall be my sole heir, but the capital from my estate shall fall to his natural or testamentary heirs. Vienna, 23 March 1827, Lu[d]wig van Beethoven.'[45] The same day Beethoven, evidently resigned to impending death, said to his friends (according to a letter written by Schindler next day, and confirmed later by Gerhard von Breuning): 'Plaudite, amici, comoedia finita est!' ('Applaud, friends, the comedy is ended'). Then or the next day he received the last sacraments, and about 1 p.m. on 24 March the wines from Schott's arrived. Thayer reports, apparently using information from Gerhard von Breuning, that Beethoven's only comment was, 'Pity, pity, too late!' and that these were his last words. That evening he lost consciousness, and remained in a coma for nearly two days.

Beethoven had once remarked that his health always suffered in the 'battle between spring and winter'[46] (perhaps a reference to the opening of Haydn's *The Seasons*). Just such a battle took place in the late afternoon of Monday 26 March, as a violent thunderstorm raged. Various people had

---

[44] The Society ultimately did receive a version of the first movement of this symphony, based entirely on these sketches, in a completion by the present writer in 1988.

[45] Facsimile in Cooper, *Compendium*, plate 36.     [46] A-360.

come and gone during the day, but now only two, Anselm Hüttenbrenner (a friend of Schubert's) and a woman (probably Beethoven's maid), were left with him. Hüttenbrenner records that at 5.45 p.m. there was suddenly a flash of lightning and loud thunder; Beethoven opened his eyes, sat up, or at least raised his arm, fist clenched, and sank back dead.

The composer who had taken Europe by storm had died during a storm. Beethoven had first revealed his talent to the world in 1778, in the late afternoon of 26 March; his talent was now lost to the world on the same date in 1827, at the same time of day, in a dramatic end to the *comoedia* of his life. The last action of this lover of nature was to respond to a phenomenon of nature. And it must have been the thunder, not the lightning. His bed was not close to a window, it was still daylight, his eyes were closed, and various curtains and shadows would have reduced the lightning's brightness. But a very close, almost deafening peal of thunder, with its reverberations, is always more startling than a flash, and could easily have produced the response described by Hüttenbrenner. Thus Beethoven, so close to complete deafness during the 1820s, must have heard sounds in the very last moments of his life. His deafness was never total.

An autopsy was performed the next day, revealing that Beethoven evidently died from liver disease, compounded in the latter stages by kidney failure. Whether the liver disease was caused by his alcohol consumption is still disputed, but alcohol was probably a contributory factor. The funeral was quickly arranged, and took place on 29 March. As the procession moved from the Schwarzspanierhaus to the Trinity Church and on to the Währing cemetery, up to 20,000 people took part—a mark of the enormous admiration felt for him. Two of his trombone Equali, arranged for voices by Seyfried, were sung, and a brass band played an arrangement of the 'Marcia funebre' from his Sonata, Op. 26. At the gates of the cemetery the actor Heinrich Anschütz read a moving funeral oration by Grillparzer, and the coffin was then lowered into the ground.

It was the end of an era—the 'Age of Beethoven' as it is sometimes known. Never since, and probably never before, has one composer been so dominant for such a long period; and his successors, though often using his ideas, had to find new paths, since he had traced his to its limits. Beethoven is still in many ways the central figure in Western music,[47] the culmination of the Classical period and an archetype for the Romantic concept of a genius—heroic, individualistic, eccentric, single-minded, and visionary. His art ranged over almost all types of music then current, and embraces the whole gamut of human emotion, from the ecstatic joy of the Ninth Symphony to the profound suffering of the *Pathétique* Sonata, and from the deep mysticism of the *Missa solemnis* to the playful humour of his many scherzos. And his compositional technique far surpasses that of most composers, manipulating themes, pitches, intervals, registers, keys,

---

[47] See Cooper, *Compendium*, 304.

instruments, rhythms, phrases, and structural patterns in ways previously unimagined—halving note values in a triple-time fugue theme, for example, or creating a form that is simultaneously both a single movement and a multi-movement structure, or exploiting the utmost extremes of the piano, or using the timpani as a melody instrument. Yet a nobility and seriousness of purpose invariably underlie his music—a desire to 'raise men to the level of gods' through his art.[48] This desire stemmed from an innate goodness and kindness that permeated his character throughout his life, and attracted noble-minded friends despite his peculiar habits and occasional insensitivity. With all his exceptional musical gifts, Antonie Brentano still described him as 'greater as a human being than as an artist'.[49] Her view is endorsed by Varnhagen's remark, 'I found the man in him even more appealing than the artist,' and by Johann Aloys Schlosser, Beethoven's first biographer, who wrote: 'Great as Beethoven's art was, his heart was yet greater.'[50] Beethoven's life and work, however, are perhaps best summed up in the central portion of Grillparzer's funeral oration, which succinctly encapsulates his unique greatness:[51]

He was an artist, and who can stand beside him? Like the behemoth storming through the seas, he rushed on to the limits of his art. From the cooing of doves to the rolling of thunder, from the most ingenious interweaving of intractable elements of art, to that dreaded point where design gives way to the arbitrary lawlessness of contending natural forces, he had traversed and grasped it all. Whoever comes after him will not continue him; he must begin anew, for his predecessor left off only where art leaves off.

Adelaide and Leonore! Celebration of the heroes of Vittoria, and devout sacrificial song of the Mass! Children of three- and four-part voices! Surging symphony! 'Freude, schöner Götterfunken', you swan-song. Muse of song and lyre. . . . He was an artist, but also a man—a human being in the most perfect sense of the word. Because he withdrew from the world, they called him hostile, and because he shunned sentimentality, unfeeling. No! One who knows himself to be firm does not flee. He who is oversensitive avoids the display of feeling. If he fled from the world, it was because in the depths of his loving nature he found no weapon against it. If he withdrew from mankind, it was because he had given his all and received nothing in return. He remained alone, because he found no second self.

Yet till death he preserved a human heart for all humanity; a fatherly affection for his kin; and his possessions and life-blood for the whole world. Thus he was, thus he died, and thus will he live for all time.

---

[48] A-376.          [49] Solomon, *Beethoven*, 182.
[50] TF, 513; Schlosser, *Beethoven*, 106.
[51] Three versions of the oration are known: see Breuning, *Memories*, 109–10, 141; Schlosser, *Beethoven*, 113–14, 179–81. The version given here is based on Schlosser's text.

# Appendix A

# Calendar

Since Beethoven was born in mid-December, his age is given as that for the main part of the year rather than the last half-month. For other musicians, the age given applies to their birthday or their actual age when they died.[1]

| Year | Age | Life | Contemporary musicians and events |
|------|-----|------|-----------------------------------|
| 1770 | | Ludwig van Beethoven baptized at Bonn, 17 Dec (born 16 Dec.?), son of Johann, Court singer, and Maria Magdalena Leym, née Keverich. | Tartini (77) dies, 26 Feb.; Reicha born, 26 Feb. Albrechtsberger aged 34, Arne 60; C. P. E. Bach 56; J. C. Bach 35; W. F. Bach 60; Boccherini 27; Boyce 59; Cherubini 10; Cimarosa 21; Clementi 18; Dittersdorf 31; Dussek 10; Förster 22; Galuppi 64; Gluck 56; Grétry 29; J. Haydn 38; M. Haydn 33; Jommelli 56; Kozeluch 23; Mozart 14; Paisiello 30; Piccinni 42; Pleyel 13; Quantz 73; Salieri 20; G. B. Sammartini 69/70; Viotti 15; Wagenseil 55; Winter 16; Zelter 12; Zumsteeg 10. |
| 1771 | | | J. B. Cramer born, 24 Feb.; Paer born, 1 June. |
| 1772 | 1 | | Daquin (78) dies, 15 June. |
| 1773 | 2 | Grandfather Ludwig or Louis (61) dies, 24 Dec. | Quantz (76) dies, 12 July. |
| 1774 | 3 | Brother Caspar Anton Carl baptized, 8 Apr. | Jommelli (59) dies, 25 Aug.; Spontini born, 14 Nov. |
| 1775 | 4 | | Sammartini (c.74) dies, 15 Jan.; Crotch born, 5 July. |
| 1776 | 5 | Brother Nikolaus Johann baptized, 2 Oct. | E. T. A. Hoffmann born, 24 Jan. Burney and Hawkins publish music histories. |

[1] Their dates are based on Sadie, *Concise Dictionary*.

*351*

| Year | Age | Life | Contemporary musicians and events |
|---|---|---|---|
| 1777 | 6 | | Wagenseil (62) dies, 1 Mar. Mozart dismissed from service in Salzburg, leaves for Munich and Mannheim. |
| 1778 | 7 | First known public performance, as pianist, Cologne, 26 Mar., playing 'various concertos and trios'. | Arne (67) dies, 5 Mar.; Hummel born, 14 Nov. Mozart in Paris for 6 months. |
| 1779 | 8 | Neefe (31) arrives in Bonn, Oct., and soon starts giving B. music tuition. | Boyce (67) dies, 7 Feb. |
| 1780 | 9 | | Empress Maria Theresa dies, succeeded by Joseph II. |
| 1781 | 10 | Leaves school. Cousin Rovantini, who had given B. violin lessons, dies Sept. | Diabelli born, 6 Sept. Mozart settles in Vienna, 16 Mar. |
| 1782 | 11 | First publication: Dressler Variations. | J. C. Bach (46) dies, 1 Jan.; Field born, July; Paganini born, 27 Oct. Haydn's Quartets, Op. 33 published. |
| 1783 | 12 | Neefe reports on B.'s progress in Cramer's *Magazin der Musik*, 2 Mar. Three piano sonatas (WoO 47) published. Visits Holland with mother, performs in The Hague. | |
| 1784 | 13 | Elector Maximilian Friedrich dies, 15 Apr., succeeded by Maximilian Franz, who reorganizes music at Bonn. B. appointed Court organist, alongside Neefe. | W. F. Bach (73) dies, 1 July; Spohr born, 5 Apr.; Onslow born, 27 July; Ferdinand Ries baptized, 28 Nov. |
| 1785 | 14 | Three piano quartets composed. | Galuppi (78) dies, 3 Jan. |
| 1786 | 15 | | Kuhlau born, 11 Sept.; Weber born, ?18 Nov. Première of *The Marriage of Figaro* by Mozart. |
| 1787 | 16 | Visits Vienna to study with Mozart but returns hastily because of mother's illness. She dies (40), 17 July. | Gluck (73) dies, 15 Nov. |
| 1788 | 17 | Count Waldstein (26) arrives in Bonn. | C. P. E. Bach (74) dies, 14 Dec.; Archduke Rudolph born, 8 Jan. |
| 1789 | 18 | B. plays viola in several operas at newly opened theatre at Bonn Court. | Outbreak of French Revolution, with storming of Bastille, 14 July. |
| 1790 | 19 | Composes *Joseph* and *Leopold* Cantatas. Haydn visits Bonn on his way to London, Dec. | Emperor Joseph II dies, succeeded by Leopold II. |

| Year | Age | Life | Contemporary musicians and events |
|------|-----|------|-----------------------------------|
| 1791 | 20 | *Ritterballett* composed and performed. Righini Variations published. Visits Aschaffenburg and Mergentheim and plays to Sterkel. | Mozart (35) dies, 5 Dec. Czerny born, 21 Feb. Meyerbeer born, 5 Sept. |
| 1792 | 21 | Haydn meets Beethoven during return journey to Vienna. B. moves to Vienna, Nov. Father dies (*c*.52), 18 Dec. | Rossini born, 29 Feb. French army invades Rhineland, Oct. Emperor Leopold II dies, succeeded by Franz II. |
| 1793 | 22 | Befriended by Prince Karl Lichnowsky (37) and others. Lessons with Haydn continue. Five new works sent to Bonn as evidence of progress. | Execution of Louis XVI and Marie Antoinette. |
| 1794 | 23 | Transfers counterpoint studies to Albrechtsberger when Haydn departs for London. | Moscheles born, 23 May. Bonn occupied by the French. |
| 1795 | 24 | First public appearance in Vienna with new piano concerto (probably No. 1), 29 Mar. Publication of Op. 1 Trios. Completion of Opp. 2–4. Conclusion of studies with Albrechtsberger. Early work on a symphony in C. | Marschner born, 16 Aug. Haydn's last symphonies composed. |
| 1796 | 25 | Visits Prague, Dresden, and Berlin. Composes *Ah! perfido* (Op. 65), Sonata, Op. 49 No. 2, Wind Sextet Op. 71, Cello Sonatas, Op. 5. | Berwald born, 23 July; Loewe born, 30 Nov. |
| 1797 | 26 | Completion of song 'Adelaide', Sonatas, Opp. 6, 7, 49 No. 1, Serenade Op. 8. | Schubert born, 31 Jan.; Donizetti born, 29 Nov. |
| 1798 | 27 | Trios, Opp. 9 and 11, Sonatas, Opp. 10 and 12 completed. Quartets, Op. 18 begun. Begins using sketchbooks. Second Piano Concerto revised. | *Allgemeine musikalische Zeitung* begun. Gaveaux's opera *Léonore* produced in Paris. |
| 1799 | 28 | Studies vocal composition with Salieri from about this time. *Pathétique* Sonata completed and published. Gives Amenda first version of Quartet, Op. 18 No. 1. Septet completed. Meets Cramer and Dragonetti. | Dittersdorf (59) dies, 24 Oct. Première of *The Creation* by Haydn. |
| 1800 | 29 | Septet and First Symphony performed in a benefit concert, | Piccinni dies, 7 May. |

| Year | Age | Life | Contemporary musicians and events |
|------|-----|------|-----------------------------------|
| | | 2 Apr. Composes Horn Sonata for Stich, who plays it with B. in Vienna and Budapest. Quartets, Op. 18 completed. Sonata, Op. 22 composed. Work on Third Piano Concerto left unfinished. | |
| 1801 | 30 | *Prometheus* composed and produced. Violin Sonatas, Opp. 23 and 24, Piano Sonatas, Opp. 26–8, Quintet, Op. 29 composed. Reveals deafness in letters to Wegeler and Amenda, June–July. Later falls in love with Giulietta Guicciardi. Ries arrives in Vienna and studies piano with B. | Cimarosa (51) dies, 11 Jan.; Lortzing born, 23 Oct.; Bellini born, 3 Nov. Napoleon makes Concordat with the Pope. |
| 1802 | 31 | Spends Apr.–Oct. at Heiligenstadt, with increasing despair of cure for deafness. Writes Heiligenstadt Testament, 6 and 10 Oct. Completes Second Symphony, composes Violin Sonatas, Op. 30, Piano Sonatas, Op. 31, Bagatelles, Op. 33, Variations, Opp. 34 and 35. | Zumsteeg (42) dies, 27 Jan. First Viennese performances of Cherubini's *Lodoïska* and *Les deux journées*. |
| 1803 | 32 | Takes up residence at the Theater an der Wien. Concert there, 5 Apr., includes premières of Third Piano Concerto, oratorio *Christus am Oelberge*, and Second Symphony. Composes 'Kreutzer' Sonata Op. 47 for violinist George Bridgetower, performed, 24 May. Composes Third Symphony, intended for Napoleon, during summer. Begins and abandons opera *Vestas Feuer*, before turning to 'Waldstein' Sonata. Erard of Paris send B. one of their pianos. | Glinka born, 1 June; Berlioz born, 11 Dec. |
| 1804 | 33 | *Christus* performed in revised version, 27 Mar. *Leonore* (later known as *Fidelio*) begun. Piano Sonatas, Op. 53 ('Waldstein') and Op. 54, Triple Concerto and Third Symphony completed. When B. hears that Napoleon has proclaimed himself Emperor he cancels the dedication of the | Paer's *Leonore* produced at Dresden. |

| Year | Age | Life events | Contemporary musicians and |
|------|-----|-------------|----------------------------|
| | | symphony. 'Appassionata' Sonata (Op. 57) begun. | |
| 1805 | 34 | B. in love with Josephine Deym, presents her with song *An die Hoffnung* (Op. 32). First public performance of Third Symphony (*Eroica*). *Leonore* completed, first performed 20 Nov. after five-week delay, and just after French occupation of Vienna. | Boccherini (62) dies, 28 May. Battles of Trafalgar and Austerlitz. |
| 1806 | 35 | *Leonore* revised, with Overture 'No. 2' replaced by 'No. 3'; performed 29 Mar. and 10 Apr. only. Brother Carl marries Johanna Reiss, 25 May; their only child, Karl, born 4 Sept. Composes Fourth Piano Concerto, Fourth Symphony, 'Razumovsky' Quartets, and Violin Concerto. Visits Silesia with Lichnowsky but returns home suddenly after dispute. Première of Violin Concerto, played by Clement, 23 Dec. | M. Haydn (68) dies, 10 Aug. |
| 1807 | 36 | Fourth Symphony, Fourth Piano Concerto, and newly written *Coriolan* Overture performed, Mar. Clementi visits Vienna and purchases British publication rights of recent works, Opp. 58–62, Apr. Mass in C, composed during the summer, performed at Eisenstadt, Sept. Much work on Fifth Symphony. | |
| 1808 | 37 | Fifth and Sixth Symphonies, Cello Sonata, Op. 69, Piano Trios, Op. 70 completed. Offered post of Kapellmeister at Kassel, Oct., but does not go there. Benefit concert at Theater an der Wien, 22 Dec., includes Fifth and Sixth Symphonies, Fourth Piano Concerto, ending with newly written Choral Fantasia, Op. 80. | Part I of Goethe's *Faust* published. |
| 1809 | 38 | Archduke Rudolph, Prince Kinsky, and Prince Lobkowitz agree to pay B. an annuity of | Albrechtsberger (73) dies, 7 Mar.; J. Haydn (77) dies, 31 May; Mendelssohn born, 3 Feb. |

355

| Year | Age | Life | Contemporary musicians and events |
|------|-----|------|-----------------------------------|
| | | 4000 fl., 1 Mar. *Lebewohl* Sonata (Op. 81a) composed for Rudolph, who is forced by French advance to leave Vienna, 4 May. B. seeks refuge with Carl during French bombardment, 11–12 May. Fifth Piano Concerto, Quartet, Op. 74, Fantasia, Op. 77, Sonatas, Opp. 78–9 completed. | |
| 1810 | 39 | Rudolph returns to Vienna and begins (or resumes) composition lessons with B. Possible marriage proposal to Therese Malfatti. Meets the Brentanos. First batch of folksong settings completed for Thomson. Music for *Egmont*, Quartet, Op. 95 and Goethe songs Op. 83 composed. | Chopin born, ?1 Mar.; Schumann born, 8 June; Nicolai born, 9 June. |
| 1811 | 40 | 'Archduke' Trio completed, Mar. Music for *König Stephan* and *Die Ruinen von Athen* composed for theatre in Pest. Visits Teplitz, Aug.–Sept. Begins work on Seventh Symphony. | Liszt born, 22 Oct. Fivefold currency devaluation in Austria, 15 Mar. |
| 1812 | 41 | Première of *König Stephan* and *Die Ruinen von Athen*, 9 Feb. Seventh Symphony completed. Revisits Teplitz; writes letter to 'Immortal Beloved', 6–7 July. Meets Goethe in Teplitz. Moves to Karlsbad and Franzensbad, back to Teplitz, then visits brother Johann in Linz, Oct., where Eighth Symphony completed. Prince Kinsky killed in riding accident, Nov. Begins a memorandum book known as his *Tagebuch*. Composes Violin Sonata Op. 96 for Rode and Archduke Rudolph, who perform it on 29 Dec. | Dussek (52) dies, 20 Mar. Napoleon invades Russia and is driven back with huge losses. |
| 1813 | 42 | Writes to Princess Kinsky about his annuity, without result. At Maelzel's suggestion, composes *Wellingtons Sieg* (the so-called Battle Symphony) to celebrate Wellington's victory at Vittoria. This is performed along with Seventh Symphony, 8 and 12 Dec. | Grétry (72) dies, 24 Sept.; Wagner born, 22 May; Verdi born, 9/10 Oct.; Alkan born, 30 Nov. Duke of Wellington victorious at Battle of Vittoria, 21 June. Napoleon defeated at Battle of Leipzig, Oct. |

| Year | Age | Life | Contemporary musicians and events |
|------|-----|------|-----------------------------------|
| 1814 | 43 | *Fidelio* again revised, and produced 23 May. First public performance of 'Archduke' Trio, Apr. Piano Sonata Op. 90 composed. Benefit concerts on 2 Jan., 27 Feb., 29 Nov. and 2 Dec., the last two including the newly completed cantata *Der glorreiche Augenblick*. | Congress of Vienna, Sept. Razumovsky's palace destroyed by fire, 31 Dec. |
| 1815 | 44 | Large number of works sold to Steiner. Cello sonatas Op. 102 composed. Pocket sketchbooks start being used regularly. 'Namensfeier' Overture and cantata *Meeresstille und glückliche Fahrt* completed after lengthy sketching. B's brother Carl dies 15 Nov. | Napoleon defeated at Waterloo. |
| 1816 | 45 | B. granted custody of nephew Karl in preference to the boy's mother, Johanna. Karl is sent to Giannatasio's boarding school, but dispute with Johanna continues. Song cycle *An die ferne Geliebte* completed, Apr.; Piano Sonata, Op. 101 completed, Nov. Prince Lobkowitz, dedicatee of several Beethoven works, dies 15 Dec. | Paisiello (76) dies, 5 June; Sterndale Bennett born, 13 Apr. Première of *The Barber of Seville* by Rossini. |
| 1817 | 46 | Persistent ill health greatly restricts B.'s output. Ries invites B. to compose two symphonies for London and to visit there the next year, but only a few sketches are made for the Ninth Symphony and the visit does not take place. Extended correspondence with Nanette Streicher, who assists B. with domestic matters. Metronome marks for the first eight symphonies published. | Gade born, 22 Feb. |
| 1818 | 47 | Karl leaves Giannatasio's school, 24 Jan., to live with B. Broadwood of London send B. one of their pianos. 'Hammerklavier' Sonata (Op. 106), and twelve sets of folk-song variations for Thomson, | Kozeluch (70) dies, 7 May; Gounod born, 17 June. |

357

| Year | Age | Life | Contemporary musicians and events |
|------|-----|------|-----------------------------------|
| | | completed. Rudolph, closely assisted by B., composes set of 40 variations on a theme by B. First conversation books. Johanna again attempts to obtain the guardianship of Karl. After B. reveals he is not of noble birth the case is transferred to a lower court, the *Magistrat*. | |
| 1819 | 48 | Johanna gains temporary custody of Karl, who then enters the Blöchlinger Institute. Beethoven's protests and counter-petition are rejected. Diabelli Variations and *Missa solemnis* begun. | Offenbach born, 20 June. |
| 1820 | 49 | Archduke Rudolph enthroned as Archbishop of Olmütz, 9 Mar., but *Missa solemnis* not ready in time. B. turns to the Court of Appeal concerning Karl's guardianship and is finally successful 8 Apr.: he and Karl Peters appointed co-guardians. Final batch of folksong settings for Thomson. Piano Sonata, Op. 109 completed. | |
| 1821 | 50 | Work on *Missa solemnis* delayed by extended illness. Josephine Deym (now Baroness Stackelberg) dies, 31 Mar. Piano Sonata, Op. 110 completed (but with early version of finale). | Première of *Der Freischütz* by Weber. |
| 1822 | 51 | Piano Sonata, Op. 111 and *Missa solemnis* completed. Visited by Rossini, whose operas had become very popular in Vienna. Reworks *Die Ruinen von Athen* as *Die Weihe des Hauses*, with new overture, for reopening of Josephstadt Theatre on 3 Oct. Prince Galitzin requests some new quartets from B. | E. T. A. Hofmann dies, 25 June; Franck born, 10 Dec. Schubert's 'Unfinished' Symphony composed. |
| 1823 | 52 | Diabelli Variations completed and published. Extensive work on Ninth Symphony. Visited by Weber, Oct. Karl leaves Blöchlinger Institute to attend university. | Förster (75) dies, 12 Nov. Schubert composes *Die schöne Müllerin*. |

| Year | Age | Life | Contemporary musicians and events |
|------|-----|------|-----------------------------------|
| 1824 | 53 | Galitzin gives première of *Missa solemnis* in St Petersburg, Apr. Première of Ninth Symphony at B.'s benefit concert (which also included parts of the *Missa solemnis*), 7 May, repeated 23 May. Bagatelles, Op. 126 and Quartet Op. 127 completed. | Viotti (68) dies, 3 Mar.; Smetana born, 2 Mar.; Bruckner born, 4 Sept. |
| 1825 | 54 | First performance of Quartet, Op. 127, 6 Mar. Serious illness, Apr., followed by composition of 'Heiliger Dankgesang' as part of Op. 132, which is completed about June. Quartet, Op. 130 composed with *Grosse Fuge* as finale. Last known sketches for unfinished Tenth Symphony. Karl transfers to the polytechnic. | Salieri (74) dies, 7 May; Winter (71) dies, 17 Oct.; J. Strauss (ii) born, 25 Oct. Schubert's 'Great' C major Symphony and Mendelssohn's Octet composed. |
| 1826 | 55 | First performance of Quartet, Op. 130, 21 Mar. B.'s attitude to Karl drives him to attempt suicide, 6 Aug. Recently completed Quartet Op. 131 sent to Schott's a few days later. B. and Karl stay in Gneixendorf with brother Johann. Quartet, Op. 135 and new finale for Op. 130 completed there. Unfinished String Quintet in C begun. B. returns home with Karl, 1 Dec. Falls ill with severe chill and pneumonia on arrival. Receives Stumpff's gift of Handel scores. | Weber (39) dies, 5 June. Mendelssohn's Overture *A Midsummer Night's Dream* composed. |
| 1827 | 56 | Karl departs for military service, 2 Jan. B. confined to bed with dropsy; his condition deteriorates despite treatment from Wawruch and Malfatti. Receives £100 from Philharmonic Society; offers them his Tenth Symphony, 18 Mar. Dies during thuderstorm at 5.45 p.m., 26 Mar. | Bellini aged 26; Sterndale Bennett 11; Berlioz 24; Berwald 31; Bruckner 3; Cherubini 67; Chopin 17; Clementi 75; J. B. Cramer 56; Crotch 52; Czerny 36; Diabelli 46; Donizetti 30; Field 45; Franck 5; Gade 10; Glinka 24; Gounod 9; Hummel 49; Kuhlau 41; Liszt 16; Loewe 31; Lortzing 26; Marschner 32; Mendelssohn 18; Meyerbeer 36; Moscheles 33; Nicolai 17; Offenbach 8; Onslow 43; Paer 56; Paganini 45; Ries 43; |

Year   Age   Life

**Contemporary musicians and events**
Rossini 35; Archduke
Rudolph 39; Schubert 30;
Schumann 17; Smetana 3;
Spohr 43; Spontini 53; J.
Strauss (ii) 2; Verdi 14;
Wagner 14; Zelter 69.

# Appendix B

# List of works

Most of Beethoven's works appeared in a nineteenth-century Complete Edition (*GA*), and almost all the remainder were included in a supplement in 1959–71 (*SGA*: see Appendix D for details). A new Complete Edition (*NA*), prepared under the auspices of the Beethovenhaus, Bonn, is still in progress. Many works were given an opus number by Beethoven himself when first published. Others, such as Op. 119, acquired their present number later, while a few numbers, such as Op. 41, have been allocated to unauthentic arrangements of his works made by someone else. In the Beethoven thematic catalogue published in 1955,[1] works that had not by then acquired an opus number were listed as 'Werke ohne Opuszahl' (works without opus-number), abbreviated to WoO. Meanwhile Willy Hess was compiling a list of all Beethoven works not included in *GA*. His list, published in 1957,[2] includes many works with a WoO number, plus many more—mostly variant versions, fragments and trivia. Those without a WoO number but sufficiently significant are listed below with their Hess number. A very small number of works do not even have a Hess number, while a few of doubtful authenticity are also included. Authentic titles of instrumental works are given in italics; unofficial nicknames are in quotation marks.

Works are listed below according to the following classification: symphonies; concertos; other orchestral music; dance music and marches; chamber music with wind; chamber music for piano and strings; string quartets; other string chamber music; piano sonatas; piano variations; other music for piano solo; piano music for four hands; stage music; works with chorus; solo voice(s) with orchestra; canons; songs; folksong settings; arrangements of his own music; miscellaneous; unfinished works. Within each category, the order is chronological as far as possible, and the date given is generally the date of completion.

SYMPHONIES

| 1800 | Op. 21 | Symphony No. 1 in C major |
| 1801–2 | Op. 36 | Symphony No. 2 in D major |
| 1803–4 | Op. 55 | Symphony No. 3 in E flat major, *Eroica* |
| 1806 | Op. 60 | Symphony No. 4 in B flat major |
| 1807–8 | Op. 67 | Symphony No. 5 in C minor |
| 1808 | Op. 68 | Symphony No. 6 in F major, *Pastorale* |
| 1812 | Op. 92 | Symphony No. 7 in A major |

---

[1] KH.    [2] Hess, *Verzeichnis*.

*Beethoven*

| 1812 | Op. 93 | Symphony No. 8 in F major |
| 1823–4 | Op. 125 | Symphony No. 9 in D minor ('Choral') |

See also **Other Orchestral Music** (*Wellingtons Sieg*) and **Unfinished Works** below.

CONCERTOS

| 1784 | WoO 4 | Piano Concerto in E flat major. Only the piano part survives, with orchestral cues. |
| 1790–2 | WoO 5 | Violin Concerto in C major. Only the first 259 bars of the autograph score survive, but Beethoven may well have completed the work. |
| 1793 | Hess 12 | Oboe Concerto in F major. Lost, but the main themes survive, and sketches for the middle movement. |
| 1793 | WoO 6 | Rondo in B flat major for piano and orchestra. Probably the original finale of Op. 19 (see next entry). |
| 1795–8 | Op. 19 | Piano Concerto No. 2 in B flat major. Perhaps originally composed as early as 1788, it was revised several times, with new second and third movements incorporated *c*.1795, a major revision and new score in 1798, and the solo part finally written out in 1801. Cadenza composed in 1809. |
| 1795–1800 | Op. 15 | Piano Concerto No. 1 in C major. Composed in 1795; revised with new score in 1800. Cadenza composed in 1809. |
| 1803 | Op. 37 | Piano Concerto No. 3 in C minor. Cadenza composed in 1809. |
| 1804 | Op. 56 | Triple Concerto in C major, for piano, violin, and cello |
| 1806 | Op. 58 | Piano Concerto No. 4 in G major. Cadenzas composed 1809. |
| 1806 | Op. 61 | Violin Concerto in D major. Also published by Beethoven as a Piano Concerto. Cadenzas composed (1809) only for the piano version. |
| 1809 | Op. 73 | Piano Concerto No. 5 in E flat major ('Emperor') |
| 1809? | WoO 58 | Two cadenzas for Mozart's Piano Concerto in D minor, K. 466 |

See also **Other Orchestral Music** (Romances) and **Unfinished Works** below.

OTHER ORCHESTRAL MUSIC

| 1786? | Hess 13 | Romance in E minor for flute, bassoon, piano, and orchestra. This incomplete movement may have been the slow movement of a now lost concerto. |
| 1798? | Op. 50 | Romance in F major for violin and orchestra. This may well have originated *c*. 1791 as the slow movement of WoO 5 (see **Concertos** above). Existing score evidently dates from 1798. |
| 1800–2 | Op. 40 | Romance in G major for violin and orchestra |

1813     Op. 91     *Wellingtons Sieg* ('Battle Symphony'). Second part originally written for Maelzel's panharmonicon (see **Miscellaneous** below).
1814–15   Op. 115    Overture in C major ('Namensfeier')
1822     WoO 3     *Gratulations-Menuett* in E flat major

For other overtures see **Stage Music** below.


DANCE MUSIC AND MARCHES

?     WoO 9     Six minuets (2 violins and bass). Probably pre-1795, but authenticity not confirmed
1795     WoO 7     Twelve minuets (orchestra, or 2 violins and bass, or piano solo)
1795     WoO 8     Twelve German dances (orchestra, or 2 violins and bass, or piano solo)
1795     WoO 10    Six minuets (only piano version survives)
1796     WoO 42    Six German dances (violin and piano)
*c.*1792–7   WoO 13    Twelve German dances (only piano version survives, in copy of *c.*1800)
1799     WoO 11    Seven ländler (only piano version survives)
1799     WoO 12    Twelve minuets: spurious, by Beethoven's brother Carl.
*c.*1791–   WoO 14    Twelve contredanses (orchestra, or 2 violins and bass, or
1801              piano solo)
1802     WoO 15    Six ländler (2 violins and bass, or piano solo)
—       WoO 16    Twelve ecossaises: unauthentic arrangements of various works.
*c.* 1806   WoO 83    Six ecossaises (only piano version survives)
1809–10   WoO 18    March in F major (military band). Trio added in 1822.
1810     WoO 19    March in F major (military band). Trio added in 1822.
*c.* 1810?   WoO 20    March in C major (military band). Trio added in 1822.
1810     WoO 21    Polonaise in D major (military band)
1810     WoO 22    Ecossaise in D major (military band)
*c.* 1810   WoO 23    Ecossaise in G major (survives only in Czerny's piano arrangement)
1816     WoO 24    March in D major (large military band)
—       WoO 17    Eleven 'Mödling' dances: spurious.

See also **Other Orchestral Music** (*Gratulations-Menuett*) above; **Other Music for Piano Solo** (various dances) and **Chamber Music with Wind** (March, WoO 29) below.


CHAMBER MUSIC WITH WIND

1786     WoO 37    Trio in G major (flute, bassoon, piano).
*c.* 1791?   —       Sonata in B flat major (flute and piano), listed in KH as Anhang 4 and perhaps spurious.
1792     WoO 26    Duo in G major (2 flutes)
—       WoO 27    Three duos (clarinet and bassoon). First published in Paris, *c.* 1810–15, but probably spurious. If genuine, probably of early date.

| | | |
|---|---|---|
| 1793 | Op. 103 | Octet in E flat major (2 oboes, 2 clarinets, 2 horns, 2 bassoons). Later recomposed as string quintet, Op. 4. |
| 1793 | WoO 25 | Rondo (Rondino) in E flat major. Intended at one time as 4th movement of Op. 103, and with same instrumentation. |
| 1793 | Hess 19 | Quintet in E flat major (oboe, 3 horns, bassoon). Partly lost. |
| 1795? | Op. 87 | Trio in C major (2 oboes, cor anglais) |
| 1795? | WoO 28 | Variations on 'Là ci darem' from *Don Giovanni* by Mozart, C major (2 oboes, cor anglais) |
| 1795? | Op. 81b | Sextet in E flat major (2 horns, string quartet) |
| 1796 | Op. 16 | Quintet in E flat major (oboe, clarinet, horn, bassoon, piano; also for violin, viola, cello, piano) |
| 1796? | Op. 71 | Sextet in E flat major (2 clarinets, 2 horns, 2 bassoons) |
| 1797 | Op. 11 | Trio in B flat major (clarinet or violin, cello, piano) |
| 1797–8 | WoO 29 | March in B flat major (2 clarinets, 2 horns, 2 bassoons) |
| 1799 | Op. 20 | Septet in E flat major (clarinet, horn, bassoon, violin, viola, cello, double bass) |
| 1800 | Op. 17 | Sonata in F major (horn or cello, piano) |
| 1801 | Op. 25 | Serenade in D major (flute, violin, viola) |
| 1812 | WoO 30 | Three Equali: D minor, D major, B flat major (4 trombones) |
| 1815 | Hess 297 | Adagio in A flat major (3 horns) |
| 1818–19 | Op. 105 | Six national airs with variations (piano and optional flute or violin) |
| 1818–19 | Op. 107 | Ten national airs with variations (piano and optional flute or violin) |

## CHAMBER MUSIC FOR PIANO AND STRINGS

| | | |
|---|---|---|
| 1785 | WoO 36 | Three piano quartets: E flat major, D major, C major (violin, viola, cello, piano) |
| 1791? | WoO 38 | Piano Trio in E flat major |
| *c.*1791 | Hess 46 | Fragment of Sonata in A major (violin and piano); authenticity not confirmed. |
| *c.*1791 | Hess 48 | Allegretto in E flat major (piano trio) |
| 1792? | Op. 44 | Variations on 'Ja, ich muss mich' from *Das rote Käppchen* by Dittersdorf, E flat major (piano trio) |
| 1793 | WoO 40 | Variations on 'Se vuol ballare' from *The Marriage of Figaro* by Mozart, F major (violin and piano) |
| 1793–4 | WoO 41 | Rondo in G major (violin and piano) |
| 1794–5 | Op. 1 | Three piano trios: E flat major, G major, C minor |
| 1796 | WoO 43–4 | Four mandolin pieces: C minor, E flat major, C major, D major (mandolin and piano) |
| 1796 | Op. 5 | Two cello sonatas: F major, G minor (cello and piano) |
| 1796 | WoO 45 | Variations on 'See the conqu'ring hero' from *Judas Maccabaeus* by Handel, G major (cello and piano) |
| 1796? | Op. 66 | Variations on 'Ein Mädchen oder Weibchen' from *The Magic Flute* by Mozart, F major (cello and piano) |

| | | |
|---|---|---|
| 1797–8 | Op. 12 | Three violin sonatas: D major, A major, E flat major (violin and piano) |
| 1800 | Op. 23 | Violin Sonata in A minor (violin and piano) |
| 1800–1 | Op. 24 | Violin Sonata in F major, 'Spring' (violin and piano) |
| 1801 | WoO 46 | Variations on 'Bei Männern' from *The Magic Flute* by Mozart, E flat major (cello and piano) |
| 1802 | Op. 30 | Three violin sonatas: A major, C minor, G major (violin and piano) |
| 1803 | Op. 47 | Violin Sonata in A major, 'Kreutzer' (violin and piano). Finale originally composed for Op. 30 No. 1. |
| 1807–8 | Op. 69 | Cello Sonata in A major (cello and piano) |
| 1808 | Op. 70 | Two piano trios: D major 'Ghost', E flat major |
| 1811 | Op. 97 | Piano Trio in B flat major, 'Archduke' |
| 1812 | WoO 39 | Allegretto in B flat major (piano trio) |
| 1812 | Op. 96 | Violin Sonata in G major (violin and piano) |
| 1815 | Op. 102 | Two cello sonatas: C major, D major (cello and piano) |
| *c.*1816 | Op. 121a | Variations on 'Ich bin der Schneider Kakadu' from *Die Schwestern von Prag* by Müller, G major (piano trio). Originally composed 1803? |

See also **Dance Music and Marches** (various dance collections) above; **Unfinished Works** (Piano Trio in F minor) below.

## STRING QUARTETS

| | | |
|---|---|---|
| *c.*1791 | Hess 33 | Minuet in A flat major |
| 1794–5 | Hess 30 | Prelude and Fugue in F major |
| 1794–5 | Hess 31 | Prelude and Fugue in C major |
| 1799– 1800 | Op. 18 | Six string quartets: F major, G major, D major, C minor, A major, B flat major. Early version of No. 1 survives as Hess 32. |
| 1806 | Op. 59 | Three string quartets, 'Razumovsky': F major, E minor, C major |
| 1809 | Op. 74 | String Quartet in E flat major, 'Harp' |
| 1810 | Op. 95 | String Quartet in F major, *Quartett serioso* |
| 1817 | — | Allegretto in B minor |
| 1824–5 | Op. 127 | String Quartet in E flat major |
| 1825 | Op. 132 | String Quartet in A minor |
| 1825–6 | Op. 130 | String Quartet in B flat major |
| 1825–6 | Op. 133 | *Grosse Fuge* in B flat major for string quartet. Originally composed as finale of Op. 130. |
| 1826 | Op. 131 | String Quartet in C sharp minor |
| 1826 | Op. 135 | String Quartet in F major |

See also **Arrangements** (quartet arrangement of Op. 14) below.

## OTHER STRING CHAMBER MUSIC

| | | |
|---|---|---|
| ? | Hess 39 | String Quintet in F major. Lost |
| *c.*1791 | — | Duo in E flat major (violin and cello). Fragment of one movement only |

| 1795? | Op. 3 | String Trio in E flat major (violin, viola, cello) |
| 1795 | Op. 4 | String Quintet in E flat major (2 violins, 2 violas, cello). Reworking of Wind Octet Op. 103. |
| 1796–7 | Op. 8 | Serenade in D major (violin, viola, cello) |
| 1796–7 | WoO 32 | Duo in E flat major *with two obbligato eye-glasses* (viola and cello). Second movement is fragmentary. |
| 1797–8 | Op. 9 | Three string trios: G major, D major, C minor (violin, viola, cello). Hess 28 is a second Trio section in C major apparently rejected from Scherzo of No. 1. |
| 1801 | Op. 29 | String Quintet in C major (2 violins, 2 violas, cello) |
| 1817 | Hess 40 | Prelude and (fragment of) Fugue in D minor (2 violins, 2 violas, cello) |
| 1817 | Op. 137 | Fugue in D major (2 violins, 2 violas, cello) |
| 1822 | WoO 34 | Duet for 2 violins. 7 bars. |

See also **Canons** (WoO 35), **Arrangements** (Op. 104), and **Unfinished Works** (WoO 62) below.

## PIANO SONATAS

| 1783 | WoO 47 | Three sonatas, 'Kurfürsten': E flat major, F minor, D major |
| 1795 | Op. 2 | Three sonatas: F minor, A major, C major |
| 1795–7 | Op. 49 | Two sonatas (or sonatinas): G minor, G major. No. 2 composed probably about a year before No. 1. |
| 1796–7 | Op. 7 | Grand Sonata in E flat major |
| 1798 | Op. 10 | Three sonatas: C minor, F major, D major |
| 1798? | Op. 13 | Grand Sonata, *Pathétique*, in C minor |
| 1798 | Op. 14 | Two sonatas: E major, G major. No. 1 later arranged as string quartet. |
| 1800 | Op. 22 | Grand Sonata in B flat major |
| 1800–1 | Op. 26 | Grand Sonata in A flat major |
| 1800–1 | Op. 27 | Two sonatas *quasi una fantasia*: E flat major, C sharp minor, 'Moonlight' |
| 1801 | Op. 28 | Grand Sonata in D major, 'Pastoral' |
| 1802 | Op. 31 | Three sonatas: G major, D minor, E flat major |
| 1803–4 | Op. 53 | Grand Sonata in C major, 'Waldstein' |
| 1804 | Op. 54 | Sonata in F major |
| 1804–6 | Op. 57 | Sonata in F minor, 'Appassionata' |
| 1809 | Op. 78 | Sonata in F sharp major |
| 1809 | Op. 79 | Sonata (or sonatina) in G major |
| 1810 | Op. 81a | Sonata in E flat major, *Lebewohl, Abwesenheit und Wiedersehn* or 'Les Adieux' |
| 1814 | Op. 90 | Sonata in E minor |
| 1816 | Op. 101 | Sonata in A major |
| 1818 | Op. 106 | Grand Sonata in B flat major, 'Hammerklavier' |
| 1820 | Op. 109 | Sonata in E major |
| 1821–2 | Op. 110 | Sonata in A flat major |
| 1822 | Op. 111 | Sonata in C minor |

## PIANO VARIATIONS

| 1782 | WoO 63 | On a March by Dressler, C minor |
|------|--------|--------------------------------|
| c.1791 | WoO 64 | On a Swiss song, F major |
| c.1791 | WoO 65 | On 'Venni amore' by Righini, D major |
| 1792 | WoO 66 | On 'Es war einmal' from *Das rote Käppchen* by Dittersdorf, A major |
| 1795 | WoO 68 | On 'Menuett à la Viganò' from *Le nozze disturbate* by Haibel, C major |
| 1795 | WoO 69 | On 'Quant' è più bello' from *La molinara* by Paisiello, A major |
| 1795 | WoO 70 | On 'Nel cor più non mi sento' from *La molinara* by Paisiello, G major |
| 1795? | WoO 72 | On 'Une fièvre brûlante' from *Richard Coeur de Lion* by Grétry, C major |
| 1796–7 | WoO 71 | On a Russian dance from *Das Waldmädchen* by Wranitzky, A major |
| 1799 | WoO 73 | On 'La stessa, la stessissima' from *Falstaff* by Salieri, B flat major |
| 1799 | WoO 76 | On 'Tändeln und Scherzen' from *Soliman II* by Süssmayr, F major |
| 1799 | WoO 75 | On 'Kind, willst du ruhig schlafen' from *Das unterbrochene Opferfest* by Winter, F major |
| 1800 | WoO 77 | On an original theme, G major |
| 1802 | Op. 34 | On an original theme, F major |
| 1802 | Op. 35 | On an original theme from *Die Geschöpfe des Prometheus*, E flat major |
| 1803 | WoO 78 | On 'God save the King', C major |
| 1803 | WoO 79 | On 'Rule, Britannia' from *Alfred* by Arne, D major |
| 1806 | WoO 80 | On an original theme, C minor |
| 1809 | Op. 76 | On an original theme, D major. The theme was reused in *Die Ruinen von Athen* |
| 1823 | Op. 120 | On a Waltz by Diabelli, C major |

## OTHER MUSIC FOR PIANO SOLO

| 1783 | WoO 48 | Rondo in C major |
|------|--------|------------------|
| c. 1783 | WoO 49 | Rondo in A major |
| 1785? | WoO 82 | Minuet in E flat major |
| 1787? | WoO 55 | Prelude in F minor |
| 1789? | Op. 39 | Two preludes, both C major |
| c. 1791 | WoO 50 | Sonatina(?) in F major. Two short pieces probably belonging together. |
| 1791–8? | WoO 51 | Sonatina in C major. End of second movement and whole of third lost; second completed by Ries in 1830. |
| c. 1793 | WoO 81 | Allemande, A major. Revised as bagatelle in 1822. On the same bifolio are four other pieces (no WoO or Hess number) also numbered as bagatelles in 1822. |
| 1795 | Op. 129 | *Alla ingharese: quasi un capriccio* in G major. Unfinished, completed probably by Diabelli, its first |

publisher, who may also have coined its popular title 'The Rage over the Lost Penny'.

| | | |
|---|---|---|
| 1795 | Hess 64 | Fugue in C major |
| c.1795 | WoO 52 | Presto in C minor. Originally for Sonata Op. 10 No. 1; revised in 1798 and 1822. |
| c.1795 | Hess 69 | Allegretto in C minor. Revised as a bagatelle in 1822. |
| 1796–7 | WoO 53 | Allegretto in C minor |
| c.1796–8 | Op. 51 | Two rondos, C major and G major. Composed and first published separately. |
| 1801–2 | Op. 33 | Seven bagatelles |
| 1802? | WoO 54 | *Lustig-Traurig* in C major |
| 1803 | WoO 57 | Andante in F major, 'Andante favori'. Originally written for 'Waldstein' Sonata. |
| 1803 | WoO 56 | Allegretto in C major. Revised as a bagatelle in 1822. |
| 1809 | Op. 77 | Fantasia in G minor to B major |
| 1810? | WoO 59 | *Für Elise* in A minor. Revised as a bagatelle in 1822. |
| 1814 | Op. 89 | Polonaise in C major |
| 1818 | WoO 60 | Bagatelle in B flat major |
| 1821 | WoO 61 | Allegretto in B minor |
| 1820–2 | Op. 119 | Eleven bagatelles. Nos. 7–11 composed as a set in 1820–1; Nos. 1–5 written earlier, revised 1822, when No. 6 was added. |
| 1824 | Op. 126 | Six bagatelles |
| 1824 | WoO 84 | Waltz in E flat major |
| 1825 | WoO 61a | Allegretto quasi andante in G minor |
| 1825 | WoO 85 | Waltz in D major |
| 1825 | WoO 86 | Ecossaise in E flat major |

See also **Dance Music and Marches** above; **Arrangements** below.

### PIANO MUSIC FOR FOUR HANDS

| | | |
|---|---|---|
| 1792? | WoO 67 | Variations on a theme by Count Waldstein, C major |
| 1796–7 | Op. 6 | Sonata in D major |
| 1803 | WoO 74 | Variations on an original theme 'Ich denke dein', D major. Originally composed 1799. |
| 1803 | Op. 45 | Three marches: C major, E flat major, D major |

See also **Arrangements** below.

### STAGE MUSIC

| | | |
|---|---|---|
| 1791 | WoO 1 | Ballet *Ritterballett* |
| c.1795 | WoO 91 | Two arias for Umlauf's singspiel *Die schöne Schusterin* |
| 1801 | Op. 43 | Ballet *Die Geschöpfe des Prometheus* |
| 1807 | Op. 62 | Overture *Coriolan* |
| 1810 | Op. 84 | *Egmont* Overture and Incidental Music |
| 1811 | Op. 117 | Singspiel *König Stephan* |
| 1811 | Op. 113 | Singspiel *Die Ruinen von Athen* |

| 1813 | WoO 2a | 'Triumph-Marsch' for *Tarpeja* |
| 1814 | WoO 94 | Chorus for singspiel *Die gute Nachricht* |
| 1814 | Op. 72 | Opera *Fidelio*. First completed 1805, with overture known as *Leonore* No. 2 (also included WoO 2b); revised 1806, with overture *Leonore* No. 3; a third overture, *Leonore* No. 1 (Op. 138), written in 1807 but replaced in 1814 by *Fidelio* overture along with other revisions to the opera. |
| 1815 | WoO 96 | Incidental Music for *Leonore Prohaska* |
| 1815 | WoO 97 | Chorus for singspiel *Die Ehrenpforten* |
| 1822 | Hess 118 | Singspiel *Die Weihe des Hauses*, adapted from *Die Ruinen von Athen* (see above). This version includes a new Overture (Op. 124), new chorus (WoO 98) and greatly revised March and Chorus (Op. 114). |

See also **Unfinished Works** (*Vestas Feuer*) below.

## WORKS WITH CHORUS

| 1790 | WoO 87 | Cantata on the Death of Emperor Joseph II |
| 1790 | WoO 88 | Cantata on the Accession of Emperor Leopold II |
| *c*. 1801–2 | WoO 99 | 19 unaccompanied Italian partsongs. Some of these also appear in earlier versions, and some additional ones are not part of WoO 99 (Hess 208–32). |
| 1801 | WoO 100 | *Lob auf den Dicken*, unaccompanied voices. Short musical joke. |
| 1802 | WoO 101 | *Graf, Graf, liebster Graf*, unaccompanied voices. Short musical joke. |
| 1803–4 | Op. 85 | Oratorio *Christus am Oelberge*. Composed 1803, revised and expanded 1804. |
| 1807 | Op. 86 | Mass in C |
| 1808 | Op. 80 | Choral Fantasia |
| 1814 | WoO 102 | *Abschiedsgesang*, unaccompanied voices |
| 1814 | WoO 103 | Cantata *Un lieto brindisi*, voices and piano |
| 1814 | Op. 118 | *Elegischer Gesang*, voices and string quartet |
| 1814 | WoO 95 | *Chor auf die verbündeten Fürsten*, voices and orchestra |
| 1814 | Op. 136 | Cantata *Der glorreiche Augenblick* |
| 1814–15 | Op. 112 | Cantata *Meeresstille und glückliche Fahrt* |
| 1817 | WoO 104 | *Gesang der Mönche*, unaccompanied voices |
| 1819 | WoO 105 | *Hochzeitslied*, voices and piano |
| 1822 | Op. 123 | *Missa solemnis* in D. Begun in 1819; completed 1822 with minor revisions thereafter. |
| 1822–4 | Op. 121b | *Opferlied*, voices and chamber orchestra. Two versions exist, from 1822 and 1824. |
| 1823 | WoO 106 | Birthday Cantata for Prince Lobkowitz, voices and piano |
| 1823–4 | Op. 122 | *Bundeslied*, voices and chamber ensemble |

See also **Symphonies** (No. 9) and **Stage Music** above; **Songs** and **Folksong Settings** below.

WORKS FOR SOLO VOICE(S) AND ORCHESTRA

| | | |
|---|---|---|
| *c.*1791 | WoO 92 | *Primo amore* |
| *c.*1791 | WoO 89 | *Prüfung des Küssens* |
| *c.*1791–2 | WoO 90 | *Mit Mädeln sich vertragen* |
| 1796 | Op. 65 | *Ah! perfido* |
| 1802 | WoO 92a | *No, non turbarti* |
| 1802 | Op. 116 | *Tremati, empi.* Revised 1814? |
| 1802 | WoO 93 | *Nei giorni tuoi felici* |

CANONS

| | | |
|---|---|---|
| *c.*1795 | WoO 159 | *Im Arm der Liebe* |
| *c.*1795 | WoO 160 | Two untexted canons, G and C major |
| *c.*1797 | Hess 276 | *Herr Graf* |
| 1803 | Hess 229 | *Languisco e moro* |
| 1803 | Hess 274–5 | Two untexted canons, G and A flat major |
| *c.*1811? | WoO 161 | *Ewig dein* |
| — | WoO 162 | *Ta ta ta ta.* Spurious: by Schindler |
| 1813 | WoO 163 | *Kurz ist der Schmerz* |
| 1814 | WoO 164 | *Freundschaft ist die Quelle* |
| 1815 | WoO 165 | *Glück zum neuen Jahr* |
| 1815 | WoO 166 | *Kurz ist der Schmerz* |
| *c.*1815 | WoO 167 | *Brauchle, Linke* |
| 1816 | WoO 168 | *Das Schweigen* and *Das Reden* |
| 1816 | WoO 169 | *Ich küsse Sie* |
| 1816 | WoO 170 | *Ars longa, vita brevis* |
| 1817 | WoO 171 | *Glück fehl' dir* |
| *c.*1818 | WoO 172 | *Ich bitt' dich* |
| 1819 | WoO 173 | *Hol' euch der Teufel* |
| 1819 | WoO 174 | *Glaube und hoffe* (not strict canon) |
| 1819 | WoO 176 | *Glück zum neuen Jahr* |
| 1819 | WoO 179 | *Seiner kaiserlichen Hoheit*; the canon itself begins with *Alles Gute* |
| 1820 | WoO 175 | *Sankt Petrus* |
| 1820 | Hess 300 | *Liebe mich* |
| 1820 | Hess 301 | *Wähner . . . es ist kein Wahn* |
| 1820 | WoO 180 | *Hoffmann, sei es ja kein Hofmann* |
| *c.*1820 | WoO 177 | *Bester Magistrat* |
| *c.*1820? | WoO 178 | *Signor Abbate* |
| 1821 | WoO 182 | *O Tobias* |
| 1822 | WoO 181 | Three canons |
| 1823 | WoO 183 | *Bester Herr Graf* |
| 1823 | WoO 184 | *Falstafferel, lass' dich sehen* |
| 1823 | WoO 185 | *Edel sei der Mensch* (2 versions) |
| 1824 | WoO 186 | *Te solo adoro* |
| 1824 | WoO 187 | *Schwenke dich* |
| 1825 | WoO 188 | *Gott ist eine feste Burg* |
| 1825 | WoO 189 | *Doktor sperrt das Tor* |
| 1825 | WoO 190 | *Ich war hier, Doktor* |

| | | |
|---|---|---|
| 1825 | WoO 35 | Untexted canon in A major (2 violins?) |
| 1825 | WoO 191 | *Kühl, nicht lau* |
| 1825 | WoO 192 | *Ars longa, vita brevis* |
| 1825 | WoO 194 | *Si non per portas* |
| 1825 | WoO 195 | *Freu' dich des Lebens* |
| *c.*1825? | WoO 193 | *Ars longa, vita brevis* |
| 1826 | — | *Bester Magistrat* (different from WoO 177) |
| 1826 | WoO 196 | *Es muss sein* |
| 1826 | WoO 197 | *Da ist das Werk* |
| 1826 | Hess 277 | *Esel aller Esel* |
| 1826 | WoO 198 | *Wir irren allesamt* |

## SONGS

| | | |
|---|---|---|
| 1783 | WoO 107 | Schilderung eines Mädchens |
| 1784 | WoO 108 | An einen Säugling |
| *c.*1790 | WoO 113 | Klage |
| *c.*1790? | WoO 110 | Elegie auf den Tod eines Pudels |
| *c.*1791 | WoO 111 | Punschlied |
| *c.*1792 | WoO 109 | Trinklied |
| *c.*1792 | WoO 112 | An Laura |
| *c.*1792 | WoO 114 | Selbstgesprach |
| *c.*1792 | WoO 115 | An Minna |
| 1792–4 | WoO 117 | Der freie Mann |
| *c.*1794 | WoO 116 | Que le temps me dure |
| *c.*1794 | WoO 119 | O care selve |
| 1794–5 | WoO 118 | Seufzer eines Ungeliebten; Gegenliebe |
| *c.*1794–5 | Op. 46 | Adelaide |
| *c.*1795 | WoO 123 | Zärtliche Liebe |
| *c.*1795–6 | WoO 124 | La partenza |
| 1796 | WoO 121 | Abschiedsgesang an Wiens Bürger |
| 1797 | WoO 122 | Kriegslied der Oesterreicher |
| 1798–9 | WoO 127 | Neue Liebe, neues Leben |
| 1798–9 | WoO 125 | La tiranna |
| 1798–9 | WoO 128 | Plaisir d'aimer |
| 1799 | WoO 74 | Ich denke dein. Followed by variations (see **Piano Music for Four Hands** above). |
| *c.* 1801 | WoO 120 | Man strebt die Flamme |
| 1801–2 | WoO 126 | Opferlied. Originally composed 1794–5. For later setting see Op. 121b under **Works with Chorus.** |
| 1801–2 | Op. 48 | Six Gellert songs: 1 Bitten; 2 Die Liebe des Nächsten; 3 Vom Tode; 4 Die Ehre Gottes aus der Natur; 5 Gottes Macht und Vorsehung; 6 Busslied |
| 1803 | WoO 129 | Der Wachtelschlag |
| 1803 | Op. 88 | Das Glück der Freundschaft |
| 1803–5 | Op. 52 | Eight songs: 1 Urians Reise um die Welt; 2 Feuerfarb; 3 Das Liedchen von der Ruhe; 4 Maigesang; 5 Mollys Abschied; 6 Die Liebe; 7 Marmotte; 8 Das Blümchen |

|  |  | Wunderhold. Most or all of these were originally composed in the 1790s or earlier. |
|---|---|---|
| 1804–5 | Op. 32 | An die Hoffnung |
| 1806 | WoO 132 | Als die Geliebte sich trennen wollte |
| 1806–7 | WoO 133 | In questa tomba oscura |
| 1807–8 | WoO 134 | Sehnsucht (four settings) |
| 1808 | WoO 136 | Andenken |
| 1809 | WoO 137 | Lied aus der Ferne |
| 1809 | WoO 138 | Der Jüngling in der Fremde |
| 1809 | WoO 139 | Der Liebende |
| 1809 | Op. 75 | Six songs: 1 Mignon; 2 Neue Liebe, neues Leben; 3 Aus Goethes Faust (Flohlied); 4 Gretels Warnung; 5 An den fernen Geliebten; 6 Der Zufriedene |
| 1809 | Op. 82 | Four ariettas and a duet: 1 Hoffnung; 2 Liebes-Klage; 3 L'amante impatiente; 4 L'amante impatiente (another setting); 5 Lebens-Genuss |
| 1810 | Op. 83 | Three Goethe songs: 1 Wonne der Wehmut; 2 Sehnsucht; 3 Mit einem gemalten Band |
| 1811–14 | WoO 140 | An die Geliebte |
| 1813 | WoO 141 | Der Gesang der Nachtigall |
| 1813 | WoO 142 | Der Bardengeist |
| 1813–15 | Op. 94 | An die Hoffnung |
| 1814 | WoO 143 | Des Kriegers Abschied |
| 1814 | WoO 144 | Merkenstein |
| 1814 | Op. 100 | Merkenstein. For 2 voices |
| *c*.1815? | WoO 135 | Die laute Klage |
| 1815 | WoO 145 | Das Geheimnis |
| 1816 | WoO 146 | Sehnsucht |
| 1816 | Op. 98 | Song cycle *An die ferne Geliebte*: 1 Auf dem Hügel; 2 Wo die Berge; 3 Leichte Segler; 4 Diese Wolke; 5 Es kehret der Maien; 6 Nimm sie hin denn |
| 1816 | Op. 99 | Der Mann von Wort |
| 1816 | WoO 147 | Ruf vom Berge |
| 1817 | WoO 148 | So oder so |
| 1817 | WoO 149 | Resignation |
| 1818 | WoO 200 | O Hoffnung. Written as a theme for variations by Archduke Rudolph. |
| 1820 | WoO 150 | Abendlied unterm gestirnten Himmel |
| 1820 | WoO 130 | Gedenke mein. Another song with the same title but now lost was written in 1804–5. |
| 1822 | Op. 128 | Der Kuss. Sketched 1798. |
| 1823 | WoO 151 | Der edle Mensch |

## FOLKSONG SETTINGS

| 1809–10 | Group 1 | 1 Merch Megan; 2 Love without Hope; 3 Oh let the Night; 4 To the Blackbird (1st setting); 5 The Monks of Bangor's March; 6 The Dream; 7 The Old Strain; 8 The Dairy House; 9 Helpless Woman; 10 TheGolden Robe; |

11 Farewell, thou Noisy Town; 12 Waken Lords; 13 Ned Pugh's Farewell; 14 Three Hundred Pounds; 15 Good Night; 16 Constancy; 17 Sweet Richard; 18 The Vale of Clwyd; 19 The Cottage Maid; 20 Cupid's Kindness; 21 The Damsels of Cardigan; 22 To the Aeolian Harp; 23 Sion, the Son of Evan; 24 [Untitled and untexted]; 25 The Fair Maid of Mona; 26 The Hapless Soldier; 27 In Vain to this Desart; 28 On the Massacre of Glencoe (1st setting); 29 Dermot and Shelah; 30 Hide not thy Anguish; 31 The Soldier's Dream; 32 They bid me Slight; 33 When Eve's Last Rays; 34 What shall I do; 35 Once more I hail thee; 36 English Bulls; 37 I'll praise the Saints (1st setting); 38 The Morning Air; 39 Sweet Power of Song; 40 Since Greybeards inform us; 41 The British Light Dragoons; 42 Paddy O'Rafferty; 43 Faithfu' Johnie (1st setting). Most listed in KH under WoO 152, 153, 155 or 158. Nos. 4, 37, and 43 are Hess 206, 196, and 203 respectively.

| | | |
|---|---|---|
| 1810 | Group 2 | 1 'Tis but in Vain (1st setting); 2 His Boat comes; 3 The Wand'ring Gypsy; 4 No Riches; 5 Lament for Owen Roe O'Neill; 6 Farewell Bliss; 7 Come Draw we Round; 8 The Return to Ulster; 9 I dream'd I lay (1st setting); 10 Let Brain-spinning Swains. Most listed in KH under WoO 152, 153, or 158. Nos. 1 and 9 are Hess 197 and 194 respectively. |
| 1812 | Group 3 | 1 The Traugh Welcome; 2 Thou Emblem of Faith; 3 Musing on the Roaring Ocean; 4 Oh Harp of Erin (1st setting); 5 The Deserter; 6 Morning a Cruel Turmoiler; 7 From Garyone (1st setting); 8 Oh! would I were (1st setting); 9 Wife, Children and Friends. Most listed in KH under WoO 152. No. 8 is Hess 198. |
| 1813 | Group 4 | 1 To the Blackbird; 2 On the Massacre of Glencoe; 3 I'll praise the Saints; 4 Faithfu' Johnie; 5 'Tis but in Vain; 6 I dream'd I lay; 7 Oh Harp of Erin; 8 From Garyone; 9 Oh! would I were. All written as replacements for settings in Groups 1–3. Most listed in KH under WoO 153–5 or Op. 108. No. 2 is Hess 192. |
| 1813 | Group 5 | 1 Put Round the Bright Wine; 2 Thy Ship must sail; 3 O might I; 4 Norah of Balamagairy; 5 The Kiss, Dear Maid; 6 Adieu my Lov'd Harp; 7 He promis'd me; 8 The Soldier in a Foreign Land; 9 The Hero may Perish; 10 The Elfin Fairies; 11 The Farewell Song; 12 The Pulse of an Irishman; 13 Save me from the Grave; 14 Oh! who, my Dear Dermot; 15 O soothe me, my Lyre; 16 No more, my Mary; 17 Come, Darby Dear; 18 Castle O'Neill; 19–20 When Far from the Home (2 settings); 21 When Mortals all; 22 Judy, Lovely. Most listed in KH under WoO 153–5 or 158. No. 20 is Hess 195. |

*373*

| 1815 | Group 6 | 1 The Wandering Minstrel; 2 A Health to the Brave; 3 By the Side of the Shannon; 4 The Soldier; 5 Cauld Frosty Morning *or* Erin! oh, Erin; 6 Sad and Luckless; 7 O Mary ye's be Clad; 8 The Parting Kiss; 9 Highland Harry; 10 Again, my Lyre; 11 Dim, dim is my Eye; 12 Bonny Laddie; 13 The Sweetest Lad; 14 Sympathy; 15 O swiftly glides. Listed in KH under WoO 153, 155–8 or Op. 108. |
|---|---|---|
| 1815 | Group 7 | 1 'Tis Sunshine; 2 Robin Adair; 3 Oh! thou art the Lad. WoO 153/13, 157/7, and Op. 108/11 respectively. |
| 1816 | Group 8 | 1 O Cruel was my Father; 2 Could this Ill World; 3 Oh, had my Fate; 4 The Lovely Lass; 5 O how can I be Blythe; 6 Schöne Minka. Listed in KH under Op. 108 or WoO 158. |
| 1816 | Group 9 | 1 Vo lesochke; 2 Akh, rechenki; 3 Kak poshli nashi podruzhki; 4 Wann i in der Früh; 5 Una paloma blanca; 6 Como la mariposa; 7 Tiranilla Española; 8 La gondoletta; 9 Yo no quiero; 10 Seus lindos olhos; 11 Horch auf, mein Liebchen; 12 Wegen meiner bleib d'Fräula; 13 An ä Bergli; 14 Da brava, Catina; 15 I bin a Tyroler Bua; 16 A Madel, ja a Madel; 17 Oj, oj upiłem; 18 Poszła baba. Listed in KH under WoO 158 (except No. 8: WoO 157/12). |
| 1816–17 | Group 10 | 1 When my Hero in Court; 2 Cease your Funning; 3 Sally in our Alley; 4 Non, non, Colette; 5 Air français; 6 God save the King; 7 The Highland Watch. Most listed in KH under WoO 156–8 or Op. 108. No. 5 is Hess 168. |
| 1816–17 | Group 11 | 1 Lilla Carl; 2 Wer solche Buema; 3 Edes kinos emlékezet; 4 Ih mag di nit nehma. Listed in KH under WoO 158. |
| 1817 | Group 12 | 1 The Maid of Isla; 2 Oh Sweet were the Hours; 3 O Mary, at thy Window; 4 Oh was not I; 5 Come fill, fill; 6 Music, Love and Wine; 7 Red gleams the Sun; 8 Jeanie's Distress; 9 Behold, my Love; 10 Sir Johnie Cope; 11 O Sanctissima; 12 Ridder Stig. Listed in KH under Op. 108 or WoO 157–8. |
| 1818 | Group 13 | 1 The Shepherd's Song; 2 Sunset; 3 Enchantress, Farewell.Op. 108 nos. 23, 2, and 18. |
| 1818 | Group 14 | 1 Lochnagar; 2 Duncan Gray; 3 Womankind; 4 Auld Lang Syne; 5 The Quaker's Wife; 6 Ye Shepherds of this Pleasant Vale; 7 From thee, Eliza; 8 Polly Stewart. Listed in KH under WoO 156 and 158. |
| 1819 | Group 15 | 1 O Charlie is my Darling. WoO 157/3 |
| 1819 | Group 16 | 1 Up! Quit thy Bower; 2 Glencoe; 3 The Banner of Buccleuch; 4 The Miller of Dee. Listed in KH under WoO 156–7. |
| 1820 | Group 17 | 1 Highlander's Lament; 2 Sleep'st thou *or* Mark yonder Pomp; 3 Bonny wee Thing (Haydn setting, with lower |

|   |   | voices added by Beethoven). Listed in KH under WoO 157–8. |
|---|---|---|
| 1820 | Group 18 | 1 Das liebe Kätzchen; 2 Der Knabe auf dem Berge. Hess133–4. |
| 1820 | Op. 108 | 25 Scottish songs. Revised versions of 25 settings listed above. |

## ARRANGEMENTS OF HIS OWN MUSIC

| | | |
|---|---|---|
| — | Hess 87–99 | Piano arrangements of various works, notably *Ritterballett* (WoO 1), *Die Geschöpfe des Prometheus* (Op. 43), and *Wellingtons Sieg* (Op. 91). |
| 1801–2 | Hess 34 | String Quartet in F major, arranged from Piano Sonata Op. 14 No. 1. |
| 1802–3 | Op. 38 | Trio for piano, clarinet or violin, and cello, arranged from Septet Op. 20. |
| 1803 | Op. 41 | Serenade for flute/violin and piano, arranged by F. X. Kleinheinz, corrected by Beethoven, from Serenade, Op. 25. |
| 1803 | Op. 42 | Notturno for viola and piano, arranged by F. X. Kleinheinz, corrected by Beethoven, from Serenade, Op. 8. |
| 1805 | (Op. 36) | Piano Trio, arranged by someone else (probably corrected by Beethoven) from Symphony No. 2. |
| 1806 | Op. 63 | Piano Trio, arranged, possibly without Beethoven's knowledge, from String Quintet, Op. 4. |
| 1807 | Op. 64 | Sonata for cello and piano, arranged, possibly without Beethoven's knowledge, from String Trio, Op. 3. |
| 1817 | Op. 104 | String Quintet in C minor, arranged by Kaufmann, corrected by Beethoven, from Piano Trio, Op. 1 No. 3. |
| 1820–1 | Hess 65 | Concert Finale in C major for piano, arranged from coda of Piano Concerto No. 3, Op. 37. |
| 1826 | Op. 134 | *Grosse Fuge* in B flat for piano duet, arranged from string quartet version Op. 133. |

See also **Concertos** (Op. 61), **Dance Music and Marches** (various works), **Chamber Music with Wind** (Opp. 16, 11, 17), and **Other String Chamber Music** (Op. 4) above.

## MISCELLANEOUS

| | | |
|---|---|---|
| 1783? | WoO 31 | Fugue in D major for organ |
| 1793–5 | Hess 233–46 | Counterpoint exercises for Haydn and Albrechtsberger |
| 1794–9 | WoO 33 | Five pieces for musical clock. Nos. 4–5 probably date from 1794; Nos. 1–3 from 1799. |
| *c.* 1798 | Hess 36 | Arrangement for string quartet of part of Overture to Handel's *Solomon* |
| 1801–2 | Hess 38 | Arrangement for string quintet of Bach's Fugue in B flat minor from *Das wohltemperirte Clavier*, book 1 |

*Beethoven*

| 1813 | Hess 108 | Original version for panharmonicon of 'Sieges-symphonie' from *Wellingtons Sieg* (Op. 91) |
| — | WoO 199, 201–5 | Various short musical jokes and quips in letters etc. |

UNFINISHED WORKS

Beethoven left large numbers of compositions unfinished, but not many progressed beyond the first few bars. The main ones with some substance are as follows.

| 1793–5 | — | Fantasia in D major for piano. Substantial sketches in the Kafka Sketch Miscellany. |
| 1795–8 | — | Symphony (No. 0) in C major. Extensively sketched in 1795–7, but eventually evolved into Symphony No. 1. |
| 1802 | — | Triple Concerto in D major. Partial score of first movement, plus sketches; replaced by Triple Concerto in C major. |
| 1803 | Hess 115 | Opera *Vestas Feuer*. One scene composed. |
| 1815 | Hess 15 | Piano Concerto No. 6 in D major. Partial score of first movement, plus sketches. |
| 1816 | — | Piano Trio in F minor. Part of first movement composed. |
| 1822–5 | — | Overture in B flat major on B-A-C-H. Various sketches. |
| 1822–5 | — | Symphony No. 10 in E flat major. Sketches for first movement, plus brief ideas for possible later movements. First-movement sketches were elaborated into complete movement by Barry Cooper in 1988. |
| 1826–7 | WoO 62 | String Quintet in C major. Sketches plus piano arrangement (by Diabelli) of first movement. |

# Appendix C

# Personalia

**Albrechtsberger,** Johann Georg (1736–1809), was a prominent organist, theorist, and composer. When Haydn left for London in 1794, Albrechtsberger began giving Beethoven tuition in counterpoint, correcting and improving his exercises with great care and imagination. Lessons continued for about 18 months, and Beethoven later modelled his own teaching of Archduke Rudolph on what he had learnt from Albrechtsberger.

**Amenda,** Karl Friedrich (1771–1836), a violinist and theologian from Courland, lived in Vienna in 1798–9 and became closely acquainted with Beethoven, who ever after retained the deepest affection for him. On Amenda's departure in 1799, Beethoven gave him a copy of his Quartet, Op. 18 No. 1 in an early version which was later revised before publication.

**Artaria & Co.,** the leading Viennese music publisher in the late 18th century, issued many of Beethoven's early works including Opp. 1–8. Notable members of the Artaria family in Beethoven's day included Francesco (1744–1808) and his son Domenico (1775–1842). Another member, Mathias (1793–1835), ran an independent firm in the 1820s and published Beethoven's Quartet, Op. 130 and *Grosse Fuge.*

**Bach,** Johann Baptist (1779–1847), was an eminent lawyer who gave Beethoven much sound advice on legal matters—most notably during Beethoven's appeal concerning the guardianship of his nephew in 1819–20.

**Beethoven,** (Caspar Anton) Carl van (1774–1815), was the elder of the composer's two surviving brothers. He moved to Vienna in 1794, and after attempts to establish himself as a musician became a clerk in the Department of Finance. During 1802–5 he gave Beethoven much secretarial assistance in dealings with publishers. On 25 May 1806 he married Johanna Reiss, who gave birth to their only child Karl on 4 September that year.

**Beethoven,** Johann van (*c.* 1740–92), father of the composer, was a professional singer at the Electoral court in Bonn, and a teacher of piano and singing. He gave Beethoven his first lessons in music, but was strict and harsh as a father. In later life he became increasingly addicted to alcohol, and was dismissed from service at the court in 1789.

**Beethoven,** Johanna van, née Reiss (*c.* 1786–1868), was wife of Beethoven's brother Carl and mother of his nephew Karl. In 1811 she was convicted of theft, an offence later used by Beethoven as evidence of her unsuitability for Karl's guardianship during their lengthy legal battles of 1815–20 after Carl's death. Beethoven sometimes referred to her as the Queen of the Night, on account of her allegedly evil influence on Karl. In 1820 she gave birth to an illegitimate daughter, Ludovika.

**Beethoven**, Karl van (1806–58), was the son of Beethoven's brother Caspar Carl and Johanna. After Carl's death in 1815, the boy initially entered a boarding school, the Giannatasio Institute, and then lived with Beethoven for a time before becoming a pupil at the Blöchlinger Institute (1819–23). Next he attended Vienna University but transferred to the Polytechnic in 1825. On 6 August 1826 he attempted suicide. After recovering he joined the army, which he left in 1832, the year of his marriage to Caroline Naske (1808–91). They had five children.

**Beethoven**, Ludwig van (1712–73), grandfather of the composer and known mainly as Louis in his early life when he lived in Mechelen (Malines). He joined the Electoral court at Bonn as a musician in 1733 and became Kapellmeister in 1761. As a young child Beethoven adored him, and in later life revered his memory.

**Beethoven**, Maria Magdalena van, née Keverich (1746–87), the composer's mother, came from Ehrenbreitstein near Koblenz. After the death of her first husband, Johann Leym, she married Johann van Beethoven on 12 November 1767. They had seven children, but four died in infancy, as did Leym's only child. She was a very serious, earnest woman, but Beethoven always spoke highly of her after her early death from tuberculosis.

**Beethoven**, (Nikolaus) Johann van (1776–1848), the composer's younger surviving brother, followed him to Vienna in 1795 and worked in a pharmacy there until 1808. He then moved Linz to run his own pharmacy, from which he became very wealthy. He married Therese Obermayer in 1812, and in 1819 he purchased an estate at Gneixendorf, which Beethoven visited in 1826.

**Beethoven**, Therese van, née Obermayer (1787–1828), became the mistress of Beethoven's brother Johann in Linz in 1812, having already given birth to an illegitimate daughter (Amalie Waldmann) five years earlier. The couple married on 8 November, but Therese had no further children.

**Bernard**, Carl Joseph (or Joseph Karl) (1780–1850), a writer who arrived in Vienna in 1800, became editor of the *Wiener Zeitung* in 1819. His first known connection with Beethoven was in 1814, as author of the patriotic *Chor auf die verbündeten Fürsten* (WoO 95). He was in close contact with the composer during the following years, and wrote for him the text of an oratorio, *Der Sieg des Kreuzes*, but Beethoven never set it.

**Bigot**, Marie, née Kiené (1786–1820), was a noted pianist, and wife of Razumovsky's librarian. The couple became friendly with Beethoven about 1806, and he presented her with the autograph score of the 'Appassionata' Sonata, but the Bigots left for Paris in 1809.

**Braun**, Baron Peter von (1758–1819), was a wealthy businessman and music lover who was for a time in charge of the two court theatres in Vienna. He rarely allowed Beethoven to use either theatre for a concert, but after taking over the Theater an der Wien he helped set up the première of *Leonore* in 1805. Beethoven dedicated his Piano Sonatas, Op. 14, and his Horn Sonata, Op. 17, to Braun's wife Josephine (1765–1838).

**Breitkopf & Härtel**, of Leipzig, a music-publishing firm since the early 18th century, was founded by the Breitkopf family. Gottfried Christoph Härtel (1763–1827) joined them in 1795, and took full control the following year. Beethoven's dealings with them, conducted through Härtel himself, began in 1801. For a while they were his favourite publishers, issuing over twenty of his works, although he was frequently displeased by their carelessness and inattention to detail. From 1798 the firm also published the *Allgemeine musikalische Zeitung*.

**Brentano,** Antonie, née von Birkenstock (1780–1869), was Viennese by birth, but married the Frankfurt merchant Franz Brentano (1765–1844) in 1798. She returned to Vienna for a three-year period (1809–12) when her father died, and became closely acquainted with Beethoven, as did Franz's half-sister Bettina (1785–1859), who married the poet Achim von Arnim in 1811. There is almost overwhelming evidence that Antonie was the intended recipient of Beethoven's famous love letter of July 1812 to the 'Immortal Beloved', but after that summer she never saw him again. The Brentanos had six children, including Maximiliane (1802–61), to whom Beethoven dedicated a short trio (WoO 39) in 1812.

**Breuning,** Stephan von (1774–1827), was a childhood friend of Beethoven, and they renewed their friendship when Stephan moved to Vienna in 1801. He revised the libretto of *Leonore* in 1806, and received the dedication of the Violin Concerto in 1808 on his marriage to Julie Vering (1791–1809), to whom the piano version of the work was dedicated. After her early death Stephan married Constanze Ruschowitz. Their son Gerhard (1813–92) often visited Beethoven during the composer's last two years, and published his recollections in 1874.

**Browne** (Browne-Camus), Count Johann Georg von (1767–1827), of Irish extraction, was one of Beethoven's most generous patrons during the 1790s, and once presented him with a horse. In return he and his wife Countess Anna Margarete received several dedications, and he also commissioned the Three Marches, Op. 45.

**Brunsvik** was the name of an aristocratic Hungarian family, several members of whom had connections with Beethoven: Therese (1775–1861), her brother Franz (1777–1849), and their sisters Josephine (see under Deym) and Charlotte (1782–1843). Therese and Josephine received daily piano lessons from Beethoven for a short time in 1799, and he dedicated to them his variations on 'Ich denke dein' (WoO 74). Therese never married. Her memoirs and correspondence are a useful source of information about Beethoven.

**Clement,** Franz (1780–1842), was a prominent Viennese violinist. His benefit concert in 1805 included the public première of Beethoven's *Eroica* Symphony, and the following year Beethoven composed his Violin Concerto for Clement, who gave its first performance that December.

**Clementi,** Muzio (1752–1832), Italian by birth, became prominent in England as a piano virtuoso and a composer, whose sonatas had a significant influence on Beethoven's. He later set up a piano-making and music-publishing firm in London, and while visiting Vienna in 1807 he negotiated a deal with Beethoven to publish several of his major works. Over a dozen of Beethoven's works were eventually issued by Clementi in editions independent of the continental ones.

**Collin,** Heinrich Joseph (1771–1811), was a Viennese poet and playwright whose *Coriolan* prompted Beethoven's overture of that name in 1807. They subsequently planned to collaborate on an opera—possibly *Macbeth* or *Bradamante*—but nothing materialized.

**Cramer,** Johann Baptist (1771–1858), though born in Mannheim, was brought up in London. He became acquainted with Beethoven during a visit to Vienna in 1799–1800, and Beethoven greatly admired his playing, according to Ries. He was unrelated to Carl Friedrich Cramer, whose *Magazin der Musik* included an early report on Beethoven's ability in 1783.

**Czerny,** Carl (1791–1857), known today mainly as a composer of piano studies, showed great ability at an early age, and was taught the piano by Beethoven from

1801 to 1803. He later taught Beethoven's nephew (as also did the pianist Joseph Czerny, who was unrelated). In Volume 4 of his *Complete Theoretical and Practical Piano Forte School*, Op. 500, he provides advice on how to perform Beethoven's piano music. His memoirs, though rather disjointed, include many interesting details about Beethoven.

**Deym**, Countess Josephine, née Brunsvik (1779–1821), first met Beethoven in 1799, when she and her sister Therese were given piano lessons by him. Later that year she married Count Joseph Deym (1751–1804), but after his death she fell in love with Beethoven, who wrote several amorous letters to her during 1805–7. In February 1810 she married Baron Christoph von Stackelberg, and gave birth to three more children to add to the four from her first marriage, but he left her in 1813. Some maintain that she was Beethoven's 'Immortal Beloved' of 1812, but there is no real evidence to support this hypothesis.

**Diabelli**, Anton (1781–1858), worked in Steiner's music-publishing firm before setting up his own firm with Pietro Cappi in 1818. The following year he invited Viennese composers to write one variation each on a waltz he had composed. 50 of them did so, but Beethoven instead wrote a set of 33 variations (Op. 120), which appeared in 1823, a year before the other 50.

**Duport**, Jean-Louis (1749–1819) and Jean-Pierre (1741–1818), were brothers and notable cellists. Beethoven met them when he visited Berlin in 1796, and probably composed his Cello Sonatas, Op. 5, and perhaps other works, for Jean-Louis.

**Erdödy**, Countess (Anna) Marie, née Niczky (1778–1837), married Count Peter Erdödy in 1796, and they had three children before separating. She was a fine pianist and Beethoven became very friendly with her by 1808, but the following year they had a violent quarrel. They apparently resumed their friendship in 1815, and Beethoven began writing a piano trio for her three children; but one of them, August, died and the work was left unfinished.

**Ertmann**, Baroness Dorothea von, née Graumann (1781–1849), was another excellent pianist and friend of Beethoven, who taught her for a time. A prominent champion of Beethoven's music, she received the dedication of his Sonata, Op. 101 in 1817.

**Esterházy**, Prince Nikolaus (1765–1833), like his father and grandfather, was Haydn's patron, but he commissioned the Mass in C from Beethoven for his wife's name-day in 1807, by which time Haydn had retired from composing. He was displeased with the result, however, and commissioned nothing more from Beethoven.

**Fischer**, Gottfried (1780–1864), was a close acquaintance of Beethoven in Bonn, and from 1838, with the help of his sister Cäcilia (1762–1845), he wrote many reminiscences of the composer's early life, which is otherwise poorly documented.

**Fries**, Count Moritz von (1777–1826), was a wealthy banker who commissioned Beethoven's String Quintet, Op. 29 in 1801, and probably also the Violin Sonatas, Opp. 23 and 24. It was through his firm Fries & Co. that Beethoven received payments for his work for George Thomson.

**Galitzin**, Prince Nikolas (1794–1866), a cello-playing Russian prince, greatly admired Beethoven's works, and wrote to him in 1822 commissioning three new quartets. These were duly written and dedicated to him (Opp. 127, 132, and 130). He also purchased a manuscript copy of the *Missa solemnis*, from which he was able to give the première of the work in April 1824, in St Petersburg.

**Gebauer**, Franz Xaver (1784–1822), was a music teacher who established a series of *Concerts Spirituels* in Vienna in 1819. The series was designed to provide performances of major orchestral works, and many of Beethoven's works were included.

**Giannatasio** (or **Giannattasio**) **del Rio,** Cajetan (1764–1828), ran a boarding school in Vienna which Beethoven's nephew Karl attended in 1816–18. His elder daughter Fanny (1790–1873) kept a diary that records many details about Beethoven's visits, and in 1819 Beethoven composed a wedding song (WoO 105) for her sister Anna (1792–1868) and her bridegroom Leopold Schmerling.

**Gleichenstein,** Baron Ignaz von (1778–1828), was a close friend of Beethoven, and during 1807–10 provided him with much secretarial assistance. A keen cellist, he received the dedication of the Cello Sonata, Op. 69. By 1811, when he married Anna Malfatti, he had ceased his secretarial help, and the couple left Vienna shortly afterwards.

**Goethe,** Johann Wolfgang von (1749–1832), the great poet and playwright, met Beethoven in July 1812 in Teplitz, although Beethoven had long admired Goethe's writings. Goethe was struck by Beethoven's rough manners, his energy, and his sincerity, as well as his amazing talent. They were in daily contact for little over a week, but Beethoven continued to admire Goethe, and his greatest ambition was to compose music for *Faust.*

**Grillparzer,** Franz (1791–1872), poet and playwright, knew Beethoven well, and together they planned to write an opera in the 1820s—either *Drahomira* or *Melusine.* When Beethoven died, Grillparzer provided the funeral oration.

**Guicciardi,** Countess Giulietta (1784–1856), cousin of the Brunsvik sisters, studied the piano with Beethoven in 1801 and evidently was in love with him for a time. In 1802 he dedicated to her the 'Moonlight' Sonata (a replacement for the Rondo, Op. 51 No. 2, that she was to have received), but the following year she married Count Wenzel von Gallenberg (1783–1839).

**Haslinger,** Tobias (1787–1842), settled in Vienna in 1810 and for many years was assistant to the music publisher Steiner, whose firm he eventually took over. He became a close friend of Beethoven, whose letters to him usually have humorous content. The canon *O Tobias* (WoO 182) was apparently composed after Beethoven had had a dream about Haslinger, and in 1825 Beethoven sent Schott's an amusing fictional biography of Haslinger; much to his dismay, they published it!

**Haydn,** (Franz) Joseph (1732–1809), evidently first met Beethoven in Bonn en route to London in 1790. Beethoven then moved to Vienna in 1792 specifically to study with Haydn, the most celebrated composer of the day. Lessons continued until early 1794, when Haydn made his second trip to London. Beethoven clearly learnt much from Haydn's music (although the lessons themselves may not have been so productive), and dedicated his Piano Sonatas, Op. 2, to him in 1795.

**Hoffmeister,** Franz Anton (1754–1812), was a composer who set up a music publishing firm in Vienna, and published Beethoven's *Pathétique* Sonata in 1799. The following year he moved to Leipzig to found another branch of the firm (which became known as Hoffmeister & Kühnel), and published four Beethoven works (Opp. 19–22) shortly thereafter, plus several others later on.

**Holz,** Karl (1799–1868), was second violinist in Schuppanzigh's quartet in the 1820s, and became a close friend of Beethoven in 1825, as well as giving him much secretarial help. His reminiscences seem generally trustworthy.

**Hotschevar,** Jakob, was a relative of Beethoven's sister-in-law Johanna, and supported her during the dispute over the guardianship of Beethoven's nephew Karl. In 1827, after Beethoven's death, he himself became Karl's guardian.

**Hummel**, Johann Nepomuk (1778–1837), was a noted pianist and composer, with a more delicate and less passionate style than Beethoven. He lived in Vienna for a time and knew Beethoven quite well. In 1814 he took part in performances of *Wellingtons Sieg*, and was a pallbearer at Beethoven's funeral.

**Kinsky**, Prince Ferdinand (1781–1812) was one of three patrons who contributed to Beethoven's annuity from 1809, although he had little direct contact with the composer. After his death in a riding accident in November 1812, payments were suspended for a time, but they were eventually renewed and backdated.

**Kreutzer**, Rodolphe (1766–1831), was a noted French violinist who visited Vienna in 1798 and made a good impression on Beethoven. The violin sonata known as the 'Kreutzer' was actually written for George Bridgetower, but was dedicated to Kreutzer in 1805. He was not related to Konradin Kreutzer (1780–1849), a composer who took part in the première of Beethoven's Ninth Symphony.

**Krumpholz**, Wenzel (1750–1817), was a violinist who settled in Vienna about 1795 and became a close friend of Beethoven. Beethoven's *Gesang der Mönche* was written to mark Krumpholz's sudden death in May 1817.

**Lichnowsky**, Prince Karl (1761–1814), was Beethoven's most prominent and generous patron during his early years in Vienna. In return, Beethoven dedicated to Lichnowsky his Opus 1 (three piano trios), and several other works. In 1806 Beethoven accompanied him to his castle at Grätz, where a violent dispute took place, after which relations were never so cordial.

**Lichnowsky**, Count Moritz (1771–1837), younger brother of Prince Karl, was also a friend and patron of Beethoven, who dedicated his *Prometheus* Variations (Op. 35) and the Piano Sonata, Op. 90, to him.

**Linke**, Joseph (1783–1837), was a cellist who played in quartets for Count Razumovsky until 1815, and later taught Countess Erdödy's children. Beethoven's cello sonatas Op. 102 were perhaps written primarily for him and the Countess. In the 1820s he was in Schuppanzigh's quartet, and took part in the premières of some of Beethoven's late quartets.

**Lobkowitz**, Prince Franz Joseph von (1772–1816), one of Beethoven's leading patrons, commissioned the String Quartets, Op. 18, and put his private orchestra at Beethoven's disposal for trials of new works—notably the *Eroica*. In 1809 he was one of three patrons who combined to give Beethoven an annuity of 4000 florins. Beethoven composed a birthday cantata for his son Ferdinand (1797–1868) in 1823.

**Maelzel**, Johann Nepomuk (1772–1838), moved to Vienna in 1792 and is most noted as the inventor of the metronome. His many other inventions include two of benefit for Beethoven—the panharmonicon, a mechanical orchestra for which Beethoven wrote part of *Wellingtons Sieg*; and a series of ear trumpets to aid Beethoven's weak hearing.

**Malfatti**, Therese (1792–1851), was probably introduced to Beethoven by Gleichenstein in 1810 as a possible bride, and for a time Beethoven planned to marry her, but her family evidently opposed the idea. Her sister Anna, however, married Gleichenstein himself, and her uncle Giovanni (1775–1859), a prominent physician, treated Beethoven from time to time, including during his last illness. Beethoven composed the popular *Für Elise* for Therese, and a short cantata *Un lieto brindisi* for Giovanni.

**Maximilian Franz** (1756–1801), brother of Emperor Joseph II, succeeded Maximilian Friedrich as Elector of Cologne in 1784 and was Beethoven's principal patron in Bonn. He sponsored Beethoven's visits to Vienna in 1787 and 1792.

**Moscheles**, Ignaz (1794–1870), composer and pianist, settled in Vienna in 1808 and knew Beethoven well, making piano arrangements (corrected by Beethoven) of several of his works. He moved to London in 1825, and in 1841 published an annotated translation of Schindler's 1840 biography.

**Mozart**, Wolfgang Amadeus (1756–91), was always held in high esteem by Beethoven, who admired Mozart's music above any other until he became acquainted with Handel's. Beethoven went to study with Mozart in Vienna in 1787, but the visit was very short and it is uncertain whether he ever heard Mozart play the piano. Mozart's operas, concertos, and wind music in particular had enormous influence on Beethoven's style.

**Neate**, Charles (1784–1877), was a pianist and composer, and a founder member of the Philharmonic Society of London. He visited Vienna in 1815–16, when he became a friend of Beethoven's, and later attempted to promote Beethoven's interests in London.

**Neefe**, Christian Gottlob (1748–98), was born in Saxony and studied law and music in Leipzig before arriving in Bonn in 1779. He soon became Court Organist there, and taught Beethoven piano, figured bass, and composition, quickly recognizing the boy's talent.

**Oliva**, Franz (1786–1848), was a banking clerk who in about 1810 succeeded Gleichenstein as Beethoven's principal unpaid secretary. He continued as a close friend of Beethoven's until 1820, when he moved to St Petersburg.

**Oppersdorff**, Count Franz von (1778–1818), commissioned Beethoven's Fourth and Fifth Symphonies. In 1806 Beethoven visited him at his castle in Upper Silesia, when the Second Symphony was performed.

**Pasqualati**, Baron Johann Baptist von (1777–1830), was a music lover and art collector who owned the house on the Mölkerbastei in which Beethoven resided during most of the period 1804–15 (Beethoven's rooms are now a memorial museum). In 1814 Beethoven wrote the *Elegischer Gesang* in memory of the Baron's wife Eleonore, and the Baron sent Beethoven some gifts of food during his final illness.

**Peters**, Karl (1782–1849), was a tutor in the Lobkowitz household, and his wife Josephine was an amateur singer. His known contact with Beethoven dates from about 1815, and he gave much assistance during the guardianship struggle, becoming co-guardian of Karl from 1820 to 1825. He was unrelated to Carl Friedrich Peters (1779–1827), the music publisher of Leipzig, who succeeded Hoffmeister & Kühnel in 1814 and attempted to obtain some of Beethoven's works in the 1820s.

**Piringer**, Ferdinand (1780–1829), a Viennese Court official, was a violinist active in the Gesellschaft der Musikfreunde and later succeeded Gebauer as director of the *Concerts Spirituels*. Beethoven wrote a short Allegretto (WoO 61) for him in 1821, and from 1823 Piringer made many entries in the conversation books.

**Pleyel**, Ignaz Joseph (1757–1831), like Beethoven, was a pupil of Haydn and also contributed settings to Thomson's folksong collection. In 1795 he settled in Paris, founding a firm of music publishers and piano makers, but he visited Vienna in 1805 and met Beethoven there.

**Razumovsky**, Count Andreas Kirillovich (1752–1836), was Russian Ambassador in Vienna, and commissioned from Beethoven the string quartets Op. 59 that are generally known by his name. He supported a permanent string quartet from 1808 to 1816, sometimes participating as second violin. His magnificent palace in Vienna was destroyed by fire on 31 December 1814 during celebrations associated with the Congress of Vienna.

**Ries**, Ferdinand (1784–1838), a prominent composer and son of Beethoven's violin teacher Franz (1755–1846), was another Bonn musician who moved to Vienna, arriving there in 1801. Beethoven gave him piano lessons and they were in close contact until Ries's departure in 1805. He returned briefly in 1808–9 before settling in London in 1813, where he did much to promote Beethoven's interests. He returned to the Rhineland in 1824, eventually moving to Frankfurt. At the end of his life he wrote important reminiscences about Beethoven, published with Wegeler's in 1838 as *Biographische Notizen über Ludwig van Beethoven*.

**Rochlitz**, Johann Friedrich (1769–1842), was founding editor of the important Leipzig music journal *Allgemeine musikalische Zeitung* from 1798. In 1803 he sent Beethoven an opera libretto which was rejected, and in 1822 he visited Vienna. After Beethoven's death Rochlitz gave a detailed account of meetings he claimed to have had with the composer, but his account is highly suspect.

**Rudolph**, Archduke of Austria (1788–1831), youngest brother of Emperor Franz, apparently became acquainted with Beethoven about 1807 (despite Schindler's claim for an earlier association). Already a fine pianist, he soon became a close friend, receiving many dedications. In 1809, together with two other patrons, he granted Beethoven an annuity of 4000 florins. He then became Beethoven's only composition pupil, and later composed several fine works. Because of poor health he chose an ecclesiastical rather than military career, and was enthroned as Cardinal Archbishop of Olmütz on 9 March 1820; Beethoven's *Missa solemnis* was intended for this occasion, but was not completed in time.

**Salieri**, Antonio (1750–1825), was a prominent opera composer in Vienna, and gave Beethoven tuition in the Italian vocal style from about 1800 to 1802. He probably also provided Beethoven with some kind of assistance before then, since Beethoven dedicated to him the Violin Sonatas, Op. 12, in 1799.

**Salomon**, Johann Peter (1745–1815), born in Bonn, settled in London in his youth, and is best known for having brought Haydn from Vienna to London in 1790. During their journey they stopped in Bonn and presumably met Beethoven, who occasionally corresponded with Salomon in later years.

**Schickh**, Johann (1770–1835), came to Vienna in 1807 and in 1816 became founding editor of the important arts journal the *Wiener Zeitschrift* (also known as the *Modenzeitung* and various other names). A few of Beethoven's songs first appeared in the *Wiener Zeitschrift*, bringing him into close contact with Schickh.

**Schikaneder**, Emanuel (1751–1812), is best known as the librettist of *The Magic Flute* (1791). As director of the Theater an der Wien he collaborated with Beethoven on the opera *Vestas Feuer* in 1803, but Beethoven abandoned the project after six months.

**Schindler**, Anton Felix (1795–1864), a violinist, acted for a time as Beethoven's unpaid secretary during the 1820s. Beethoven appreciated his help but did not regard him highly. Immediately after Beethoven's death Schindler acquired about 140 conversation books, into which he inserted numerous fake entries during the next few years to give the impression he had known Beethoven far better than was the case. In 1840 he published a biography, which he greatly revised and expanded in 1860, but both versions are extremely unreliable, containing much fabrication as well as plain errors.

**Schlemmer**, Mathias (1783–1827), a court official in Vienna, was landlord of Beethoven's nephew Karl during 1825–6, when he made several entries in the conversation books. He was probably unrelated to Beethoven's chief copyist Wenzel Schlemmer (1760–1823).

**Schubert**, Franz Peter (1797–1828), greatly admired Beethoven's music, and some of his own works show Beethoven's direct influence, but although they were living in the same city, there was little personal contact, and they had different circles of friends.

**Schuppanzigh**, Ignaz (1776–1830), a prominent Viennese violinist, became acquainted with Beethoven shortly after the composer's arrival in Vienna. The friendship continued right up to Beethoven's final year, and Schuppanzigh took part in premières of many Beethoven's works, except during a period when he was in St Petersburg (1816–23). His large girth prompted Beethoven to nickname him 'Falstaff'.

**Sebald**, Amalie (1787–1846), a Berlin singer, met Beethoven at Teplitz in 1811 and again in 1812, and he became very fond of her. She has even been proposed as his 'Immortal Beloved', but can be ruled out as she was not in Karlsbad at the right time.

**Seyfried**, Ignaz Ritter von (1776–1841), was, like Beethoven, a pupil of Albrechtsberger, and he was a composer at the Theater an der Wien from 1797 to 1825. He knew Beethoven over a long period, without being an intimate friend, and in 1832, in his role as a music pedagogue, he published a rather inaccurate account of Beethoven's studies in composition, adding some interesting recollections.

**Simrock**, Nikolaus (1751–1832), was initially (from 1775) a horn player in the Bonn orchestra, and therefore well acquainted with Beethoven. He later set up as a music publisher, issuing several of Beethoven's works, and the business was continued by his son Peter Joseph (1792–1868).

**Smart**, Sir George (1776–1867), organist, conductor, and composer, was a founder member of the Philharmonic Society of London. He conducted the London première of Beethoven's Ninth Symphony, commissioned by the Society, in March 1825, and visited Vienna later that year, meeting Beethoven several times. He later wrote a detailed account of the visit.

**Spohr**, Louis (1784–1859), was a prominent composer and violinist, who lived in Vienna during 1812–15, when he was leader of the orchestra at the Theater an der Wien. His autobiography contains several reminiscences of Beethoven, including an account of his unorthodox conducting style.

**Stadler**, Abbé Maximilian (1748–1833), a priest and composer, lived in Vienna during 1796–1803 and from 1815. Beethoven nearly dedicated his *Prometheus* Variations, Op. 35, to him, but had a late change of mind. In 1826 Stadler sent Beethoven a copy of his monograph on Mozart's Requiem, and Beethoven was greatly appreciative.

**Starke**, Friedrich (1774–1835), a composer and horn player, was a long-standing but not particularly close friend of Beethoven. In 1819–21 he published a piano method that contained new works by several composers, including Beethoven's set of five bagatelles Op. 119 Nos. 7–11.

**Steiner**, Sigmund Anton (1773–1838), published many of Beethoven's works from 1815 onwards, and occasionally gave Beethoven financial help. His assistants included Haslinger and Diabelli, and his music shop in the Paternostergasse became a common meeting place for Beethoven and his friends.

**Stich**, Johann Wenzel (1746–1803), was a prominent horn player from Bohemia, and was often known by the Italian form of his name, Giovanni Punto. He visited Vienna in 1800, and Beethoven wrote for him the Horn Sonata, Op. 17.

**Streicher**, Nanette (1769–1833), the daughter of the famous Augsburg piano maker Johann Andreas Stein, married another piano maker, Johann Andreas Streicher, in 1794. The couple moved to Vienna and became close friends of Beethoven, who for a time preferred their pianos to any others. Nanette gave Beethoven much domestic advice and assistance, especially in 1817 as he prepared to take Karl into his home.

**Stumpff**, Johann Andreas (1769–1846), though German by birth, moved to London about 1792 and worked principally as a harp maker. He visited Beethoven in 1818 to tune his new Broadwood piano, and again in 1824 when he resolved to send him Arnold's edition of Handel's music.

**Swieten**, Baron Gottfried van (1733–1803), was one of Mozart's staunchest supporters and a great admirer of the works of Bach and Handel. He was also one of Beethoven's early patrons in Vienna, and received the dedication of the First Symphony in 1800.

**Thomson**, George (1757–1851), worked in the civil service in Edinburgh, but was an avid collector of folksongs. He befriended Robert Burns, publishing many of his poems, and for settings of the melodies he turned first to Pleyel, then Kozeluch, Haydn, Beethoven, and, later, Weber. Beethoven's contribution amounted to 176 settings, most of which were published by Thomson.

**Treitschke**, Georg Friedrich (1776–1842), a playwright and poet, settled in Vienna in 1800, working mainly at the Kärntnertor Theatre. He knew Beethoven from 1811 or earlier, and in addition to his masterly reworking of the libretto of *Fidelio* in 1814, he provided the texts for a few shorter works.

**Umlauf**, Michael (1781–1842), was son of the composer Ignaz (1746–96) whose singspiel *Die schöne Schusterin* was furnished with two arias by Beethoven (WoO 91) about 1795. Michael was prominent mainly as a conductor, and gave the premières of the 1814 version of *Fidelio* and, ten years later, Beethoven's Ninth Symphony.

**Varena**, Joseph von (1769–1843), lived in Graz, but met Beethoven at Teplitz in 1811 and persuaded him to send several unpublished scores for charity concerts in Graz.

**Varnhagen von Ense**, Karl August (1785–1858), was a writer and diplomat who met Beethoven at Teplitz in 1811. While living in Prague in 1812 he tried to help Beethoven obtain from Prince Kinsky the full value of his annuity, and his memoirs of 1837 contain a detailed description of his encounters with Beethoven.

**Waldstein**, Count Ferdinand von (1762–1823), was one of Beethoven's leading patrons in Bonn, and apparently commissioned the *Ritterballett* (WoO 1), which was at first passed off as Waldstein's own composition. Like Beethoven, he later moved to Vienna, and in 1805 he received the dedication of the sonata (Op. 53) that customarily bears his name.

**Wegeler**, Dr Franz Gerhard (1765–1848), was a close friend of Beethoven in Bonn, and they renewed their friendship while Wegeler was studying medicine in Vienna in 1794–6. In 1802 he married Eleonore von Breuning (1771–1841), sister of Beethoven's friend Stephan, and the couple later settled in Koblenz. In 1838 he published important recollections about Beethoven, in collaboration with Ries, and added a supplement in 1845.

**Zelter**, Carl Friedrich (1758–1832), was a noted song composer of the North German school, and a friend of Goethe. He encountered Beethoven during a visit to Vienna in 1819.

**Zmeskall von Domanovecz,** Nikolaus (1759–1833), was an official in the Hungarian Chancellery, and a long-standing friend of Beethoven. A fine cellist and amateur composer, he received the dedication of the String Quartet, Op. 95 (of which he also made a manuscript copy still in existence). He often provided Beethoven with practical help in such matters as finding a servant, accommodation, or quills. In the 1820s he became bedridden, but managed to attend the première of Beethoven's Ninth Symphony.

# Appendix D

# Select bibliography

With the vast literature on Beethoven increasing rapidly, this bibliography is necessarily extremely selective, restricted mainly to works actually cited. Fuller bibliographies, though still highly selective, can be found in Cooper ed., *Compendium*, Kerman and Tyson, *Beethoven*, Kinderman, *Beethoven* (with commentary), Solomon, *Beethoven* (with commentary), and elsewhere. The fullest bibliography is that being compiled at the Ira F. Brilliant Center for Beethoven Studies, San Jose State University, California, currently accessible via the Internet.

## EDITIONS OF THE WORKS

The main edition of Beethoven's works is the old *Gesamtausgabe* (*GA*), and its *Supplemente* (*SGA*), which are gradually being superseded by the *Neue Ausgabe* (*NA*). These are listed below, but there are many other useful editions of selections of works, plus facsimiles of autograph scores and sketchbooks.

GA     *Ludwig van Beethoven's Werke: Vollständige kritisch durchgesehene überall berechtigte Ausgabe*, 25 vols (Leipzig, 1862–5, 1888).

NA     *Ludwig van Beethoven: Werke: Neue Ausgabe sämtlicher Werke* (Munich and Duisburg, 1961– ).

SGA    *Ludwig van Beethoven: Supplemente zur Gesamtausgabe*, ed. Willy Hess, 14 vols (Wiesbaden, 1959–71).

## MAJOR REFERENCE WORKS AND SOURCE STUDIES

A      Emily Anderson, ed. and tr., *The Letters of Beethoven*, 3 vols (London, 1961). [Letters are referred to in the present study by A- followed by Anderson's number.]

Alb    Theodore Albrecht, ed. and tr., *Letters to Beethoven and Other Correspondence*, 3 vols. (Lincoln Ne. and London, 1996). [Letters etc. are referred to in the present study by Alb- followed by Albrecht's number.]

BB    Sieghard Brandenburg, ed., *Ludwig van Beethoven: Briefwechsel Gesamtausgabe*, 7 vols (Munich, 1996–8).

BKh   Karl-Heinz Köhler and others, eds, *Ludwig van Beethovens Konversationshefte*, 10 vols to date (Leipzig, 1968– ).

Hess   Willy Hess, *Verzeichnis der nicht in der Gesamtausgabe veröffentlichte Werke Ludwig van Beethovens* (Wiesbaden, 1957).

JTW    Douglas Johnson, Alan Tyson, and Robert Winter (ed. Douglas Johnson), *The Beethoven Sketchbooks: History, Reconstruction, Inventory* (Oxford, 1985).

KH    Georg Kinsky (completed Hans Halm), *Das Werk Beethovens* (Munich, 1955).

N-I    Gustav Nottebohm, *Beethoveniana* (Leipzig, 1872, repr. New York, 1970).

N-II    —— *Zweite Beethoveniana* (Leipzig, 1887; repr. New York, 1970).

TDR    Alexander Wheelock Thayer (rev. Hermann Deiters and Hugo Riemann), *Ludwig van Beethovens Leben*, 5 vols (Leipzig, 1907–23).

TF    Elliot Forbes, ed., *Thayer's Life of Beethoven* (Princeton, 2/1967).

## BIOGRAPHY, REMINISCENCES, GENERAL STUDIES

Breuning, Gerhard (ed. Maynard Solomon), *Memories of Beethoven*, tr. Henry Mins and Maynard Solomon (Cambridge, 1992).

Cooper, Barry, ed., *The Beethoven Compendium: A Guide to Beethoven's Life and Music* (London, 2/1996).

Czerny, Carl (ed. Paul Badura-Skoda), *On the Proper Performance of all Beethoven's Works for the Piano* (Vienna, 1970).

Goldschmidt, Harry, *Um die Unsterbliche Geliebte: Eine Bestandsaufnahme* (Leipzig, 1977).

Kagan, Susan, *Archduke Rudolph, Beethoven's Patron, Pupil, and Friend: His Life and Music* (Stuyvesant, 1988).

Kerman, Joseph, and Tyson, Alan, *The New Grove Beethoven* (London, 1983).

Kinderman, William, *Beethoven* (Oxford and Berkeley, 1995).

Küster, Konrad, *Beethoven* (Stuttgart, 1994).

Landon, H. C. Robbins, *Beethoven: A Documentary Study* (London, 1970).

—— *Haydn: Chronicle and Works*, 5 vols (London, 1976–80).

Sadie, Stanley, ed., *The Grove Concise Dictionary of Music* (London, 3/1994).

Schiedermair, Ludwig, *Der junge Beethoven* (Leipzig, 1925).

Schlosser, Johann Aloys (ed. Barry Cooper), *Beethoven: The First Biography [1827]*, tr. Reinhard G. Pauly (Portland, 1996).

Schmidt-Görg, Joseph, ed., *Des Bonner Bäckermeisters Gottfried Fischer Aufzeichnungen über Beethovens Jugend* (Bonn, 1971).

Solomon, Maynard, *Beethoven* (New York, 1977).

Sonneck, O. G., ed., *Beethoven: Impressions of Contemporaries* (New York, 1926, repr. 1967).

Sterba, Editha and Richard, *Beethoven and his Nephew* (New York, 1954).

Tellenbach, Marie-Elisabeth, *Beethoven und seine 'unsterbliche Geliebte' Josephine Brunswick* (Zurich, 1983).

Wegeler, Franz Gerhard, and Ries, Ferdinand, *Remembering Beethoven*, tr. Frederick Noonan (Arlington, 1987).

Wolf, Stefan, *Beethovens Neffenkonflikt* (Munich, 1995).

## THE MUSIC

Arnold, Denis, and Fortune, Nigel, eds, *The Beethoven Companion* (London, 1971).

Bockholdt, Rudolf, and Weber-Bockholdt, Petra, eds, *Beethovens Klaviertrios: Symposion München 1990* (Munich, 1992).

Brandenburg, Sieghard, and Loos, Helmut, eds, *Beiträge zu Beethovens Kammermusik: Symposion Bonn 1984* (Munich, 1987).

Broyles, Michael, *Beethoven: The Emergence and Evolution of Beethoven's Heroic Style* (New York, 1987).

Cook, Nicholas, *Beethoven: Symphony No. 9* (Cambridge, 1993).

Cooper, Barry, *Beethoven's Folksong Settings: Chronology, Sources, Style* (Oxford, 1994).

Dahlhaus, Carl, *Ludwig van Beethoven: Approaches to his Music*, tr. Mary Whittall (Oxford, 1991).

Del Mar, Jonathan, *Ludwig van Beethoven: Symphony No. 9 in D minor Op. 125: Critical Commentary* (Kassel, 1996).

Drabkin, William, *Beethoven: Missa solemnis* (Cambridge, 1991).

Hess, Willy, *Das Fidelio-Buch* (Winterthur, 1986).

Hopkins, Antony, *The Nine Symphonies of Beethoven* (London, 1981).

Jones, David Wyn, *Beethoven: Pastoral Symphony* (Cambridge, 1995).

Kallick, Jenny, *A Study of the Advanced Sketches and Full Score Autograph for the First Movement of Beethoven's Ninth Symphony* (Ph.D. diss., Yale Univ., 1987).

Kerman, Joseph, *The Beethoven Quartets* (New York, 1967).

Kinderman, William, *Beethoven's Diabelli Variations* (Oxford, 1987).

Levy, Janet, *Beethoven's Compositional Choices: The Two Versions of Opus 18, No. 1, First Movement* (Philadelphia, 1982).

Marston, Nicholas, *Beethoven's Piano Sonata in E, Op. 109* (Oxford, 1995).

Münster, Arnold, *Studien zu Beethovens Diabelli-Variationen* (Munich, 1982).

Reti, Rudolph, *Thematic Patterns in Sonatas of Beethoven* (London, 1967).

Tovey, Donald Francis, *A Companion to Beethoven's Pianoforte Sonatas* (London, 1931).

—— *Essays in Musical Analysis: Chamber Music* (London, 1944).

Winter, Robert, *Compositional Origins of Beethoven's Opus 131* (Ann Arbor, 1982).

## SPECIAL STUDIES, ESSAY COLLECTIONS

Brandenburg, Sieghard, and Gutiérrez-Denhoff, Martella, eds, *Beethoven und Böhmen* (Bonn, 1988).

Brenneis, Clemens, ed., *Ein Skizzenbuch aus dem Jahre 1809 (Landsberg 5)*, 2 vols. (Bonn, 1993).

Cooper, Barry, *Beethoven and the Creative Process* (Oxford, 2/1992).

Dorfmüller, Kurt, ed., *Beiträge zur Beethoven-Bibliographie* (Munich, 1978).

Goldschmidt, Harry, ed., *Zu Beethoven: Aufsätze und Annotationen* (Berlin, 1979); *Zu Beethoven 2: Aufsätze und Dokumente* (Berlin, 1984); *Zu Beethoven 3: Aufsätze und Dokumente* (Berlin, 1988).

Johnson, Douglas, *Beethoven's Early Sketches in the 'Fischhof Miscellany': Berlin, Autograph 28*, 2 vols (Ann Arbor, 1980).

Kerman, Joseph, ed., *Ludwig van Beethoven: Autograph Miscellany from circa 1786 to 1799*, 2 vols (London, 1970).

Kinderman, William, ed., *Beethoven's Compositional Process* (Lincoln Ne. and London, 1991).

Klein, Hans-Günter, *Ludwig van Beethoven: Autographe und Abschriften*

(Staatsbibliothek Preussischer Kulturbesitz: Kataloge der Musikabteilung, I/2), (Berlin, 1975).

Lockwood, Lewis, *Beethoven: Studies in the Creative Process* (Cambridge, Mass., 1992).

—— and Benjamin, Phyllis, eds, *Beethoven Essays: Studies in Honor of Elliot Forbes* (Cambridge, Mass., 1984).

Lühning, Helga, and Brandenburg, Sieghard, eds, *Beethoven: Zwischen Revolution und Restauration* (Bonn, 1989).

Mikulicz, Karl Lothar, ed., *Ein Notierungsbuch von Beethoven aus dem Besitze der Preussischen Staatsbibliothek zu Berlin* (Leipzig, 1927, repr. Hildesheim and New York, 1972). [A transcription of the sketchbook Landsberg 7]

Nottebohm, Gustav, *Beethoven's Studien* (Leipzig and Winterthur, 1873).

—— *Ein Skizzenbuch von Beethoven aus dem Jahre 1803* (Leipzig, 1880, repr. New York, 1970).

Solomon, Maynard, *Beethoven Essays* (Cambridge, Mass., 1988).

Stowell, Robin, ed., *Performing Beethoven* (Cambridge, 1994).

Tyson, Alan, *The Authentic English Editions of Beethoven* (London, 1963).

—— ed., *Beethoven Studies* (New York, 1973, London, 1974); *Beethoven Studies 2* (London, 1977); *Beethoven Studies 3* (Cambridge, 1982).

Van der Zanden, Jos, *Beethoven: Nieuwe onthullingen* (Hilversum, 1993).

Virneisel, Wilhelm, ed., *Beethoven: Ein Skizzenbuch zu Streichquartetten aus Op. 18, SV 46*, 2 vols (Bonn, 1972–4).

Wallace, Robin, *Beethoven's Critics* (Cambridge, 1986).

Winter, Robert, and Carr, Bruce, eds, *Beethoven, Performers, and Critics: The International Beethoven Congress Detroit 1977* (Detroit, 1980).

ARTICLES

Albrecht, Theodore, and Schwensen, Elaine, 'More than just Peanuts: Evidence for December 16 as Beethoven's Birthday', *BN*, iii (1988), 49, 60–3.

Beahrs, Virginia, '"My Angel, My All, My Self": A Literal Translation of Beethoven's Letter to the Immortal Beloved', *BN*, v (1990), 29, 34–9.

Block, Geoffrey, 'Some Gray Areas in the Evolution of Beethoven's Piano Concerto in B flat major, Op. 19', in Lockwood and Benjamin, eds, *Beethoven Essays*, 108–26.

Brandenburg, Sieghard, 'Beethovens Streichquartette op. 18', in Brandenburg and Gutiérrez, eds, *Beethoven und Böhmen*, 259–309.

—— 'The First Version of Beethoven's G major Quartet, Op. 18 No. 2', *ML*, lviii (1977), 127–52.

—— 'The Historical Background to the *Heiliger Dankgesang* in Beethoven's A minor Quartet Op. 132', in Tyson, ed., *Beethoven Studies 3*, 161–91.

—— 'Die Quellen zur Entstehungsgeschichte von Beethovens Streichquartett Es-dur op.127', *BeJb*, x (1978–81), 221–76.

—— 'Die Skizzen zur Neunten Symphonie', in Goldschmidt, ed., *Zu Beethoven 2*, 88–129.

Busch-Weise, Dagmar von, 'Beethovens Jugendtagebuch', *Studien zur Musikwissenschaft*, xxv (1962), 68–88.

Cook, Nicholas, 'Beethoven's Unfinished Piano Concerto: A Case of Double Vision?', *JAMS*, xlii (1989), 338–74.

Cooper, Barry, 'Beethoven's Immortal Beloved and Countess Erdödy: A Case of Mistaken Identity?', *BJo*, xi/2 (1996), 18–24.

—— 'Beethoven's Oratorio and the Heiligenstadt Testament', *BJo*, x (1995), 19–24.

—— 'Beethoven's Revisions to his Fourth Piano Concerto', in Stowell, ed., *Performing Beethoven*, 23–48.

—— 'The Ink in Beethoven's "Kafka" Sketch Miscellany', *ML*, lxviii (1987), 315–32.

—— 'Newly Identified Sketches for Beethoven's Tenth Symphony', *ML*, lxvi (1985), 9–18.

—— 'Schindler and the *Pastoral* Symphony', *BN*, viii (1993), 2–6.

—— 'Subthematicism and Metaphor in Beethoven's Tenth Symphony', *The Music Review* (forthcoming).

De Roda, Cecile, 'Un quaderno di autografi di Beethoven del 1825', *Rivista musicale italiana*, xii (1905), 63–108, 592–622, 734–67.

Dorfmüller, Kurt, 'Beethovens Schaffen für Klaviertrio und der Musikmarkt seiner Zeit', in Bockholdt and Weber-Bockholdt, eds, *Beethovens Klaviertrios*, 23–34.

—— 'Beethovens "Volksliederjagd" ', in Stephan Hörner and Bernhold Schmid, eds, *Festschrift Horst Leuchtmann* (Tutzing, 1993), 107–25.

Drabkin, William, 'The Agnus Dei of Beethoven's *Missa Solemnis*: The Growth of Its Form', in Kinderman, ed., *Beethoven's Compositional Process*, 130–59.

Edelmann, Bernd, 'Wenzel Müllers Lied vom "Schneider Wetz" und Beethovens Trio-Variationen op. 121a', in Bockholdt and Weber-Bockholdt, eds, *Beethovens Klaviertrios*, 76–102.

Hanson, Alice M., 'Incomes and Outgoings in the Vienna of Beethoven and Schubert', *ML*, lxiv (1983), 173–82.

Johnson, Douglas, '1794–1795: Decisive Years in Beethoven's Early Development', in Tyson, ed., *Beethoven Studies 3*, 1–28.

—— 'Music for Prague and Berlin: Beethoven's Concert Tour of 1796', in Winter and Carr, eds, *Beethoven, Performers, and Critics*, 24–40.

Kerman, Joseph, '*An die ferne Geliebte*', in Tyson ed., *Beethoven Studies*, 123–57.

Kirby, F.E., 'Beethoven's Pastoral Symphony as a *Sinfonia Caracteristica*', *MQ*, lvi (1970), 605–23.

Kirkendale, Warren, 'New Roads to Old Ideas in Beethoven's *Missa Solemnis*', *MQ*, lvi (1970), 665–701.

Kojima, Shin-Augustinus, 'Die Solovioline-Fassungen und -Varianten von Beethovens Violinkonzert op. 61—ihre Entstehung und Bedeutung', *BeJb*, viii (1971–2), 97–145.

Kropfinger, Klaus, 'Das gespaltene Werk—Beethovens Streichquartett Op. 130/133', in Brandenburg and Loos, eds, *Beiträge zu Beethovens Kammermusik*, 296–335.

Küthen, Hans-Werner, 'Neue Aspekte zur Entstehung von *Wellingtons Sieg*', *BeJb*, viii (1971–2), 73–92.

Loos, Helmut, 'Beethoven in Prag 1796 und 1798', in Brandenburg and Gutiérrez-Denhoff, eds, *Beethoven und Böhmen*, 63–90.

Lühning, Helga, 'Florestans Kerker in Rampenlicht. Zur Tradition des Soterraneo', in Lühning and Brandenburg, eds, *Beethoven: Zwischen Revolution und Restauration*, 137–204.

—— 'Gattungen des Liedes', in Brandenburg and Loos, eds, *Beiträge zu Beethovens Kammermusik*, 191–204.

Marston, Nicholas, 'Beethoven's "Anti-organicism"? The Origins of the Slow Movement of the Ninth Symphony', in Broude Bros. (publ.), *Studies in the History of Music 3: The Creative Process* (New York, 1992), 169–200.

—— 'Beethoven's Sketches and the Interpretative Process', *BF*, i (1992), 225–42.

May, Jürgen, 'Beethoven and Prince Karl Lichnowsky', *BF*, iii (1994), 29–38.

Meredith, William, 'The Origins of Beethoven's Op. 109', *MT*, cxxvi (1985), 713–16.

Meredith, William, 'Conference Report: "Rethinking Beethoven's Late Period: Sources, Aesthetics, and Interpretation," Harvard University Department of Music, November 1–3, 1996', *BJo*, xii (1997), 32–41.

Platen, Emil, 'Über Bach, Kuhlau und die thematisch-motivische Einheit der letzten Quartette Beethovens', in Brandenburg and Loos, eds, *Beiträge zu Beethovens Kammermusik*, 152–64.

Röder, Thomas, 'Beethovens Sieg über die Schlachtenmusik. Opus 91 und die Tradition der Battaglia', in Lühning and Brandenburg, eds, *Beethoven: Zwischen Revolution und Restauration*, 229–58.

Schmidt, Hans, 'Verzeichnis der Skizzen Beethovens', *BeJb*, vi (1965–8), 7–128.

Smyth, David H., 'Beethoven's Revision of the Scherzo of the Quartet, Opus 18, No. 1', *BF*, i (1992), 147–63.

Solomon, Maynard, 'Beethoven's Tagebuch of 1812–1818', in Tyson, ed., *Beethoven Studies 3*, 193–288 (rev. version in Solomon, *Beethoven Essays*).

—— 'The Ninth Symphony: A Search for Order', in Solomon, *Beethoven Essays*, 3–32.

—— 'Recherche de Josephine Deym', *BN*, ii (1987), 21–6.

Stadlen, Peter, 'Possibilities of an Aesthetic Evaluation of Beethoven's Sketches', in Carl Dahlhaus *et al.*, eds, *Bericht über den Internationalen Musikwissenschaftlichen Kongress Bonn 1970* (Kassel, 1971), 111–17.

Tellenbach, Marie-Elisabeth, 'Beethoven and the Countess Josephine Brunswick, 1799–1821', *BN*, ii (1987), 41–51.

—— 'Psychoanalysis and the Historiocritical Method: On Maynard Solomon's Image of Beethoven', *BN*, viii-ix (1993–4), 84–92, 119–27.

Timbrell, Charles, 'Notes on the Sources of Beethoven's Op. 111', *ML*, lviii (1977), 204–15.

Tyson, Alan, 'The Authors of the Op. 104 String Quintet', in Tyson, ed., *Beethoven Studies*, 158–73.

—— 'Beethoven in Steiner's Shop, *The Music Review*, xxiii (1962), 119–27.

—— 'Beethoven to the Countess Susanna Guicciardi: A New Letter', in Tyson ed., *Beethoven Studies*, 1–17.

—— 'The Problem of Beethoven's "First" Leonore Overture', *JAMS*, xxviii (1975), 292–334.

—— 'The "Razumovsky" Quartets: Some Aspects of the Sources', in Tyson, ed., *Beethoven Studies 3*, 107–40.

—— 'Stages in the Composition of Beethoven's Piano Trio Op. 70, No. 1', *Proceedings of the Royal Musical Association*, xcvii (1970–1), 1–19.

—— 'The 1803 Version of Beethoven's *Christus am Oelberge*', *MQ*, lvi (1970), 551–84.

—— 'Yet Another "Leonore" Overture?', *ML*, lviii (1977), 192–204.

Volek, Tomislav, and Macek, Jaroslav, 'Beethoven's Rehearsals at the Lobkowitz's', *MT*, cxxvii (1986), 75–80.

Weber-Bockholdt, Petra, 'Beethovens Opus 44', in Bockholdt and Weber-Bockholdt, eds, *Beethovens Klaviertrios*, 103–17.

Webster, James, 'The Falling-Out between Haydn and Beethoven: The Evidence of the Sources', in Lockwood and Benjamin, eds, *Beethoven Essays*, 3–45.

—— 'The Form of the Finale of Beethoven's Ninth Symphony', *BF*, i (1992), 25–63.

Weill, Hanna, 'The Two Versions of the *Adagio* of Beethoven's String Quartet, Opus 18, No. 1: Revisions in Dynamics, Harmony, and Rhythm', *BJo*, x (1995), 60–5.

Winter, Robert, 'Reconstructing Riddles: The Sources for Beethoven's *Missa Solemnis*', in Lockwood and Benjamin, eds, *Beethoven Essays*, 217–50.

—— 'The Sketches for the "Ode to Joy" ', in Winter and Carr, eds, *Beethoven*, 176–214.

# Index

## Beethoven